Measuring Economic Sustainability and Progress

Studies in Income and Wealth
Volume 72

National Bureau of Economic Research
Conference on Research in Income and Wealth

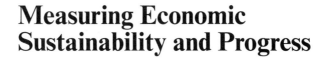

Measuring Economic Sustainability and Progress

Edited by **Dale W. Jorgenson, J. Steven Landefeld, and Paul Schreyer**

The University of Chicago Press

Chicago and London

DALE W. JORGENSON is the Samuel W. Morris University Professor
in the Department of Economics at Harvard University. J. STEVEN
LANDEFELD is director of the Bureau of Economic Analysis at the US
Department of Commerce. PAUL SCHREYER is deputy chief statistician
at the Organisation for Economic Co-operation and Development.

The University of Chicago Press, Chicago 60637
The University of Chicago Press, Ltd., London
© 2014 by the National Bureau of Economic Research
All rights reserved. Published 2014.
Printed in the United States of America

23 22 21 20 19 18 17 16 15 14   1 2 3 4 5
ISBN-13: 978-0-226-12133-8 (cloth)
ISBN-13: 978-0-226-12147-5 (e-book)
DOI: 10.7208/chicago/9780226121475.001.0001

Library of Congress Cataloging-in-Publication Data

Measuring economic sustainability and progress / edited by Dale W.
    Jorgenson, J. Steven Landefeld, and Paul Schreyer.
        pages cm — (Studies in income and wealth ; volume 72)
    "This volume contains revised versions of most of the papers and
    discussions presented at the Conference on Research in Income and
    Wealth entitled 'Measuring Economic Sustainability and Progress,'
    held in Cambridge, Massachusetts, on August 6–8, 2012."—
    Prefatory note.
        ISBN 978-0-226-12133-8 (cloth : alkaline paper) —
    ISBN 978-0-226-12147-5 (e-book) 1. Economics—Measurement—
    Congresses. 2. Economics—Statistical methods—Congresses.
    3. Economic development—Measurement—Congresses.
    I. Jorgenson, Dale W. (Dale Weldeau), 1933– editor. II. Landefeld,
    J. Steven, editor. III. Schreyer, Paul, editor. IV. Series: Studies in
    income and wealth ; v. 72.
    HB135.M426 2014
    338.9'27—dc23

                                                                2013040583

⊗ This paper meets the requirements of ANSI/NISO Z39.48-1992
(Permanence of Paper).

Relation of the Directors to the
Work and Publications of the
National Bureau of Economic Research

1. The object of the NBER is to ascertain and present to the economics profession, and to the public more generally, important economic facts and their interpretation in a scientific manner without policy recommendations. The Board of Directors is charged with the responsibility of ensuring that the work of the NBER is carried on in strict conformity with this object.

2. The President shall establish an internal review process to ensure that book manuscripts proposed for publication DO NOT contain policy recommendations. This shall apply both to the proceedings of conferences and to manuscripts by a single author or by one or more co-authors but shall not apply to authors of comments at NBER conferences who are not NBER affiliates.

3. No book manuscript reporting research shall be published by the NBER until the President has sent to each member of the Board a notice that a manuscript is recommended for publication and that in the President's opinion it is suitable for publication in accordance with the above principles of the NBER. Such notification will include a table of contents and an abstract or summary of the manuscript's content, a list of contributors if applicable, and a response form for use by Directors who desire a copy of the manuscript for review. Each manuscript shall contain a summary drawing attention to the nature and treatment of the problem studied and the main conclusions reached.

4. No volume shall be published until forty-five days have elapsed from the above notification of intention to publish it. During this period a copy shall be sent to any Director requesting it, and if any Director objects to publication on the grounds that the manuscript contains policy recommendations, the objection will be presented to the author(s) or editor(s). In case of dispute, all members of the Board shall be notified, and the President shall appoint an ad hoc committee of the Board to decide the matter; thirty days additional shall be granted for this purpose.

5. The President shall present annually to the Board a report describing the internal manuscript review process, any objections made by Directors before publication or by anyone after publication, any disputes about such matters, and how they were handled.

6. Publications of the NBER issued for informational purposes concerning the work of the Bureau, or issued to inform the public of the activities at the Bureau, including but not limited to the NBER Digest and Reporter, shall be consistent with the object stated in paragraph 1. They shall contain a specific disclaimer noting that they have not passed through the review procedures required in this resolution. The Executive Committee of the Board is charged with the review of all such publications from time to time.

7. NBER working papers and manuscripts distributed on the Bureau's web site are not deemed to be publications for the purpose of this resolution, but they shall be consistent with the object stated in paragraph 1. Working papers shall contain a specific disclaimer noting that they have not passed through the review procedures required in this resolution. The NBER's web site shall contain a similar disclaimer. The President shall establish an internal review process to ensure that the working papers and the web site do not contain policy recommendations, and shall report annually to the Board on this process and any concerns raised in connection with it.

8. Unless otherwise determined by the Board or exempted by the terms of paragraphs 6 and 7, a copy of this resolution shall be printed in each NBER publication as described in paragraph 2 above.

Contents

Prefatory Note

This volume contains revised versions of most of the papers and discussions presented at the meeting of the Conference on Research in Income and Wealth entitled "Measuring Economic Sustainability and Progress," held in Cambridge, Massachusetts, on August 6–8, 2012.

We gratefully acknowledge the financial support for this conference provided by the Bureau of Economic Analysis. Support for the general activities of the Conference on Research in Income and Wealth is provided by the following agencies: Bureau of Economic Analysis, Bureau of Labor Statistics, Census Bureau, Board of Governors of the Federal Reserve, Internal Revenue Service, and Statistics Canada.

We thank Dale Jorgenson, J. Steven Landefeld, and Paul Schreyer, who served as conference organizers and editors of this volume. We are also grateful to the staff of the NBER (with special thanks to Carl Beck, Brett Maranjian, and Helena Fitz-Patrick) and to the Bureau of Economic Analysis conference working group managed by Shaunda Villones for their excellent work.

Executive Committee, September 2013

John M. Abowd	Michael W. Horrigan
Susanto Basu	Charles R. Hulten (chair)
Andrew Bernard	Ron Jarmin
Ernst R. Berndt	J. Steven Landefeld
Carol A. Corrado	Brent Moulton
W. Erwin Diewert	Valerie Ramey
Robert C. Feenstra	Mark J. Roberts
John Greenlees	Daniel Sichel
John C. Haltiwanger	William Wascher

Introduction

Dale W. Jorgenson, J. Steven Landefeld,
and Paul Schreyer

Since the creation of national accounts during the Great Depression there have been calls to expand macroeconomic statistics to better account for economic growth, the sustainability of growth, and the effect of growth on economic well-being. The Great Recession, the increasing concentration of income, and the importance of education, human capital, health, and the environment have underlined the urgency of moving forward on a measurement agenda of expanding the scope of national accounts.

This volume would be the latest in a long series of Studies in Income and Wealth and earlier National Bureau of Economic Research (NBER) publications dating back to the 1930s that have played a key role in the development of the US national accounts and those of other nations. The most recent NBER volume on national accounts was *A New Architecture for the National Accounts*, which laid out a plan for integrating the existing systems of accounts, identifying gaps and inconsistencies, and expanding and integrating systems of nonmarket accounts into the core system. That 2006 volume (a) helped efforts to better integrate the Bureau of Economic Analysis's own national and industry accounts; (b) fostered collaborative research that produced three integrated accounts (Integrated Federal Reserve Board/BEA Income, Product, and Financial Accounts; Integrated Bureau of Labor Statistics /BEA Productivity Accounts; and Prototype Integrated BLS/BEA Industry-Level Production Accounts); (c) advanced

Dale W. Jorgenson is the Samuel W. Morris University Professor in the Department of Economics at Harvard University. J. Steven Landefeld is director of the Bureau of Economic Analysis at the US Department of Commerce. Paul Schreyer is deputy chief statistician at the Organisation for Economic Co-operation and Development.

For acknowledgments, sources of research support, and disclosure of the authors' material financial relationships, if any, please see http://www.nber.org/chapters/c12824.ack.

further work on the integration of micro- and macrodata; (d) contributed to significant extensions and improvements in key census data used in these new integrated accounts; and (e) laid the groundwork for extensions of the accounts in the areas of household production, health, education, and the environment.

This volume provides a framework for building on the accomplishments associated with the 2006 *New Architecture* volume by extending the work on integration and extensions of the accounts begun with that volume and stimulated by the new international System of National Accounts (SNA) framework introduced in 2008. This volume also begins to address long-standing gaps, including those related to economic welfare and sustainability that became increasingly apparent during the recent recession. Work in this volume shows advances within a national accounts framework, and so contributes to other national and international initiatives such as those pursued by the Organisation for Economic Co-operation and Development (OECD) that aim at developing better indicators of material well-being and the quality of life.

The NBER research on the national accounts has been important in leading innovation and has been a unique and long-standing forum for collaboration between academia and government. Just as the creation of the national accounts in the 1930s in response to the Great Depression was a collaborative effort between academia and government, so too is the statistical response to the Great Recession outlined in this volume.

The Great Recession and the associated financial crisis provide an opportunity, as economic calamities of the past have, to make substantive progress in our understanding of the economy. As one looks to the United States and other countries' gross domestic product (GDP) and other national accounts statistics, over time, most major innovations have been collaborations between academic, business, and government researchers.

Moving forward, there is also a need to fill the following gaps in our statistical coverage revealed by the recession and the period leading up to the recession:

- The increasing share of income going to those at the top, that for many households resulted in disconnects between their personal experiences and the reported growth in official statistics like GDP and disposable personal income.
- The failure of many of the existing macroeconomic and financial statistics to provide a consistent and clear set of new "leading" financial indicators on the unsustainability of trends in saving, spending, debt, and housing and equity prices.
- The lack of data on health care, the environment, education, and human capital and their increasing importance to the rate and sustainability of economic growth.

The introductory talk by Federal Reserve Bank (FRB) chairman Bernanke lays out a persuasive argument for extending the economic measurement beyond income, wealth, and consumption to encompass economic well-being and its distribution and determinants.

The first set of chapters in the volume addresses conceptual and empirical proposals for extending the accounts to better measure economic sustainability and welfare by extending the boundaries of national accounts. The chapter by former Council of Economic Advisors (CEA) member Abraham provides an inside look at how extended market and nonmarket estimates can be of importance in fact-based economic policy. The chapter by Jorgenson and Slesnick provides a theoretical and empirical methodology for incorporating distributional information into the accounts, along with Paul Schreyer and Erwin Diewert who develop a theoretical framework for valuing household production along the lines suggested by Nordhaus, Mackie, and Abraham in the 2006 volume. The fourth chapter in this set is by Christopher Carroll, who argues that in order to understand aggregate household spending behavior, it is necessary to augment the existing national accounts with satellite accounts that provide information at less aggregated levels.

Although there is a broad consensus about the usefulness of distributional information, the user is sometimes confronted with differences in evidence, depending on whether administrative or survey data is used. Part II of the volume addresses this issue. The chapters by McCully, Harris, and Sammartino as well as Fixler and Johnson offer practical solutions to the problems associated with reconciling tax, household, and business data on the distribution of income and spending and on filling gaps in coverage that have been the subject of over fifty years of research (including a two-volume NBER study of the issue in the 1940s directed by Milton Friedman). A related issue is covered by Alice Henriques and Joanne Hsu in the area of consumer finances, savings, and wealth.

Part III of the volume remains within the existing boundaries of national accounts and demonstrates how integrated economic accounts can provide consistent information for policymakers. The chapter by Cagetti, Holmquist, Lynn, McIntosh, and Wasshausen on the integrated macroeconomic accounts produced jointly by BEA and the Federal Reserve Board is the latest extension of the integrated accounts originally presented in the 2006 volume. The chapter illustrates the usefulness of such data for issues such as the evolution of household net worth and its role in the financial crisis, brings the US accounts closer into alignment with the framework laid out in the 2006 volume and to the SNA 2008, and lays out an agenda for further extensions of the financial sector. Fleck, Rosenthal, Russell, Strassner, and Usher showcase a prototype for US industry-level productivity accounts that have been developed by the BLS and the BEA. The chapter by Shrestha presents a framework for filling gaps in the financial data identified during the financial crisis.

The fourth set of chapters presents conceptual and empirical solutions to better capture medical-care costs, human capital, innovation, and the environment. Muller's chapter builds on work in environmental accounting by Nordhaus (and Rob Mendelsohn) and adjusts GDP for damages due to air pollution. Christian develops human capital estimates based on the framework developed by Jorgenson and Fraumeni, and Corrado and Hulten lay out the necessary steps in building an innovation satellite account. The chapters by Dunn, Liebman, and Shapiro, and by Gu and Morin illustrate the type of estimates that might be incorporated in health accounts extensions suggested by Mackie and Abraham in 2006. These papers provide concrete examples of how such values can be developed in consistency with national accounts and thereby provide key baseline data for better understanding such issues as the sources of growth in medical spending, the returns to investments in education, and the relationship between the environment and economic growth.

Summary of Papers

"Expanded Measurement of Economic Activity: Progress and Prospects" (Abraham)

In her remarks, Abraham provides an overview of recent efforts to expand economic accounting in order to improve the measurement of resource utilization and production in key sectors. These efforts include accounting for investment in education, accounting for investment in health, and improving the measurement of government output. Abraham notes that the growing interest in these topics within the statistical community has been paralleled by a growing interest among policy officials.

A major barrier to expanding the accounting for education, health, and government output is the lack of comprehensive source data. For example, few data sources exist that allow student outcomes to be monitored. Without such data sources, it is difficult to evaluate the performance of the education sector as a whole or of different types of educational institutions or programs. Similarly, the lack of comprehensive data on health care that allow health spending to be linked to patient outcomes makes it difficult to determine how to achieve better health outcomes at the lowest cost. The lack of evidence on outcomes resulting from government spending makes it difficult for governments to assess how to make efficient use of available resources. Developments that should improve the data available to measure education, health, and government output include the planned construction of student-level longitudinal data systems, the formation of the Health Care Cost Institute (which provides researchers access to a database including over five billion claims records from four large insurers), and guidance from the Office of Management and Budget to federal agencies calling for them to demonstrate a commitment to expanding the use of evidence in carrying out agency operations, respectively.

Abraham briefly discusses aggregate measures of welfare and well-being. Proposed approaches to measuring well-being include adjusting the existing GDP measure by adding the value of household production and subtracting defense expenditures, developing composite indicators that weight measures for several individual dimensions of interest (e.g., the United Nations Human Development Index and the Genuine Progress Indicator), and developing aggregate measures of subjective well-being, such as global measures of life satisfaction or time accounts that track variation in time spent in pleasant or unpleasant activities. However, Abraham notes that aggregate well-being measures are intellectually interesting, but it is unclear if and how they will be used to guide policy decisions.

"Measuring Social Welfare in the US National Accounts"
(Jorgenson and Slesnick)

Jorgenson and Slesnick develop measures of individual and social welfare within a new architecture for the US national accounts. This new architecture comprises a set of income statements, balance sheets, flow of funds statements, and productivity estimates for the economy, and by sector, that are more accurate and internally consistent than the existing accounts. The new architecture makes it possible to avoid confusing the measurement of production and welfare, which was a key concern of the Stiglitz, Sen, and Fitoussi's 2009 "Report by the Commission on Measurement of Economic Performance and Social Progress."

Jorgenson and Slesnick present measures of the cost and standard of living and inequality that are integrated with the national accounts, in contrast to the BLS' Consumer Price Index and the Census Bureau's statistics on standard of living, poverty, and inequality. For the entire postwar period (1948–2010), the authors obtain a measure of the standard of living with a growth rate of 2.69 percent. Within this period, they find that growth in the standard of living peaked during 1948 to 1973 at 3.62 percent and then declined to around 2 percent after 1973. They find that all of the growth in equity over the postwar period occurred during the period 1948 to 1973. The surge in economic growth from 1995 to 2000 was largely offset by the sharp decline in equity.

The authors conclude by recommending that national statistical agencies develop satellite accounts as a first step to incorporating distributional information into the national accounts.

"Household Production, Leisure, and Living Standards"
(Schreyer and Diewert)

Household production is an important nonmarket activity that is largely outside the production boundary of the System of National Accounts

(SNA). The SNA generally excludes most services produced by households because there are no market prices available to value them. However, it acknowledges that for purposes of measuring economic welfare, it is useful to estimate the value of household production.

Most studies on how to value the services produced by households have used an input cost approach; the time household members spend on household production has been the primary focus of research. The two main methods to valuing labor input into own-account household production have been the opportunity cost approach and the replacement cost approach. Schreyer and Diewert develop a model of the household as producer and consumer that provides a theoretical justification for these two main methods. They provide justifications for the replacement cost approach but show that, for households that are active in labor markets, the opportunity cost method should be used when the purpose of valuing time spent on household production is to capture full consumption, as opposed to capturing only the value of own-account household production.

Schreyer and Diewert also develop a cost-of-living index for full consumption and full household income. Finally, they perform a cross-country comparison of full consumption across a selection of OECD countries and compare material living standards using the volume of full consumption per capita. They find that, on average, household production (and the equivalent additional consumption) with labor valued at replacement costs, adds about 50 percent to the value of actual final consumption, although there are significant variations between countries. They also find that the vast majority of countries improve their position against the United States when material living standards are measured using full consumption as opposed to actual individual consumption; for example, Norway's living standards become higher than the United States'.

"Representing Consumption and Saving without a Representative Consumer" (Carroll)

This chapter argues that, in order to understand aggregate household spending behavior, it is necessary to augment the existing national accounts with satellite accounts that provide high-quality information at less aggregated levels. These satellite accounts would need to include measures that reflect the microeconomic heterogeneity in expenditures, income, assets, debt, and beliefs among households and that are consistent with aggregate statistics in the existing National Income and Product Accounts.

Carroll argues that the existing data sources are inadequate for answering key questions about household spending behavior. Microeconomic representations of households' choices should be based on the household's dynamic budget constraint, but existing data sources measure only pieces of that budget constraint, or provide only snapshots of households' balance sheets. Furthermore, the quality of the existing data has been deteriorating.

Carroll identifies some promising strategies to obtaining more complete and dynamic microeconomic data on households' balance sheets, including negotiating with the Federal Reserve Board to expand the scope of the existing Survey of Consumer Finances and collecting financial records kept by households using personal financial accounting software.

"Integration of Micro- and Macrodata on Consumer Income and Expenditures" (McCully)

McCully examines macroeconomic and microeconomic sources of information on household income and expenditures. The BEA produces macroestimates of personal income and outlays that are part of the US national accounts. The Current Population Survey from the Census Bureau and the Consumer Expenditure Survey program from BLS are household surveys used to produce microeconomic estimates of household income and expenditures. The Current Population Survey collects detailed data on household income and on health insurance coverage. The Consumer Expenditure Survey collects data on direct household expenditures, as well as on household income and financial assets.

Although the National Income and Product Accounts (NIPA) estimates of household income and expenditures are generally considered to be more accurate and broader measures than estimates derived from the household surveys, they have no distributional information. McCully reconciles the differences in these estimates through the integration of microeconomic data from household surveys with national accounts data, developing measures of income distribution and of other breakdowns of household income and consumption for the years 2006 and 2010 that are consistent with national accounts values and definitions.

McCully finds that the share of disposable household income accounted for by the lowest quintile increased from 4.9 percent in 2006 to 5.4 percent in 2010, while the share accounted for by the highest quintile decreased from 48.4 percent to 47.1 percent. For all income groups, there was a significant increase from 2006 to 2010 in the share of income accounted for by government social benefits and other transfers. In particular, the share of income accounted for by government social benefits and other transfers for the lowest quintile increased by 8.4 percentage points. McCully also finds that the consumption shares by income quintile show much less dispersion than for disposable income. Mean expenditures per household for the highest quintile were slightly more than twice as high for the top quintile as for the lowest quintile, compared with a disposable household income ratio of nearly 9 to 1.

"Trends in the Distribution of Household Income, 1979–2010"
(Harris and Sammartino)

Harris and Sammartino examine changes in the distribution of household income in the United States between 1979 and 2010 using Statistics of Income (SOI) data from the Internal Revenue Service and Current Population Survey (CPS) data from the Census Bureau. Because each data set lacks certain types of information needed for estimating and comparing household income over time, each SOI record is statistically matched to a corresponding CPS record on the basis of demographic characteristics and income. This results in a new record that takes on the demographic characteristics of the CPS record and the income reported in the SOI.

Using this approach, the authors find that income after transfers and federal taxes (or "after-tax income") rose much more rapidly between 1979 and 2007 for households at the higher end of the income scale than for households at the middle and lower end of the income scale. As a result, the distribution of after-tax household income was substantially more unequal in 2007 than in 1979, with the share of income received by the top 1 percent more than doubling over the period and the share received by low and middle-income households declining.

The primary reason for the growing inequality in the after-tax income distribution was that higher-income households increased their share of market income (i.e., income measured before government transfers and taxes). The two factors that accounted for this increase were: (a) an increase in the concentration of each source of market income, including labor income, business income, capital gains, capital income, and other income; and (b) a shift in the composition of that income that reflected increases in the share of income coming from capital gains and business income.

"Accounting for the Distribution of Income in the
US National Accounts" (Fixler and Johnson)

There is considerable disagreement regarding the relationship between inequality and growth. As stated in a recent OECD report (OECD 2012, 14), "Despite a vast theoretical literature on the link between inequality and growth, no general consensus has emerged and the empirical evidence is rather inconclusive."

The focus of this chapter is to have comparable measures of growth and inequality in order to evaluate the relationship between them. The chapter examines the distribution and movement of household income, as measured by personal income, and how it influences the movements of gross domestic income (GDI), and hence GDP. As proposed by the BEA (BEA 2012, 47), Fixler and Johnson undertake "a decomposition of personal income that presents median as well as mean income and other measures of the distribution of income across households."

Fixler and Johnson provide methods to produce a median personal income (and its Gini coefficient) that is more consistent with the national accounts measure of personal income. These methods yield a variety of results on the growth of median income and inequality depending on the definition of income used and the method used to obtain the distribution. The authors show that adjusting for underreporting in household survey (Current Population Statistics) data yields a larger level and increase in the trend of the mean and median between 1999 and 2010. This, in turn, yields a larger increase in inequality. The authors use distributional information from the IRS' Statistics of Income (SOI) to perform a further adjustment that allows for different households having different levels of underreporting for each source of income. This results in a lower increase in inequality between 1999 and 2009 (the latest year for which SOI data are available). Including imputed employer- or government-provided health-care benefits in the measure of personal income decreases inequality, as such benefits are more likely to accrue to low-income households.

The authors also provide applications of their results to calculating a social welfare function and evaluating fiscal multipliers.

"Analysis of Wealth Using Micro- and Macrodata:
A Comparison of the Survey of Consumer Finances
and Flow of Funds Accounts" (Henriques and Hsu)

Researchers use different types of household balance sheet data to study different aspects of life cycle saving and wealth accumulation behavior. Macrodata from the Flow of Funds Accounts (FFA) are produced quarterly and are available in a timely manner, but they can only be used to study the behavior of the household sector as a whole. Microdata from the Survey of Consumer Finances (SCF) are available every three years and only with a lag, but they can be used to address questions that involve differences in behavior over time and across various types of households.

Henriques and Hsu find that, despite the very different approaches to estimating household net worth, the FFA and the SCF data sets show the same general patterns of wealth changes over the past twenty-five years. Levels of net worth are nearly identical in the period 1989 to 1998. Beginning in 2001 and through 2010, the SCF estimates of net worth exceed the FFA estimates by approximately 20 percent. The gap that emerged in the early twenty-first century is a combination of higher values for tangible assets in the SCF, in particular noncorporate business equity and owner-occupied housing, and larger values of liabilities in the FFA, especially for consumer credit. These areas of divergence between the SCF and FFA appear to be largely attributable to methodological decisions used in the production of the data, but they do not dramatically alter one's perceptions of household wealth dynamics leading up to and following the Great Recession.

"The Integrated Macroeconomic Accounts of the United States"
(Cagetti, Holmquist, Lynn, McIntosh, and Wasshausen)

The integrated macroeconomic accounts (IMAs), produced jointly by
BEA and the Federal Reserve Board (FRB), present a sequence of accounts
that relate income, saving, investment in real and financial assets, and asset
revaluations to changes in net worth. They were developed as part of an effort
to further harmonize the BEA's National Income and Product Accounts
and the FRB's flow of funds accounts. This chapter provides background
information on the IMAs and on their construction. It describes the usefulness of the IMAs, including for analyzing the evolution of household net
worth and its components, a set of series that has appeared frequently in
discussions of the causes and effects of the recent financial crisis. Some of
the challenges associated with integrating nonfinancial and financial data
sources are also discussed. These data sources include the current and capital
accounts statistics from BEA's National Income and Product Accounts and
the financial account statistics from FRB's flow of funds accounts. In the
final section, the chapter describes future plans for improving the IMAs,
including a proposed framework and methodology for breaking out the
financial business sector into three subsectors: (a) central bank, (b) insurance and pension funds, and (c) other financial business.

"A Prototype BEA/BLS Industry-Level Production Account for the
United States" (Fleck, Rosenthal, Russell, Strassner, and Usher)

Gross domestic product (GDP) by industry statistics provide detailed
information on the industry sources of aggregate value added growth, but
do not include estimates of the contributions of capital and labor inputs and
multifactor productivity (MFP) to economic growth. It captures the part of
output growth that cannot be explained by changes in the combined contribution of capital, labor, energy, materials, and services inputs (KLEMS).
The official MFP measures for the United States provide information on
components of economic growth in the market economy, but they do not
report detailed information on the nonmarket economy. While these two
sets of statistics share a common economic accounting framework, they are
prepared by two separate agencies. The GDP statistics are published by the
Bureau of Economic Analysis (BEA), US Department of Commerce, and
MFP and labor productivity statistics are published by the Bureau of Labor
Statistics (BLS), US Department of Labor.

This chapter builds on the GDP by industry statistics produced by the
BEA and the capital, labor, and MFP statistics produced by the BLS to
assemble a consistent industry-level production account for the United
States that is consistent with GDP. This set of accounts allows one to decompose the industry contributions of inputs and MFP to the sources of GDP
growth at the aggregate level.

The initial results of the prototype account show that over the period 1998 to 2010, capital accounted for about 60 percent of US economic growth, labor accounted for about 10 percent, and MFP accounted for about 30 percent of growth. In forty-eight out of sixty-three industries, at least one KLEMS input to production was a more important source of real gross output growth than was MFP.

"Toward the Development of Sectoral Financial Positions and Flows in a From-Whom-to-Whom Framework" (Shrestha)

The global crisis of 2008 highlighted the need to understand financial interconnectedness among the various sectors of an economy and between them and their counterparties in the rest of the world. In addition, the financial interconnectedness is also to be understood as an integral part of the linkages between real and financial economies. Although the System of National Accounts (SNA) provides an overarching framework for the development of such macroeconomic statistics, application of this kind of analysis has been hampered by the lack of adequate data.

This chapter reviews the attributes of the SNA as a framework for integrated macroeconomic accounts, explores application of SNA principles for developing data on intersectoral financial linkages, reviews some important experiences that will be of use in the development of fully integrated macroeconomic accounts, and outlines activities and steps to implement sectoral accounts and balance sheets, including sectoral financial positions and flows in a from-whom-to-whom framework in the future.

"Toward the Measurement of Net Economic Welfare: Air Pollution Damage in the US National Accounts—2002, 2005, 2008" (Muller)

Time-series environmental accounting estimates rates of growth (or contraction) in the stocks of valuable natural resources and the magnitude of environmental damage from market production. Including these measures into augmented accounts is a critical step in closing the gap between the current production-based measures of output and a more complete picture of national economic welfare.

In this chapter, Muller employs environmental accounting methodology to measure the gross external damage (GED) due to air pollution emissions in the US economy in 2002, 2005, and 2008. The chapter measures three indices: the GED, the ratio of GED to value added (GED/VA), and net value added (NVA), defined as value added minus the GED. Each of these indices is computed for each sector of the US economy in 2002, 2005, and 2008. Real GED is estimated to be $480 billion in 2002, $430 billion in 2005, and $350 billion in 2008. Most of the reduction in GED from 2005 to 2008 is due to fewer emissions in the utility, manufacturing, agriculture, and transportation sectors. The GED/VA begins in 2002 at 0.054, drops to 0.039 in 2005, and then declines significantly to 0.03 in 2008. The empirical time-series estimation of environmentally adjusted value added (EVA) is an important augmentation to standard measures of growth. From 2002 to 2005 VA grew at an annual rate of 2.76 percent. Over the same period EVA grew at 3.07 percent. Between 2005 and 2008 VA grew at 1.118 percent while the EVA increased by 1.47 percent. Thus, the reduction in the GED over these time periods results in growth rates in the EVA greater than VA by about 0.30 percent.

"Human Capital Accounting in the United States: Context, Measurement, and Application" (Christian)

Christian's (2010) human capital account for the United States measured the human capital stock and human capital investment in both nominal and real terms over the period between 1994 and 2006. The account broke down net human capital investment among five components: investment from births, depreciation from deaths, investment from education net of the aging of enrolled persons, depreciation from the aging of nonenrolled persons, and a residual component that takes into account both migration and measurement error.

This chapter updates Christian's (2010) work to the year 2009, refining the underlying data and putting the account into international context by reviewing applications in the rest of the world. It also measures the sensitivity of human capital measures to alternative assumptions about income growth rates, discount rates, the treatment of taxes, smoothing and imputation of labor force and school enrollment data, and the valuation of nonmarket time. It concludes with an application to the measurement of the output of the education sector.

"Measuring the Stock of Human Capital for International and Intertemporal Comparisons" (Liu)

Despite the wide interest in human capital, there has been no agreement on how to measure its stock. A variety of indicators have been used by analysts to measure the stock of human capital; these indicators include average school years, shares of the population having reached various levels of educational attainment, measures of people's competencies, expenditures in the education system, and lifetime earnings. This diversity of approaches has made it difficult to draw policy implications from comparisons of the stock of human capital across countries and highlights the need to develop broader and more consistent methodologies.

The OECD human capital project was launched in order to identify common methodologies for measuring the stock of human capital for comparative analysis and to implement these methods using existing OECD data. This chapter summarizes the outcomes of the first phase of the project and shows the feasibility of applying the lifetime income approach to measuring human capital for comparative analysis across countries and over time using categorical data that are typically available within the OECD statistics system.

In this chapter, monetary estimates of the stock of human capital were computed for fourteen OECD countries (Australia, Canada, Denmark, France, Israel, Italy, Korea, the Netherlands, New Zealand, Norway, Poland, Spain, the United Kingdom, and the United States), and one nonmember country (Romania). These estimates indicate that the estimated value of human capital is substantially larger than that of traditional physical capital. Ratios of human capital to nominal GDP are in a range from around eight to over ten across the countries included in the study. The distributions of human capital by age, gender, and education show that men dominate women in terms of their human capital holdings. In addition, people with higher education are better off than those with lower education, and the same is true for younger people compared to their older counterparts, although the detailed patterns vary across countries.

Volume measures of the stock of human capital were developed for all fifteen countries included in the study. Temporal volume indices, including the volume of human capital per capita, were developed for twelve of the countries. These temporal volume indices show that human capital volume increased for all twelve countries during the observed period, but that in some countries, the volume of human capital in per capita terms fell. For countries that experienced increases in the volume of human capital per capita (Italy, Poland, Spain, and the United Kingdom), the positive contribution from education was larger than the negative effect from population aging. For countries that experienced broadly stable volumes of human capital per capita (Australia, Canada, France, and New Zealand), these two effects almost cancelled out each other. For countries that experienced decreases in the volume of human capital per capita (Israel, Korea, Norway, and the United States), the contribution from age exceeded that from education.

The chapter concludes that the lifetime income approach, by bringing together the influence of a broad range of factors (demography, mortality, and educational attainment, as well as labor market aspects) allows comparing the relative importance of these factors and drawing useful policy implications from the estimates.

"Developing a Framework for Decomposing Medical-Care
Expenditure Growth: Exploring Issues of Representativeness"
(Dunn, Liebman, and Shapiro)

Despite the importance of health-care spending to economic growth in the United States, there are many areas within this sector in which the understanding of expenditure growth is incomplete. This is especially true of the commercial health-care sector, where the primary data sources are often nonrandom convenience samples (i.e., available claims data from contributing insurers and employers). The goal of this chapter is to better understand issues related to using convenience samples to obtain nationally representative estimates of the various components of expenditure growth. The authors find similar qualitative findings by applying a multitude of strategies, including weighted and unweighted estimates. In general, they find that prevalence and service price are the key drivers of spending growth, with utilization per episode being flat. However, they also find that estimates that incorporate population weights tend to be more aligned with national benchmarks of expenditure and price growth.

"Experimental Measures of Output and Productivity in the
Canadian Hospital Sector, 2002 to 2010" (Gu and Morin)

The volume of output of the hospital sector in the existing Canadian System of National Accounts is measured by the volume of inputs. This approach to measuring output assumes that there is no productivity growth in the hospital sector.

The goal of this chapter is to develop an experimental index of output for the Canadian hospital sector that can be compared with inputs in order to measure the productivity performance of the hospital sector. It uses the approach outlined in the OECD Handbook on the measurement of the volume output of education and health services and constructs a direct output measure of the hospital sector in Canada. The volume index of the output of the hospital sector is estimated from aggregating the number of inpatient cases and outpatient cases using their cost share as weights. It also examines two potential sources of bias in this cost-weighted volume index: substitution bias and aggregation bias. The analysis reveals a large substitution bias in the volume index when inpatient treatment and outpatient treatment of the same medical disease or condition are aggregated using their respective unit costs as weights. The volume index of the hospital sector output corrected for substitution bias increased 4.3 percent annually during the 2002 to 2010 period. Labor productivity based on the direct output measure increased 2.6 percent annually over the period.

"Innovation Accounting" (Corrado and Hulten)

National accounting practice has traditionally linked inputs of capital and labor to the output of consumption, investment, net exports, and government with no explicit account being taken of the innovations in technology and the organization of production that led to a greater quantity of output from a given base of inputs (or improvements in the quality of the inputs and outputs). Corrado and Hulten have found in previous research that innovation investment, or "intangibles," has been the largest systematic driver of economic growth in business sector output over the last fifty years and that US businesses currently invest more in intangibles than they do in traditional fixed assets. Despite the importance of intangibles, most are excluded from national and financial accounting practice.

This chapter describes some of the steps involved in building a more comprehensive national innovation account as a satellite to the main national accounting framework, with a primary focus on business intangible capital and its measurement. The authors find that, when the asset boundary is extended to include investments in innovation, capital deepening becomes the dominant factor explaining the growth of labor productivity (measured as output per hour). Intangible capital deepening alone explains about 1/4 of the growth in output per hour since 1979 and nearly 1/3 since 2000. The importance of the quality dimension of intangible investment is also discussed. This issue has been largely absent from previous literature on intangibles.

Summary of Statistical Agency Panel Remarks

Steven Landefeld describes how the chapters contained in this volume highlight ways in which the BEA and other statistical agencies can address the urgent need to update and extend economic statistics in the face of daunting budgetary challenges in the United States and abroad. He suggests that through new source data methods and source data statistical agencies may be able to cut and improve at the same time. Examples drawn from the conference papers include: (a) collaborative work on the integration of micro- and macrodata in developing more timely, comprehensive, and consistent estimates of the distribution of income and spending; (b) coordination in the development and use of new financial data collections for both regulatory and statistical purposes; and (c) use of existing health insurance records to improve and expand existing measures of medical-care prices, output, and productivity.

Shirin Ahmed discusses efforts at the US Census Bureau to fill data gaps in services, intellectual property, offshore production, and capital spending. She also underlined the importance of sharing data between the BEA, BLS, and Census Bureau, while protecting the confidentiality of that data. Such sharing has the potential of significantly improving accuracy and consistency, and increasing efficiency. Finally, Shirin discussed the need to build upon and expand the collaboration between the BEA, BLS, and Census Bureau in the current budget environment. These updates and extensions to the US statistical infrastructure produced by the Census Bureau are key to efforts to update and extend the existing accounts.

John Ruser described work underway at the Bureau of Labor Statistics that will address a broad range of the challenges raised by the chapters included in this volume. These include efforts to improve the Consumer Expenditure Survey, update and expand data on medical-care prices and output, the development of integrated industry-level production accounts, and the addition of a well-being model to the American Time Use Survey.

Finally, Adelheid Burgi-Schmelz provided an international agency perspective by discussing efforts at the International Monetary Fund to play a leadership role in efforts to plug data gaps revealed by the financial crisis. She described the G-20 and the IMF Data Gaps Initiative and the collaborative work underway around the globe to five major systemic issues raised by the G-20 report.

References

BEA. 2012. "Economic and Statistical Analysis Budget Estimates, Fiscal Year 2012, as Presented to Congress." February.
OECD. 2012. "Reducing Income Inequality While Boosting Economic Growth: Can It Be Done?" In *Economic Policy Reforms 2012: Going for Growth*, 181–202. Paris: OECD Publishing.

1

Economic Measurement

Ben S. Bernanke

I appreciate the opportunity to speak at a conference with the important theme of economic measurement. In many spheres of human endeavor, from science to business to education to economic policy, good decisions depend on good measurement. More subtly, what we decide to measure, or are able to measure, has important effects on the choices we make, since it is natural to focus on those objectives for which we can best estimate and document the effects of our decisions. One great pioneer in this subject area, of course, is Simon Kuznets, who was awarded the Nobel Prize in 1971 for his work on economic measurement, including the national income accounts. Over the years many economists have built on his work to further improve our ability to quantify aspects of economic activity and thus to improve economic policymaking and our understanding of how the economy works. The remarkably broad and ambitious research program of this conference and the impressive expertise that has been assembled illustrate the continued vitality of this field. Evolving technologies that allow economists to gather new types of data and to manipulate millions of data points are just one factor among several that are likely to transform the field in coming years.

As we think about new directions for economic measurement, we might start by reminding ourselves of the purpose of economics. Textbooks describe economics as the study of the allocation of scarce resources. That definition may indeed be the "what," but it certainly is not the "why." The ultimate purpose of economics, of course, is to understand and promote

Ben S. Bernanke is the former chairman of the Board of Governors of the Federal Reserve System.

For acknowledgments, sources of research support, and disclosure of the author's material financial relationships, if any, please see http://www.nber.org/chapters/c12833.ack.

the enhancement of well-being. Economic measurement accordingly must encompass measures of well-being and its determinants.

In the tradition of national income accounting, economic policymakers have typically focused on variables such as income, wealth, and consumption. The Federal Reserve has a statutory mandate to foster maximum employment and price stability, which motivates our extensive efforts to monitor and forecast measures of employment and inflation. Substantial research and the development of data collection infrastructures have, over the years, greatly enhanced our ability to receive timely and accurate measures of those variables. Aggregate measures, such as gross domestic product and personal consumption expenditures, are useful for monitoring people's ability to meet basic material needs and for tracking cyclical and secular changes in the economy as a whole. Indeed, the experience of the recent financial crisis and the ensuing recession was strongly reflected in nearly all of these aggregate measures, indicating the severe economic stress felt by millions of people and hundreds of communities across the country.

But, as many of you will discuss this week, aggregate statistics can sometimes mask important information. For example, even though some key aggregate metrics—including consumer spending, disposable income, household net worth, and debt service payments—have moved in the direction of recovery, it is clear that many individuals and households continue to struggle with difficult economic and financial conditions. Exclusive attention to aggregate numbers is likely to paint an incomplete picture of what many individuals are experiencing. One implication is that we should increase the attention paid to microeconomic data, which better capture the diversity of experience across households and firms. Another implication, however, is that we should seek better and more-direct measurements of economic well-being, the ultimate objective of our policy decisions.

Although the field is still young, there have been interesting developments in the measurement of economic well-being. In a commencement address two years ago titled "The Economics of Happiness," I spoke about the concepts of happiness and life satisfaction from the perspective of economics and other social science research.[1] Following the growing literature, I define "happiness" as a short-term state of awareness that depends on a person's perceptions of one's immediate reality, as well as on immediate external circumstances and outcomes. By "life satisfaction" I mean a longer-term state of contentment and well-being that results from a person's experiences over time. Surveys and experimental studies have made progress in identifying the determinants of happiness and life satisfaction. Interestingly, income and wealth do contribute to self-reported happiness, but the relationship is more complex and context-dependent than standard utility theory would

1. See Bernanke (2010).

suggest.[2] Other important contributors to individuals' life satisfaction are a strong sense of support from belonging to a family or core group and a broader community, a sense of control over one's life, a feeling of confidence or optimism about the future, and an ability to adapt to changing circumstances. Indeed, an interesting finding in the literature is that the overwhelming majority of people in the United States and in many other countries report being very happy or pretty happy on a daily basis—a finding that researchers link to people's intrinsic abilities to adapt and find satisfaction in their lives even in very difficult circumstances.[3]

This line of research has generated alternative measures of well-being that are frequently survey-based and incorporate elements such as psychological wellness, the level of education, physical health and safety, community vitality and the strength of family and social ties, and time spent in leisure activities. These measures have begun to inform official statistics and have started to be discussed in policy debates. An interesting and unique case is the Kingdom of Bhutan, which abandoned tracking gross national product in 1972 in favor of its Gross National Happiness index based on a survey that incorporates these types of indicators. Taking the measurement of well-being in a cross-country framework, the Organisation for Economic Co-operation and Development (OECD), as part of its OECD Better Life Initiative, has created a "better life index" that allows a side-by-side comparison of countries according to various quality-of-life indicators that could, at least in principle, be followed over time.[4] Other somewhat-more-conventional economic indicators that bear on quality of life, and that accordingly might be developed and followed in more detail, include changes in the distribution of income, wealth, or consumption; the degree of upward mobility in material measures of well-being; indications of job security and confidence about future employment prospects; and households' liquidity buffers or other measures of their ability to absorb financial shocks. All of these indicators could be useful in measuring economic progress or setbacks as well as in explaining economic decision-making or projecting future economic outcomes.

Continued work on the measurement of economic well-being will likely lead to greater recognition by economists of the contributions of psychology—an area that has been explored by pioneers like 2002 Nobel laureate Daniel Kahneman. One topic on the frontier of economics and psychol-

---

2. Canonical models of economic decision-making presume individual maximization of "utility," or well- being. They tend to focus on the consumption of goods or services and assume that more consumption is preferred to less. For example, see Mas-Colell et al. (1995)

3. For examples drawn from Organisation for Economic Co-operation and Development countries from the mid-1970s to the mid-1990s, see Di Tella and MacCulloch (2008). For a survey of evidence on adaptability, see Frederick and Loewernstein (1999), pp. 302–29.

4. See Organisation for Economic Co-operation and Development (2011).

ogy is the neurological basis of human decisions, including decisionmaking under risk and uncertainty, intertemporal choice, and social decisionmaking.[5] Researchers are investigating behavioral tendencies in a variety of circumstances—for instance, by examining human responses to perceived inequality, losses, risk, and uncertainty; the need for autonomy; and the importance for well-being of social ties and community. For example, brain imaging research has documented differences in the brain regions that light up in response to losses and gains—a clear physical manifestation of the "loss aversion" documented in the earlier behavioral studies in economics and psychology.[6] Evolutionary psychologists suggest that humans experienced evolutionary benefits from brain developments that included aversion to loss and risk, and from instincts for cooperation that helped strengthen communities.

Measurement of well-being is an important direction, but just one of many new directions for economic measurement being explored in the field generally and at this conference in particular. I am glad to see scholars and practitioners continuing to push the frontiers of economic measurement with a broad perspective and with open minds. As Arthur Conan Doyle's immortal character Sherlock Holmes aptly put it, "It is a capital mistake to theorize before one has data."[7] As I said at the beginning, good economic analysis and policymaking depend on good measurement, and the work you are doing will accordingly yield significant benefits. I thank you for the opportunity to give these short remarks, and I wish you the best for a productive and stimulating conference.

References

Bernanke, Ben S. 2010. "The Economics of Happiness." Speech delivered at the University of South Carolina commencement ceremony, Columbia, South Carolina, May 8. www.federalreserve.gov/newsevents/speech/bernanke20100508a.htm.

Di Tella, Rafael, and Robert MacCulloch. 2008. "Gross National Happiness as an Answer to the Easterlin Paradox?" *Journal of Development Economics* 86(April): 22–42.

Doyle, Arthur Conan. ([1892] 1900). "A Scandal in Bohemia." In *The Adventures of Sherlock Holmes.* New York: Harper & Brothers. http://books.google.com/books?id=RxAJAAAAIAAJ&printsec=frontcover&dq=adventures+of+sherlock+holmes&source=bl&ots=tr8SxsUQhJ&sig=8d1uYsv-D13W5iU5T66tnzUFbOc&hl=en#v=onepage&q=It%20is%20a%20capital%20mistake%20to%20theorize%20before%20one%20has%20data&f=false.

Frederick, Shane, and George Loewenstein. 1999. "Hedonic Adaptation." In *Well-*

5. For example, see Loewenstein et al. (2008).
6. See Tom et al. (2007).
7. See Doyle ([1892] 1900), p. 7.

Being: The Foundations of Hedonic Psychology, edited by Daniel Kahneman, Ed Diener, and Norbert Schwarz. New York: Russell Sage Foundation.

Loewenstein, George, Scott Rick, and Jonathan D. Cohen. 2008. "Neuroeconomics." *Annual Review of Psychology* 59(January): 647–72.

Mas-Colell, Andrew, Michael D. Whinston, and Jerry R Green. 1995. *Microeconomic Theory*. New York: Oxford University Press.

Organisation for Economic Co-operation and Development. 2011. *How's Life? Measuring Well- Being*. Washington: OECD Publishing.

Tom, Sabrina M., Craig R. Fox, Christopher Trepel, and Russell A. Poldrack. 2007. "The Neural Basis of Loss Aversion in Decision-Making under Risk." *Science* 315(January): 515–8.

I

**Expanded Measures of Economic
Sustainability and Welfare:
Retrospect and Prospect**

2

Expanded Measurement of Economic Activity
Progress and Prospects

Katharine G. Abraham

Too much and too long, we seem to have surrendered community excellence and community values in the mere accumulation of material things. Our gross national product . . . if we should judge America by that—counts . . . ambulances to clear our highways of carnage. It counts special locks for our doors and the jails for those who break them. It counts the destruction of our redwoods and the loss of our natural wonder in chaotic sprawl. It counts napalm and the cost of a nuclear warhead, and armored cars for police who fight riots in our streets. It counts Whitman's rifle and Speck's knife, and the television programs which glorify violence in order to sell toys to our children.

Yet the gross national product does not allow for the health of our children, the quality of their education, or the joy of their play. It does not include the beauty of our poetry or the strength of our marriages; the intelligence of our public debate or the integrity of our public officials. It measures neither our wit nor our courage; neither our wisdom nor our learning; neither our compassion nor our devotion to our country; it measures everything, in short, except that which makes life worthwhile. And it tells us everything about America except why we are proud that we are Americans.

—Robert F. Kennedy (1968)

Katharine G. Abraham is professor of economics and survey methodology at the University of Maryland and a research associate of the National Bureau of Economic Research.

For acknowledgments, sources of research support, and disclosure of the author's material financial relationships, if any, please see http://www.nber.org/chapters/c12838.ack.

During the Great Depression of the 1930s, the absence of systematic information on economic activity was a significant impediment to the development of sound economic policy. Recognition of policymakers' critical need for better information about current economic conditions gave impetus to work then underway in the United States to develop the nascent National Income and Product Accounts (NIPAs). The NIPAs, produced by the Bureau of Economic Analysis (BEA), have come to be recognized as a signature accomplishment. In the words of then secretary of commerce William Daley, speaking in December 1999 about the work of the Department of Commerce during the twentieth century, "As we searched for our greatest achievement, something . . . that had the greatest impact on America, it was the invention of the national economic accounts" (Daley 1999).

The NIPAs were designed from the start to serve the needs of policymakers for current information on economic conditions and continue to be critical in meeting those needs. While the importance of the NIPAs is widely recognized, the limitations inherent in their design also are well known. Simon Kuznets, the person most responsible for the early work to develop the NIPAs, himself noted that, "the welfare of a nation can scarcely be inferred from a measurement of national income as defined [by the GDP]" (Kuznets 1934). This does not imply that the existing accounts lack value or should be replaced. The existing accounts, however, may be seen as providing a framework on which a set of expanded accounts designed to meet additional needs can be built.

2.1   Building on the Existing Economic Accounts

In an influential paper, Nordhaus and Tobin (1972) discussed the limitations of the gross domestic product (GDP) as a welfare measure. They went on to suggest the rough outlines of an alternative measure that, among other things, would treat certain expenditures such as spending on police or defense as intermediate rather than final outputs (necessary for the production of output but not of value in and of themselves) and account for the services of household labor and consumer durables. Pioneering work by Kendrick (1976) and Eisner (1985, 1988, 1989) proposed expanded accounts that incorporated investments in human as well as physical capital. Interest in expanded economic accounting has been reinvigorated over the past decade, with two major reports on the subject issued in 2005 and 2009, respectively.

The first of these reports, a 2005 National Research Council volume titled *Beyond the Market*, laid out a framework for a set of satellite accounts for home production, education, health, government and the nonprofit sector, and the environment that would complement the existing NIPAs. Key recommendations concerning the development of these satellite accounts included: (a) measuring the value of outputs separately from the value of inputs (including nonmarket time); (b) using monetary rather than physical metrics; and (c) assigning marginal valuations wherever possible based on the outcomes of market activities (Abraham and Mackie 2005, 2006).

The 2009 report of the Stiglitz-Sen-Fitoussi Commission—more formally, the "Commission on the Measurement of Economic Performance and Social Progress"—was broader in scope. A portion of this report was focused on what its authors termed classical GDP issues—broadening measures of household activity, improving measures of government services, and examining income, consumption, and wealth as well as production. The report also stressed the importance of considering distribution as well as average or aggregate levels, for example, looking at the median in addition to the mean of family income. In addition, however, it discussed measures of the quality of life and of the sustainability of economic development and environmental health. With respect to the quality of life, the Stiglitz-Sen-Fitoussi Commission's report encouraged the measurement of subjective well-being together with consideration of objective factors such as education, health, time use, political voice, social connections, and insecurity that affect subjective well-being. With respect to sustainability, it argued for the development of a dashboard that focused on the "stocks" that underpin well-being, with separate measures for economic and environmental sustainability (Stiglitz, Sen, and Fitoussi 2009).

As these reports suggest, there are multiple possible objectives for an expanded set of economic accounts. First, expanded accounts might provide more complete measures of investment in capital—broadly speaking, any stock that contributes to the nation's future productive capacity. Traditional measures of investment reflected spending only on physical plant and equipment. In a knowledge economy, however, business investment in intangible capital has become increasingly important. Taking an even broader perspective, households may make substantial investments in intangible human capital that are not captured as such in the existing accounts. Second, expanded accounts could provide more accurate measures of output and productivity in key sectors such as education, health, and government. Third, most closely in the spirit of the remarks by Robert Kennedy quoted at the beginning of this chapter, expanded accounts could contribute to the assessment of trends in societal welfare or well-being. Information on how the output of a society is distributed could be an important part of this. Finally, something I will not address here but that undoubtedly merits further exploration, an appropriately structured set of expanded accounts could contribute to an assessment of sustainability, especially environmental sustainability.

2.2   Accounting for Investment in Education

Even within the existing NIPAs, as the importance of intangible capital has grown, the treatment of investment in such capital has evolved. Investment in software was incorporated in the NIPAs in 1999 and investment in research and development in 2013 (Aizcorbe, Moylan, and Robbins 2009; Bureau of Economic Analysis 2013). In principle, other forms of business investment in intangibles, such as firm-specific human capital or organizational capital associated with the adoption of productivity-enhancing business practices, also could be incorporated (see, for example, Corrado, Hulten, and Sichel 2005, 2006).

The fact that the existing accounts are structured to reflect only business and government investment would make it more difficult to incorporate the investments in human capital made by members of households. Perhaps more importantly, the data needed to measure household investments generally are not available in "real time" or at quarterly frequencies. In any case, information about household investment arguably is important primarily for understanding long-term trends rather than short-term fluctuations in output and productivity, meaning that quarterly accounting for such investment would serve little value. Satellite accounts for investments in human capital, and in particular for investments in education and health, offer a possible path forward.

Table 2.1, adapted from a similar table that appeared in *Beyond the Market*, shows the potential elements of a double-entry satellite account for education. The costs of investing in education are shown on the left-hand side of the table; these include not only items whose acquisition involves market transactions and whose costs thus should already be reflected in the NIPAs, such as the paid labor of teachers and support staff, the cost of books and other materials, and expenditures on school buildings, computers, and other equipment (all shown in normal font), but also the unpaid time of students, their parents, and school volunteers (shown in italics). The outputs associated with investments in education are shown on the right-hand side; these

Table 2.1   **Elements of a double-entry education satellite account**

Input	Output
Paid labor	Educated individuals
Teachers	Higher workplace productivity
Support staff	*Higher nonmarket productivity*
Volunteer labor	*Intangibles: Better informed citizens,*
Students' and parents' time	*improved individual and societal well-*
Materials: Books and other	*being*
Fixed capital: School buildings and other	
structures, equipment, and computer	
software	
Social capital	

Source: Adapted from Abraham and Mackie (2005).

include not only the higher market productivity of more educated workers, but also the higher *nonmarket* productivity of more educated individuals together with a broader set of intangible benefits associated with having a more educated citizenry.

The two sides of table 2.1 correspond to the alternative approaches that have been taken in the literature for measuring the value of educational investments. One strand of this literature, exemplified by Schultz (1961), Kendrick (1976), and Eisner (1985, 1988, 1989), has quantified investment in education based on the costs of the associated inputs, including both market and nonmarket time. The other strand in the literature, tracing back to Weisbrod (1961) and developed more fully by Jorgenson and Fraumeni (1989, 1992a, 1992b), measures the investment in education based on the estimated present value of the increment to earnings that is associated with additional education, presumed to reflect the higher productivity of more educated workers. The two approaches yield very different answers: estimates of the present value of the increments to earnings attributable to education generally are *much* larger than estimates of the cost of providing that education. These estimates can be reconciled in an accounting sense by treating the excess of returns over costs as "profits" accruing to the household sector, but this is not entirely satisfactory.

Over the last five years, the Organisation for Economic Co-operation and Development (OECD) has begun a major project to measure national investments in human capital. The project seeks in its first phase to build Jorgenson-Fraumeni-type estimates of the value of investment in education and the resulting stock of human capital across many of the OECD member countries (Liu 2011). Data inputs to the project include labor force surveys and country-specific mortality tables that provide information on school enrollment rates by age, gender, and previous educational attainment up to age forty; employment rates and annual earnings by age, gender, and educational attainment; and survival rates by age and gender. The project is focused on the returns to education realized in work by persons age sixteen to sixty-four; whereas nonmarket returns (higher productivity of more educated persons in nonmarket activities) are a large part of the returns to education estimated in Jorgenson and Fraumeni's work, the OECD estimates do not incorporate nonmarket returns. Early results show that, even restricting attention to market returns, the estimated value of the stock of educational human capital generally is much larger than the value of traditional physical capital in those same countries.

Given the early stage of the OECD initiative, there are, not surprisingly, still a number of outstanding issues concerning the resulting estimates to be resolved (see Abraham [2010] for further discussion of many of these issues). As in the Jorgenson-Fraumeni papers, the OECD estimates of how educational attainment affects earnings begin with data for a synthetic cohort of individuals whose current earnings are used to infer the life-cycle pattern of earnings for people with different amounts of education. To the extent that the relative earnings of those with different amounts of education vary over time due to changes in demand conditions or that the quality of education has changed, however, using synthetic cohort data to proxy for expected future earnings could be misleading. It is also possible that those with higher education tend to benefit more from other sorts of investment in human capital—early childhood investments, investments in on-the-job training, or investments in health—and that this confounds the estimates of the return to education. Even leaving these potential issues aside, estimates of the present value of the anticipated returns to education are sensitive to assumptions about future earnings growth, the discount rate, and the effect of failing to complete a year of schooling on expected educational attainment. Given the nature of the data on which they are based, the estimates produced to date have been relatively aggregated; there are many purposes for which estimates disaggregated by level and type of schooling would be of value. Finally, estimates of investment in education based on anticipated future earnings ultimately should be reconciled with estimates based on the costs of obtaining that education. These many challenges notwithstanding, the OECD project is an important step forward.

The growing interest within the statistical community in the measurement of investment in education has been paralleled by a growing interest among policy officials in better understanding what we are spending on education and what we are getting for that money. All levels of education, including early childhood and K–12 education, have attracted policymakers' attention, but for tractability I will restrict my attention here to higher education policy. As someone with ties to both the policy world and the data world, I am struck by the strong potential linkages between policymakers' interest in college affordability and the college value proposition on the one hand, and the work already underway within the statistical community to develop an educational satellite account on the other.

By way of background, average published tuition and fees at public US four-year colleges and universities—the schools that most students who pursue a bachelor's degree attend—have grown rapidly over the past decade, increasing 5.2 percent per year in real terms between 2002/3 and 2012/13, from \$5,210 per year in 2002/3 to an estimated \$8,660 per year in 2012/13, an increase of \$3,450 (2012 dollars, exclusive of room and board) (College Board 2012). Thanks in large part to growth in federal educational assistance in the form of Pell grants and the American Opportunity Tax Credit (AOTC), the net prices actually paid by students have grown much less than sticker prices over this period. Pell grant expenditures totaled an estimated \$35.6 billion in 2010/11, with awards reaching about 9.3 million undergraduates, or roughly half of the student population, compared to \$14.7 billion in Pell grants and 5.5 million students assisted in 2007/8 (US Department of the Treasury and US Department of Education 2012). The AOTC was introduced in 2009; compared to the Hope Credit it replaced, the AOTC can be claimed for four years rather than just two years, is partially refundable rather than entirely nonrefundable, and has higher family income limits. In 2010, the latest year for which data are available, the combined value to American households of federal education tax credits totaled $24.1 billion, versus $8.2 billion in 2008 just prior to the advent of the AOTC (both in 2012 dollars) (US Department of the Treasury 2012). After adjusting for grants (from all sources) and tax credits, average net tuition at public four-year colleges and universities grew from $1,490 in 2002/3 to $2,910 in 2012/13 (both in 2012 dollars), an increase of $1,420, less than half as large as the $3,450 increase in sticker prices at the same schools noted above (College Board 2012).

While federal financial aid for education has played a critical role in helping to keep college affordable, future increases in the costs of higher education are unlikely to be offset by further growth in federal financial assistance. College graduates continue to earn substantially more than those with lower levels of education and college enrollments have remained high, but the large amounts of both public and private money flowing into higher education have lead to increasing discussion in the policy sphere of whether this money is being well spent. As a result, there is growing interest in tracking the labor market outcomes of those who attend and graduate from institutions of higher education.

It turns out that the information needed to construct the higher education component of an education satellite account is very similar to the information that policymakers are now seeking in order to evaluate the performance of the higher education sector as a whole and, at a more disaggregated level, the performance of different types of schools and even the performance of individual higher education institutions and programs. This confluence of interests creates both new opportunities and new urgency for work to develop an education satellite account.

A major barrier to satisfying both objectives—the statistical analysts' interest in developing an education satellite account and the policymakers' interest in holding the educational sector accountable for the labor market success of its students—has been the lack of data that allow student outcomes to be monitored, but this is beginning to change. Starting in 2005, the Department of Education has awarded several rounds of grants to states for work to develop student-level longitudinal education data systems. When fully realized, these longitudinal data systems will allow students to be tracked from the K–12 grades through the higher education institutions they may attend. Complementing the Department of Education's activities, the Department of Labor has funded grants to states through its Workforce Data Quality Initiative to support improvements in the linkages between education and employment in existing longitudinal data systems, as well as improvements to the longitudinal data systems that track individuals through their working years.

More directly related to the desire to hold institutions of higher education accountable for their performance, earlier this year the Department of Education released the initial version of a College Scorecard that is intended to make it easier for students and their families to make comparisons across the different institutions they may be considering. The version of the scorecard released in February includes measures of the annual cost of attendance, the graduation rate, the median debt incurred by students who attend the institution, and the loan default rate among student borrowers at the school. Once student-level information about those who attend a particular institution can be linked to administrative information about their employment and earnings in the years following graduation, a measure of the average earnings of former undergraduates will be added to the scorecard. The measure currently planned for the scorecards refers to relatively short-term earnings outcomes, but longer-term earnings outcome measures also could, in principle, be produced.

These developments in the policy sphere can be expected to lead to improvements in the data available to those working to develop satellite accounts for education. The state longitudinal data systems, for example, may help analysts to identify the return to higher education separately from the return to earlier school experiences. Data that relate labor market outcomes to the institution attended or even the course of study pursued should be useful for producing more disaggregated estimates of the return to education. Further, the intense policy interest in understanding what we are getting from our investments in higher education implies that there is likely to be an appetite for aggregated statistical measures of the sort that would be embodied in a satellite account for education.

2.3   Accounting for Investment in Health

Table 2.2, adapted from a similar table that appeared in *Beyond the Market*, shows the potential elements of a double-entry health satellite account. The costs of investing in health are shown on the left-hand side of the table; these include not only items whose costs should already be reflected on the product side of the NIPAs, such as payments to health-care providers (shown in normal font), but also items that are not reflected in the NIPAs, such as the value of the time that individuals invest in their own health and the time of unpaid family caregivers (shown in italics). On the output side, better health is associated not only with higher market productivity and earnings, but also with the enjoyment of longer lives and a higher quality of life made possible by reduced mortality and morbidity.

Table 2.2   Elements of a double-entry health satellite account

Input	Output
Medical care	*Measures of health status, and valuations of*
Market labor/capital	*changes where possible*
Volunteer labor	Income from being healthier
Time invested in individual's own health, time	
of family caregivers	
Other consumption items	
Research and development	
Quality of environment	

Source: Adapted from Abraham and Mackie (2005).

Efforts to develop a satellite account for health have begun in recent years. If successful, these efforts will help to fill the information gaps that preclude a comprehensive assessment of output and productivity in the health-care sector and of that sector's contribution to the overall economy. A major limitation of existing data for the purpose of feeding a health satellite account is that both the NIPA data on health-care expenditures and the Bureau of Labor Statistics (BLS) data on medical prices are organized by type of product or service (e.g., pharmaceuticals, other medical products, physical services, paramedical services, or hospital services) rather than by disease. Developing an understanding of the efficiency and effectiveness of health care, however, requires data that are organized by disease. More specifically, development of a health-care satellite account will require information about the resources used to treat diseases and the outcomes achieved for people with those diseases.

While much remains to be done, the federal statistical agencies have made progress over the past five years toward developing these data. Research at the BEA has focused on developing disease-based measures of household medical care expenditure (Aizcorbe et al. 2012). Research at the BLS has focused on the development of disease based price indexes that begin to account for shifts in treatment patterns (Bradley et al. 2010). The BLS price indexes will be of value to the BEA for breaking out the contributions of price and quantity to the growth of overall medical care expenditures.

As work to develop disease-based measures of medical spending and outcomes has progressed, some of the decisions and challenges that will need to be confronted to develop such data have become more apparent (National Research Council 2010; Aizcorbe et al. 2012). A necessary first step will be to agree upon a scheme for categorizing diseases. A major question here will be the appropriate level of specificity to use in organizing the data. Second, better and more comprehensive sources of data on health spending will need to be developed. Much of the work done to date in this area has made use of the Medical Expenditure Panel Survey (MEPS), which has a nationally representative sample but is too small to represent unusual conditions. Perhaps not surprisingly, given the large share of health-care spending that occurs among those at the end of life, the MEPS also appears to underrepresent the highest spending individuals. Third, methods to allocate spending across diseases will need to be developed. Options that have been proposed include the encounter-based approach; the episode-based approach; and the person-based approach. As described by Aizcorbe et al. (2012), the encounter-based approach is relatively easy to implement, but does not deal well with co-morbidities and leaves out spending with no diagnosis code. The episode-based approach uses a natural-seeming unit of observation, but defining what constitutes a health-care episode can be difficult, and comorbidities and spending without a diagnosis code again are problematic. Aizcorbe et al. (2012) suggest that, while it is more complex, the person-based approach, in which regression analysis is used to relate health spending by an individual to that individual's diagnoses, may be the most promising. Finally, in order to adjust appropriately for changes in the quality of treatment, evidence on treatment effectiveness and agreed-upon metrics for valuing improvements in health outcomes will need to be developed.

As with education, efforts by economic statisticians to develop a health satellite account have been paralleled by significant and growing policy interest in health-care spending and productivity. Health-care spending has grown much faster than overall GDP and, as a result, health care has represented an ever-growing fraction of total national output. There is enormous policy interest in what is driving per capita health-care costs—improvements in care versus increases in the price of care—and in finding ways to slow the growth of those costs without adversely affecting the quality of care. Health-care experts have suggested a variety of possible means of "bending the cost curve," such as taking steps to reduce administrative overhead; increasing the availability of preventive care; redesigning payment schemes to provide doctors and hospitals with stronger incentives to control costs while maintaining the quality of care; and providing better information to patients and their providers on best-treatment practices to inform their health-care decisions. Much research is needed, however, to determine how well these strategies work and how they can be implemented most effectively.

Similar to the situation with respect to education, a major barrier to satisfying both the statistical analysts' interest in developing a health satellite account and the policymakers' interest in achieving better health outcomes at the lowest possible cost has been the lack of comprehensive data that allow health spending to be linked to health outcomes. Individual research teams have done interesting work based on insurance claims records; Cutler et al. (2001), for example, used Medicare claims data to study changes in the effectiveness of the treatment of heart attack patients over time, and Berndt,

Busch, and Frank (2001) used data on claims obtained from four large self-insured employers to examine changes over time in the treatment of depression. Better answers to the questions policymakers are asking about health care, however, will require more comprehensive data.

In this regard, efforts currently underway to develop health-care claims databases that can be used for analytic purposes are an exciting development. A number of individual states have passed legislation to establish state-specific All-Payer Claims Databases that can be used to provide cost information to consumers, inform the development of insurance products, determine provider competitiveness, and serve other purposes, potentially including research purposes (Miller et al. 2010). The Health Care Cost Institute (HCCI), a nonprofit organization that has as one of its primary objectives to foster a better understanding of the drivers of health-care costs, is developing a national claims database that is intended to be broadly accessible to bona fide researchers who need detailed data on health-care spending for their work. Researcher access to the HCCI data repository will take place under controlled conditions that protect the confidentiality of individual patients. The database, rolled out in May 2012, includes more than five billion claims records from four large insurers that, taken together, provide health insurance coverage for thirty-three million people, and there are plans to add claims records from additional insurers as well as Medicaid claims records (Kliff 2012). The HCCI repository could, in time, provide reasonably comprehensive coverage of the health-care sector, especially if, as expected, the implementation of the Affordable Care Act leads to a decline in the number of uninsured patients whose interactions with the health-care sector do not leave a trail of insurance claims (and who thus are not represented in insurance claims databases).

Another relevant development is the funding provided under the Affordable Care Act for comparative effectiveness research. Under the terms of the act, the agenda for this research is to be set by the Patient-Centered Outcomes Research Institute after broad public consultation. The first such review was recently completed. The language of the act states that estimates of cost-effectiveness will not be used "as a threshold to determine coverage, reimbursement, or incentive payments" under Medicare, but it is to be hoped that better information on what works and what does not will help to move spending toward more effective treatments over time.

These developments in the policy sphere can be expected to improve the information available to those working to develop health satellite accounts. Insurance claims data, such as those contained in the repository being developed by the HCCI, can help with allocating spending by disease category and also with tracking the experiences of individuals who may have multiple interactions with the health-care system. Better information about the effectiveness of alternative treatments can help with making appropriate adjustments for changes in the quality of care over time. Further, as with education, the intense policy interest in understanding what we are getting from our investments in health care imply that there is likely to be an appetite for aggregate measures of the sort that would be embodied in a satellite account for health.

2.4   Improving the Measurement of Government Output

While this chapter has been focused primarily on the development of satellite accounts for education and health, there may be broader synergies between economic accountants and policymakers with regard to the measurement of government activity. The existing NIPAs measure government output based on the cost of the inputs (largely labor) that it employs. By construction, a measure based on the assumption that the output of the government sector grows in line with the labor it employs will show no improvement in labor productivity. Because they are based on an embedded assumption about productivity growth, such measures obviously cannot serve the growing policy interest in assessing and improving the efficiency of the government sector.

In the European Union, Eurostat has called for national statistical agencies to develop direct measures of the volume of government services provided to individuals (European Commission 2001). An influential report prepared for the Office of National Statistics in the United Kingdom (Atkinson 2005) offers one set of more specific guidelines for how such measures might be developed. Efforts to date in several countries have concentrated on education and health, using measures such as the number of students served and indexes of the number of health-care procedures performed. There also has been some work on public safety and social services, using measures such as the number of prisoner nights, the number of fires attended, and the number of adults and children in care.

For someone charged with managing the resources of a government department in order to provide a particular set of services, using available resources more efficiently in order to provide a larger volume of services is a positive accomplishment. Viewed from that perspective, volume measures of the sort recommended by Eurostat and in the Atkinson report make a great deal of sense. For a policymaker who is concerned more broadly with how well the government is doing its job, however, these seem like the wrong sort of metrics on which to focus. Ultimately, assessments of the value of government services should be based on outcomes rather than on outputs. Questions of interest might include, for example, whether public schooling raises students' subsequent earnings; whether the provision of publicly supported health services leads to longer lives and better health; and whether the activities of the criminal justice system are helping to lower the crime rate. The measurement of outcomes is, of course, a considerably more difficult task than the measurement of the sort of outputs envisioned by the Eurostat guidance and in the Atkinson report.

Consider as an illustrative example the activities of an agency charged with protecting the safety of workers on the job. A first step for the agency is to develop an appropriate set of workplace regulations. Given those regulations, the agency can use its resources in a number of different ways—offering compliance assistance to firms subject to its regulations; conducting inspections to identify violations of the regulations; assessing fines or other penalties against those found to be in violation of the regulations; or engaging in broader public communications about the regulations and enforcement actions undertaken by the agency, designed to affect the behavior of a larger number of firms. The number of workplace inspections that the agency carries out would be a natural volume measure of this agency's activities, but conducting more inspections will not necessarily lead to better outcomes. The impact of an inspection program will depend, for example, on how it is targeted. Further, even if inspections tend to lower injury and illness rates at the workplaces that are inspected, at the margin there may be other things the agency could do with its resources that would have a larger impact, for example, engaging in broader employer outreach and education efforts. There is at present relatively little research evidence available to guide the resource allocation decisions this enforcement agency must make, but it seems clear that simply counting the number of inspections the agency performs—or even tracking some weighted average of the counts of all of the agency's various activities—could be a very misleading indicator of the value of its activities. As a conceptual matter, measures of value added and productivity for government based on outcomes rather than outputs—in this case, how the agency's activities have affected the incidence of occupational injuries and illnesses in the economy as a whole—seem clearly to be a more legitimate basis on which to evaluate the government's performance.

Here, too, the measurement challenges that confront the economic statistician overlap significantly with the concerns of policymakers. In an era of tightening government budgets, making efficient use of available resources is becoming increasingly important to government managers. Doing this well requires good evidence on what works and what does not work to produce desired outcomes. In May of 2012, Jeff Zeints, the acting director of the Office of Management and Budget (OMB), issued guidance to federal agencies calling for them to document how they use evidence to allocate their resources and to demonstrate a commitment to expanding the use of evidence in carrying out their operations. Specific suggestions mentioned in the guidance memorandum included seeking opportunities for low-cost evaluations using administrative data; expanding evaluation efforts within existing programs; using comparative cost-effectiveness data to allocate resources; tying grant awards to evidence; using evidence to inform the enforcement of criminal, environmental, and workplace safety laws; and appointing a high-level official to strengthen the agency's evaluation capacity. The message that federal agencies increasingly will be expected to use evidence to improve the efficiency and effectiveness of their operations was reinforced in a July 2013 guidance memorandum cosigned by OMB director Sylvia Burwell. These are powerful documents—because OMB is responsible for developing and overseeing the president's budget, its stated view on how agencies should be allocating their resources carries great weight. The goal of this nascent initiative is to develop and apply a stronger body of evidence about the impacts of the full range of government activities.

As with education and health, then, there is hope for complementarities between the policymakers' interest in improving the functioning of government and the statistical analysts' interest in producing better measures of government output. Further, more meaningful measures of government output are apt to be of considerable interest to government policymakers and managers.

2.5   What about Measures of Well-Being?

My focus thus far has been on steps that could be taken to improve the measurement of resource utilization and production in key sectors that are characterized poorly or incompletely in the current accounts. Such improvements would be of great value to policymakers, but they would not fully address the somewhat separate interest that has been expressed in measuring the well-being of individuals in our society.

Producing better information about distributions as well as totals would be one path toward satisfying the interest in measures of well-being. Even in an economy that is growing, there is no guarantee that everyone in the economy or even the typical person in the economy will experience an improvement in material welfare. In the United States, for example, the distribution of income has become substantially more unequal since the mid-1970s, with a disproportionate share of the growth in total income flowing to those at the very top of the income distribution (see, for example, Piketty and Saez [2003] and subsequent updates to their estimates). Better information on the distribution of income, consumption, and wealth that sheds light on the experience of the typical member of society would be a natural complement to the existing aggregates reported in the National Income and Product Accounts. The announcement by the Bureau of Economic Analysis of long-term plans to work toward the development of such measures is welcome news and it is to be hoped that similar efforts underway in other countries also will bear fruit.

Finding a way to measure well-being directly is another path that has attracted considerable interest. Several alternative approaches to measuring well-being have been proposed (Smith [2011] provides a useful review). First, the existing GDP measure can be adjusted so that it comes closer to capturing the output that one would expect to contribute to well-being; for example, the value of household production could be added to the conventional estimate of GDP and defensive expenditures could be subtracted. Second, composite indicators that weight measures for several individual dimensions of interest can be constructed; examples of this approach include the United Nations Human Development Index and the Genuine Progress Indicator. As a variant on this approach, indicator dashboards can be developed that leave the weighting of the various dimensions to the user of the data; the OECD Better Life Initiative, which provides measures for a range of domains, together with a tool that allows data users to construct their own aggregate measure, is a nice example. Development of aggregate measures of subjective well-being is a third approach. There is a growing literature about how best to do this, whether using global measures of life satisfaction, measures of affect at particular points in time, or time accounts designed to track the hours spent in pleasant or unpleasant activities, as proposed by Krueger (2009).

It is easy to see in principle how information about subjective well-being could be useful for policy evaluation. For example, in deciding whether it is worthwhile to build a new bridge, it might be important to know how the bridge would affect the amount of time drivers spend in traffic as opposed to doing other more enjoyable things. There has been considerable discussion in the United Kingdom about using subjective measures for policy assessment and the Office for National Statistics (ONS) has made notable investments in this approach. It remains unclear, however, whether the development of subjective measures—and especially the development of broad aggregate measures of well-being—will in fact have the desired effect of changing the way that policy officials make their decisions.

The experience of the ONS with developing an experimental satellite account for household production in the early twenty-first century may be illuminating. The impetus for the development of this account was the recognition that there is a great deal of nonmarketed production that is omitted from the conventional economic accounts. The ONS put a fair amount of work into developing estimates of the value of nonmarketed output produced by households, and the estimates showed the value of household production to be sizable as compared to conventionally measured GDP (see Holloway, Short, and Tamplin [2002] for details). Despite the high quality of the work to produce the experimental account, however, there turned out to be no real demand for the estimates, and the exercise has not been repeated.

The jury is still out, I think, on whether the aggregate measures of well-being currently being developed by various statistical agencies will fare better. Like the ONS household production estimates, the aggregate well-being measures are intellectually interesting, but it is less clear how they might be used to guide day-to-day policy decisions.

2.6 Conclusion

Our existing economic accounts have many users, but exist primarily to serve the public policy process. Similarly, I would argue, the opportunities and potential rewards for the development of expanded economic accounts are greatest in those spheres where there is a compelling public policy interest in the information that would be produced. There are good arguments, I believe, for the development of satellite accounts for education and for health. Policymakers care a great deal about the magnitude of our investments in these forms of human capital and about the performance of the education and health sectors. Further, data being developed to meet immediate policy needs should help to inform the construction of such satellite accounts. The same may be true with respect to improved measurement of government more generally. A key test for the broader measures of welfare and well-being that have received so much discussion in recent years will be whether they prove to be not only intellectually interesting but also useful for policy purposes.

References

Abraham, Katharine G. 2010. "Accounting for Investments in Human Capital." *Survey of Current Business* June:42–53.
Abraham, Katharine G., and Christopher Mackie, eds. 2005. *Beyond the Market: Designing Nonmarket Accounts for the United States.* Washington, DC: National Academies Press.
———. 2006. "A Framework for Nonmarket Accounting." In *A New Architecture for the US National Accounts*, Studies in Income and Wealth, vol. 66, edited by Dale W. Jorgenson, J. Steven Landefeld, and William D. Nordhaus, 161–92. Chicago: University of Chicago Press.
Aizcorbe, Ana M., Eli B. Liebman, David M. Cutler, and Allison B. Rosen. 2012. "Household Consumption Expenditures for Medical Care: An Alternative Presentation." *Survey of Current Business* 92 (6): 34–48.
Aizcorbe, Ana M., Carol E. Moylan, and Carol A. Robbins. 2009. "Toward Better Measurement of Innovation and Intangibles." *Survey of Current Business* 89 (1): 10–23.
Atkinson, Tony. 2005. "Measurement of Government Output and Productivity for the National Accounts." In *Atkinson Review: Final Report.* United Kingdom: Palgrave Macmillian.
Berndt, Ernst R., Susan H. Busch, and Richard G. Frank. 2001. "Treatment Price Indexes for Acute Phase Major Depression." In *Medical Care Output and Productivity*, edited by David M. Cutler and Ernst R. Berndt, 463–508. Chicago: University of Chicago Press.
Bradley, Ralph, Elaine Cardenas, Daniel H. Ginsburg, Lyubov Rozental, and Frankie Velez. 2010. "Producing Disease-Based Price Indexes." *Monthly Labor Review* 133 (February): 20–8.

Bureau of Economic Analysis. 2013. "Preview of the 2013 Comprehensive Revision of the National Income and Product Accounts: Changes in Definitions and Presentations." *Survey of Current Business* 93 (3): 13–39.

College Board. 2012. *Trends in College Pricing.* College Board Advocacy and Policy Center, Trends in Higher Education Series. http://trends.collegeboard.org/college -pricing.

Corrado, Carol, Charles Hulten, and Daniel Sichel. 2005. "Measuring Capital and Technology: An Expanded Framework." In *Measuring Capital in the New Economy,* Studies in Income and Wealth, vol. 65, edited by C. Corrado, J. Haltiwanger, and D. Sichel, 11–46. Chicago: University of Chicago Press.

———. 2006. "Intangible Capital and Economic Growth." NBER Working Paper no. 11948, Cambridge, MA.

Cutler, David M., Mark B. McClellan, Joseph P. Newhouse, and Dahlia K. Remler. 2001. "Pricing Heart Attack Treatments." In *Medical Care Output and Productivity,* edited by David M. Cutler and Ernst R. Berndt, 306–62. Chicago: University of Chicago Press.

Daley, William M. 1999. "Press Conference Announcing the Commerce Department's Achievements of the Century." Secretary, US Department of Commerce. December 7.

Eisner, Robert. 1985. "The Total Incomes System of Accounts." *Survey of Current Business* 65 (1): 24–48.

———. 1988. "Extended Accounts for National Income and Product." *Journal of Economic Literature* 26 (2): 1611–94.

———. 1989. *The Total Incomes System of Accounts.* Chicago: University of Chicago Press.

European Commission. 2001. *Handbook on Price and Volume Measures in National Accounts.* http://epp.eurostat.ec.europa.eu/portal/page/portal/product_details /publication?p_product_code=KS-41-01-543.

Holloway, Sue, Sandra Short, and Sarah Tamplin. 2002. *Household Satellite Account (Experimental) Methodology.* London: UK Office for National Statistics.

Jorgenson, Dale W., and Barbara M. Fraumeni. 1989. "The Accumulation of Human and Nonhuman Capital." In *The Measurement of Saving, Investment, and Wealth,* edited by Robert E. Lipsey and Helen Stone Tice, 227–81. Chicago: University of Chicago Press.

———. 1992a. "Investment in Education and US Economic Growth." *Scandinavian Journal of Economics* 94 (supplement): S51–S70.

———. 1992b. "The Output of the Education Sector." In *Output Measurement in the Service Sectors,* edited by Zvi Griliches, 303 38. Chicago: University of Chicago Press.

Kendrick, John W. 1976. *The Formation and Stocks of Total Capital.* New York: Columbia University Press.

Kennedy, Robert F. 1968. "Remarks of Robert F. Kennedy at the University of Kansas." University of Kansas, March 18. http://www.jfklibrary.org/Research/Research -Aids/Ready-Reference/RFK-Speeches/Remarks-of-Robert-F-Kennedy-at-the -University-of-Kansas-March-18-1968.aspx.

Kliff, Sarah. 2012. "What Could Revolutionize Health Care? This Database." *Washington Post,* May 21.

Krueger, Alan B., ed. 2009. *Measuring the Subjective Well-Being of Nations: National Accounts of Time Use and Well-Being.* Chicago: University of Chicago Press.

Kuznets, S. 1934. *National Income 1929–1932.* Senate Document No. 124, 73rd Congress, 2nd Session. Washington, DC: US Government Printing Office.

Liu, Gang. 2011. "Measuring the Stock of Human Capital for Comparative Analysis: An Application of the Lifetime Income Approach to Selected Countries." Working Paper no. 41, Statistics Directorate, Organisation for Economic Co-operation and Development.

Miller, Patrick B., Denise Love, Emily Sullivan, Jo Porter, and Amy Costello. 2010. "All-Payer Claims Databases: An Overview for Policymakers." Academy Health and Robert Wood Johnson Foundation. May.

National Research Council. 2010. *Accounting for Health and Health Care: Approaches to Measuring the Sources and Costs of Their Improvement,* Washington, DC: National Academies Press.

Nordhaus, W., and J. Tobin. 1972. "Is Growth Obsolete?" In *Economic Research: Retrospect and Prospect, Volume 5, Economic Growth,* 1–80. New York: Columbia University Press.

Piketty, Thomas, and Emmanuel Saez. 2003. "Income Inequality in the United States, 1913–1998." *Quarterly Journal of Economics* 118 (1): 1–39.

Schultz, Theodore W. 1961. "Investment in Human Capital." *American Economic Review* 51 (1): 1–17.

Smith, Conal. 2011. "Alternative Measures of Well-Being: The OECD Better Life Initiative." Unpublished presentation slides. December 2.

Stiglitz, Joseph E., Amartya Sen, and Jean-Paul Fitoussi. 2009. *Report by the Commission on the Measurement of Economic Performance and Social Progress.* http://www.stiglitz-sen-fitoussi.fr/en/index.htm.

US Department of the Treasury. 2012. *Statistics of Income 2010, Individual Income Tax Returns.* Publication 1304. Internal Revenue Service. August.

US Department of the Treasury, and US Department of Education. 2012. *The Economics of Higher Education.* December. Washington, DC.

Weisbrod, Burton A. 1961. "The Valuation of Human Capital." *Journal of Political Economy* 69 (5): 425–36.

Measuring Social Welfare in the US National Accounts

Dale W. Jorgenson and Daniel T. Slesnick

3.1 Introduction

At the meeting of the Conference on Research in Income and Wealth in April 2004, D. Jorgenson, J. Steven Landefeld, William D. Nordhaus, and their coauthors proposed a new architecture for the US national accounts.[1] The initial step in implementing the new architecture was the integrated macroeconomic accounts for the United States, developed by the Bureau of Economic Analysis (BEA) and the Board of Governors of the Federal Reserve System (FRB).[2] In this chapter we employ the integrated macroeconomic accounts as the starting point for measuring social welfare.[3]

Our measure of potential social welfare is based on personal consumption expenditures. Actual social welfare depends on the distribution of consumption over the population, and we refer to this as the *standard of living*. Our measure of *inequality* is the difference between potential and actual social

Dale W. Jorgenson is the Samuel W. Morris University Professor in the Department of Economics at Harvard University. Daniel T. Slesnick is professor of economics at the University of Texas at Austin.

We are indebted to J. Steven Landefeld, Lawrence J. Lau, and Thomas M. Stoker for their collaboration on earlier phases of this research. Thanks are due to Jon D. Samuels for his excellent work on the national accounts and helpful comments. Finally, we are indebted to Dennis Fixler and Timothy Smeeding for their comments on an earlier draft. Financial support by the Donald B. Marron Fund for Research at Harvard University is gratefully acknowledged. The usual disclaimer applies. For acknowledgments, sources of research support, and disclosure of the authors' material financial relationships, if any, please see http://www.nber.org/chapters /c12825.ack.

1. Jorgenson, Landefeld, and Nordhaus (2006).
2. Teplin et al. (2006). For current data from the integrated macroeconomic accounts, see http://www.bea.gov/national/nipaweb/Ni_FedBeaSna/Index.asp.
3. Plans for developing these accounts are discussed by Cagetti et al., chapter 10, this volume.

welfare.[4] Our measures of the cost and standard of living and inequality are consistent with the integrated macroeconomic accounts and the US National Income and Product Accounts (NIPAs).[5]

In September 2009, Joseph E. Stiglitz, Amartya K. Sen, and Jean-Paul Fitoussi presented the "Report by the Commission on the Measurement of Economic Performance and Social Progress" to the former president of France Nicolas Sarkozy.[6] The report called for a shift in the focus of economic measurement from production toward "people's well-being." The report contained twelve specific recommendations, including the use of consumption, income, and wealth, rather than production, for this purpose.[7]

The recommendations of the Stiglitz-Sen-Fitoussi Commission's report are complementary to those of the nearly contemporaneous 2008 System of National Accounts (United Nations 2009), which includes consumption, income, and wealth.[8] In response to the Stiglitz-Sen-Fitoussi Commission's report, the Organisation for Economic Co-operation and Development (OECD) has established an international expert group chaired by the Australian Bureau of Statistics to develop new international standards and guidelines for microeconomic data on income, consumption, and wealth.[9] The OECD has established a second international expert group on disparities in the national accounts chaired by Eurostat to consider the role of distributional statistics in the national accounts.[10]

The new architecture for the US national accounts avoids confusion between production and welfare, a key concern of the Stiglitz-Sen-Fitoussi Commission's report. By augmenting personal consumption with its distribution over the population, we are able to incorporate detailed measures of the cost and standard of living and inequality into the NIPAs.[11] By including production, as measured by the gross domestic product (GDP) and gross domestic income (GDI), we can also include measures of output, input, and

4. For more details see Jorgenson (1990) and Slesnick (1998).

5. See Jorgenson (1997b) and Slenick (2001).

6. Stiglitz, Sen, and Fitoussi (2010). For more detail on the commission and its reports, see http://www.stiglitz-sen-fitoussi.fr/en/index.htm. For a discussion of the implications of the Stiglitz-Sen-Fitoussi Commission's report for the NIPAs, see Landefeld et al. (2010).

7. A more technical presentation of issues in the measurement of welfare or "social well-being" is given in Fleurbaey (2009). This is partly based on Fleurbaey's report to the commission. For more details, see http://www.stiglitz-sen-fitoussi.fr/documents/Individual_Well-Being _and_Social_Welfare.pdf. Fleurbaey's own proposal for welfare measurement is presented in Fleurbaey and Maniquet (2011).

8. United Nations (2009).

9. OECD (2013a, b).

10. Fesseau, Wolff, and Mattonetti (2013) and Fesseau and Mattonetti (2013).

11. The measurement of household income in the United States is discussed by Harris (chapter 7, this volume). The measurement of household wealth in the United States is discussed by Henriques and Hsu (chapter 9, this volume). The integration of household consumption and income data into the US national accounts is discussed by Fixler and Johnson (chapter 8, this volume) and McCully (chapter 6, this volume).

productivity in the national accounts, as pointed out in chapters 19 and 20 of the 2008 SNA.

In section 3.2 we introduce measures of individual and social welfare within the new architecture for the US national accounts. The key feature of our measures of individual welfare is that they are cardinal and interpersonally comparable. We aggregate these measures by means of a social welfare function. In section 3.3 we employ individual and social expenditure functions to provide money measures of individual and social welfare appropriate for the national accounts.

Our measures of individual welfare incorporate three types of information. We use personal consumption to represent the size of the household budget. We express the household's consumption in constant prices. We then divide real consumption by household size. Finally, we express individual welfare as the logarithm of real consumption per capita, so that increments of individual welfare are equal to proportional increases in consumption. These features are commonly employed in the literature on consumer behavior.

We combine measures of individual welfare into a measure of social welfare. We emphasize that the validity of social welfare evaluations depends on the normative conditions of horizontal and vertical equity, as well as information on consumer preferences. We consider a class of social welfare functions that combines the mean of individual welfare with a measure of dispersion that gives additional weight to equity considerations.

In section 3.4 we present the empirical counterparts of individual and social expenditure functions, exploiting an econometric model of aggregate consumer behavior described in greater detail in the appendix. In section 3.5 we summarize the new architecture and update the key accounting magnitudes for consumption and production presented by Jorgenson (2009).[12] We link our measure of welfare to personal consumption expenditures and our measure of production to the GDP.

In section 3.6 we present measures of the cost and standard of living and inequality within the US national accounts. We incorporate distributional information into the measurement of inequality and the standard of living. The Consumer Price Index (CPI) produced by Bureau of Labor Statistics (BLS) can be interpreted as a measure of the cost of living. The Bureau of the Census generates official statistics on the standard of living, poverty, and inequality. However, these statistics are not integrated with the NIPAs.

While our welfare measures are consistent with the 2008 SNA and the proposals of the Stiglitz-Sen-Fitoussi Commission's report, we emphasize links to the NIPAs and the integrated macroeconomic accounts for the United States. In section 3.7 we discuss possible extensions of the national accounts to include nonmarket activities. Examples are household production and

---

12. Jorgenson (2009).

consumption, the accumulation of human capital, the enhancement of environmental quality, and health care.

We conclude by recommending that national statistical agencies experiment with the incorporation of measures of social welfare into the national accounts. The availability of properly constructed welfare measures would address concerns about the misuse of the GDP as a measure of welfare. However, there is little justification for treating welfare measures as a substitute for income, consumption, wealth, or other economic aggregates that appear in the national accounts.

3.2   Measuring Individual and Social Welfare

Despite the exclusion of social welfare from the national accounts, welfare measurement is well established in both economic theory and economic statistics.[13] Sen's (1970) magisterial *Collective Choice and Social Welfare* was a crucial turning point in the theory of social choice.[14] Sen greatly broadened the scope of welfare measurements by mapping out the alternatives to the traditional assumptions of ordinal measures of individual welfare that are not comparable among individuals. This led to an explosion of research on "possibility theorems" during the following decade.[15] For example, measures of inequality based on social welfare functions by Anthony B. Atkinson and Serge C. Kolm were given a rigorous foundation in the theory of social choice summarized by Roberts (1980).[16]

Following the elaboration of new conceptual possibilities for welfare measurement, we developed an econometric methodology to eliminate the gap between the theory of social choice and measures of welfare used in economic statistics. This gap arises from the fact that surveys of consumer expenditures are based on households rather than individuals, a distinction almost absent from the theoretical literature. We presented the results in a series of papers on the cost and standard of living, inequality, and poverty.[17] Our approach to welfare measurement is summarized in Jorgenson's (1990) presidential address to the Econometric Society, Slesnick's (1998) survey article in the *Journal of Economic Literature*, and Slesnick's (2001) book.

Econometric models of consumer behavior have long been used in measuring individual welfare.[18] The challenge we faced was to extend this approach to social welfare by comparing levels of welfare among individuals and aggregating over them. Our solution to this problem was to exploit the

13. The measurement of social welfare is discussed by Jorgenson (1997b) and Slesnick (2001).
14. Sen (1970).
15. For a summary of this literature and many new results, including the framework used for our social welfare measures, see Roberts (1980). Fleurbaey and Maniquet (2011) have proposed an approach to welfare measurement that retains the traditional assumptions.
16. See Atkinson (1970) and Kolm (1969).
17. These papers are collected in Dale W. Jorgenson (1997b).
18. See Deaton and Muellbauer (1980, ch. 9, 214–40) and Slesnick (1998).

econometric model of aggregate demand introduced by Jorgenson, Lawrence Lau, and Thomas Stoker (1982).[19]

Aggregation over individuals is obviously the key to social welfare measurement. It is straightforward to incorporate the restrictions on individual consumer behavior required for aggregation. The necessary framework is provided by the theory of household behavior of Gary S. Becker, Pollak, and Paul A. Samuelson.[20] However, this is beyond the scope of the traditional theory of consumer behavior based on individuals.

Jorgenson, Lau, and Stoker showed how to recover the models of individual demand that underlie their model of aggregate demand. In Jorgenson and Slesnick (1983, 1984) we derived cardinal measures of individual welfare that are interpersonally comparable from these models of individual demand. We introduced the normative assumptions employed by Roberts (1980) and aggregated our measures of individual welfare by means of a social welfare function.

Our final step was to convert individual and social welfare into money measures appropriate for the national accounts, using the individual expenditure function introduced by Lionel McKenzie (1957) and the social expenditure function originated by Robert Pollak (1981).[21] We used these tools in developing a "dashboard" of detailed measures of social welfare, later recommended by Stiglitz, Sen, and Fitoussi (2010). We also developed measures of welfare for groups within the population and showed how to aggregate them into overall measures of social welfare.

Our empirical research used observations on households from the Consumer Expenditure Survey (CEX), conducted by BLS on a quarterly basis since 1980.[22] An important feature of the CEX, like other consumer expenditure surveys, is that observations are available for households, but not for individuals. To generate interpersonal comparisons based on households, we employed a long-established concept in economic statistics, household equivalence scales.[23]

The concept of household equivalence scales has been used to establish family needs for income support programs and assess the cost of additional children. We derived household equivalence scales econometrically from household expenditure functions.[24] These household equivalence scales, like traditional scales, depend on the demographic characteristics of households.

19. Jorgenson, Lau, and Stoker (1982). This paper is included in Jorgenson (1997a, 203–359).

20. See Becker (1981), Pollak (1981), and Samuelson (1956).

21. McKenzie (1957) and Pollak (1981).

22. In 2009 the BLS launched the Gemini Project to improve the quality of data reported on the survey. For details on important limitations of the current CEX, see http://www.bls.gov/cex/geminiproject.htm.

23. See Jorgenson and Slesnick (1987). This paper is included in Dale W. Jorgenson (1997b). Alternative approaches to household equivalence scales are summarized by Slesnick (2001, 88–121) and OECD (2013a, 152–57).

24. This approach to modeling household behavior was originated by Barten (1964).

Unlike traditional scales, our household equivalence scales also depend on prices faced by households.

The introduction of household equivalence scales into the measurement of social welfare bridged the gap between the economic theory and economic statistics. The conceptual basis for this link was established by Arthur Lewbel (1989) in a paper on the economic theory of household equivalence scales.[25] Lewbel began by clarifying the role of exact aggregation in deriving cardinal measures of individual welfare that are interpersonally comparable.

Lewbel demonstrated that household equivalence scales can be identified under the assumptions that these scales are independent of household welfare, depending only on household characteristics and prices. These are precisely the assumptions employed in our household equivalence scales. Using the possibility theorems summarized by Roberts (1980), Lewbel combined these household equivalence scales with cardinal measures of individual welfare, using our approach as a key illustration.

Our cardinal and interpersonally comparable measures of household welfare fit neatly into the framework of the theory of social choice. This has provided a rigorous approach to measuring social welfare that successfully exploits econometric methods for modeling consumer behavior. However, official measures of the cost and standard of living and inequality in the United States have been unaffected by these econometric methods.[26]

3.3   Money Measures of Individual and Social Welfare

In this section we assume that household expenditures are allocated to maximize a household welfare function. As demonstrated by Samuelson (1956) and Pollak (1981), the household behaves in the same way as an individual maximizing a utility function. We treat households as individuals in measuring social welfare. All subsequent references to individuals are to households considered as consuming units.

We present money measures of individual and social welfare. Our measures of individual welfare are based on the preference orderings of consumers. We represent these orderings by real-valued individual welfare functions. Our measure of social welfare is based on preferences over social states by all individuals. We represent a social ordering by means of a real-valued social welfare function, defined on the distribution of individual welfare over the population.

To provide a money measure of individual welfare, we represent prefer-

25. Lewbel (1989). For more details, see Fleurbaey and Hammond (2004).
26. Recommendations for revisions of the official measures have been provided by Jorgenson (1990) and Slesnick (2001). Supplemental measures of poverty based on income have been proposed by the Bureau of the Census (2011). See http://www.census.gov/hhes/povmeas/. These are based on a 1995 report by the National Academy of Sciences. See Citro and Michael (1995).

ences by means of an individual expenditure function, using the following notation:

p_n: price of the nth commodity, assumed to be the same for all consuming units.

$p = (p_1, p_2, \ldots, p_N)$: vector of prices of all commodities.

x_{nk}: quantity of the nth commodity consumed by the kth consuming unit $(n = 1, 2, \ldots, N; k = 1, 2, \ldots, K)$.

$x_k = (x_{1k}, x_{2k}, \ldots, x_{Nk})$: vector of quantities of all commodities consumed by the kth consuming unit $(k = 1, 2, \ldots, K)$.

$M_k = \sum_{n=1}^{N} p_n x_{nk}$: total expenditure of the kth consuming unit $(k = 1, 2, \ldots, K)$.

A_k: vector of attributes of the kth consuming unit $(k = 1, 2, \ldots, K)$.

The *individual expenditure function* gives the minimum total expenditure M_k required for the kth consuming unit to achieve the welfare level W_k at the prices $p(k = 1, 2, \ldots, K)$. More formally, the individual expenditure function $M_k(p, W_k, A_k)$ is defined by:

(1) $$M_k(p, W_k, A_k) = \min\{M_k = \sum_{n=1}^{N} p_n x_{nk} : W_k(x_k, A_k) \geq W_k\}.$$

Individual welfare W_k is the maximum attainable at total expenditure M_k. This is a money measure of individual welfare at the current price system p.

We employ the individual welfare function and the individual expenditure function to construct measures of the standard of living and its cost. We illustrate these concepts geometrically in figure 3.1. This represents the indifference map for a consuming unit with expenditure function $M_k(p, W_k, A_k)$. For simplicity we consider the case of two commodities $(N = 2)$. Consumer equilibrium in the base period is represented by the point A. The corresponding level of individual expenditure $M_k(p^0, W_k^0, A_k)$, divided by the price of the second commodity p_2^0, is given on the vertical axis. This provides a representation of individual expenditure in terms of units of the second commodity.

Consumer equilibrium in the current period is represented by the point C. To translate welfare W_k^1 into total expenditure at the prices of the base period, we evaluate the individual expenditure function (1) at this level of welfare and the base period price system p^0. The resulting total expenditure $M_k(p^0, W_k^1, A_k)$ corresponds to consumer equilibrium at the point B. The ratio between levels of total expenditure $M_k(p^0, W_k^1, A_k)$ and M_k^0 is the household standard of living. The price index given by the ratio between levels of total expenditure M_k^1 and $M_k(p^0, W_k^1, A_k)$ is the household cost of living.

Under the Pareto principle, a social state represents an improvement over an alternative state if all consuming units are as well off as under the alternative, and at least one unit is better off. The Pareto principle provides a partial ordering of social states. This ordering is invariant with respect to monotone increasing transformations of individual welfare that differ among consuming units. Only welfare comparisons that are ordinal and noncomparable among consuming units are required.

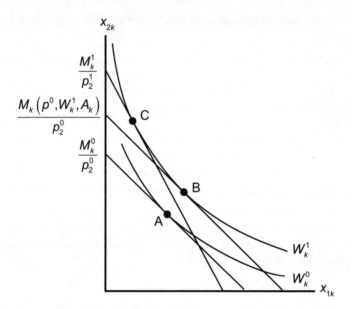

Fig. 3.1   Household standard of living and its cost

The money measure of individual welfare provided by the expenditure function (1) is a monotone increasing transformation of individual welfare. This transformation depends on the prices faced by the consuming unit and on attributes of the consumer. Considered as a measure of individual welfare in its own right, this measure provides the information about preferences required for applications of the Pareto principle. To obtain a complete ordering of social states we next introduce a social welfare function.

We consider orderings over the set of social states and the set of real-valued individual welfare functions. To describe these social orderings in greater detail we introduce the following notation:

x: matrix with $N \times K$ elements $\{x_{nk}\}$ describing the social state.
$u = (W_1, W_2, \ldots, W_K)$: vector of individual welfare functions of all K consuming units.

To represent social orderings in a form suitable for measuring social welfare we consider a class of social welfare functions $W(u, x)$ incorporating a notion of horizontal equity. We require that individuals with identical individual welfare functions enter the social welfare functions in the same way. We also incorporate a notion of vertical equity by requiring that the social welfare functions are equity-regarding in the sense of Hammond (1977). This imposes a version of Dalton's (1920) principle of transfers: A transfer from a household with a higher welfare level to a household with a lower welfare level that does not reverse their relative positions must increase the level of social welfare.[27]

To provide a money measure of individual welfare, we have expressed individual welfare in terms of total expenditure. Similarly, we can express social welfare in terms of aggregate expenditure. For this purpose we introduce the *social expenditure function*, defined as the minimum level of total expenditure, $M = \sum_{k=1}^{K} M_k$, required to attain a given level of social welfare, say W, at a specified price system p. More formally, the social expenditure function $M(p,W)$ is defined by

$$(2) \qquad M(p,W) = \min\{M = \sum_{k=1}^{K} M_k : W(u,x) \geq W\}.$$

For a given price system we translate social welfare into monetary terms by evaluating the social expenditure function. To determine the level of social welfare we first evaluate the individual welfare functions $\{W_k\}$ for all consuming units at the price system p and the distribution of total expenditure $\{M_k\}$. We then evaluate the social welfare function $W(u,x)$. Finally, we express the level of social welfare in terms of the price system by means of the social expenditure function $M(p,W)$.

We can decompose our money measure of social welfare into money measures of equity and efficiency. Equity reflects the gain in welfare from a more egalitarian distribution of a given total expenditure. Efficiency is the maximum level of social welfare that can be attained by lump-sum redistributions, so that welfare losses from an inequitable distribution of total expenditure are eliminated.

To define money measures of equity and efficiency we evaluate the social welfare function at the maximum that can be attained through lump-sum redistributions. This maximum is our measure of *efficiency*. Evaluating the social expenditure function at the potential level of welfare, we obtain aggregate expenditure M. This is our money measure of efficiency at the price system p.

Given a money measure of efficiency, we define a corresponding money measure of *equity* as the ratio between the money measure of actual social welfare $M(p,W)$ and the money measure of efficiency M. This measure of equity increases as the distribution of total expenditure approaches perfect equality. We express our money measure of social welfare as the product of efficiency and equity:

$$(3) \qquad M(p,W) = M \cdot \left(\frac{M(p,W)}{M}\right).$$

The critical feature of this decomposition is that all three measures are expressed in terms of the price system p.

27. Dalton (1920) and Hammond (1977).

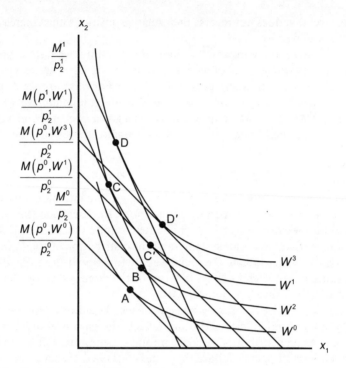

Fig. 3.2   Social standard of living and its cost

The social welfare function and the social expenditure function can be employed in defining measures of the standard of living and its cost. We illustrate these concepts geometrically in figure 3.2. The figure represents the indifference map of a representative consumer with preferences corresponding to the social expenditure function $M(p,W)$. This concept of a representative consumer was proposed by Samuelson (1956) and Pollak (1981).

For simplicity we consider the case of two commodities ($N = 2$), as before. Consumer equilibrium at the actual level of social welfare in the base period W^0 is represented by the point A. The corresponding level of aggregate expenditure $M(p^0,W^0)$, divided by the price of the second commodity p_2^0, is given on the vertical axis. This level provides a representation of aggregate expenditure in terms of units of the second commodity. Consumer equilibrium at the level of social welfare in the current period W^1 is represented by the point C.

To translate the level of social welfare W^1 into aggregate expenditure at the prices of the base period, we evaluate the social expenditure function at the price system p^0. Aggregate expenditure $M(p^0,W^1)$ corresponds to consumer equilibrium at the point C'. The value of the social expenditure function at the potential level of welfare W^2, expressed in terms of the price system p^0, is M^0. The corresponding consumer equilibrium is represented by the point B.

Similarly, consumer equilibrium at the potential level of social welfare in the current period, say W^3, is presented by the point D. This is the maximum social welfare that can be attained through lump-sum redistributions of aggregate expenditure M^1 at current prices p^1. We translate this level of social welfare into expenditure at the base period price system p^0 by evaluating the expenditure function $M(p^0, W^3)$ at the consumer equilibrium represented by the point D'.

The quantity index given by the ratio between levels of aggregate expenditure $M(p^0, W^0)$ and $M(p^0, W^1)$ is a measure of the *actual standard of living*. Similarly, the index represented by the ratio of the levels of aggregate expenditure $M(p^0, W^3)$ and M^0 is the measure of the *potential standard of living*. The ratio of the actual to the potential standard of living is the measure of equity. Finally, the price index given by the ratio between levels of expenditure M^1 and $M(p^0, W^3)$ is the measure of the social cost of living proposed by Pollak (1981).

3.4 Implementing Measures of Individual and Social Welfare

Our next objective is to implement money measures of individual and social welfare empirically.[28] We require individual welfare functions that reflect the preference orderings of individual consuming units. For this purpose we employ an updated version of the econometric model of consumer behavior in the United States presented by Jorgenson and Slesnick (1987).[29] This model is described in the appendix.

Our econometric model incorporates integrability restrictions that assure the existence of an indirect utility function. In the following section we construct indirect utility functions for all consuming units. In combining these utility functions with assumptions about horizontal and vertical equity, we develop numerical counterparts for the money measures of individual and social welfare in figures 3.1 and 3.2.

Our system of aggregate demand functions is obtained by summing over individual demand systems. Our model of individual demand incorporates cross-section data on quantities consumed, total expenditure, and attributes of households such as demographic characteristics. The aggregate quantities consumed depend on the attributes and total expenditure of individual consuming units through summary statistics of the joint distribution of total expenditure and attributes of individual households.

Exact aggregation is useful in simplifying the econometric modeling of

28. Implementation of measures of individual and social welfare is discussed by Slesnick (2001, 201–14).

29. This model was updated by Slesnick (2001, 96).

aggregate consumer behavior. In fact, the special formulations of exact aggregation developed by William M. Gorman (1953) and Muellbauer (1976) were designed precisely for this purpose.[30] We exploit the exact aggregation restrictions in constructing cardinal measures of individual welfare and defining interpersonal comparability in terms of household equivalence scales. We combine these measures of individual welfare with the assumptions on horizontal and vertical equity discussed below to measure social welfare.

To construct an econometric model based on exact aggregation, we first represent individual preferences by means of an indirect utility function for each consuming unit, using the following notation:

$w_{nk} = p_n x_{nk}/M_k$: expenditure share of the nth commodity in the budget of the kth consuming unit ($n = 1,2,...,N; k = 1,2,...,K$).

$w_k = (w_{1k}, w_{2k},...,w_{Nk})$: vector of expenditure shares for the kth consuming unit ($k = 1,2,...,K$).

$\ln(p/M_k) = [\ln(p_1/M_k), \ln(p_2/M_k)..., \ln(p_N/M_k)]$: vector of logarithms of ratios of prices to expenditure by the kth consuming unit ($k = 1,2,...,K$).

$\ln p = (\ln p_1, \ln p_2,..., \ln p_N)$: vector of logarithms of prices.

We assume that the kth consuming unit allocates expenditures in accord with the transcendental logarithmic or translog indirect utility function, say V_k, where:

$$(4) \qquad \ln V_k = G\left(\ln\frac{p'}{M_k}\alpha_p + \frac{1}{2}\ln\frac{p'}{M_k}B_{pp}\ln\frac{p}{M_k} + \ln\frac{p'}{M_k}B_{pA}A_k, A_k \right),$$

$$(k = 1,2,...,K).$$

In this representation the function G is a monotone increasing function of its first argument. The vector α_p and the matrices B_{pp} and B_{pA} are constant and the same for all consuming units. In addition, the function G depends directly on the attribute vector A_k. This form of the indirect utility function is ordinal and noncomparable among consuming units. Measurability and interpersonal comparability of individual preferences are not required in modeling consumer behavior.

The expenditure shares of the kth consuming unit can be derived by the logarithmic form of Roy's (1943) identity[31]

$$(5) \qquad w_{nk} = \frac{(\partial\ln V_k)/[\partial\ln(p_n/M_k)]}{\sum_{n=1}^{N}\{(\partial\ln V_k)/[\partial\ln(p_n/M_k)]\}}, (n = 1,2,...,N; k = 1,2,...,K).$$

Applying this identity to the translog indirect utility function (4), we obtain the system of individual expenditure shares

30. Gorman (1953) and Muellbauer (1976).
31. Roy (1943).

(6) $w_k = \dfrac{1}{D_k(p)}\left(\alpha_p + B_{pp}\ln\dfrac{p}{M_k} + B_{pA}A_k\right), (k = 1,2,\ldots,K),$

where the denominators $\{D_k(p)\}$ take the form

(7) $D_k(p) = i'\alpha_p + i'B_{pp}\ln\dfrac{p}{M_k} + i'B_{pA}A_k, (k = 1,2,\ldots,K),$

and i is a vector of ones.

The individual expenditure shares are homogeneous of degree zero in the unknown parameters α_p, B_{pp}, B_{pA}. By multiplying a given set of parameters by a constant we obtain another set of parameters that generates the same system of individual budget shares. Accordingly, we can normalize the parameters without affecting observed patterns of individual expenditure allocation. We find it convenient to employ the normalization

$$i'\alpha_p = -1.$$

Under this restriction any change in the unknown parameters will be reflected in changes in individual expenditure patterns.

The conditions for exact aggregation are that the individual expenditure shares are linear in functions of the attributes $\{A_k\}$ and total expenditures $\{M_k\}$ for all consuming units.[32] These conditions will be satisfied if and only if the terms involving the attributes and expenditures do not appear in the denominators of the expressions for the individual expenditure shares, so that:

$$i'B_{pA} = 0, \text{ and } i'B_{pp}i = 0.$$

The exact aggregation restrictions imply that the denominators $\{D_k(p)\}$ reduce to:

$$D(p) = -1 + i'B_{pp}\ln p,$$

where the subscript k is no longer required, since the denominator is the same for all consuming units. Under these restrictions the individual expenditure shares can be written:

(8) $w_k = \dfrac{1}{D(p)}(\alpha_p + B_{pp}\ln p - B_{pp}i \cdot \ln M_k + B_{pA}A_k), (k = 1,2,\ldots,K).$

The individual expenditure shares are linear in the logarithms of expenditures $\{\ln M_k\}$ and the attributes $\{A_k\}$, as required by exact aggregation.

To construct an econometric model of aggregate consumer behavior based on exact aggregation we obtain aggregate expenditure shares, say w, by multiplying individual expenditure shares (8) by expenditure for each consuming unit, adding over all consuming units, and dividing by aggregate expenditure, $M = \sum_{k=1}^{K} M_k$ and

32. Details are given by Jorgenson, Lau, and Stoker (1982, 280–6).

$$(9) \qquad w = \frac{\Sigma M_k w_k}{M}.$$

The aggregate expenditure shares can be rewritten

$$(10) \qquad w = \frac{1}{D(p)}\left(\alpha_p + B_{pp}\ln p - B_{pp}i\frac{\Sigma M_k \ln M_k}{M} + B_{pA}\frac{\Sigma M_k A_k}{M}\right).$$

Aggregate expenditure patterns depend on the distribution of expenditure over all consuming units through summary statistics of the joint distribution of expenditures and attributes—$\Sigma M_k \ln M_k/M$ and $\{\Sigma M_k A_k/M\}$. Under exact aggregation systems of individual expenditure shares (8) for consuming units with identical demographic characteristics can be recovered in one and only one way from the system of aggregate expenditure shares (10). We next define cardinal measures of individual welfare that are fully comparable among individuals.

Under exact aggregation and integrability, the translog indirect utility function for the kth consuming unit V_k can be written:

$$(11) \qquad \ln V_k = \ln p' \alpha_p + \frac{1}{2}\ln p' B_{pp} \ln p - D(p)\ln\left[\frac{M_k}{m_0(p, A_k)}\right],$$

$$(k = 1,2,\ldots,K).$$

In this representation the function $m_0(p, A_k)$ is the *general household equivalence scale* and can be interpreted as the number of household equivalent members.

The general household equivalence scale takes the form:

$$(12) \quad \ln m_0(p, A_k) = \frac{1}{D(p)}$$

$$\cdot\left[\ln m(A_k)'\alpha_p + \frac{1}{2}\ln m(A_k)'B_{pp}\ln m(A_k) + \ln m(A_k)'B_{pp}\ln p\right],$$

$$(k = 1,2,\ldots,K),$$

where:

$$(13) \qquad \ln m(A_k) = B_{pp}^{-1}B_{pA}A_k, (k = 1,2,\ldots,K).$$

This household equivalence scale has the key property identified by Lewbel (1989); namely, independence of the level of household welfare. We refer to the scales $\{m(A_k)\}$ as the *commodity-specific translog household equivalence scales.*[33]

Given the indirect utility function (11) for each consuming unit, we can

---

33. Alternative approaches to household equivalence scales are summarized by Slesnick (2001, 88–121).

express total expenditure as a function of prices, the general household equivalence scale, and the level of utility:

$$(14) \qquad \ln M_k = \frac{1}{D(p)}\left[\ln p'\left(\alpha_p + \frac{1}{2}B_{pp}\ln p\right) - \ln V_k\right] + \ln m_0(p, A_k),$$

$$(k = 1,2,\ldots,K).$$

We refer to this function as the *translog individual expenditure function*. The translog expenditure function gives the minimum level of expenditure required for the kth consuming unit to achieve the utility level V_k, given the prices $p(k = 1,2,\ldots,K)$.

The first step in measuring social welfare is to select representations of the individual welfare functions. We define individual welfare for the kth consuming unit, say $W_k (k = 1,2,\ldots,K)$, as the logarithm of the translog indirect utility function (11)

$$(15) \qquad W_k = \ln V_k = \ln p'\alpha_p + \frac{1}{2}\ln p'B_{pp}\ln p - D(p)\ln\left[\frac{M_k}{m_0(p, A_k)}\right],$$

$$(k = 1,2,\ldots,K).$$

It is important to emphasize that we have utilized the exact aggregation restrictions in establishing that the household equivalence scale is independent of the level of welfare.

At an intuitive level, the appeal of our measures of individual welfare is that they incorporate three types of information that are relevant to welfare measurement. Total expenditure M_k corresponds to size of the household budget, while the number of household equivalent member $m_0(p, A_k)$ is an indicator of the size of the consuming unit. The budget and the size of the household are combined into a "per capita" measure of total expenditure.

Transforming expenditure per capita logarithmically implies that increments in individual welfare correspond to proportional changes in the resources of the household. Prices faced by the household enter through a linear transformation that is the same for all consuming units. Household size also depends on prices since the preferences of household members are not necessarily identical.

More formally, individual welfare is a linear function of the logarithm of total expenditure per household equivalent member $\ln[M_k/m_0(p, A_k)]$ with an intercept and slope coefficient that depends only on prices $p(k = 1,2,\ldots,K)$. This property is invariant with respect to positive affine transformations that are the same for all consuming units, so that the individual welfare function provides a cardinal measure of individual welfare that is fully comparable among units. The incorporation of measures of individual welfare into a social welfare function requires a normative judgment about horizontal equity. We assume that every individual should be treated symmetrically with any other individual having the same welfare function.[34]

To represent social orderings in a form suitable for measuring social welfare, we consider the class of social welfare functions introduced by Jorgenson and Slesnick (1983):

$$(16) \qquad W(u,x) = \ln \bar{V} - \gamma(x) \left[\frac{\sum_{k=1}^{K} m_0(p, A_k) |\ln V_k - \ln \bar{V}|^{-\rho}}{\sum_{k=1}^{K} m_0(p, A_k)} \right]^{-1/\rho}.$$

The first term in the social welfare functions (16) corresponds to an average of individual welfare levels over all consuming units:

$$\ln \bar{V} = \frac{\sum_{k=1}^{K} m_0(p, A_k) \ln V_k}{\sum_{k=1}^{K} m_0(p, A_k)}$$

$$= \ln p' \left(\alpha_p + \frac{1}{2} B_{pp} \ln p \right) - D(p) \frac{\sum_{k=1}^{K} m_0(p, A_k) \ln \{M_k / [m_0(p, A_k)]\}}{\sum_{k=1}^{K} m_0(p, A_k)}.$$

The second term is a linear homogeneous function of deviations of levels of individual welfare from the average and is a measure of dispersion in individual welfare levels. These social welfare functions are invariant with respect to positive affine transformations and provide cardinal measures of social welfare.

The parameter ρ determines the curvature of the social welfare function in the individual welfare functions $\{W_k(x)\}$. We refer to this parameter as the *degree of aversion to inequality*. The range of admissible values of ρ is from negative unity to negative infinity. By selecting an appropriate value of this parameter, we can incorporate ethical judgments about vertical equity into the social welfare function.

The measure of dispersion vanishes in the limiting case where the degree of aversion to inequality ρ is equal to negative infinity. The social welfare function reduces to an average of welfare levels over all consuming units. We refer to this as the *utilitarian* social welfare function. This limiting case gives the least possible weight to equity considerations.

We also consider the limiting case where ρ is equal to negative unity in order to give the greatest weight to equity considerations. We refer to this as the *egalitarian* social welfare function. For the applications in the following section, we present measures of social welfare for both utilitarian and egalitarian cases in order to highlight the role of normative considerations in social welfare measurements.

At this point we have generated a class of social welfare functions capable of expressing the implications of a variety of normative judgments. The Pareto principle requires that an increase in individual welfare must increase

---

34. Lewbel (1989) suggested that this approach could also be employed for the AIDS system proposed by Deaton and Muellbauer (1980). Details are provided by Fleurbaey and Hammond (2004).

social welfare. This condition implies that the increase in the average level of individual welfare must exceed the increase in the dispersion in individual welfare. We assume that the function $\gamma(x)$ must take the maximum value consistent with the Pareto principle. This assumption gives maximum weight to the second term in equation (16), representing equity considerations.

The intuition underlying the class of social welfare functions (16) is that we augment the mean of individual welfare with a measure of dispersion. This class includes the utilitarian social welfare functions based on average social welfare and frequently used in policy evaluation. Allowing for dispersion makes it possible to give additional weight to equity considerations.

In order to determine the form of the social expenditure function $M(p, W)$, we maximize the social welfare function (16) for a fixed level of aggregate expenditure by equalizing total expenditure per household equivalent member $M_k/[m_0(p, A_k)]$ for all consuming units. For the translog indirect utility function, this takes the form:

$$(17) \qquad \ln \overline{V} = \ln p'\left(\alpha_p + \frac{1}{2} B_{pp} \ln p\right) - D(p)\ln\left[\frac{M}{\sum_{k=1}^{K} m^0(p, A_k)}\right].$$

The maximum level of welfare that is potentially available is our measure of efficiency and does not depend on the degree of aversion to inequality ρ.

If aggregate expenditure is distributed so as to equalize total expenditure per household equivalent member, the level of individual welfare is the same for all consuming units and the social welfare function reduces to the average level of individual welfare $\ln \overline{V}$. The value of social welfare is obtained by evaluating the translog indirect utility function at total expenditure per household equivalent member $M/[\sum_{k=1}^{K} m_0(p, A_k)]$ for the economy as a whole. This is an algebraic representation of the preferences of the representative consumer depicted in figure 3.2.

We can express aggregate expenditure as a function of the level of social welfare and prices:

$$(18) \quad \ln M(p, W) = \frac{1}{D(p)}\left[\ln p'\left(\alpha_p + \frac{1}{2} B_{pp} \ln p\right) - W\right] + \ln[\sum_{k=1}^{K} m_0(p, A_k)].$$

The value of aggregate expenditure is obtained by evaluating the translog individual expenditure function (14) at the level of social welfare W and the number of household equivalent members $\sum_{k=1}^{K} m_0(p, A_k)$ for the economy as a whole. This is the social expenditure function used in constructing the measures of the social standard of living and its cost represented in figure 3.2.

3.5   Measuring Welfare in the US National Accounts

We turn next to the measurement of social welfare in the US national accounts. The first issue to be addressed is: Why incorporate welfare into the national accounts? The advantages stem from the accuracy and reliability of estimates carried out within a system of national accounts. Finally, the results can be reported with other estimates from the national accounts on a regular basis—annually, quarterly, or even monthly.

The next issue to be addressed is: Why use the new architecture? The national accounts incorporate the double-entry bookkeeping associated with systems of private accounts. Each account in the new architecture is expressed in both current and constant prices, so that the benefits of double-entry bookkeeping are multiplied by a factor of two. This "quadruple entry" bookkeeping is characteristic of national accounting, but is not usually employed in private accounting.

Another advantage of measuring welfare within the national accounts is the establishment of international standards like those that underlie the 2008 SNA. The resulting uniformity of methods is essential for international comparability. The 2008 SNA rules out a welfare interpretation of the national accounts, but systems of satellite accounts, such as environmental accounts, are often given a welfare interpretation.[35] Based on experience with the 2008 SNA and its predecessors, the incorporation of welfare measures into the national accounts will require lengthy international consultations.

As an illustration of international comparability, the World Bank's estimates of poverty and inequality are very valuable in comparing economic performance and social progress across countries.[36] These estimates are based on hundreds of microeconomic data sets for different countries providing information on income and consumption for individuals and households. The estimates also incorporate purchasing power comparisons of production in the World Bank's International Comparisons Project.[37]

In January 2008, the new architecture was endorsed by the Advisory Committee on Measuring Innovation in the Twenty-first Century Economy to the US secretary of commerce Carlos Guttierez:[38]

> The proposed new "architecture" for the NIPAs (US national income and product accounts) would consist of a set of income statements, balance sheets, flow of funds statements, and productivity estimates for the entire economy and by sector that are more accurate and internally consistent.[39]

In response to the recommendations of the Advisory Committee on Innovation, the Bureau of Economic Analysis (BEA) and the Bureau of Labor Statistics (BLS) produced an integrated production account in May 2009,

35. See 2008 SNA, United Nations (2009, ch. 2, 12–13; ch. 29, 534–8). This issue will be discussed in more detail below.
36. See Chen and Ravallion (2010). A recent summary is provided by Ravallion (2012). A critique of the World Bank's approach is given by Deaton (2010).
37. World Bank (2008).
38. Advisory Committee on Measuring Innovation in the Twenty-First Century Economy (2008).
39. The Advisory Committee on Measuring Innovation in the Twenty-First Century Economy (2008, 8).

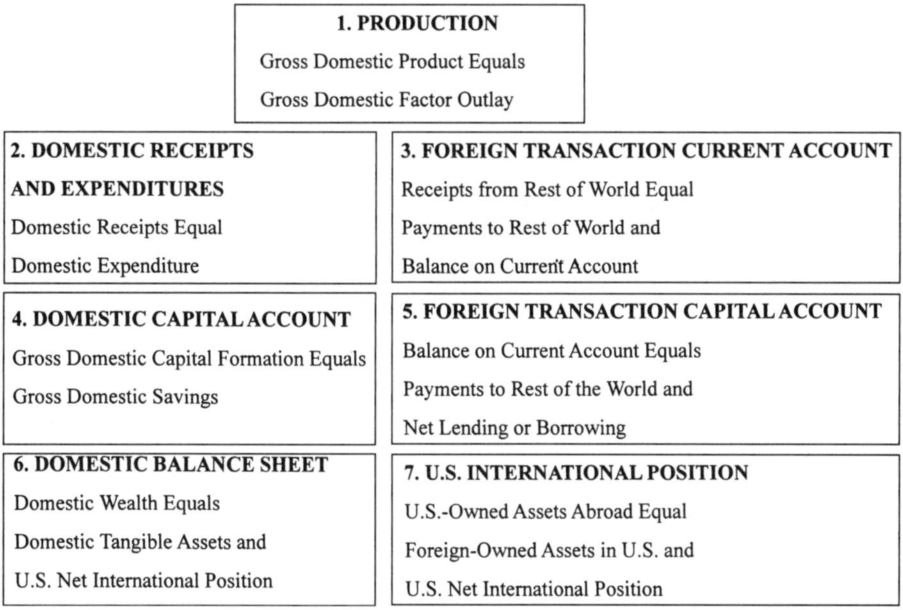

1. PRODUCTION
Gross Domestic Product Equals
Gross Domestic Factor Outlay

2. DOMESTIC RECEIPTS AND EXPENDITURES	3. FOREIGN TRANSACTION CURRENT ACCOUNT
Domestic Receipts Equal	Receipts from Rest of World Equal
Domestic Expenditure	Payments to Rest of World and
	Balance on Current Account

4. DOMESTIC CAPITAL ACCOUNT	5. FOREIGN TRANSACTION CAPITAL ACCOUNT
Gross Domestic Capital Formation Equals	Balance on Current Account Equals
Gross Domestic Savings	Payments to Rest of the World and
	Net Lending or Borrowing

6. DOMESTIC BALANCE SHEET	7. U.S. INTERNATIONAL POSITION
Domestic Wealth Equals	U.S.-Owned Assets Abroad Equal
Domestic Tangible Assets and	Foreign-Owned Assets in U.S. and
U.S. Net International Position	U.S. Net International Position

Fig. 3.3   New architecture for an expanded and integrated set of national accounts for the United States

linking multifactor productivity with the NIPAs.[40] This was a critical step in implementing the new architecture.[41] The omission of productivity statistics from the NIPAs and the United Nations' System of National Accounts (SNA) had been a serious barrier to application of the national accounts in assessing the sources of economic growth. Estimates of productivity are also essential for projecting potential economic growth.[42]

In August 2008, four years after the meeting of the Conference on Research in Income and Wealth devoted to the new architecture, Jorgenson presented an update of the prototype system of national accounts he had developed with Landefeld. The occasion was Jorgenson's Richard and Nancy Ruggles Memorial Lecture to the Thirtieth General Conference of the International Association for Research on Income and Wealth.[43] Jorgenson linked the new architecture presented in figure 3.3 to the integrated macroeconomic accounts developed by the BEA and the FRB.

Jorgenson presented the GDP as a measure of production and personal consumption expenditures, and as a component of potential social welfare.

40. Harper et al. (2009). For current data from the integrated production account, see http://www.bea.gov/national/integrated_prod.htm.
41. For a more detailed discussion, see Jorgenson (2011).
42. See Jorgenson, Ho, and Stiroh (2008).
43. Dale W. Jorgenson (2009).

He emphasized that consumption is a measure of the current flow of welfare. Saving, the second component of domestic expenditures, is a measure of current contributions to future welfare through consumption.[44]

Jorgenson's Ruggles lecture focused primarily on integrating productivity measures into the national accounts.[45] The Domestic Income and Product Account is presented in table 3.1. In the prototype system of national accounts this account is modeled after Jorgenson's presidential address to the American Economic Association.[46] Like the BEA/BLS Integrated Production Account, this conforms to the standards presented in Schreyer's (2001) OECD productivity manual.

A key innovation in the new architecture for the US national accounts is the inclusion of prices and quantities of capital services for all productive assets in the US economy. The process that led to the 2008 SNA was formally initiated by the United Nations Statistical Commission in March 2004, almost simultaneously with the development of the new architecture for the US national accounts. Issues related to the measurement of capital were assigned to an expert group, designated Canberra II after the site of the initial meeting in Canberra, Australia.

The incorporation of the price and quantity of capital services into the 2008 SNA was recommended by the Canberra II expert group and approved by the United Nations Statistical Commission at its February-March 2007 meeting. Schreyer, then head of national accounts at the OECD, prepared an OECD manual titled *Measuring Capital*.[47] Schreyer's manual provided detailed recommendations on methods for the construction of prices and quantities of capital services.

Estimates of capital services like those used in the new architecture were discussed in chapter 20 of the 2008 SNA:

> By . . . associating estimates of capital services with the standard breakdown of value added, the contributions of both (labor) and capital to production can be portrayed in a form ready for use in the analysis of productivity in a way entirely consistent with the accounts of the SNA.[48]

Jorgenson concluded that the Domestic Income and Product Account of the new architecture is consistent with the 2008 SNA. The volume measure of input is a quantity index of capital and labor services, while the volume

---

44. This interpretation has been developed by Samuelson (1961), Nordhaus and Tobin (1973), Weitzman (1976), and Weitzman (2003).

45. Issues in measuring productivity were considered by a statistical working party of the OECD Industry Committee, headed by Edwin Dean, former associate commissioner for productivity and technology of the BLS. The working party established international standards for productivity measurement at both aggregate and industry levels. The results are summarized in Schreyer (2001).

46. Jorgenson (2001).

47. Schreyer (2009).

48. 2008 SNA, United Nations (2009, ch.20, 415).

Table 3.1   Production account 2010

A. Output

Line	Product	Source	Total
1	GDP (NIPA)	NIPA 1.1.5 line 1	14,526.5
2	+ Services of consumers' durables	our imputation	1,396.6
3	+ Services of household land (net of BEA estimate)	our imputation	174.6
4	+ Services of durables held by institutions	our imputation	49.9
5	+ Services of durables, structures, land, and inventories held by government	our imputation	500.4
6	+ Private land investment	our imputation	0.0
7	+ Government land and inventory investment	our imputation	−62.6
8	− General government consumption of fixed capital	NIPA 3.10.5 line 5	278.6
9	− Government enterprise consumption of fixed capital	NIPA 3.1 line 38–3.10.5 line 5	55.4
10	− Federal taxes on production and imports	NIPA 3.2 line 4	101.5
11	− Federal current transfer receipts from business	NIPA 3.2 line 16	48.7
12	− S&L taxes on production and imports	NIPA 3.3 line 6	952.6
13	− S&L current transfer receipts from business	NIPA 3.3 line 18	50.3
14	+ Capital stock tax	—	0.0
15	+ MV tax	NIPA 3.5 line 28	9.1
16	+ Property taxes	NIPA 3.3 line 8	430.6
17	+ Severance, special assessments, and other taxes	NIPA 3.5 line 29,30,31	74.5
18	+ Subsidies	NIPA 3.1 line 25	57.3
19	− Current surplus of government enterprises	NIPA 3.1 line 14	−15.7
20	= Gross domestic product		15,685.5

(*continued*)

Table 3.1   (continued)

B. Factor outlay

Line	Income	Source	Total
1	+ Consumption of fixed capital	NIPA 5.1 line 13	1,874.9
2	+ Statistical discrepancy	NIPA 5.1 line 26	0.8
3	+ Services of consumers' durables	our imputation	1,396.6
4	+ Services of household land (net of BEA estimate)	our imputation	174.6
5	+ Services of durables held by institutions	our imputation	49.9
6	+ Services of durables, structures, land, and inventories held by government	our imputation	500.4
7	+ National income adjustment for land investment	our imputation	−62.7
8	− General government consumption of fixed capital	NIPA 3.10.5 line 5	278.6
9	− Government enterprise consumption of fixed capital	NIPA 3.1 line 38–3.10.5 line 5	55.4
10	= National income	NIPA 1.7.5 line 16	12,840.1
11	− ROW income	NIPA 1.7.5 line 2–3	189.4
12	− Sales tax	Product Account	638.9
13	+ Subsidies	NIPA 3.1 line 25	57.3
14	− Current surplus of government enterprises	NIPA 3.1 line 14	−15.7
15	= Gross domestic income		15,685.4

measure of output is a quantity index of investment and consumption goods. Productivity is the ratio of output to input.

The interpretation of output, input, and productivity requires the production possibility frontier introduced by Jorgenson (1966):[49]

$$Y(I, C) = A X(K, L),$$

gross domestic product in constant prices Y consists of outputs of investment goods I and consumption goods C. These products are produced from capital services K and labor services L. These factor services are components of gross domestic income in constant prices X and are augmented by multifactor productivity A.

The key feature of the production possibility frontier is the explicit role for changes in the relative prices of investment and consumption outputs. The aggregate production function is a competing methodology, but there is no role for separate prices of investment and consumption goods. Under the assumption that product and factor markets are in competitive equilibrium, the share-weighted growth of outputs is the sum of the share-weighted growth of inputs and growth in multifactor productivity:

$$\bar{w}_I \Delta I + \bar{w}_C \Delta \ln C = \bar{v}_K \Delta \ln K + \bar{v}_L \Delta \ln L + \Delta \ln A,$$

where w and v denote average shares of the outputs and inputs, respectively, in the value of GDP.

Table 3.2 presents accounts for the sources of US economic growth during 1948 to 2010 and various subperiods. For the period as a whole, the contribution of capital services accounted for 51.6 percent of economic growth. Labor services contributed 31.6 percent, while multifactor productivity growth contributed only 19.0 percent. The first subperiod ends with the business cycle peak in 1973. After strong output and productivity growth in the 1950s, 1960s, and early 1970s, the growth of GDP dropped from 3.95 percent from 1948 to 1973 to only 2.68 percent from 1973 through 1995.

A powerful resurgence in US economic growth began in 1995 but ended abruptly in 2000 with the dot-com crash. United States economic growth surged to 4.14 percent during the period 1995 to 2000. This reflected the investment boom of the late 1990s, as businesses, households, and governments poured resources into plant and equipment, especially computers, software, and communications equipment. Between 1973 and 1995 and 1995 to 2000, the contribution of capital input to US economic growth jumped by 0.80 percentage points, accounting for more than half the increase in output growth of 1.45 percent. The contribution of labor input increased by a modest 0.17 percent, while multifactor productivity growth accelerated by 0.49 percent.

After the dot-com crash in 2000, GDP growth slowed to 2.87 percent per

49. Jorgenson (1966).

Table 3.2   Contributions to output and growth, 1948–2010

	1948–2010	1948–1973	1973–1995	1995–2000	2000–2005	2005–2010
	Output					
Gross domestic product	3.18	3.95	2.68	4.14	2.87	0.94
Contribution of consumption	2.29	2.79	1.96	2.33	2.26	1.27
Contribution of investment	0.89	1.16	0.72	1.81	0.61	–0.33
	Growth					
Gross domestic income	2.59	2.93	2.52	3.49	2.05	1.07
Contribution of capital services	1.64	1.88	1.40	2.20	1.58	1.05
Contribution of labor services	0.95	1.06	1.12	1.29	0.24	0.03
Multifactor productivity	0.59	1.02	0.16	0.65	0.83	–0.14

year and the relative importance of investment in information technology declined sharply. The contribution of capital services to economic growth dropped by 0.62 percent per year. The growth of multifactor productivity increased to 0.83 percent, while the contribution of labor input sank by more than a full percentage point to 0.24 percent per year. The GDP growth plunged to only 0.94 percent during 2005 to 2010, a subperiod that includes the Great Recession of 2007 to 2009.

The results presented in table 3.2 highlight the importance of the new architecture. In the absence of an integrated production account, like that published by the BEA and BLS in 2009, the analysis of sources of economic growth would have had to rely on a mixture of estimates from different sources, combined with estimates of missing information, such as growth in labor input per hour worked. Different analysts could readily produce conflicting interpretations of events such as the spurt in productivity growth after 1995, and the collapse of output and productivity growth during the Great Recession.

The Domestic Income and Product Account of the new architecture has been disaggregated to the level of sixty-five industries by Susan Fleck, Steven Rosenthal, Matthew Russell, Erich Strassner, and Lisa Usher (chapter 11, this volume).[50] Jorgenson, Ho, and Samuels (2012) have extended this industry-level account to cover the period 1947 to 2010.[51] The methodology follows that of Jorgenson, Ho, and Stiroh (2008), and conforms to the international standards established in Schreyer's (2001) OECD productivity

50. Fleck et al. (chapter 11, this volume). For data covering 1998–2010, see http://www.bea.gov/industry/pdf/Prototype%20BEA-BLS%20Industry-Level%20Production%20Account%20for%20the%20United%20States%201998-2010_Final.pdf.
51. Jorgenson, Ho, and Samuels (2012).

manual. Jorgenson and Schreyer (2013) have shown how to integrate the industry-level production account of Jorgenson, Ho, and Samuels (2012) into the 2008 SNA.[52]

Industry-level production accounts have been incorporated into the national accounts in seven countries in addition to the United States. The EU KLEMS project has developed systems of production accounts for the economies of twenty-five of the twenty-seven European Union (EU) member states.[53] For major EU countries this project includes accounts for seventy-two industries, covering the period 1970 to 2005. The World KLEMS Initiative will extend the EU KLEMS framework to important developing and transition economies, including Argentina, Brazil, Chile, China, India, Indonesia, Mexico, Russia, Turkey, and Taiwan.[54]

We employ the Domestic Income and Expenditures Account presented in table 3.3 in measuring individual and social welfare in the new architecture. The key accounting identity for the Domestic Income and Expenditures Account is that net income is equal to net expenditures. Net income includes gross income from sales of capital and labor services from the Domestic Income and Product Account, less depreciation. Net income also contains net receipts from the rest of the world, including taxes and transfers. Net expenditures are the sum of personal consumption expenditures, government consumption expenditures, and net saving.[55]

Economic growth creates opportunities for both present and future consumption. These opportunities are generated by expansion in the supply of capital and labor services, augmented by changes in the level of living:

$$Z(C,S) = BW(L,N),$$

net domestic expenditures in constant prices Z consist of consumption expenditures C and saving S, net of depreciation. These expenditures are generated by net incomes in constant prices W, comprising labor incomes L and property incomes N, net of depreciation.

The level of living B must be carefully distinguished from multifactor productivity A. An increase in the level of living implies that for given supplies of the factor services that generate labor and property incomes, the US economy generates greater opportunities for present and future consumption. The share-weighted growth of expenditures is the sum of the share-weighted growth of incomes and growth in the level of living:

52. Jorgenson and Schreyer (2013).

53. The EU KLEMS project was completed on June 30, 2008. A summary of the findings is presented by Timmer et al. (2010), and Mas and Stehrer (2012). For current estimates see www.euklems.net/.

54. Jorgenson (2012). See http://www.csls.ca/ipm/24/IPM-24-Jorgenson.pdf. Jorgenson summarizes the prototype industry-level production account for the United States developed by Jorgenson, Ho, and Samuels (2012).

55. Jorgenson (2009, table 3, 15), expresses the Domestic Income and Expenditures Account in terms of the US National Income and Product Accounts.

Table 3.3   **Domestic receipts and expenditures, 2010**

A. Receipts

Line	Income	Source	Total
1	+ Gross income	Product account	15,685.4
2	+ Production taxes	Product account	638.9
3	– Subsidies	NIPA 3.1 line 25	57.3
4	+ Current surplus of government enterprises	NIPA 3.1 line 14	–15.7
5	= Gross domestic income at market prices		16,251.3
6	+ Income receipts from the rest of the world	NIPA 1.7.5 line 2	702.9
7	– Income payments to the rest of the world	NIPA 1.7.5 line 3	513.5
8	– Current taxes and transfers to the rest of the world (net)	NIPA 4.1 line 25	151.6
9	= Gross income		16,289.1
10	– Depreciation	our imputation	2,776.3
11	= Net income		13,512.8

B. Expenditures

Line	Expenditures	Source	Total
1	+ Personal consumption expenditures		10,781.1
2	PCE nondurable goods (NIPA)	NIPA 2.3.5 line 6	2,301.5
3	PCE services (NIPA)	NIPA 2.3.5 line 13	6,858.5
4	PCE services less space rental value of inst. building and nonfarm dwellings	our imputation	5,729.2
5	Services of consumers' durables	our imputation	1,396.6
6	Services of structures and land	our imputation	1,303.9
7	Services of durables held by institutions	our imputation	49.9
8	+ Government consumption expenditures		2,663.9
9	Government consumption nondurable goods	NIPA 3.10.5 line 8	271.1
10	Government intermediate purchases, durable goods	NIPA 3.10.5 line 7	75.6
11	Government consumption services total		369.1
12	Government consumption services	NIPA 3.10.5 line 9	758.1
13	Less sales to other sectors	NIPA 3.10.5 line 11	389.0
14	Services of durables, structures, land, and inventories held by government	our imputation	500.4
15	Less government enterprise consumption of fixed capital	NIPA 3.1 line 38–3.10.5 line 5	55.4
16	Government compensation of employees excluding force account labor	NIPA 3.10.5 line 4–10	1,503.1
17	+ Gross national saving and statistical discrepancy	Capital account	2,844.0
	– Depreciation	our imputation	2,776.3
18	= Net domestic expenditures		13,512.8

$$\bar{w}_C \Delta \ln C + \bar{w}_S \Delta S = \bar{v}_L \Delta \ln L + \bar{v}_N \Delta \ln N + \Delta \ln B,$$

where w and v denote average value shares for expenditures and incomes, respectively.

Table 3.4 presents a decomposition of the uses of economic growth for the period 1948 to 2010. The growth rate of expenditures is a weighted average of growth rates of personal consumption expenditures, government consumption expenditures, and net saving. The contribution of each category of expenditures is the growth rate weighted by the relative share. Similarly, the contributions of labor and property incomes are the growth rates weighted by the relative shares. Growth in the level of living is the difference between growth rates of expenditures and incomes.

The growth of net expenditures largely reflects the pattern of output growth, but averaged 0.25 percent lower for the period 1948 to 2010. Strong growth in expenditures during the period 1948 to 1973 was followed by a slowdown after 1973. A sharp revival occurred after 1995, but the boom was followed by another slowdown after 2000 and a collapse after 2005. Personal consumption expenditures, a key component of our measure of potential welfare, greatly predominated as a source of growth in the net expenditures. The contribution of net saving added 0.16 percent to growth of expenditures for the period as a whole, but this contribution declined sharply after 2000.

Table 3.4   Contributions to growth of net expenditures, 1948–2010

	Average annual growth rates					
	1948–2010	1948–1973	1973–1995	1995–2000	2000–2005	2005–2010
	Receipts					
Domestic receipts	2.24	2.70	2.15	3.02	1.14	0.68
Contribution of labor income	1.08	1.19	1.29	1.48	0.28	0.02
Contribution of net property income	1.16	1.51	0.86	1.54	0.86	0.66
Level of living	0.74	1.03	0.56	0.90	1.17	−0.46
	Expenditures					
Net expenditures	2.99	3.73	2.71	3.91	2.31	0.23
Contribution of consumption	2.82	3.34	2.44	3.34	2.72	1.50
Contribution of personal consumption	2.36	2.69	2.07	3.12	2.45	1.12
Contribution of government consumption	0.46	0.65	0.37	0.21	0.27	0.37
Contribution of net saving	0.16	0.39	0.27	0.57	−0.42	−1.27

3.6   Standard of Living and Its Cost

In this section we integrate distributional measures for personal consumption expenditures into the US national accounts for the period 1948 to 2010. Measurement of the standard of living and its cost are classic problems in the application of normative economics.[56] Measurement of the standard of living is the objective of the approach to evaluating national income introduced by John Hicks (1940) and discussed by Samuelson (1950).[57] John Chipman and James Moore have demonstrated that the compensation principle proposed by Hicks provides a valid indicator of social welfare only if preferences are identical and homothetic for all consuming units.[58] Sen (1976, 1979) has revived interest in this problem, applying rank-order weights to elements of the matrix x that describes the social state.[59] Hammond (1978) has shown that Sen's approach requires preferences of the type considered by Gorman (1953) for its validity.[60]

Fisher, Johnson, and Smeeding (2012) provide a detailed survey of the recent literature on the measurement of inequality in consumption and income.[61] Their estimates of inequality employ data from the Consumer Expenditure Survey (CEX) and cover the period 1984 to 2010. Other recent and comprehensive studies of welfare measurement based on the CEX include Attanasio, Hurst, and Pistaferri (2012) and Meyer and Sullivan (2009).[62] Our approach is complementary to the work of Fixler and Johnson (chapter 8, this volume), who consider the integration of distributional measures for income from the Current Population Survey (CPS) into the US national accounts.[63]

We next implement the approach to normative economics presented in section 3.2. Our measure of potential social welfare is personal consumption expenditures from the Domestic Income and Expenditures Account of figure 3.3, expressed in constant prices per household equivalent member. Actual social welfare also depends on the distribution of personal consumption expenditures over the population.

We first introduce a quantity index of social welfare, say Q_A, as a measure of the standard of living. We define this index as the ratio of two levels of aggregate expenditure per capita

---

56. Measurement of the standard of living and its cost is discussed by Jorgenson and Slesnick (1983), Jorgenson and Slesnick (1990), and Slesnick (2001, 67–121).

57. See Hicks (1940) and Samuelson (1950).

58. Chipman and Moore (1973, 1980).

59. Sen (1976, 1979).

60. Hammond (1978).

61. See Fisher, Johnson, and Smeeding (2012).

62. See Attanasio, Hurst, and Pistaferri (2012) and Meyer and Sullivan (2009). This short list of references is far from exhaustive.

63. Fixler and Johnson (chapter 8, this volume).

(19) $$Q_A(p^0,W^0,W^1) = \frac{M(p^0,W^1)/\sum_{k=1}^{K^1}m_0(p^0,A_k)}{M(p^0,W^0)/\sum_{k=1}^{K^0}m_0(p^0,A_k)}.$$

The numerator is the expenditure per capita required to attain the current level of social welfare W^1 at base period prices p^0. The denominator is the expenditure per capita required for the base period level of welfare W^0. Our measure of the size of the population is the number of household equivalent members.

We obtain the base level of social welfare W^0 by evaluating the social welfare function at the price system p^0 and the distribution of total expenditure $\{M_k^0\}$. To obtain the current level of social welfare W^1 we evaluate the social welfare function at the current price system p^1 and the distribution of total expenditure $\{M_k^1\}$. Using the social expenditure function (18), we express the quantity index of social welfare (19) in the form

(20) $$\ln Q_A(p^0,W^0,W^1) = \frac{1}{D(p^0)}(W^0 - W^1).$$

We refer to the index Q_A as the *translog standard-of-living index*. If this index is greater than unity, actual social welfare has increased; otherwise, social welfare has remained the same or decreased.

Next, we decompose the index of social welfare (20) into the product of efficiency and equity. We first determine the maximum level of welfare, say W^3, that can be attained through lump-sum redistributions of aggregate total expenditure $M^1 = \sum M_k^1$. Expenditure must be distributed so as to equalize individual expenditure per capita, so that the social welfare function reduces to average individual welfare (17)

(21) $$W^3 = \ln \bar{V}^1 = \ln p^{1\prime}\left(\alpha_p + \frac{1}{2}B_{pp}\ln p^1\right) - D(p^1)\ln[M^1/\sum_{k=1}^{K^1}m_0(p^1,A_k)].$$

This is our measure of efficiency and does not depend on the degree of aversion to inequality ρ.

We define efficiency, say Q_p, as the ratio of two levels of aggregate expenditure per capita

(22) $$Q_p(p^0,W^2,W^3) = \frac{M(p^0,W^3)/\sum_{k=1}^{K^1}m_0(p^0,A_k)}{M(p^0,W^2)/\sum_{k=1}^{K^0}m_0(p^0,A_k)}$$

$$= \frac{M(p^0,W^3)/\sum_{k=1}^{K^1}m_0(p^0,A_k)}{M^0/\sum_{k=1}^{K^0}m_0(p^0,A_k)},$$

where M^0 is base period expenditure.

The quantity index of efficiency (22) is the ratio of money measures of efficiency in the current period and the base period, both evaluated at the base period price system p^0. The numerator is the per capita expenditure required to attain the potential level of social welfare in the current period

W^3. The denominator of (22) is the expenditure per capita required for the potential level of welfare in the base period W^2.

We express potential levels of social welfare in the base period W^2 and the current period W^3 in terms of average individual welfare (17). Using the social expenditure function, we express the quantity index of efficiency (22) in the form

$$(23) \qquad \ln Q_p(p^0, W^2, W^3) = \frac{1}{D(p^0)}(W^2 - W^3).$$

We refer to the index Q_p as the *translog efficiency index*. If this index is greater than unity, potential social welfare has increased; otherwise, potential welfare has remained the same or decreased.

Finally, we define equity, say Q_E as the ratio of the index of social welfare to the index of efficiency

$$(24) \qquad Q_E = \frac{Q_A}{Q_p} = \frac{M(p^0, W^1)/M(p^0, W^3)}{M(p^0, W^0)/M^0}.$$

The numerator of our quantity index of equity (24) is a money measure of equity in the current period. Similarly, the denominator is the money measure of equity in the base period. Since measures of equity depend on the degree of aversion to inequality ρ, we present indexes for both utilitarian and egalitarian social welfare functions.

Using the social expenditure function, we express the quantity index of equity (24) in the form

$$(25) \qquad \ln Q_E(p^0, W^0, W^1, W^2, W^3) = \frac{1}{D(p^0)}[(W^0 - W^1) - (W^2 - W^3)],$$

and refer to the index Q_E as the *translog equity index*. If this index is greater than unity, equity has increased; otherwise, equity has remained the same or decreased.[64]

The social welfare function (16) provides a cardinal measure of social welfare. Since the translog indexes of the standard of living, efficiency, and equity are proportional to differences between values of this social welfare function, they also provide cardinal measures. Growth rates of these indexes are cardinal measures of changes in social welfare.

To define a social cost-of-living index we first consider the ratio of nominal expenditure per capita, as follows:

$$(26) \qquad \ln \frac{M^1/\sum_{k=1}^{K^1} m_0(p^1, A_k)}{M^0/\sum_{k=1}^{K^0} m_0(p^0, A_k)} = \ln \frac{M(p^1, W^3)/\sum_{k=1}^{K^1} m_0(p^1, A_k)}{M(p^0, W^2)/\sum_{k=1}^{K^0} m_0(p^0, A_k)}.$$

---

64. This approach to the measurement of inequality was introduced by Jorgenson and Slesnick (1984), and is discussed by Jorgenson (1990), Jorgenson and Slesnick (1990), Slesnick (1994), and Slesnick (2001, 122–55).

Base period expenditure M^0 is a money measure of potential social welfare, evaluated at base period prices p^0. Similarly, current expenditure M^1 is a measure of potential welfare at current prices p^1.

Next, we decompose nominal expenditure (26) into the product of an index of efficiency and a social cost-of-living index,

$$\ln \frac{M^1/\sum_{k=1}^{K^1} m_0(p^1, A_k)}{M^0/\sum_{k=1}^{K^0} m_0(p^0, A_k)} = \ln Q_p + \ln P,$$

where Q_p is the translog index of efficiency (23) and the index P is the translog social cost-of-living index introduced by Jorgenson and Slesnick (1983),

$$(27) \quad \ln P(p^1, p^0, W^3) = \ln M^1 - \frac{1}{D(p^0)}[\ln p^{0\prime}(\alpha_p + B_{pp}\ln p^0) - W^3]$$

$$+ \ln \sum_{k=1}^{K^1} m_0(p^0, A_k).$$

The social cost-of-living index is the ratio of the aggregate expenditure required to attain the potential level of welfare in the current period W^3 at current prices p^1 to the expenditure required to attain this level of welfare at base period prices p^0. This depends only on potential social welfare W^3 and is independent of the degree of aversion to inequality ρ. If the translog social cost-of-living index is greater than unity and aggregate expenditure is constant, then social welfare is decreased by the change in prices.

As an illustration of the standard of living Q_A in (19) and the cost-of-living P in (27), we assess the impact of changes in the price system p and the distribution of total expenditure $\{M_k\}$ on the standard of living for both utilitarian and egalitarian social welfare functions. In the first column of table 3.5 we present personal consumption expenditures for the United States in nominal terms for the period 1948 to 2010. This is aggregate expenditure M, the sum of total expenditure over all US households $\sum_{k=1}^{K} M_k$.

In the second column of table 3.5, we present the translog social cost-of-living index P from equation (27). We divide consumption in nominal terms by the social cost-of-living index to obtain personal consumption expenditures in constant prices of 2005 in the third column. In the fourth column of table 3.5 we present the number of household equivalent members $\sum_{k=1}^{K} m_0(p, A_k)$ of the US population. We divide personal consumption expenditures in real terms by the number of household equivalent members to express real consumption in per capita terms. This results in a measure of potential social welfare that is proportional to the translog efficiency index Q_p in (22).

In table 3.6 we present indexes of the US standard of living for both utilitarian and egalitarian social welfare functions to emphasize the role of normative conditions in measuring social welfare. In the first column of table 3.6 we present the translog equity index Q_E in (24), evaluated for the

Table 3.5   **Personal consumption expenditures, 1948–2010**

Year	Personal consumption expenditures (billions)	Cost-of-living index (2005 = 1.0000)	Personal consumption expenditures, quantity (2005 dollars)	Number of household equivalent members (millions)	Personal consumption expenditures, quantity per household equivalent member (thousands of 2005 dollars)
1948	176.1	0.1483	1,187.7	247.4	4.80
1949	179.2	0.1472	1,217.8	245.8	4.95
1950	191.3	0.1490	1,284.0	248.1	5.18
1951	210.1	0.1563	1,344.3	250.8	5.36
1952	223.5	0.1597	1,399.8	252.6	5.54
1953	235.8	0.1634	1,443.1	256.1	5.63
1954	244.5	0.1654	1,478.0	262.3	5.63
1955	261.4	0.1678	1,557.9	269.8	5.77
1956	274.8	0.1702	1,614.4	272.4	5.93
1957	290.4	0.1750	1,659.5	276.0	6.01
1958	302.0	0.1783	1,693.6	280.4	6.04
1959	323.2	0.1827	1,768.9	280.2	6.31
1960	337.8	0.1861	1,815.2	290.9	6.24
1961	350.3	0.1883	1,860.0	296.1	6.28
1962	370.1	0.1916	1,932.0	295.2	6.54
1963	388.5	0.1943	1,998.9	295.3	6.77
1964	417.5	0.1982	2,105.8	298.3	7.06
1965	449.8	0.2024	2,221.7	298.1	7.45
1966	486.9	0.2080	2,340.2	299.2	7.82
1967	514.3	0.2130	2,414.4	303.5	7.96
1968	558.6	0.2210	2,528.1	306.5	8.25
1969	606.7	0.2312	2,624.0	309.8	8.47
1970	654.1	0.2417	2,706.2	312.9	8.65
1971	703.6	0.2526	2,785.1	317.6	8.77
1972	771.0	0.2628	2,934.1	320.7	9.15
1973	847.1	0.2755	3,075.2	328.5	9.36
1974	932.2	0.3011	3,095.7	329.5	9.40
1975	1,036.5	0.3265	3,174.3	332.7	9.54
1976	1,156.7	0.3490	3,314.2	335.0	9.89
1977	1,283.0	0.3727	3,442.8	339.0	10.16
1978	1,434.3	0.3985	3,599.6	342.4	10.51
1979	1,599.5	0.4298	3,721.3	350.6	10.61
1980	1,775.2	0.4712	3,767.1	352.0	10.70
1981	1,969.3	0.5153	3,822.0	348.7	10.96
1982	2,118.6	0.5474	3,870.2	344.6	11.23
1983	2,317.9	0.5749	4,031.6	342.5	11.77
1984	2,524.2	0.6008	4,201.5	355.6	11.82
1985	2,720.8	0.6183	4,400.7	360.6	12.20
1986	2,876.0	0.6318	4,551.8	353.1	12.89
1987	3,092.6	0.6545	4,725.3	364.9	12.95
1988	3,344.1	0.6811	4,910.1	375.2	13.09
1989	3,593.7	0.7097	5,063.4	375.3	13.49
1990	3,848.6	0.7412	5,192.6	377.0	13.78
1991	4,025.9	0.7671	5,248.3	388.5	13.51

(continued)

Table 3.5   (continued)

Year	Personal consumption expenditures (billions)	Cost-of-living index (2005 = 1.0000)	Personal consumption expenditures, quantity (2005 dollars)	Number of household equivalent members (millions)	Personal consumption expenditures, quantity per household equivalent member (thousands of 2005 dollars)
1992	4,270.7	0.7902	5,404.2	385.3	14.03
1993	4,491.3	0.8057	5,574.3	389.1	14.32
1994	4,759.0	0.8248	5,770.0	393.8	14.65
1995	5,001.9	0.8422	5,939.2	410.9	14.45
1996	5,295.4	0.8631	6,135.4	411.6	14.91
1997	5,588.1	0.8794	6,354.7	422.0	15.06
1998	5,888.7	0.8835	6,665.1	423.3	15.75
1999	6,267.9	0.8955	6,999.2	435.0	16.09
2000	6,720.3	0.9150	7,344.9	445.2	16.50
2001	7,020.8	0.9270	7,573.4	449.8	16.84
2002	7,312.7	0.9376	7,799.5	453.8	17.19
2003	7,662.7	0.9534	8,036.9	460.8	17.44
2004	8,086.0	0.9731	8,309.7	467.8	17.76
2005	8,620.1	1.0000	8,620.1	472.0	18.26
2006	9,118.1	1.0245	8,900.1	476.6	18.67
2007	9,618.3	1.0535	9,130.1	481.4	18.97
2008	10,008.0	1.0894	9,186.6	489.5	18.77
2009	10,019.0	1.1062	9,057.5	496.1	18.26
2010	10,383.1	1.1273	9,210.4	501.6	18.36

egalitarian social welfare function (16) with ρ equal to negative unity. The egalitarian measure of social welfare is proportional to the translog social welfare index Q_A in (20),[65] expressed in constant prices of 2005. Similarly, the utilitarian standard of living presented in the fifth column of table 3.6 is evaluated for the utilitarian social welfare function with ρ equal to negative infinity. This is our utilitarian measure social welfare, expressed in constant prices of 2005.

Finally, in the third column of table 3.6 we present the egalitarian index of relative inequality. This is defined as the proportional loss in money metric social welfare due to an unequal distribution of household welfare:

$$(28) \qquad I(p^0, W^1, W^3) = 1 - \frac{M(p^0, W^1)}{M(p^0, W^3)}.$$

Like the familiar Gini coefficient, this index of relative inequality lies between zero and one with zero defining perfect equality. We present the utilitarian index of relative inequality in the sixth column of table 3.6.

---

65. For measures covering the years 1947–1985, see Jorgenson (1990) and Jorgenson and Slesnick (1990).

Table 3.6   **Standard of living, 1948–2010**

	Egalitarian			Utilitarian		
Year	Equity (2005 = 1.0000)	Standard of living (thousands of 2005 dollars)	Relative inequality	Equity (2005 = 1.0000)	Standard of living (thousands of 2005 dollars)	Relative inequality
1948	0.881	2.56	0.4658	0.941	3.58	0.2538
1949	0.880	2.64	0.4666	0.940	3.69	0.2547
1950	0.905	2.84	0.4516	0.955	3.92	0.2423
1951	0.904	2.94	0.4517	0.955	4.06	0.2422
1952	0.906	3.05	0.4504	0.956	4.20	0.2418
1953	0.899	3.07	0.4548	0.951	4.25	0.2454
1954	0.897	3.07	0.4559	0.950	4.25	0.2463
1955	0.896	3.14	0.4570	0.948	4.35	0.2476
1956	0.911	3.27	0.4475	0.957	4.50	0.2403
1957	0.907	3.31	0.4500	0.955	4.56	0.2425
1958	0.912	3.34	0.4471	0.957	4.59	0.2404
1959	0.952	3.64	0.4229	0.981	4.91	0.2219
1960	0.990	3.75	0.3998	1.003	4.97	0.2045
1961	0.990	3.77	0.3997	1.003	5.00	0.2044
1962	0.999	3.96	0.3944	1.008	5.23	0.2004
1963	1.006	4.13	0.3900	1.012	5.43	0.1973
1964	1.013	4.33	0.3859	1.015	5.69	0.1945
1965	1.018	4.60	0.3825	1.018	6.02	0.1922
1966	1.023	4.85	0.3796	1.021	6.33	0.1904
1967	1.028	4.96	0.3769	1.023	6.46	0.1886
1968	1.032	5.16	0.3741	1.025	6.71	0.1868
1969	1.036	5.32	0.3716	1.027	6.90	0.1852
1970	1.040	5.46	0.3691	1.029	7.06	0.1837
1971	1.046	5.56	0.3660	1.031	7.18	0.1817
1972	1.050	5.82	0.3635	1.034	7.50	0.1799
1973	1.071	6.08	0.3507	1.044	7.75	0.1719
1974	1.064	6.06	0.3547	1.041	7.76	0.1743
1975	1.060	6.13	0.3570	1.038	7.86	0.1761
1976	1.057	6.34	0.3588	1.037	8.14	0.1775
1977	1.053	6.49	0.3613	1.034	8.33	0.1795
1978	1.049	6.69	0.3640	1.031	8.60	0.1818
1979	1.044	6.72	0.3672	1.028	8.66	0.1843
1980	1.039	6.74	0.3701	1.025	8.70	0.1869
1981	1.051	6.99	0.3626	1.033	8.98	0.1807
1982	1.056	7.19	0.3596	1.035	9.23	0.1785
1983	1.040	7.42	0.3693	1.025	9.57	0.1869
1984	1.025	7.35	0.3783	1.016	9.53	0.1936
1985	1.020	7.55	0.3815	1.013	9.81	0.1961
1986	1.026	8.02	0.3778	1.017	10.40	0.1934
1987	1.030	8.09	0.3753	1.019	10.47	0.1914
1988	1.018	8.08	0.3825	1.010	10.49	0.1984
1989	1.037	8.48	0.3713	1.022	10.94	0.1893

(continued)

Table 3.6 (continued)

	Egalitarian			Utilitarian		
Year	Equity (2005 = 1.0000)	Standard of living (thousands of 2005 dollars)	Relative inequality	Equity (2005 = 1.0000)	Standard of living (thousands of 2005 dollars)	Relative inequality
1990	1.032	8.62	0.3744	1.018	11.12	0.1925
1991	1.0393	8.51	0.3698	1.0258	10.99	0.1862
1992	1.0323	8.78	0.3741	1.0189	11.34	0.1916
1993	1.0396	9.03	0.3697	1.0247	11.64	0.1872
1994	1.0466	9.30	0.3654	1.0277	11.94	0.1848
1995	1.0456	9.16	0.3661	1.0277	11.78	0.1848
1996	1.0401	9.40	0.3693	1.0240	12.11	0.1877
1997	1.0249	9.36	0.3785	1.0152	12.13	0.1946
1998	1.0280	9.82	0.3767	1.0167	12.70	0.1934
1999	1.0101	9.86	0.3875	1.0035	12.81	0.2039
2000	1.0107	10.11	0.3871	1.0052	13.16	0.2025
2001	1.0069	10.28	0.3894	1.0017	13.38	0.2053
2002	1.0304	10.74	0.3752	1.0165	13.86	0.1936
2003	1.0119	10.70	0.3865	1.0085	13.95	0.2000
2004	1.0207	10.99	0.3811	1.0112	14.25	0.1978
2005	1.0000	11.07	0.3936	1.0000	14.49	0.2067
2006	1.0022	11.35	0.3923	1.0008	14.82	0.2061
2007	1.0020	11.52	0.3924	0.9993	15.04	0.2072
2008	0.9956	11.33	0.3963	0.9965	14.84	0.2095
2009	1.0029	11.10	0.3919	1.0017	14.51	0.2053
2010	0.9815	10.93	0.4049	0.9885	14.40	0.2158

In table 3.7 we present average growth rates for personal consumption expenditures in constant prices per household equivalent member, our measure of efficiency, for the postwar period 1948 to 2010, and for five subperiods. We also present growth rates of egalitarian and utilitarian measures of equity and the standard of living. The average annual growth rate of efficiency for the period as a whole was 2.16 percent. The average growth rate of the egalitarian measure of the standard of living was 2.34 percent, reflecting a modest gain in equity of 0.17 percent per year. For the utilitarian measure of the standard of living the growth rate was 2.24 percent and the growth rate of equity was only 0.08 percent.

Growth of equity was limited to the subperiod 1948 to 1973 for both egalitarian and utilitarian measures. Equity declined modestly during 1973 to 1995, 0.11 percent per year for the egalitarian measure, and 0.07 for the utilitarian measure. For the subperiod 2000 to 2005, these rates of decline were 0.21 for the egalitarian measure and 0.10 for the utilitarian measure. For both measures equity plunged during the investment boom of 1995 to 2000 and again during the Great Recession of 2005 to 2010. The egalitarian

Table 3.7   **Contributions to growth of the standard of living, 1948–2010**

	Average annual growth rates					
	1948–2010	1948–1973	1973–1995	1995–2000	2000–2005	2005–2010
	Egalitarian					
Standard of living	2.34	3.45	1.87	1.96	1.82	−0.27
Efficiency	2.16	2.67	1.97	2.65	2.03	0.11
Equity	0.17	0.78	−0.11	−0.68	−0.21	−0.37
	Utilitarian					
Standard of living	2.24	3.09	1.90	2.20	1.93	−0.12
Efficiency	2.16	2.67	1.97	2.65	2.03	0.11
Equity	0.08	0.42	−0.07	−0.44	−0.10	−0.23

measure declined by 0.68 percent per year during 1995 to 2000 and 0.37 percent during 2005 to 2010. For the utilitarian measure these rates were 0.44 and 0.23 percent per year, respectively, for these two subperiods.

The growth rate of efficiency was highest during the period 1948 to 1973. Since this is the only period when the growth of equity was positive, the growth rates of the standard of living were also highest for both egalitarian and utilitarian measures. The growth rate of efficiency dropped during the subperiod 1973 to 1995. Combined with the modest declines in equity, this resulted in a substantial decline in the growth rates of both egalitarian and utilitarian measures of the standard of living.

The growth rate of efficiency revived briefly during the investment boom of 1995 to 2000, falling short of its postwar peak. This growth rate dropped again during 2000 to 2005 and was barely positive during the Great Recession period of 2005 to 2010. For the egalitarian measure of equity the investment boom growth in efficiency was more than offset by the substantial decline in equity, so that the growth rate of the standard of living continued its downward course. This continued during 2000 to 2005 and became negative during the Great Recession after 2005. The decline in equity was less substantial for the utilitarian measure, so that the growth rate of the standard of living rose modestly during 1995 to 2000 before falling in 2000 to 2005 and becoming negative during the Great Recession.

The modest differences between egalitarian and utilitarian growth rates of the standard of living illustrate the importance of value judgments in measuring social welfare. However, the qualitative picture is very similar for the two measures. High growth rates during 1948 to 1973 were followed by lower but relatively stable growth rates for 1973 to 2005, and by a collapse during the Great Recession period of 2005 to 2010. For both measures, the investment boom of 1995 to 2000 was largely offset by an accelerated decline in equity. Finally, substantial declines in equity contributed to the collapse of the standard of living during the Great Recession for both measures.

3.7   Conclusion

We conclude by recommending that distributional information should be incorporated into the US national accounts. This process could begin with a satellite system for measuring social welfare that would include the two polar opposite social welfare functions that we have considered. The egalitarian social welfare function gives maximum weight to equity considerations, while the utilitarian social welfare functions gives these considerations minimum weight.

The satellite system for measuring social welfare could include a breakdown of our measures of social welfare by family size, age of head of household, region, race, and urban versus rural residence and gender of head of household. A breakdown could also be provided by personal consumption expenditures per family. Using data sets on consumption from sources such as the World Bank and the Luxembourg Income Study, together with prices of consumption from sources like the World Bank's International Comparison Project, the satellite system could provide international comparisons.[66]

Incorporating normative judgments into the national accounts is a substantial departure from a long tradition. This tradition, as reflected in SNA 2008, excludes normative judgments that are essential for interpreting distributional information. The traditional view is that economists have little to contribute to these judgments. Our view is that the development of the economic theory of social choice and its many applications has made many economists expert in using normative perspectives in the evaluation of economic policy. These perspectives should be reflected in the US national accounts.

The strengths of the traditional approach to the national accounts could be preserved by presenting distributional information in a satellite system and considering a number of alternatives. Well-established aggregates from the production, income and expenditure, and wealth accounts, such as the GDP, personal consumption expenditures, and national wealth should be retained in the core system of national accounts. These are essential for developing and interpreting distributional information within the framework of the new architecture for the US national accounts.

The boundary of social welfare could be extended to include nonmarket goods and services and measures of subjective well-being. Alan B. Krueger (2009) and his coauthors have developed a detailed system of national time accounting. This includes both market and nonmarket uses of time, combined with evaluations based on measures of subjective well-being.[67]

A comprehensive review of nonmarket accounts is provided by Kath-

66. See the following for data from the World Bank: http://web.worldbank.org/WBSITE /EXTERNAL/TOPICS/EXTPOVERTY/EXTPA/0,,contentMDK:20202198~menuPK :435055~pagePK:148956~piPK:216618~theSitePK:430367,00.html.
For data from the Luxembourg Income Study, see http://www.lisdatacenter.org/.
67. See Krueger (2009).

arine B. Abraham and Christopher Mackie (2005, 2006) and their co-authors.[68] This includes accounts for household production, investments in education and health, activities of nonprofit organizations and governments, and environmental assets and services. Erwin Diewert and Paul Schreyer (chapter 4, this volume) provide a model of household production and consumption and an international comparison.[69] Michael B. Christian (chapter 14, this volume) presents human capital accounts for the United States, and Gang Liu (chapter 15, this volume) presents these accounts for sixteen countries, including fifteen OECD members.[70] Nicholas Muller,[71] Robert Mendelsohn, and William Nordhaus (2011) have constructed a system of environmental accounts for the United States.[71] Allison B. Rosen and David M. Cutler (2007) have proposed a system of national health accounts for the United States.[72]

Jorgenson and Slesnick (2008) have extended the model of consumer behavior presented in the appendix to include the demand for leisure, as well as goods and services.[73] This concept of leisure includes the nonmarket time used for household production, investments in education and health, and volunteer activities. Leisure time based on the CEX could be included in measures of individual and social welfare like those we have presented for market goods and services.

The next step in integrating the NIPAs with the Flow of Funds Accounts will be to extend the national balance sheet for the US economy. The prototype system of national accounts generated by Jorgenson, Landefeld, and Nordhaus (2006) could incorporate balance sheets for the individual sectors identified in the Flow of Funds Accounts. This could be used as the basis of intertemporal measures of individual and social welfare. For this purpose a representation of consumer behavior like that employed by Jorgenson and Slesnick (2008) would be required.

Appendix
Modeling Consumer Behavior

The system of individual expenditure shares (6) can be fitted without requiring that it is generated from an indirect utility function of the form (4). We

---

68. Abraham and Mackie (2005). A summary is provided by Abraham and Mackie in Jorgenson, Landefeld, and Nordhaus, eds. (2006, 161–92). The conceptual basis for nonmarket accounting is discussed by Nordhaus in Jorgenson, Landefeld, and Nordhaus (2006, 143–60). Abraham (chapter 2, this volume) presents a survey of expanded measures of welfare.

69. Diewert and Schreyer (2013).

70. Christian (chapter 14, this volume) and Liu (chapter 15, this volume).

71. Muller, Mendelsohn, and Nordhaus (2011). Additional results are given by Muller (chapter 13, this volume).

72. Rosen and Cutler (2007).

73. Jorgenson and Slesnick (2008).

say that the system is *integrable* if it can be generated from such an indirect utility function. Since we utilize the indirect utility functions for all consuming units in measuring social welfare, we impose conditions for integrability on the individual demand functions. A complete set of conditions for integrability[74] is the following:

Homogeneity. The individual expenditure shares are homogeneous of degree zero in prices and total expenditure.

We can write the individual expenditure shares in the form

$$w_k = \frac{1}{D(p)}(\alpha_p + B_{pp}\ln p - \beta_{pM}\ln M_k + B_{pA}A_k), (k = 1,2,...,K),$$

where the vector of parameters β_{pM} is constant and the same for all consumer units. Homogeneity implies that this vector must satisfy the restrictions

(A1) $\beta_{pM} = B_{pp}i.$

Given the exact aggregation restrictions, there are $N - 1$ restrictions implied by homogeneity.

Summability. The sum of the individual expenditure shares over all commodity groups is equal to unity

$$i'w_k = 1, (k = 1,2,...,K).$$

We can write the denominator $D(p)$ in (1.3.5) in the form

$$D = -1 + \beta_{Mp}\ln p,$$

where the vector of parameters β_{Mp}, is constant and the same for all commodity groups and all consuming units. Summability implies that this vector must satisfy the restrictions

(A2) $\beta_{Mp} = i'B_{pp}.$

Given the exact aggregation restrictions, there are $N - 1$ restrictions implied by summability.

Symmetry. The matrix of compensated own- and cross-price substitution effects must be symmetric.

If the system of individual expenditure shares can be generated from an indirect utility function of the form (4), a necessary and sufficient condition for symmetry is that the matrix B_{pp} must be symmetric. Without imposing this condition, we can write the individual expenditure shares in the form:

$$w_k = \frac{1}{D(p)}\left(\alpha_p + B_{pp}\ln\frac{p}{M_k} + B_{pA}A_k\right), (k = 1,2,...,K).$$

---

74. This set of conditions is based on the classic formulation of the theory of consumer behavior by Chipman et al. (1971). Details are presented by Jorgenson, Lau, and Stoker (1982, 287–301).

Symmetry implies that the matrix of parameters B_{pp} must satisfy the restrictions:

(A3) $$B_{pp} = B'_{pp}.$$

The total number of symmetry restrictions is $(1/2)N(N-1)$.

Nonnegativity. The individual expenditure shares must be nonnegative. By summability the individual expenditure shares sum to unity, so that we can write:

$$w_k \geq 0, (k = 1,2,...,K),$$

where $w_k \geq 0$ implies $w_{nk} \geq 0 (n = 1,2,...,N)$, and $w_k \neq 0$.

Since the translog indirect utility function is quadratic in the logarithms of prices, we can always choose the prices so that the individual expenditure shares violate the nonnegativity conditions. Accordingly, we cannot impose restrictions on the parameters of the translog indirect utility functions that would imply nonnegativity of the individual expenditure shares for all prices and total expenditure. Instead we consider restrictions on the parameters that imply monotonicity of the system of individual demand functions for all data points in our sample.

Monotonicity. The matrix of compensated own- and cross-price substitution effects must be nonpositive definite.

We introduce the definition, due to Martos (1969), of a *strictly merely positive subdefinite matrix*; namely, a real symmetric matrix S such that:

$$x'Sx < 0$$

implies $Sx > 0$ or $Sx < 0$.[75] A necessary and sufficient condition for monotonicity is either that the translog indirect utility function is homothetic or that B_{pp}^{-1} exists and is strictly merely positive subdefinite.

In implementing the econometric model of consumer behavior we divide consumer expenditures among five commodity groups. These groups are aggregates defined on a much more detailed classification of commodities, as described by Jorgenson, Slesnick, and Stoker (1987).[76] We assume that the indirect utility functions are homothetically separable in prices of the commodities within each group:

1. *Energy*: expenditures on electricity, natural gas, heating oil, and gasoline
2. *Food*: expenditures on all food products, including tobacco and alcohol
3. *Consumer goods*: expenditures on all other nondurable goods
4. *Capital services*: the service flow from consumer durables and housing
5. *Consumer services*: expenditures on consumer services, such as car repairs, medical services, entertainment, and so on

---

75. Martos (1969).
76. Jorgenson, Slesnick, and Stoker (1987).

We employ the following demographic characteristics as attributes of individual households:

1. *Family size*: 1, 2, 3, 4, 5, 6, and 7 or more persons
2. *Age of head of household*: 16–24, 25–34, 35–44, 45–54, 55–64, 65 and over
3. *Region of residence*: Northeast, North-Central, South, and West
4. *Race*: white, nonwhite
5. *Type of residence*: urban, rural
6. *Gender of head of household*: male, female

We treat expenditure shares for the five commodity groups as endogenous variables, so that we estimate four equations. As unknown parameters we have four elements of the vector α_p, four expenditure coefficients of the vector $B_{pp}i$, seventeen attribute coefficients for each of the four equations in the matrix B_{pA}, and ten price coefficients in the matrix B_{pp} which is constrained to be symmetric. The expenditure coefficients are sums of price coefficients in the corresponding equation, so that we have a total of eighty-six unknown parameters. Jorgenson and Slesnick (1987) estimated the complete model by pooling time-series and cross-section data. This model was revised to include gender of head of household and updated by Slesnick (2001). Our cross-section observations on consumption expenditures for each commodity group and demographic characteristics of individual households are from the Survey of Consumer Expenditures (CEX).[77]

References

Abraham, Katharine G., and Christopher Mackie, eds. 2005. *Beyond the Market: Designing Nonmarket Accounts for the United States*. Washington, DC: National Academies Press.

———. 2006. "A Framework for Nonmarket Accounting." In *A New Architecture for the US National Accounts*, edited by Dale W. Jorgenson, J. Steven Landefeld, and William D. Nordhaus, Studies in Income and Wealth 66:161–92. Chicago: University of Chicago Press.

Advisory Committee on Measuring Innovation in the Twenty-First Century Economy. 2008. *Innovation Measurement: Tracking the State of Innovation in the 21st Century Economy*. Washington, DC: Department of Commerce. January.

Atkinson, Anthony B. 1970. "On the Measurement of Inequality." *Journal of Economic Theory* 2 (3): 244–63.

Attanasio, Orazio, Erik Hurst, and Luigi Pistaferri. 2012. "The Evolution of Income, Consumption, and Leisure Inequality in the U.S., 1980–2010." NBER Working Paper no. 17982, Cambridge, MA.

77. Our measures of personal consumption expenditures and consumption at the microeconomic level are discussed in detail by Slesnick (2001, 47–66) and Jorgenson and Slesnick (2008).

Barten, Anton P. 1964. "Family Composition, Prices, and Expenditure Patterns." In *Econometric Analysis for Economic Planning: 16th Symposium of the Colston Society*, edited by Peter Hart, Gareth Mills, and John D. Whitaker, 277–92. London: Butterworth.

Becker, Gary S. 1981. *A Treatise on the Family*. Cambridge, MA: Harvard University Press.

Chen, Shaohua, and Martin Ravallion. 2010. "The Developing World is Poorer than We Thought, but No Less Successful in the Fight Against Poverty." *Quarterly Journal of Economics* 125 (4): 1577–629.

Chipman, John S., Leonid Hurwicz, Marcel K. Richter, and Hugo F. Sonnenschein, eds. 1971. *Preferences, Utility, and Demand*. New York: Harcourt, Brace, Jovanovich.

Chipman, John S., and James C. Moore. 1973. "Aggregate Demand, Real National Income, and the Compensation Principle." *International Economic Review* 14 (1): 153–81.

———. 1980. "Real National Income with Homothetic Preferences and a Fixed Distribution of Income." *Econometrica* 48 (2): 401–22.

Citro, Constance, and Robert Michael, eds. 1995. *Measuring Poverty: A New Approach*. Washington, DC: National Academies Press.

Dalton, Hugh. 1920. "The Measurement of the Inequality of Income." *Economic Journal* 30 (119): 361–84.

Deaton, Angus. 2010. "Price Indexes, Inequality, and the Measurement of World Poverty." *American Economic Review* 100 (1): 5–34.

Deaton, Angus, and John Muellbauer. 1980. *Economics and Consumer Behavior*. Cambridge: Cambridge University Press.

Fesseau, Maryse, and Maria Liviana Mattonetti. Forthcoming. "Distributional Measures among Household Groups in a National Accounts Framework: Results from an Experimental Cross-Country Exercise on Household Income, Consumption, and Saving." OECD Statistics Working Paper no. 2013/4, Organisation for Economic Co-operation and Development, Paris.

Fesseau, Maryse, Florence Wolff, and Maria Liviana Mattonetti. Forthcoming. "A Cross-Country Comparison of Household Income, Consumption and Wealth between Micro Sources and National Accounts Aggregates." OECD Statistics Working Paper no. 2013/3, Organisation for Economic Co-operation and Development, Paris.

Fisher, Jonathan, David Johnson, and Timothy Smeeding. 2012. "Inequality of Income and Consumption: Measuring the Trends in Inequality from 1985–2010 for the Same Individuals." Thirty-Second General Conference, International Association for Research in Income and Wealth, Boston, Massachusetts, August, pp. 6–9.

Fleurbaey, Marc. 2009. "Beyond the GDP: The Quest for Measures of Social Welfare." *Journal of Economic Literature* 47 (4): 1029–75.

Fleurbaey, Marc, and Peter J. Hammond. 2004. "Interpersonally Comparable Utility." In *Handbook of Utility Theory: Extensions*, edited by Salvador Barbera, Peter J. Hammond, and Christian Seidl, 1179–285. Heidelberg: Springer.

Fleurbaey, Marc, and Francois Maniquet. 2011. *A Theory of Fairness and Social Welfare*. Cambridge: Cambridge University Press.

Gorman, William M. 1953. "Community Preference Fields." *Econometrica* 21 (1): 63–80.

Hammond, Peter J. 1977. "Dual Interpersonal Comparisons of Utility and the Economics of Income Distribution." *Journal of Public Economics* 7 (1): 51–71.

———. 1978. "Economic Welfare with Rank Order Price Weighting." *Review of Economic Studies* 45 (2): 381–4.

Harper, Michael, Brent Moulton, Steven Rosenthal, and David Wasshausen. 2009. "Integrated GDP-Productivity Accounts." *American Economic Review* 99 (2): 74–9.

Hicks, John R. 1940. "The Valuation of Social Income." *Economica* N.S. 7:105–24.

Jorgenson, Dale W. 1966. "The Embodiment Hypothesis." *Journal of Political Economy* 74 (1): 1–17.

———. 1990. "Aggregate Consumer Behavior and the Measurement of Social Welfare." *Econometrica* 58 (5): 1007–40.

———. 1997a. *Aggregate Consumer Behavior*. Cambridge, MA: The MIT Press.

———. 1997b. *Measuring Social Welfare*. Cambridge, MA: The MIT Press.

———. 2001. "Information Technology and the US Economy." *American Economic Review* 91 (1): 1–32.

———. 2009. "A New Architecture for the US National Accounts." *Review of Income and Wealth* 55 (1): 1–42.

———. 2011. "Innovation and Productivity Growth: T. W. Schultz Lecture." *American Journal of Agricultural Economics* 93 (2): 276–96.

———. 2012. "The World KLEMS Initiative." *International Productivity Monitor* 24 (Fall): 5–19.

Jorgenson, Dale W., Mun S. Ho, and Samuels. 2012. "A Prototype Industry-Level Production Account for the United States, 1947–2010." Presented to the Final Conference of the World Input-Output Database project, Groningen, The Netherlands, April 25. http://www.economics.harvard.edu/faculty/jorgenson/files/12_0425_WIOD.pdf.

Jorgenson, Dale W., Mun S. Ho, and Kevin J. Stiroh. 2008. "A Retrospective Look at the US Productivity Growth Resurgence." *Journal of Economic Perspectives* 22 (1): 3–24.

Jorgenson, Dale W., J. Steven Landefeld, and William D. Nordhaus, eds. 2006. *A New Architecture for the US National Accounts*, Studies in Income and Wealth, vol. 66. Chicago: University of Chicago Press.

Jorgenson, Dale W., Lawrence J. Lau, and Thomas M. Stoker. 1982. "The Transcendental Logarithmic Model of Aggregate Consumer Behavior." In *Advances in Econometrics,* vol. 1, edited by Robert L. Basmann and George Rhodes, 97–238. Greenwich, CT: JAI Press.

Jorgenson, Dale W., and Paul Schreyer. 2013. "Industry-Level Productivity Measurement and the 2008 System of National Accounts." *Review of Income and Wealth* 59 (2): 185–211.

Jorgenson, Dale W., and Daniel T. Slesnick. 1983. "Individual and Social Cost-of-Living Indexes." In *Price Level Measurement*, edited by W. Erwin Diewert and Claude Montmarquette, 241–323. Ottawa: Statistics Canada.

Jorgenson, Dale W., and Daniel T. Slesnick. 1984. "Aggregate Consumer Behavior and the Measurement of Inequality." *Review of Economic Studies* 51 (3): 369–91.

Jorgenson, Dale W., and Daniel T. Slesnick. 1987. "Aggregate Consumer Behavior and Household Equivalence Scales." *Journal of Business and Economic Statistics* 5 (2): 219–32.

Jorgenson, Dale W., and Daniel T. Slesnick. 1990. "Inequality and the Standard of Living." *Journal of Econometrics* 43 (1–2): 103–20.

Jorgenson, Dale W., and Daniel T. Slesnick. 2008. "Consumption and Labor Supply." *Journal of Econometrics* 127 (1): 326–35.

Jorgenson, Dale W., Daniel T. Slesnick, and Thomas M. Stoker. 1987. "Two-Stage Budgeting and the Consumer Demand for Energy." In *Advances in the Economics of Energy and Resources,* vol. 6, edited by John R. Moroney, 125–62. Greenwich, CT: JAI Press.

Kolm, Serge C. 1969. "The Optimal Production of Social Justice." In *Public Economics*, edited by Julius Margolis and Henri Guitton, 145–200. London: Macmillan.

Krueger, Alan B. 2009. *Measuring the Subjective Well-Being of Nations: National Accounts of Time Use and Well-Being.* Chicago: University of Chicago Press.

Landefeld, J. Steven, Brent Moulton, Joel D. Platt, and Shaunda M. Villones. 2010. "GDP and Beyond: Measuring Economic Progress and Sustainability." *Survey of Current Business* 90 (4): 12–25.

Lewbel, Arthur. 1989. "Household Equivalence Scales and Welfare Comparisons." *Journal of Public Economics* 39 (3): 377–91.

Martos, Bela. 1969. "Subdefinite Matrices and Quadratic Forms." *SIAM Journal of Applied Mathematics* 17 (6): 1215–23.

Mas, Matilde, and Robert Stehrer, eds. 2012. *Industrial Productivity in Europe: Growth and Crisis.* Cheltenham, UK: Edward Elgar.

McKenzie, Lionel W. 1957. "Demand Theory without a Utility Index." *Review of Economic Studies* 24 (65): 185–9.

Meyer, Bruce, and James Sullivan. 2009. "Five Decades of Consumption and Income Poverty." NBER Working Paper no. 14827, Cambridge, MA.

Muellbauer, John. 1976. "Community Preferences and the Representative Consumer." *Econometrica* 44 (5): 979–99.

Muller, Nicholas, Robert Mendelsohn, and William Nordhaus. 2011. "Environmental Accounting for Pollution in the United States." *American Economic Review* 100 (3): 1649–75.

Nordhaus, William D., and James Tobin. 1973. "Is Growth Obsolete?" In *The Measurement of Economic and Social Performance*, edited by Milton Moss, 509–64. Princeton, NJ: Princeton University Press.

Organisation for Economic Co-operation and Development. 2013a. *Framework for Statistics on the Distribution of Household Income, Consumption, and Wealth.* Paris: OECD.

———. 2013b. *Guidelines for Micro Statistics on Household Wealth.* Paris: OECD.

Pollak, Robert A. 1981. "The Social Cost of Living Index." *Journal of Public Economics* 15 (3): 311–36.

Ravallion. 2012. "More Relatively-Poor People in a Less Absolutely-Poor World." Nancy and Richard Ruggles Memorial Lecture, International Association for Research in Income and Wealth, Boston, Massachusetts, August.

Roberts, Kevin W. S. 1980. "Possibility Theorems with Interpersonally Comparable Welfare Levels." *Review of Economic Studies* 47 (147): 409–20.

Rosen, Allison B., and David M. Cutler. 2007. "Measuring Medical Care Productivity: A Proposal for US National Health Accounts." *Survey of Current Business* 87 (6): 54–8.

Roy, Rene. 1943. *De l'Utilité. Contribution à la Théorie des Choix.* Paris: Hermann & Cie.

Samuelson, Paul A. 1950. "Evaluation of Real National Income." *Oxford Economic Papers* N.S. 1:1–29.

———. 1956. "Social Indifference Curves." *Quarterly Journal of Economics* 70 (1): 1–22.

———. 1961. "The Evaluation of 'Social Income.'" In *The Theory of Capital*, edited by F. A. Lutz and D. C. Hague, 32–57. London: Macmillan.

Schreyer, Paul. 2001. *Measuring Productivity.* Paris: Organisation for Economic Co-operation and Development.

———. 2009. *Measuring Capital.* Paris: Organisation for Economic Co-operation and Development.

Sen, Amartya K. 1970. *Collective Choice and Social Welfare*. San Francisco: Holden-Day.
———. 1976. "Real National Income." *Review of Economic Studies* 43 (133): 19–40.
———. 1979. "The Welfare Basis for Real Income Comparisons: A Survey." *Journal of Economic Literature* 17 (1): 1–45.
Slesnick, Daniel T. 1994. "Consumption, Needs, and Inequality." *International Economic Review* 35 (3): 677–703.
———. 1998. "Empirical Approaches to the Measurement of Welfare." *Journal of Economic Literature* 36 (4): 2108–65.
———. 2001. *Consumption and Social Welfare: Living Standards and Their Distribution in the United States*. Cambridge: Cambridge University Press.
Stiglitz, Joseph E., Amartya Sen, and Jean-Paul Fitoussi. 2010. *Mismeasuring Our Lives: Why GDP Doesn't Add Up*. New York: The New Press.
Teplin, Albert M., Rochelle Antoniewicz, Susan Hume McIntosh, Michael Palumbo, Genevieve Solomon, Charles Ian Mead, Karin Moses, and Brent Moulton. 2006. "Integrated Macroeconomic Accounts for the United States: Draft SNA-USA." In *A New Architecture for the US National Accounts*, Studies in Income and Wealth, vol. 66, edited by Dale W. Jorgenson, J. Steven Landefeld, and William D. Nordhaus, 471–540. Chicago: University of Chicago Press.
Timmer, Marcel P., Robert Inklaar, Mary O'Mahony, and Bart van Ark. 2010. *Economic Growth in Europe: A Comparative Industry Perspective*. Cambridge: Cambridge University Press.
United Nations. 2009. *2008 System of National Accounts*. New York: United Nations. http://unstats.un.org/unsd/nationalaccount/sna2008.asp.
Weitzman, Martin. 1976. "On the Welfare Significance of National Product in a Dynamic Economy." *Quarterly Journal of Economics* 90 (1): 156–62.
———. 2003. *Income, Wealth, and the Maximum Principle*. Cambridge, MA: Harvard University Press.
World Bank. 2008. *Global Purchasing Power Parities and Real Expenditures: 2005 International Comparison Program*. Washington, DC: World Bank. http://site resources.worldbank.org/ICPEXT/Resources/ICP_2011.html.

4

Household Production, Leisure, and Living Standards

Paul Schreyer and W. Erwin Diewert

4.1 Introduction

Households are economic units that act as both consumers and producers of goods and services. The System of National Accounts (SNA) records mainly those acts of consumption and production that are subject to monetary transactions, leaving out of the picture the consumption and production that households undertake on their own account or for other economic units, but without a monetary market transaction. In particular, the nonmarket production of services by households such as cooking or child care (but not dwelling services provided by owner-occupiers of houses) is outside the SNA production boundary. The reasons why most services produced by households are outside the SNA production boundary are mainly rooted in practical considerations. Absent market prices, it is "[. . .] therefore extremely difficult to estimate values not only for the outputs of services but also for the associated incomes and expenditures" (SNA 2008, paragraph 6.29). At the same time, the SNA acknowledges that for purposes of measuring economic welfare, it is useful to estimate the value and evolution of comprehensive household production. The 2009 report of the Stiglitz-Sen-Fitoussi Commission also advocates comprehensive measures of produc-

Paul Schreyer is deputy chief statistician at the Organisation for Economic Co-operation and Development. W. Erwin Diewert is professor of economics at the University of British Columbia and at the Australian School of Business at the University of New South Wales and a research associate of the National Bureau of Economic Research.

We thank David Johnson and the participants at the 2012 CRIW "Measuring Economic Progress and Economic Sustainability" conference in Cambridge, Massachusetts, for valuable comments. The views expressed in this chapter are those of the authors and do not necessarily reflect the views of the OECD or its member countries. For acknowledgments, sources of research support, and disclosure of the authors' material financial relationships, if any, please see http://www.nber.org/chapters/c12826.ack.

tion and consumption and a look at the literature shows that researchers have produced estimates for a number of countries and time periods.[1]

Absent market transactions on own-account household production, the question of how to value these services is central. A vast majority of studies has used an input cost approach, valuing outputs by the costs of inputs, of which, the time household members spend on the task of production is the most prominent element. Two variants of valuing labor input have been prevalent: valuation with a market-wage rate (the opportunity cost approach) of the household member that carries out household production, and valuation with a wage rate for a household employee (the replacement cost approach). The former responds to the question, "What is the earning foregone by the household member due to the fact that he or she produces services at home rather than offering labor services on the labor market?" The latter responds to the question, "How much would it cost to hire someone on the labor market to produce the household services *in lieu* of the household member?" Hill (2009) summarizes the discussion as follows:

> The procedure adopted in national accounts is to value nonmarket flows of goods and services whenever possible at the prices at which the same goods and services are sold on the market. To be consistent with this general principle, the labor inputs should be valued using the market wages payable to employees doing the same kind of work. However, a case can also be made for valuing at internal opportunity costs . . . . Valuing at internal opportunity costs is not generally favored in studies on household production, because it makes the value of the labor inputs depend on who does the work, rather than on the nature of the work done. . . . A further complication is that people may engage in certain household productive activities, such as child care, because they enjoy it. . . . The motivation behind some household activities may be quite complex. For example, the activity of gardening is recognized to be a good form of exercise, so it may be undertaken as a substitute for going to the gym. . . . The concept of the opportunity cost in these kinds of circumstances is not altogether clear. On balance, it seems preferable to value work done in household production at the corresponding market wage rate for that type of work. (440)

Although the literature has discussed this choice from conceptual and practical perspectives, such a discussion has not been framed in a formal economic model and with a clear distinction between household work as an input into production and household work as a potential source of utility (or disutility) *in itself*. Also, standard optimizing models of household

1. For valuations of household work see Bridgman, Dugan, Lal, Osborne, and Villones (2012), Ahmad and Koh (2011), Roy (2011), Landefeld, Fraumeni, and Vojtech (2005), Ruger and Varjonen (2008), Fraumeni (2008), Abraham and Mackie (2005), Landefeld and McCulla (2000), Goldschmidt-Clermont (1993), Folbre and Wagman (1993), Fouquet and Chadeau (1981), and Reid (1934). For the valuation of child care more specifically, see Folbre and Yoon (2008).

production à la Becker (1965) would always suggest an opportunity cost approach as the appropriate valuation, thus being at variance with the above reasoning. The first and main contribution of the present chapter consists of a generalization of Becker's (1965) full consumption model and shows how such an extended model can provide guidance to the valuation issue. We conclude that two elements condition the choice between an opportunity-cost and a replacement-cost approach:

- In the general case of an unconstrained household, a first element enters the considerations: Is the purpose of valuing time spent on household production to capture full consumption (a welfare-related concept) or is the purpose more narrowly defined at capturing only the value of own-account household production (not necessarily a welfare-related concept)? In the second case, the replacement cost method applies; whereas in the first case, household time should be valued using the opportunity-cost method.
- The second element is whether the household under consideration is constrained in its allocation of time between selling its labor services and other usages of time. If the answer is to the affirmative, as it would be in the case of an unemployed or retired person in our present model, the replacement-cost method will constitute the correct valuation for own-account household services as well as for other components of full consumption, in particular leisure.

(Current price) valuation of nonmarket activities is but one objective of research in this area. At least as much interest lies in comparing living standards over time or across countries. The evolution of living standards or their comparison across countries is intimately related to the construction of price indices (over time or across countries) that reflect a cost-of-living concept. These price indices are the appropriate vehicle to deflate the nominal values of full consumption. The second major contribution of this chapter is the development of a cost-of-living index for full consumption in line with our theoretical model. We show how the expenditure functions of constrained and unconstrained households can be combined to provide the theoretical basis for the derivation of an exact cost-of-living index for full consumption in the sense of Diewert (2001).

We conclude by providing some calculations of full income and household production for a cross section of OECD countries. As the main focus and contributions of the chapter are of a theoretical nature, these calculations are of an illustrative nature only. By the same token, no attempt is made here to provide a comprehensive picture of the empirical issues arising in measuring household production— such as the measurement of capital input or methods of quality adjustment—the reader will be referred to the relevant literature. Some of the implementation issues will no doubt constitute the object of future research.

4.2   The Model

We start by providing some intuition for our modeling. Essentially, we consider a household that faces two decisions: (a) the allocation of monetary income between various purchases, including final consumption products, but also purchases of labor services for household work; (b) the allocation of time between working in the labor market, time spent on household work, or production and leisure. In the simplest of all worlds, the household is only constrained by the twenty-four hours of the day and the various prices and wages it faces on the market. Under these conditions, when deciding on the amount of household production, a utility-maximizing household following Becker's (1965) model of the allocation of time will compare his or her own (after tax) wage rate w with the wage rate of a household employee w_N. If w exceeds w_N, it *always* pays to hire a household employee and no own-account household work takes place. In the opposite case, it *never* pays to hire a household employee, and the value of household work equals the market wage rate in this simple opportunity-cost approach. But this simple setup is not compatible with the observation that in practice there are households (probably many) whose wage rate w exceeds the wage rate of a household employee *and* they spend time on household production.

A more elaborate setting is thus needed and we introduce two extensions. The first extension acknowledges that household work may produce utility in itself.[2] By allowing, for instance, for the fact that parents value the time spent with children, the implicit price of child care—a household production activity—changes. Indeed, time spent on child care becomes a joint product: labor input into household production and a "commodity" with intrinsic value. As we will demonstrate, the joint product should be valued at opportunity costs, but the labor input part at replacement costs. The second extension considers the case where households are constrained in their free allocation of time. The example we use is unemployment, where no time can be allocated to supplying labor to the labor market. Absent an opportunity cost on the labor market, the correct valuation of household production turns out to be the replacement cost. With both extensions we are able to define a measure of full consumption that comprises traditional consumption, the consumption value of household production, the commodity value of household production, and the value of leisure. The following sections present these arguments in a more rigorous form.

4.2.1   Unconstrained Households

Our formal setup starts with a household that is unconstrained in its allocation of consumer expenditure and in its allocation of time. In particular, there are no constraints in offering labor services on the labor market at the

---

2. This first extension is due to Pollak and Wachter (1975, 266).

going wage rate. The household consumes the following types of commodities: (a) a final consumption product q_1 that is purchased on the market at price p_1 and directly serves to satisfy consumer needs, such as ice cream or a haircut (the product undergoes no transformation by the consumer); and (b) a service Q_N such as washing or child care that the household produces itself.[3] The own-account production process of this service is captured by the production function:

(1) $$Q_N = f_N(t_N + q_N, q_2),$$

where t_N is the amount of time the household spends on producing the service. We assume that instead of spending time on production, the household can also hire labour q_N that is perfectly substitutable to t_N as in input.[4] The variable q_2 is the quantity of intermediate inputs and/or capital services from consumer durables used in production. The variable f_N will be taken to be an increasing, concave, and linearly homogenous function of $t_N + q_N$, and q_2 over suitable domains of definition. An important and rather restrictive assumption is implicit in the absence of disembodied productivity growth in the production of household services.[5]

Turning to the household's time constraint, we let T be the total time per period available to the household, after accounting for matters of personal care. Variable T can then be either spent on t_L hours of work in the labor market, t_N hours of work in own-account production, or t_F hours of leisure so that

(2) $$T = t_L + t_N + t_F.$$

Next we specify the household's utility function as $U(q_1, Q_N, t_L, t_F, t_N)$. Variable U contains the items that the household "consumes" and values

3. The distinction between q_1 and Q_N is not strictly necessary, but helpful. In a general setup such as Becker (1965) and Lancaster (1966), all "goods" that the household purchases on the market (including ice cream) are combined with time or other inputs in a household production function to produce "commodities." The difference between q_1 and Q_N is that the time input for a work-type activity can be purchased on the market, whereas the time spent on consuming ice cream has to be allocated by the consumer.

4. This is a simplification. The empirical literature (for instance, Abraham and Mackie [2005]) has discussed whether one hour spent by a household member to accomplish a particular task such as plumbing equals one hour spent on the same task by a professional. In many cases, the answer will be "no," and a quality adjustment will be required. This is rather straightforward to introduce into the theoretical model. For instance, labor input into household production could be specified as $\mu t_N + q_N$ where $\mu > 0$ is a quality adjustment factor for household labor. The μ would be less than unity, if household labor is less proficient than purchased labor, and vice versa. It is also clear from the empirical literature that μ is hard to measure. For the theoretical purpose at hand, and to save on notation, we stick to the simple case of $\mu = 1$. If the quality adjustment term were carried throughout the analysis, all results for the valuation with replacement costs would carry over for the valuation with quality-adjusted replacement costs μw_N.

5. As with the case of quality adjustment of labor input spelled out in the preceding footnote, ignoring productivity change is in anticipation of the empirical problems associated with its estimation rather than a reflection of introducing productivity change into the theoretical model.

positively or negatively. In particular, U will be taken as a concave function, that is increasing in q_1, Q_N, and t_F, of unknown sign in t_N, and decreasing in t_L.[6] The explicit appearance of the time variable in the utility function allows for situations where households are not indifferent between spending time on household work, market work, or leisure above and beyond the fact that they generate consumption possibilities. Thus, in addition to serving as an input into own-account production, the household also consumes t_N directly. For example, time spent with a child not only constitutes an input to the service "child care" but may be valued *as such* by households. Along a similar vein, the household consumes leisure t_F—that is, the time not spent on paid work, on household work, and on personal care. This point had already been made by Pollak and Wachter (1975) who argue in favor of keeping separate time variables in the utility function:

> In particular, we object to the implied but crucial assumption that time spent cooking and time spent cleaning are "neutral" from the standpoint of the household and that only the "outputs" of these production processes enter the household's utility function. A more plausible assumption is that the household is not indifferent among all situations which involve the same output of home cooked meals and clean houses but involve different amounts of hired labor and household labor. Instead, we suggest that household time spent cooking or cleaning is a direct source of utility or disutility to the household. (270)[7]

Before going further, note two further shortcuts in the present formulation. The first shortcut consists in the use of scalars for each type of commodity. Obviously, in reality we shall be dealing with vectors of final consumption products, and several types of own-account produced services. An extension from scalars to vectors is fairly straightforward but comes at the expense of more complicated notation, which we want to avoid at this stage. The second shortcut is empirically motivated and lies in our labelling of Q_N as a service. In practice households produce not only services, but also goods for their own account. The empirical difference is that own-account produced goods *are* included in countries' national accounts, whereas own-account produced services (with the exception of own-produced dwelling services) are outside the national accounts production boundary and do not figure in data on private consumption. As all conceptual considerations regarding own-account production of services that will follow carry over directly to own-account produced goods, we chose to restrict ourselves to the discussion of services because they are both produced on own-account

---

6. We shall, however, assume monotonicity so that the derivative is nondecreasing or nonincreasing everywhere over the domains of interest.

7. For a more general debate on Pollak and Wachter's approach toward modeling household production, see Barnett (1977) and Pollak and Wachter's (1977) reply.

and outside the conventional measurement boundary. This is without consequences for the theoretical exposition.

Having dealt with consumption commodities and own-account production, we now come to consumption expenditure, monetary transactions, and income. Note the difference between consumption and consumption expenditures that arises in the present context. Hill (2009) explains this as follows:

> In the present context, it is necessary to underline the fundamental distinction between consumption and consumption expenditures, even though the two terms are often casually used interchangeably. . . . Household final consumption is a particular type of economic activity in which members of households use goods or services to satisfy their personal needs, wants or desires. By definition, a final consumption good or service provides utility to the person or household that consumes it. . . . Household consumption expenditures may be defined as expenditures incurred by households to *acquire* goods and services that they intend to use for purposes of final consumption. (432)

In our setup, the household's consumption expenditure consists of (a) final consumption goods q_1, purchased at price p_1; (b) intermediate products q_2, purchased at price p_2; (c) labor services q_N, purchased at price w_N; and (d) consumer durables. Consumer durables are capital goods that deliver capital service above and beyond the period during which they are purchased. Although the national accounts, in principle, recognize the capital character of consumer durables, by convention, they are treated as final goods; that is, as if they were consumed during the period of purchase. This convention cannot be sustained in a model of household production, and for empirical purposes we shall construct a stock of consumer durables that delivers capital services to household production. The formal model can easily capture capital services as a particular version of q_2. Also, in the special case where all consumer durables are rented, the capital services become intermediate inputs. Our conceptual considerations will therefore be limited to q_1, q_2, and q_N.

To define household consumption and consumption expenditure in our setup, we start by stating the monetary budget constraint that the household faces. Let w be the household's (after tax) wage rate on the labor market, so that (after tax) wage income is given by wt_L. Let Y stand for all other forms of money revenues (for instance, property income) that are spent during the period under consideration.[8] Then the monetary budget constraint faced by the household (and pictured in the national accounts) indicates that households' disposable income equals consumption expenditure:

---

8. If the household's market purchases of goods and services during the period is less than its after tax labor income, then Y would be negative and would represent savings out of labor income.

(3) $wt_L + Y = p_1q_1 + p_2q_2 + w_Nq_N.$

Substituting the time constraint into the monetary budget constraint yields the following extended budget constraint:

(4) $w(T - t_N - t_F) + Y = p_1q_1 + p_2q_2 + w_Nq_N.$

The above constraint can be rewritten as follows:

(5) $FI \equiv wT + Y = p_1q_1 + p_2q_2 + w_Nq_N + wt_N + wt_F.$

The left-hand side of equation (5) now shows a *nominal* measure of Becker's *full income* $FI \equiv wT + Y$. The first term in this full income expression is total time available to the household, T, which has been valued with the household's labor market wage rate w. Becker (1965) reasons as follows:

> Households in richer countries do, however, forfeit money income in order to obtain additional utility, i.e., they exchange money income for a greater amount of psychic income. For example, they might increase their leisure time, take a pleasant job in preference to a better-paying unpleasant one, employ unproductive nephews or eat more than is warranted by considerations of productivity. In these and other situations the amount of money income forfeited measures the cost of obtaining additional utility. Thus the full income approach provides a meaningful resource constraint and one firmly based on the fact that goods and time can be combined into a single overall constraint because time can be converted into goods through money income. It also incorporates a unified treatment of all substitutions of non-pecuniary for pecuniary income, regardless of their nature or whether they occur on the job or in the household. (498)

The right-hand side of equation (5) shows a measure of consumption of the consumer-producer household. In what follows, we shall refer to the sum of direct consumption, the value of intermediate products, work at home, hired labor services, and leisure as *full consumption* $FC \equiv p_1q_1 + p_2q_2 + w_Nq_N + wt_N + wt_F.$

To make a statement about the valuation of the different components of household time, it will be necessary to move from definitional relationships to behavioural relationships. We start by using the time constraint to eliminate t_L from the utility function and define a reduced form utility function f as

(6) $f(q_1, Q_N, t_F, t_N) \equiv U(q_1, Q_N, t_F, t_N, T - t_N - t_F).$

The household's maximisation problem is then

(7) $\max_{q_1, q_2, q_N, t_N, t_F} \{ f : p_1q_1 + p_2q_2 + w_Nq_N + wt_F + wt_N \leq FI;$

$$Q_N = f_N(t_N + q_N, q_2) \}.$$

In words, households maximize utility given their monetary and time budget constraints and given a technology for the production of own-account household services. Assume that q_1^*, q_2^*, q_N^*, t_F^* and t_N^* are positive and solve equation (7). With a monotonicity condition on the utility function f, the budget constraint will hold with equality so one has $p_1 q_1^* + p_2 q_2^* + w_N q_N^* + w t_N^* + w t_F^* = FI = FC$. The first-order conditions for an interior solution to the utility maximisation problem are:

(8) $$\lambda^* p_1 = \partial f^*/\partial q_1;$$

(9) $$\lambda^* p_2 = [\partial f^*/\partial Q_N][\partial f_N^*/\partial q_2];$$

(10) $$\lambda^* w = [\partial f^*/\partial Q_N][\partial f_N^*/\partial t_N] + \partial f^*/\partial t_N;$$

(11) $$\lambda^* w_N = [\partial f^*/\partial Q_N][\partial f_N^*/\partial q_N];$$

(12) $$\lambda^* w = \partial f^*/\partial t_F;$$

where f_N^* and f^* denote functions evaluated at the utility-maximizing variables and λ^* is the corresponding marginal utility of income. We can now interpret the conditions for utility-maximizing behavior. From equation (12) it is clear that for a household that is not constrained in its supply of hours to the labor market, the implicit price of leisure is its opportunity cost or the hourly market wage rate w: households will adjust leisure time until the marginal utility from leisure ($\partial f^*/\partial t_F$) equals the marginal utility from offering an extra hour of paid work at the rate w. Comparison of equations (10) and (12) indicates that time will be allocated to leisure and household work such that, at the margin, they yield the same utility.

Next consider equations (10) and (11)—they contain information about the implicit price for time spent on household production t_N and on the optimal hiring of household labor q_N. Equation (10) indicates that the total shadow price of time spent in household work is the market wage w. But remember that t_N is a joint product that is both an input into household production and a commodity in itself (it constitutes an argument in the utility function), and consequently the total shadow price of t_N has two components as can be seen from the right-hand side of equation (10). The first component is the shadow price of t_N as an input into household production, the second component is the shadow price of the commodity t_N. As t_N and q_N are perfect substitutes, it must be true that the marginal product of t_N just equals the marginal product of q_N: $[\partial f^*/\partial Q_N][\partial f_N^*/\partial t_N] = [\partial f^*/\partial Q_N][\partial f_N^*/\partial q_N]$. Inserting this equality into equations (10) and (11) tells us that the shadow price of the commodity t_N is $(w - w_N)$, and consequently, the shadow price of household labor as a production input is w_N:

(13) $$\lambda^* w_N = [\partial f^*/\partial Q_N][\partial f_N^*/\partial t_N].$$

This provides a theoretical justification for the common practice of valuing household work *as an input into household production* by the wage rate of a comparable household employee. Note, however, that this remains a partial approach—when welfare-relevant full consumption is to be valued, comprising all aspects of t_N (as well as leisure) the correct price for an unconstrained household is w.

The shadow price of the commodity t_N is:

(14) $$\lambda^*(w - w_N) = \partial f^*/\partial t_N.$$

This expression determines the allocation of time worked at home. If there is negative marginal utility to housework so that $\partial f^*/\partial t_N < 0$, a necessary condition for an interior solution, that is, a positive supply of t_N, is $w - w_N < 0$: it implies that the opportunity cost of housework is less than the cost of hiring someone to provide household labor services. If w were larger than w_N, no time would be spent on household work. Conversely, if the marginal utility from household work is positive ($\partial f^*/\partial t_N > 0$), a necessary condition for an interior solution is that w exceeds w_N. Thus, the household will increase time worked at home even if the market wage that it could earn is higher than the costs of hiring a domestic employee as long as the difference between w and w_N (in utility terms) is smaller than the direct utility derived from working at home. For example, a person may be willing to take care of a child even if the wage foregone on the labor market exceeds the costs of hiring a nanny. One can think of corner solutions where either no or a maximum amount of t_N is supplied. A corner solution will arise in particular when household labor is not an argument in the utility function but *only* an input into household production. In this case, all household work will be carried out by the household itself ($t_N > 0$, $q_N = 0$) if the wage rate of domestic labor exceeds the household's wage rate on the labor market ($w_N > w$) and the correct valuation of t_N is the market wage rate w. In the opposite case of ($w_N < w$), there would be no time spent on household production ($t_N = 0$, $q_N > 0$) and the issue of valuation of t_N does not arise. In the more complex case where household work is an argument in the utility function, a corner solution may arise when market wages exceed wages of a household employee ($w > w_N$) *and* the household derives disutility from home production ($\partial f^*/\partial t_N < 0$). No time would be spent on household production and a maximum of time would be spent on supplying labor to the labor market.[9] Conversely, if a household whose market wage rate is less than the wage rate of a household employee at the same time derives positive utility from household work, a corner solution arises where the household would spend a maximum of time on household production.[10] Although we have no evidence regarding the prevalence of corner solutions, we focus on interior

9. There are natural limits to supplying labor (minimum leisure, sleeping) that have not been modeled here. Institutional and legal limits such as maximum hours for full-time employment would bring us to the case of constrained households dealt with below.

10. The household's budget and time constraints imposes a limit to the time spent on household production, as the household needs a minimum market income to purchase q_1-type products in line with the condition in equation (8). At this point, the only remaining trade-off is between household work and leisure. Such a situation may be relevant for low-income households with potentially important distributional implications.

solutions in what follows, assuming that they are the rule rather than the exception.

Having established that the implicit price of t_N in its usage as an input into producing Q_N is w_N, we can take a closer look at the household's own account production function in equation (1). In particular, we are interested in defining an implicit price of the own-account product Q_N, given that in practice it will rarely be possible to directly observe such a price. Define the cost function that is dual to this production function as follows:[11]

$$(15) \quad C_N(Q_N, w_N, p_2) \equiv \min_{q_2, q_N, t_N} \{w_N(t_N + q_N) + p_2 q_2 : f_N(t_N + q_N, q_2) \geq Q_N\}$$

$$= Q_N C_N(1, w_N, p_2)$$

$$= Q_N P_N.$$

In the first line of equation (15), we have made use of equation (11) that essentially determined the input price of t_N. The second equation follows from the linear homogeneity of f_N; that is, total cost is equal to total output times unit cost, $C_N(1, w_N, p_2)$, where the latter is independent of the level of production/consumption Q_N. For the third equation, the implicit price of own-account production has been defined as its unit cost: $P_N \equiv C_N(1, w_N, p_2)$. For utility-maximizing levels of household production, Q_N^*, one gets

$$(16) \qquad C_N(Q_N^*, w_N, p_2) = Q_N^* C_N(1, w_N, p_2) = w_N(t_N^* + q_N^*) + p_2 q_2^*.$$

Multiplication of both sides of equation (9) by q_2^*, of both sides of equation (11) by q_N^* and of both sides of equation (14) by t_N^* gives

$$(17) \quad \lambda^* p_2 q_2^* + \lambda^* w_N(t_N^* + q_N^*)$$

$$= (\partial f^*/\partial Q_N)[(\partial f_N^*/\partial q_2)q_2^* + (\partial f_N^*/\partial t_N)(t_N^* + q_N^*)]$$

$$= (\partial f^*/\partial Q_N)Q_N^* \qquad \text{using the linear homogeneity of } f_N.$$

Next, combine equations (17) and (16) in order to obtain the following equations:

$$(18) \qquad \lambda^*[p_2 q_2^* + w_N(t_N^* + q_N^*)] = \lambda^* Q_N^* C_N(1, w_N, p_2) = \lambda^* Q_N^* P_N$$

$$= (\partial f^*/\partial Q_N)Q_N^* \text{ and } \lambda^* P_N = (\partial f^*/\partial Q_N).$$

The last line of the expression above suggests that the implicit price P_N, defined as the unit cost of producing Q_N, is indeed the shadow price of household production: P_N (times the marginal utility of income λ^*) equals the marginal utility that households derive from own-account services Q_N^*.

The final step toward deriving measures of full income and full consumption is accomplished by invoking minimum expenditure of the consumer/producer's activity. Formally, we capture the cost side by an expenditure

---

11. See Diewert (1993) for additional material and references to the literature on duality theory.

function e that is dual to the utility function f. Note that we use equation (14) to put a shadow price to the commodity t_N that directly shows up in the utility function.

$$(19) \quad e(u^*, p_1, P_N, w, w_N) \equiv \min\nolimits_{q_1, q_2, q_N, t_N, t_F} \{p_1 q_1 + P_N Q_N + (w - w_N)t_N + w t_F :$$
$$f(q_1, Q_N, t_F, t_N) \geq u^*\}.$$

Under the regularity conditions imposed on f and household behavior, actual expenditure equals minimum expenditure so that $e(u^*, p_1, P_N, w, w_N) = FC = FI$. Here, u^* is the utility level commensurate with the cost-minimising choice of q_1^*, Q_N^*, t_F^* and t_N^*, given prices p_1, P_N, w_N, and w. Thus,

$$(20) \quad e(u^*, p_1, P_N, w, w_N) = p_1 q_1^* + P_N^* Q_N^* + (w - w_N)t_N^* + w t_F^*$$
$$= p_1 q_1^* + p_2 q_2^* + w_N q_N^* + w t_N^* + w t_F^* \qquad \text{by using equation (18)}$$
$$= FC = FI.$$

Note that t_N^* is valued at its shadow price, so in considering full consumption and substituting $P_N^* Q_N^*$ for $p_2 q_2^* + w_N q_N^* + w_N t_N^*$, we end up with $w t_N^*$ as the value of time spent on household work. We can now draw some conclusions concerning the case of an unconstrained household that supplies market labor services:

- In the absence of corner solutions, the replacement-cost approach is the relevant valuation of time spent on household work *as in input into producing the own-account service* Q_N. This lends support to many studies that have proceeded along these lines.
- The opportunity-cost valuation is, however, the appropriate approach toward valuing time spent on household labor when the objective is valuing *full consumption*, above and beyond household production Q_N. Full consumption also captures the value of t_N as a commodity and leisure, lending a welfare interpretation to time allocated by the household. Leisure should be valued with an opportunity-cost approach.

4.2.2 Households That Are Constrained in Their Labor Supply

To this point, we have dealt with a representative household that is free in its choice of allocating income and time between different uses. While this may be true for some households, it is certainly not true for all households. We therefore now examine the part of the population that is not active on the labor market due to some institutional or economic constraint and study the consequences for the valuation of household time.[12] One situation that characterises a constrained household is unemployment—a person seeking employment at a given wage rate without success. Similarly, a person with

---

12. Note that the approach that we followed in the previous section, which essentially follows that of Becker (1965), cannot be used when the household has no opportunity to supply market labor services.

involuntary part-time work is faced with a constraint to supply additional labor. In principle, a constraint on labor supply can also arise when there are legal limits to the maximum hours of work per week. Fully employed persons who wish to extend their labor supply would then not be able to do so.[13] Similarly, persons who have reached retirement age and wish to keep supplying labor to the labor market may be constrained in their choice if retirement age is compulsory. While these and similar cases are covered by our model, it is apparent that identifying the existence of these constraints household by household is difficult in practice. Our empirical illustration below will, therefore, be confined to the most apparent case of constrained labor supply—unemployment.

For purposes of the theoretical exposition, we start with a general utility function $U(q_1, Q_N, t_F, t_N)$ from which the labor supply variable has been eliminated since it is fixed at zero. As before, U is increasing in q_1, Q_N, t_F, and either decreasing or increasing in t_N. Nothing changes with regard to the production function f_N. The new time constraint is

(21) $$t_F + t_N = T.$$

Absent labor market income, the new household budget constraint is:

(22) $$Y = p_1 q_1 + p_2 q_2 + w_N q_N.$$

The variable t_N can be eliminated from the utility function using the time constraint in equation (21), so as before we define a *reduced form utility function, F*:

(23) $$F(q_1, Q_N, t_F) \equiv U(q_1, Q_N, t_F, T - t_F).$$

The consumer's utility maximization problem can be written as follows:

(24) $$\max_{q_1, q_2, q_N, t_F} \{F(q_1, Q_N, t_F) : p_1 q_1 + p_2 q_2 + w_N q_N \leq Y; Q_N = f_N(t_N + q_N, q_2)\}.$$

As before we assume that q_1^*, q_2^*, q_N^* and t_F^* are all positive and solve equation (24). With a monotonicity condition on the utility function F, the budget constraint will hold with equality so we will have $p_1 q_1^* + p_2 q_2^* + w_N q_N^* = Y$. When F is differentiable, the first-order necessary conditions are:

(25) $$\lambda^* p_1 = \partial F^* / \partial q_1;$$

(26) $$\lambda^* p_2 = [\partial F^* / \partial Q_N][\partial f_N^* / \partial q_2];$$

(27) $$\lambda^* w_N = [\partial F^* / \partial Q_N][\partial f_N^* / \partial q_N];$$

(28) $$0 = -[\partial F^* / \partial Q_N][\partial f_N^* / \partial q_N] + \partial F^* / \partial t_F.$$

Expression (28) describes the choice between own-account production and leisure: at the margin, the utility from producing extra own-account

---

13. If one follows this reasoning, a necessary condition to be unconstrained in the choice of labor supply is to be in a situation of part-time work (or exactly at the optimising path with full-time employment).

output Q_N by spending an additional hour on household work has to equal the marginal utility from extra household work as a commodity minus the marginal utility lost by sacrificing an hour of leisure. The latter two effects are captured by $\partial F^*/\partial t_F$ (assumed to be nonnegative, otherwise we would face a corner solution with all time allocated to household production). Adding equations (27) and (28) gives us the following equation:

$$(29) \qquad \lambda^* w_N = \partial F^*/\partial t_F.$$

Equation (29) tells us that the shadow price of leisure, t_F, is now equal to w_N, the market price for purchased labor services. As noted earlier, $\partial F^*/\partial t_F$ is a net effect, combining the direct effects of leisure on utility and the direct effects on utility of the change in t_N, that is necessarily associated with the time constraint in equation (21). Since $\partial f_N^*/\partial q_N$ equals $\partial f_N^*/\partial t_N$, equation (27) implies also that

$$(30) \qquad \lambda^* w_N = [\partial F^*/\partial Q_N][\partial f_N^*/\partial t_N].$$

Thus, for a constrained household, the correct valuation of the labor input into household production is the replacement-cost method. Now multiply both sides of equation (26) by q_2^*, both sides of equation (27) by q_N^*, both sides of equation (30) by t_N^* to obtain the following equation:

$$(31) \quad \lambda^*[p_2 q_2^* + w_N q_N^* + w_N t_N^*]$$
$$= [\partial F^*/\partial Q_N][(q_N^* + t_N^*)(\partial f_N^*/\partial q_N) + q_2^*(\partial f_N^*/\partial q_2)]$$
$$= [\partial F^*/\partial Q_N] f_N^* \qquad \text{using the linear homogeneity of } f_N$$
$$= [\partial F^*/\partial Q_N]\, Q_N^* = \lambda^* P_N^* Q_N^*. \quad \text{using equations (1) and (18).}$$

There is no difference between the constrained and the unconstrained household as far the household's production function and cost function is concerned. Thus, it is still the case that P_N, the implicit price of own-account production, equals unit costs of household production. From equations (25), (15), and (29) it can be seen that the three first-order partial derivatives of $F(q_1^*, Q_N^*, t_F^*)$ are proportional to the prices p_1, P_N^*, and w_N and we have:

$$(32) \quad E(u^*, p_1, P_N, w_N)$$
$$= p_1 q_1^* + P_N^* Q_N^* + w_N t_F^*$$
$$= p_1 q_1^* + p_2 q_2^* + w_N q_N^* + w_N t_N^* + w_N t_F^* \qquad \text{using equation (15),}$$

where E is the expenditure function that is dual to the utility function $F(q_1, Q_N, t_F)$. Finally, along with (22), the two equations in (32) imply the following equations:

$$(33) \quad p_1 q_1^* + P_N Q_N^* + w_N t_F^* = Y + w_N t_N^* + w_N t_F^*$$
$$= Y + w_N T \qquad \text{using the time constraint (21)}$$

where the last expression is again *nominal full consumption and full income*, except that we are using the wage rate for market home services w_N in place of the opportunity market wage rate as was the case for an unconstrained household.[14]

We conclude the following in the case of a constrained household:

- In the absence of corner solutions, the replacement-cost approach is the relevant valuation of time spent on household work *as in input into producing the own-account service Q_N*. This valuation for valuing household work is the same as our suggested valuation for the case of an unconstrained household.
- Unlike unconstrained households, however, the replacement-cost valuation is also the appropriate approach toward valuing time spent on household labor when the objective is valuing full consumption, above and beyond Q_N. Full consumption also captures the value of t_N as a commodity and leisure, both of which are valued with replacement costs in the case of a constrained household.

4.2.3 Cost-of-Living Index

This is not the end of the story, however. Two analytical questions are now of interest. First, given the value of full consumption, how should its movements be split into a price and a volume component? And second, is the associated price index a cost-of-living index? This is important because a cost-of-living index is the conceptually appropriate tool for deflation of consumption or income flows when making intertemporal or interspatial welfare-based comparisons of standards of living.

A cost-of-living index gauges the relative cost of achieving the same level of utility when households face different sets of prices for the components of full consumption. For a single type of household, the Konüs (1924) cost-of-living index is defined as the ratio of two expenditure functions, each evaluated at price vectors for the comparison periods and for a reference set of utility levels. For the purpose at hand, we have two types of households, and need to develop a group cost-of-living index. We start by simplifying our notation and define the following vectors:

(34) $\mathbf{u} \equiv [u_a, u_p, n_a, n_p]$

$\mathbf{P}_a \equiv [p_1, P_{N,a}, w_N, w]$; $\mathbf{P}_p \equiv [p_1, P_{N,a}, w_N]$;

$\mathbf{Q}_a \equiv [q_{1,a}, Q_{N,a}, t_{N,a}, t_{F,a}]$; $\mathbf{Q}_p \equiv [q_{1,p}, Q_{N,p}, t_{N,p} + t_{F,p}]$;

$\mathbf{p}_a \equiv [p_1, p_2, w_N, w]$; $\mathbf{p}_p \equiv [p_1, p_2, w_N, w_N]$;

$\mathbf{q}_a \equiv [q_{1,a}, q_{2,a}, q_{N,a}, t_{N,a} + t_{F,a}]$; $\mathbf{q}_p \equiv [q_{1,p}, q_{2,p}, q_{N,p}, t_{N,p} + t_{F,p}]$.

---

14. This concept for full income could be labeled as *restricted full income* in order to distinguish it from Becker's full income.

The subscripts a and p stand for the active and nonactive (passive) part of the population with regard to their involvement in the labor market. Vectors in uppercase letters indicate prices and quantities including the (often unobserved) prices and quantities of household production. Vectors in lowercase letters indicate prices and quantities including the (typically observable) prices and quantities of the inputs into household production. Variables n_a and n_p are the number of active and inactive households, respectively. Combine the expenditure functions of the active and nonactive households developed earlier into an aggregate expenditure function ε by weighting each expenditure function by the number of households:

$$(35) \qquad \varepsilon(\mathbf{u}, \mathbf{P}_a, \mathbf{P}_p) \equiv n_a e(u_a, \mathbf{P}_a) + n_p E(u_p, \mathbf{P}_p).$$

We then follow Pollak (1980) and Diewert (1983) and call P^* a plutocratic cost-of-living index between period 1 and period 0:

$$(36) \qquad P^*(\mathbf{u}, \mathbf{P}_a^0, \mathbf{P}_p^0, \mathbf{P}_a^1, \mathbf{P}_p^1) \equiv \varepsilon(\mathbf{u}, \mathbf{P}_a^1, \mathbf{P}_p^1)/\varepsilon(\mathbf{u}, \mathbf{P}_a^0, \mathbf{P}_p^0)$$

In equation (36), the price index P^* is the ratio of the minimum expenditure of the two groups of households, given prices in period 1 and in period 0, and given reference utility measures and household numbers $\mathbf{u}$. Time periods have been indicated via superscripts. Diewert (1983, 2001) shows how the Laspeyres and the Paasche-type index form the upper and the lower bound of the true group price index P^*. The Fisher index constitutes the point estimate for the change in cost of living:

$$(37) \qquad P^*(\mathbf{u}^0, \mathbf{P}_a^0, \mathbf{P}_p^0, \mathbf{P}_a^1, \mathbf{P}_p^1)$$

$$\leq \Sigma_{j=a,p} n_j \mathbf{P}_j^1 \cdot \mathbf{Q}_j^0 / \Sigma_{j=a,p} n_j \mathbf{P}_j^0 \cdot \mathbf{Q}_j^0$$

$$= \Sigma_{j=a,p} n_j \mathbf{p}_j^1 \cdot \mathbf{q}_j^0 / \Sigma_{j=a,p} n_j \mathbf{p}_j^0 \cdot \mathbf{q}_j^0 \equiv P_L^* \quad \text{using equation (20);}$$

$$(38) \qquad P^*(\mathbf{u}^1, \mathbf{P}_a^0, \mathbf{P}_p^0, \mathbf{P}_a^1, \mathbf{P}_p^1)$$

$$\geq \Sigma_{j=a,p} n_j \mathbf{P}_j^1 \cdot \mathbf{Q}_j^1 / \Sigma_{j=a,p} n_j \mathbf{P}_j^0 \cdot \mathbf{Q}_j^1$$

$$= \Sigma_{j=a,p} n_j \mathbf{p}_j^1 \cdot \mathbf{q}_j^1 / \Sigma_{j=a,p} n_j \mathbf{p}_j^0 \cdot \mathbf{q}_j^1 \equiv P_L^* \quad \text{using equation (32);}$$

$$(39) \qquad P_F = (P_L^* P_P^*)^{1/2}.$$

Variable P_F^* provides the price change that is required to break down the value change of full consumption into a price and a volume component. Thus, by applying the Fisher price index P_F^* to the measure of full consumption as defined earlier, we obtain a Fisher *volume index Q_F of full consumption*:

$$(40) \qquad Q_F \equiv [FC^1/FC^0]/P_F,$$

where $FC^0 = \Sigma_{j=a,p} n_j \mathbf{p}_j^0 \cdot \mathbf{q}_j^0$ and $FC^1 = \Sigma_{j=a,p} n_j \mathbf{p}_j^1 \cdot \mathbf{q}_j^1$.

This completes our theoretical considerations concerning the valuation of household work and leisure as well as the measurement of full consumption in real terms over time and across countries. The remainder of the chapter will deal with an empirical illustration of these concepts.

4.3   An Illustrative Cross-Country Comparison of Full Consumption

Recent work by the OECD (Ahmad and Koh 2011) has produced estimates of the value of own-account household production, using both a replacement-cost and an opportunity-cost method. Extended measures of household consumption were shown by the authors after adding the value of own-account household production to the value of actual final consumption (as available from the national accounts). Their conclusion, confirming other results from the literature, is that there are large differences in the resulting extended measures of consumption, depending on the valuation method chosen. Valuation methods matter in particular when results are expressed as a percentage of conventional measures of consumption of GDP. Our theoretical findings above lend support to giving preference to a replacement-cost valuation, as long as the purpose is measuring the value of household production.

The present empirical section will build on the authors' data and go one step further toward providing a valuation of full consumption, thus also incorporating the value of household work as a commodity and leisure. We rely on the model set out earlier and distinguish between unconstrained and constrained households before aggregating across these two types of households. To keep things manageable empirically, only unemployment is used as a criterion for identifying a constrained household. We then construct a spatial cost-of-living index in the form of an extended purchasing power parity to compare volume measures of full consumption across countries. It is important to stress that the resulting calculations are of an illustrative nature only. Full implementation requires separately identifying actual individual consumption of constrained and unconstrained households, an improved time use information of these two groups of households, and resolving additional conceptual issues such as the distinction between a household and a person that we have conveniently ignored here. A number of additional shortcuts were necessary, and consequently, the results presented here are orders of magnitude rather than precise estimates. Also, as we heavily rely on the data provided by Ahmad and Koh (2011) for our calculations, no attempt is made here to replicate the discussion of the various measurement issues that these authors provide, such as the statistical sources for the various wage rates and time use surveys. Consequently, the following section only presents the most salient features of the data work involved.

4.3.1   Valuing Labor and Capital Services

Ahmad and Koh (2011) start with empirical information from the latest time-use surveys of OECD countries as compiled by the OECD. People's activities during a typical day are classified into time devoted to (a) paid work or study (work-related activities); (b) unpaid work (household activities); (c) personal care; (d) leisure; and (e) other activities not included elsewhere. Allocation of time across these categories is not always straightforward; in particular, the cases of multiple activities and activities that can constitute both acts of production and leisure activities, such as cooking. For the purposes of measuring household production of nonmarket services, the relevant activity is unpaid work, which comprises the following six subcategories: routine housework, shopping, care for household members, care for nonhousehold members, volunteer work, and travel related to household activities.

The time-use data used by Ahmad and Koh (2011) makes no distinction between constrained and unconstrained households or persons. We derive a set of data that makes this distinction by separating each country's population (of persons sixteen years and older) into unemployed persons (that is, those seeking and available for employment), persons older than sixty-five, and all other persons (that is, persons in employment and persons of working age that are not in the labor force such as persons in education). In a rather stark simplification, the first two groups are considered constrained, and the third group is considered unconstrained in their time allocation.[15] We next combine the statistics on time-use patterns for all households as in Ahmad and Koh (2011) with supplementary information from Krueger and Mueller (2008) on time use of unemployed and employed persons to approximate time-use patterns of constrained and unconstrained persons. Again this entails a number of shortcuts and, consequently, a likely source of measurement imprecision (differences in years, country coverage, classifications of activities, etc.).

Valuation with replacement costs (w_N) of household labor as an input into production uses the data developed by Ahmad and Koh (2011), an average posttax, and the hourly wage rate of a general household employee deemed to be representative of the broad range of activities covered in the production of household production of nonmarket services.

As time spent on household production t_N and hired time q_N were considered perfect substitutes in the theoretical setup, the valuation of hourly labor w_N under the replacement-cost approach should ideally be the quality adjusted price of a specialist worker in the activity being measured, where the quality is adjusted to reflect the productivity of nonspecialized individuals. In practice, however, many studies do not adjust for such quality differences, and those that do generally do so using relatively simple estimates that assume that the quality/productivity of the nonspecialist is likely to be lower

15. For instance, all employed persons are considered nonconstrained. This is clearly not true as persons may be employed and yet constrained, for instance, in their choice of working time. Also, discouraged workers who no longer seek employment are considered unconstrained in our classification, which may be subject to debate. It is also questionable whether persons outside the working age should be considered constrained in their choices, as we do.

by a certain ratio. Landefeld, Fraumeni, and Vojtech (2005), for example, assume that the average hourly wage, used as a proxy for the replacement cost, is 75 percent of the specialist hourly wage in a number of activities.

Measurement of the costs of labor used in the production of household nonmarket services for own use can simply be described as follows: value of annual labor used in household production of nonmarket services = average hourly posttax labor costs of household employee * average hours worked per day * 365 (in 2008) * population sixteen years and older. Where valuation of time with opportunity costs is called for (as would be the case for leisure of unconstrained households), we use Ahmad and Koh's (2011) average posttax wage rates for the economy.

Like any other activity, both capital and labor are used in the production of household nonmarket services. Capital is measured as the services of consumer durables, which includes household appliances, motor vehicles, and also categories of consumer durables, such as furniture, that provide capital services related to dwelling services.[16] The usual approach, also followed by the authors, is to create estimates of the value of capital services by estimating the productive stock of consumer durables constructed using the perpetual inventory method and valuing the flow of capital services (Jorgenson and Griliches 1967) as unit user costs multiplied by the productive stock.[17]

To get a sense for the orders of magnitude involved, table 4.1 presents results for the nominal value of household production that do not discriminate between types of households—average time-use patterns are applied. Two valuations of labor input are presented, at replacement costs and at opportunity costs. It is apparent (see last column) that results vary critically with the choice of valuation methods. Similarly, any ratio of household production over GDP or over actual individual consumption would vary strongly, depending on the method. However, as our theoretical considerations have shown, in an extended model of households, if the measurement purpose is valuation of household production only (rather than full consumption), the replacement-cost method is the correct way to proceed. As the same replacement-cost wage rate is applied to constrained and unconstrained households, our results for the value of household production are identical to Ahmad and Koh's (2011) computations at replacement costs.

But full consumption goes beyond the value of household production and includes the value of household production, both directly and as a commodity, the value of direct consumption $p_1 q_1$ as well as the value of leisure. We use actual individual consumption as shown in the System of

16. It is important to note that the estimates of capital services produced below will be biased upward, since some consumer durables, such as cars, also provide capital services to commuting and leisure activities, and not just household nonmarket services.

17. Unit user costs were measured as a real rate of return plus a rate of depreciation times the price index of new consumer durables.

Table 4.1   Household production valued at replacement costs and at opportunity costs, 2008

	Value of own-account household production	Population above 15 years of age	Value of labor spent on own-account household production		Value of capital services after tax	Value of own-account household production		
	Hours per day per person	1,000 persons, total	At replacement costs, millions of national currency	At opportunity costs, millions of national currency	Millions of national currency	At replacement costs, millions of national currency	At opportunity costs, millions of national currency	Replacement costs in % of opportunity costs
Australia	4.1	17,483	532,333	698,303	54,715	587,048	753,018	78
Austria	3.4	7,067	68,128	115,441	15,232	83,359	130,673	64
Belgium	3.3	8,937	79,302	144,912	15,410	94,713	160,323	59
Canada	3.3	27,718	238,817	636,099	102,054	340,870	738,153	46
Germany	3.5	71,204	584,718	1,177,610	168,311	753,029	1,345,921	56
Denmark	3.6	4,483	533,829	962,602	120,165	653,994	1,082,767	60
Spain	3.3	38,898	390,689	512,213	56,939	447,628	569,152	79
Finland	3.4	4,421	48,208	92,730	8,580	56,788	101,311	56
France	3.3	52,406	549,396	1,022,856	96,109	645,505	1,118,964	58
United Kingdom	3.5	50,488	368,906	981,179	92,433	461,338	1,073,612	43
Hungary	3.3	8,537	8,405,457	8,487,291	1,371,325	9,776,782	9,858,616	99
Ireland	3.5	3,526	49,501	86,458	7,043	56,544	93,500	60
Italy	3.6	51,382	466,069	702,785	98,135	564,203	800,920	70
Japan	2.7	110,358	193,979,541	266,309,877	19,679,898	213,659,439	285,989,774	75
Korea	2.3	40,149	162,559,680	431,270,701	37,275,187	199,834,867	468,545,888	43
Mexico	4.2	75,282	2,259,048	4,518,096	628,361	2,887,409	5,146,457	56
Netherlands	3.6	13,512	115,997	265,669	28,542	144,539	294,211	49
Norway	3.1	3,859	430,376	1,121,691	118,672	549,048	1,240,363	44
New Zealand	3.8	3,390	68,213	98,196	12,187	80,400	110,383	73
Poland	3.8	32,253	240,406	480,812	43,085	283,490	523,896	54
Portugal	3.7	8,996	74,815	87,626	13,402	88,218	101,028	87
Sweden	3.5	7,678	787,176	1,725,291	124,042	911,219	1,849,334	49
United States	3.4	243,169	2,590,250	6,925,596	870,534	3,460,784	7,796,130	44
Estonia	3.9	1,110	54,211	108,423	9,340	63,551	117,763	54
Slovenia	3.8	1,695	11,445	12,255	2,075	13,519	14,330	94

Source: Ahmad and Koh (2012).

National Accounts to capture $p_1 q_1$, the value of household production $P_N Q_N$ is measured at replacement costs and the value of household production as a commodity plus leisure are valued at opportunity costs or replacement costs, depending on the type of household. Table 4.2 presents the results. It starts by discriminating between constrained and unconstrained households in their time use regarding household production and leisure. This is unnecessary for the computation of the nominal value of household production, but matters for the valuation of leisure as well as for the construction of price indices. The final columns in table 4.2 present the nominal values of household production and of full consumption as a percentage of actual individual consumption. On average, household production (and the equivalent additional consumption) with labor valued at replacement costs, adds about 50 percent to the value of actual final consumption, although there are significant variations between countries. Full consumption—a welfare-related measure—is considerably higher. On average, full consumption is more than 2.5 times the value of actual individual consumption. It is of note that the spread of these ratios declines as one moves from comparing the relative size of household production to the relative size of full consumption.

An important step involves moving from nominal to real considerations. To compare real full consumption across countries, the cost-of-living index derived in the theoretical part of this chapter takes the form of a new set of purchasing power parity (PPP)s. The new PPPs were constructed by introducing additional "products" into the traditional set of PPP calculations. These products are the labor input to household production, capital input to household production, t_N as a commodity, and leisure, where a distinction is made between constrained and unconstrained persons. The monetary value for each item relative to full consumption provides the relevant weight. As would be expected, the set of adjusted PPPs turns out to be quite different from the official PPPs for actual individual consumption.

The final step consists of applying the new set of PPPs to obtain a volume comparison of per capita full consumption. Results are shown in table 4.3. Given the empirical shortcuts, these should be interpreted with caution. However, it is notable that the vast majority of countries improve their position against the United States when material living standards are measured using full consumption as opposed to actual individual consumption. We are also in a position to compare our results for real full consumption with those shown by Ahmad and Koh (2012). The authors do not account for leisure and the intrinsic value of household production. The last column in table 4.3 shows the difference in volume indices. It is apparent that moving from actual individual consumption plus household production to full consumption tends to improve the position of high-income countries such as Norway, Denmark, and Australia, whereas it tends to worsen the position of lower-income countries such as Mexico, Poland, or Estonia. This is

Table 4.2   Household production with differentiated households, 2008

Country/Unit	Own-account household production (hours per day per person)			Millions of national currency (all persons)			Leisure (hours per day per person)			Value of leisure and household work as commodity (millions of national currency)			Millions of national currency (all persons)		Share of actual individual consumption (percentages)	
	All persons[a]	Unconstrained persons[a]	Constrained persons[a]	Value of labor spent on own-account household production, at replacement costs	Value of capital services after tax	Value of own-account household production at replacement costs	All persons	Unconstrained persons[a]	Constrained persons[a]	All persons	Unconstrained persons[a,b]	Constrained persons[a,c]	Actual individual consumption (AIC)	Full consumption	Own-account household production	Full consumption
Australia	4.1	3.5	6.2	532,333	54,715	587,048	4.7	4.4	6.1	877,512	725,439	152,072	821,563	2,286,122	71	27
Austria	3.4	2.9	5.1	68,128	152,32	83,359	4.7	4.3	5.9	172,047	144,959	27,088	178,867	434273	47	243
Belgium	3.3	2.8	5.0	79,302	15,410	94,713	5.4	5.0	6.8	244,817	205,041	39,776	229,307	568,837	41	248
Canada	3.3	2.9	4.8	238,817	102,054	340,870	5.1	4.6	7.1	1,087,743	982,332	105,411	1,081,953	2,510,567	32	232
Germany	3.5	2.9	5.2	584,718	168,311	753,029	5.6	5.1	7.0	1,896,523	1,571,243	325,280	1,683,560	4,333,112	45	257
Denmark	3.6	3.2	5.3	533,829	120,165	653,994	5.5	5.2	6.6	1,586,427	1,375,908	210,519	1,172,094	3,412,515	56	291
Spain	3.3	2.7	4.9	390,689	56,939	447,628	4.9	4.5	6.2	780,546	589,300	191,246	745,804	1,973,978	60	265
Finland	3.4	2.9	4.8	48,208	8,580	56,788	5.8	5.4	6.9	166,819	142,989	23,830	122,863	346,470	46	282
France	3.3	2.8	4.9	549,396	96,109	645,505	4.1	3.7	5.1	1,391,613	1,182,053	209,561	1,407,097	3,444,215	46	245
United Kingdom	3.5	3.0	5.4	368,906	92,433	461,338	5.3	4.9	6.7	1,621,522	1,464,127	157,396	1,122,561	3,205,422	41	286
Hungary	3.3	2.8	5.1	8,405,457	1,371,325	9,776,782	4.6	4.3	5.9	11,817,518	8,417,602	3,399,915	17,625,878	39,220,178	55	223
Ireland	3.5	3.1	5.6	49,501	7,043	56,544	5.3	4.9	6.8	142,870	126,430	16,441	111,887	311,301	51	278
Italy	3.6	3.0	5.3	466,069	98,135	564,203	4.7	4.3	5.9	966,044	763,302	202,742	1,115,941	2,646,189	51	237
Japan	2.7	2.3	4.0	193,979,541	19,679,898	213,659,439	3.8	3.4	4.8	378,730,840	283,964,970	94,765,870	344,176,400	936,566,679	62	272
Korea	2.3	2.0	3.6	162,559,680	37,275,187	199,834,867	4.9	4.6	6.4	1,023,260,163	956,985,704	66,274,460	628,693,900	1,851,788,931	32	295
Mexico	4.2	3.9	6.9	2,259,048	628,361	2,887,409	3.7	3.5	4.9	5,559,494	5,294,570	264,924	8,502,337	16,949,239	34	199
Netherlands	3.6	3.2	5.7	115,997	28,542	144,539	5.3	4.9	6.8	435,079	392,072	43,007	360,925	940,543	40	261
Norway	3.1	2.8	4.6	430,376	118,672	549,048	6.1	5.8	7.4	2,347,841	2,145,686	202,156	1,316,045	4,212,934	42	320
New Zealand	3.8	3.3	5.8	68,213	12,187	80,400	4.1	3.8	5.3	119,204	101,368	17,837	130,520	330,125	62	253
Poland	3.8	3.3	5.9	240,406	43,085	283,490	4.9	4.6	6.3	709,594	631,352	78,242	918,554	1,911,638	31	208
Portugal	3.7	3.1	5.5	74,815	13,402	88,218	4.0	3.7	5.0	98,277	72,420	25,857	134,650	321,144	66	239
Sweden	3.5	3.0	5.1	787,176	124,042	911,219	5.2	4.9	6.2	2,720,205	2,371,463	348,743	2,113,194	5,744,618	43	272
United States	3.4	2.9	5.5	2,590,250	870,534	3,460,784	4.9	4.5	6.2	11,212,133	10,297,205	914,928	11,020,000	25,692,917	31	233
Estonia	3.9	3.4	5.7	54,211	9,340	63,551	4.8	4.5	5.8	153,936	136,528	17,408	167,338	384,825	3	230
Slovenia	3.8	3.3	6.0	11,445	2,075	13,519	5.2	4.8	6.6	16,798	12,994	3,803	23,832	54,149	57	227

Source: Authors' calculations.

[a] Unconstrained persons = population sixteen to sixty-four years, minus unemployed persons. Constrained persons = unemployed persons plus persons sixty-five years and older. Time-use data by type of person are first-order approximations only and should be interpreted with great caution. Estimates using data by Krueger and Mueller (2008).

[b] Valued at opportunity costs.

[c] Valued at replacement costs.

Table 4.3   Full consumption in real terms, 2008

Reference group	Value of own-account household production			Value of leisure and household work as commodity			Actual individual consumption (AIC)	Full consumption	Actual individual consumption (AIC) as share of full consumption	PPPs for AIC	PPPs for full consumption	AIC per capita relative to the USA	Full consumption per capita relative to the USA (1)	Own-account production at replacement costs plus AIC, volumes as in Ahmad and Koh (2012) (2)	Difference (1)−(2)
Country\Unit	All persons[b]	Unconstrained persons[a]	Constrained persons[a]	All persons[b]	Unconstrained persons[a]	Constrained persons[a]	All persons	All persons	All persons	All persons	All persons	All persons	USA = 100	USA = 100	Percentage points
	Millions of national currency			Millions of national currency			Millions of national currency		Percentages	National currency per US dollar		USA = 100			
Australia	587,048	420,906	166,141	877,512	725,439	152,072	821,563	2,286,122	36	1.4614	1.569	71.9	79.9	67.8	12.1
Austria	83,359	56,432	26,928	172,047	144,959	27,088	178,867	434,273	41	0.8584	0.867	69.1	71.2	74.1	−2.9
Belgium	94,713	61,831	32,881	244,817	205,041	39,776	229,307	568,837	40	0.8976	0.894	66.0	70.5	73.4	−3.0
Canada	340,870	248,009	92,862	1,087,743	982,332	105,411	1,081,953	2,510,567	43	1.2439	1.203	72.2	74.3	84.6	−10.3
Germany	753,029	465,168	287,861	1,895,523	1,571,243	325,280	1,683,560	4,333,112	39	0.8078	0.802	70.2	78.0	79.6	−1.6
Denmark	653,994	460,731	193,263	1,585,427	1,375,908	210,519	1,172,094	3,412,515	34	8.3938	8.657	70.3	85.2	71.8	13.4
Spain	447,628	280,929	166,698	780,546	589,300	191,246	745,804	1,973,978	38	0.7462	0.778	60.6	66.0	62.7	3.3
Finland	56,788	38,150	18,639	165,819	142,989	23,830	122,863	346,470	35	0.9482	0.962	67.5	80.4	71.6	8.8
France	645,505	420,996	224,510	1,391,613	1,182,053	209,561	1,407,094	3,444,215	41	0.8806	0.899	68.9	70.9	71.0	−0.1
United Kingdom	461,338	315,245	146,093	1,621,522	1,464,127	157,396	1,122,561	3,205,422	35	0.6418	0.648	78.8	95.5	82.8	12.7
Hungary	9,776,782	6,529,313	3,247,469	11,817,518	8,417,602	3,399,915	17,625,872	39,220,178	45	126.0816	122.681	38.5	37.8	55.2	−17.4
Ireland	56,544	41,786	14,758	142,870	126,430	16,441	111,884	311,301	36	1.0392	1.065	67.0	78.0	69.1	8.9
Italy	564,203	355,660	208,543	966,044	763,302	202,742	1,115,940	2,646,189	42	0.8156	0.818	63.3	64.1	72.3	−8.2
Japan	213,659,439	129,612,328	84,047,112	378,730,840	283,964,970	94,765,870	344,176,400	936,566,679	37	119.0859	129.349	62.7	67.4	55.9	11.5
Korea	199,834,867	157,375,415	42,459,452	1,023,260,163	956,985,704	66,274,460	628,693,900	1,851,788,931	34	816.3230	796.801	43.8	56.7	52.7	4.0
Mexico	2,887,409	2,454,010	433,399	5,559,494	5,294,570	264,924	8,502,337	16,949,239	50	7.0863	6.574	31.1	28.7	61.0	−32.3
Netherlands	144,539	103,109	41,431	435,079	392,072	43,007	360,925	940,543	38	0.8336	0.828	72.9	82.0	81.6	0.3
Norway	549,048	399,440	149,607	2,347,841	2,145,686	202,156	1,316,045	4,212,934	31	9.4273	9.631	81.0	108.8	78.7	30.1
New Zealand	80,400	58,478	21,923	119,204	101,368	17,837	130,520	330,125	40	1.4336	1.472	58.8	62.2	64.3	−2.2
Poland	283,490	201,572	81,919	709,594	631,352	78,242	918,556	1,911,638	48	1.7617	1.606	37.8	37.0	68.7	−31.7
Portugal	88,218	56,370	31,847	98,277	72,420	25,857	134,650	321,144	42	0.6792	0.691	51.6	51.9	62.0	−10.1
Sweden	911,219	596,738	314,480	2,720,205	2,371,463	348,743	2,113,194	5,744,618	37	8.9600	9.005	70.8	82.1	76.7	5.4
United States	3,460,784	2,474,378	986,405	11,212,133	10,297,205	914,928	11,020,000	25,692,917	43	1.0000	1.000	100.0	100.0	100.0	0.0
Estonia	63,551	44,554	18,997	153,936	136,528	17,408	167,338	384,825	43	8.8065	8.160	39.2	41.7	66.3	−24.5
Slovenia	13,519	9,691	3,828	16,798	12,994	3,803	23,832	54,149	44	0.6387	0.633	51.0	50.2	65.8	−15.6

Source: authors' calculations.

[a]Unconstrained persons = population sixteen to sixty-four years, minus unemployed persons. Constrained persons = unemployed persons plus persons sixty-five years and older. Time-use data by type of person are first-order approximations only and should be interpreted with great caution. Estimates using data by Krueger and Mueller (2008).

[b]Results for all persons are sourced from Ahmad and Koh (2011).

consistent with the idea that the volume and value of leisure tends to rise with rising income.

4.4 Summary and Conclusion

This chapter has established a theoretical framework and identified conditions for the validity of the two most widely used approaches to value household labor. The first approach toward valuing time spent on household work is the replacement-cost approach that imputes a wage rate for labor services that could be purchased by the household for household work. This valuation is warranted when households are constrained in their supply of labor to the labor market. For unconstrained households, the replacement cost approach is also correct if the sole objective is valuing household production but with no commodity value of time spent on household production.

Our theoretical model also demonstrates that full consumption goes beyond measuring household production and should include the value of leisure and the intrinsic value of the time spent on household work. We show that these items should be valued at opportunity costs in the case of unconstrained households and valued at replacement costs in the case of constrained households.

Another main element of this chapter is the definition of a cost-of-living index of full consumption. We use the economic approach toward index numbers to define this price index with a view to measuring volume changes in full consumption.

Finally, we apply the findings empirically and compute comparative measures of the volume of full consumption per capita across a selection of OECD countries, thereby combining valuation and cost-of-living indexes. We conclude that moving from a comparison of actual final consumption to a comparison of full consumption has a marked influence on the relative position of countries.

Many research and measurement issues remain; for instance, the treatment of joint production within households, measuring productivity change in household production, and differentiating between types of expenditures such as educational investments and consumption. Another policy-relevant question is whether moving toward full consumption and full income affects distributional measures such as the Gini coefficient or the difference between average and median income.

References

Abraham, K. G., and C. Mackie, eds. 2005. *Beyond the Market; Designing Nonmarket Accounts for the United States*. Washington, DC: National Academies Press.

Ahmad, N., and S. Koh. 2011. "Incorporating Estimates of Household Production of Non-Market Services into International Comparisons of Material Well-Being." OECD Statistics Working Papers, 2011/07, Organisation for Economic Co-operation and Development, http://dx.doi.org/10.1787/5kg3h0jgk87g-en.

Barnett, W. 1977. "Pollak and Wachter on the Household Production Function Approach." *Journal of Political Economy* 85 (5): 1073–108.

Becker, G. S. 1965. "A Theory of the Allocation of Time." *Economic Journal* 75 (299): 493–517.

Bridgman, B., A. Dugan, M. Lal, M. Osborne, and S. Villones. 2012. "Accounting for Household Production in the National Accounts, 1965–2010." *Survey of Current Business* May:23–36.

Diewert, W. E. 1983. "The Theory of the Cost of Living Index and the Measurement of Welfare Change." In *Price Level Measurement*, edited by W. E. Diewert and C. Montmarquette, 163–239. Ottawa: Statistics Canada.

———. 1993. "Duality Approaches to Microeconomic Theory." In *Essays in Index Number Theory*, vol. 1, edited by W. E. Diewert and A. Nakamura 105–75. London: Emerald Publishing Group.

———. 2001. "The Consumer Price Index and Index Number Purpose." *Journal of Economic and Social Measurement* 27:167–248.

European Commission, IMF, OECD, World Bank, and United Nations. 2009. *2008 System of National Accounts*. New York: United Nations.

Folbre, N., and Barnet Wagman. 1993. "Counting Housework: New Estimates of Real Product in the United States, 1800–1860." *Journal of Economic History* 53 (2): 275–88.

Folbre, N , and J. Yoon. 2008. "The Value of Unpaid Child Care in the United States in 2003." In *How Do We Spend Our Time? Evidence from the American Time Use Survey*, edited by Jean Kimmel, 31–56. Kalamazoo, MI: W. E. Upjohn Institute for Employment Research.

Fouquet, A., and A. Chadeau. 1981. *Le Travail Domestique: Essai de Quantification*. Paris: French National Institute for Statistics and Economic Studies.

Fraumeni, B. M. 2008. "Household Production Accounts for Canada, Mexico, and the United States: Methodological Issues, Results, and Recommendations." Paper presented at the 30th General Conference of the International Association for Research in Income and Wealth, Slovenia.

Goldschmidt-Clermont, L. 1993. "The Monetary Valuation of Non-Market Productive Time: Methodological Considerations." *Review of Income and Wealth* 39 (4): 419–33.

Hill, T. P. 2009. "Consumption of Own Production and Cost of Living Indices." In *Price Index Concepts and Measurement*, Studies in Income and Wealth, vol. 70, edited by W. E. Diewert, J. S. Greenlees, and C. R. Hulten, 429–44. Chicago: University of Chicago Press.

Jorgenson, Dale W. and Zvi Griliches. 1967. "The Explanation of Productivity Change." *Review of Economic Studies* 34 (3): 249–83.

Konüs, Alexander A. 1924. "The Problem of the True Index of the Cost of Living." *Econometrica* 7:10–29.

Krueger, A., and A. Mueller. 2008. "The Lot of the Unemployed: A Time Use Perspective." IZA Discussion Paper no. 3490, Institute for the Study of Labor.

Lancaster, K. J. 1966. "A New Approach to Consumer Theory." *Journal of Political Economy* 74 (2): 132–57.

Landefeld, S., B. Fraumeni, and C. Vojtech. 2005. "Accounting for Nonmarket Production: A Prototype Satellite Account Using the American Time Use Survey." BEA Paper no. 0056, Bureau of Economic Analysis.

Landefeld, S., and S. McCulla. 2000. "Accounting for Nonmarket Household Production within a National Accounts Framework." *Review of Income and Wealth* 46 (3): 289–307.

Pollak, R. A. 1980. "Group Cost-of-Living Indexes." *American Economic Review* 70:273–8.

Pollak, R. A., and M. L. Wachter. 1975. "The Relevance of the Household Production Function and Its Implications for the Allocation of Time." *Journal of Political Economy* 83 (2): 255–77.

———. 1977. "Reply: 'Pollak and Wachter on the Household Production Approach.'" *Journal of Political Economy* 85 (5): 1083–6.

Reid, M. G. 1934. *Economics of Household Production*. New York: Wiley and Sons.

Roy, D. 2011. "La Contribution du Travail Domestique au Bien-être Matériel des Ménages: Une Quantification à Partir de l'enquête Emploi du Temps." Document de Travail INSEE F 1104. Paris: French National Institute for Statistics and Economic Studies.

Ruger, Y., and J. Varjonen. 2008. "Value of Household Production in Finland and Germany." Working Paper no. 112, National Consumer Research Centre, Helsinki.

Representing Consumption and Saving without a Representative Consumer

Christopher D. Carroll

5.1 Introduction

One entry in Aristotle's famous 350 BC catalog of logical errors is the "Fallacy of Division," in which the characteristics of a whole are improperly attributed to its parts. A Google search for a contemporary example yields: "America is rich. Z is an American. Therefore Z is rich."

This hits home following an economic crisis widely blamed on an unsustainable run-up of household debt. Before the crisis, many macroeconomists (in particular, adherents of the "representative agent" school) argued that the rising ratio of debt to household income was nothing to worry about: aggregate assets had risen more than debt, so the balance sheet of "the representative consumer" was healthy.[1] This view was often buttressed by graphical exhibits like figure 5.1, which plots total net worth (aggregate assets minus aggregate debt) and personal saving.[2] The striking negative relationship between wealth and saving was interpreted as indicating that the low American saving rate was appropriate because, thanks to rising asset

Christopher D. Carroll is professor of economics at Johns Hopkins University. He is on the board of directors of the National Bureau of Economic Research.

This chapter was written for the NBER-CRIW "Measuring Economic Stability and Progress" conference held August 6–8, 2012, in Cambridge, MA. For acknowledgments, sources of research support, and disclosure of the author's material financial relationships, if any, please see http://www.nber.org/chapters/c12830.ack.

1. While a few well-known economists like Krugman (2005) and Shiller (2005) argued that much of the measured asset valuation reflected a housing bubble, a review of the public record concludes "the pessimistic case was a distinctly minority view, especially among professional economists." See, for example, Himmelberg, Mayer, and Sinai (2005) for a "no bubble" view published in the leading "popular" journal of the *American Economic Association*.

2. Both variables are measured as ratios to income.

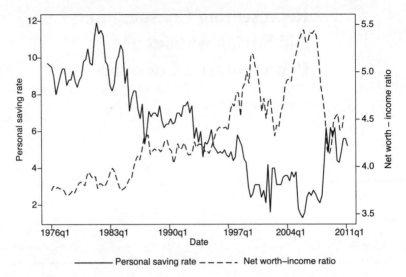

Fig. 5.1   The personal saving rate versus the ratio of wealth to income
Source: BEA and FFA.

prices, the representative consumer's wealth had increased so much that there was no *net* need to save (in the aggregate).

The implicit assumption that would justify this conclusion is that debtors and creditors are identical in a key respect: either group responds to a one dollar change in its net wealth by changing annual spending by some small amount like two or three cents (estimated from aggregate historical data).

Of course, this defies common sense. As James Tobin (1980) remarked long ago in an extended critique of representative agent modeling (cited in International Monetary Fund [2012]), "the population is not distributed between debtors and creditors randomly. Debtors have borrowed for good reasons, most of which indicate a high marginal propensity to spend from wealth or from current income or from any other liquid resources they can command." And microeconomic evidence has long borne out the proposition that marginal propensities to consume (MPCs) differ sharply for people with different financial circumstances.

Given these points, it is not surprising that estimated versions of representative agent models did a poor job explaining the collapse in household spending following the crisis. According to one estimate (Carroll, Slacalek, and Sommer 2012), the drop in wealth can explain only about half of the increase in saving in the crisis.

When economists' and policymakers' attention turned to the consideration of fiscal and monetary options to prevent the crisis from turning into a second Great Depression, representative consumer models proved even less useful. Such models gave implausible answers to questions about the likely response of household spending to the main available policy instruments: fiscal "stimulus" measures, and changes in real interest rates. As section 5.2 of the chapter will argue, off-the-shelf representative agent models tend to imply that virtually all of a one-time stimulus check will be saved, a proposition strongly at odds with the microeconomic empirical evidence (e.g., from the earliest, Kreinin [1961] and Friedman [1963], to the latest, Parker and Broda [2011] and Parker et al. [2011]; henceforth, PB and PSJM). Representative agent models also tend to predict that monetary policy should be extremely potent, because according to such models, household spending decisions should be hypersensitive to interest rates (a proposition for which there is essentially no empirical evidence at either the micro- or the macro-level—and not for lack of looking). A final defect is that off-the-shelf closed-economy representative agent models do not admit any sensible role for the financial sector, really, to exist: The essence of finance is the channeling of funds from those who want to lend to those who want to borrow, but if everyone is identical (as effectively assumed in representative agent models), then everybody follows Polonius's advice: "Neither a borrower nor a lender be."[3] With neither borrowers or lenders, finance is irrelevant.

Given such manifest inadequacies, why has representative agent modeling been the main tool of macroeconomic analysis for many years? In my view, the answer lies largely in the fact that the data required by representative agent models are easily available, are produced regularly, and are of high quality, while the data necessary to explore more sensible models that take account of microeconomic heterogeneity have mostly been of low quality, are difficult to work with, and (perhaps most importantly) do not paint a picture of the aggregate economy that is consistent with macroeconomic facts that we know from other sources. For example, data from the principal microeconomic survey of household expenditures in the United States show a personal saving rate that has been rising steadily for many years, in flagrant contradiction to reasonably well-measured facts from a host of more credible sources (see, e.g., Aguiar and Bils 2011).

The thesis of this chapter is that our only hope of making progress in being able, in real time, to answer questions like "is the recent rapid debt buildup sustainable" or "how would different stimulus plans affect consumer spending" is to augment the existing national accounts with satellite accounts that provide high-quality information at less aggregated levels. Specifically, what is needed is supplementary data that has two characteristics: (a) it is well measured at the level of some microeconomic unit; and (b) it adds up to, or at least makes recognizable contact with, aggregate facts as measured in the existing National Income and Product Accounts (NIPA). As we shall see, the existing disaggregated data sources satisfy neither of these criteria.

The chapter proceeds in three main parts. The first section sketches a

---

3. A quip I have shamelessly stolen from Bob Hall.

modern microfounded framework for saving and balance sheet decisions that I will use to illustrate what will be needed from any expansion of the national accounts that aspires to remedy the problems outlined above. Next comes a précis of the implications of that framework for the measurement of consumption and saving. This provides a natural introduction to a discussion of the problems with existing data sources, as well as to a penultimate section that discusses some promising approaches that are emerging from a variety of nontraditional sources, ranging from personal finance apps to Scandinavian registry data.

5.2   Framework

5.2.1   The Household's Dynamic Budget Constraint

Adopting the notational convention that returns on tradable assets accrue between the end of period t and the beginning of period $t + 1$ and indexing the different kinds of such assets by j, we can represent the evolution of a consumer's balance sheet between the end of period t and the "decision moment" in period $t + 1$ by

$$(1) \qquad m_{t+1,j} = a_{t,j} \mathcal{R}_{t+1,j} + y_{t+1,j},$$

where $a_{t,j}$ represents the asset positions after all period-t actions have been accomplished, and the return factor $\mathcal{R}_{t+1,j}$ includes interest payments, capital gains, and depreciation. $y_{t+1,j}$ represents the net income in category j that is not interpretable as a rate of return; the main example will be cash non-capital (labor and transfer) income, assigned (arbitrarily) to asset category $j = 0$. The processes of receiving returns and earning income combine to yield a balance sheet m_{t+1} that summarizes the consumer's market resources at the moment when consumption and portfolio allocation decisions must be made.

It is thus useful to separate these return-and-income-earning processes from the other steps in the evolution of the household's balance sheet from an initial set of values $m_{t,j}$. Using $x_{t,j}$ for the net eXpenditures paid out from a given asset category yields the within-period accounting equation

$$(2) \qquad a_{t,j} = m_{t,j} - x_{t,j}$$

for all $j > 0$ (assuming that consumption spending is paid for with cash, which is category 0),

$$(3) \qquad a_{t,0} = m_{t,0} - x_{t,0} - c_t.$$

Without a j subscript $a_t = \sum_j a_{t,j}$ and similarly for m_t and x_t, a_t and m_t are measures of the household's total net tradable wealth position after and before period t's choices of sales and purchases (asset-related net expenditures x_t). Within the period the household's tradable net worth thus evolves according to

(4) $$a_t = m_t - x_t - c_t,$$

where c_t is total expenditures on nondurables and services, and can in principle be decomposed into arbitrarily many $c_{t,k}$ categories that sum to c_t. Note that rearrangements of the portfolio (selling one asset whose proceeds are used to buy another) will yield no net contribution to expenditures $x_t = 0$ because purchases of one asset are financed by sales of the other (if there are transactions costs, e.g., brokerage fees, associated with such rearrangements, those will be captured as a positive net value of x_t).[4]

Using $\mathfrak{R}_{t+1}$ as the portfolio-weighted rate of return, a combination of equation (4) and equation (1) yields an aggregated household-level dynamic budget constraint

(5) $$m_{t+1} = (m_t - x_t - c_t)\mathfrak{R}_{t+1} + y_{t+1}.$$

5.2.2   Household Income

The key insight of Friedman (1957) was that households' responses to income shocks ought to depend on whether they perceive those shocks to be transitory or permanent. Since Friedman's time, a vast literature has found that his dichotomy between transitory and permanent shocks provides a good description of household-level income data (for a recent treatment, see Hryshko [2012]). Data also support the proposition that households' spending response to permanent shocks is much greater than the response to transitory shocks (recently, see Blundell, Pistaferri, and Preston [2008]).

The literature thus suggests that household income dynamics can reasonably be captured by

(6) $$p_{t+1} = p_t \Gamma_{t+1}$$

(7) $$y_{t+1} = p_{t+1} \theta_{t+1},$$

where Γ_{t+1} is the growth of permanent income; it incorporates both the predictable (say, age-related) and the unpredictable (say, receiving tenure— or not). The θ_{t+1} is a mean-one transitory shock.

Some readers might wonder whether it is wise to impose such a specific description of income dynamics; the answer, gleaned through painful experience, is that even the most basic correlations in cross-section or short-panel empirical data cannot be meaningfully interpreted unless the analyst knows whether the correlation in question is between the object of interest and transitory income or between that object and permanent income (or at least, some highly persistent component of income that is reasonably

---

4. It is common to measure transactions costs as an element in $c_{t,k}$ but for our purposes this seems inappropriate because presumably brokerage fees and similar expenses are instrumental expenses that do not directly yield utility, and we will later be interpreting c as reflecting the spending that yields utility.

approximable by permanent income).[5] Some method for distinguishing the transitory from the persistent components of income is therefore entirely appropriate as a requirement for any useful measurement of household balance sheets.

5.2.3   A Specific Model

Utility Maximization with CRRA Utility

A standard approach to the analysis of consumer behavior is to make the further assumption that household preferences are time separable and that the period utility function is in the constant relative risk aversion class,

$$u(\bullet) = \left(\frac{\bullet^{1-\rho}}{1-\rho}\right).$$

This specialization to CRRA utility is likely not necessary for most of the points emphasized below, but will be assumed henceforth for convenience.

In the CRRA case, the problem can be normalized by permanent income; using nonbold variables to indicate the corresponding bold variable defined above so normalized, optimal behavior will be characterized by a consumption function $c_t(m_t)$, where the time subscript indicates the dependence of optimal behavior on age, and the function will differ for each different configuration of preferences.

The decision problem for the household in period t can be written using normalized variables; the consumer's objective is to choose consumption function $c(m)$ that satisfies:

(8) $$v(m_t) = \max_{\{c_t, x_t\}} u(c_t) + \beta \mathbb{E}_t[\Gamma_{t+1}^{1-\rho} v(m_{t+1})]$$

s.t.

$$m_{t+1} = (m_t - x_t - c_t)\mathfrak{R}_{t+1}/\Gamma_{t+1} + \theta_{t+1},$$

where the nonbold (ratio) variables are defined as the bold (level) variables divided by the level of permanent income p_t. The only state variable is (normalized) cash-on-hand m_t.

The principal difference between this framework and typical representative agent models is that household income is assumed to follow a Friedmanesque structure with transitory and permanent shocks whose characteristics are calibrated using microeconomic rather than macroeconomic data.

It is not implausible to expect this calibration to make a big difference,

---

5. As of this writing, the best measurement of household income dynamics is that of DeBacker et al. (2013), who use newly available IRS tax data and conclude that the serial correlation of the "persistent" component of household income shocks is about 0.98; close enough to 1 as to be nearly equivalent to a specification with a truly permanent component.

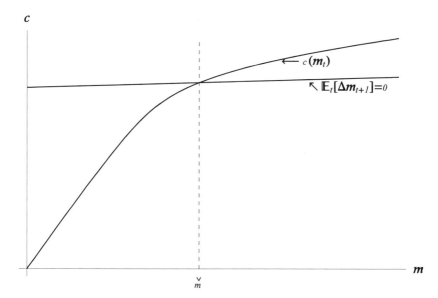

Fig. 5.2   Concave consumption function

since the estimated variance of permanent shocks to household income in the Panel Study of Income Dynamics is about 100 times as large as the estimated variance of permanent shocks to NIPA disposable personal income (Carroll, Slacalek, and Tokuoka 2011).[6]

Implications of the Baseline Model

The generic characteristics of the solution to models like this are captured in figure 5.2, which shows the consumption function for a model described in Carroll (2011), along with the "sustainable consumption" locus. The place where the two loci meet defines a "target" such that, if $m < \bar{m}$ then the cash-on-hand ratio m will rise (in expectation), and vice versa if m exceeds its target.

It is worth emphasizing that the target $\bar{m}$ is a *ratio* of market resources to permanent income. If at some date t, everyone were at their target $\bar{m}$, then the degree of inequality in the level of market resources m would mirror the degree of inequality in permanent income p.

In practice, the baseline version of the model implies that a set of households indexed by i, all of whom have identical $\bar{m}$ values, will have actual $m_{t,i}$'s s distributed stochastically around that $\bar{m}$, with the differences across house-

---

6. Comparison of the relative magnitudes of transitory shocks is more difficult because a substantial proportion of what is measured as transitory shocks in microeconomic data is likely to be measurement error instead.

holds attributable to their differing histories of idiosyncratic shocks. While various nonlinearities in the model prohibit any proof of an exact correspondence between the model's implied distribution of *m* and the simulated population's distribution of *p*, the intuition that the baseline model implies a degree of *m* inequality similar to the degree of *p* inequality is roughly right. Since any sensible method of measurement shows a high degree of inequality in permanent income, the model makes a good start toward explaining the high degree of wealth inequality measured in the empirical sources like the Survey of Consumer Finances.

However, figure 5.3 (taken from Carroll, Slacalek, and Tokuoka [2011]) shows that the version of the model in which all households have the same time preference rate (the β-Point version), and thus identical $\bar{m}$ targets, produces a wealth distribution that is far more equal than the actual distribution in the empirical data (US data). This reflects the empirical fact that wealth inequality is much greater than permanent income inequality. Thus, in order for a model of this kind to match the degree of wealth heterogeneity observed in the data, it is necessary to introduce some reason for behavioral heterogeneity beyond simply the fact that different households experience different shocks.

Many kinds of heterogeneity are plausible candidates. For example, the model that generated the results in the figure assumes that all agents have the same remaining life expectancy, and the same expected profiles for income growth. Introducing an empirically realistic profile for income over the lifetime and for mortality probabilities would introduce life cycle motives for saving that are absent from that model.

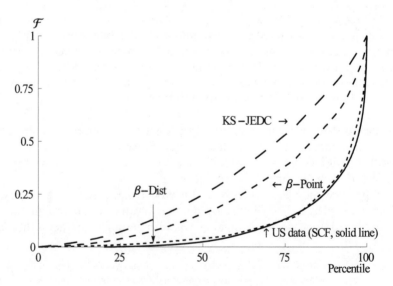

Fig. 5.3   Cumulative wealth distribution (models and data)

But the literature experimenting with such models is increasingly reaching the conclusion that the vast heterogeneity in outcomes in microeconomic data even among people of the same age and with similar life histories cannot be explained without some degree of heterogeneity in preferences (or, nearly equivalently, in beliefs).

Preference Heterogeneity

Specifically, the recent macroeconomic literature has begun grudgingly to explore the consequences of differences in characteristics like risk aversion or time preference rates. Preference heterogeneity matters for macroeconomic analysis insofar as it results in an equilibrium in which different consumers have profoundly different responses to any given given shock, so that the distribution of that shock across agents will determine its aggregate impact.

Even without taking a stand on which are the most important kinds of preference heterogeneity for macroeconomics, it is clear that a statistical framework that hopes to represent the data faithfully will need to measure some of the dimensions along which such heterogeneity produces different outcomes. Differences in the structure of households' balance sheets are likely to be a revealing indicator of differences in their preferences; this by itself would be a compelling reason to measure the structure of household balance sheets, even if there were not other reasons to do so.

It is not hard to see why preference differences might be expected to matter. Different degrees of patience, or different risk aversion, or differences in many other kinds of household characteristics should lead households to different values of $\bar{m}$. Since theory implies that macroeconomic outcomes are likely to depend heavily on the distribution of consumers across values of m, it seems inevitable that the distribution of preferences will make a big difference to macroeconomic predictions.

Carroll, Slacalek, and Tokuoka (2011) perform a simple experiment to determine whether their baseline model's failure to fit the degree of inequality can be remedied by the simple expedient of allowing time preference rates to vary across individuals. Although plenty of experimental evidence supports the proposition that time preference rates do differ in the population, their preferred interpretation is that the variation they consider should be viewed as also proxying for a host of other kinds of heterogeneity: in age, growth expectations, demographic structure, and so forth.

Whatever might be the proper interpretation of the estimated degree of time preference heterogeneity, the solid locus labeled β-Dist in figure 5.3 plots the results when the distribution of time preference rates in the simulated population is assumed to be uniform, so that its width can be estimated by a single parameter. The model targets the proportions of wealth held by the 40th, 60th, and 80th percentiles in the population, but the model's simulated distribution fits the empirical data quite well across the entire spectrum of wealth's distribution (except at the very top; the model does not

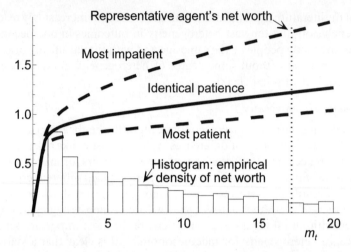

Fig. 5.4   Consumption and the _m_ distribution (ratios to quarterly income)

include opportunities for entrepreneurship, which is the source of much of the income of the richest 1 percent of households).

The estimated difference in time preference rates between the least and the most patient agents in the model is only 4 percentage points (at an annual rate). Nevertheless, the optimal consumption rules of those categories of agents differ strikingly, as shown in figure 5.4 (taken from the same source). That figure also superimposes a histogram of values of _m_ calculated from the 1998 Survey of Consumer Finances (SCF), which shows that a very substantial portion of the population is concentrated at values of _m_ at which impatient households would have a high MPC.

5.3   Implications for Measurement of Consumption and Saving

One way of evaluating any proposal for how to augment the NIPA accounts to permit better measurement of heterogeneity in saving is by asking whether the resulting data would permit researchers to construct the empirical analogue of figure 5.4.

Using the notation for a household's dynamic budget constraint articulated in section 5.2.1, the data set would need, at a minimum, to contain for each household:

- measures of total household market resources in successive years: $m_{t,i}$ and $m_{t+1,i}$;
- a measure of the household's actual income received in one year $y_{t+1,i}$;
- a measure of the household's perceived permanent income $p_{t,i}$;
- measures of transactions costs related to financial investments $x_{t,i}$; and

- a measure of the rate of return earned on each of the household's assets $\mathfrak{R}_{t+1,i}$.

Notably absent from this enumeration is a direct measure of the household's consumption expenditures c_t. For reasons articulated below, my proposal is that consumption should be calculated as a residual; equation (5) can be solved for c_t to yield

$$(9) \qquad c_t = (m_{t+1} - y_{t+1})\mathfrak{R}_{t+1}^{-1} + m_t - x_t.$$

Considerable value would be gained by having a third year of panel information, so that two successive years of expenditures could be constructed. Friedman (1957) emphasized the importance of accounting for transitory expenditures (a child's wedding, or unanticipated home repairs after a hurricane) in attempting to assess the validity of his permanent income hypothesis, and although transitory expenditures have not received as much attention as transitory income in the subsequent literature, there can be little doubt that they are substantial. Having an extra year (or, better, two) of spending data would allow the analyst to smooth through such episodes.

A further motivation for the collection of several years of consumption data is that almost all standard empirical macroeconomic models today incorporate some form of habit formation in order to capture the substantial degree of sluggishness apparent in aggregate spending dynamics. But to date, the microeconomic literature has found little evidence of habit formation. One interpretation of the lack of microeconomic support for habits, unfortunately, is that the microeconomic data on total household spending are of such poor quality that habit formation may exist but be undetectable using those data. Since a substantial number of important questions in macroeconomic theory, welfare analysis, and public policy depend on whether or not habits exist, the ability to resolve the question by collecting several years' worth of panel household balance sheet data provides a powerful further motivation for a substantial panel component to any such survey. It seems likely that at least three years' worth of spending data would be necessary to have a shot at resolving this question, which would require a minimum of four panel wealth interviews. (Though best of all would be an ongoing panel like the Panel Study of Income Dynamics.)

A panel data set that included only household totals (for example, net worth, total income, and investment transactions) would be an enormous improvement on available data sources. But such a data set would still be unable to answer some vital questions. A particularly interesting such question at present is the extent to which the internal structure of a household's balance sheet influences its spending decisions. That is, for a given level of total net market wealth, to what extent (if any) does it matter whether that net worth is held in the form, say, of $100,000 in a bank account versus, say, a house whose value is $600,000 along with a $500,000 mortgage (and cash holdings near zero)? In a world with imperfect capital markets, there are good reasons why the behavior of two such households might be different, including the consequences of house price risk, refinancing risk, risk to various interest rates, and so on.

The breakdown of the household's assets by categories (particularly between debt [secured and unsecured], liquid assets, and illiquid assets) may yield very useful further insights. For example, a recent paper by Kaplan and Violante (2011) argues that even many households with high permanent income have a large proportion of their assets in illiquid forms; they show that if this is the case even households with high wealth-to-income ratios might have a high marginal propensity to consume out of a fiscal stimulus check.

A further reason to probe the allocation of assets across categories is that allocation decisions may yield indirect information about the distribution of household preferences (like the time preference rate). For example, it is easy to show that a household's degree of risk aversion with respect to investments in risky assets should be directly related to its expected future marginal propensity to consume. (Variation in future returns that does not translate into much variation in future consumption should not generate much risk aversion.) Theories about the nature of preference heterogeneity can thus be probed by looking at the interrelationships between net worth, permanent income, consumption, and portfolio allocation. Theories like the "hyperbolic discounting" model of Laibson (1997) that depart from the frictionless optimization paradigm sketched above, may have even stronger predictions for balance sheet structure; for example, Laibson, Repetto, and Tobacman (2007) propose to explain the simultaneous presence of credit card balances and low-return assets on the balance sheets of many households by allowing different short-term and long-term discount factors. It can be argued that the principal reason their view has not been universally adopted is the absence of the kinds of panel data on household balance sheets that can decisively prove that the kinds of behavior they observe in the cross section are not transitory episodes but instead persistently characterize the behavior of the same households over many successive periods.

5.4   Problems with Existing Data Sources

This chapter's overarching argument is that the household's dynamic budget constraint is the bedrock on which attempts at microeconomic representations of households' global choices (like decisions about how much to save, or how to structure a balance sheet between assets and liabilities, or choices about investments in risky versus riskless assets) should rest.

In large part, this view reflects a perception that all other approaches have been tried, and have failed.

A host of existing microeconomic sources attempt to measure slivers of the household's budget constraint. The Current Population Survey (CPS), the Survey of Income and Program Participation (SIPP), IRS tax panel data, and other sources widely used by labor economists provide a window on households' incomes but provide little or no information about consumption or assets. The triennial Survey of Consumer Finances has measured the cross section of household balance sheets, but until very recently has not provided dynamic (panel) information (the crisis provoked a 2009 reinterview of the 2007 respondents—a valuable, but perhaps unique, experiment).[7] The Panel Study of Income Dynamics provides a rich sampling of income data every two years and recently has added considerable data on expenditures, but provides nothing approximating the careful accounting of the evolution of households' balance sheets that is required for a thorough understanding of saving decisions.

This situation reflects the fact that all of the objects in equation (5) are difficult to observe. For example, a series of influential papers (e.g., Meyer and Sullivan 2009) have argued that even income, in principle perhaps the easiest element of the equation to observe, is seriously and systematically mismeasured by existing microdata sources for households in the lower part of the distribution. Given the formidable difficulties in measuring each item, surveys have (reasonably enough) tended to pick one object in the budget constraint for special attention while neglecting the others.

The survey that focuses on the c component of the budget constraint (and neglects the others) is the Consumer Expenditure Survey, which has been conducted in approximately its current form on a continuous basis since the early 1980s. Until recently, no other data source for the United States attempted to get much information about household expenditures.[8]

Unfortunately, the quality of the CE data (like that of data obtained from many other household surveys) has been deteriorating steadily over time. The principal reason for this decline is not hard to guess: Imagine a surveyor arriving at your doorstep and asking "Would you be willing to spend several hours being interviewed about the details of your household spending, and then having us come back and repeat the process four more times over the following year? And, by the way, would you also be willing to keep a complete diary of all of your household's expenditures for a two-week period?" The number of households contacted who ultimately participate in all five interviews is now only about 40 percent, and no amount of weighting or other statistical wizardry is likely to be able to transform these data into something that is representative of the other households who (understandably) decline to subject themselves to the full course of torture. Further-

---

7. The 1983 to 1989 panel was such a difficult and problematic enterprise that no panel was attempted again until the Great Recession.

8. A few surveys, most notably the Panel Study of Income Dynamics, have recently been augmented to obtain more data on spending; but those data, while potentially useful, do not offer any real hope of resolving the many problems I will dwell on with the CE survey.

more, even among the participating households, there is strong evidence of differential reporting bias; Aguiar and Bils (2011) argue, in particular, that expenditures are differentially underreported by high-income households and that this problem has been growing worse over time, leading (they argue) to serious biases like the survey's implication that saving rates have increased over time and that consumption inequality has increased less than income inequality.

From the perspective of macroeconomic analysis, perhaps an even more serious problem is the failure of the total spending growth data from the CE survey to show much correlation with macroeconomic aggregates. Attanasio, Battistin, and Padula (2010) show that the correlation of annual changes in expenditures as measured in the CE, and the changes in the corresponding spending categories in the NIPA accounts, is close to zero and statistically insignificant. This result is deeply discouraging for macroeconomists who might want to use CE data to delve into the microfoundations of aggregate fluctuations. If the aggregate fluctuations that are such a prominent feature of the macroeconomic data cannot be reliably *detected* when the microdata is aggregated, the whole microfoundations research program becomes problematic.[9]

Recognizing these and other problems, the Bureau of Labor Statistics has recently embarked on an ambitious program to redesign the CE survey from the ground up (see Bureau of Labor Statistics [2011] for an overview). To provide advice, the BLS commissioned a panel of experts (see Horrigan 2010) from the Committee on National Statistics, which issued its report in October of 2012 (see National Research Council 2012). As in many prior analyses, however, the report was better at documenting the problems of the existing approach than at clarifying how the problems it identifies could be solved.

While the BLS has been commendably open in acknowledging those problems, and has articulated an impressive vision for how to address them, waiting for the CE redesign process to be completed before embarking on an attempt to add disaggregated household satellite accounts to the NIPA data would be costly.[10] According to current projections, the CE redesign may not be fully operational for another ten years—assuming it is pursued despite the lean budgets that are likely to prevail in the coming decade. Furthermore, even if the redesigned CE is an improvement in many dimensions on the current survey, there is no guarantee that it will exhibit a major improvement

9. This depiction is perhaps a bit too bleak; Parker and Vissing-Jorgensen (2009) have done some impressive work that makes some progress in determining how the spending of different groups varies over the business cycle, arguing in particular that high-income and low-income households seem to bear more of the fluctuations than do middle-income households. But the amount of effort required to extract results of this kind from such a highly imperfect data set is a formidable barrier to entry for other scholars, and skeptics can argue that other factors (like variation in survey participation over the cycle) could drive the results.

10. See http://www.bls.gov/cex/ce_gemini_redesign.pdf.

in coherence with NIPA data. The CE survey's principal statutory purpose is to determine expenditure weights for the Consumer Price Index, and it is possible (perhaps even likely) that the CE redesign might reasonably meet that goal without satisfying the goals articulated above as the chief priorities for NIPA distributional satellite accounts (though see Parker, Souleles, and Carroll [2013] for an argument that a survey that does not get the totals right cannot be taken seriously as a means of producing weights for the components of those totals).

There is little disagreement with the principle that equation (5) is the proper framework for accounting for the "true" evolution of a household's balance sheet. To restate this chapter's main thesis: Extensive and painful experience in trying to learn about the marginal propensity to consume, portfolio choice, the evolution of household balance sheets, and other "global" characteristics of households' behavior using instruments designed to measure only partial slivers or snapshots of the balance sheet have demonstrably failed. It seems likely at this point that the only approach that offers a reasonable chance of success is one that embraces the dynamic budget constraint rather than ignoring it.

5.5   Practicalities

However fervent it may be, an injunction to measure household-level dynamic budget constraints is not likely to be heeded if the task is viewed as impossible. Fortunately, several promising strategies are available.

5.5.1   The SCF+ Strategy

The most straightforward approach would be to negotiate with the Federal Reserve to expand the scope and mission of its existing Survey of Consumer Finances. The SCF is widely viewed as one of the premier microeconomic surveys in the world, and a deep and broad base of research already exists using the SCF to address a host of important topics.

Most importantly, the economic crisis prompted the Fed to sponsor a reinterview (panel) survey in 2009 of the 2007 respondents, and that reinterview survey could be reinterpreted as a pilot study for the move to a truly panel structure for the SCF.

To achieve the full vision that has been laid out, the reinterviews would need to become annual, and the sample size would need to be augmented. But if the survey were modified to take advantage of the explosion of personal financial tracking tools available for smartphones and web-based accounts, the burden on respondents might become substantially lighter than in the past.

These considerations also suggest the possibility of designing a new measurement instrument from scratch that could be tailored to the specific needs of the Bureau of Economic Analysis (BEA).

5.5.2   Personal Financial Accounting Software

I like to think of myself as a public-spirited person. But I shudder at the thought of being asked to participate in the Survey of Consumer Finances or the Consumer Expenditure Survey. Little in modern life appeals less than the idea of than spending hours trying to answer the sorts of questions that make up the substance of such surveys—especially the Consumer Expenditure Survey, much of which I could not answer because I simply do not know how much I spent on the various categories of items the survey takers want to measure.

But my guilt at this reaction is tempered by the self-justifying thought that if the survey takers would be willing to settle for receiving a copy of the excellent financial records I keep using personal financial accounting software, I would happily participate. It is hard not to suspect that anyone else who has such records would have the same reaction (though perhaps this reflects a bias identified more recently than 350 BC; modern psychological evidence suggests that individuals tend to think that other people are more like them than those other people actually are).

While the majority of households may not keep such accurate records, it seems plausible that even among people who do not, many would be happy to agree to an offer by the survey taker to organize their financial records for them (in exchange for the surveyor being allowed to keep an anonymized version for research purposes).

A closely related idea would be to contract with one of the proliferating personal finance websites to which millions of people have entrusted their financial account login ID's and passwords for online access. These "aggregator" sites then construct balance sheets for their customers that incorporate many of the elements needed for BEA's purposes. Such sites are typically free, paid for with advertising revenue. It seems that it would be a short leap for the BEA to advertise for volunteers on such a site, at least for a pilot project to see how much could be learned from such a source.

Another starting point might be to approach the firms that constitute the "wealth management" industry, who have developed their own systems for measuring the household balance sheets of their customers. The software systems used by firms in this industry are more focused on capturing the complex details of the balance sheets of wealthy households than on measuring details of spending, so an approach that began with wealth management software would probably need to be augmented for some method of constructing a reasonably reliable measure of expenditures as well, but again a customized version of the software could surely be commissioned for this purpose.

Any of these strategies would, of course, require efforts to deal with the obvious sample selection problems reflected in the fact that the users of personal finance software or websites (or wealth management services!) are not a random sampling of the population. It is not obvious, however, that these sampling problems are more difficult than the crippling problems already afflicting many surveys. Indeed, it is not at all implausible to suppose that many respondents would be pleased to receive free software and training in exchange for release of their (anonymized) financial information.

5.5.3   Data from Scandinavian Countries

A number of Scandinavian countries have undertaken initiatives to pull together all of their governments' records about individual citizens into a single database. The amalgamated data set includes tax and property records, demographic information, earnings, and a smorgasbord of other information.

In Sweden, as a legacy of a now-abolished wealth tax, the national database even includes highly detailed data on real estate values, mortgage debt, and financial information, including security-by-security transactions data. A fascinating recent paper by Koijen, Van Nieuwerburgh, and Vestman (2013) pulls together these data to construct a measure of household expenditures along precisely the lines sketched above (proving, if nothing else, that such a scheme is practical enough to be implemented, at least in Sweden). Of the many interesting results in the paper, one stands out: The correlation is not particularly high between expenditures as measured in this way, and expenditures are measured using a traditional expenditure survey (respondents' answers are linkable to their national registry records). Since the authors have high-quality data on virtually every component of the dynamic budget constraint as specified above, these results suggest that the expenditure survey data are of even lower quality than one might have hoped. (See also the related paper by Kreiner, Lassen, and Leth-Petersen [2013] on a similar exercise Danish registry data, which does not contain wealth transactions information).

Of course, the BEA needs to measure balance sheets in the United States, not Sweden. But the existence of the Scandinavian registry data could nevertheless be useful in several ways. First, joint initiatives with such countries could provide an invaluable way for the BEA to answer many questions whose resolution might be nearly impossible in the United States (such as determining which questions, if any, households can accurately answer in a survey context). Second, sponsored research (either jointly between BEA and the other country's statistical bureau, or by academic researchers with access to the data) could explore the extent to which data of this kind really satisfy the needs of the BEA. A particular question that could be addressed is the extent to which measures of aggregate expenditures constructed using the balance sheet approach resemble spending dynamics obtained using traditional methods like retail sales surveys. Another target would be to match aggregate Flow of Funds accounts.

If research of this kind demonstrated that administrative data are the "holy grail" of national income statistics, perhaps progress could be made in moving toward a similar system in the United States. At present, privacy rules and other impediments have prevented the kinds of data sharing across government agencies that has allowed the Swedes (and the Danes, and Norwegians) to construct their impressive databases. With concerted and sustained efforts (and careful rules about privacy), it is possible that many of these rules could be relaxed for the purpose of producing anonymized national accounts data.

An alternative might be to combine such adminstrative data with survey data. This could be done either by compiling a large database of administrative data and then sampling the households in that data set to ask the crucial questions needed to fill out the balance sheets, or the approach could be the inverse: begin with transactions data from an online or personal finance source, then augment those with administrative data.

One key contribution that administrative data might be able to make in either of these cases would be to help in constructing a measure of permanent income for the individuals constituting a household. Social Security earnings histories could be enormously helpful in measuring permanent income, which is unlikely to be easy to measure using the time-limited data that can be obtained using either of the other approaches.

5.6   Conclusions

If the purpose of national accounts is to provide the data needed to understand the workings of the economy at the aggregate level, it seems clear that this mission is not satisfactorily accomplished by the existing NIPA accounts. Both economic theory and practical experience indicate that detailed microeconomic information on household balance sheets and their dynamics will be essential for making progress. While the challenge is formidable, a variety of recent developments suggest it is not infeasible. The remarkable data available in Scandinavian countries provide a test bed for research on the measurement of balance sheets. Recent advances in electronic data resources, along with the successful recent reinterview survey by the Survey of Consumer Finances, point to alternative paths for accomplishing the goal in the United States.

If a successful set of satellite accounts on the distribution and evolution of household balance sheets could be constructed, that would constitute arguably the most important advance in national income accounting since the glory days of the 1950s, when the accounts were first created in their present form. It is a big challenge, and one that will require collaboration with academia, with other countries, and with the private sector (as happened in the 1950s). But it is a challenge that has the potential to make national accounting exciting in a way that has not been true for fifty years.

References

Aguiar, Mark A., and Mark Bils. 2011. "Has Consumption Inequality Mirrored Income Inequality?" NBER Working Paper no. 16807, Cambridge, MA.

Aristotle. 350 BC. *On Sophistical Refutations*. The Wikipedia Foundation. http://en.wikipedia.org/wiki/Sophistical_Refutations.

Attanasio, Orazio, Erich Battistin, and Mario Padula. 2010. *Inequality in Living Standards Since 1980: Evidence from Expenditure Data*. Washington, DC: American Enterprise Institute for Public Policy Research.

Blundell, Richard, Luigi Pistaferri, and Ian Preston. 2008. "Consumption Inequality and Partial Insurance." *American Economic Review* 98 (5): 1887–921.

Bureau of Labor Statistics. 2011. "Consumer Expenditure Survey (CE) Gemini Project." http://www.bls.gov/cex/geminiproject.htm.

Carroll, Christopher D. 2011. "Theoretical Foundations of Buffer Stock Saving." Unpublished manuscript, Department of Economics, Johns Hopkins University. http://econ.jhu.edu/people/ccarroll/papers/BufferStockTheory.

Carroll, Christopher D., Jiri Slacalek, and Martin Sommer. 2012. "Dissecting Saving Dynamics: Measuring Wealth, Precautionary, and Credit Effects." Unpublished manuscript, Johns Hopkins University. http://econ.jhu.edu/people/ccarroll/papers/cssUSSaving/.

Carroll, Christopher D., Jiri Slacalek, and Kiichi Tokuoka. 2011. "Digestible Microfoundations: Buffer Stock Saving in a Krusell-Smith World." Unpublished manuscript, Johns Hopkins University. http://econ.jhu.edu/people/ccarroll/papers/BSinKS.pdf.

DeBacker, Jason, Bradley Heim, Vasia Panousi, Shanthi Ramnath, and Ivan Vidangos. 2013. "Rising Inequality: Transitory or Permanent? New Evidence from a Panel of US Tax Returns." *Brookings Papers on Economic Activity* 2013 (1): 67–142.

Friedman, Milton A. 1957. *A Theory of the Consumption Function*. Princeton, NJ: Princeton University Press.

———. 1963. "Windfalls, the 'Horizon,' and Related Concepts in the Permanent Income Hypothesis." In *Measurement in Economics*, edited by Carl Christ, 1–28. Stanford: Stanford University Press.

Himmelberg, Charles, Christopher Mayer, and Todd Sinai. 2005. "Assessing High House Prices: Bubbles, Fundamentals and Misperceptions." *Journal of Economic Perspectives* 19 (4): 67–92.

Horrigan, Michael. 2010. "Official Charge to the CNSTAT Panel on Redesign of the Consumer Expenditure Survey." http://www.bls.gov/cex/redpanl1_horrigan.pdf.

Hryshko, Dmytro. 2012. "Labor Income Profiles are not Heterogeneous: Evidence from Income Growth Rates." *Quantitative Economics* 3 (2): 177–209.

International Monetary Fund. 2012. *World Economic Outlook, 2012* (chap. 3). Washington, DC: International Monetary Fund. http://www.imf.org/external/pubs/ft/weo/2012/01/pdf/text.pdf.

Kaplan, Greg, and Giovanni L. Violante. 2011. "A Model of the Consumption Response to Fiscal Stimulus Payments." NBER Working Paper no. 17338, Cambridge, MA.

Koijen, Ralph, S. Van Nieuwerburgh, and Roine Vestman. Forthcoming. "Judging the Quality of Survey Data by Comparison with Truth as Measured by Administrative Records: Evidence from Sweden." In *Improving the Measurement of Consumer Expenditures*, Studies in Income and Wealth, edited by Christopher D. Carroll, Thomas Crossley, and John Sabelhaus. Chicago: University of Chicago Press.

Kreiner, Claus Thustrup, David Dreyer Lassen, and Søren Leth-Petersen. Forthcoming. "Examples of Combining Administrative Records and Survey Data in Validation Studies." In *Improving the Measurement of Consumption Expenditure*, Studies in Income and Wealth, edited by Christopher D. Carroll, Thomas Crossley, and John Sabelhaus. Chicago: University of Chicago Press.

Kreinin, Mordecai E. 1961. "Windfall Income and Consumption: Additional Evidence." *American Economic Review* 51:388–90.

Krugman, Paul. 2005. "That Hissing Sound." *New York Times*. August 8.

Laibson, David. 1997. "Golden Eggs and Hyperbolic Discounting." *Quarterly Journal of Economics* CXII (2): 443–77.

Laibson, David, Andrea Repetto, and Jeremy Tobacman. 2007. "Estimating Discount Functions with Consumption Choices over the Lifecycle." NBER Working Paper no. 13314, Cambridge, MA.

Meyer, Bruce D., and James X. Sullivan. 2009. "Five Decades of Consumption and Income Poverty." Working Paper, Harris School of Public Policy Studies, University of Chicago.

National Research Council. 2012. *Measuring What We Spend: Toward a New Consumer Expenditure Survey*, edited by Don A. Dillman and Carol C. House. Panel on Redesigning the BLS Consumer Expenditure Surveys; Committee on National Statistics; Division of Behavioral and Social Sciences and Education. Washington, DC: National Academies Press.

Parker, Jonathan, and Christian Broda. 2011. "The Economic Stimulus Payments of 2008 and the Aggregate Demand for Consumption." Unpublished manuscript, Northwestern University.

Parker, Jonathan A., Nicholas S. Souleles, and Christopher D. Carroll. Forthcoming. "The Benefits of Panel Data in Consumer Expenditure Surveys." In *Improving the Measurement of Consumption Expenditure*, Studies in Income and Wealth, edited by Christopher D. Carroll, Thomas Crossley, and John Sabelhaus. Chicago: University of Chicago Press.

Parker, Jonathan A., Nicholas S Souleles, David S. Johnson, and Robert McClelland. 2011. "Consumer Spending and the Economic Stimulus Payments of 2008." NBER Working Paper no. 16684, Cambridge, MA.

Parker, Jonathan A., and Annette Vissing-Jorgensen. 2009. "Who Bears Aggregate Fluctuations and How?" NBER Working Paper no. 14665, Cambridge, MA.

Shiller, Robert. 2005. "Yale Professor Predicts Housing 'Bubble' Will Burst." Interview by Madeleine Brand, *Day by Day*, National Public Radio, June 3. http://www.npr.org/templates/story/story.php?storyId=4679264.

Tobin, James. 1980. *Asset Accumulation and Economic Activity: Reflections on Contemporary Macroeconomic Theory*. Oxford: Basil Blackwell.

II

Reconciling Administrative and Survey Data on the Distribution of Income and Wealth

6

Integration of Micro- and Macrodata on Consumer Income and Expenditures

Clinton P. McCully

6.1 Introduction

There has been increasing recognition in recent years of the importance of the distribution of income as an indicator of economic well-being, amid concerns about the widening of income disparities. Macroestimates of household income and expenditures in the National Income and Product Accounts (NIPAs) produced by the Bureau of Economic Analysis (BEA) measure aggregates and per capita averages, but these estimates are limited as measures of social and economic progress because they contain no information on the distribution of income or other household income breakdowns such as by age and by household type.[1] Microestimates of household money income and expenditures from the Census Bureau's Current Population Survey Annual Social and Economic Supplement (CPS-ASEC) and from the Bureau of Labor Statistics' Consumer Expenditure Survey (CE) provide distributional information, including measures of median household income, but income and expenditures are more narrowly defined than in the NIPAs and there are issues with underreporting, nonreporting, and the underrepresentation of high-income households.[2]

Clinton P. McCully recently retired as chief of the research group in the National Income and Wealth Division at the Bureau of Economic Analysis.

National income and product accounts (NIPA) data cited in this chapter reflect published estimates prior to the revised estimates for 2009 and 2010 released in July 2012. Kevin J. Furlong of BEA's NIWD research group made a major contribution to the development of the integrated estimates. For acknowledgments, sources of research support, and disclosure of the author's material financial relationships, if any, please see http://www.nber.org/chapters/c12831.ack.

1. Data from the NIPAs are available here: http://www.bea.gov/iTable/iTable.cfm?ReqID=9&step=1#reqid=9&step=1&isuri=1.

2. Detailed data tables from the Census Bureau's Current Population Survey Annual Social and Economic Supplement (CPS-ASEC) are available here: http://www.census.gov/hhes/www

The macro- and microdata have provided conflicting signals in recent years about changes in the economic status of US households. Macroestimates of real per capita disposable personal income (DPI) showed moderate increases from 2000 to 2008, followed by a sharp decline in 2009 and a small increase in 2010 that left it at about the 2006 level, as shown in figure 6.1. Real median household money income derived from CPS-ASEC was little changed between 2000 and 2007, and has since steadily declined. Real per capita DPI was 12 percent higher in 2010 compared to 2000, while real median income declined by 7 percent, for a cumulative difference of 19 percentage points over the ten-year period.

Consumer expenditure data have shown similar differences between the BEA estimates and those based on the CE. These differences have been the source of much discussion and debate. The faster growth in the national accounts measures, which rely mainly on business surveys, tax information, and administrative data, have been attributed to a number of factors, including:

- inclusion of in-kind supplements to wages and salaries in the NIPA estimates, which have grown faster than wage and salary income;
- inclusion of in-kind government social benefits such as Medicare and Medicaid in the NIPA estimates, which have grown very rapidly in recent years;
- better coverage of high income individuals, whose incomes have been growing faster than other groups, in national accounts than in household surveys; and
- overstatement by NIPA data of the condition of most households through the use of average rather than median or quintile data.

Integration of the micro- and macroestimates would reconcile these differences and provide valuable information that none of the sources by themselves can provide. Integrated estimates would combine the more accurate and more broadly defined NIPA estimates of household income and expenditures with the distributional information contained in the microestimates.[3]

/income/data/incpovhlth/2011/dtables.html. For user documentation on the Bureau of Labor Statistics' Consumer Expenditure Survey (CE) see http://www.bls.gov/cex/2010/csxintvw .pdf.

3. The BEA and its predecessor agency, the Office of Business Economics, periodically published estimates of the size distribution of national accounts personal income in the United States from the 1950s to the 1970s using CPS, Internal Revenue Service, and Federal Reserve Board data, and such estimates were published as part of the National Income and Product Accounts from 1959 to 1964. More recently, the Expert Group on Disparities in National Accounts, sponsored by the Organisation for Economic Co-operation and Development (OECD) and Eurostat, has been working to develop internationally comparable estimates of the breakdown of household income and consumption on a national accounts basis, and Fixler and Johnson (2012) have done work to account for the distribution of income in the US national accounts.

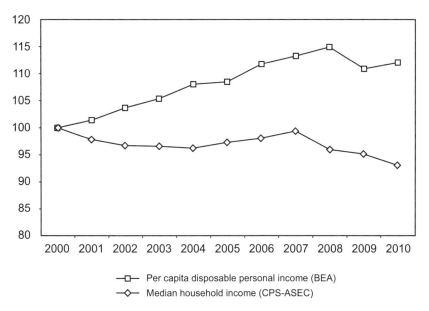

Fig. 6.1   **Micro- and macroincome (Real income: 2000 = 100)**

Controlling the detailed component estimates in the microsources to the macrovalues would account for the varying degrees of underreporting in the microcomponents. Inclusion of third-party payments and imputations from the macroestimates would account for the 30 percent of personal consumption expenditures not captured in the out-of-pocket expenditures from the CE (Passero, Garner, and McCully 2011). Third-party payments are particularly important for health care, where the majority of care is financed by employer-sponsored health insurance and by government programs such as Medicare and Medicaid rather than by out-of-pocket expenditures captured in the CE. The integration of the micro- and macroestimates is consistent with recommendations made in the "Report by the Commission on the Measurement of Economic Performance and Social Progress," which stated that "distributional measures should be compatible in scope with average measures from the national accounts" (Stiglitz, Sen, and Fitoussi 2009, I.43).

   This chapter compares the micro- and macromeasures of income and expenditures and describes the process of deriving the integrated estimates, which are developed for the years 2006 through 2010. The results of the integration are discussed, and the distribution of household income is compared to results from the CPS-ASEC and the Internal Revenue Service (IRS). The chapter concludes with a discussion of the issues raised by the integration and the direction of future research.

6.2   Micro- and Macromeasures of Income and Consumption

6.2.1   Microsources

The CPS-ASEC collects data on income, while the CE collects data on both income and expenditures. The CPS-ASEC and the CE surveys are nationwide household surveys designed to represent the US civilian non-institutional population. There are differences between the surveys in the unit of measure and significant differences in frequency and design.[4] The CPS-ASEC is an interview survey conducted annually to collect data on household money income and health insurance coverage for the previous calendar year.

The CE consists of an Interview Survey and of a Diary Survey. The Interview Survey collects data on income and on expenditures that are large, such as for property and motor vehicles, or that occur on a fairly regular basis, such as utility or insurance payments. The Diary Survey collects data on small, frequently purchased items that are difficult to recall. Though there are items unique to the Interview Survey and to the Diary Survey, there is considerable overlap in the coverage of the two surveys. The published CE estimates combine data from the Interview and Diary Surveys. When data are covered in both surveys, the more reliable of the two based on statistical criteria are used.[5]

6.2.2   Macrosources

The sources used for the NIPA estimates of personal income and outlays are many and diverse, but can be characterized in general as being based on reports by businesses and governments. Business data are collected administratively, such as from tax records for business income, from trade sources such as motor vehicle industry publications for motor vehicle sales, in sample surveys such as the Census Bureau surveys of retail trade and service industries, and in economic censuses conducted at five-year intervals by the Census Bureau. Estimates of government social benefits included in personal income come from federal agencies and from state and local governments as reported in annual Census Bureau surveys of government finances. Estimates of Social Security and Medicare taxes are based on data from the Social Security Administration, estimates of federal income taxes are based on data from the IRS, and estimates of state and local taxes are

---

4. The unit of measure in the CE is the consumer unit, and households in some instances have more than one consumer unit based on the criteria of financial independence. The differences are small, however (about 2 percent), and BLS uses the term households in its *Handbook of Methods* chapter about the CE, so households are used in this chapter in describing the CE.

5. Details on the conduct of the CPS-ASEC and CE surveys are in a longer version of this chapter available here: http://www.bea.gov/papers/pdf/integration_of_micro_and_macro _data_on_consumer_expenditures.pdf.

based on annual Census Bureau surveys of government finance. Use of data from CPS-ASEC and CE is very limited: data on self-employment income from the CPS are used to develop adjustments for tax return nonfilers in the NIPA estimates of proprietors income and in personal consumption expenditures (PCE), CE data for categories such as motor vehicle leasing are used, constituting less than one-half of one percent of the total PCE value.

The NIPA estimates are generally considered more accurate than aggregate values derived from household surveys (Attanasio, Battistin, and Leicester 2006; Bee, Meyer, and Sullivan 2011; Bosworth 2010; Roemer 2000; Ruser, Pilot, and Nelson 2004). Reports from businesses collected in economic censuses, sample surveys, and administratively are more reliable than household surveys, which for the CE Interview Survey and CPS-ASEC have issues with recalling income and expenditures and are subject to deliberate underreporting of certain items. For the CE Diary Survey, there are issues of what is sometimes called "diary fatigue," which refers to the drop-off in recording of expenditures over time, evidenced by a persistent pattern of lower-reported expenditures for the second of the one-week surveys compared to the first (BLS 1983; Stephens 2003). Businesses are required to account for all of their receipts and expenditures on an ongoing basis. The NIPA estimates are not considered "the truth" because the data on which they are based are subject to nonsampling error such as underreporting of income and, in many instances, to sampling error as well. However, NIPA expenditure estimates are periodically benchmarked to estimates based on the economic censuses, which are not subject to sampling error, and estimates are adjusted for misreporting and undercoverage, particularly for business income. Microestimates of income and expenditures are generally lower than macroestimates, often by significant amounts.

For the overall economy, NIPA estimates of gross domestic product (GDP) are conceptually identical to gross domestic income (GDI), which measures the incomes generated and the costs incurred in generating GDP. The GDP and GDI measures are derived independently, and as such, provide a means of verifying the validity of each measure. Differences between the two, known as the statistical discrepancy, have ranged from minus two percent to plus two percent of GDP over time.

6.2.3 Coverage

The civilian noninstitutional population is covered in both the CPS-ASEC and CE. Personal income and outlays (PI&O) estimates in the NIPAs cover the income and expenditures of those defined as US residents in the national accounts, which includes nonprofit institutions serving households (NPISHs), the institutionalized population, federal civilian and military personnel stationed abroad, and persons whose usual place of residence is the United States, but who are private employees working abroad for a period of less than one year.[6] Excluded from the NIPA definition of residents are foreign nationals who work and reside in the United States for part of the year, foreign nationals employed by international organizations, and foreign nationals studying in the United States. Also, NIPA estimates include the income and expenditures of those who died during the preceding year, which are not captured in CPS-ASEC, and is an annual survey collecting income data from households for the previous calendar year. Excluding NPISHs income and outlays from the PI&O and accounting for transfers between households and NPISHs gives a measure of household income and outlays (HI&O), which will be referenced during the remainder of the chapter and used for the integration of the micro- and macroestimates.[7]

6.3   Integration Steps

The first step in the integration process is the merging of the microdata sets for income from CPS-ASEC and for income and expenditures from the CE. Following the merging of the data sets, the integration steps for both income and expenditures are as follows:

- Adjusting the scope of the macroestimates to match the civilian non-institutional population covered in the microsources.
- Matching the macro- and microcomponent estimates.
- Determining indicators for noncomparable macrocomponents.
- Calculating macro-to-micro ratios for each matched component.
- Scaling household-level matched components in the microdata by the macro-to-micro ratios.
- Using indicators to distribute unmatched macrovalues to households.
- Classifying households by income group, main source of income, and household type using the scaled and distributed household-level estimates.

6.3.1   Merging of Microdata Sets

A data set combining CPS-ASEC and CE household-level data was constructed using a procedure that linked household units in CPS-ASEC to units in the CE through the use of "common" variables that exist in both surveys. This process is known as "statistical matching" and it was necessary because neither the CPS-ASEC source nor CE contained all the information necessary for the analysis, either for income or for consumption. The synthetic data created through this procedure contained all income components necessary to construct household-level income and outlays.

In total, twenty common variables were identified in the CPS and the CE.

6. The inclusion of NPISHs in PI&O is treated as a scope difference rather than as a definitional difference.
7. Separate estimates of household and NPISHs income and outlays are published annually in NIPA, table 2.9.

These variables were used in the unconstrained statistical matching procedure to link the two surveys.

Common income variables:

- wages and salaries
- nonfarm income
- farm income
- Social Security and railroad retirement benefits
- Supplemental Security Income
- unemployment compensation
- workers' compensation
- welfare
- pensions
- alimony received
- child support received
- Food Stamps

Common demographic variables:

- household size
- number of children
- number of persons older than sixty-five
- marital status of reference person
- education level of reference person
- location in a metropolitan statistical area with a population greater than one million
- race of reference person
- housing tenure (rent, own, no cash rent)

A distance function based on the differences in the common variables in the two data sets was used to match records from the CPS-ASEC and CE. The matching was "unconstrained" in that a given record could be used multiple times.[8]

6.4   Income Integration

6.4.1   Definitions

Money income from CPS-ASEC is essentially a measure of cash income from the following sources:

- wages and salaries
- self-employment income
- rental income from leasing of residential properties

8. Further details on the statistical matching procedure is available in a longer version of this chapter available here: http://www.bea.gov/papers/pdf/integration_of_micro_and_macro _data_on_consumer_expenditures.pdf.

- royalties
- interest and dividends
- government transfers
- transfers from households and other private sources
- pensions[9]

Household income in the NIPAs includes, with the exception of transfers from households and pension income, these forms of cash income, but is a broader measure of income in that it includes the following imputations and third-party payments:

- employer contributions to employee pension and insurance funds
- in-kind government social benefits
- imputed interest received by depositors and insurance policyholders
- interest and dividends received by entities holding household assets
- the imputed rental income of owner-occupied housing
- current transfers from business
- in-kind income provided to employees
- farm products consumed on farms
- margins on owner-built housing

In addition, NIPA household income subtracts employee and self-employed contributions for social insurance, which is not done in the case of money income.[10]

Employer contributions to employee pension and insurance funds include contributions to private and publicly administered retirement plans and to group health and life insurance, workers' compensation, and supplemental unemployment (NIPA, table 6.11D). In-kind government social benefits include Medicare, Medicaid, other state and local government medical care, Supplemental Nutrition Assistance Program (SNAP) benefits, Women, Infants, and Children (WIC) food benefits, energy assistance, and part of education benefits.[11] Though not included in money income, employer contributions for health insurance and in-kind government social benefits for Medicare, Medicaid, food stamps, and energy assistance are measured in CPS-ASEC for use in alternate income estimates.

Imputed interest is received from banks and other depository institutions, from regulated investment companies, from life insurance carriers, and

9. See DeNavas-Walt, Proctor, and Smith (2011) for a listing of components of money income and Census Bureau (1998, appendix A) for definitions of income components in a longer version of this chapter available: http://www.bea.gov/papers/pdf/integration_of_micro_and_macro_data_on_consumer_expenditures.pdf.

10. Employer contributions for social insurance (primarily Social Security and Medicare) are included in supplements to wages and salaries in compensation of employees, but are subtracted in deriving household income. (See NIPA, table 2.1 and table 3.6.)

11. SNAP was formerly known as food stamps, which is the term still used in the CPS-ASEC estimates.

from property-casualty insurance companies. Imputed interest received by depositors at commercial banks and other depository institutions is income attributed to depositors to pay for services furnished without payment, such as for bookkeeping or check clearing. It is equal for commercial banks to the difference between what is known as a "reference rate"—essentially a riskless interest rate such as on US government securities—and the interest rate paid on deposits applied to the value of deposits held by households. For other depository institutions, the difference between the interest rate received and that paid on deposits is used. Imputed interest received by regulated investment company (RIC) shareholders is income attributed to shareholders to pay for RIC services, as measured by their expenses, which are primarily for portfolio management. Imputed interest received by life insurance policyholders measures the life insurers' income receipts on policy reserves, which are deemed to belong to households. Imputed interest received by property-casualty insurance policyholders is measured by income receipts on what are known as "technical reserves," which are reserves on unearned premiums and unpaid losses, and which are treated as supplements to premiums paid by policyholders.

Interest and dividends in the NIPAs include the property income of pension plans. Dividends also include S corporation income reported on Schedule E of the federal individual income tax return (BEA 2011b).[12] The S corporation income equals passive and nonpassive gains less passive and nonpassive losses and certain expenses. Since this income is not dividends for tax-reporting purposes, it is likely that it is not reported as such in CPS-ASEC, though it may be reported as part of self-employment income. Similarly, interest income received by nonfinancial sole proprietorships and partnerships is not included in interest reported on federal income tax returns, and may be reported as part of self-employment income in CPS-ASEC. Interest and dividends in the NIPAs also include property income of individual retirement arrangements (IRAs) and Keogh and other self-employed plans. This property income is not reported on individual income tax returns and is therefore unlikely to be included in interest and dividends reported in CPS-ASEC.

To derive disposable household income, household current taxes are subtracted from household income. The great majority of these taxes are federal and state income taxes, and other taxes include motor vehicle licenses, personal property taxes, and hunting, fishing, and other personal licenses. They do not include estate and gift taxes, which are classified in the NIPAs as capital transfers. Federal and state income taxes are estimated in CPS-ASEC; though they are not a subtraction in deriving money income,

---

12. S corporations allow income and expenses to pass through to the shareholders, who are responsible for any resulting tax liability (Luttrell 2006).

they are subtractions in alternate income definitions used by CPS-ASEC in determining the effects of benefits and taxes on income and poverty.

6.4.2   Scope Adjustments

Scope adjustments to household income are shown on table 6.1. The *institutionalized adjustment* removes the income of those living in institutionalized group quarters, including correctional institutions, nursing homes, mental hospitals, hospitals or wards for the chronically ill and for those who have no usual home elsewhere, and institutions for the mentally retarded, physically handicapped, and drug/alcohol abusers. Cash income of the institutionalized population is estimated using income of the institutionalized and total US income from the 2000 Census of Population and Housing 5 Percent Microdata Sample.[13] Income shares for the following categories were calculated from the census data:

- wages and salaries
- self-employment
- interest, dividends, rental income, royalty income, income from estates and trusts
- Social Security and railroad retirement
- Supplemental Security Income
- public assistance
- other income, including veterans benefits, unemployment compensation, child support, and alimony[14]

The income shares from the 2000 census were applied to the appropriate household income categories. The wages and salaries share was applied to the components of compensation of employees, including employer contributions for employee pension and insurance funds and for government social insurance (the latter not included in household income). The self-employment income share was applied to farm and nonfarm proprietors' income. Interest, dividends, and related income shares were applied to household interest income and dividend income. Social Security, railroad retirement, and Supplemental Security Income shares were applied to the respective government social benefits categories. The public assistance share was applied to the family assistance and general assistance categories of government social benefits. The other income share was applied to workers' compensation, unemployment compensation, other government social benefits except Medicare and Medicaid, and current transfer receipts from

13. For technical documentation on the 2000 Census of Population and Housing, see http://www.census.gov/prod/cen2000/doc/pums.pdf and http://www.census.gov/prod/cen2000/doc/sf1.pdf.
14. Retirement income for the institutionalized and for the total population are also available from the 2000 census, but are not used in the scope adjustments because NIPA household income does not include non–Social Security retirement income.

Table 6.1   **Scope adjustments to household income and outlays by type and component (billions of dollars)**

Label	Published[a]	Scope adjustments	Scope-adjusted
		2010	
Household income	12,400.1	443.0	11,957.1
Compensation of employees, received	7,971.4	80.7	7,890.6
Proprietors' income with inventory valuation and capital consumption adjustments	1,036.4	9.2	1,027.2
Rental income of households with capital consumption adjustment	343.6	7.4	336.2
Household income receipts on assets	1,678.4	37.1	1,641.3
Household current transfer receipts	2,357.2	318.5	2,038.7
Government social benefits	2,221.1	316.8	1,904.3
Other household current transfer receipts	136.1	1.7	134.5
Less: Contributions for government social insurance, domestic	986.8	9.8	977.0
Less: Household current taxes	1,193.9	41.6	1,152.2
Equals: Disposable household income	11,206.3	401.4	10,804.9
Less: Household outlays	10,547.9	345.3	10,202.5
Household consumption expenditures	9,965.3	326.1	9,639.2
Household interest payments	173.4	6.2	167.2
Household transfer payments	409.2	13.0	396.2
Equals: Household saving	658.4	56.1	602.3
Household saving as a percentage of household disposable income	5.9%	—	5.6%
Scope adjustments to household income by type	—	443.0	—
Institutionalized	—	163.4	—
Medicare & Medicaid	—	78.1	—
Other	—	85.3	—
Decedents	—	248.6	—
Medicare & Medicaid	—	195.5	—
Other	—	53.1	—
US residents not physically present in United States	—	28.2	—
Federal civilian and military personnel stationed abroad	—	27.1	—
Wages of private US residents abroad	—	1.1	—
Domestic military living on post	—	15.5	—
Foreign students and foreign temporary workers in United States	—	–12.7	—
Addendum:			
Medicare and Medicaid	—	273.6	—

[a]Differs from values published in NIPA table 2.9 by amount of alimony and child support received (income) and paid (outlays).

business and from nonprofit institutions. Income shares ranged from less than 1 percent for wages and salaries and self-employment income to 9.4 percent for public assistance. Adjustments for institutionalized cash income were $85.3 billion in 2010, 0.7 percent of household income. Medicare and Medicaid benefits for nursing home residents, which are not included in the

2000 census income, totaled $78.1 billion in 2010, 0.6 percent of household income, so that the total institutional adjustment to household income was $163.4 billion, 1.3 percent of household income. Personal current taxes, disposable household income, and household outlays were also reduced by 1.3 percent.

The *decedent adjustment* removes the income of those who died during the reference year. Cash income of decedents was estimated using mortality rates by age, sex, and race, applied using Monte Carlo simulations to CPS databases for 2006 to 2009 matched on sex and race combinations to estimate decedents and their income. The weighted sum of the income variables was divided by two to represent decedent income for the year. Adjustments for decedent cash income were $53.1 billion in 2010, 0.4 percent of household income.

Estimates of in-kind social benefits received by decedents from the Medicare and Medicaid programs are based on the results of studies that have estimated the share of Medicare and Medicaid expenditures for persons in the last year of life (Hoover et al. 2002; Riley and Lubitz 2010). The first study, based on data from the 1992 to 1996 Medicare Beneficiary Study, showed 25 percent of Medicare expenditures and 26 percent of Medicaid expenditures were for those in the last year of life. The more recent study also shows that expenditures for those in the last year of life account for 25 percent of all Medicare spending. Percentages were adjusted to 24 percent for Medicare and 18 percent for Medicaid to account for nursing home care captured in the institutionalized adjustment. These benefits totaled $195.5 billion in 2010, 1.6 percent of household income, so that the total decedent adjustment was $248.6 billion, 2.0 percent of household income. Personal current taxes, disposable household income, and household outlays were also reduced 2.0 percent.

The following income items of US government civilian and military personnel stationed abroad were removed:

- wage and salary disbursements
- supplements to wages and salaries
- dividends, interest, and rent on federal retirement plans
- less: contributions for government social insurance

These adjustments are the same as those made in BEA's state personal income estimates, and are calculated as the difference between NIPA estimates for those income components and the state personal income components (BEA 2011a).[15] Earnings of private US residents employed abroad for a period of less than one year, from unpublished data in BEA's international transactions accounts, are also excluded. The 2010 adjustments for federal

---

15. The values used in this chapter are slightly different from those published in October 2011, based on more up-to-date data.

workers were $27.1 billion in 2010, and for private workers $1.1 billion. Personal taxes are estimated as the difference between state personal current taxes and NIPA personal current taxes.

The *adjustment for domestic military personnel living on post* removes the following income components: wages and salaries, employer contributions for government social insurance, employer contributions for military retirement, employer contributions for group life insurance, and interest income on military retirement. The wages and salaries of domestic military personnel living on post are estimated as the product of the number of personnel and an average rate of pay. Estimates of the number of military personnel living on post are based on counts of these personnel from the 2000 and 2010 Decennial Censuses of Population and Housing, calculated as a percentage of total active duty military personnel, with the percentage interpolated between 2000 and 2010 and applied to the total number of military personnel in each year. Data on total active duty military personnel are from the Department of Defense's Personnel and Military Casualty Statistics.[16] Average pay was estimated using pay scale data from the Department of Defense's Defense Finance and Accounting Service.[17] Average wages and salaries equaled basic monthly pay and basic allowance for subsistence for military pay grade E-4, the pay grade for enlisted personnel believed to reflect the average pay grade of personnel living on post.

Employer contributions for social insurance for domestic military personnel living on post were estimated using the Social Security/Medicare tax rate. Employer contributions for military retirement were estimated using military retirement contributions as a percentage of total military wages and salaries and applying this percentage to estimated wages and salaries for military living on post. Contributions for government social insurance, a subtraction in deriving household income, were calculated as twice the employer contributions for government social insurance. Personal current taxes, a subtraction in deriving disposable household income, were estimated by applying the overall tax rate on household income to basic pay.

Adjustments for foreign workers studying at colleges and universities in the United States, foreign professionals temporarily residing in the United States, and foreign temporary agricultural and nonagricultural workers in the United States add their compensation, and are based on unpublished detail from the US international transactions accounts. Income of these groups was $12.7 billion in 2010 (shown on table 6.1 as a negative $12.7 billion scope adjustment).

The scope adjustments reduced 2010 household income by 3.6 percent, equal to $443.0 billion. The reduction to disposable household income was

16. Data retrieved from https://www.dmdc.osd.mil/appj/dwp/getLinks.do?category=dod&subCat=reports&tab=3&clOn=reps.
17. Data retrieved from http://www.dfas.mil/militarymembers/payentitlements/militarypaytables.html.43.

also 3.6 percent, equal to $401.4 billion. Adjustments to Medicare and Medicaid for the institutionalized and decedents were $273.6 billion, 62 percent of the total household income adjustment. Other institutionalized and decedent adjustments were $138.4 billion, while net residency adjustments and the adjustment for domestic military living on post were each $15.5 billion.

6.4.3   Matches and Indicators

The integration of scope-adjusted macroincome estimates with microestimates required the identification of microseries that matched the macroseries as defined in the NIPAs as closely as possible. For NIPA series, which could not be matched to microvariables, indicators were developed from the microdata to distribute the macrovalues. Most cash income included in household income was matched to CPS-ASEC series. Series were treated as matches if they referred to the same type of income, even if there were significant differences in coverage and measurement. An example of an indicator is the use of participants in a government program to distribute the government social benefits for that program. "Coverage ratios" were calculated as the microvalues divided by the scope-adjusted macrovalues. Table 6.2 shows scope-adjusted NIPA values for major household income series, with microvalues and coverage ratios for matched categories and identification of categories using indicators; in most instances, matching was done at a more detailed level than shown in the table.

For *compensation of employees*, wages and salaries matched definitionally and had very high coverage ratios: 2010 CPS wages and salaries were 97 percent of the NIPA value. For supplements to wages and salaries, data on payroll taxes and on employer contributions for health insurance collected in CPS-ASEC for use in alternative measures of income were matched to the two largest components. The health insurance contributions are a direct match, while the payroll taxes paid by employees for Social Security and Medicare (FICA) were assumed to be the same as employer payments and matched to employer contributions for old age, survivors, disability, and hospital insurance.[18] For military medical insurance, which provides coverage to dependents of active duty military personnel at nonmilitary facilities, the number of family households with one or more members in the armed forces and participating in military health care was used as the indicator. For supplemental unemployment benefits, CPS-ASEC benefits received were used as the indicator. Wages and salaries were used as indicators for the remaining components. For employer contributions to pension plans, wages and salaries of those participating in employer-sponsored pension plans were used. Private wages and salaries were used as the indicator for employer contributions to private workers' compensation, and total wages and salaries

18. The employer and employee tax rates were the same through 2010, the latest year covered in this study.

Table 6.2   Household income and micromatches and indicators, 2010

NIPA series	NIPA scope-adjusted values	Micromatches		
		Source	Value	Ratio to adjusted NIPA value
Household income	11,957.1	—	—	—
Compensation of employees, received	7,890.6	—	—	—
Wage and salary disbursements	6,353.7	CPS	6,137.4	0.966
Supplements to wages and salaries	1,537.0	—	—	—
Employer contributions for employee pension and insurance funds	1,068.7	—	—	—
Group health insurance	553.4	CPS	402.0	0.726
Other	515.3	CPS	I	—
Employer contributions for government social insurance	468.2	—	—	—
Old-age, survivors, disability, and hospital insurance	394.5	CPS	458.9	1.163
Other	73.8	CPS	I	—
Proprietors' income	1,027.2	CPS	363.2	0.354
Rental income of households with capital consumption adjustment	336.2	—	—	—
Tenant-occupied housing and royalties	111.1	CPS	68.3	0.614
Imputed rental income for owner-occupied housing	225.1	CEI	310.7	1.380
Household income receipts on assets	1,641.3	—	—	—
Household interest income	950.4	—	—	—
Monetary interest	503.9	—	—	—
Monetary interest received by pensions plans	172.7	CPS	I	—
Monetary interest received by households	331.2	CPS	159.7	0.482
Imputed interest received by households	446.5	CEI	I	—
Household dividend income	690.8	CPS	96.6	0.140

(continued)

Table 6.2 (continued)

NIPA series	NIPA scope-adjusted values	Micromatches		
		Source	Value	Ratio to adjusted NIPA value
Household current transfer receipts	2,038.7	—	—	—
Government social benefits	1,904.3	—	—	—
Benefits from social insurance funds	1,196.3	—	—	—
Social security and railroad retirement	665.1	CPS	581.0	0.873
Medicare	366.1	CPS	320.8	0.876
Unemployment insurance	136.9	CPS	99.1	0.724
Other benefits from social insurance funds	28.1	CPS	I	—
Other government social benefits	708.0	—	498.9	0.705
Medicaid	299.0	CPS	202.1	0.676
Other	409.0	CPS	296.8	0.726
Other household current transfer receipts	134.5	—	—	—
From business (net)	24.2	CEI	I	—
From nonprofit institutions	78.9	CPS	19.2	0.244
From other households	31.4	CPS	31.4	1.000
Less: Contributions for government social insurance, domestic	977.0	—	—	—
Employer and employee social contributions	873.2	CPS	917.8	1.051
Self-employed contributions	46.6	CPS	I	—
Supplementary medical insurance (Medicare)	57.2	CEI	50.2	0.878
Less: Household current taxes	1,152.2	—	1,170.9	1.016
Federal and state and local income taxes	1,122.7	CPS	1,144.9	1.020
Licenses and personal property taxes	29.5	CEI CED	26.0	0.878
Equals: Disposable household income	10,804.9	—	—	—
Addendum: Matched household income items	9,590.8	—	7,408.3	0.772

Notes: CPS-ASEC and CE series may be combinations of variables. CPS = Current Population Survey Annual Social and Economic Supplement, CEI = Consumer Expenditure Interview Survey, CED = Consumer Expenditure Diary Survey, and I = Indicator.

were used as indicators for group life insurance and for government social insurance contributions other than Social Security and Medicare and military medical insurance. These social insurance contributions consist primarily of unemployment insurance and state workers' compensation.

For *proprietors' income*, farm and nonfarm proprietors' income were matched to their respective self-employment counterparts in CPS-ASEC. The measures of income from self-employment differ definitionally and have low coverage ratios: CPS-ASEC self-employment income is 35 percent of the NIPA value in 2010, with a dollar difference of $664.0 billion. The low self-employment ratio is affected by significant adjustments made in the NIPAs. The CPS-ASEC nonfarm self-employment income is expected to be consistent with that reported on individual income tax returns, and for 2009, nonfarm self-employment income in CPS-ASEC was $337.5 billion, 78 percent of nonfarm proprietorship and partnership income of $431.9 billion reported to the IRS.[19] Nonfarm proprietors' income reported in the NIPAs was $902.0 billion in 2009. The NIPA estimates use the IRS data as a starting point, but make substantial adjustments to align the estimates with NIPA definitions, to account for entities not captured in the IRS data, and to account for misreporting (NIPA, table 7.14). The largest NIPA adjustments were $444.1 billion for misreporting and a capital consumption adjustment of $155.2 billion. The capital consumption adjustment changes depreciation from a tax-reported basis to a current replacement cost basis.

Rental income of households is measured in the NIPAs as rental income on tenant-occupied dwellings, royalties, and the imputed rental income of owner-occupied housing. The CPS-ASEC series for rents, royalties, estates or trusts is matched to the sum of tenant-occupied dwellings income and royalties, with a coverage ratio of 61 percent. The match is clearly not exact because of the inclusion of estate and trust income in the CPS-ASEC series, which in the NIPAs are primarily included in income receipts on assets. The NIPA value for the imputed rental income of owner-occupied housing, which has no CPS-ASEC counterpart, was derived by subtracting expenses from the gross rental value of housing, including intermediate expenses, property taxes, net interest, and consumption of fixed capital. A match was constructed using data from the CE Interview Survey, including the rental equivalence of owned homes and expenses for insurance, maintenance and repairs, closing costs, mortgage interest, and property taxes. Homeowners' insurance premiums were used as indicators for insurance net of losses and for net insurance settlements, each a part of intermediate expenses in the NIPA estimates.[20] Maintenance and repair expenditures and closing costs, also included in intermediate expenses, were matched exactly, as were prop-

---

19. Comparisons are made for 2009 because at the time of the published 2010 NIPA estimates discussed in this chapter (prior to the July 2012 revised estimates for 2009 and 2010), 2010 IRS estimates were not yet available.

20. Net insurance settlements measure the difference between actual and expected losses.

erty taxes. Mortgage interest reported in the CE was used as an indicator for net interest and for borrower services included in intermediate expenses. Net interest and borrower services sum to mortgage interest paid; in the NIPAs, part of the nominal mortgage interest paid is deemed to be payments for services provided to borrowers. Consumption of fixed capital, with no CE match, used owners' equivalent rent as an indicator.

For *income receipts on assets*, household interest and dividend income were broken out into monetary interest received by publicly administered government employee retirement plans, monetary interest received by private noninsured pension plans, other monetary interest, imputed interest by type of financial institution, and dividend income. Because household monetary interest and dividend income in the NIPAs are estimated as residuals, and because only interest received by publicly administered government employees retirement plans is reported separately, separately identifying interest and dividends received by entities holding household assets from income received directly by households is difficult. For monetary interest, only interest received by employer-sponsored pension plans (for government and private employees) was estimated separately. Scope-adjusted monetary interest was $503.9 billion in 2010, of which pension plan interest was $172.7 billion; the remaining $331.2 billion in interest includes that received directly by households and by nonfinancial sole proprietorships and partnerships, fiduciaries, IRAs and other tax-deferred savings accounts. The remaining interest income was matched to CPS-ASEC interest, and all of NIPA dividends were matched to CPS-ASEC dividends, though a portion of NIPA dividends was received by pension plans. For publicly administered government employee pension plans and for private pension plans, wages and salaries of government workers and of private workers participating in pension plans were used as indicators.

For imputed interest, indicators were used in all instances. For depository institutions, interest was distributed using the value of savings and checking accounts held by consumer units from the CE. For RICs, interest received by private pension plans used the wages and salaries of private employee pension plan participants from CPS-ASEC, while for other interest received from RICs, the market value of all securities held from the CE Interview Survey was used. For imputed interest received from life insurance carriers, premiums for life, endowment, annuities, and other insurance policies providing death benefits from the CE Interview Survey were used. For property-casualty insurance companies, premiums for vehicle insurance and homeowners' insurance from the CE Interview Survey were used as the indicator.

Government social benefits were separated into cash and in-kind benefits. Almost all of the cash benefits were matched to CPS-ASEC variables, including Social Security, railroad retirement, unemployment insurance, Supplemental Security Income, refundable tax credits, temporary disability insurance, family and general assistance, and veterans' pensions and disability. Medicare and Medicaid, the largest of the in-kind benefits, were matched to the "person market value" of each of these programs in CPS-ASEC, which measures the average government cost per recipient and is akin to the insurance cost of coverage. The SNAP benefits were matched to the CPS-ASEC food stamps value. For other in-kind social benefits, including energy assistance, other state and local medical care, Women, Infants, and Children (WIC) food benefits, and dependent and retiree military medical insurance, benefits were distributed using the number of participants by household. Government social benefits, which are a combination of cash and in-kind benefits, including veterans' education and training benefits, workers' compensation, and educational assistance, were matched to the cash benefits in CPS-ASEC.

Other current transfer receipts include receipts from business and from NPISHs, and alimony and child support payments from other households. Receipts from business, which include payments by insurance to persons and business losses due to fraud and theft, have no counterpart in CPS-ASEC. Insurance reimbursements from the CE for stolen or total loss vehicles were used as an indicator, though the link is weak, in that payments from commercial motor vehicle policies are only a portion of the transfer receipts from business, and reimbursements reported in the CE are probably overwhelmingly from private passenger policies rather than from commercial policies. Current transfer receipts from business were $24.2 billion in 2010, 0.2 percent of total household income. For current transfer receipts from NPISHs, the matched CPS-ASEC series was private educational assistance, though this is only a partial match, since transfers from educational institutions account for only part of receipts from NPISHs. Receipts from NPISHs were $78.9 billion in 2010, 0.7 percent of total household income. For alimony and child support, the CPS-ASEC values were used directly, and equaled $31.4 billion in 2010, 0.3 percent of household income.

For *contributions for government social insurance*, a subtraction in deriving household income, the employer contributions are the same as for compensation of employees. Payroll taxes from CPS-ASEC, used for the employer contributions match, are nearly an exact match for the NIPA employee contributions; FICA contributions accounted for 98 percent of the $405.0 billion in NIPA employee contributions for 2010. The indicator used for self-employed contributions was CPS-ASEC farm and nonfarm self-employment income. For contributions for Medicare supplementary medical insurance, CE values for Medicare payments and for Medicare Prescription Drug premiums were matched to the NIPA values.

For *household current taxes*, CPS-ASEC taxes after credits for federal income taxes and for state and local income taxes were matched to the NIPA values. For motor vehicle licenses, CE values for state and local registration and for drivers licenses were matched to the NIPA values. For other taxes, including hunting, fishing, and other personal licenses, CE fees for participant sports were used as the indicator, though the link is weak, in that sporting licenses are a relatively small part of the overall fees for participant sports.

Overall, coverage ratios for comparable series were high for wages and salaries and other employment-related variables, for rental income, for government social benefits, for supplementary medical insurance (Medicare) contributions, and for taxes. They were much lower for proprietors' income, for household income receipts on assets, and for current transfer receipts from nonprofit institutions.

6.5   Expenditures Integration

6.5.1   Definitions

Household outlays in the NIPAs consist of household consumption expenditures, household interest payments, and household current transfer payments. Household consumption expenditures (HCE) consist of direct household expenditures for goods and services, expenditures financed by government social benefits, imputed expenditures, and expenses of financial institutions holding household assets.

Most direct household expenditures are comparable to CE consumer expenditures. A significant exception is financial services. Securities commissions, portfolio management and investment advice services, penalty fees on bank and credit card accounts, and trust, fiduciary, and custody activity fees are not captured in CE consumer expenditures.[21] Expenditures financed by government, such as for health care, education, and energy assistance, are not captured in the CE, but have their exact counterparts in the government social benefits included in household income. Food expenditures financed by the SNAP (food stamp) program are included in CE food expenditures, though not separately identified. Imputed expenditures that have no counterparts in CE consumer expenditures include the following:

- employer contributions for group health insurance and workers' compensation
- gross rental value of owner-occupied housing[22]
- financial services furnished without payment to depositors and borrowers
- premium supplements for property and casualty insurance
- food products produced and consumed on farms

---

21. Late fees paid on credit cards and other credit sources are reported on the CE Interview Survey, but are not reported separately from finance charges and interest.

22. In NIPA 7.12, the imputed rental value is net of the intermediate expenses and investment in owner-occupied residential structures and the imputation also nets out investment in owner-occupied residential structures.

Financial services furnished without payment to depositors have their counterparts in household imputed interest received by commercial bank, savings institution, and credit union depositors and by shareholders in regulated investment companies. Borrower services are those provided on nonmortgage loans from commercial banks, and are that part of monetary interest paid that are payments for services; household interest payments in household outlays are net of the value of these services. Employer contributions for health insurance, which have their counterpart in household income, are captured in two parts of HCE: benefit payments are included in health expenditures, and premiums net of benefits are included in health insurance. The net cost of private workers' compensation is included in HCE for health insurance, while medical benefit payments are included in HCE for health; cash payments for private workers' compensation are included in CPS-ASEC money income. Premium supplements for property and casualty insurance have their counterpart in imputed interest received by property-casualty insurance policyholders in household income. Farm products produced and consumed on farms measures the gross value of farm own-consumption; the value net of intermediate inputs is included in household income. The values of food and lodging furnished to employees, which are imputed values in HCE, have their counterparts in imputed wages and salaries in household income, and these are captured in the CE as "food as pay" and "rent as pay."

Household interest payments in NIPA household outlays are nonmortgage monetary interest payments net of borrower services. The CE Interview Survey captures monetary interest payments, late fees, and other penalty fees in consumer expenditures. Household current transfer payments consist of payments to government, contributions to nonprofit institutions, and net transfers to the rest of the world. Payments to government consist of contributions, fees, and fines paid to federal, state, and local governments. Contributions are captured in CE consumer expenditures, though contributions to nonprofit institutions and to government (such as public universities) are not separately identified. Net transfers to the rest of the world consist of US households' transfers to foreign residents less foreign transfers to US resident households. The US households' transfers to foreign residents are probably included in "other cash gifts" in CE consumer expenditures, though there is no differentiation between gifts sent to resident households and those sent to nonresident households. Transfers by foreign residents to US households are very small.

6.5.2 Scope Adjustments

Adjustments to overall expenditures were generally made first, followed by allocations of the adjustments to individual expenditure categories. For the *institutional adjustment*, the household outlays' components—consumption expenditures, interest, and current transfer payments—were assumed to be in the same proportions to the adjustments to disposable household income as for the overall values. For the *decedent adjustment*, household outlays were assumed to be equal to DHI. For *US government civilian and military personnel stationed abroad* and for *civilian workers temporarily stationed abroad*, their expenditures were removed from HCE. For *foreign students and workers* in the United States, these expenditures, which are a subtraction in the calculation of total HCE, were added back in. Consumption expenditures and interest payments for *domestic military living on post* were assumed to be in the same proportions to the DHI adjustment as for the overall values.

Allocations of the HCE adjustments to individual categories varied by type of adjustment. For the *institutional adjustment*, the Medicare and Medicaid adjustments were allocated entirely to HCE for nursing homes. The remaining adjustment was allocated to other categories in proportion to their shares of HCE, excluding nursing homes. For the *decedent adjustment*, the Medicare and Medicaid adjustments were allocated to HCE health, medical, and hospitalization insurance, and social services. The remaining adjustment was allocated to other categories in proportion to their shares of HCE, excluding all Medicare and Medicaid expenditures. For *US government and private workers abroad*, no allocation was necessary, because these are separate estimates within HCE. For *domestic military living on post*, categories on which expenditures were unlikely, such as housing and health care, were first excluded and then the expenditures were allocated proportionately to the remaining categories. For *foreign students in the United States* and for *foreign nationals working in the United States*, there is no need to allocate to individual categories, because their expenditures are already included in those categories (in HCE, the total value of their expenditures is removed).

Scope adjustments to household outlays were 3.3 percent for 2010, equal to $345.3 billion, as shown in table 6.1. As with household income, the largest contributors to the scope adjustment were Medicare and Medicaid payments, which significantly affected health, insurance, and social services expenditures. For Medicare and Medicaid, expenditure adjustments exactly match income adjustments.

6.5.3   Matches and Indicators

For household consumption expenditures, near or exact matches from the CE data were made for the great majority of direct household expenditures. For a number of HCE categories, in order to align expenditures with the CE values, adjustments had to be made to account for expenditures by residents while out of the country and to exclude expenditures by nonresidents traveling in the United States. This was done primarily using data from the US travel and tourism satellite accounts.

For the *imputed rental value of owner-occupied housing*, the CE rental equivalence of owned dwellings is an exact match.

For *health care*, CPS-ASEC values for employer contributions for health insurance were used as indicators for health benefits paid by employer-paid health insurance. For health benefits paid by employee and self-paid insurance, the CE values for health insurance premiums paid were used as indicators. For Medicare, Medicaid, and other state and local medical care, the CPS-ASEC values were used as indicators. Out-of-pocket and other expenditures were matched to CE values.

For *motor vehicles and recreational vehicles*, sales were netted from CE values and trade-in values were added to net expenditures to align them with NIPA values.

For *motor vehicle maintenance and repair*, NIPA values were disaggregated into motor vehicle body repair and other motor vehicle maintenance and repair. The CE motor vehicle insurance premiums were used as the indicator for motor vehicle body repair, while CE expenditures for motor vehicle maintenance and repair were matched to other motor vehicle maintenance and repair.

Postsecondary education includes higher education and commercial and vocational schools. The CPS-ASEC values used for government social benefits were matched to the portion of the NIPA expenditures financed by government. The CE values for tuition expenditures were matched to the remaining NIPA expenditures.

Financial services has no CE matches, so indicators from CPS-ASEC or CE were used in all instances. For financial services furnished without payment by depository institutions and by regulated investment companies, the indicators are the values of deposits and of securities holdings from the CE, the same indicators used for imputed interest income in household income. For pension fund expenses, wages and salaries of those participating in employer-sponsored pension plans from CPS-ASEC were used, the same indicator as that used for employer contributions to pension plans in household income. For financial service charges and fees, an indicator consisting of safe deposit box rental, checking account fees, credit card membership fees, and finance charges excluding mortgages and vehicles—which includes late charges—from the CE was used. For securities commissions, an indicator consisting of the sum of the purchase price of securities including brokerage fees and the sale price of securities net of brokerage fees from the CE was used as an indicator. For portfolio management, investment advice, trust, fiduciary, and custody activities, the market value of all securities held was used as an indicator.

For *insurance*, indicators were used in most instances. For life insurance, which is measured by the expenses of insurers and the profits of stock life insurance companies in the NIPAs, premiums for life, endowment, annuities, and other insurance policies providing death benefits from the CE were used as an indicator. Household insurance, which is insurance on household contents and is net of losses, was disaggregated into two parts: net tenants' insurance and net homeowners' insurance on household contents. Premiums for tenants' insurance from the CE were used as the indicator for the former, and premiums for homeowners' insurance were used for the latter; coverage for household contents is generally a portion of homeowners' insurance. Medical care and hospitalization insurance, which is measured as premiums net of benefits, was disaggregated into five parts: employer-paid insurance, employee and self-paid insurance, Medicare, Medicaid, and other state and local medical care. Employer-paid premiums from CPS-ASEC was used as the indicator for employer-paid insurance, and CE health insurance premiums (excluding Medicare supplement premiums) were used as the indicator for employee and self-paid insurance. The person market values of Medicare and of Medicaid from CPS-ASEC were used as indicators for the respective parts of medical and hospitalization insurance, and the indicator for other state and local medical insurance was the number of children by household enrolled in the State Children's Health Insurance Program (SCHIP) from CPS-ASEC. For income loss insurance and for private workers' compensation, wages and private wages, respectively, from CPS-ASEC were used as indicators. For motor vehicle insurance, premiums for auto insurance and auto repair service policies were used as an indicator.

For *social services and religious activities*, indicators were used in most instances. For child care, CE other expenses for day care centers and nursery schools, including tuition, and expenditures for babysitting and child care were used as an indicator. This is considered an indicator because nursery school expenditures are classified with education expenditures in the NIPAs. Social assistance was broken down into Medicare, Medicaid, other state and local medical care, and out-of-pocket and other expenditures. The person market values for Medicare and Medicaid from CPS-ASEC were used as indicators for the respective components, and the number of children by household enrolled in the SCHIP program from CPS-ASEC were used as the indicator of other state and local medical care. The remaining social assistance expenditures and expenditures for social advocacy and civic and social organizations, religious organizations, and foundations and grant making and giving services were distributed evenly to all households because of the lack of indicators. These expenditures equaled $68.1 billion in 2010, 0.7 percent of household consumption expenditures.

For *professional and other services*, wages and salaries from CPS-ASEC were used as an indicator for two series: employment agency services and professional association dues. Expenditures for these categories were less than 0.1 percent of HCE in 2010. Labor organization dues were distributed using labor union members by households.

Nonmortgage interest payments from the CE were the indicators for both monetary interest paid and imputed interest paid, which is a negative value that removes borrower services from monetary interest. For transfers to government, which consists largely of gifts such as those to higher education institutions, the CE indicator is cash contributions to educational institutions. This is a somewhat weak indicator, in that the CE value includes gifts to private educational institutions, and household current transfers includes other items, such as fines. The CE indicator for household transfer payments to the rest of the world is the CE series other cash gifts. The indicator for transfers to NPISHs is the combination of CE cash contributions to religious organizations, charities, educational institutions, and political organizations. CE alimony and child support expenditures are used directly. Coverage ratios for household outlays shown on table 6.3 were gener-

Table 6.3   Household outlays and micromatches and indicators, 2010

		Micromatches		
NIPA series	NIPA scope-adjusted values	Source	Value	Ratio to adjusted NIPA value
Household outlays	10,202.5	—	—	—
Household consumption expenditures	9639.2	—	—	—
Food and beverages purchased for off-premises consumption	756.5	CED	465.9	0.616
Clothing, footwear, and related services	345.5	CEI, CED	174.5	0.505
Housing, utilities, and fuels	1,906.6	CEI	1,952.9	1.024
Furnishings, household equipment, and routine household maintenance	411.1	CEI, CED	238.7	0.581
Health	1,770.3	—	—	—
Health insurance	800.7	CPS, CEI	—	—
Medicare, Medicaid, and other state and local health care	586.3	CPS	—	—
Out-of-pocket and other expenditures	383.3	CEI, CED	163.1	0.426
Transportation	1,000.6	CEI, CED	729.6	0.729
Communication	235.4	CEI, CED	189.2	0.804
Recreation	904.1	CEI, CED	367.0	0.406
Education	247.4	CEI, CPS	134.5	0.544
Food services and accommodations	610.6	CEI, CED	363.5	0.595
Financial services and insurance	776.5	CEI, CPS	—	—
Other goods and services	674.6	—	—	—
Personal care and personal items	277.8	CEI, CED	112.7	0.406
Social services and religious activities	141.2	CEI, CPS	—	—
Professional and other services	162.5	CEI, CPS	46.1	0.284
Tobacco	93.1	CED(I)	43.8	0.471
Household interest payments	167.2	CEI	32.5	0.195
Household transfer payments	396.2	CEI	205.0	0.517
Addendum: Matched household outlays items	7,897.9	—	5,219.0	0.661

Notes: Matches may have been made at a more detailed level than shown in the table. CED = Consumer Expenditure Diary Survey, CEI = Consumer Expenditure Interview Survey, CED(I) = Consumer Expenditure Diary and Interview Survey, CPS = Current Population Survey Annual Social and Economic Supplement.

ally lower than those for household income. For comparable categories, the overall coverage ratio was 66 percent, compared to 77 percent for comparable income categories. The coverage ratio was highest for housing, utilities, and fuels, where the microvalues slightly exceeded the scope-adjusted NIPA values. The coverage ratios for transportation and communication were 80 percent and 73 percent, respectively, while coverage ratios for the remaining categories were significantly lower.

6.6   Household Breakdowns

The household-level integrated income and outlays values were broken down along three dimensions:

- quintiles of disposable income
- household type
- main source of income

Quintiles of income were based on "equivalized disposable income," which adjusts for differences in household size and composition. Equivalized disposable income for each household was calculated for each household by dividing their disposable income by the number of consumption units in the household. Households were then grouped in quintiles based on their equivalized income. The number of consumption units for each household was calculated using the Oxford (sometimes called the OECD) modified scale, in which a weight of 1.0 is given for the household head, a weight of 0.5 for each additional adult household member, and a weight of 0.3 for each child. The weighting reflects how households share resources and take advantage of economies of scale. It has similarities to the three-parameter scale used to produce equivalence-adjusted income in CPS-ASEC. For quintiles, income shares by primary source of income were broken down as follows:

- earned income
- property income
- government social benefits and other transfers

Earned income combines employee compensation and self-employment income and nets out employer, employee, and self-employed contributions for government social insurance. Government social benefits and other transfers equal transfers and other income less contributions for Medicare supplementary medical insurance.

Household types were the following:

- single up to sixty-five
- single older than sixty-five
- single with children under eighteen
- two adults up to sixty-five
- two adults with at least one older than sixty-five

- two adults with children under eighteen
- other household types

The "other" household type includes children eighteen or older living with parents.

The *main sources of income* distinguished were:

- employee compensation
- self-employment income
- property income
- transfers and other income

Property income includes rental income, interest, and dividends. Transfers and other income include government social benefits and transfers from NPISHs, businesses, and other households.

6.7   Results

6.7.1   Income Quintiles

The share of disposable household income accounted for by the lowest quintile increased from 4.9 percent in 2006 to 5.4 percent in 2010, while the share accounted for by the highest quintile decreased from 48.4 percent to 47.1 percent; the shares accounted for by the other quintiles showed little change (table 6.4). For all income groups during this period, there was a significant increase in the share of income accounted for by government social benefits and other transfers, and corresponding decreases in the shares accounted for by earned income and property income. The shift in sources of income was especially pronounced for the three lowest quintiles. In particular, the share of income accounted for by earned income for the lowest quintile fell by 7.7 percentage points from 2006 to 2010, and the share accounted for by government social benefits and other transfers increased by 8.4 percentage points.

For 2010, the share of disposable household income accounted for by earned income increased from 51.8 percent in the lowest quintile to 74.0 percent in the 4th quintile, while the earned income share of the highest quintile was somewhat lower at 69.1 percent. The shares of household income accounted for by transfers and by property income move in opposite directions: the share accounted for by transfers fell progressively through the income quintiles from 45.6 percent for the lowest quintile to 7.0 percent for the highest quintile, while property income shares rose with income, ranging from 2.5 percent for the lowest quintile to 23.9 percent for the highest quintile.

The consumption shares by income quintile show much less dispersion than does income (table 6.5). Mean expenditures per household for the highest quintile were a bit more than twice as high for the top quintile as for the

Table 6.4   **Income quintiles**

	2006	2010	Change
Shares of disposable household income of quintiles			
Lowest	4.9	5.4	0.5
Second	10.1	10.5	0.4
Third	14.8	15.0	0.2
Fourth	21.8	22.0	0.2
Highest	48.4	47.1	(1.3)
Mean disposable household income of quintiles			
Lowest	20,110	24,424	4,314
Second	41,798	47,742	5,944
Third	61,345	68,254	6,910
Fourth	90,253	100,193	9,940
Highest	200,521	214,330	13,810
Overall	82,805	90,989	8,184
Mean disposable household income of quintiles in 2010 dollars			
Lowest	21,808	24,424	2,616
Second	45,328	47,742	2,414
Third	66,525	68,254	1,729
Fourth	97,874	100,193	2,318
Highest	217,454	214,330	(3,124)
Overall	89,798	90,989	1,191
Earned income shares by quintile			
Lowest	59.6	51.8	(7.7)
Second	60.6	53.7	(6.8)
Third	69.5	63.0	(6.4)
Fourth	77.1	74.0	(3.1)
Highest	70.1	69.1	(1.0)
Overall	70.1	66.9	(3.2)
Property income share by quintile			
Lowest	3.2	2.5	(0.7)
Second	7.8	7.4	(0.4)
Third	10.2	9.7	(0.5)
Fourth	12.4	12.1	(0.3)
Highest	24.5	23.9	(0.6)
Overall	17.2	16.5	(0.6)
Government social benefits/other transfers share by quintile			
Lowest	37.2	45.6	8.4
Second	31.7	38.9	7.3
Third	20.3	27.2	6.9
Fourth	10.5	14.0	3.4
Highest	5.4	7.0	1.5
Overall	12.7	16.6	3.8

Table 6.5   Household consumption expenditures by income quintiles

			2010			
	Lowest	Second	Third	Fourth	Highest	Overall
(billions of dollars)						
Total	1,354.8	1,567.7	1,824.4	2,139.8	2,752.5	9,639.2
Food and beverages purchased for off-premises consumption	140.8	146.1	141.9	157.5	170.1	756.5
Clothing, footwear, and related services	61.8	62.4	61.0	64.6	95.6	345.5
Housing, utilities, and fuels	286.4	329.4	376.2	427.1	487.6	1906.6
Furnishings, household equipment, and routine household maintenance	58.3	61.1	70.7	94.1	126.9	411.1
Health	198.4	333.3	391.5	403.4	443.7	1770.3
Transportation	139.2	157.9	189.8	245.0	268.7	1000.6
Communication	39.3	45.3	47.4	52.1	51.3	235.4
Recreation	146.5	128.8	155.2	211.7	261.9	904.1
Education	25.5	19.1	27.7	49.0	126.1	247.4
Food services and accommodations	83.8	87.6	106.8	135.1	197.4	610.6
Financial services and insurance	66.6	83.1	117.0	156.8	353.0	776.5
Other goods and services	108.2	113.7	139.2	143.4	170.1	674.6
Mean expenditures per household						
Total	57,049	66,004	76,822	90,097	115,893	81,173
Food and beverages purchased for off-premises consumption	5,930	6,152	5,977	6,632	7,161	6,371
Clothing, footwear, and related services	2,603	2,628	2,571	2,718	4,027	2,909
Housing, utilities, and fuels	12,060	13,867	15,840	17,982	20,529	16,056
Furnishings, household equipment, and routine household maintenance	2,454	2,571	2,978	3,963	5,343	3,462
Health	8,352	14,034	16,486	16,985	18,682	14,908
Transportation	5,862	6,647	7,993	10,316	11,314	8,427
Communication	1,655	1,909	1,996	2,192	2,161	1,983
Recreation	6,169	5,424	6,534	8,914	11,027	7,614
Education	1,074	803	1,166	2,064	5,309	2,083
Food services and accommodations	3,530	3,687	4,496	5,689	8,310	5,142
Financial services and insurance	2,806	3,497	4,925	6,602	14,865	6,539
Other goods and services	4,555	4,786	5,861	6,040	7,163	5,681

(continued)

Table 6.5   (continued)

			2010			
	Lowest	Second	Third	Fourth	Highest	Overall
Share of consumption by quintile						
Total	14.1	16.3	18.9	22.2	28.6	100.0
Food and beverages purchased for off-premises consumption	18.6	19.3	18.8	20.8	22.5	100.0
Clothing, footwear, and related services	17.9	18.1	17.7	18.7	27.7	100.0
Housing, utilities, and fuels	15.0	17.3	19.7	22.4	25.6	100.0
Furnishings, household equipment, and routine household maintenance	14.2	14.9	17.2	22.9	30.9	100.0
Health	11.2	18.8	22.1	22.8	25.1	100.0
Transportation	13.9	15.8	19.0	24.5	26.9	100.0
Communication	16.7	19.3	20.1	22.1	21.8	100.0
Recreation	16.2	14.2	17.2	23.4	29.0	100.0
Education	10.3	7.7	11.2	19.8	51.0	100.0
Food services and accommodations	13.7	14.3	17.5	22.1	32.3	100.0
Financial services and insurance	8.6	10.7	15.1	20.2	45.5	100.0
Other goods and services	16.0	16.9	20.6	21.3	25.2	100.0
Consumption shares within quintiles						
Total	100.0	100.0	100.0	100.0	100.0	100.0
Food and beverages purchased for off-premises consumption	10.4	9.3	7.8	7.4	6.2	7.8
Clothing, footwear, and related services	4.6	4.0	3.3	3.0	3.5	3.6
Housing, utilities, and fuels	21.1	21.0	20.6	20.0	17.7	19.8
Furnishings, household equipment, and routine household maintenance	4.3	3.9	3.9	4.4	4.6	4.3
Health	14.6	21.3	21.5	18.9	16.1	18.4
Transportation	10.3	10.1	10.4	11.4	9.8	10.4
Communication	2.9	2.9	2.6	2.4	1.9	2.4
Recreation	10.8	8.2	8.5	9.9	9.5	9.4
Education	1.9	1.2	1.5	2.3	4.6	2.6
Food services and accommodations	6.2	5.6	5.9	6.3	7.2	6.3
Financial services and insurance	4.9	5.3	6.4	7.3	12.8	8.1
Other goods and services	8.0	7.3	7.6	6.7	6.2	7.0

lowest quintile, versus a disposable household income ratio of nearly 9 to 1. The largest differences in consumption between the lowest and highest quintiles were for education and for financial services and insurance. Mean expenditures for food and beverages purchased for home use showed only modest differences between the lowest and highest quintiles, while mean expenditures for food services and accommodations were 135 percent higher for the highest quintile compared to the lowest quintile. Mean expenditures for health ranged from $8,352 for the lowest quintile to $18,682 for the highest quintile. Within quintiles, the shares of expenditures accounted for by food, clothing, and housing and utilities decreased in moving from the lowest to the highest quintile, while the share accounted for by financial services and insurance increased steadily.

6.7.2   Household Type

The share of disposable household income accounted for by households with children fell by 3.0 percentage points from 2006 to 2010, from 31.1 percent to 28.1 percent (table 6.6). Their real mean disposable household income fell, while the mean income of households with at least one member over age sixty-five increased significantly. The earned income shares of disposable household income fell and the government social benefits and other transfers shares rose between 2006 and 2010 for all of the household types except for single households over age sixty-five Property income shares of income fell for all household types except two adults with children between 2006 and 2010.

Mean expenditures were highest for households with two adults and at least one older than sixty-five, followed by households with two adults and children (table 6.7). The consumption shares accounted for by health expenditures were highest for households with at least one members older than sixty-five. These household types also had the highest shares of consumption accounted for by housing, utilities, and fuels and by financial services and insurance.

6.7.3   Main Source of Income

The share of income accounted for by households in which government social benefits and other transfers were the main source of income increased by 3.3 percentage points between 2006 and 2010, to 12.8 percent, while the income shares accounted for by households whose main source of income was earned income and property income each fell (table 6.8). Mean disposable income was highest for households whose main source of income was self-employment income or property income, and lowest for households whose main source of income was transfers and other sources. Real mean disposable household income fell between 2006 and 2010 for households where self-employment income was the largest source, while it rose for each of the other groups, including a 13.0 percent increase for households whose main source of income was property income.

Table 6.6   Disposable household income by household type

	2006	2010	Change
Shares of disposable household income			
Single up to 65	10.3	10.4	0.1
Single older than 65	4.3	4.8	0.5
Single w/children	3.4	3.1	(0.3)
Two adults up to 65	24.0	24.6	0.6
Two adults at least one more than 65	9.3	9.6	0.3
Two adults w/children	27.7	25.0	(2.7)
Other	21.0	22.4	1.4
Mean disposable household income			
Single up to 65	48,774	52,616	3,841
Single older than 65	36,605	46,105	9,500
Single w/children	48,704	51,993	3,288
Two adults up to 65	92,202	101,771	9,570
Two adults at least one more than 65	81,665	99,932	18,267
Two adults w/children	106,256	112,817	6,562
Other	113,297	127,091	13,794
Overall	82,805	90,989	8,184
Mean disposable household income in 2010 dollars			
Single up to 65	52,893	52,616	(277)
Single older than 65	39,696	46,105	6,408
Single w/children	52,817	51,993	(825)
Two adults up to 65	99,988	101,771	1,783
Two adults at least one more than 65	88,561	99,932	11,370
Two adults w/children	115,229	112,817	(2,411)
Other	122,864	127,091	4,227
Overall	89,798	90,989	1,192
Earned income shares of total disposable household income			
Single up to 65	74.5	72.7	(1.8)
Single older than 65	10.9	13.6	2.7
Single w/children	65.0	58.2	(6.8)
Two adults up to 65	76.2	74.8	(1.3)
Two adults at least one more than 65	24.9	22.9	(2.1)
Two adults w/children	83.1	79.4	(3.7)
Other	75.5	71.5	(4.0)
Overall	70.1	66.9	(3.2)
Property income shares of total disposable household income			
Single up to 65	16.0	14.1	(2.0)
Single older than 65	39.5	37.7	(1.8)
Single w/children	7.7	7.0	(0.7)
Two adults up to 65	17.3	14.9	(2.5)
Two adults at least one more than 65	39.7	39.6	(0.1)
Two adults w/children	10.8	11.4	0.5
Other	13.2	12.7	(0.5)
Overall	17.2	16.5	(0.6)
Government social benefits/other transfers shares of total disposable household income			
Single up to 65	9.5	13.2	3.7
Single older than 65	49.6	48.7	(0.9)

Table 6.6   (continued)

	2006	2010	Change
Single w/children	27.3	34.8	7.5
Two adults up to 65	6.5	10.3	3.8
Two adults at least one more than 65	35.4	37.6	2.2
Two adults w/children	6.1	9.2	3.1
Other	11.3	15.7	4.4
Overall	12.7	16.6	3.8

Mean consumption expenditures were highest for households where property income was the main source of income, and lowest for those whose principal source was government social benefits and other transfers (table 6.9). Expenditures for the transfers group exceeded their disposable income, while the opposite was true for all other groups. A disproportionate share of health expenditures were accounted for by the group whose primary source was government social benefits and other transfers, and for this group, health expenditures were the highest share of consumption. For this group, 82.2 percent of their health expenditures were accounted for by in-kind government social benefits, including Medicare, Medicaid, State Children's Health Insurance Program (SCHIP), and other state and local medical care.

6.8   Comparison to Other Measures

The income distribution measures on a NIPA basis may be compared to the CPS-ASEC measures and also to measures produced by the IRS in their Statistics of Income (SOI) data.[23] Differences between the measures reflect both definitional and measurement differences. Among the definitional differences are the following:

- The NIPA estimates are after tax, while money income and IRS-adjusted gross income (AGI) measures are pretax.
- The NIPA estimates include both cash and in-kind social benefits, while money income only includes cash benefits and AGI excludes the great majority of social benefits.
- AGI includes capital gains (and losses), excluded from NIPA income and money income.
- Money income and AGI include pension and annuity income and IRA distributions, which are excluded from the NIPA measure.
- NIPA estimates and money income measure the distribution of household income, while IRS estimates measure the distribution of income by tax-filing unit.

23. Detailed SOI data from the IRS are available here: http://www.irs.gov/uac/Tax-Stats-2.

Table 6.7   Household consumption expenditures by household type

	Single up to 65	Single older than 65	Single w/children	Two adults up to 65	Two adults at least one more than 65	Two adults w/children	Other	Overall
	(Billions of dollars)							
Total	1,330.9	580.2	377.4	2,029.5	1,113.7	2,381.2	1,826.2	9,639.2
Food and beverages purchased for off-premises consumption	78.4	37.4	30.1	156.1	81.8	203.5	169.3	756.5
Clothing, footwear, and related services	35.7	10.6	19.4	70.4	28.2	110.3	70.8	345.5
Housing, utilities, and fuels	271.8	140.8	75.5	387.0	232.6	441.4	357.6	1906.6
Furnishings, household equipment, and routine household maintenance	45.0	23.0	13.8	92.4	54.6	108.5	73.7	411.1
Health	246.5	155.0	76.3	347.0	233.9	398.7	313.1	1770.3
Transportation	122.3	33.7	39.2	234.6	95.1	267.3	208.4	1000.6
Communication	31.6	12.0	11.7	49.8	24.6	55.9	49.8	235.4
Recreation	150.1	38.5	33.6	185.1	98.1	243.1	155.5	904.1
Education	38.4	5.3	7.4	51.9	6.2	67.0	71.1	247.4
Food services and accommodations	97.1	22.8	18.1	148.2	57.3	150.7	116.4	610.6
Financial services and insurance	104.0	64.9	18.0	177.3	133.0	157.9	121.2	776.5
Other goods and services	110.0	36.1	34.2	129.5	68.4	177.0	119.4	674.6
	Mean expenditures per household							
Total	62,061	51,276	58,149	77,557	107,243	99,533	96,013	81,173
Food and beverages purchased for off-premises consumption	3,656	3,302	4,631	5,966	7,874	8,506	8,902	6,371
Clothing, footwear, and related services	1,663	940	2,993	2,691	2,719	4,609	3,724	2,909
Housing, utilities, and fuels	12,673	12,441	11,638	14,789	22,397	18,448	18,798	16,056
Furnishings, household equipment, and routine household maintenance	2,096	2,037	2,130	3,532	5,259	4,536	3,872	3,462
Health	11,494	13,696	11,757	13,259	22,520	16,664	16,459	14,908
Transportation	5,702	2,982	6,037	8,966	9,160	11,171	10,957	8,427
Communication	1,473	1,060	1,805	1,905	2,365	2,339	2,617	1,983
Recreation	7,000	3,405	5,181	7,073	9,445	10,162	8,177	7,614
Education	1,793	470	1,141	1,984	594	2,801	3,738	2,083
Food services and accommodations	4,529	2,018	2,786	5,665	5,516	6,297	6,120	5,142
Financial services and insurance	4,851	5,733	2,780	6,777	12,811	6,602	6,373	6,539
Other goods and services	5,130	3,192	5,270	4,950	6,583	7,400	6,275	5,681

Share of consumption by household type

Total	13.8	6.0	3.9	21.1	11.6	24.7	18.9	100.0
Food and beverages purchased for off-premises consumption	10.4	4.9	4.0	20.6	10.8	26.9	22.4	100.0
Clothing, footwear, and related services	10.3	3.1	5.6	20.4	8.2	31.9	20.5	100.0
Housing, utilities, and fuels	14.3	7.4	4.0	20.3	12.2	23.1	18.8	100.0
Furnishings, household equipment, and routine household maintenance	10.9	5.6	3.4	22.5	13.3	26.4	17.9	100.0
Health	13.9	8.8	4.3	19.6	13.2	22.5	17.7	100.0
Transportation	12.2	3.4	3.9	23.4	9.5	26.7	20.8	100.0
Communication	13.4	5.1	5.0	21.2	10.4	23.8	21.1	100.0
Recreation	16.6	4.3	3.7	20.5	10.8	26.9	17.2	100.0
Education	15.5	2.2	3.0	21.0	2.5	27.1	28.7	100.0
Food services and accommodations	15.9	3.7	3.0	24.3	9.4	24.7	19.1	100.0
Financial services and insurance	13.4	8.4	2.3	22.8	17.1	20.3	15.6	100.0
Other goods and services	16.3	5.4	5.1	19.2	10.1	26.2	17.7	100.0

Consumption shares for each household type

Total	100.0	100.0	100.0	100.0	100.0	100.0	100.0	100.0
Food and beverages purchased for off-premises consumption	5.9	6.4	8.0	7.7	7.3	8.5	9.3	7.8
Clothing, footwear, and related services	2.7	1.8	5.1	3.5	2.5	4.6	3.9	3.6
Housing, utilities, and fuels	20.4	24.3	20.0	19.1	20.9	18.5	19.6	19.8
Furnishings, household equipment, and routine household maintenance	3.4	4.0	3.7	4.6	4.9	4.6	4.0	4.3
Health	18.5	26.7	20.2	17.1	21.0	16.7	17.1	18.4
Transportation	9.2	5.8	10.4	11.6	8.5	11.2	11.4	10.4
Communication	2.4	2.1	3.1	2.5	2.2	2.3	2.7	2.4
Recreation	11.3	6.6	8.9	9.1	8.8	10.2	8.5	9.4
Education	2.9	0.9	2.0	2.6	0.6	2.8	3.9	2.6
Food services and accommodations	7.3	3.9	4.8	7.3	5.1	6.3	6.4	6.3
Financial services and insurance	7.8	11.2	4.8	8.7	11.9	6.6	6.6	8.1
Other goods and services	8.3	6.2	9.1	6.4	6.1	7.4	6.5	7.0

Table 6.8   Household income by main source of income

	2006	2010	Change
Shares of household disposable income	100.0	100.0	—
Compensation of employees	68.3	67.6	(0.6)
Self-employment income	11.1	9.0	(2.1)
Property income	11.1	10.5	(0.6)
Transfers and other	9.6	12.8	3.3
Mean disposable household income (dollars)	82,805	90,989	8,184
Compensation of employees	84,737	96,189	11,452
Self-employment income	182,491	189,606	7,115
Property income	129,638	158,862	29,223
Transfers and other	38,472	46,853	8,381
Mean disposable household income in 2010 dollars	89,798	90,989	1,191
Compensation of employees	91,893	96,189	4,296
Self-employment income	197,902	189,606	(8,296)
Property income	140,586	158,862	18,276
Transfers and other	41,721	46,853	5,133

Income taxes have some redistributive effects, so that after-tax income will be more evenly distributed than pretax income. An indication of this is that the 50 percent of taxpayers with the lowest AGIs, accounting for 12.8 percent of total AGI in 2009, paid only 2.3 percent of the income taxes. Similarly, government social benefits are received disproportionately by those in the lower income ranges. In 2010, the 40 percent of households with the lowest disposable income accounted for 40 percent of all social benefits, even though they accounted for 16 percent of total disposable income. Capital gains, of course, work in the opposite direction. In 2009, the 12 percent of taxpayers with AGIs of $100,000 or more accounted for 94 percent of all capital gains. Capital gains declined precipitously from $779.5 billion in 2006 to $231.5 billion in 2009. The use of the number of taxpayers in the IRS data has the effect of lowering the share of AGI accounted for by those in the lowest income groups, because many of those reporting low incomes are in the same households as higher-income filers. Often, those reporting low incomes are the children of those reporting much higher incomes. Consolidation of these into single households with the higher-earning parents would reduce the number of low-income reporters and raise the share of income reported by the lowest quintile.

Table 6.10 shows the distributions for 2006, 2009, and 2010. For the lowest quintile, the NIPA shares of income are significantly higher than the CPS-ASEC and IRS shares.[24] Compared to CPS-ASEC, much of the difference

24. There are no published IRS estimates of AGI by quintiles. The quintile distribution of AGI was estimated using IRS data on the number of returns and AGI by income-size class. These estimates are based on only those returns with positive AGI. (The IRS does produce AGI distributions by cumulative percentiles.)

Table 6.9   Household consumption expenditures by main source of income

	2010				
	Compensation of employees	Self-employment income	Property income	Transfers and other	Total
(Billions of dollars)					
Total	6,665.4	365.1	690.0	1,918.7	9,639.2
Food and beverages purchased for off-premises consumption	535.6	30.4	40.0	150.5	756.5
Clothing, footwear, and related services	264.0	15.8	16.1	49.5	345.5
Housing, utilities, and fuels	1,337.0	68.9	135.7	365.0	1906.6
Furnishings, household equipment, and routine household maintenance	290.6	16.4	35.1	68.9	411.1
Health	1,061.7	62.3	117.2	529.2	1770.3
Transportation	762.6	35.6	59.6	142.8	1000.6
Communication	173.3	7.7	12.8	41.6	235.4
Recreation	646.4	38.3	55.0	164.4	904.1
Education	168.2	8.6	7.3	63.3	247.4
Food services and accommodations	469.9	21.5	38.2	81.0	610.6
Financial services and insurance	483.9	29.8	135.9	127.0	776.5
Other goods and services	472.2	29.7	37.1	135.6	674.6
Mean expenditures per household					
Total	90,056	68,635	93,095	59,952	81,173
Food and beverages purchased for off-premises consumption	7,237	5,720	5,394	4,702	6,371
Clothing, footwear, and related services	3,567	2,979	2,177	1,546	2,909
Housing, utilities, and fuels	18,064	12,957	18,307	11,404	16,056
Furnishings, household equipment, and routine household maintenance	3,926	3,092	4,742	2,153	3,462
Health	14,345	11,704	15,808	16,535	14,908
Transportation	10,304	6,690	8,044	4,462	8,427
Communication	2,342	1,456	1,724	1,299	1,983
Recreation	8,734	7,191	7,424	5,136	7,614
Education	2,272	1,609	989	1,979	2,083
Food services and accommodations	6,349	4,046	5,155	2,531	5,142
Financial services and insurance	6,537	5,601	18,329	3,967	6,539
Other goods and services	6,380	5,589	5,003	4,237	5,681

(continued)

Table 6.9 (continued)

	2010				
	Compensation of employees	Self-employment income	Property income	Transfers and other	Total
Share of consumption by main source of income					
Total	69.1	3.8	7.2	19.9	100.0
Food and beverages purchased for off-premises consumption	70.8	4.0	5.3	19.9	100.0
Clothing, footwear, and related services	76.4	4.6	4.7	14.3	100.0
Housing, utilities, and fuels	70.1	3.6	7.1	19.1	100.0
Furnishings, household equipment, and routine household maintenance	70.7	4.0	8.6	16.8	100.0
Health	60.0	3.5	6.6	29.9	100.0
Transportation	76.2	3.6	6.0	14.3	100.0
Communication	73.6	3.3	5.4	17.7	100.0
Recreation	71.5	4.2	6.1	18.2	100.0
Education	68.0	3.5	3.0	25.6	100.0
Food services and accommodations	77.0	3.5	6.3	13.3	100.0
Financial services and insurance	62.3	3.8	17.5	16.4	100.0
Other goods and services	70.0	4.4	5.5	20.1	100.0
Consumption shares for each main source of income type					
Total	100.0	100.0	100.0	100.0	100.0
Food and beverages purchased for off-premises consumption	8.0	8.3	5.8	7.8	7.8
Clothing, footwear, and related services	4.0	4.3	2.3	2.6	3.6
Housing, utilities, and fuels	20.1	18.9	19.7	19.0	19.8
Furnishings, household equipment, and routine household maintenance	4.4	4.5	5.1	3.6	4.3
Health	15.9	17.1	17.0	27.6	18.4
Transportation	11.4	9.7	8.6	7.4	10.4
Communication	2.6	2.1	1.9	2.2	2.4
Recreation	9.7	10.5	8.0	8.6	9.4
Education	2.5	2.3	1.1	3.3	2.6
Food services and accommodations	7.0	5.9	5.5	4.2	6.3
Financial services and insurance	7.3	8.2	19.7	6.6	8.1
Other goods and services	7.1	8.1	5.4	7.1	7.0

Table 6.10   Estimates of income distribution (percentage of total)

	National accounts disposable household income (DHI)	CPS-ASEC measures				DHI differences with other measures			
		Money income	Equivalence-adjusted money income	Money income less taxes plus noncash transfers	Internal Revenue Service (IRS) adjusted gross income[a]	Money income	Equivalence-adjusted money income	Money income less taxes plus noncash transfers	IRS adjusted gross income
				2006					
Lowest quintile	4.9	3.4	3.7	—	2.0	1.5	1.2	—	2.9
Second quintile	10.1	8.6	9.4	—	4.7	1.5	0.7	—	5.4
Middle quintile	14.8	14.5	15.0	—	10.8	0.3	-0.2	—	4.0
Fourth quintile	21.8	22.9	22.5	—	19.0	-1.1	-0.7	—	2.8
Highest quintile	48.4	50.5	49.4	—	63.6	-2.1	-1.0	—	-15.2
				2009					
Lowest quintile	5.1	3.4	3.4	4.6	2.2	1.7	1.7	0.5	2.9
Second quintile	10.4	8.6	9.2	10.8	6.4	1.8	1.2	-0.4	4.0
Middle quintile	15.1	14.6	15.0	16.3	11.6	0.5	0.1	-1.2	3.5
Fourth quintile	22.0	23.2	22.9	23.9	20.5	-1.2	-0.9	-1.9	1.5
Highest quintile	47.4	50.3	49.4	44.4	59.3	-2.9	-2.0	3.0	-11.9
				2010					
Lowest quintile	5.4	3.3	3.3	—	—	2.1	2.1	—	—
Second quintile	10.5	8.5	9.2	—	—	2.0	1.3	—	—
Middle quintile	15	14.6	15.1	—	—	0.4	-0.1	—	—
Fourth quintile	22	23.4	23.2	—	—	-1.4	-1.2	—	—
Highest quintile	47.1	50.2	49.3	—	—	-3.1	-2.2	—	—
				2006–2009 Change					
Lowest quintile	0.2	0.0	-0.3	—	0.2	0.2	0.5	—	0.0
Second quintile	0.3	0.0	-0.2	—	1.7	0.3	0.5	—	-1.4
Middle quintile	0.3	0.1	0.0	—	0.8	0.2	0.3	—	-0.5
Fourth quintile	0.2	0.3	0.4	—	1.5	-0.1	-0.2	—	-1.3
Highest quintile	-1.0	-0.2	0.0	—	-4.3	-0.8	-1.0	—	3.3
				2006–2010 Change					
Lowest quintile	0.5	-0.1	-0.4	—	—	0.6	0.9	—	—
Second quintile	0.4	-0.1	-0.2	—	—	0.5	0.6	—	—
Middle quintile	0.2	0.1	0.1	—	—	0.1	0.1	—	—
Fourth quintile	0.2	0.5	0.7	—	—	-0.3	-0.5	—	—
Highest quintile	-1.3	-0.3	-0.1	—	—	-1.0	-1.2	—	—

[a]Returns with positive adjusted gross income.

is accounted for by the presence of in-kind social benefits in the NIPA estimates and by the effects of income taxes on the distribution. Compared to a money income measure that excludes taxes and adds noncash government social benefits, the difference is much smaller. The rapid growth in in-kind social benefits between 2006 and 2010 contributed to the growth in the shares of the two lowest quintiles, while the shares in CPS-ASEC money income and equivalence-adjusted money income declined over this period. For the highest quintile, there are large differences between the NIPA and CPS-ASEC shares and the IRS shares. This is clearly related to the inclusion of capital gains (net of losses) in the IRS measure. The 4.3 percentage point drop in the highest quintile share of income in the IRS data between 2006 and 2009 is primarily accounted for by the very large drop in capital gains income.

6.9   Issues and Future Directions

The results presented in this chapter are based on NIPA definitions and measures of income and expenditures. Strict application of the NIPA definitions in deriving estimates of income distribution yields some anomalous results, which are addressed below, along with consideration of the use of IRS data on individual income tax returns.

6.9.1   Pensions

In the NIPAs, employer contributions to pension plans and interest and dividends earned on pension plan assets are part of household income. Pension payments are not recognized in the NIPAs because they are treated as withdrawals from assets owned by households. Pension payments and IRA and self-employed retirement plan withdrawals are part of money income in the CPS-ASEC estimates, and taxable pensions and annuities and IRA distributions are part of AGI in the IRS estimates. A consequence of the NIPA treatment of pensions in developing estimates of income distribution is that households with pension income, who use that income to provide funds for their expenditures, have expenditures that exceed their income, often by large amounts. Disposable (after-tax) income is negative in some instances, when taxes exceed income from other sources, and the income estimates do not reflect the households' economic circumstances. As a result, such households are often placed into the lowest income quintile. Payments from collective pension plans are significant: they equaled $836.4 billion in 2010, 7.5 percent of disposable household income. For purposes of measuring income distribution, the NIPA treatment should be changed, so that payments from collective pension funds are accounted for as part of household income and pension plan contributions and earnings excluded. This is consistent with the treatment in the 2008 System of National Accounts, where collective pension fund payments are treated as social benefits.[25]

6.9.2   Capital Gains Taxes

In the NIPAs, capital gains (net of losses) are not included in household income, but capital gains taxes are included in the federal and state income taxes netted against household income to derive disposable household income. At the microlevel, this means that households with significant capital gains income may record low or even negative disposable income, in many instances placing them in the lowest income quintile. If possible, capital gains taxes should be removed from income taxes in deriving the income distribution estimates.

6.9.3   IRS Data

The IRS data on individual income tax returns from the SOI program have a number of elements in common with NIPA household income, including wages and salaries, proprietors' income, interest and dividends including S corporation income, rents and royalties, Social Security benefits, and unemployment compensation. A motivation for using the data is that the IRS data better capture high-income households than do the CPS-ASEC data, which is especially important for estimates of property income and proprietors' income. There are two primary issues with the use of IRS data in deriving NIPA-based estimates of income distribution: timeliness and reporting unit differences.

The most recent IRS public-use microdata on individual income tax returns are for 2008. Data for 2009 and 2010 by source of income and AGI bracket have been published by IRS. The reporting unit for the IRS data is the tax-filing unit rather than the household. A household may have more than one tax filer, and conversely, some households have no tax filers. The number of tax-filing units in 2010 was 142.9 million, versus 118.7 million households covered in CPS-ASEC. An IRS study of data for 1993 showed that the consolidation of tax filers into households overwhelmingly affected those tax returns reporting the lowest AGI (Sailer and Weber 1997). Of the 115 million returns filed that year, 9 million were filed by dependents of other taxpayers, and the overwhelming majority of these taxpayers reports AGIs of less than $10,000.

To use the IRS data, some means would have to be found to consolidate taxpayer units into households so that the IRS data could be statistically matched to the CPS-ASEC/CE data set. Alternatively, it may be possible

25. In earlier estimates of the distribution of personal income (BEA 1973), employer contributions to pension, health, and welfare funds were excluded from personal income and private pension and annuity payments were added to personal income to derive "family personal income" used for the income distribution estimates.

using tax status and family- and person-level CPS-ASEC data to construct a data set that could be statistically matched with the IRS taxpayer-unit data, although in this case the matched data would then have to be converted back into household units. If the taxpayer-household issue can be resolved, a means of carrying forward estimates from the last year of IRS public-use data would have to be found, using the CPS-ASEC/CE data set alone or in combination with published IRS data by income bracket.

References

Attanasio, Orazio P., Erich Battistin, and Andrew Leicester. 2006. "From Micro to Macro, from Poor to Rich: Consumption and Income in the UK and the US." Prepared for the National Poverty Center Conference, The Well-Being of Families and Children as Measured by Consumption Behavior, Washington, DC. http://www.homepages.ucl.ac.uk/~uctpjrt/Files/Attanasio-Battistin-Leicester.pdf .
Bee, Adam, Bruce D. Meyer, and James X. Sullivan. 2011. "The Validity of Consumption Data: Are the Consumer Expenditure Interview and Diary Surveys Informative?" Prepared for Conference on Improving Measures of Consumer Expenditures, sponsored by Conference for Research in Income and Wealth and National Bureau of Economic Research, Washington, DC, December 2–3. http://www.nber.org/chapters/c12662.pdf.
Bosworth, Barry. 2010. "Price Deflators, the Trust Fund Forecast, and Social Security Solvency." Working Paper no. 2010-12, Center for Retirement Research at Boston College. http://crr.bc.edu/working-papers/price-deflators-the-trust-fund-forecast-and-social-security-solvency/.
DeNavas-Walt, Carmen, Bernadette D. Proctor, and Jessica C. Smith. 2011. Current Population Reports, P60-239, Income, Poverty, and Health Insurance Coverage in the United States: 2010. US Census Bureau. http://www.census.gov/prod/2011pubs/p60-239.pdf .
European Commission, International Monetary Fund, Organisation for Economic Co-operation and Development, United Nations, World Bank. 2009. System of National Accounts 2008. New York. http://unstats.un.org/unsd/nationalaccount/img/pdf.gif.
Fixler, Dennis, and David Johnson. 2012. "Accounting for the Distribution of Income in the U.S. National Accounts." Prepared for NBER Conference on Research in Income and Wealth: Measuring Economic Sustainability and Progress, Boston, Massachusetts, August 6–8. http://www.nber.org/confer/2012/CRIWf12/Fixler_Johnson.pdf .
Hoover, Donald R., Stephen Crystal, Rizie Kumar, Usha Sambamoorthi, and Joel C. Cantor. 2002. "Medical Expenditures during the Last Year of Life: Findings from the 1992–1996 Medicare Current Beneficiary Survey." Health Services Research HSR 37 (6): 1625–42. http://www.ncbi.nlm.nih.gov/pmc/articles/PMC1464043/
Luttrell, Kelly. 2006. "S Corporation Returns, 2003." Statistics of Income (SOI) Bulletin—Spring 2006. Internal Revenue Service. http://www.irs.gov/file_source/pub/irs-soi/03scorp.pdf.
Passero, William, Thesia I. Garner, and Clinton McCully. 2011. "Understanding the Relationship: CE Survey and PCE." Prepared for Conference on Improving Measures of Consumer Expenditures sponsored by Conference for Research in

Income and Wealth and National Bureau of Economic Research, Washington, DC, December 2–3. http://www.nber.org/chapters/c12659.pdf.

Roemer, Marc I. 2000. "Assessing the Quality of the March Current Population Survey and the Survey of Income and Program Participation Income Estimates, 1990—1996." US Bureau of the Census, June. http://www.census.gov/hhes/www/income/publications/assess1.pdf.

Riley, Gerald F., and James D. Lubitz. 2010. "Long-Term Trends in Medicare Payments in the Last Year of Life." *Health Services Research* 45 (2): 565–76. http://www.ncbi.nlm.nih.gov/pmc/articles/PMC2838161/.

Ruser, John, Adrienne Pilot, and Charles Nelson. 2004. "Alternative Measures of Household Income: BEA Personal Income, CPS Money Income, and Beyond." US Bureau of Economic Analysis and US Census Bureau. Prepared for Federal Economic Statistics Advisory Committee, November. http://www.bea.gov/about/pdf/AlternativemeasuresHHincomeFESAC121404.pdf.

Sailer, Peter, and Michael Weber. 1997. "Household and Individual Income Data from Tax Returns." Internal Revenue Service. http://www.irs.gov/file_source/pub/irs-soi/petasa98.pdf.

Stephens, Melvin, Jr. 2003. "3rd of the Month: Do Social Security Recipients Smooth Consumption Between Checks?" *American Economic Review* 93 (1): 406–22.

Stiglitz, Joseph E., Amartya Sen, and Jean-Paul Fitoussi. 2009. "Report by the Commission on the Measurement of Economic Performance and Social Progress." Commission on the Measurement of Economic Performance and Social Progress, September. http://www.stiglitz-sen-fitoussi.fr/documents/rapport_anglais.pdf.

US Bureau of Economic Analysis (BEA). 1973. *Size Distribution of Family Personal Income: Methodology and Estimates for 1964.* Bureau of Economics Staff Paper no. 21, June.

———. 2011a. "Regional Quarterly Report." *Survey of Current Business* 91 http://www.bea.gov/scb/pdf/2011/10%20October/1011_regreport.pdf .

———. 2011b. *State Personal Income and Employment Methodology.* September. US Department of Commerce, Bureau of Economic Analysis. http://www.bea.gov/regional/pdf/spi2010.pdf.

US Bureau of Labor Statistics (BLS). 1983. "Consumer Expenditure Survey: Diary Survey, 1980–81." Bulletin 2173, September. US Department of Labor.

US Census Bureau. 1998. Current Population Reports, P60-200, 1998. *Money Income in the United States: 1997.* August. Washington: US Government Printing Office. http://www.census.gov/prod/3/98pubs/p60-200.pdf.

Trends in the Distribution of Household Income, 1979–2010

Edward Harris and Frank Sammartino

7.1 Introduction

Numerous studies have found that the distribution of income in the United States has become increasingly unequal—in particular, the share of income accruing to the highest-income households has increased, whereas the share accruing to other households has declined. That finding is robust across numerous methodologies, income definitions, and data sources. Other developed economies have experienced a similar long-term trend toward greater inequality in household income (OECD 2008).

The primary source for information on the income distribution in the United States is the Annual Social and Economic Supplement to the Census Bureau's Current Population Survey (CPS). That survey captures the demographic characteristics and income for a large sample of households. As computed by the Census Bureau, the Gini index for household money income—a before-tax income measure that includes some government transfers—rose from 0.397 in 1967 to 0.469 in 2010, though some of that increase reflects changes in data collection methodology (Jones and Weinberg 2000; DeNavas-Walt, Proctor, and Smith 2010; Burkhauser et al. 2008).

In an influential paper, Thomas Piketty and Emmanuel Saez used data from tax returns to examine market income inequality in the United States over almost a century (Piketty and Saez 2003). They found that income con-

Edward Harris is principal analyst at the Congressional Budget Office. Frank Sammartino is assistant director for tax analysis at the Congressional Budget Office.

The authors would like to thank Edward Wolff, Dale Jorgenson, Alice Henriques, and Paul Schreyer for their helpful comments. The views presented here are those of the authors and do not necessarily reflect those of the Congressional Budget Office. For acknowledgments, sources of research support, and disclosure of the authors' material financial relationships, if any, please see http://www.nber.org/chapters/c12827.ack.

centration dropped dramatically following World War I and World War II, remained roughly unchanged for the next few decades, and then rose starting in 1975, reaching pre–World War I levels by 2000. Increases within the top percentile of the income distribution were especially dramatic.

Each of those data sources has strengths and limitations.[1] The key advantage of tax return data is richness at the top of the income distribution, where much of the change in the income distribution has occurred, owing to very high sampling rates among high-income taxpayers. Tax return data are not subject to the traditional forms of measurement error found in household surveys, though taxpayers certainly face incentives to report their income in a way that minimizes their tax liability. Tax return data, however, is of limited usefulness in describing the bottom of the income distribution: it lacks information on individuals who do not file a federal tax return, does not report income from many government cash transfer programs, and has no information about the receipt of in-kind government transfers and benefits. In contrast, the CPS better represents the whole population and generally captures income from a broader array of sources, although income from government transfer programs tends to be underreported. However, the CPS is weaker for describing the top of the income distribution, as it does not oversample high-income households and topcodes their incomes. The CPS also does not report capital gains income, significantly underreports other income from capital, and lacks information on deductions and adjustments necessary to accurately compute income taxes.

This chapter presents estimates of the distribution of household income in the United States derived from a statistical combination of data from the Current Population Survey and from samples of income tax returns. This combined series overcomes some limitations of estimates produced from either the CPS or the income tax data alone: it covers the full population while maintaining the richness at the top of the income distribution, and can yield comprehensive estimates of the effect of the tax and transfer system on the full income distribution. The chapter focuses on the inequality of income after taxes and transfers, and decomposes the effects of the market income distribution, the tax system, and the transfer system on the inequality of household income after government transfers and federal taxes.[2]

7.2 Methodology

7.2.1 Data

This analysis draws its information on income from two primary sources. The core data come from the Statistics of Income (SOI), a nationally repre-

1. For a more complete description of the advantages and disadvantages of income statistics derived from tax returns and from household surveys, see Atkinson, Piketty, and Saez (2011).
2. These estimates have also been presented in Congressional Budget Office papers (Congressional Budget Office 2011, 2012).

sentative sample of individual income tax returns collected by the Internal Revenue Service.[3] The number of returns sampled has grown over the time period studied, ranging from roughly 90,000 in some of the early years to more than 300,000 in the later years. In the later years of the analysis, those tax returns are matched to certain information returns, such as W-2 and 1099 forms. Information returns provide data not available on the tax returns, such as the split of wages between spouses in married couples, contributions to deferred compensation plans, and Social Security benefits for filers with income below the level at which they are required to report those benefits.

Tax return information is supplemented with data from the Annual Social and Economic Supplement to the Census Bureau's Current Population Survey, which contains survey data on the demographic characteristics and income of a large sample of households. The two sources are combined by statistically matching each SOI record to a corresponding CPS record on the basis of demographic characteristics and income. Each pairing resulted in a new record that takes on some characteristics of the CPS record and some characteristics of the SOI record.[4]

The first step in the matching process is to align the unit of analysis by constructing tax-filing units from CPS households. A tax-filing unit is a single person or a married couple plus their dependents, and often differs from a CPS family. To construct tax units, household heads and their spouses are considered to be primary filing units. We apply tax rules to see if other members of the household can be claimed as dependents (in order to be a dependent, a person must meet certain age, relationship, and income requirements). We assign people who meet the dependent tests as dependents while those not meeting the test we classify as separate tax units. In cases where multiple people could potentially claim a dependent, we assume that the household chooses the arrangement that results in the most advantageous tax situation—for example, an unmarried cohabiting couple with two children might each claim a child and file as a head of household if it lowers their combined taxes.

Next, we divide tax-filing unit records in each file into fifteen demographic subgroups, based on marital status, the number of dependents, and whether the primary taxpayer or their spouse is age sixty-five or older. Records from the two files are then matched within the same demographic cell, with certain exceptions. Because the CPS contains fewer head of household (single parent with children) tax-filing units than the SOI, we match some single childless CPS records, and some married CPS records with head-of-household filers on the SOI. The deficit in head-of-household filers on the CPS likely reflects some combination of misreporting of filing status on the SOI and

---

3. For a complete description of the SOI file, see Internal Revenue Service (2012).
4. For a general description and evaluation of statistical matching, see Cohen (1991) and D'Orazio, Di Zio, and Scanu, (2006).

a failure of the algorithm that creates tax units for the CPS to account for complex living arrangements.

Within each demographic subgroup, we fit an ordinary least squares regression model on the SOI. The model predicts total income as a function of all the income items that are common to both the SOI and the CPS (wages, interest, dividends, rental income, business income and losses, pension income, and unemployment insurance). We apply the coefficients from that regression to the records in both files to construct a predicted income variable, and sort records in both files in descending order by the predicted value. The SOI record with the highest predicted income is matched to the CPS record with the highest predicted income. Of the two records, the one with the lower weight is matched to only one corresponding record. The record with the higher weight is "split," and is available (with its weight reduced) to be matched to the next record in the other file. (In practice, the highest income SOI records have very low weights, so the top CPS record can be matched to many SOI records). We repeat that process until all the SOI records are exhausted. Residual CPS records (those with the lowest predicted income) are assumed to represent households that did not file a tax return.

Each matched pairing results in a new record with the demographic characteristics of the CPS record and the income reported in the SOI. Some types of income, such as certain transfer payments and in-kind benefits, appear only in the CPS; values for those items were drawn directly from that survey. Income values for CPS records that represent nonfiling units are taken directly from the CPS.

Next, we rebuild households from tax-filing units based on the relationships as reported in the CPS. In general, CPS tax filing units will have been split or matched to multiple SOI records. In households where multiple split tax units are present, multiple instances of the household are created, covering all possible combination of tax units, with the weight appropriately allocated.

7.2.2   Measuring Income

This analysis uses three measures of household income: market income; market income plus government transfers (referred to as before-tax income); and market income plus government transfers, minus federal taxes paid (referred to as after-tax income).

Market income includes the following components:

- *Labor income*: Cash wages and salaries, including those allocated by employees to 401(k) plans; employer-paid health insurance premiums (as measured by the CPS); the employer's share of Social Security, Medicare, and federal unemployment insurance payroll taxes; and the share of corporate income taxes borne by workers.

- *Business income*: Net income from businesses and farms operated solely by their owners, partnership income, and income from S corporations.
- *Capital gains*: Profits realized from the sale of assets. Increases in the value of assets that have not been realized through sales are not included in market income.
- *Capital income (excluding capital gains)*: Taxable and tax-exempt interest, dividends paid by corporations (but not dividends from S corporations, which are considered part of business income), positive rental income, and the share of corporate income taxes borne by capital owners.
- *Other income*: Income received in retirement for past services and other sources of income.

Government transfers consist of cash payments from Social Security, unemployment insurance, Supplemental Security Income, Temporary Assistance for Needy Families ([TANF] and its predecessor, Aid to Families with Dependent Children [AFDC]), veterans' programs, workers' compensation, and state and local government assistance programs. It also includes the value of in-kind benefits such as Supplemental Nutrition Assistance Program vouchers (formerly known as food stamps), school lunches and breakfasts, housing assistance, energy assistance, and benefits provided by Medicare, Medicaid, and the Children's Health Insurance Program (measured by the Census Bureau's estimates of the average cost to the government of providing that insurance).

After-tax income is the sum of market income and government transfers, minus federal taxes paid. This analysis includes four federal taxes: individual and corporate income taxes, social insurance (payroll) taxes, and excise taxes. Those taxes have generally accounted for over 95 percent of federal revenues. Some smaller tax sources (estate and gift taxes, customs duties, Federal Reserve earnings, miscellaneous receipts) are omitted, either because of uncertainty surrounding their incidence or difficulties in estimating their distribution.

7.2.3   Incidence of Federal Taxes

Households are assumed to bear the economic cost of the taxes they pay directly, such as individual income taxes and the employee's share of payroll taxes. Employers are assumed to pass on their share of payroll taxes to employees by paying lower wages than they would otherwise pay, so the employer's share of payroll taxes is included in household before-tax income and in household taxes.

Excise taxes are generally assumed to fall on households according to their consumption of taxed goods (such as tobacco and alcohol). Excise taxes on intermediate goods, which are paid by businesses, were attributed to households in proportion to their overall consumption. We assume that each household spends the same amount on taxed goods as the average for households with comparable income and demographics as reported on the Bureau of Labor Statistics' Consumer Expenditure Survey.

Far less consensus exists about how to allocate corporate income taxes (and taxes on capital income generally). In this analysis, we allocated 75 percent of the burden of corporate income taxes to owners of capital in proportion to their income from interest, dividends, rents, and adjusted capital gains. Capital gains are adjusted by scaling them to their long-term historical level given the size of the economy and the tax rate that applies to them—rather than actual capital gains so as to smooth out any large year-to-year variations in the total amount of gains realized. We allocated 25 percent of the burden of corporate income taxes to workers in proportion to their labor income.

7.2.4   Adjusting for Household Size

Households are the unit of analysis. A household includes all people living in a single housing unit. The presumption is that households make joint economic decisions, which may not be true in every case (in a group house, for example). Households may comprise more than one taxpaying unit, such as a married couple and their adult children living together. In those cases, the income and taxes of each taxpaying unit are added together.

Larger households need more income to achieve the same standard of living as smaller ones. At the same time, there are some economies of scale in consumption, especially in housing consumption. To account for varying needs of different size households, and following a standard practice in the income inequality literature, income is adjusted for household size by dividing income by an adjustment factor equal to the square root of the number of people in the household, counting adults and children equally.

Some results are presented for various subgroups of the population, such as the lowest 20 percent or the top 1 percent. In constructing those subgroups, households are ranked by income that is adjusted for household size. Each subgroup of the population contains an equal number of people, but because households vary in size, subgroups generally contain unequal numbers of households.

7.3   Limitations of the Analysis

We strive to measure income, transfers, and taxes as broadly as possible. However, there are several conceptual and measurement issues that limit the analysis.

7.3.1   Annual Income

This study presents a series of annual snapshots of household income. Because annual income is only one perspective for evaluating economic well-being, focusing exclusively on that measure may provide an incomplete picture. For example, a household's income in any given year may not accurately represent its economic well-being over a longer period. Measuring income over a longer time frame, even over a lifetime, might provide a better indicator of a household's economic circumstances. Likewise, a household's consumption—rather than its income—may present a more accurate picture of its welfare or economic well-being (Slesnick 2001).

Household income measured over a multiyear period is more equally distributed than income measured over one year, although only modestly so (Congressional Budget Office 2005; Kopczuk, Saez, and Song 2010). That is somewhat surprising given the fairly substantial year-to-year movement of households across income groups, but much of the movement involves relatively small changes in income that, although sufficient to push households into a different income group, are not large enough to greatly affect the overall distribution of income. Multiyear income measures also show the same pattern of increasing inequality over time as is observed in annual measures.

Household consumption is more equally distributed than household income. The question of trends in consumption inequality is less settled, however. Several influential studies have documented that consumption inequality has not increased as much as income inequality (Slesnick 2001; Krueger and Perri 2006). Later studies have employed new techniques to account for errors in the measurement of consumption, and found much greater increases in consumption inequality (Aguiar and Bils 2011; Attanasio, Hurst, and Pistaferri 2012). An important measurement issue is the degree to which data on the consumption of US households adequately capture consumption by high-income households, a group whose rising income accounts for much of the observed increase in annual income inequality.

7.3.2 Capital Gains and Pensions

Two aspects of our income definition bear further discussion—capital gains and pensions. We measure capital gains income when realized, rather than as it accrues. For pensions, we measure the income when received or withdrawn (in the case of defined-contribution type retirement accounts). That decision is partly based on data availability, and partly from a desire to use the same accounting framework when measuring income and taxes.

Benchmark definitions of income differ in their treatment of these income sources (see Johnson and Fixler, chapter 8, this volume, for more detailed discussion). Under a comprehensive Haig-Simons income definition, often operationalized by defining income as equal to consumption plus the change in net worth, both capital gains and pensions would be counted when accrued. Under the Bureau of Economic Analysis definition of personal income, both realized and unrealized capital gains are excluded. Pension payments are excluded, but employer contributions to pension funds are included when made, and the interest and dividends (but not capital gains) earned by pension funds are included as they accrue. The measure of household income recommended by the Canberra Group excludes capital gains, and counts pension income when received (Canberra 2011).

In practice, efforts to measure pensions and gains on an accrual basis are hampered by data constraints. Existing household surveys and administrative data simply do not capture well the increase in personal assets at the household level. The value of benefits promised under defined-benefit plans are particularly difficult to measure as they accrue. While there has been some progress on measuring capital income at the household level as it accrues, based on asset holdings and the assumption that all households receive the same rate of return on a given asset type, those estimates are limited to certain years (Armour, Burkhauser, and Larrimore 2013; Smeeding and Thompson 2010).

Our view is that, in the absence of lifetime income data, it is impossible to accurately apportion the capital gains realized in a single year over multiple years, and that the practical choice is between counting the gain as income when realized or allotting only part or none of it to current income.[5] Omission seems the worse choice, especially because the favorable tax treatment of capital gains income has created strong incentives for high-income taxpayers to recharacterize ordinary income as capital gains. Excluding capital gains would reduce the market income Gini by 0.014 in 1979 and by 0.011 in 2010. Excluding the gains shifting in 1986 and 1987, the maximum effect of capital gains occurred in 2007 (0.027 Gini points) and 2005 (0.025 Gini point).

The desire to examine the joint distribution of income and taxes also argues for including pension and capital gains income upon realization. The US income tax is assessed on such income when realized; there is some logic to using the same accounting principles for the measurement of income and taxes. Otherwise the misalignment in timing would show, for instance, very high tax rates on pensioners or on taxpayers whose primary income is capital gains. While in theory one could compute the taxes on such income on an accrual basis as well, doing so would making assumptions about future tax law, household economic circumstances, and the timing of pension receipt and the sale of assets.

7.3.3   State and Local Taxes

This analysis excluded state and local taxes because of the difficulty of estimating them for individual households over a long period. State sales taxes would be particularly challenging, as no major survey collects data on

5. Extensive examination of tax data on the sales of capital assets indicates that apportioning gains across years on the basis of a single year's realizations would lead to significant error. See Congressional Budget Office, *Perspectives on the Ownership of Capital Assets and the Realization of Capital Gains* (May 1997).

sales taxes paid by households. It is unclear how the omission of those taxes affects conclusions about trends in the progressivity of the entire tax system.

In the time frame studied here, state and local taxes have ranged between 8.2 percent and 9.3 percent of gross domestic product—equal to about 40 percent to 50 percent of total federal taxes. State and local taxes have three primary components, and the composition of receipts has been fairly stable over time. Sales taxes are the largest source, accounting for 34 percent of state and local revenue in 2010. Those taxes are generally assumed to be roughly proportional to consumption, making the tax regressive with respect to income (because lower-income households consume a greater proportion of their income than do higher-income households). Property taxes accounted for 33 percent of state and local revenues in 2010. The progressivity of those taxes depends critically on the assumptions about the incidence of the taxes, which is a matter of considerable debate. State individual income taxes, which accounted for 21 percent of state and local revenues in 2010, are much less progressive than the federal individual income tax because the rate structures for state-level income taxes are flatter than those at the federal level and any refundable credits are small. Thus, though different analysts have reached different conclusions about whether state and local taxes on net are proportional, progressive, or regressive, they are clearly less progressive than the federal tax system (Phares 1980; Pechman 1985; Chamberlain and Prante 2007; and ITEP 2009). Consequently, analysis of the entire tax system would show less progressivity than analysis of the federal tax system alone. It is more difficult to know how state and local taxes have affected trends in tax progressivity, however.

7.3.4 Misreporting of Transfer Income

For most transfer payments, estimates of participation and benefit amounts are taken from the CPS. For Social Security and unemployment insurance benefits, which are partially taxable, estimates come from a combination of tax and information returns and survey reporting. Unfortunately, reporting rates for transfer payments, especially means-tested transfers, on the CPS are relatively low, and have generally been declining over time. For example, the percentage of annual food stamp benefit dollars captured in the CPS declined from 67 percent in 1993 to 55 percent in 2005 (Wheaton 2007). For TANF/AFDC, reporting rates declined from 75 percent in 1993 to 57 percent in 2005.

We have corrected for some misreporting of transfers in some years, using data from the Transfer Income Model (TRIM3).[6] That model applies the

6. The model was developed and is maintained by the Urban Institute, with funding primarily from the Department of Health and Human Services, Office of the Assistant Secretary for Planning and Evaluation. TRIM3 requires users to input assumptions and interpretations about economic behavior and the rules governing federal programs. Therefore, the conclusions presented here are attributable only to the authors.

rules of several transfer programs to each household in the CPS to determine if households are eligible for benefits and, if so, the size of the benefit they can receive. Households that report receiving benefits, and who appear eligible, are given the computed amount of the benefit. Households that are ineligible are assumed to receive no benefits, even if they report receiving them. New participants are created from eligible households who did not report receiving benefits in such a way as to match the size and characteristics of recipients on the basis of agencies' program data. The model targets the number of recipients rather than the overall amount of benefits, but the estimated benefit amounts approximate the agencies' totals.

To assess the sensitivity of its main analysis to the misreporting of transfers, we combined estimates of transfer payments using TRIM3 with our merged data file. For the programs covered by TRIM3—food stamps, SSI, TANF/AFDC, and housing subsidies—we replaced benefits as reported in the CPS with benefits as estimated using TRIM3, and recomputed our inequality measures. We made those estimates for 1993 and 2004, the earliest and latest years for which TRIM3 estimates are available at the time of the analysis.

Adjusting for the misreporting of transfer payments adds income to the bottom of the distribution. Consequently, the Gini index adjusted for misreporting is lower than the unadjusted Gini index. For 1993, reporting adjustments cause the Gini index to fall from 0.005, or by about 1 percent. For 2004, reporting adjustments lower the Gini index by 0.004, or by 0.8 percent. The adjustment had a smaller impact in the latter year, despite the fact that underreporting of transfer income grew, because transfer income was a smaller share of household income in that year. Specifically, the misreporting adjustments were larger in 2004 as a share of transfer income but smaller as a share of total household income. Even for households at the bottom of the distribution, transfer income grew more slowly than other income over the 1993 to 2004 period, mitigating the effect of increased misreporting on the observed degree of inequality.

While that result suggests that misreporting of transfers have not had a large impact on our measures of income inequality, that result is not definitive because of the limited number of transfer programs covered and the limited timeframe. Importantly, no adjustments have been made for non-means-tested transfers (such as Medicare) or for Medicaid. While Medicare has fairly high reporting rates, misreporting of Medicaid is a significant issue. A planned extension of our work is to make a full set of misreporting adjustments, to cover all major transfer programs and years.

7.4 The Distribution of Household Income

This section begins with an examination of trends in the distribution of income after transfers and federal taxes. It then examines changes in the market income distribution in more detail, and finally isolates the effect of taxes and transfers on the income distribution.

7.4.1   The Distribution of Income after Federal Taxes and Transfers

Income after taxes and transfers is the income measure that most closely corresponds to the ultimate resources available to households. From 1979 to 2010, mean after-tax household income grew much more rapidly for the highest-income households than for the rest of the income distribution (see figure 7.1).[7] Over the full thirty-two-year period, annual real income growth for the top percentile averaged 3.4 percent. For other households in the highest-income quintile (the 81st through 99th percentiles), average after-tax income grew at an average annual rate of 1.6 percent. That rate somewhat exceeded that of the lowest quintile (1.1 percent) and the middle three quintiles (1.2 percent).

Income for the top percentile has been quite volatile: after a period of strong growth in the early 1980s, it spiked in 1986 and fell in 1987, reflecting an acceleration of capital gains realizations into 1986 in anticipation of the scheduled increase in tax rates the following year. Income growth for the top 1 percent of the population rebounded in 1988 but fell again with the onset of the 1990 to 1991 recession. By 1994, after-tax household income was 51 percent higher than it had been in 1979. Income growth accelerated in 1995, averaging more than 20 percent per year through 2000. After falling sharply during the recession and stock market drop in 2001, average real after-tax income for the top 1 percent of the population almost doubled between 2002 and 2007. Large declines in capital income associated with the recession in 2008 and 2009 caused a steep decline in top incomes between 2007 and 2009. Top incomes partially rebounded in 2010.

As a result of that uneven income growth, shares of total after-tax income shifted in favor of higher-income households. Measured across business cycle peaks, the share of income received by the top 1 percent more than doubled, from about 8 percent in 1979 to over 16 percent in 2007, before declining to 13 percent in 2010. The share received by other households in the highest income quintile remained relatively flat over the 1979 to 2010 period, while the share of income accruing to each of the four lowest-income quintiles fell by over a percentage point.

The upward shift in after-tax income shares is reflected in the Gini coefficient for after-tax income (see figure 7.2). That index rose by 0.106 points from 1979 to 2007, before falling 0.030 points from 2007 to 2010. The index increased in almost every year during that span, declining only with the recessions in 1990 to 1991, 2001, and 2007 to 2009. It also declined in 1987 largely due to income shifting associated with the Tax Reform Act of 1986. The rate of increase was not constant, however. The Gini index increased

---

7. Inflation is measured using the personal consumption expenditures price index.

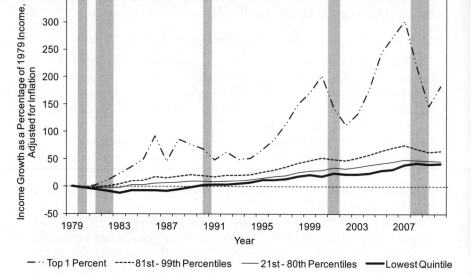

Fig. 7.1 Cumulative growth in average after-tax income by income group, 1979–2010

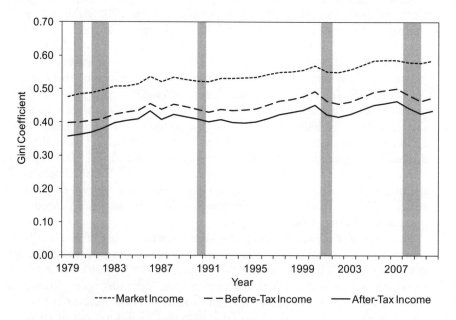

Fig. 7.2 Gini coefficients, 1979–2010

at a rate of about 0.003 points per year in the 1980s expansion, 0.006 points per year in the 1990s expansion, and 0.010 points per year during the expansion in the 2000s.

7.4.2   The Distribution of Market Income

An increase in the inequality of market income was the primary cause of the widening inequality of after-tax income. With a few exceptions, the Gini coefficient for after-tax income parallels that of market income. From 1979 to 2007, the increase in the Gini for market income was almost identical to the increase in the Gini for after-tax income (though those measures deviated somewhat in the recession of 2008 to 2009, discussed later).

A useful property of the Gini index is that it is possible to determine the contribution of different income sources to the increase in overall income inequality through a simple decomposition. The contribution of each income source to the Gini index for total market income is the product of the concentration index (often called a pseudo-Gini) for that income source and the share of total market income attributable to that source.[8] Thus, changes in the concentration of income from a source such as labor income will have a much greater effect on overall income concentration than an equivalent change in the concentration of another income source (such as capital income) because labor income is a much larger share of total income. Changes in the Gini for market income can be decomposed into changes in the weight placed on each source, and changes in the concentration index for each source.

A concentration index differs from a Gini index for each source because in calculating the concentration index, the population is ranked by total market income rather than by income from that source, as they would be in calculating the Gini index for that source. The concentration index captures two effects: the concentration of income from that source, and the correlation of that income source with income from other sources (and hence with total income). The latter effect arises because households are sorted by total income when computing the metric. Thus, for example, the concentration index for labor compensation has increased over time both because compensation has become more unevenly distributed in favor of higher-compensation households and because compensation has become more highly correlated with other unevenly distributed sources of income, such as capital income.[9]

---

8. This derivation is reported in Shorrocks (1982) and Fei, Ranis, and Kuo (1978).

9. Lerman and Yitzhaki (1985) propose an alternative three-factor decomposition that decomposes the pseudo-Gini for each income source into the Gini coefficient for that source and a factor they term the Gini correlation, which measures the relationship between an income source and total income.

Decomposing Changes in Market Income Inequality by Income Source

Looking first at the concentration of different income sources, it is clear that labor income is more evenly distributed across the income spectrum than capital income, and both are more evenly distributed than capital gains or business income (see figure 7.3). Concentration indexes for the major sources of income all increased—albeit irregularly—from 1979 to 2010, indicating rising inequality in the distribution of each source of income. Labor income became steadily more concentrated from 1979 through 1988, and then again in 1992 following the 1990 to 1991 recession. After remaining mostly unchanged during the rest of the 1990s, the concentration of labor income increased again from 1999 through 2002. From 2002 to 2005 the concentration was has declined slightly, before rising with the 2008 to 2009 recession.

Capital income (excluding capital gains) became increasingly concentrated beginning in the mid-1980s. Its concentration shows a clear cyclical pattern, rising in expansions and falling in recessions, probably reflecting differences in asset holdings across the income spectrum. Capital gains also became increasingly concentrated beginning in the early 1990s; unlike other income from capital, however, the degree of concentration of capital gains continued to rise through 2003 but fell thereafter. The concentration of business income was quite variable in the early part of the 1980s. Some of that variability might reflect changes in tax law in that period. After 1986, the concentration of business income rose steadily through 1991, declined

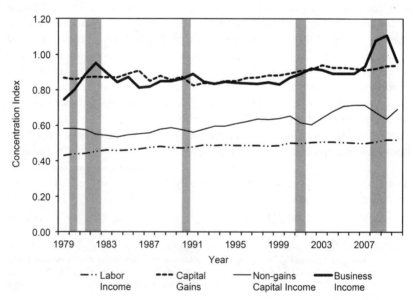

Fig. 7.3   Income concentration, by major source

through much of the 1990s, before rising in the 2000 to 2002 period. Especially noteworthy is the large jump in the concentration of business income in 2008 and 2009, which was largely due to large business losses in that period.

Turning to the composition of market income, labor income is the largest income component, accounting for more than 70 percent of market income in most years between 1979 and 2007. The labor share of total income was at its high point, 75 percent, at the beginning of the period. That share generally rose in recessions (as other income sources are more cyclical) and fell in expansions, and by 2007 had reached a nadir of 66 percent. The 2008 to 2009 recession caused sharp drops in capital gains and other capital income, and consequently pushed the labor share back near its high points in 2009 and 2010. Capital income (excluding capital gains) is the next largest source, but even at its peak in 1981 it was only about 14 percent of market income. Since then, the share of total income from capital has declined to about 10 percent of total income in 2007, and to 8 percent in 2010. Income from capital gains rose from about 4 percent of market income in 1979 to about 9 percent in 2007, before falling to 4 percent in 2010. Business income and income from other sources (primarily private pensions) each accounted for about 8 to 9 percent of total income at the end of the period, up from about 4 percent apiece in 1979.

The relative importance of changes in the concentration of particular income sources and shifts in the shares of market income represented by those sources in explaining trends in market income inequality varied over time (see table 7.1). Subperiods are defined here by whether the Gini coefficient rose or fell, and they loosely correspond with business cycles. From 1979 to 1988, almost all of the increase of 0.059 points in the Gini index for total market income resulted from an increasing concentration of separate income sources, primarily labor income. Small shifts in the share of market income from less to more highly concentrated sources—in particular, from labor income to business and other income—explain only a small portion of the increase in the concentration of total market income over that period.

In contrast, from 1991 to 2000—a period that saw an increase of 0.049 points in the Gini index—a shift to more concentrated sources explains about 45 percent of the overall increase in market income inequality, and an increase in the concentration within each source accounts for the other 55 percent. In that case, a decrease in the percentage of total income from labor and capital and an increase in the share from capital gains was a major factor, as was an increase in the concentration of both labor and capital income.

The reasons for the increase of 3.8 percentage points in the Gini index for total market income between 2002 and 2007 differ yet again. More than three-quarters of the total increase in the Gini index stemmed from an increase in the share of total income coming from more highly concentrated

Table 7.1 Sources of change in Gini index for selected years

	1979–1988	1988–1991	1991–2000	2000–2002	2002–2007	2007–2010	1979–2010
Change in Gini index for market income	0.059	-0.013	0.049	-0.021	0.038	-0.001	0.110
Change due to							
Increased share of income from more concentrated sources	0.004	-0.008	0.021	-0.022	0.029	-0.025	-0.003
Increased concentration of income sources	0.055	-0.005	0.027	0.001	0.009	0.024	0.113
Labor income	0.039	-0.002	0.016	0.003	-0.005	0.015	0.066
Business income	0.005	0.002	-0.001	0.003	0.001	0.002	0.012
Capital gains	0.001	-0.002	0.004	0.001	0.000	0.002	0.003
Capital income	0.000	-0.002	0.010	-0.004	0.010	-0.002	0.011
Other income	0.011	-0.001	-0.002	-0.002	0.003	0.008	0.020
Percentage change due to							
Increased share of income from more concentrated sources	0.06	0.63	0.44	1.06	0.77	23.97	-0.02
Increased concentration of income sources	0.94	0.37	0.56	-0.06	0.23	-22.97	1.02

capital gains. An increase in the concentration of capital income accounts for most of the remaining increase. Labor income became somewhat less concentrated over that period, but the effect on overall income dispersion was small.

The 2007 to 2010 period saw little net change in the Gini for market income. That reflects two offsetting effects. First, capital and business income declined sharply, pushing up the labor share of market income. By itself, that effect would have caused the Gini coefficient to rise by 0.025 points. At the same time, however, labor income and other income grew more concentrated, largely offsetting the effect of the changing mix of incomes.

Over the 1979 to 2007 period as a whole, the increased concentration of the individual sources of market income accounted for more than 100 percent of the total increase in the Gini index, as all major sources of market income became more highly concentrated in favor of higher-income households. Labor income was the biggest contributor because it is by far the largest source of income, even though the increase in the concentration of labor income was smaller than the increase in concentration for other sources.[10]

7.4.3   Income Changes for the Top 1 Percent of the Population

The rapid growth of average market income for the 1 percent of the population in households with the highest income was a major contributing factor to the increase in household income inequality between 1979 and 2010. Without the income growth at the very top of the distribution, income dispersion still would have increased, but not by as much. Recalculating the Gini index by excluding the 1 percent of the population in households with the highest income in each year reduces the level of the measured market income inequality (from .586 to 0.515 in 2010) and also the measured increase in market income inequality over the full 1979 to 2010 period (from 0.110 to 0.082).

Average market income for the highest income grew very rapidly over that period. At its peak in 2007, mean income for that group had almost quadrupled. The pattern of market income growth is similar to the pattern of after-tax income growth: tremendous growth in the late 1990s, sharp declines during the recession and stock market decline in 2001, followed by another period of rapid growth between 2002 and 2007. Large declines in capital income associated with the recession in 2008 and 2009 caused a steep decline in top incomes between 2007 and 2009. Top incomes partially rebounded in 2010.

Between 1979 and 2010, the composition of household income for the 1 percent of the population in households with the highest income changed

---

10. Many studies have documented the increasing inequality of labor income. Despite a voluminous literature on the subject, the causes of this are still a somewhat unsettled matter. See for example, Lemieux (2010) and the references therein.

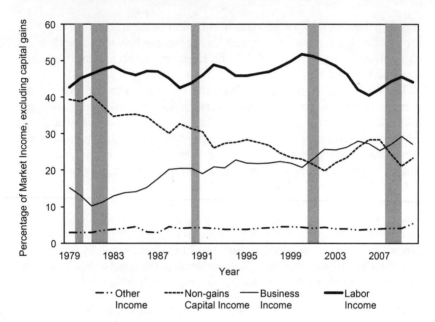

Fig. 7.4   Shares of market income, by source, for the top 1 percent of households, 1979–2010

significantly. Because of the volatile nature of income from capital gains realizations and its significance for the highest-income households, it is more illuminating to look at sources of income as shares of market income excluding capital gains. From 1979 through 2010, wages and other labor compensation varied from 40 percent to 50 percent of total income excluding capital gains, with no apparent trend (see figure 7.4). Interestingly, the labor share rose while top incomes grew rapidly during the late 1990s, but declined as top incomes grew rapidly during the middle of the first decade of the twenty-first century.

Capital income excluding capital gains—in other words, interest, dividends, and rents—has generally been a declining source of income among the highest-income households. Its share dropped from 40 percent of market income excluding capital gains in 1979 to 20 percent in 2002 and then increased to about 28 percent by 2007. It then declined in the 2008 to 2009 recession, before rebounding somewhat in 2010. Over the same period, the share of income from business activities has grown sharply and fairly steadily, increasing from a low of 10 percent of total market income excluding capital gains in 1981 to nearly 30 percent in 2010.

Capital gains are the most volatile source of income, and their importance as a share of household income for the top 1 percent of the population has fluctuated. That fluctuation appears to reflect movements in stock prices and changes in tax law. Between 1979 and 1985, capital gains were equal to 20 percent to 30 percent of market income excluding capital gains for the top 1 percent; in 1986, they spiked to more than twice that share. The ratio of income from capital gains to other market income declined throughout the late 1980s and then began to pick up in the mid-1990s before entering a period of rapid growth starting in 1995. That ratio peaked at 34 percent of market income in 2000 before falling to 15 percent in 2002 and then rebounding to 36 percent in 2007 and falling to 11 percent in 2011.

The fall in capital income and the increase in business income may in part reflect a recharacterization of income. Following the Tax Reform Act of 1986, which lowered the top statutory tax rate on individual income below the top rate on corporate income, many C corporations (which are taxed separately from their owners under the corporate income tax) were converted to S corporations (which pass corporate income through to their shareholders, where it is taxed under the individual income tax). As a result, corporate dividend income and capital gains from the sale of corporate stock were converted into S corporation income, which is counted here as part of business income. Business income jumped in the 1986 to 1988 period as those conversions began and it continued to grow rapidly throughout the 1990s and early twenty-first century as more conversions occurred and new businesses were formed as S corporations rather than C corporations.

The changing composition of income for the highest-income households reflects a much longer trend. Over the entire twentieth century, capital income declined sharply in importance for high-income taxpayers. The wage share of income for the top income groups was higher in 2007 than before World War II, as highly compensated workers have replaced people whose income is from property or securities at the top of the income distribution (Piketty and Saez 2003).

Numerous explanations for the rise of the highest incomes have been proffered, though it is a unsettled issue.[11] One theory is that that the compensation of "superstars" (such as actors, athletes, and musicians) may be especially sensitive to technological changes. Another line of research has focused on the very large pay increases for top corporate executives, with some arguing that weaknesses in corporate governance have enabled corporate executives to overpay themselves and others arguing that increases in corporate size and complexity have made firms more willing to pay large salaries to attract and keep the best executives. Still others have focused on the form of compensation, arguing that the increasing importance of stock options in executive compensation has caused that compensation to grow rapidly during periods of rapid appreciation in the stock market.

7.5   The Effect of the Tax and Transfer System on Income Inequality

Changes in the distribution of after-tax household income were primarily driven by changes in the market income distribution. However, changes in

---

11. For a review of that literature, see Gordon and Dew-Becker (2007).

the distribution of government transfer payments and federal taxes played some role.

Overall, transfers and federal taxes reduce income inequality. Transfers that are a decreasing percentage of market income as income rises (progressive transfers) lower the Gini index by boosting income for people at the bottom of the scale. Taxes that are an increasing percentage of before-tax household income as income rises (progressive taxes) make income more equal by reducing income by more for higher-income households. In addition, the earned income tax credit, which in this analysis is included with federal taxes (though some of its benefits are conveyed in the form of government payments), has an effect on the income distribution similar to that of transfers by raising the after-tax income of lower-income households.

The equalizing effect of transfers and taxes depends on their degree of progressivity and on their size relative to household income. Holding the size of transfers and taxes constant, an increase in the progressivity of transfers and taxes will reduce income inequality. Holding the degree of progressivity constant, an increase in the size of a progressive transfers and tax system will also reduce inequality.

The effect of transfers and taxes on the dispersion of household income can be seen by comparing the Gini index for market income with the Gini index for after-transfer, before-tax income and the Gini index for after-transfer, after-tax income. A proportional transfer and tax system would leave the Gini index for after-transfer, after-tax income equal to that for household market income. Because both transfers and taxes are progressive in the United States, they reduce the Gini index. The dispersion of after-tax income in 2010 is about three-fourths as large as the dispersion of market income. Transfers have been more redistributive than taxes, and their effect has fluctuated more.

The redistributive effect of the tax and transfer system has varied over the period (see figure 7.5). In 1979, transfers and taxes reduced the Gini index by 0.118. The effect of taxes and transfers rose and fell over ensuing years, varying with economic conditions and changes in tax and transfer policy. In 2007, immediately before the recession, transfers and taxes reduced the Gini index by 0.122, almost identical to the effect in 1979. The effect of taxes and transfers rose rapidly in the 2008 to 2010 period, so by 2010, taxes and transfers reduced the Gini index by 0.152 points, the largest reduction seen in the period. Much of that increase reflects temporary policy responses to the recession, which are not expected to persist.

7.5.1   Government Transfer Payments

In 2010, transfers reduced the income inequality by 0.11. Prior to the 2008 to 2009 recession, the redistributive effect of transfers fluctuated within a fairly narrow band, reducing the Gini coefficient by between 0.08 and 0.10 points. The effect of transfers was flat for most of the 1980s, rose in the early

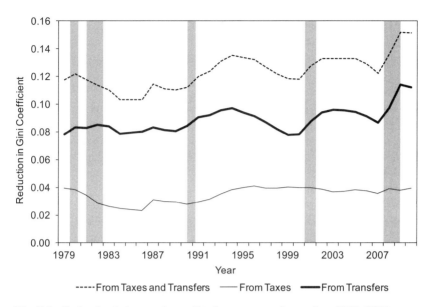

Fig. 7.5   Reduction in income inequality from taxes and transfers, 1979–2010

1990s, then declined in the latter part of that decade. The effect of transfers rose again around the 2001 recession and the 2008 to 2009 recession. Most of those movements reflected changes in the overall size of the transfer system.

The amount of government transfer payments—including federal, state, and local transfers—fluctuated with the business cycle (see figure 7.6). Measured peak to peak—1979 to 2007—transfers rose from around 10.9 percent of market income to 13.5 percent. Transfers then rose sharply as a share of market income in 2008 to 2010, reflecting several factors. First, transfers rose because some programs, such as unemployment insurance and the Supplemental Nutrition Assistance Program (SNAP), function as automatic stabilizers, naturally rising in recession as market incomes decline. Additionally, several policy changes temporarily increased the generosity of transfer programs—unemployment benefits were increased and the maximum number of months recipients could receive benefits was expanded; and the maximum benefit for SNAP was increased. Finally, even without an increase in transfer payments the steep decline in market income caused the ratio of transfers to market income to rise. All of these effects should fade as the economy recovers.

Social Security is the largest transfer program, equaling about 6.6 percent of household market income on average over the period studied. Benefits have been a fairly stable percentage of market income, with the most notable increase occurring in 2008 and 2009. Even though average Social Security benefits have grown more slowly than average income, the population receiv-

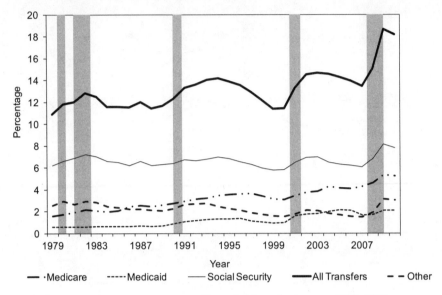

Fig. 7.6   Transfers as a percentage of household market income, 1979–2010

ing benefits has grown faster than the overall population, holding benefits fairly flat as a share of market income. Medicare and Medicaid benefits have both grown rapidly as a share of market income, by about 3.5 and 1.5 percentage points respectively. This reflects rapid growth in health-care costs and, in the case of Medicaid, expanded eligibility. Other transfers (including SNAP and unemployment benefits) declined from nearly 3 percent of household market income at their peak in 1982 to under 2 percent by 2007 before rebounding during the recent recession.

The shifts in the relative importance of different transfer programs since 1979 moved the distribution of transfer benefits away from households in the lower part of the income spectrum to some extent (see figure 7.7). Rapid growth in Medicare, which is not means-tested, tended to shift more transfer income to middle- and upper-income people. At the same time, spending on Aid to Families with Dependent Children and its successor, Temporary Assistance for Needy Families, has declined relative to market income; benefits from those means-tested programs are heavily concentrated at the bottom of the income scale. As a result, households in the lowest-income quintile received 56 percent of federal transfer payments in 1979 and 42 percent in 2010. The upward shift in the distribution of transfers tended to reduce the redistributive effect of the transfer system.

In sum, the transfer system grew somewhat larger over the three-plus decades studied, measured peak to peak, while becoming less skewed to the bottom of the income distribution. This larger, less targeted transfer system

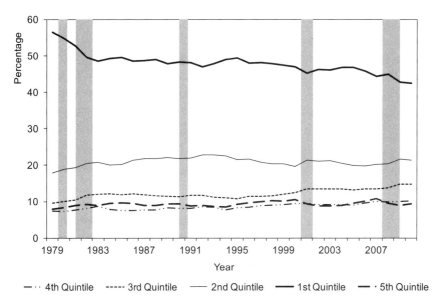

Fig. 7.7   Share of total transfers, by market income group, 1979–2010

had a roughly similar effect on income inequality in 2007 as the system in place at the beginning of the period. The effect of transfers on inequality rose quite a bit in the recent recession as the size of the transfer system, relative to market income, grew strongly; however, much of that effect is expected to fade as the economy recovers.

7.5.2   Federal Taxes

The effect of taxes on the distribution of after-tax income has been remarkably stable. In many ways, trends in the tax system are the mirror image of those seen in the transfer system. Over the three decades studied, the tax system grew smaller, but tax payments grew more skewed to the top of the distribution. Those effects approximately netted out, leaving a tax system that reduces inequality by about the same amount—0.04 Gini points—at the beginning and the end of the period.

Average Federal Tax Rates

The overall average federal tax rate has declined from 22 percent of household income in 1979 to 18 percent in 2010 (see figure 7.8). The average tax rate declined in the early 1980s then rose through much of the 1980s and 1990s. It peaked at 23 percent in 2000, and then dropped sharply following the 2001 recession and tax legislation enacted in 2001 and 2003, falling to just under 20 percent in 2003, lower than any year since 1979. The rate fell again substantially in the 2008 to 2010 period, as a new round of tax reduc-

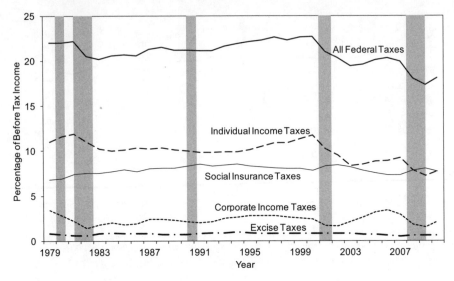

Fig. 7.8   Average tax rates for all households by tax source, 1979–2010

tions, coupled with the recession, reduced federal taxes as a share of GDP to post-WWII lows.

The composition of federal taxes changed notably over the period. The reduction in average rates has come about primarily because of reductions in average individual income taxes rates, which fell by over 3 percentage points over the period, while the average payroll tax rate rose by about a percentage point. By the end of the period, payroll taxes were about as large as individual income taxes. Those variations stemmed from a combination of legislative changes and economic developments.

The average individual income tax rate peaked at 12 percent of household income in 1981. The individual income tax rate then fell as the tax rate reduction enacted in 1981 took effect. The rate rose in the late 1990s because of legislation enacted in 1993 and because of rapidly rising incomes. After 2000, the rate fell as a result of the 2001 and 2003 tax reductions and the recession in 2001. The Economic Stimulus Act of 2008 (which provided a partially refundable payment to almost all taxpayers) and the American Recovery and Reinvestment Act (ARRA) of 2009 (which introduced new refundable income tax credits and expanded existing one) both reduced income taxes further in the late 2010s.

The increase in the payroll tax rate came about in the 1980s as a result of increases in the cap on earnings subject to the Social Security payroll tax and legislation enacted in 1983 that accelerated previously scheduled increases in the Social Security payroll tax rate. Subsequent legislation in the early 1990s first increased and then eliminated the cap on earnings subject

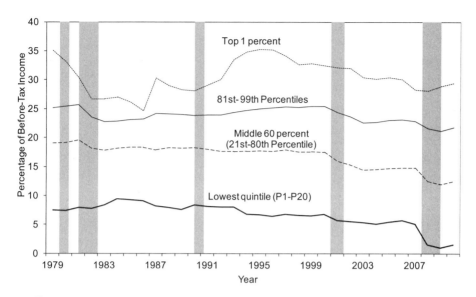

Fig. 7.9   **Average federal tax rate by pretax income group, 1979–2010**

to the hospital insurance payroll tax (which is used to finance a portion of Medicare). The payroll tax rate declined in the late 1990s and middle of the first decade of the twenty-first century as labor income grew more slowly than other income sources and as earnings above the Social Security taxable maximum grew more rapidly than earnings below the maximum. Those trends reversed around the recessions in 2001 and 2008 to 2009, pushing up average payroll tax rates.

Taken as a whole, the federal tax system is progressive—that is, average tax rates generally rise with income. In 2010, households in the bottom fifth of the before-tax income distribution paid 1.5 percent of their before-tax income in federal taxes, households in the middle quintile paid 11.5 percent, and households in the highest quintile paid 24.0 percent percentile (see figure 7.9). Average rates rose within the top quintile, and households in the top 1 percent of the before-tax income distribution faced an average rate of 29.4 percent while those in the 81st to 99th percentiles paid 21.8. Much of the progressivity of the federal tax system derives from the individual income tax, where average rates ranged from –9.2 percent for the bottom income quintile to 1.6 percent for the middle quintile, 13.8 percent for the highest quintile, and 20.1 percent for the top 1 percent.[12]

For most income groups, the average federal tax rates in the 2008 to 2010 period were the lowest observed in the 1979 to 2010 period. The pattern in

12. A negative average rate occurs when refundable tax credits exceed the income taxes owed by an income group.

the intervening years is more varied, reflecting the interaction of numerous changes to tax law and changes in the composition and distribution of income.

For the lowest income group, the average rate fell from 7.5 percent in 1979 to 1.5 percent in 2010. Almost two-thirds of that decline came between 2007 and 2009, largely as a result of new refundable tax credits introduced by the ARRA. The largest of those credits, the Making Work Pay credit, expired at the end of 2010. Declines in earlier years were mainly caused by increases in the earned income tax credit, especially in the 1990s. Payroll tax rates rose steadily for the lowest income group, offsetting some of the decline in their individual income tax rate.

Households in the middle three income quintiles saw their average tax rate fall by 6.6 percentage points over the thirty-two years studied, from 19.1 percent in 1979 to 12.5 percent in 2010. That decline was due primarily to declines in individual income taxes. The average tax rate for this group fell somewhat in the early 1980s and then fluctuated within a fairly narrow band through the 1980s and 1990s. Over the 2001 to 2003 period, the rate declined by 3.1 percentage points, reflecting numerous changes in law enacted in 2001—such as the expansion of the child tax credit, reductions in tax rates, and increases in the standard deduction for married couples—that lowered taxes for households in the middle quintiles. The rate fell 2.8 percentage points from 2007 to 2009, largely because of changes enacted in ARRA.

The average tax rate for households in the 81st to 99th percentiles of the income distribution also reached a low point in 2009, about 4 percentage points below its 1979 level, before rising slightly in 2010. That rate fell in the early 1980s and then crept up over the remaining part of that decade and the 1990s, such that by 2000 it slightly exceeded its 1979 level. The average tax rate for this group fell 2.9 percentage points between 2000 and 2003, rose modestly from 2003 to 2007, and then fell another 1.7 percentage point from 2007 to 2009, before rising 0.7 percentage points in 2010.

In contrast, the average tax rate in 2010 for households in the top 1 percent of the before-tax income distribution was above its low point, reached in the early 1980s. The average tax rate for those households fell in the early 1980s and then rose following enactment of the Tax Reform Act of 1986. The average tax rate for that group then fell somewhat again in the latter half of the 1980s before climbing in the 1990s. That climb reflected changes in law that raised tax rates for that group as well as rapid increases in their income, which caused their average tax rate to rise as more income was taxed in higher tax brackets. Tax rates for households in the top percentile declined after 2000. The decline was especially rapid in 2003, when a reduction in the tax rate for the top tax bracket enacted in 2001 took effect and further changes in law reduced tax rates on dividends and realized capital gains. The tax rate fell again in 2007, mostly due to declines in corporate income taxes, and then rose somewhat from 2007 to 2009, as sharp declines in capital gains income caused a larger portion of the income of that group to be subject to the ordinary income tax rates. Their tax rate continued to rise in 2010 because of increased corporate income taxes, muted somewhat by declining individual income tax rates.

Progressivity of Federal Taxes

Because tax rates were lower for all income groups in 2007 than in 1979, it is not immediately apparent from examining tax rates alone whether combined federal taxes became more or less progressive over that period. To measure the level and change over time in the progressivity of taxes, researchers have developed various approaches to summarizing the distribution of taxes into a single number. One such measure, often called the Reynolds-Smolensky index, is simply the difference between the Gini for before-tax income and after-tax income. As seen earlier (figure 7.5), that measure was very stable over the thirty-two years studied. Federal taxes reduced the Gini coefficient by about 0.04 points at the beginning of that period. The redistributive effect of the tax system fell throughout the early 1980s, reaching a nadir of 0.023 points in 1986, then rose back to around 0.04 in the mid-1990s. From then on, it has varied within a very narrow range.

Another measure, the Kakwani index, is the difference between the tax concentration index, ranking households by their before-tax income, and the Gini index for before-tax income (Kakwani 1976). That index is effectively based on a comparison of shares of taxes paid with the share of income earned, and defines progressivity as the degree to which the former are more concentrated. Positive values indicate a progressive tax (shares of taxes are more skewed than shares of income) and a negative value indicates a regressive tax. An important property of that index is that it is unaffected by the size of the tax system. The Kakwani index is mathematically related to the Reynolds-Smolensky index. Specifically, the Reynolds-Smolensky index is equal to the Kakwani index multiplied by the average tax rate, plus a (usually small) term for reranking of households (Creedy 1999). The two indexes reflect different concepts of progressivity, and can move in different directions.

The Kakwani index for the tax system as a whole has increased somewhat over the period studied here (see figure 7.10). While pretax income has grown more skewed, the skewness of tax payments has increased even more. After an initial period of decline, that progressivity measure reached its 1979 level by 1994, and has continued to increase since then. The measure jumped notably in 2001 and 2008, in large part because of legislative action.

At the same time, the tax system grew smaller over the three decades studied here, as indicated by the average tax rate. That effect approximately netted out the increased concentration of tax payments, and produced a tax system that reduces inequality by about the same amount—0.04 Gini points—at the beginning and the end of the period.

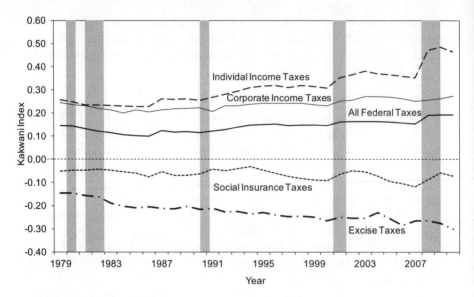

Fig. 7.10   Progressivity index by tax source, 1979–2010

Progressivity of Federal Taxes by Source

Another useful property of the Kakwani index is that it can be decomposed by tax source. The index for the entire tax system is equal to the average of the indexes for each source, weighted by the size of each tax source.

By that measure of tax concentration, individual income taxes are the most progressive source. Average federal income tax rates in 2010 ranged from −5.6 percent for households in the lowest income quintile to 18.8 percent for the 1 percent of the population with the highest income. The lowest income quintile has a negative average tax rate because, as a group, households in that quintile qualify for more in refundable tax credits than they owe in income taxes (before the credits are applied).

Those taxes became notably more progressive over the past twenty-nine years, particularly from 1990 through 1995 and again between 2000 and 2003 and finally post-2007. Tax law changes account for much of those periods of growth. The early 1990s saw increases in tax rates for higher income taxpayers, as well as large expansions of the earned income tax credit, which reduced taxes at the bottom of the income distribution. The first tax reductions enacted in the early twenty-first century also reduced taxes by more (relative to income) for lower income taxpayers. Finally, the changes enacted in ARRA provided bigger tax reductions relative to income in the lower portions of the income distribution.

Corporate income taxes are progressive, and have become more so. Those taxes are allocated in proportion to income from capital (75 percent) and labor (25 percent). Any change in the measured progressivity of those taxes simply indicates shifts in the underlying income distribution used to allocate the taxes, not structural features of the taxes themselves.

The Kakwani index for payroll is negative, indicating that those taxes are regressive.[13] Average rates for payroll taxes are fairly flat across most of the income distribution but are lower at the top in part because more of the earnings for those households are above the maximum income subject to Social Security taxes and in part because earnings are a smaller share of their income. Payroll taxes have become more regressive largely because labor income (the base of the tax) for households at the bottom grew more rapidly than their other sources of income over the period, pushing up their payroll taxes. Legislated increases to the maximum taxable amount for hospital insurance payroll taxes in the early 1990s offset some of that decline.

Excise taxes are also regressive. Lower-income households tend to spend a large share of their income on such goods as gasoline, alcohol, and tobacco, which are subject to federal excise taxes. Excise taxes have grown more regressive over time. As incomes have increased among the highest-income taxpayers, their spending on excise-taxed goods has fallen as a share of income.

Taken together, the tax system as a whole became somewhat more progressive. While the progressivity of the individual income tax increased, that tax source also became less important. Payroll taxes, a slightly regressive tax source, grew in importance.

7.6 Conclusions

The distribution of after-tax income has grown more unequal over the thirty-two years covered in this analysis. Virtually all of that increase occurred because of a growing inequality in market income. The shift in market income, in turn, was primarily due to increases in inequality of various income sources, especially labor income, rather than a changing mix of income sources. Outside of the recent recession, the tax and transfer system did little to offset the growing inequality, reducing the income inequality by roughly constant amounts over most of the period. The transfer system became larger, but less targeted to the bottom of the income distribution. The tax system became smaller, but more concentrated at the top of the income distribution.

The transfer system did become more redistributive in the 2008 to 2010 period, but much of that effect reflects temporary growth in transfer programs, and we do not expect that to persist once the economy recovers. The

---

13. Although Social Security payroll taxes are not progressive, the program as a whole is generally thought to be progressive because the ratio of the lifetime benefits received from Social Security to the lifetime payroll taxes paid for the program is higher for people with lower lifetime earnings than for people with higher earnings.

tax system also became more progressive in those years as average tax rates for lower-income households fell as the result of new refundable tax credits enacted during the recession and average tax rates for the high-income groups rose as the share of their income from dividends and capital gains, which are taxed at lower rates that other income, declined during the recession. We expect that some of those changes also will be temporary as a significant portion of the new refundable credits expired after 2010, and the share of income from dividends and capital gains for high-income households is likely to return to more normal levels.

References

Aguiar, M. A., and M. Bils. 2011. "Has Consumption Inequality Mirrored Income Inequality?" NBER Working Paper no. 16807, Cambridge, MA.

Armour, Philip, Richard V. Burkhauser, and Jeff Larrimore. 2013. "Levels and Trends in United States Income and Its Distribution: A Crosswalk from Market Income towards a Comprehensive Haig-Simons Income Apporach." NBER Working Paper No. 19110, Cambridge, MA, June.

Atkinson, A. B., T. Piketty, and E. Saez. 2011. "Top Incomes in the Long Run of History." *Journal of Economic Literature* 49 (1) 3–71.

Attanasio, O., E. Hurst, and L. Pistaferri. 2012. "The Evolution of Income, Consumption, and Leisure Inequality in the US, 1980–2010." NBER Working Paper no. 17982, Cambridge, MA.

Burkhauser, R. V., S. Feng, S. P. Jenkins, and J. Larrimore. 2008. "Estimating Trends in US Income Inequality Using the Current Population Survey: The Importance of Controlling for Censoring." NBER Working Paper no. 14247, Cambridge, MA.

Canberra Group. 2011. *Handbook on Household Income Statistics*, 2nd ed. United Nations Economic Commission for Europe. http://www.unece.org/index.php ?id=28894.

Chamberlain, A., and G. Prante. 2007. "Who Pays Taxes and Who Receives Government Spending? An Analysis of Federal, State, and Local Tax and Spending Distributions, 1991–2004." Working Paper 1, Tax Foundation, Washington, DC.

Cohen, M. L. 1991. "Statistical Matching and Microsimulation models." In *Improving Information for Social Policy Decisions: The Use of Microsimulation Modeling*, vol. II: Technical Papers, edited by Citro and Hanushek. Washington, DC: National Academy Press.

Congressional Budget Office (CBO). 2005. "Effective Tax Rates: Comparing Annual and Multiyear Measures." Report. Washington, DC: CBO. http://www.cbo.gov /publication/16212.

———. 2011. "Trends in the Distribution of Household Income Between 1979 and 2007." Report. Washington, DC: CBO. http://www.cbo.gov/publication/42729.

———. 2012. "The Distribution of Household Income and Federal Taxes, 2008 and 2009." Report. Washington, DC: CBO. http://www.cbo.gov/publication/43373.

Creedy, J. 1999. "Taxation Redistribution and Progressivity: An Introduction." *Australian Economic Review* 32 (4): 410–22.

D'Orazio, M., M. Di Zio, and M. Scanu. 2006. *Statistical Matching: Theory and Practice*. Hoboken, NJ: Wiley Press.

DeNavas-Walt, C., B. D. Proctor, and J. C. Smith. 2010. "Income, Poverty, and Health Insurance Coverage in the United States: 2009, Current Population Reports, Series P60-238." Washington, DC: US Bureau of the Census.

Fei, J. C. H., G. Ranis, and S. Kuo. 1978. "Growth and the Family Distribution of Income by Factor Components." *Quarterly Journal of Economics* 92 (1): 17–53.

Gordon, R. J., and I. Dew-Becker. 2007. "Selected Issues in the Rise of Income Inequality." *Brookings Papers on Economic Activity* 2:169–90.

Institute on Taxation and Economic Policy (ITEP). 2009. "Who Pays? A Distributional Analysis of the Tax Systems in All 50 States." http://www.itep.org/whopays/.

Internal Revenue Service. 2012. "Statistics of Income—2010 Individual Income Tax Returns Publication 1304 and Earlier Years." http://www.irs.gov/uac/SOI-Tax -Stats-Individual-Income-Tax-Returns-Publication-1304-(Complete-Report).

Jones, A. F., Jr., and D. H. Weinberg. 2000. "The Changing Shape of the Nation's Income Distribution, 1974–1998." Current Population Reports, Series P60-204. US Bureau of the Census. http://www.census.gov/main/www/cprs.html.

Kakwani, N. 1976. "Measurement of Tax Progressivity, An International Comparison." *Economic Journal* 87 (345): 71–80.

Kopczuk, W., E. Saez, and J. Song. 2010. "Earnings Inequality and Mobility in the United States: Evidence from Social Security Data Since 1937." *Quarterly Journal of Economics* 125 (1): 91–128.

Krueger, Dirk, and Fabrizio Perri. 2006. "Does Income Inequality Lead to Consumption Inequality? Evidence and Theory." *Review of Economic Studies* 73 (1): 163–93.

Lemieux, T. 2010. "What Do We Really Know About Changes in Wage Inequality?" In *Labor in the New Economy*, Studies in Income and Wealth, vol. 71, edited by Katharine G. Abraham, James R. Spletzer, and Michael J. Harper. Chicago: University of Chicago Press.

Lerman, R. I., and S. Yitzhaki. 1985. "Income Inequality Effect by Income Source: A New Approach and Applications to the United States." *Review of Economics and Statistics* 67:151–6.

OECD. 2008. "Growing Unequal? Income Distribution and Poverty in OECD Countries." Paris: Organisation for Economic Co-operation and Development.

Pechman, J. A. 1985. *Who Paid the Taxes: 1966–85?* Washington, DC: Brookings Institution.

Phares, D. 1980. *Who Pays State and Local Taxes?* Cambridge, MA: Oelgeschlager, Gunn, and Hain.

Piketty, T., and E. Saez. 2003. "Income Inequality in the United States, 1913–1998." *Quarterly Journal of Economics* 118 (1): 1–39.

Shorrocks, A. F. 1982. "Inequality Decomposition by Factor Components." *Econometrica* 50 (1): 193–211.

Slesnick, D. T. 2001. *Consumption and Social Welfare: Living Standards and Their Distribution in the United States*. Cambridge: Cambridge University Press.

Smeeding, T. M., and J. P. Thompson. 2010. "Recent Trends in the Distribution of Income: Labor, Wealth and More Complete Measures of Well Being." Working Paper, University of Massachusetts, June.

Wheaton, L. 2007. "Underreporting of Means-Tested Transfer Programs in the CPS and SIPP." 2007 Proceedings of the American Statistical Association, Social Statistics Section, Alexandria, Virginia. American Statistical Association. pp. 3622–9.

8

Accounting for the Distribution of Income in the US National Accounts

Dennis Fixler and David S. Johnson

> The welfare of a nation can, therefore, scarcely be inferred from a measurement of national income.
> —Simon Kuznets (1934, 7)

> Measured GDP growth is not the only contributor to the quality of life that Americans seek to enjoy.
> —"Economic Report of the President" (2012)

Frequent headlines present rising per capita gross domestic product (GDP) and frequent newspaper articles present people who have not shared equally in this growth (see Gertner 2010; Reinhardt 2011). This disconnect between aggregate output or income growth and its distribution to individuals has motivated a movement to examine measures of individual well-being that go beyond GDP per capita. For example, the United Nations voted (in resolution 65/309) to create a Gross National Happiness index[1] because "the gross domestic product does not adequately reflect the happiness and well-being of people." Relatedly, the Organisation for Economic Co-operation and Development (OECD) recently released a guide on the measurement of subjective well-being.

Seventy years ago Kuznets (1934), in his original report on the national accounts, suggested that growth in GDP was not sufficient to evaluate social welfare. This view is echoed in the recent "Economic Report of the Presi-

Dennis Fixler is chief statistician of the Bureau of Economic Analysis. David S. Johnson is chief economist of the BEA.

Research conducted while David S. Johnson was a visiting scholar at the Russell Sage Foundation and as staff at the US Census Bureau. The authors would like to thank Ed Wolff, Chris Carroll, Steve Landefeld, and participants in the NBER Conference on Research in Income and Wealth "Measuring Economic Stability and Progress" conference. The views expressed in this chapter, including those related to statistical, methodological, technical, or operational issues, are solely those of the authors and do not necessarily reflect the official positions or policies of the Census Bureau or the Bureau of Economic Analysis, or the views of other staff members. The authors accept responsibility for all errors. This chapter is released to inform interested parties of ongoing research and to encourage discussion of work in progress. For acknowledgments, sources of research support, and disclosure of the authors' material financial relationships, if any, please see http://www.nber.org/chapters/c12828.ack.

1. See http://www.grossnationalhappiness.com for a description of the gross national happiness index developed by the Center for Bhutan studies.

dent" and is the theme of the "Report by the Commission on the Measurement of Economic Performance and Social Progress" (or the Stiglitz, Sen, and Fitoussi [2009] report). The Stiglitz, Sen, and Fitoussi report, largely motivated by the financial crisis that started in 2007 and the consequent Great Recession, suggests that the "time is ripe for our measurement system to shift emphasis from measuring economic production to measuring people's well-being" (12).

Recent data (from 1980 to 2010) show that real per capita GDP increased 65 percent in the past thirty years, while median household income rose only 11 percent. In the past decade (between 1999 and 2010), real mean household income (from the Census Bureau) fell 5.7 percent, while real per capita personal income (from the Bureau of Economic Analysis [BEA]) increased 11.1 percent (see figure 8.1). And the recent Congressional Budget Office (CBO 2012) report shows that using a comprehensive income measure, average income decreased 0.5 percent between 1999 and 2009. Reconciling these divergent trends is one goal of this chapter.

Since its inception, the Conference on Research in Income and Wealth (CRIW) of the National Bureau of Economic Research (NBER) has been a leader in the evaluation of the distribution of income and its relationship to the national accounts.[2] This chapter follows in that tradition and contributes to it by bringing together the relevant literature on the distribution of national accounts and the measurement issues associated with household income compared to national income, creating alternative measures of the median and distribution of personal income and suggesting simple methods that could be reproduced regularly. This chapter provides distributional measures of personal income, which can then inform research to determine whether the growth rate of gross domestic income (GDI) depends on changes in the income distribution.

A primary contribution of the chapter is the presentation of simple methods that adjusts the household survey (Current Population Survey [CPS]) to more closely match the national accounts measure of personal income. Using the underlying distribution in the CPS along with these adjustments yields a higher mean and median adjusted household income than the reported household income, and yields a larger increase in inequality. Adjusting the distribution by the income distribution available from tax records increases inequality further, but does not change the trend. Finally, creating a more complete measure of personal income by imputing the value of in-kind health-care benefits yields a decrease in inequality.

We include two applications that discuss how income inequality might matter in determining social welfare and gauging the efficacy of fiscal policy. Sen's (1973) original social welfare function requires estimates of both income growth and inequality; we use our estimates to examine Sen-type

---

2. In fact, the first NBER volume (Mitchell et al. 1921) was devoted to income distribution.

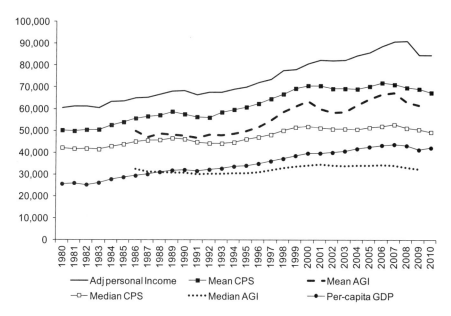

Fig. 8.1   Mean and median real household (or taxpayer) income from various measures (in 2010$ using the PCE deflator)

social welfare functions. We also examine how income inequality bears on the measurement of the average propensity to consume and by implication the marginal propensity to consume. These measures are important to forecasting the impacts of fiscal policy on GDP. In an appendix we provide a simple model that provides an illustration of the impacts. The next section of this chapter presents alternative measures of income, previous research, and the implications of measurement error in the household data. The second section discusses the data and the results. The third and fourth sections provide applications of our results to calculating a social welfare function and examining the distribution of income and consumption, and the final section concludes this chapter.

8.1   Measuring Income

The BEA is responsible for producing the aggregate statistics on income growth, while the Census Bureau releases the distributional measures along with the growth in median household income. Each agency, however, uses a different measure of income. Income distribution and aggregate growth were not always separate estimates (see Goldsmith 1955, 1958 and 1960); the Office of Business Economics (the predecessor to the BEA) produced annual estimates of the income distribution from 1950 to 1962. The BEA's national accounts measures are often interpreted at the microeconomic level as information on the behavior of representative consumers; however, most of the economic well-being literature requires (and measures of inequality require) more information about households across the income distribution. The question is whether the changes in the aggregate levels of economic activity are adequate indicators of the changes in individual well-being.

Since the development of national accounts, income distribution has been important in examining growth. Kuznets (1955, 27), in his famous paper on inequality and growth, stated: "The distribution of national product among the various groups is a subject of acute interest to many and is discussed at length in any half-articulate society." The Canberra report, the report of an expert group recommending an income measure to use in income distribution estimates, stated that the original "intention of the SNA (System of National Accounts) was to include a disaggregation of household income by socioeconomic group as a standard part of national accounts output" (Canberra Group 2011, 5).

This relationship between macroeconomic growth and income inequality has been the focus of many recent studies (see OECD 2011; Boushey and Hersh 2012). The concern is whether a rising tide is lifting all boats equally. While most studies agree that "the rich have gotten richer," the issue is whether those on the lower levels of the distribution have also experienced an improvement in their economic well-being. The question is, If growth and inequality have both increased, how has overall economic well-being changed?[3]

There is considerable disagreement regarding the relationship between inequality and growth. As suggested in a recent OECD report (OECD 2012), there is no agreement in the economics literature concerning the relationship between inequality and growth and there is no conclusive empirical evidence. The Stiglitz, Sen, and Fitoussi (2009, 8) report states: "If inequality increases enough relative to the increase in average per capita GDP, most people can be worse off even though average income is increasing." However, Lucas (2004, 13) disagrees stating: "But of the vast increase in the well-being of hundreds of millions of people that has occurred in the 200-year course of the industrial revolution to date, virtually none of it can be attributed to the direct redistribution of resources from rich to poor." Blinder (1975) provides conditions under which a redistribution would lead to increased aggregate consumption. His empirical results suggest, however, that a rise in income inequality, holding disposable income constant, would either have no effect on consumption or would actually increase it.

In order to fully evaluate the distribution and growth in income, however, we need comparable measures of income. As discussed in CRIW (1943),

---

3. In this chapter we focus on income, but many look to the distribution of consumption as the measure of well-being. See, for example, Meyer and Sullivan (2011) and Fisher, Johnson, and Smeeding (forthcoming).

there are many choices that need to be made in determining the appropriate components of income to include in a measure of income distribution. We examine the distribution and movement of household income, as measured by personal income, and how it influences the movements of gross domestic income (GDI), and hence GDP. As proposed by the BEA (BEA 2012, 47), we undertake "a decomposition of personal income that presents median as well as mean income and other measures of the distribution of income across households." With the distributional aspects of personal income, one can examine how various changes in policy may impact households at various points in the distribution. Just as the BEA creates a decomposition of personal income across states and geography, this chapter provides a decomposition across the income distribution.[4]

The most inclusive concept of income and consumption derives from the suggestions of Haig and Simons. Haig (1921, 27) stated that income was "the money value of the net accretion to one's economic power between two points of time" and Simons (1938, 50) defined personal income as "the algebraic sum of (1) the market value of rights exercised in consumption and (2) the change in the value of the store of property rights between the beginning and end of the period in question."

Economists have used the equation that income (Y) equals consumption (C) plus the change in net worth (ΔW) as the working definition of Haig-Simons income ($Y = C + \Delta W$). No household survey, however, has the necessary variables to create a full measure of Haig-Simons income. In an attempt to relate all three components, the Canberra Group *Handbook on Household Income Statistics* (2011, 10) states: "Household income receipts are available for current consumption and do not reduce the net worth of the household through a reduction of its cash, the disposal of its other financial or non-financial assets or an increase in its liabilities." Similarly, the Systems of National Accounts (SNA 2009, 160) defines household income as "the maximum amount that a household or other unit can afford to spend on consumption goods or services during the accounting period without having to finance its expenditures by reducing its cash, by disposing of other financial or non-financial assets or by increasing its liabilities." To create international standards on this Haig-Simons equation, the OECD has organized two expert groups on (a) microstatistics on household income, consumption, and wealth; and (b) disparities in the national accounts.[5]

The focus of this chapter is to evaluate the level, trend, and distribution of personal income (as measured by the BEA). Personal income, which consists mainly of compensation, transfer payments received, and investment income, has averaged about 85 percent of GDI over the period 1980

4. In fact, one could use the geographic decomposition to estimate a national distribution, which is the focus of future research.
5. Armour, Burkhauser, and Larrimore (2013) examine the distribution of a Haig-Simons income measure.

to 2010. Assuming that the distribution of the extra components in GDI (beyond those in personal income) are similarly distributed, one can use the distribution of personal income to examine how various changes in policy may affect households at various points in the distribution of GDI.[6]

There are a multitude of income measures used by researchers and the government. Table 8.1 compares personal income, census money income, the CBO income measure, the adjusted gross income (AGI), and the Survey of Consumer Finances (SCF) income measure to a Haig-Simons measure and the international measure recommended by the Canberra Group (Canberra 2011).[7] As table 8.1 shows, there are many components of income that are included in the measures. The first column shows those included in a Haig-Simons definition of income. Only three components are included in all income measures—employment income, investment income, and cash transfers from the government.

Looking at table 8.1, the main differences in the income definitions are the treatment of imputed income, retirement income, capital gains (realized and unrealized), unrealized interest on property income, and the inclusion of government and in-kind transfers. Even the Canberra definition, which is viewed as the standard in international comparisons, is different than the BEA definition, which follows the SNA. The values in table 8.2 provide an indication of some of the relative importance of the differences between the income measures.

Since the Census Bureau has issued its first reports on income, the bureau has distinguished between the BEA's personal income measures and the CPS household income measures.[8] Personal income is the income received by persons from participation in production, from government and business transfers, and from holding interest-bearing securities and corporate stocks. Personal income also includes income received by nonprofit institutions serving households, by private noninsured welfare funds, and by private trust funds. The CPS measure of money income, produced by the Census Bureau, is defined as the total pretax money income received by people on a regular basis, excluding certain lump-sum payments and excluding capital gains.

One of the main differences among the various definitions is the treatment of retirement income. Consider an elderly person with both a savings

---

6. Figure 8.2 shows that the ratio between personal income and GDI has remained fairly constant between 1999 and 2010.

7. For the CBO measure see Harris and Sammartino (chap. 7, this volume) and for the SCF measure see Henriques and Hsu (chapter 9, this volume).

8. The first P60 reports (Census 1948, 11) stated: "The purpose of the census data is to show the distribution of families and persons by income levels. They do not show estimates of aggregate income. The Office of Business Economics estimates, on the other hand, provide information on aggregate income received by the population. If an estimate of aggregate income were derived from Census Bureau data, it would be smaller than that shown in the personal income series ."

Table 8.1   Comparison of income concepts

SOURCE	Haig/Simons	Census	PI/NIPA (BEA)	CBO	SOI (AGI)	Canberra	SCF
Employment income	Yes	Yes	Yes	Yes	Yes	Yes	Yes
Employer contribution to Soc. Sec.[a]	Yes	No	Yes	Yes	No	Yes	No
Employer-provided benefits[a]	Yes	No	Yes	Yes	No	Yes	Yes
Investment income	Yes	Yes	Yes	Yes	Yes	Yes	Yes
Imputed investment income	Yes	No	Yes	No	No	No	No
Government cash transfers	Yes	Yes	Yes	Yes	Yes (taxable)	Yes	Yes
Employee contribution to Soc. Sec.	Yes	Yes	No (subtract)	Yes	Yes	Yes	No
Retirement income	Yes	Yes	No (only int.)	Yes	Yes	Yes	Yes
Cash assistance from others	Yes	Yes	No	Yes	No	Yes	Yes
Realized capital gains	Yes	No	No	Yes	Yes	No	Yes
Lump sum (IRA disbursements)[a]	Yes	No	No	Yes	Taxable	Yes	Yes
In-kind government transfers[a]	Yes	No	Yes	Yes	No	No[b]	Yes (housing only)
Other in-kind transfers[a]	Yes	No	No	No	No	No[b]	No
Home production	Yes	No	No	No	No	In concept	No
Imputed rent[a]	Yes	No	Yes	No	No	Yes	No
Unrealized capital gains	Yes	No	No	No	No	No	Yes (stock only)
Savings withdrawals	Yes[c]	No	No	No	No	No	No

[a]Estimates are imputed in the CPS.

[b]Included in the final measure of disposable income.

[c]Included in the Haig-Simons equation; depletions in savings will simply increase consumption.

Table 8.2   Katz (2012) categories included in adjusted personal income

	Adjustment to personal income, selected years		
	1999	2007	2010
Personal income	10,030	12,546	12,374
Employer health benefits	(450)	(637)	(620)
Employer pensions benefits	(267)	(396)	(470)
Imputed interest	(433)	(480)	(457)
Imputed rent for home owners	(187)	(68)	(236)
Government transfers in-kind	(676)	(9,919)	(1,132)
Adjustment for social security contributions	428	526	514
Adjustment for pension treatment	(148)	123	257
Other adjustments	(100)	(92)	(167)
Total adjustments	(1,731)	(1,943)	(2,311)
Adjusted personal income	8,299	10,603	10,062
Census money income	7,387	8,316	8,015

account and a defined contribution retirement account. The interest on these accounts will be counted as income in all measures. Planned pension disbursements will also be included in all measures except personal income. If the person makes an irregular/lump-sum withdrawal from his retirement accounts, this will be recorded as income only in the Haig-Simons, CBO, and Canberra measures. Finally, if the retiree withdraws money from his or her savings account, this will only be included in Haig-Simons income because these savings withdrawals are actually decreases in net worth that will be spent. However, with other definitions of income, one would observe consumption increases with no change in income.

Most studies of income and its distribution include the money income, but do not examine changes in assets, and only a few examine the impact of capital gains (e.g., CBO 2011, 2012; Piketty and Saez 2003; Smeeding and Thompson 2011; Wolff et al. 2012; Armour, Burkhauser, and Larrimore 2013). Two recent papers present alternative measures of a more comprehensive income. Wolff et al. (2012) construct the Levy Institute Measure of Economic Well-Being (LIMEW) as the sum of census money income, income from wealth, net government expenditures (both cash and noncash transfers and public consumption, net of taxes), and household production. The "more complete income" (MCI) concept in Smeeding and Thompson (2011) is based on Haig-Simons income and estimated using Survey of Consumer Finance data. They define MCI as earnings and net transfers and include that portion of capital income received as capital gains and royalties. They subtract reported interest, rent, and dividends and include an imputed return to all forms of net worth in order to capture the concept of the change in net worth. This combines the two approaches used by the BEA and CBO regarding capital income, including both capital gains and imputed interest. Using MCI, Smeeding and Thompson (2011) find a larger concentration of income at the top of the distribution. Wolff et al. (2012) also show a larger increase in the mean and median using more comprehensive measures of income (see also Armour et al. 2013).

8.1.1 Adjustments for "Real" and Equivalent Income

Once a measure of income is determined, there are two key measurement choices that must be made in evaluating the trends and distribution in income. These choices are crucial to making comparisons over time with changing cost of living and changing demographics. The cost-of-living adjustments are made by converting dollars into constant terms using a price index, while the demographic changes are made by adjusting by household size with an equivalence scale that adjusts for the economies of scale in a household.

Slesnick (2001), Meyer and Sullivan (2011), and Broda and Weinstein (2009) show the important impact that alternative price indexes have on the increase in the mean and median, and on the inequality measures. The Census Bureau uses the CPI-U-RS to deflate household income and produce a series of mean and median income in constant dollars, and the BEA uses the personal consumption expenditure (PCE) deflator. For example, real median household income, using the CPI-U-RS, increased 10.8 percent between 1980 and 2010. However, because the PCE deflator increases less than the CPI-U-RS, if the PCE deflator is used to convert income into constant dollars, the respective increase in median household income would be 17.3 percent. Meyer and Sullivan (2011) and Boskin et al. (1996) suggest that the CPI-U (and hence, CPI-U-RS) is biased upward by 0.8 to 1.2 percentage points per year. Meyer and Sullivan (2011) use an alternative price index that adjusts the CPI-U-RS downward by 0.8 percentage points per year. Using this alternative index to create real median income yields a 40 percent increase between 1980 and 2010. Because our focus is on producing a national accounts-based income distribution, we use the PCE to convert all income into constant 2010 dollars.[9]

The second adjustment that is required is to account for the changes in household size over time and the respective economies of scale that may occur within households. Using a simple per capita measure (as in per capita personal income) does not deal with the economies of scale in the household, and the household measure produced by the Census Bureau simply assumes perfect economies of scale in the household. Since household size has fallen over the past thirty years, one should use a measure of household

9. The new CBO report on household income, CBO (2012), changed to using the PCE deflator to adjust for inflation instead of the CPI-U-RS.

income adjusted for the household size. In this chapter, we use an equivalized measure of income using the square root of household size as the equivalence scale (see Fisher, Johnson, and Smeeding, forthcoming; Buhmann et al. 1988). Using this equivalized income shows an increase in the real median income of 17.1 percent (compared to 10.8 percent without an adjustment). Using both the equivalence-adjusted median and the PCE deflator yields a 23.9 percent increase between 1980 and 2010.

8.1.2   Reconciling Household and Aggregate Income

During the first years of the CRIW, a conference was organized and a volume produced on the size distribution of income (CRIW 1943). That volume began with a chapter by Kuznets entitled "The Why and How of Distributions of Income by Size." The volume also includes a chapter that presents one of the first uses of multiple data sources to provide an estimate of the distribution of income for the United States.

The CRIW has been involved in evaluating income distribution and its impact on the national accounts for its entire history. A few volumes have been devoted to distributional issues and this new conference will produce a volume with continued research on this topic.[10] In the 1975 volume, Budd and Radner (1975) present a method to use both CPS and IRS data to construct a distributional measure for the national accounts. By adjusting income by tax records, they find higher mean income and more families with high income than in the survey data. However, the income distribution shifts in such a manner as to yield a lower inequality measure than that found in the survey data.[11]

In the spirit of these first volumes, from 1950 to 1962, the Office of Business Economics produced annual measures of the income distribution in the United States. Goldsmith (1955) creates a distribution measure and continues with regular releases in the Survey of Current Business (see also Goldsmith 1960). These estimates also show higher mean incomes than those in the CPS, but the inequality measures, both levels and trends, are similar to those in the CPS data.

There are various methods to obtain a distribution of aggregate data. In all cases, one needs both the aggregate data and a household survey. Fesseau, Bellamy, and Raynaud (2009) and Accardo et al. (2009) use distribution of survey data to create a distribution for national account data in France. This relies on the assumption that the distribution in the household survey is the same as in the national accounts. Landefeld et al. (2010) create a median

10. Juster edited the 1975 CRIW volume The Distribution of Economic Well-Being," and in 1980, Smith edited *Modeling the Distribution and Intergenerational Transmission of Wealth*, and David and Smeeding edited H*orizontal Equity, Uncertainty, and Economic Well-Being* in 1985.
11. For example, using their tables shows that the adjusted Gini is lower than the Gini from the CPS. The adjustment basically shifts the entire distribution to the right.

discretionary income measure using the distribution in the IRS Statistics of Income (SOI) tables. Coli and Tartamella (2010) and McColl et al. (2010) both attempt to reconcile survey and national accounts data for Italy and Australia. Other methods are to create a social accounting matrix (as in Mussard and Savard 2010) or to use a reweighting procedure to adjust the survey estimates of inequality. The method presented in this chapter uses a household survey and benchmarks it to the aggregate totals.

8.1.3   Underreporting in Household Surveys

Katz (2012) shows that the changes in census household income are similar to a comparable measure of personal income between 1980 and 1999, but diverge in recent years. He suspects that much of the difference occurs because of property (or capital) income (interest, dividends, etc.). One possible reason for the difference in both the distribution and the growth rates can be the underreporting of income in the CPS. Meyer, Mok, and Sullivan (2008) show that for all surveys examined (including the CPS) there is evidence of income under-reporting, which has tended to increase over time.

Recently, there have been papers that attempted to reconcile differences between the BEA and census measures of household income. Weinberg (2006) and Ruser, Pilot, and Nelson (2004) examine the quality of CPS data. Ruser, Pilot, and Nelson (2004), a joint effort between the BEA and Census Bureau, demonstrates that the CPS underestimates the income in the national accounts data for many components. They construct a reconciliation between BEA personal income and census household income, and show that most of the discrepancy is due to definitional differences. However, the remaining differences can be due to the different sources, which could suggest that the administrative tax data may better represent the distributional aspects of GDI.

The presence of underreporting (measured as the difference between the survey data and the aggregate data) will not only affect the means and growth rates of income, but will also impact the change in inequality. As shown in Bound, Brown, and Mathiowitz (2001) and Gottschalk and Huynh (2010), if measurement error is classical, independent of income (or consumption), then an increase in error will increase inequality (and measured inequality could be biased upward). Gottschalk and Huynh (2010), however, extend this result to nonclassical measurement error, which could be mean reverting. In this case, it is not clear whether measurement error (or an increase in error) increases inequality. Hence, increased measurement error can imply an increase or a decrease in inequality of the reported resource measure. If the measurement error is correlated with income, such that higher income households are increasingly likely to underreport their income, then mean reversion in measurement error increases. As a result, measured inequality (and increases in inequality) could be biased downward.

8.2   Data and Results

To construct measures of income and its distribution, we use the CPS Annual Social and Economic Supplement (ASEC). The CPS/ASEC includes about 100,000 households who are interviewed from February to April of each year and asked about the previous year's income. While some of the tables and figures depict income and inequality since 1980, we focus on the 1999 to 2010 period. During this period, the ratio of aggregate CPS money income to adjusted personal income (explained below) fell from 89 percent (in 1999) to 80 (see figure 8.2 and Katz [2012]).

There are important conceptual differences between the BEA's measure of real personal income and the Census Bureau's measure of real money income. Many components of personal income are not included in money income and a number of components of money income are not included in personal income (see Katz 2012). Conceptually, the BEA personal income measures the income of the entire household sector and nonprofit institutions serving households (NPISHs). In contrast, the money income concept at the Census Bureau measures the incomes of individual families and persons, which can be used to examine the distribution of income across all families and persons (excluding people in institutions).

To directly compare the income estimates in the CPS to those in the national accounts, we need to use comparable income measures. We follow Katz (2012) to construct an adjusted personal income measure (see table 8.2) that matches the money income measure from the CPS. As shown in

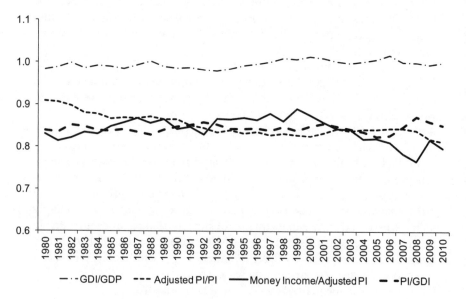

Fig. 8.2   The ratios of various measures of real aggregate income

table 8.2, most of the adjustments take various types of in-kind income out of personal income, including employer benefits, government in-kind transfers, imputed rent from owner-occupied housing, and imputed interest from life insurance reserves. In addition, pensions are measured by benefits paid rather than by employer contributions to pension funds, and the income earned on the plan assets (reserves) and employee contributions to social insurance are added back into personal income because they are included in money income, but not personal income. Adjustments are also made to take out the income of nonprofit institutions and to add in transfers between and among households.[12]

With these adjustments, the levels are more similar (as shown in table 8.2 and figure 8.2) and the trends from 1980 to 2010 show both series increasing at similar rates between 1980 and 1999, but diverging between 1999 and 2010, with the ratio falling from 89 percent to 80 percent. Table 8.2 shows that personal income increased 23.4 percent between 1999 and 2010, while adjusted income increased 21.2 percent because the adjustments increased 33.5 percent between 1999 and 2010, with one of the largest increases being the doubling of government transfers of health care.[13]

We assume that the household survey data are underreported because the aggregate estimates are less than those obtained in the national accounts data. A simple method to obtain a distribution of personal income from the national accounts is to use the income distribution in the CPS. In this case, the mean and median are simply ratio adjusted by the same amount (and hence, inequality remains unchanged).

Another simple method would be to use the median-adjusted gross income (AGI) in the SOI tables. Figure 8.1 shows the changes in the mean and median AGI from the SOI tables between 1999 and 2009 (the latest year available) and compares these to the CPS income measures. As shown, the median AGI falls 1.5 percent compared to a fall of 3.3 percent for CPS median income. In addition, similar to the CPS mean income, mean AGI falls by 2.9 percent and is much more volatile than personal income (mainly due to the inclusion of capital gains in AGI).

Landefeld et al. (2010) follows a different approach and uses the distributional tax tables to obtain a change in median AGI by finding the income category that contains the median of the number of returns and then computing the mean of the category. They also adjust the reported income from the SOI tables to include additional income sources that are included in personal income, but excluded from AGI. These adjustments are small and increase at a similar rate to the unadjusted income sources. Hence, we

12. Semega (2012) shows a similar comparison between the Canberra income and household income.
13. Table 9 in Katz (2012) provides details on the components of income in the BEA measure and the CPS. This table can also be compared to a similar method used by McCully (chapter 6, this volume).

Table 8.3   Shares for components on CPS money income, by total income

Income level	Wages (%)	Business income (%)	Property income (%)	Government transfers (%)	Retirement income (%)
Less than 50,000	57	5	3	29	6
50,000–200,000	84	4	4	4	4
200,000 or more	84	6	7	1	2
All	83	5	5	9	4

can compare this approach to the overall changes in the median AGI presented in figure 8.1. In contrast to the results in figure 8.1 that suggest a decrease of 0.2 percent between 2000 and 2007, Landefeld et al. (2010, 18) find, for 2000 to 2007, "a rough measure of real after-tax income for the median income taxpayer rose at a 1.2 percent annual rate," which implies an approximate 8 percent increase. In fact, if we were to use a comparable measure of taxpayer income, the methods used in Landefeld et al. (2010) suggest an increase of 8.2 percent between 2000 and 2007 (and the adjusted income increases 7.4 percent), which is much higher than that shown using the median AGI reported by SOI.[14]

In order to change the distribution in the CPS, different factors are needed for different households. Since the income composition varies at different points in the distribution, we could use alternative factors to ratio adjust the various sources of income. These adjustments could then change the overall distribution of income. Table 8.3 shows the income component shares by total income level in the CPS for 2010. This table shows that the share of property and interest income is higher for the highest income group.

We consider two adjustment methods. First, consider, household i, with income, $y_i = \sum_j \alpha_j y_{ji}$ (y_{ji} is the jth component of household i's income), where the adjustment factors, α_j, depend on the source, j, of income (e.g., wages or interest/dividends) and are given by the ratio of aggregate personal income to aggregate CPS income ($\alpha_j = Y_j/X_j$, where Y_j is the aggregate for source j in the personal income measure [in the NIPAs] and X_j is the aggregate for source j in the CPS). This procedure increases each household's income by source and the new adjusted household data is then used to obtain distribution measures.[15]

To illustrate, consider only one source of income, such as wages. Then the adjusted income for household i would be given by [NIPA wages/CPS wages] × CPS wages for household i, and similarly add additional sources of income. This procedure generates a NIPA-based adjusted income series for households in the CPS and thereby yields an NIPA-based income distribution.

14. Estimates calculated using underlying tables provided by the BEA.
15. The simple ratio-adjustment mentioned above is for $\alpha_j = \alpha$ for all sources.

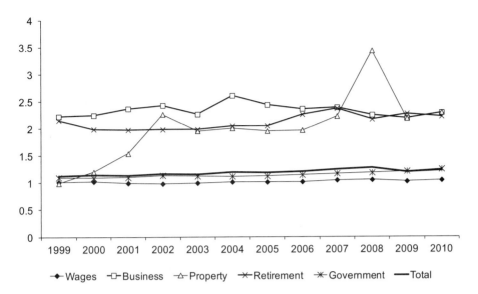

Fig. 8.3   Ratio of CPS aggregate income to NIPA income, adjustment factors $-\alpha_j$
(Katz 2012)

These NIPA adjustments are shown in figure 8.3. The adjustments for wages are fairly small, but the adjustments for property income (interest and dividends) are large and increase over time.[16] As shown in table 8.3, higher-income households have more property income, which also has a larger factor (see figure 8.3). Hence, these households obtain a larger increase in their adjusted income, which can increase inequality.

One limitation of the above approach is that every household receives the same adjustment for each source of income even though it is likely that different households have different levels of underreporting. In addition, research has shown that there is a large underreporting at the top of the distribution (see Sabelhaus et al., forthcoming). To assess these differences, we compare the distribution of income in the CPS to that in the SOI published tables.[17]

To illustrate the way we remove the limitation of a constant adjustment factor for each household source of income, we include another factor that adjusts for different income groups. Again, considering just wages, the adjusted income for household i, y_i becomes

16. Comparing the wage distribution (and levels) shows that the trend of wages in the CPS is similar to that in NIPA and SOI (see also Nichols, Smith, and Wheaton [2011]; Turek et al. [2012]; and Roemer [2000]).

17. The adjustments used in this chapter compare the average income by source for taxpayers ranked by their total AGI and compares these to the aggregate income by source for households in the CPS. Households and taxpayers are slightly different. Nichols, Smith, and Wheaton (2011) attempt to correct for the unit of analysis, and obtain similar ratios.

$$y_i = \frac{NIPAwages}{CPSwages} \times \frac{\frac{SOIwages}{CPSwages}\Big|_{incomegroupk}}{\sum_k \frac{SOIwages}{CPSwages}\Big|_{incomegroupk}} \times wages_{CPS,i},$$

where income group k follows from the level of CPS income for household i. In general, household i has income $y_i = \sum_{jk}\gamma_{jk}\alpha_j y_{jki}$, where the adjustment factors, α_j, depend on the source (as above), and $\gamma_{jk} = (Y_{jk}/X_{jk})/(Y_j/X_j)$, where Y_{jk} is the aggregate for source, j, for income group, k, in SOI tables and X_{jk} is the aggregate for source, j, for income group, k. As a result, the first adjustment factor, α_j, is augmented by the distributional information for the source-income combination from SOI data. Other sources of income would be added to the right-hand side of the above equation in a similar manner, yielding NIPA-based adjusted income series that derives from the CPS income data. From this series another distribution of income is obtained. As shown in figure 8.4, the ratio of income in the CPS to that in the SOI tables falls with income and is 1.3 for the highest income.

To adjust income by different factors for each source and income level in our second adjustment method, we use the aggregate income by source for various levels of total AGI in the SOI tables.[18] We allow the γ_{jk} to depend on various income levels (that is, the factors for each source can vary for different households across the income distribution). Since we want to benchmark to the aggregate personal income, the distribution factors are only used to redistribute income and are normalized so that the average factor is 1.

The results of these methods are shown in table 8.4. As expected, the NIPA adjustments yield a higher mean and median, and increase the changes over time. For example, in 2010, the mean NIPA-adjusted household income is 21.4 percent higher than the census money income, and the median is 17.5 percent higher. Although census median household income falls 3.6 percent between 1999 and 2010, the NIPA-adjusted household income increases 1.9 percent. The increase in the NIPA-adjusted mean income exceeds the increase in the NIPA-adjusted median by more than the corresponding increase with census money income, which suggests that inequality increases more under the NIPA-adjusted income.[19]

Using the SOI-adjusted data increases the volatility of the mean and median (as can be seen in figure 8.1), and hence, increases the volatility of the Gini coefficient shown in table 8.6. Although the distribution of property income is highly skewed in the SOI data, the large factors for high-income households are offset by similarly large factors for low-income households (see figure 8.4). This U-shaped pattern for wages and business income in

---

18. See "SOI Tax Stats—Individual Statistical Tables by Size of Adjusted Gross Income" at http://www.irs.gov/taxstats/indtaxstats/article/0,,id=96981,00.html.
19. With a log normal distribution, the ratio of mean to median income represents a measure of inequality.

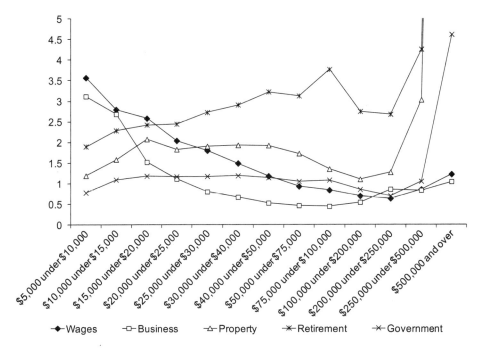

Fig. 8.4 SOI factors used to adjust CPS income (ratio of aggregate income by source for level of AGI), factors, $-\gamma_{jk}$

Table 8.4   Mean and median real household income using alternative adjustments (in 2010$)

	Mean money income	Median money income	Mean NIPA-adjusted income	Median NIPA-adjusted income	Mean SOI dist-adjusted income	Median SOI dist-adjusted income	Adjusted personal income per household
1999	69,110	50,945	77,773	56,674	78,237	66,006	80,474
2000	70,100	51,820	79,586	57,294	80,778	65,806	82,697
2001	70,341	50,986	79,726	56,539	81,511	63,644	83,442
2002	68,981	50,472	79,621	56,705	80,471	66,012	83,196
2003	69,287	50,609	79,529	56,718	81,273	66,010	83,139
2004	68,829	50,339	81,688	57,474	82,795	68,179	85,262
2005	70,042	51,043	82,748	57,507	83,230	65,987	86,262
2006	71,672	51920	85,801	59,190	86,410	68,074	88,734
2007	70,934	52,660	87,574	61,472	88,467	69,085	90,648
2008	69,458	50,995	88,071	60,664	90,319	67,831	90,445
2009	68,840	50,279	81,907	58,137	82,678	66,535	84,536
2010	67,516	49,109	81,946	57,739			84,769
Percent change (1999–2010)	–2.3%	–3.6%	5.4%	1.9%	5.7%[a]	0.8%[a]	5.3%

[a]From 1999 to 2009.

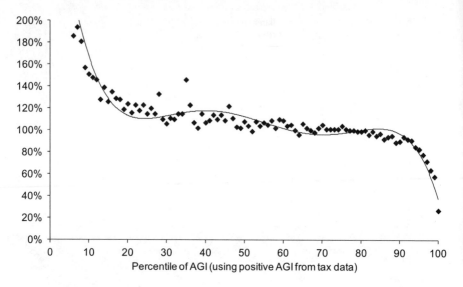

Fig. 8.5   Ratio of CPS AGI income to tax form 1040 AGI income, by AGI percentile, 2010

figure 8.4 is due partly to the use of households in the CPS and taxpayers in the SOI data, which may yield smaller AGI levels at the lower end of the distribution for the SOI taxpayers.[20] Since the SOI data are only used to redistribute income, and the NIPA adjustments are used to benchmark income, the SOI-adjusted mean increases at a rate similar to the NIPA-adjusted mean. However, because of the slight U-shaped pattern in the factors shown in figure 8.4, the median SOI-adjusted income increases only 0.8 percent between 1999 and 2009 (the latest year for which SOI data are available), compared to a 2.5 percent increase for the NIPA-adjusted median.[21]

A more accurate method for adjusting for underreporting in the CPS would be to use the actual tax records data matched to the CPS.[22] Using the 2010 IRS 1040 data linked to the CPS data, we can compare the income distributions. Figure 8.5 shows that the ratio of CPS to IRS income is fairly constant until the higher levels of income. Similar to Sabelhaus et al. (forthcoming), the largest differences are in the high income categories and using the tax data yields a larger Gini coefficient.[23]

20. Future work includes creating a more comparable measure of AGI using tax-filing units in the CPS.
21. Some of the differences between the Gini coefficients using the SOI adjusted income and the SOI tables is due to the differences between households and taxpayers.
22. Sabelhaus et al. (forthcoming) demonstrate that high-income households are missing from the Consumer Expenditure Survey, and suggest that the CPS similarly suffers.
23. The Gini coefficient in 2010 for the matched AGI tax income is .489 as compared to .449 for the AGI from the CPS. Further research includes obtaining data for 1999, and additional years to compare trends.

Table 8.5   **Mean and median real household income, adjusted to include noncash benefits (in 2010$)**

	Mean (NIPA-adjusted with health benefits)	Median (NIPA-adjusted with health benefits)	Mean (NIPA-adjusted with all imputations)	Median (NIPA-adjusted with all imputations)
1999	86,709	65,113	97,850	70,351
2000	88,892	66,550	100,177	71,706
2001	89,725	66,227	97,949	70,195
2002	90,078	66,926	95,757	69,955
2003	90,500	67,155	96,844	70,795
2004	93,066	68,435	98,882	71,690
2005	94,573	69,144	100,684	72,498
2006	97,824	71,264	103,828	74,531
2007	99,846	73,406	105,920	76,662
2008	100,422	72,982	103,921	75,625
2009	94,867	71,243	103,032	75,085
2010	95,028	71,013	103,197	74,945
Percent change (1999–2010)	9.6%	9.1%	5.5%	6.5%

While the money income measure produced by the Census Bureau excludes many of the components of income included in personal income, the Census Bureau attempts to impute some of these components. We can use these imputed values to obtain a measure of household income in the CPS that is more comparable to personal income, which contains items denoted in table 8.1 (Table 8.1 denotes these items by footnote a, which includes the market value of Medicare and Medicaid, employer contributions to health insurance, and imputed value of home equity for home owners.) Similar to Burkhauser, Larrimore, and Simon (2010) and Meyer and Sullivan (2011), including the imputations for health-care benefits yields an even greater increase in the mean and median and a smaller increase in inequality.[24]

All of these adjusted measures can then be used to determine inequality. The Gini coefficient is the most commonly used measure (see CBO 2011; Burkhauser, Larrimore, and Simon 2010; and Fisher, Johnson, and Smeeding, forthcoming). Table 8.6 shows the Gini coefficients from these adjusted measures. Similar to the relationship between the mean and medians, the NIPA-adjusted measure yields a larger increase in inequality (a 2.7 percent increase between 1999 to 2010 compared to 1.9 percent for the household income measure).

As shown in table 8.5, the inclusion of imputed health-care benefits (either from the employer or government) not only increases income, but

24. Burkhauser, Larrimore, and Simon (2010) and Meyer and Sullivan (2011) show that the median has increased between 25 percent and 50 percent between 1979 and 2007; CBO (2011) shows a 20 percent increase.

Table 8.6   Gini coefficients using alternative definitions of income

	Money income	NIPA-adjusted income	SOI dist-adjusted Income	NIPA adj, with health, retirement, and imputed interest	Money income with health benefits	Census research income (definition 14)[a]
1999	0.425	0.441	0.427	0.428	0.400	0.408
2000	0.426	0.443	0.443	0.431	0.400	0.410
2001	0.430	0.452	0.459	0.426	0.399	0.412
2002	0.426	0.451	0.445	0.416	0.395	0.405
2003	0.428	0.451	0.450	0.416	0.396	0.394
2004	0.429	0.456	0.440	0.419	0.393	0.404
2005	0.433	0.460	0.452	0.423	0.395	0.402
2006	0.435	0.461	0.451	0.424	0.396	0.405
2007	0.426	0.455	0.456	0.417	0.394	0.403
2008	0.430	0.465	0.468	0.417	0.396	0.392
2009	0.434	0.452	0.433	0.419	0.399	0.392
2010	0.433	0.453		0.417	0.398	
Percent change (1999–2010)	1.9%	2.7%	1.4%[b]	−2.6	−0.5%	−3.9%

[a]See http://www.census.gov/hhes/www/cpstables/032010/rdcall/toc.htm. For a complete description of definition 14, see http://www.census.gov/hhes/www/poverty/prevcps/p60-186rd.pdf.
[b]From 1999 to 2009.

also increases the change in income between 1999 and 2010. In addition, table 8.6 shows that these income sources decrease inequality (and lower the increase in the trend) as they are more likely to accrue to low-income households. The Census Bureau constructs an alternative income measure of after-tax-and-transfer income that also includes the imputed value of Medicare, Medicaid, employer-provided health insurance (definition 14), and shows a decrease in inequality between 1999 and 2009 (the latest year available).[25]

Burkhauser, Larrimore, and Simon (2010) show that including the value of government health-care benefits causes the change in inequality between 2000 and 2007 to increase less than the inequality using money income. Similarly, CBO (2011) shows that including health-care benefits yields a smaller increase in inequality between 1999 and 2007. Using a more comprehensive income measure, Wolff et al. (2012) find a larger increase in the median income between 2000 and 2004 (an increase of 0.6 percent) compared to a decrease of 1 percent for the standard money income definition. Wolff et al. (2012) also find a smaller increase in inequality during this period.

25. See http://www.census.gov/hhes/www/cpstables/032010/rdcall/toc.htm. For a complete description of definition 14, see http://www.census.gov/hhes/www/poverty/prevcps/p60-186rd.pdf.

To obtain a closer approximation of personal income, we could use the same adjustments to account for the imputed interest and employer-provided retirement benefits.[26] As shown in table 8.2, these components account for most of the remaining difference between adjusted personal income and personal income. If we assume that these are distributed similar to wages and reported property income, we simply increase these two factors, α_{Wage} and $\alpha_{property}$. Table 8.5 shows that this more comprehensive measure yields an increase in the mean of 5.5 percent and in the median of 6.5 percent.[27]

In sum, we began with the fact that over the past decade (between 1999 and 2010) the mean household income (from the Census Bureau) fell 5.7 percent, while per capita personal income (from the Bureau of Economic Analysis [BEA]) increased 11.1 percent, which can be construed as a difference of 16.8 percentage points with the assumption that persons per household is constant over time. Using a more comparable definition of income and national accounts data, we found that the mean-adjusted real personal income per household increased 5.3 percent during this period. In comparison, using the CPS data and after taking into account differences in the price index, accounting for underreporting and incorporating distributional information from both the CPS and SOI data, we obtain an increase of 5.7 percent (between 1999 and 2009) so that the adjustments reduce the difference between national accounts and census data on mean household income to 0.4 percent. In addition, with the adjusted measures of income there are larger increases in the median, yielding larger increases in inequality. However, as discussed above, the comparison is not straightforward when one considers imputations such as those for health benefits. Thus, to determine comparable changes in inequality there are two dimensions to the analysis: the reconciliation of published data and the definition of the "best" concept of income to use in determining well-being. Since the choice of the income measure depends on the use of the measure, we do not recommend one particular income measure for use in assessing inequality.

8.3   Determining a Social Welfare Function: An Application

There has been much research on obtaining independent measures of various social welfare functions that depend on both the level of aggregate income and its distribution (see Sen [1973]; Jorgenson [1990]; Jones and

---

26. Future work will include measures of imputed rent as measured by the return on home equity.

27. An additional method to obtain a Gini is to decompose the Gini using alternative measures of the income components. Using Lerman and Yitzhaki (1985) and Liberati and Yitzhaki (2011), the Gini can be decomposed by source as $G = \Sigma S_j G_j R_j$, where is the share of source, S_j, in income, G_j is the Gini for source, j, and R_j is the correlation between the source and the total income. Using a variety of sources can then be used to estimate the separate factors, S, R, and the source-specific Ginis. One can then aggregate these factors to obtain the overall Gini.

Klenow [2011]; Jorgenson and Slesnick, chapter 3, this volume). All of these measures attempt to aggregate the mean level of growth with changes in the distribution as measured by an inequality index (like the Gini).

Over the past three decades, the Gini coefficient increased along with per capita GDP, with a correlation of .92. Sen (1973) recommends a social welfare function (SWF) that is simply the product of mean income, μ, and a measure of equality given by (1-Gini). Many studies have recommended using a similar SWF or indicator of social welfare. Jorgenson (1990, 1012) constructs a consistent SWF such that "the individual welfare function and the individual expenditure function can be used to construct measures of the household standard of living and its cost." He then uses the same data and structure to estimate an equity index to obtain a SWF measure as the product between adjusted expenditures and equity, which is similar to Sen's SWF (see also Jorgenson and Slesnick, chapter 3, this volume).

Jones and Klenow (2011) follow a different approach and construct a SWF for a variety of countries using GDP, the Gini indexes, and other factors. Their data suggest that the Sen SWF (using the product of per capita GDP and [1-Gini]) yields a correlation (for a variety of countries) between the Jones and Klenow (2011) SWF and Sen's measure of .95.

If aggregate income growth is the result of increases in the income for households at the top of the distribution, then this growth may be offset by increases in inequality, which could yield a smaller increase in the SWF. That is, if inequality increases, then the equity index (using 1-G) falls, which diminishes the growth of SWF. For example, using a simplified SWF as the product of real per capita GDP and (1-the census Gini for money income), SWF increases about 48 percent between 1980 and 2009 (per capita GDP increases 65 percent and the Gini increases 16 percent). However, using the more comprehensive measure of household income from CBO (2012), which increases 20 percent, yields a 35 percent increase in SWF.

In order to completely evaluate the relationship between inequality and growth, we need measures of both using similar concepts (as in Jorgenson 1990). Many attempts have been made to create a summary welfare measure using GDP growth and distributional measures from household surveys. However, if there is measurement error, then inequality can be biased upward or downward, depending on the level of mean reversion. And if error is increasing over time, then inequality increases could be biased downward, while growth could be more accurate.

We can examine the recent decade (from 1999 to 2010) by using the results in the previous section (and tables 8.5 and 8.6) and construct consistent SWFs. Using per capita GDP and the census household Gini (as mentioned above) yields an increase in the SWF of 5.9 percent between 1999 and 2010. Using the household-adjusted personal income measure (as the μ) and the respective Gini (using the similarly adjusted data) yields an increase in SWF of 3.1 percent. However, using the more complete income measure that includes health benefits yields a 7.4 percent increase in SWF mainly because of a fall in inequality (shown in table 8.6).[28]

8.4   Distribution of Income and Consumption: An Application

Inasmuch as consumption is the major component of GDP, macroeconomic theory has focused, from its inception, on consumer behavior. A key indicator of this behavior is the average propensity to consume (APC). Keynes (1964) maintained that the APC declines with income. But Kuznets (1946) did not find such a decline in the data and in fact found that the APC was relatively stable with income. Friedman's (1957) permanent income hypothesis nor the Modigliani and Brumberg (1954) life cycle model sought to explain the stability of the APC. All of these discussions, however, were in the context of average or representative consumers.

The presence of heterogeneous agents, however, suggest that there is a distribution of income across them and hence, a distribution of propensities to consume. More specifically, if the propensities to consume differ by income groups then there is both a cross-sectional and time series dimension to the APC. Accordingly, two questions are of interest. First, at a point in time, how does the APC change across income categories? Second, over time, as incomes change, how does the APC for different income categories behave? We can use our methods to provide insight into the second question and leave the first question for future research.

Using the ratio of personal consumption expenditures (PCE) to personal disposable income, we can see an increase over time in the aggregate APC, with a recent fall. Between 1999 and 2010, the aggregate APC fell from 93 percent to 92 percent (see figure 8.6).[29] Alternatively, Fisher, Johnson, and Smeeding (forthcoming) calculate the APC using household-level data from the Consumer Expenditure (CE) Survey, and find a similar slight decrease from 83 to 82 percent between 1999 and 2010.

Information on APC by income quintile is not readily available; however, Fisher, Johnson, and Smeeding (forthcoming) create the APCs by quintile using the CE data. For 2010, they find APCs of 1.4, 1.0, 0.9, 0.8, and 0.7 for quintiles one to five, respectively (with an overall APC of .82). We can also use the results in McCully (chapter 6, this volume) to create adjusted income and expenditures by quintile and obtain APCs that would be consistent with personal income and PCE. Using tables 6.4 and 6.5 from McCully (chapter

---

28. These changes in the SWF can be compared to a similar measure presented in Jorgenson and Slesnick (chapter 3, this volume). They obtain a standard-of-living index using their equity index and their measure of real PCE per equivalent household member. This measure increases 14.5 percent between 1999 and 2010 mainly due to a large increase in equivalence-adjusted PCE, which increases 18 percent (as compared to the 10 percent increase in per capita GDP).

29. Using personal income instead of disposable income yields a similar result, but with lower APCs.

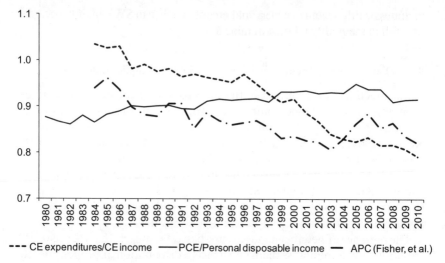

--- CE expenditures/CE income   ——PCE/Personal disposable income   — APC (Fisher, et al.)

Fig. 8.6   Various average propensities to consume (APC)

6, this volume), we obtain APCs by quintiles of 2.3, 1.4, 1.1, 0.9, and 0.5 for an overall APC of 0.89 (which is still lower than the aggregate APC given above).

Figure 8.6 provides a sense of how information on consumption by income quintile can matter. First, observe the relative stability of the aggregate APC using national income account data relative to the aggregate APC using CE data. Since the income and consumption components of the latter differ from those in the former, the difference provides further evidence on the importance of the domains of consumption and income. As shown above, using the Fisher, Johnson, and Smeeding (forthcoming) and McCully (chapter 6, this volume) APCs by income quintile demonstrate that the average APC is quite different from that obtained using aggregate NIPA data. This difference provides further evidence of the need to determine the distribution of consumption and income using national income account data, which will be the subject of future work. Finally, an implication of these different APCs by income quintile is examined further in the appendix.

8.5   Conclusion

Since their beginnings, the NBER and the CRIW have been concerned about the distribution of income and its relationship to the national accounts. Sixty years ago in his American Economic Association presidential address, Kuznets began by asking the question: "Does inequality in the distribution of income increase or decrease in the course of a country's economic growth?" He continued by arguing that the distribution of income must be linked to the measure of national income. Using previous work on creating a comparable measure of personal income in the CPS, we have provided a couple simple methods to produce a median personal income and its Gini coefficient.

These methods yield a variety of results on the growth of median income and inequality, depending on the definition of income used and the method used to obtain the distribution. Stiglitz, Sen, and Fitoussi (2009, 13) argued that averages must "be accompanied by indicators that reflect their distribution. Median consumption (income, wealth) provides a better measure of what is happening to the 'typical' individual or household than average consumption (income or wealth)." We showed that adjusting for the underreporting in the CPS yields a larger level and increase in the trend of the mean and median between 1999 and 2010. This, in turn, yields a larger increase in inequality. Using a more comprehensive income measure that includes the government- and employer-provided health benefits yields a flatter trend in inequality.

In future work we will improve the methods presented in this chapter by evaluating other methods to adjust for nonreports in the CPS data. That is, the current method only adjusts for the underreporting given a positive report of income; however, some "zero" reports may also be underreported income. In addition, the concordance used to compare the CPS measure to the personal income measure (described in table 8.2 and presented in Katz [2012]) needs to be compared to the methods presented in McCully (chapter 6, this volume).

Another method to obtain an improved measure of underreporting involves analysis of the matched household data with the tax records. A more complete method of determining the aggregate impacts of the joint distribution of income and consumption requires similar decompositions of PCE and personal income that rely on the distribution of the household survey data.

There are two dimensions to the analysis: the reconciliation of published data and the definition of the "best" concept of income to use in determining well-being. The results in this chapter may provide a framework for developing measures of median personal income, GDI, and their distribution that could be produced on a regular basis.

Appendix

A Simple Multiplier Analysis for the Different APCs by Income Quintile

One chief application of the APC is constructing an autonomous expenditure multiplier. If propensities to consume are higher for lower-income groups, then the autonomous expenditure multipliers might be higher, which in turn suggests that the efficacy of government expenditures in enhancing economic growth might be improved by income redistribution.

The multiplier analysis presented here is but one facet of the identification of the relationship between income inequality and growth.[30] Regarding the linkage between the propensity to consume, the income distribution, and macroeconomic analysis, Keynes (1964) thought that:

> The amount that the community spends on consumption obviously depends (i) partly on the amount of its income, (ii) partly on the other objective attendant circumstances, and (iii) partly on the subjective needs and the psychological propensities and habits of the individuals composing it and the principles on which the income is divided between them (which may suffer modification as output is increased) . . . . But, in general, we shall in what follows take the subjective factors as given; and we shall assume that the propensity to consume depends only on changes in the objective factors.[31]

Keynes places the income distribution in the category of a subjective factor.[32] Stone and Stone (1938), in support of Keynes, also examine the relationship between the marginal propensity to consume and the income distribution and find no relationship. Haavelmo (1945) looked at the same question in terms of the impact on the balanced budget multiplier. Goodwin (1949) and Chipman (1950) looked at the multiplier as a matrix across sectors, the latter allowing for income redistribution, and Conrad (1955) used a similar method to look at the income effects of redistribution.

To illustrate how our estimates can be used to evaluate an autonomous expenditure multiplier, we consider a very simple model that abstracts from many of the complexities to estimating multipliers that have been addressed in recent studies of the magnitude of multipliers.[33] In particular, we do not consider the dynamic complexities of consumer behavior, the role of uncertainty, the stance of monetary policy, or the stage of the business cycle. The purpose of the example below is not to add to the discussion about the magnitude of the multiplier, but rather to show in a simplified way how the incorporation of income distribution might impact an expenditure multiplier.

We consider a very simple closed Keynesian model (similar to Chipman [1950]) in which the autonomous expenditure component captures all expenditures save a consumption expenditure that is a fraction of income. We ignore taxes as well as that can be viewed as simply a change in income. Let Y_i

30. The relationship between income inequality and growth has been the focus of many studies. Both positive and negative relationships have been posited and supported by empirical evidence (see, for example, Forbes [2000] and Berg and Ostry [2011]).

31. Book III, chapter 8, page 91.

32. It should be pointed out that in other parts of Keynes (1964), there are references to the potential efficacy of income redistribution. See, for example, section II in chapter 19 and chapter 24.

33. See, for example, Auerbach and Gorodnichenko (2012), Christiano, Eichenbaum, and Rebelo (2011), and Ramey (2012).

denote income, A_i autonomous expenditure, and c_i the marginal propensity to consume for the ith income class

$$Y_i = A_i + c_iY_i \quad i = 1...N.$$

$$dY_i = dA_i + c_idY_i$$

The model shows that for income category, its marginal propensity to consume determines the sector expenditure multiplier and thereby the aggregate multiplier. Specifically, for N income categories, we can compute the impact of a change in autonomous expenditures in each category and then add up across categories to obtain the aggregate expenditure multiplier.

The system can be written as

$$(1 - c_i)dY_i = dA_i.$$

or in matrix form

$$\begin{bmatrix} dY_1 \\ \vdots \\ dY_N \end{bmatrix} = [I - C]^{-1} \begin{bmatrix} dA_1 \\ \vdots \\ dA_N \end{bmatrix},$$

where

$$C = \left[\begin{pmatrix} c_1 & \cdots & 0 \\ \vdots & \ddots & \vdots \\ 0 & \cdots & c_N \end{pmatrix} \right].$$

Let I denote the identity matrix and D be the determinant of $[I - C]$, and let D_i be the determinant of the matrix resulting from the substitution of

$$\begin{bmatrix} dA_1 \\ \vdots \\ dA_N \end{bmatrix}$$

into the ith column of $[I - C]$, then $dY_i = D_i/D$ and $dY = \sum_{i=1}^{N}(D_i/D)$.

Using quintiles, we have

$$D = \Pi_i(1 - c_i), \text{ and } D_i = (\Pi_{j \neq i}(1 - c_j)).$$

If $c = c_i$ for all i, then we obtain the usual expenditure multiplier, $5/(1 - c)$.[34] The implication is that taking into account different propensities to consume by income category can have significant effects on the

---

34. Suppose $N = 2$. Then have the total change multiplier arising from all the dAi and $dY = (2 - c_1 - c_2)/(1 - c_1 - c_2 - c_1c_2)$, and a finite solution requires $c_1 + c_2 + c_1c_2 < 1$. If $c_1 = c_2 = c$ then we obtain the usual expenditure multiplier $(2/1 - c)$, where the 2 derives from there being two sectors.

value of the autonomous expenditure multiplier. To compare this with the simple textbook multiplier that assumes constant MPC we would divide the N-sector multiplier by $1/N$ so as to obtain the textbook $1/(1 - c)$.

Using the APCs discussed in the text, the MPC can be found by assuming that the elasticity of consumption with respect to income, ε, is constant across income categories and over time and given by 0.1 (as in Dynan 2012 and Oh and Reis 2011).[35] Since $\varepsilon = $ MPC/APC, then the MPCs are basically one-tenth of the APCs. Using the average APC above yields an average MPC of .092.

Recall that Fisher, Johnson, and Smeeding (forthcoming) find for 2010 APCs of 1.4, 1.0, 0.9, 0.8, and 1.7 for quintiles one to five, respectively (with an overall APC of 0.82). Using an elasticity of 0.1 yields MPCs of 0.14, 0.10, 0.09, 0.08, and 0.07. Using the simple expenditure multiplier equations given above yields a multiplier of 1.11 compared to the multiplier for constant MPCs of 1.09, for a difference of 0.02.[36] As a result, an equalizing redistribution will have a small positive impact on the change in income.

We can use the results in McCully (chapter 6, this volume) to create adjusted income and expenditures by quintile and obtain APCs that would be consistent with personal income and PCE. Using tables 6.1 and 6.2 from McCully (chapter 6, this volume), we obtain a steeper pattern of APCs, which yields a larger divergence in MPCs between the top and bottom quintiles, and hence, a slightly larger change in the multipliers with a transfer multiplier of 0.05.

It is reasonable to ask how sensitive these findings are to the selected income consumption elasticity. Consider again the APCs from Fisher, Johnson, and Smeeding (forthcoming). If the elasticity is increased from 0.1 to 0.4 the difference between the multiplier using the average MPC and the one that uses the quintile MPCs rises from 0.02 to 0.18; a huge increase.[37] This result further demonstrates the point we made earlier; namely, that we are considering a very simple model.

References

Accardo, J., V. Bellamy, G. Consales, M. Fesseau, S. Laidier, and E. Raymaud. 2009. "Inequalities between Households in the National Accounts—Breakdown of Household Accounts." INSEE Working Paper, National Institute of Statis-

35. Oh and Reis (2011) use an average MPC of 0.11 in their estimates of the effectiveness of government transfers, and Parker et al. (2013) find MPCs ranging from .12 to .30.
36. Oh and Reis (2011), using a more robust model of redistribution and MPCs that are decreasing with income, find a similarly small positive impact of redistribution.
37. The elasticity of 0.4 is chosen because it is near the maximum that preserves a positive determinant for the I-C matrix. The impact of the increase in the elasticity qualitatively holds for the other APCs as well.

tics and Economic Studies. http://www.insee.fr/en/themes/document.asp?ref_id =ECOFRA09d.

Armour, P., R. V. Burkhauser, and J. Larrimore. 2013. "Deconstructing Income and Income Inequality Measures: A Crosswalk from Market Income to Comprehensive Income." *American Economic Review* 103 (3): 173–7.

Auerbach, A., and Y. Gorodnichenko. 2012. "Measuring the Output Responses to Fiscal Policy." *American Economic Journal: Economic Policy* 4:1–27.

BEA (Bureau of Economic Analysis). 2012. "Economic and Statistical Analysis Budget Estimates, Fiscal Year 2012, as Presented to Congress." February 2011.

Berg, A., and J. D. Ostry. 2011. "Inequality and Unsustainable Growth: Two Sides of the Same Coin?" International Monetary Fund, IMF Staff Discussion Note, SDN/11/08. April 8. http://www.imf.org/external/pubs/cat/longres.aspx ?sk=24686.0.

Blinder, A. 1975. "Distribution Effects and the Aggregate Consumption Function." *Journal of Political Economy* 83 (3): 447–75.

Boskin, M., E. Dulberger, R. Gordon, Z. Grilliches, and D. Jorgenson. 1996. "Toward a More Accurate Measure of the Cost of Living." Final Report to the Senate Finance Committee, December 4. http://www.ssa.gov/history/reports/boskin rpt.html.

Bound, J., C. Brown, and N. Mathiowitz. 2001. "Measurement Error in Survey Data." In *Handbook of Econometrics*, edited by J. J. Heckman and E. Leamer, 3707–45. Amsterdam: Elsevier Science B.V.

Boushey, H., and A. Hersh. 2012. "The American Middle Class, Income Inequality, and the Strength of Our Economy New Evidence in Economics." Center for American Progress report, May. http://www.americanprogress.org/issues/economy /report/2012/05/17/11628/the-american-middle-class-income-inequality-and-the -strength-of-our-economy/.

Broda, C., and D. E. Weinstein. 2008. *Prices, Poverty, and Inequality: Why Americans Are Better Off than You Think*. Washington, DC: AEI Press.

Budd, E., and D. Radner. 1975. "The Bureau of Economic Analysis and Current Population Survey Size Distributions: Some Comparisons for 1964." In *The Personal Distribution of Income and Wealth*, edited by James D. Smith. New York: National Bureau of Economic Research.

Buhmann, B., L. Rainwater, G. Schmauss, and T. Smeeding. 1988. "Equivalence Scales, Well-being, Inequality, and Poverty: Sensitivity Estimates across Ten Countries Using the Luxembourg Income Study Database." *Review of Income and Wealth* 34:115–42.

Burkhauser, R., J. Larrimore, and K. Simon. 2010. "A 'Second Opinion' On The Economic Health Of The American Middle Class." NBER Working Paper no. 17164, Cambridge, MA.

Canberra Group. 2011. *Handbook on Household Income Statistics*, 2nd ed. United Nations Economic Commission for Europe. http://www.unece.org/index.php ?id=28894.

Census Bureau. 1948. "Current Population Reports, Consumer Income, 1947." Series P-60, Number 4.

Chipman, J. 1950. "The Multisector Multiplier." *Econometrica* 18 (4): 355–74.

Christiano, L., M. Eichenbaum, and S. Rebelo. 2011. "When Is the Government Spending Multiplier Large?" *Journal of Political Economy* 119:78–121.

Coli, A., and F. Tartamella. 2010. "Micro-Macro Integration: Survey Data on Household Income for the Estimate of the Italian GDP." IARIW Conference Paper, International Association for Research in Income and Wealth. http://www .iariw.org/abstracts/2010/7A/coli.pdf.

Conference on Research in Income and Wealth. 1943. "Comparability and Deficiencies of Existing Data and the Construction of a Size Distribution for the United States." In *Income Size Distributions in the United States*, Part I, Conference on Research in Income and Wealth. New York: National Bureau of Economic Research.

———. 2011. "Trends in the Distribution of Household Income Between 1979 and 2007." CBO Report.

———. 2012. "The Distribution of Household Income and Federal Taxes, 2008 and 2009." CBO Report.

Conrad, Alfred. 1955. "The Multiplier Effects of Redistributive Public Budgets." *Review of Economics and Statistics* 37 (2): 160–73.

Council of Economic Advisors. 2012. *Economic Report of the President, 2012*. Washington, DC: GPO. http://www.whitehouse.gov/administration/eop/cea/economic -report-of-the-President.

Dynan, K. 2012. "Is a Household Debt Overhang Holding Back Consumption?" *Brookings Papers on Economic Activity* Spring: 229–344.

Fesseau, M., V. Bellamy, and E. Raynaud. 2009. "Inequality between Households in the National Accounts." International Institute of Statistics and Economic Studies, INSEE Premier No. 1265A. http://www.insee.fr/en/themes/document.asp ?ref_id=ip1265.

Fisher, J., D. Johnson, and T. Smeeding. Forthcoming. "Inequality of Income *and* Consumption in the US: Measuring the Trends in Inequality from 1984–2010 for the Same Individuals." *Review of Income and Wealth*.

Forbes, K. J. 2000. "A Reassessment of the Relationship Between Inequality and Growth." *American Economic Review* 90 (4): 869–87.

Friedman, M. 1957. "The Permanent Income Hypothesis." In *A Theory of the Consumption Function*, edited by M. Friedman. Princeton, NJ: Princeton University Press.

Gertner, J. 2010. "The Rise and Fall of GDP." *New York Times*, May 13.

Goldsmith, S. 1955. "Income Distribution in the United States, 1950–53." *Survey of Current Business*, March. Washington, DC: GPO.

———. 1958. "The Relation of Census Income Distribution Statistics to Other Income Data." In *An Appraisal of the 1950 Census Income Data*, Studies in Income and Wealth, vol. 23, Conference on Research in Income and Wealth. New York: National Bureau of Economic Research.

———. 1960. "Size Distribution of Personal Income, 1956–59." *Survey of Current Business*, April. Washington, DC: GPO.

Goodwin, R. M. 1949. "The Multiplier as Matrix." *Economic Journal* 59 (236): 537–55.

Gottschalk, P., and M. Huynh. 2010. "Are Earnings Inequality and Mobility Overstated? The Impact of Non-Classical Measurement Error." *Review of Economics and Statistics* 92 (2): 302–15.

Haavelmo, Trygve. 1945. "Multiplier Effects of a Balanced Budget." *Econometrica* 13 (4): 311–8.

Haig, Robert M. 1921. "The Concept of Income—Economic and Legal Aspects." *Federal Income Tax*, 1–28. New York: Columbia University Press.

Holdren, A. E., and B. Grimm. 2008. "Gross Domestic Income: Revisions and Source Data." *Survey of Current Business*, December. Washington, DC: GPO.

Jones, C., and P. Klenow. 2011. "Beyond GDP? Welfare across Countries and Time." NBER Working Paper no.16352, Cambridge, MA.

Jorgenson, D. W. 1990. "Aggregate Consumer Behavior and the Measurement of Social Welfare." *Econometrica* 58 (5): 1007–40.

Katz, A. 2012. "Explaining Long-term Differences between Census and BEA Measures of Household Income." BEA Working Paper.

Keynes, John, M. 1964. *The General Theory of Employment, Interest and Money.* New York: Harcourt, Brace & World, Inc. First published in 1936.

Kuznets, Simon. 1934. "National Income, 1929–1932." 73rd US Congress, 2nd session, Senate document no. 124.

Kuznets, S. 1955. "Economic Growth and Income Inequality." *American Economic Review* 45 (1): 1–28.

Landefeld, S. J., B. R. Moulton, J. D. Platt, and S. M. Villones. 2010. "GDP and Beyond: Measuring Economic Progress and Sustainability." *Survey of Current Business*, April. Washington, DC: GPO.

Lerman, R., and S. Yitzhaki. 1985. "Income Inequality Effects by Income Source: A New Approach and Applications to the United States." *Review of Economics and Statistics* 67 (1): 151–6.

Liberati, P., and S. Yitzhaki. 2011. "GDP and Beyond: An Implementation of Welfare Considerations to the Distribution of Earnings in Italy." Department of Economics, University Roma Tre, Unpublished manuscript.

Lucas, R. E., Jr. 2004. "The Industrial Revolution: Past and Future." *The Region*, Minneapolis Federal Reserve Bank, May.

McColl, B., J. Billing, B. Kindermann, and H. Burgess. 2010. "Micro and Macro Economic Estimates for Australian Households: Recent Developments and Future Directions." Paper presented at the International Association for Research in Income and Wealth (IARIW) annual meetings, St. Gallen, Switzerland. August.

Meyer, B., and J. Sullivan. 2011. "The Material Well-Being of the Poor and Middle Class Since 1980." AEI Working Paper no. 2011-04.

Meyer, Bruce D., Wallace K. C. Mok, and James X. Sullivan. 2008. "The Under-Reporting of Transfers in Household Surveys: Its Nature and Consequences." Working Paper, University of Chicago.

Mitchell, W. C., W. King, F. Macaulay, and O. Knauth. 1921. *Income in the United States: Its Amount and Distribution, 1909–1919, Vol. 1.* New York: National Bureau of Economic Research.

Modigliani, Franco, and Richard H. Brumberg. 1954. "Utility Analysis and the Consumption Function: An Interpretation of Cross-Section Data." In *Post-Keynesian Economics*, edited by Kenneth K. Kurihara, 388–436. New Brunswick: Rutgers University Press.

Mussard, S., and L. Savard. 2010. "Macro/Micro-Economic Modeling and Gini Multi-Decomposition: An Application to the Phillippines." *Journal of Income Distribution* 19 (2): 51–78.

Nichols, A., K. Smith, and L. Wheaton. 2011. "Analysis of Income Data Quality on the CPS ASEC." Preliminary report from Urban Institute under contract with the US Census Bureau.

Organisation for Economic Co-operation and Development (OECD). 2011. *How's Life? Measuring Well-Being*. Paris: OECD Publishing.

———. 2012. "Reducing Income Inequality While Boosting Economic Growth: Can it be Done?" In *Economic Policy Reforms 2012*. Paris: OECD Publishing.

Oh, H., and R. Reis. 2011. "Targeted Transfers and the Fiscal Response to the Great Recession." NBER Working Paper no. 16775, Cambridge, MA.

Parker, J., N. Souleles, D. Johnson, and R. McClelland. 2013. "Consumer Spending and the Economic Stimulus Payments of 2008." *American Economic Review* 103 (6): 2530–53.

Piketty, T., and E. Saez. 2003. "Income Inequality in the United States, 1913–1998." *Quarterly Journal of Economics* 118 (1): 1–39.

Ramey, V. 2012. "Government Spending and Private Activity." Manuscript, University of California, San Diego.

Reinhardt, U. E. 2011. "What Does 'Economic Growth' Mean for Americans?" *New York Times*, September 2.

Roemer, M. 2000. "Assessing the Quality of the March Current Population Survey and the Survey of Income and Program Participation Income Estimates, 1990–1996." US Census Bureau Working Paper.

Ruser, J., A. Pilot, and C. Nelson. 2004. "Alternative Measures of Household Income: BEA Personal Income, CPS Money Income, and Beyond." US Census Bureau Working Paper.

Sabelhaus, J., D. Johnson, S. Ash, D. Swanson, T. Garner, J. Greenlees, and S. Henderson. Forthcoming. "Is the Consumer Expenditure Survey Representative by Income?" In *Improving the Measurement of Consumer Expenditures*, edited by C. Carroll, T. Crossley, and J. Sabelhaus..

Semega, J. 2012. "Evaluating the Construct of a Canberra Household Income Definition Using the Annual Social and Economic Supplement to the Current Population Survey (CPS ASEC)." Paper presented at Joint Statistical meetings, August. American Statistical Association.

Sen, A. 1973. *On Economic Inequality*. Oxford: Clarendon Press. Expanded edition, 1997.

Simons, H. 1938. *Personal Income Taxation: The Definition of Income as a Problem of Fiscal Policy*. Chicago: University of Chicago Press.

Slesnick, D. T. 2001. *Consumption and Social Welfare: Living Standards and Their Distribution in the United States*. Cambridge: Cambridge University Press.

Smeeding, T. M., and J. P. Thompson. 2011. "Recent Trends in the Distribution of Income: Labor, Wealth and More Complete Measures of Well Being." *Research in Labor Economics* May:1–49.

SNA (System of National Accounts). 2009. "System of National Accounts 2008." New York: European Communities, International Monetary Fund, Organisation for Economic Co-operation and Development, United Nations, and World Bank.

Stiglitz, J. E., A. Sen, and J. Fitoussi. 2009. *Report by the Commission on the Measurement of Economic Performance and Social Progress*. New York: United Nations Press.

Stone, J. R., and W. M. Stone. 1938. "The Marginal Propensity to Consume and the Multiplier." *Review of Economic Studies* 6:1–24.

Turek, J., K. Swenson, B. Ghose, F. Scheuren, and D. Lee. 2012. "How Good Are ASEC Earnings Data? A Comparison to SSA Detailed Earning Records." Paper presented at the Federal Committee on Statistical Methodology (FCSM).

Weinberg, D. 2006. "Income Data Quality Issues in the CPS." *Monthly Labor Review* June.

Wolff, E., A. Zacharias, T. Masterson, S. Eren, A. Sharpe, and E. Hazell. 2012. "A Comparison of Inequality and Living Standards in Canada and the United States Using an Expanded Measure of Economic Well-Being." Levy Economics Institute of Bard College Working Paper no. 703.

Analysis of Wealth Using Micro- and Macrodata
A Comparison of the Survey of Consumer Finances and Flow of Funds Accounts

Alice M. Henriques and Joanne W. Hsu

9.1 Introduction

Household balance sheets are key inputs into macroeconomic analysis and forecasting, and thus the Federal Reserve Board allocates substantial resources toward two major data products that are used to independently generate estimates of household net worth over time. The Federal Reserve Board is responsible for the most widely used macrolevel estimates of US household sector net worth, generated as part of the quarterly Flow of Fund Accounts (FFA).[1] The Federal Reserve Board is also responsible for the microlevel Survey of Consumer Finances (SCF), used extensively to study household behavior.[2] Previous studies have looked at the relationship between SCF and FFA aggregate net worth over time. See, in particular, Avery and Kennickell (1991), Avery, Elliehausen, and Kennickell (1988), Curtin, Juster, and Morgan (1989), and Antoniewicz (2000).

Alice M. Henriques and Joanne W. Hsu are economists at the Board of Governors of the Federal Reserve System.

This chapter was prepared for the National Bureau of Economic Research Summer Institute meeting of the Conference on Research in Income and Wealth in Cambridge, Massachusetts, August 6–8, 2012. We are grateful to Joshua Gallin, James Kennedy, Arthur Kennickell, John Sabelhaus, Paul Smith, Kevin Moore, and Marco Cagetti for helpful suggestions on earlier drafts. We also thank Robert Argento for excellent research assistance. The analysis and conclusions set forth are those of the authors and do not indicate concurrence by other members of the research staff of the Board of Governors of the Federal Reserve System. For acknowledgments, sources of research support, and disclosure of the authors' material financial relationships, if any, please see http://www.nber.org/chapters/c12829.ack.

1. The FFA data are available for download at http://www.federalreserve.gov/releases/z1.

2. Results of the most recent SCF, conducted in 2010, are discussed in Bricker et al. (2012). The SCF microdata are available for download or online tabulation and analysis at http://www.federalreserve.gov/econresdata/scf/scfindex.htm. Longer term trends in wealth on the SCF are discussed in Wolff (2011, 1998) and Kennickell (2011).

In light of more recent economic developments, we revisit trends in household wealth using these two data sources to better understand how households have fared. Despite substantial differences in the goals and methods used to produce the two measures of household net worth, the patterns of aggregate household wealth change over the past twenty-five years are similar. The differences that do exist in a few subcomponents of the household balance sheet—such as owner-occupied housing, noncorporate equity, and credit cards—are attributable to methodological differences made in the production of the data. These differences do not fundamentally alter the pattern of household wealth changes leading up to and following the Great Recession.

Macro- and microwealth data are used to answer different types of questions about life cycle saving and wealth accumulation. Macrowealth data from the FFA, drawn primarily from various administrative sources, are often used in conjunction with macroincome and macroconsumption data to study household-sector saving and spending over time.[3] One might ask, for example, whether the dramatic decline in aggregate personal consumption expenditures during the Great Recession and subsequent slow growth have been unusual, given what happened to aggregate household wealth and income.[4] This sort of aggregate time-series analysis leads to estimates of key macroeconomic forecasting parameters, such as the marginal effect of wealth change or the effects of permanent and transitory income shocks on personal consumption expenditures. Answering such questions requires high-frequency, timely, and comprehensive data of the sort provided by the FFA.

The drawback to using macrodata is that the aggregate behavior of the household sector is modeled as though households are a monolithic entity, rather than generated by summing the behavior across the millions of households actually making the spending and saving decisions.[5] In a world of perfect household data (a world where this chapter would never have to be written) the macrowealth data would be aggregated from household-level wealth data, and that underlying household-level data would also have the key income, demographic, socioeconomic, labor force, credit market experiences, and expectation attributes of the individual households that theory tells us should affect their saving and spending decisions. Microdata is desirable for studying behavior both because households differ in terms of these underlying characteristics, but also because any given set of changes to the macroeconomic environment will have differential effects across households, depending on their initial conditions.[6]

---

3. For example, see Wilson et al. (1989).

4. This issue has been addressed in a number of papers. See, for example, Lettau and Ludvigson (2004).

5. One exception is Maki and Palumbo (2001), who use the SCF to provide evidence of heterogeneity inherent in the FFA values.

6. See, for example, De Nardi, French, and Benson (2012) and Petev, Pistaferri, and Eksten (2011).

The SCF is a widely used microdata set for studying saving and wealth accumulation behavior across different types of households. The popularity of the SCF among economic researchers is attributable to a unique sampling and data production strategy, and because the SCF collects both comprehensive balance sheet data and the extensive income, demographic, and other supplemental information that researchers want.[7] The SCF data have been used in several different ways for studying basic life cycle saving and wealth accumulation behavior. For example, one important use of the SCF is to calibrate structural life cycle models. Given income dynamics, realistic budget constraints, and assumptions about utility functions, deep parameters, and intertemporal optimizing behavior, one can solve for the predicted net worth outcomes of different types of households in different situations and then compare those predictions to actual outcomes in the SCF.[8] A second example of how the SCF has been used to study life cycle behavior is the so-called "synthetic cohort" approach, where observations are grouped within the independent cross sections in such a way as to make it possible to measure wealth changes for those groups between survey waves.[9]

The SCF has much of the household-level balance sheet and other information that researchers desire for studying saving and wealth accumulation behavior, but the primary drawbacks are the triennial frequency, the lag between data collection and data release, and the relatively small sample sizes.[10] These limitations arise because the SCF is a complicated household survey, and (like every data collection effort) faces a budget constraint. Conducting and processing the data from even a few thousand household interviews is a substantial undertaking, and survey resources are allocated to balance competing objectives of data quality, frequency, and timeliness.

The FFA data are collected in a very different way and with different goals in mind, and thus there is a different set of tradeoffs. To a large extent, the

7. The sampling strategy of the SCF involves combining a standard area-probability sample with a special "list" sample of (probabilistically) high-wealth households. The list sample is chosen based on statistical records derived from income tax returns. Other household surveys that collect measures of household net worth, such as the Survey of Income and Program Participation (SIPP), Panel Survey of Income Dynamics (PSID), and Health and Retirement Study (HRS), generally find wealth levels comparable to the SCF for much of the wealth distribution, but they fall far short for the wealthiest households. Given the high concentration of wealth, this also means those other microdata sets fall well short of producing aggregate net worth estimates that would match estimates of aggregate household net worth generated by the FFA.

8. See, for example, Hubbard, Skinner, and Zeldes (1994). Browning and Lusardi (1996) provide an extensive overview of how different types of microdata have been used to study saving and wealth accumulation in different ways.

9. See, for example, Gale and Pence (2006) and Sabelhaus and Pence (1999).

10. Another potential drawback is that the SCF has been almost exclusively a cross section since 1989, with the one exception being a 2009 reinterview of 2007 respondents that the Federal Reserve Board undertook in order to study the financial effects of the Great Recession; see Bricker et al. (2011). Bosworth (2012) shows that measuring saving (and thus consumption, solved for by subtracting saving from income) by first-differencing wealth levels in the PSID is extremely problematic and probably uninformative. Rather than relying on measured wealth changes, Dynan (2012) uses the direct expenditure estimates now being collected by the PSID to study the effect of housing wealth on consumption.

FFA are based on data found in aggregate government reports and filings that provide comprehensive coverage of sectors or entities. For example, Call Reports provide the source data for banks, and regulatory filings with the Securities and Exchange Commission are source data for brokers, dealers, money market mutual funds, and government-sponsored enterprises. Other key government sources of data for the FFA are obtained from agencies including the Bureau of Economic Analysis (BEA), the Census Bureau, and the Internal Revenue Service (IRS). In addition, the FFA use trade association data. For example, data from the Investment Company Institute (ICI) are used to compile balance sheets for the mutual fund sector. Other data are provided by private vendors.

A heavy reliance on government filings works very well when estimating the size of some sectors. However, quarterly data are not available for households. Many components of the FFA's balance sheet for the household sector, found in table B.100, are estimated as residuals. These residuals are derived by estimating the economy-wide total, and removing the estimated values of all other sectors, which results in the value of the last remaining sector, households. Components estimated in this manner include households' holdings of checkable deposits and currency, time and savings deposits, bonds, and mutual funds.

High-quality data do not exist to estimate a balance sheet for nonprofit organizations; thus, by default, they are included in the household sector.[11] In addition, some entities, such as domestic hedge funds and some privately held trusts, for which virtually no comprehensive source data are available, are also partially included in the household sector's residual calculations. The FFA historical series are frequently revised when source data themselves are revised, when new data are available, and when Federal Reserve Board staff change their methodology. Despite the very different approaches to estimating household net worth, the two data sets show the same general patterns of saving and wealth accumulation over the past twenty-five years. Levels of net worth are nearly identical in the period 1989 to 1998. Beginning in 2001, and through 2010, the SCF estimates of net worth exceed the FFA estimates by approximately 20 percent. The gap that emerged in the early twenty-first century is a combination of higher values for tangible assets in the SCF, in particular noncorporate business equity and owner-occupied housing, and larger values of liabilities in the FFA, especially for consumer credit.

These areas of divergence between the SCF and FFA in aggregate owner-occupied housing, noncorporate business, and credit card balances appear to be largely attributable to methodological differences in the production of the data, but they do not dramatically alter one's perceptions of household

---

11. The FFA previously reported a separate accounting for the financial assets and liabilities of most nonprofit organizations in supplementary table L.100.a, but this series was discontinued in 2000 due to source data quality concerns. The annual average of the total financial assets of nonprofit organizations reported in L.100.a was 1.2 trillion dollars.

net worth changes leading up to and following the Great Recession (see tables 9.1 and 9.2). The most prominent aggregate trend in household wealth of the past decade or so is the boom and bust in owner-occupied housing. The aggregate values of owner-occupied housing in the FFA and SCF were nearly identical in 1995. Between 1995 and 2007, the FFA value increased nearly 170 percent, while the SCF value increased nearly 250 percent. Between 2007 and 2010, the FFA value fell 22 percent, while the SCF value fell 17 percent. The boom and bust in housing is clearly evident in both data sets, but the more dramatic boom and slightly less dramatic bust has left the SCF value some 40 percent higher than that in the FFA as of 2010. This pattern is unsurprising given methodological differences between the two estimates, and it is not immediately clear how these differences should be interpreted. A comprehensive explanation of why these differences exist is beyond the scope of this chapter.

According to responses to the SCF, noncorporate businesses are the tangible asset held by the fewest households, and the distribution of business values is extremely skewed. Differences in the valuation methods used by the SCF and FFA, along with a high degree of sampling variability because of the skewed distribution of owned business values possessed in the survey, combine to generate a volatile measure in which SCF business values typically exceed those in the FFA. However, as with owner-occupied housing, the general pattern of boom and bust in recent years is evident in both data sets.

Another example of apparent divergence between the SCF and FFA is in the category of consumer credit outstanding, especially credit card balances.[12] The SCF estimate of total consumer credit in any given year is generally only about two-thirds of the FFA value, and in the period of rapidly rising household debt leading up to the Great Recession, this divergence in levels contributed modestly to the widening of the gap in net worth. Again, however, a substantial fraction of this divergence appears possibly due to methodological differences. In particular, the SCF asks about credit card balances as of the time the respondent made their last payment (and thus excludes charges incurred in the interim) while the FFA measure balances at a discrete point in time without reference to the payment cycle. Both measures have their merits from the perspective of studying household behavior, and the overall impression of rapidly growing (then slowing or falling) consumer credit is evident using either concept. In order to shed light on whether additional differences between SCF and FFA aggregates are due to the micronature versus aggregate nature of the two data sets, or due to survey versus administrative sources of data, we also compare the SCF to a third source of data, the Consumer Credit Panel, a microdata set drawn from administrative records.

12. See, for example, Zinman (2009) and Brown et al. (2011).

Table 9.1   Household balance sheet (FFA data billions of dollars, levels outstanding)

	1989	1992	1995	1998	2001	2004	2007	2010
Net worth	**16,396.3**	**18,421.2**	**22,041.3**	**28,059.9**	**33,043.0**	**41,668.1**	**53,332.2**	**44,919.7**
Assets	19,390.6	22,018.1	26,439.8	33,423.7	40,064.9	51,425.1	66,246.8	57,404.9
Tangible assets and business equity	11,393.2	12,395.0	14,006.7	16,577.2	21,954.9	29,426.8	35,375.6	28,221.2
Real estate, value of residences	6,543.9	7,186.3	7,982.7	9,459.7	13,307.1	18,323.5	21,442.8	16,719.2
Consumer durable goods	1,896.2	2,171.6	2,506.3	2,799.9	3,306.4	3,830.5	4,421.6	4,571.5
Equity in noncorporate business	2,953.0	3,037.1	3,517.7	4,317.6	5,341.5	7,272.8	9,511.2	6,930.5
Financial assets	7,997.4	9,623.0	12,433.1	16,846.5	18,110.0	21,998.4	30,871.2	29,183.7
Safe assets	4,713.3	5,151.6	5,726.0	6,380.2	7,372.2	9,295.9	12,114.4	13,217.3
Deposits and MMMF shares	3,246.7	3,313.4	3,348.3	3,792.1	4,831.3	5,643.0	7,223.4	7,858.5
Bonds	1,466.6	1,838.3	2,377.7	2,588.1	2,540.9	3,652.9	4,890.9	5,358.8
Risky Assets	2,603.3	3,542.8	5,341.2	8,519.6	8,632.7	10,137.8	14,866.5	12,392.3
Directly held corporate equity	2,090.2	2,743.4	4,088.2	6,167.8	6,018.1	6,710.1	10,268.6	7,820.7
Long-term mutual funds	513.0	799.4	1,253.0	2,351.8	2,614.6	3,427.7	4,597.9	4,571.7
Assets inside 401(k)	680.9	928.6	1,365.8	1,946.6	2,105.1	2,564.6	3,890.4	3,574.2
Liabilities	2,994.2	3,596.9	4,398.4	5,363.8	7,021.9	9,757.1	12,914.6	12,485.3
Home mortgages	2,210.0	2,795.0	3,288.8	3,963.0	5,207.5	7,592.2	10,435.3	10,101.9
Consumer credit	784.2	801.9	1,109.6	1,400.7	1,814.4	2,164.9	2,479.3	2,383.4

Table 9.2   Household balance sheet (SCF data billions of dollars, levels outstanding)

	1989	1992	1995	1998	2001	2004	2007	2010
Net worth	**16,094.2**	**16,238.8**	**19,351.4**	**27,039.7**	**39,772.8**	**47,401.0**	**61,164.9**	**54,524.2**
Assets	18,486.3	19,218.4	22,853.4	31,689.4	45,494.3	56,157.6	72,369.8	65,929.5
Tangible assets and business equity	11,600.8	11,860.1	12,820.5	16,379.4	22,818.2	31,859.6	42,478.7	36,391.3
Real estate, value of residences	6,812.4	7,245.8	8,052.5	10,313.8	14,242.3	21,522.6	28,039.0	23,360.5
Consumer durable goods	1,069.4	1,033.5	1,443.0	1,611.8	2,080.1	2,509.7	2,734.3	2,751.6
Equity in noncorporate business	3,719.0	3,580.9	3,325.1	4,453.8	6,495.8	7,827.3	11,705.4	10,279.2
Financial assets	6,885.5	7,358.3	10,032.8	15,310.0	22,676.0	24,297.9	29,891.0	29,538.2
Safe assets	3,000.5	2,874.4	3,061.7	3,686.5	5,671.0	6,751.8	7,200.4	8,508.7
Deposits and MMMF shares	2,064.5	1,975.0	2,028.0	2,432.5	3,420.7	4,964.6	5,596.8	6,774.5
Bonds	936.0	899.4	1,033.7	1,254.1	2,250.4	1,787.3	1,603.6	1,734.2
Risky assets	3,089.2	3,569.2	5,369.1	9,512.6	13,933.9	13,539.4	17,108.5	15,203.5
Directly held corporate equity	2,757.1	3,065.8	4,224.5	7,805.3	11,456.1	8,679.6	10,606.2	8,675.5
Long-term mutual funds	332.1	503.4	1,144.5	1,707.3	2,477.8	4,859.8	6,502.4	6,528.0
Assets inside 401(k)	795.8	914.6	1,602.1	2,110.8	3,071.1	4,006.7	5,582.1	5,826.0
Liabilities	2,392.1	2,979.6	3,502.0	4,649.7	5,721.5	8,756.6	11,204.9	11,405.2
Home mortgages	1,873.6	2,513.6	2,911.9	3,816.8	4,780.3	7,455.6	9,617.9	9,688.4
Consumer credit	518.6	465.9	590.1	832.9	941.2	1,301.0	1,586.9	1,716.8

9.2   Comparing SCF and FFA Net Worth

The SCF measure of net worth, as found in Bricker et al. (2012), and FFA's measure of net worth reported in the B.100 table of the Z.1 release are conceptually different in several ways. We perform adjustments to each measure to reconcile the two concepts as much as possible, given the available data, for comparability. While the adjustments affect aggregate levels of net worth, trend and cyclical patterns of net worth are relatively unaffected.

9.2.1   Conceptual Adjustments to FFA Net Worth

First, FFA household net worth includes the nonprofit sector. Where possible, we remove values that are attributable to the nonprofit sector. Certain categories are separately collected for nonprofit holdings, and therefore these can be directly removed. Other categories of household net worth are calculated as residuals after subtracting other sectors from the economy-wide total. For these categories, we cannot separate holdings of nonprofits from those of households, so the values associated with nonprofits remain in the FFA measure of net worth.

Second, pension wealth is treated differently in the two measures. Assets accruing through defined-benefit (DB) pensions plans are an important component of overall household wealth but one whose levels cannot be determined unambiguously using the SCF. Pension recipients, and the SCF by extension, cannot put a value on the assets associated with future or current DB pension payouts without numerous assumptions.[13] We therefore do not include DB pensions in the measure of household wealth using the SCF, and we must also remove these assets from the FFA household balance sheet.

Lastly, we also remove a few small categories of assets and liabilities that are difficult to measure or compare. On the asset side these categories are life insurance reserves and other financial assets (listed as security credit in FFA). We also remove margin loans and loans against life insurance policies from total liabilities. See table 9A.2 of the appendix for published and adjusted household wealth values.

The impact of these three adjustments can be found in figure 9.1, which presents household net worth measured by FFA from 1989 to 2010.[14] The top-most series is the net worth as reported on the B.100 table; the second line removes nonprofits where possible, and the lowest line is the FFA net worth that is adjusted for comparability with the SCF. These adjustments lower the level but do not substantially alter the time trend of FFA net worth. The FFA net worth climbs steadily between 1989 and 1999, after

---

13. The SCF asks whether respondents have DB pensions and their source, but collects no additional information about the magnitude of future payments.
14. We present third-quarter (Q3) data from FFA as that period matches most closely the average interview date in the SCF, particularly for high-wealth households.

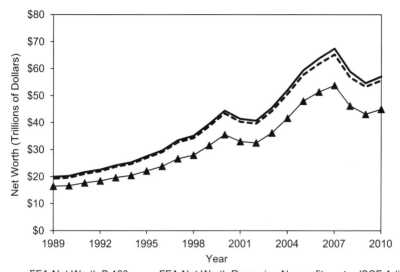

Fig. 9.1   Flow of Funds Accounts, measures of household net worth

Note: The "SCF adjusted" FFA net worth removes nonprofit assets, defined-benefit pension assets, and a few small categories as discussed in the text such as life insurance reserves. See appendix table 9A.2 for full details.

which it levels off for two years. The FFA net worth then climbs steeply until 2007, declines between 2007 and 2009, then recovers somewhat in 2010.

9.2.2   Conceptual Adjustments to SCF Net Worth

There are a few small adjustments made to the SCF to make the aggregates more comparable with FFA.[15] We allocate assets from trusts and IRAs to their component asset types. We remove the smaller categories of assets and liabilities as is done with FFA. These categories include expected payments like lottery winnings or proceeds from a lawsuit, and IRA assets in mineral rights. The FFA does not estimate the hedge fund sector separately, so we remove hedge funds from the SCF net worth. Much of the hedge fund assets will be included in the FFA household sector due to the residual nature of its measurement, but this will not provide full coverage of hedge funds held by households. Removing these hedge fund assets from the SCF household measure does not necessarily bring the two sources more in line with one another, but we do so since we are unable to compare the FFA and SCF on this dimension. Furthermore, SCF questions on hedge funds do not ask about the nature of these assets, which is a component of our

15. The difference between aggregate net worth that corresponds to the concept used by Bricker et al. (2012) and the values reported here range from 5 percent to 9 percent.

comparison of asset holdings in the SCF and FFA. Life insurance and any loans against the policy are removed from assets and liabilities, respectively. Finally, we remove second homes that collect rental income but are not reported as investment properties by the respondent.

These adjustments yield more comparable administrative and survey-based measures of net worth. Figure 9.2 shows that the fully adjusted net worth measures from the two sources track each other closely in the 1990s, with SCF generally coming in just shy of the FFA aggregates. In 2001, SCF net worth is about 25 percent higher than FFA net worth, and this difference persists in all subsequent waves. The leveling between 2000 and 2002 of the FFA is driven by a decline in corporate equity over this time period, and is partially offset by increases in house values. If corporate equity is excluded, the two series match up better between 1998 and 2004, but the SCF still shows higher growth in net worth, particularly from 1998 to 2001. Similarly, because the SCF is conducted every three years, it cannot capture the dynamics between 2008 and 2010 reflected in the FFA. However, both data sources show a similar three-year trend between 2007 and 2010.

The ratio of SCF to FFA net worth was very consistent and close to unity between 1989 and 1998. The ratio increased beginning in 2001, after which

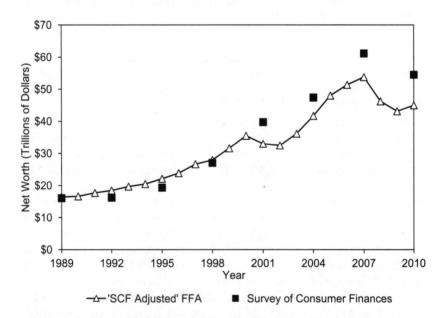

Fig. 9.2   **Net worth in comparable terms, Flow of Funds Accounts (FFA) and Survey of Consumer Finances (SCF)**

Note: The "'SCF adjusted" FFA net worth removes nonprofit assets, defined-benefit pension assets, and a few small categories as discussed in the text such as life insurance reserves. See appendix table 9A.2 for full details.

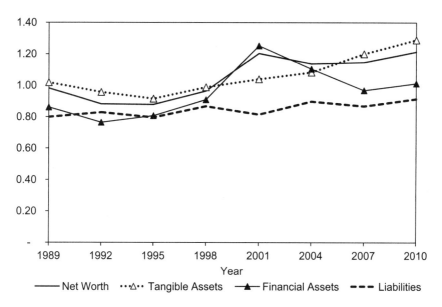

Fig. 9.3   Ratio of SCF aggregate to FFA aggregate value

the SCF shows at least 10 percent more household wealth (figure 9.3). The patterns differ by broad categories of net worth: tangible assets, financial assets, and liabilities. After 1995, there is a steady upward trend in tangible assets represented in the SCF compared to FFA. In 2001, there is a sharp break in financial assets patterns; while SCF financial assets were previously less than FFA financial assets, after 2001 SCF levels exceeded FFA, due to very little growth in the FFA between 1998 and 2001.[16] In 2007 and 2010, the SCF shows similar levels of financial assets as the FFA. The SCF-to-FFA ratio of total liabilities is relatively flat in comparison, remaining between 77 percent and 87 percent for all periods before reaching 90 percent in 2010.

9.3   Tangible Assets

Tangible assets consist of three categories: (a) owner-occupied residential real estate, (b) consumer durable goods, and (c) noncorporate business equity. In general, the level of tangible assets measured in the SCF grad-

16. The numbers for 2001 may appear to be outliers due to the substantial intrayear volatility of corporate equity prices that year. The SCF typically collects data from May to December, while the FFA values are point-in-time estimates, in our case at the close of the third quarter. For instance, the S&P 500 index declined 18 percent between May 1st and September 30th of 2001, then increased 10 percent between October 1st and December 31st. However, since list sample respondents of the SCF, which are chosen due to their high levels of wealth and therefore their large share of households' holdings of equity, are typically interviewed at the end of the field period, the timing of interviews is unlikely to be the sole reason for these outliers.

ually increases compared to the FFA after 1995 and continuing through 2010 (figure 9.3). This is a combination of relatively faster increases in both housing and noncorporate business values reported by households in the SCF. Although the SCF and FFA use fundamentally different approaches to valuing these infrequently traded assets, the overall pattern of boom and bust in asset values during the period leading up to and following the Great Recession is evident in both data sources.

9.3.1   Owner-Occupied Real Estate

The SCF and FFA once took relatively similar approaches to valuing owner-occupied real estate, but diverge methodologically in recent periods. The SCF collects owner-reported values in every survey year, which reflects respondents' subjective valuations at that point in time. The FFA also rely on owners' self-reported house values, from the American Housing Survey (AHS), which is conducted every two years. In between AHS surveys, the FFA use a national housing price index (HPI) from CoreLogic and net investment from the Bureau of Economic Analysis (BEA) to interpolate between the AHS reference points.[17] The AHS data from 2007, 2009, and 2011 were not incorporated into the FFA. At the time of their release, AHS owner-reported values were deemed unreliable relative to house price indices in measuring in changes in the aggregate value of the housing stock during the housing bust. In particular, respondents to the AHS indicated that house prices had continued to increase at a fairly rapid rate, on average, in 2006 and 2007. By contrast, market-based measures of house prices showed that prices leveled off in 2006 and fell sharply in 2007. In constructing the FFA, Federal Reserve Board staff decided not to incorporate survey-based information until they had conducted more research on the issue; such research is ongoing. Thus, since 2005, a perpetual inventory equation has been used to estimate the value of residential real estate in the FFA; the CoreLogic national house price index is used as a proxy for price changes for the existing stock, and net investment is from BEA.

Throughout most SCF survey years since 1989, the SCF and FFA measures of aggregate home values are very close. This is not surprising, as both are grounded in owner-reported values of homes.[18] The SCF asks home owners how much their house would be worth if sold at the time of the interview. The AHS poses a question with the exact same wording as the SCF. The primary difference between the AHS and the SCF is that the AHS is a sample of *homes*, not households, and is collected in odd-numbered years,

---

17. The CoreLogic HPI is calculated using multiple sales of the same property to remove unobserved heterogeneity associated with each property. http://www.corelogic.com/products /corelogic-hpi.aspx.

18. Following the FFA approach of measuring owner-occupied residential real estate for comparability, we remove any residential property that collects rental income from aggregate SCF measures. The SCF also measures vacation homes more accurately than the AHS, which is another reason why the SCF values are larger than the FFA.

while the SCF is collected every three years. Given these minor differences, it is not surprising that from 1989 through 2001, the levels of owner-occupied real estate observed in the SCF and the FFA (which is benchmarked to the AHS) match well. In 1998 and 2001, there is a slight divergence, with the SCF reporting higher values by almost 10 percent (see table 9.3 and figure 9.4).

Table 9.3 Household balance sheet (ratio of SCF aggregate to FFA aggregate)

	1989	1992	1995	1998	2001	2004	2007	2010
Net worth	0.98	0.88	0.88	0.96	1.20	1.14	1.15	1.21
Assets	0.95	0.87	0.86	0.95	1.14	1.09	1.09	1.15
Tangible assets and business equity	1.02	0.96	0.92	0.99	1.04	1.08	1.20	1.29
Real estate, value of residences	1.04	1.01	1.01	1.09	1.07	1.17	1.31	1.40
Consumer durable goods	0.56	0.48	0.58	0.58	0.63	0.66	0.62	0.60
Equity in noncorporate business	1.26	1.18	0.95	1.03	1.22	1.08	1.23	1.48
Financial assets	0.86	0.76	0.81	0.91	1.25	1.10	0.97	1.01
Safe assets	0.64	0.56	0.53	0.58	0.77	0.73	0.59	0.64
Deposits and MMMF shares	0.64	0.60	0.61	0.64	0.71	0.88	0.77	0.86
Bonds	0.64	0.49	0.43	0.48	0.89	0.49	0.33	0.32
Risky assets	1.19	1.01	1.01	1.12	1.61	1.34	1.15	1.23
Directly held corporate equity	1.32	1.12	1.03	1.27	1.90	1.29	1.03	1.11
Long-term mutual funds	0.65	0.63	0.91	0.73	0.95	1.42	1.41	1.43
Assets inside 401(k)	1.17	0.98	1.17	1.08	1.46	1.56	1.43	1.63
Liabilities	0.80	0.83	0.80	0.87	0.81	0.90	0.87	0.91
Home mortgages	0.85	0.90	0.89	0.96	0.92	0.98	0.92	0.96
Consumer credit	0.66	0.58	0.53	0.59	0.52	0.60	0.64	0.72

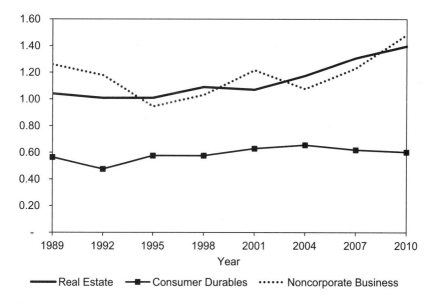

Fig. 9.4 Ratio of SCF aggregate to FFA aggregate value: Tangible assets

The comparability between SCF and AHS owner-reported house values is evident at all points in the distribution of house values and across survey years. Comparison of values over time requires harmonizing the SCF values with the top-coding of high values in the AHS. The public-use AHS is topcoded at $350,000 through 2003, but that topcode limit was increased in 2005 and is now tied to house price growth. In order to facilitate a direct comparison across the house price distributions, we artificially cap the AHS values at $350,000 in 2005, so that the increase in the topcode effectively occurs in 2007 when the next wave of the SCF was conducted. We topcode SCF home values at the same thresholds as the AHS in every year. The FFA adjust down the aggregate AHS value of residential real estate 5.5 percent in 2001, 2003, and 2005 to account for the apparent upward bias in reported home values in survey responses shown in Goodman and Ittner (1992) and others.

After making the topcode adjustments, owner-reported house values across survey years line up very well both in terms of the aggregate (figure 9.5) and at various percentiles in the distribution of house values (figure 9.6).[19] One small difference is the value at the 90th percentile in the AHS is slightly smaller than in the SCF beginning in the late 1990s. Thus, even though the sampling approach is very different between the two surveys, the picture of housing values and trends is very similar. That is, the boom and bust in house prices leading up to and following the Great Recession is evident in both surveys.

Beginning with the 2004 SCF survey, there is a growing divergence between the SCF and FFA; in 2007 and 2010, the SCF estimate was more than 30 percent larger than the FFA estimate. The 2004 FFA value combines information from the 2003 AHS, the CoreLogic index between 2003 and 2004, and net investment in housing between those two years. It was a period of rapidly rising house prices, with the growth in 2004 exceeding the gains in 2002 and 2003 according to the national CoreLogic HPI. Between 2001 and 2004, the SCF reported total growth of 50 percent while the FFA and CoreLogic HPI report a change of approximately 40 percent. It is unclear whether the divergence is happening more in the early period (2001–2002) than the later period (2003–2004). According to CoreLogic, the growth from 2003 to 2004 was 50 percent larger than in the two preceding years (about 15 percent compared to annual growth rates of about 10 percent).

In the most recent period, 2007 to 2010, the SCF data show much higher aggregate housing values than the FFA. The divergence in 2007 and 2010 may not be surprising given the differences in estimation methodology. Since the FFA have not been benchmarked to the AHS since 2005, the estimates

19. The 90th percentile in 2005 is missing because it corresponds to a topcoded value. Beginning in 2005, AHS observations with values above the topcode value are given the mean of all properties above the threshold.

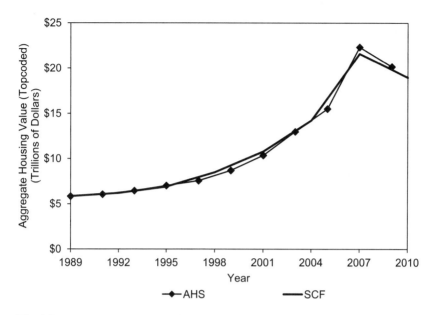

Fig. 9.5   Aggregate owner-occupied real estate, SCF and AHS, topcoded

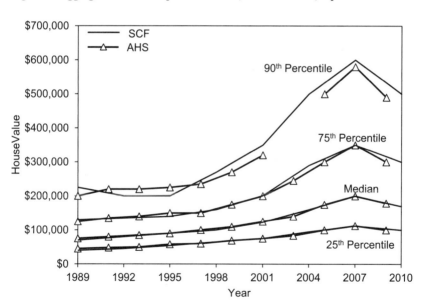

Fig. 9.6   Percentiles from distribution of home values, SCF and AHS

are now driven by transaction-based measures of home values rather than owners' reports. The CoreLogic HPI represents changes in the value of houses that transact in a given period, whereas the SCF is a sample of households, most of which did not engage in a recent transaction. As a result, the SCF and FFA are now using different conceptual frameworks to measure changes in house prices over time.

Most of the increased gap between SCF and FFA aggregate house values occurred between 2004 and 2007. During this period, the housing price boom continued through 2005 before leveling off in 2006 and declining in 2007, the year leading up to the Great Recession. In the period 2007 to 2010, the decline in SCF self-reported house values was less than the value indicated by the CoreLogic transaction-based index, and thus the gap between SCF and FFA aggregates continued to widen, albeit at a slower pace.

9.3.2   Durable Goods

The second category of tangible assets common to the SCF and FFA is durable goods. The FFA obtain values directly from the BEA. The SCF's method of measuring durable goods remains the same over the full time period.[20] The ratio of SCF to FFA is fairly constant over the full time period, averaging 60 percent representation of what the FFA reports. This difference is confirmed using BEA tables that show categories not measured by the SCF account for more than 30 percent of all consumer durable goods. As a result, both sources show similar trends in households' holdings of durable goods.

9.3.3   Equity in Noncorporate Business

Among tangible assets, noncorporate businesses are held by the fewest number of households, and the distribution of the holdings is extremely skewed.[21] The nonfinancial noncorporate business sector consists of partnerships and limited liability companies, sole proprietorships, and properties that receive rental income. Noncorporate farms are included in this sector. For noncorporate financial firms, the FFA include security brokers and dealers. Differences in the valuation methods used by the SCF and FFA along with a high degree of sampling variability (see appendix) because of the distribution of owned business values combine to generate a volatile measure in which SCF business values typically exceed those in the FFA.

The FFA rely on intermediary sources for noncorporate financial and nonfinancial noncorporate business values. For noncorporate financial businesses the FFA get their estimates from SEC filings of security brokers and dealers. For noncorporate nonfinancial businesses, financial assets are estimated using IRS estimates based on business income reported on tax

---

20. Durable goods measured by the SCF include vehicles, which comprise the majority of this category, small valuables, and other collectibles.
21. Fewer than 15 percent of households held noncorporate equity in 2007 and 2010.

returns, nonfinancial assets are estimated using data from BEA, and data on noncorporate farms primarily come from the US Department of Agriculture (USDA).[22] The FFA estimates of real estate holdings incorporate data from CoStar. As with owner-occupied housing, the SCF asks noncorporate business owners how much they believe their business would sell for today.

The SCF finds higher aggregate values for noncorporate equity than the FFA in every year except for 1995.[23] From 1989 to 1995, the two series moved closer together, and in fact, the FFA estimate exceeded the SCF aggregate in 1995. Since then, the two series have diverged substantially, but the overall pattern of boom and bust leading up to and following the Great Recession is evident in both data sets. The value of noncorporate business grew roughly 80 percent in both data sets between 2001 and 2007, though the growth during the boom underscores the difficulties with getting precise estimates. The ratio of SCF to FFA noncorporate equity fell from 122 percent to 108 percent between 2001 and 2004, before rising to 123 percent by 2007. Since the FFA show that real estate holdings comprise much of the net worth of noncorporate businesses, differences in owner-reported and index-based values might explain why SCF measures tend to exceed FFA measures. Sampling variability may also be an issue in the latest comparison (see appendix), but methodological differences may also have played a role. The aggregate value of noncorporate businesses fell about 27 percent in the FFA between 2007 and 2010, while the corresponding decline in the SCF was 12 percent. Thus, the gap between the two estimates widened substantially in the most recent survey. One possible explanation for this recent divergence is that FFA values are tied more directly to realized business incomes, which took a substantial hit during the Great Recession.

9.4   Financial Assets

Financial assets are a large component of total assets and net worth. These assets, which include risky assets like corporate equity, and other assets like deposits, which we will call safe assets, can be held in various types of accounts. High-level FFA-SCF comparisons across account types and risk types tell the same story over time, though we see divergence in detailed drilldowns of portfolio allocation. In both data sets, the aggregate level of financial assets reached about 30 trillion dollars in 2010 (see tables 9.1 and 9.2). In the first half of our study period, the SCF reported lower levels of

22. A description of the data sources and limitations can be found at http://www.irs.gov /taxstats/bustaxstats/article/0,,id=214346,00.html.

23. Antoniewicz's (2000) values for noncorporate equity in the SCF are much lower for 1989 to 1998. As a result, she finds that either FFA and SCF are very comparable or that SCF is smaller. Antoniewicz (2000) includes our definition of other residential real estate (vacation homes) as investment real estate instead of net nonresidential real estate. From 1989 through 1998, the value of net nonresidential real estate is more than twice the value of other residential properties.

financial assets than the FFA. The trend has a large break in 2001, after which the ratio of SCF to FFA financial assets fell.[24] In the past two SCF surveys, both SCF and FFA show similar levels of financial assets. However, patterns for detailed asset types are not as close for the two data sets, which can be expected due to the very different methods used by the FFA and SCF for allocating financial assets to asset classes.

9.4.1   Assets inside and outside Retirement Accounts

The highest-level breakdown within financial assets is the distinction between assets held inside and outside 401(k)-type accounts and other defined contribution plans, trusts, and managed investment trusts (MIAs). For simplicity, we will refer to these as 401(k)-type plans. Since data on 401(k)-type accounts are collected separately from other financial assets for both the SCF and the FFA, we will consider these assets on their own. Figure 9.7 displays the SCF-FFA ratio of safe and risky assets held outside 401(k)-type accounts and assets inside 401(k)-type accounts over time. While the time trend of measurement of safe and risky assets outside 401(k)-type accounts on the two data sets are similar, the SCF level of 401(k)-type assets has grown relative to the FFA since 1998.

For financial assets outside 401(k)-type accounts the FFA values are residuals, so they include assets held by nonprofits and hedge funds.[25] The FFA data on IRA holdings are reported in their respective asset class: deposits, bonds, corporate equity, and mutual funds. Making the SCF comparable to the FFA here requires allocating assets to the same asset categories. Furthermore, the SCF methodology for estimating the value of non-401(k)-type holdings of detailed asset types has changed over time so we will instead focus primarily on analyzing risky assets, which include corporate equity and mutual funds, versus safe assets, which include deposits and bonds.

9.4.2   Deposits and Bonds outside 401(k)-Type Accounts

The SCF levels of safe assets (deposits and bonds) are consistently lower than FFA levels. One explanation is that the residual nature of FFA safe assets likely increases their value relative to the SCF since the FFA include assets held by nonhousehold entities, such as churches and other nonprofits, which are likely to have significant holdings of deposits and bonds.[26] The SCF-FFA ratio of safe assets is generally between 0.53 and 0.64, with slightly elevated ratios in 2001 to 2004. Deposits in the SCF are consistently lower than in the FFA. The levels of deposits measured by the SCF were

24. Refer to footnote 17 for more information about 2001 data.
25. Hedge funds are also included in FFA residuals as they do not have direct reporting requirements that could be used to remove them. As mentioned above, some of these assets are held by households.
26. See footnote 11 for more information on FFA data on nonprofit organizations.

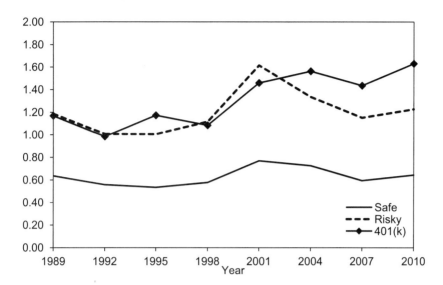

Fig. 9.7   Ratio of SCF aggregate to FFA aggregate value: Financial assets

Notes: Safe assets include deposits and bonds while risky assets include corporate equity and mutual funds.

stable at about 60 percent of FFA deposits until 1998. The SCF-FFA ratio rose to about 70 percent in 2001 and since has stabilized around 80 percent. Some of the reasons for this persistent gap between the SCF and FFA have been established. Avery, Elliehausen, and Kennickell (1988) discuss some of these explanations. For instance, unlike the FFA, the SCF measure does not include currency. Also, check float and the holdings of churches could account for some of the discrepancy.

The SCF also reports much lower bond holdings than the FFA. The SCF-FFA ratio of bonds has declined somewhat from 59 percent in 1989 to 50 percent or below in all years except 2001. In 2001, the ratio reached over 80 percent. Furthermore, the pattern is also partially driven by no growth in bond holdings in the FFA between 1998 and 2001 with a large increase measured in the SCF, which saw almost 100 percent increase. Lastly, SCF respondents are likely to report the face value of their bonds, which may differ from the book values or other types of valuations used in the FFA (see Antoniewicz 2000).[27]

27. Our analysis yields different findings than Antoniewicz (2000) due to large upward revisions that have been made since 2000 to the FFA historical series.

9.4.3   Mutual Funds and Corporate Equity
outside 401(k)-Type Accounts

Risky financial assets consist of mutual funds and corporate equities. The SCF-FFA ratio is close to one in the 1990s. However, the ratio jumps from 1.12 in 1998 to 1.61 in 2001. This is likely attributable to new SCF questions on asset allocations within IRAs added during the 2001 wave.[28] In previous waves, IRA accounts were allocated to risky and safe assets based on simple rules-of-thumb drawn from brief follow-up survey questions.[29] After 2001, the SCF-FFA ratio came down to lower levels.

Comparing SCF and FFA measure of the two subcomponents of risky assets requires even more detailed allocation of SCF assets. All risky assets held in IRAs, trusts, and MIAs were allocated to corporate equities for survey waves prior 2004, but were subsequently allocated to mutual funds from 2004 onward. Therefore, we expect that the SCF will understate true household holdings of corporate equity and overstate holdings of mutual funds prior to 2004, and vice versa thereafter.

The FFA levels of the value of publicly traded corporate equities are drawn from direct measures of publicly traded shares. For closely held corporations, the FFA combine information from IRS revenue data on S corporations, data from *Forbes* on private C corporations, and data from Compustat. In all survey waves, SCF levels of corporate equity exceed FFA levels. With one exception, the typical difference between SCF and FFA levels is approximately 15 percent. Like the SCF-FFA ratio of bonds, the ratio of corporate equity spiked in 2001, reaching 1.90. Similar to the trend between 1998 and 2001 for net worth, SCF and FFA measures of corporate equities diverge between these two waves. The FFA do not show an increase in corporate equity between these two waves, whereas the SCF levels increase over 40 percent.

The value of mutual funds in the SCF has increased relative to the FFA over the course of the study period. Initially, the SCF-FFA ratio of long-term mutual funds was approximately 0.65. It rose to 0.91 in 1995, dropped in 1998, and in 2001 rose to 0.95. Since 2004, the SCF levels of mutual funds have exceeded 1.4 times that of the FFA. This is consistent with the change in IRA allocations on the SCF discussed above.

9.4.4   Assets inside 401(k)-Type Accounts

Holdings in 401(k)-type accounts are collected separately from other financial assets in both the SCF and the FFA. Prior to 2001, the SCF and

28. Unlike assets held within 401(k)-type accounts and IRA accounts, SCF respondents are queried specifically about holdings of particular asset classes held outside these accounts during all waves.
29. Antoniewicz (2000) assigns the assets in SCF based on the type of institution holding the account. However, this approach is no longer realistic due to consolidation in the banking industry.

FFA show very similar levels of assets in 401(k)-type accounts. Starting in 2001, the SCF reports levels of 401(k) holdings that are over 40 percent higher than those reported by the FFA. Some of this divergence may be due to data coverage. The SCF changed its questionnaire in 2001 to include current and future work-related defined contribution plans.

Consequently, the SCF level of 401(k) holdings has exceeded that on the FFA persistently since 2001. The SCF-FFA ratio held relatively steady between 2001 and 2007 and increased in 2010. This is due to the fact that the SCF shows an increase in the value of assets between 2007 and 2010, whereas the FFA show a modest decline.

9.5   Liabilities

Household liabilities cover home mortgages and consumer credit and debt. Levels of liabilities have increased over time, as shown both in the FFA and SCF data (see tables 9.1 and 9.2). However, we do not expect aggregate levels of liabilities as measured on the FFA to perfectly match SCF aggregate levels due to major differences in their methods. Like the SCF's approach to collecting data on assets, the survey asks respondents about their liabilities account by account. The FFA collects data on liabilities by type of institution, including savings institutions, credit unions, government-sponsored enterprises, and finance companies. Data on mortgages, consumer credit, and other liabilities are collected separately, and subtypes are not drilled down. In contrast, SCF asks respondents about various types of outstanding debt within those three categories. For instance, respondents are asked separately about mortgages and home equity lines of credit on primary and second homes, credit cards, education loans, vehicle loans, and so forth. Furthermore, the two sets of data measure fundamentally different concepts. The FFA collect data on consumer *credit*, which includes current balances that consumers may pay off in full without incurring interest—so-called "convenience credit," whereas SCF focuses on outstanding consumer *debt*, which excludes convenience credit.

As can be seen in figure 9.3, the ratio of total liabilities from the SCF and FFA has been relatively stable during this time period. Liabilities on the SCF were about 77 percent of those measured by the FFA in 1992, and this ratio subsequently hovered around 80 percent, ending at 88 percent in 2010. As shown in figure 9.8, the SCF-FFA ratios of the two major categories of liabilities (mortgages and consumer credit/debt) have been relatively stable over time.

9.5.1   Home Mortgages

Overall, the SCF and FFA measures of home mortgages track each other quite well. The SCF levels of home mortgages have become modestly closer to FFA levels over time. The SCF levels of mortgages were between 85

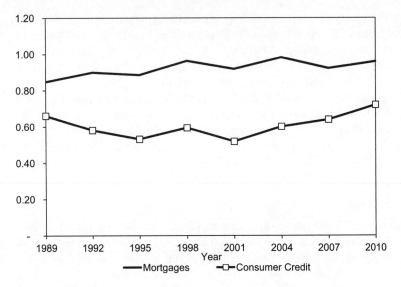

Fig. 9.8   **Ratio of SCF aggregate to FFA aggregate value: Liabilities**

and 98 percent, settling at 96 percent in 2010. This comparison suggests that administrative and survey measures of home mortgages exhibit similar trends over time. The similarities are likely attributable to the fact that the FFA and SCF have relatively consistent conceptual definitions and data collection methods throughout the sample period. The results are consistent with Bucks and Pence's (2008) findings that the mortgage terms reported by home owners on the SCF match administrative records as well for fixed-rate mortgages. Both data sets show a growth in home mortgages over time, with a leveling off between 2007 and 2010.

9.5.2   Consumer Credit and Debt

While the SCF measures outstanding consumer *debt*, the FFA explicitly measures consumer *credit*, which includes current balances, whether or not they are paid off in full without incurring interest. Therefore, SCF measures of consumer debt should, due to definitional differences, be smaller than FFA measures. Furthermore, the discrepancy between the two sources of data may change over time depending on the importance of convenience credit.[30] The greater the convenience use of consumer credit, the greater the definitional discrepancy between the SCF and FFA measures of liabilities. Lastly, some differences may arise due to difficulties in separating spending for personal versus business purposes.

---

30. Johnson (2004) presents evidence that levels of convenience credit have increased over time.

The SCF consumer debt was about two-thirds the level of consumer credit measured by the FFA in 1992, falling to half in 2001, then rose to 71 percent in 2010. This is consistent with previous studies documenting the gap between credit card measures, one of the primary components of consumer credit/debt, on the SCF and FFA. Zinman (2009) has shown a gap in aggregate credit card debt between the SCF and G.19 release, the FFA's main source for credit card data.[31]

9.5.3 Credit Card Balances on Administrative and Household Microdata

The G.19 data used by the FFA are aggregates from administrative data, and the SCF collects microdata using survey responses. To investigate whether discrepancies between the two data sources arise because one source uses macrodata whereas the other uses microdata, or because one uses administrative sources rather than survey responses, we turn to a third data set. The Federal Reserve Bank of New York's Consumer Credit Panel (CCP) provides administrative microdata on household liabilities for individuals with credit reports (Lee and van der Klaauw 2010). In a comparison of 2007 data from the SCF and the CCP, Brown et al. (2011) find that the levels of overall debt from the two data sources are fairly close, as are levels of overall home-secured debt and education loans. However, the authors find that rates and levels of holding credit card debt are lower on the SCF than the CCP.[32]

In particular, Brown et al. find that about 46 percent of SCF respondents report outstanding credit card debt, whereas the Consumer Credit Panel/Equifax implies 76 percent of households have credit card balances on their credit reports. The 46 percent rate calculated in the SCF is the proportion of households presumed to have credit reports that report outstanding balances on credit cards after the last payments on those accounts. However, the 76 percent of households with credit card balances from the CCP is computed using any credit card balances from credit reports and cannot distinguish between convenience usage and such outstanding balances. Adding in the additional 28 percentage points of SCF 2007 households who report having new credit card charges (but no outstanding balances) yields an estimated 74 percent of credit-report generating households with credit card charges, compared to the 76 percent found in the CCP.

Including new credit card charges as well as outstanding balances on credit cards on the SCF, which makes the SCF measure of credit card balances more comparable to the administrative data, also substantially increases SCF aggregate credit card levels. This broader measure would increase SCF

---

31. See Furletti and Ody (2006) for more details on the G.19 estimate of consumer credit.

32. Their results are consistent with Zinman (2009), which is unsurprising given that the CCP and G.19 both measure credit from credit cards, not outstanding balances alone.

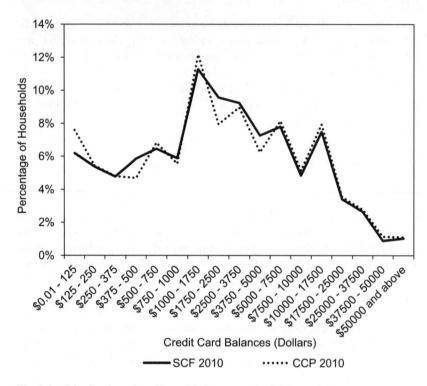

Fig. 9.9   Distribution of credit card balances on the SCF and CCP, 2010

levels of credit card debt by 28 percent in 2001 and 2004, 21 percent in 2007, and 25 percent in 2010.

Figure 9.9 shows the distribution of credit card balances by household, conditional on having any credit card spending, in the CCP and the SCF (using the broader definition including new charges) in 2010. The distributions are quite close across the four waves of the SCF that overlap with the CCP data.[33] Therefore, the distributions of comparable concepts are very close for administrative and survey-based microdata.

Table 9.4 shows the proportion of total balances attributable to new charges for waves between 2001 and 2010. In all waves, the greater the total balance on credit cards, the smaller the proportion attributable to new charges. For instance, the vast majority of balances under $1,000 are attributable to new charges rather than revolved debt. Both mean and median proportions of total balances attributable to new charges have declined in

33. In 2001 and 2004, the CCP shows greater mass between $7,500 and $17,500, but the distributions line up remarkably for this range in 2007 and 2010. The figures for 2001 to 2007 are available upon request.

Table 9.4   Proportion of total credit card spending attributable to new charges, SCF

Balances (dollars)	2001		2004		2007		2010	
	Mean (%)	Median (%)	Mean (%)	Median (%)	Mean (%)	Median (%)	Mean (%)	Median (%)
0.01–125	88.9	100	92.0	100	82.4	100	87.5	100
125–250	80.0	100	79.2	100	71.7	100	75.9	100
250–375	75.7	100	68.7	100	64.9	100	72.8	100
375–500	69.8	100	70.4	100	63.8	100	70.8	100
500–750	62.6	77.6	61.4	68.1	58.3	69.2	66.8	100
750–1,000	62.6	68.7	63.7	100	59.5	82.2	65.2	100
1,000–1,750	54.5	51.1	56.0	53.8	55.0	58.9	56.3	59.8
1,750–2,500	49.7	44.7	54.0	52.5	50.2	48.9	59.4	83.4
2,500–3,750	40.1	21.3	41.0	18.4	43.3	27.0	53.0	50.0
3,750–5,000	36.8	10.4	40.6	24.6	40.1	16.7	45.6	26.3
5,000–7,500	26.5	7.7	33.2	13.1	34.7	9.8	39.3	11.7
7,500–10,000	21.2	7.3	22.2	4.8	25.4	5.9	33.9	6.7
10,000–17,500	17.4	3.8	18.9	5.1	16.2	3.8	19.8	3.9
17,500–25,000	17.6	3.5	19.5	4.5	12.5	2.3	14.3	2.2
25,000–37,500	24.5	4.1	17.7	2.5	13.6	3.2	11.0	1.6
37,500–50,000	12.7	0.9	24.7	2.8	11.0	5.1	11.3	1.3
50,000 and above	29.2	7.0	18.8	5.2	6.4	1.4	11.0	2.1

2007 to 2010 for high balances over $25,000, which would be consistent with the narrowing gap in consumer credit and debt on the SCF and FFA in recent waves.

Further research is needed to investigate if other characteristics of consumer debt are sources of discrepancies between survey and administrative data. In addition to conceptual differences between consumer credit on the FFA and consumer debt on the SCF, differences in credit card measures might be attributable to the individual nature of such accounts. Whereas mortgages might be considered household-level loans, credit card accounts are often held separately by different members of the family, and information on the account-level charges and debts may be shared across family members differently in different households. Since the SCF only interviews one respondent per household, such heterogeneity may lead to some respondents producing highly accurate levels of outstanding balances and new charges, if they are single or are fully aware of the credit card behavior of all other members of the family. Other respondents may not be able to accurately report credit card behavior on behalf of their relatives. In addition, the SCF asks respondents to exclude business credit cards. Individuals may use business cards for personal spending, and personal spending for business purposes, which makes it difficult for both the survey and administrative side to isolate personal debt of households. Further investigation can shed light on the relative importance of these factors in explaining why SCF aggregate liabilities have been 80 to 91 percent of FFA aggregate liabilities.

9.6 Conclusions

The period leading up to the Great Recession can be characterized by a dramatic increase in asset prices, especially for tangible assets like owner-occupied housing and noncorporate businesses, and to some extent in the value of corporate equities and other risky assets as well. The other dominant feature of the decade or so preceding the recent financial crisis was an explosion in household debt, especially mortgages, associated with that boom in asset prices. The financial crisis itself was, of course, driven by the subsequent collapse in asset prices, which combined with elevated debt levels, has left many household balance sheets in distress.

These overarching patterns of boom and bust in asset prices and debt accumulation along with the consequent effects on household balance sheets are evident in both the macrolevel FFA and the microlevel SCF. There is some divergence between the SCF and FFA in terms of asset prices increases during the boom, and to a lesser extent in the severity of asset price declines in the most recent period, but the general implications for household behavior one takes away from the long-term trends and fluctuations is basically the same. The different patterns that do exist in categories such as owner-occupied real estate, noncorporate businesses, and credit cards are attributable, at least in part, to methodological differences in the production of the two data sets.

Researchers using the SCF and FFA to study various aspects of household behavior need to appreciate the different strengths of each data set. Maki and Palumbo (2001) incorporate household heterogeneity in income and educational attainment measured by the SCF with the aggregate trends found in the FFA and exploit the strengths of both data sets in tandem. Similarly, Gale and Pence (2006) use the SCF to show that the aggregate increase in wealth that occurred in the 1990s accrued favored older households over younger ones. Likewise, researchers should keep those methodological differences in mind when drawing conclusions.

Appendix

Table 9A.1   Household balance sheet (SCF data standard errors)

	1989	1992	1995	1998	2001	2004	2007	2010
Net worth	**898.0**	**409.3**	**523.9**	**652.7**	**710.4**	**1,292.4**	**927.2**	**1,076.3**
Assets	955.0	425.8	541.2	644.8	741.5	1,348.5	939.8	1090.6
Tangible assets and business equity	720.7	234.6	266.3	316.6	475.7	745.4	783.6	634.1
Real estate, value of residences	250.1	166.5	148.6	216.4	241.5	501.9	448.8	384.8
Consumer durable goods	50.7	29.5	38.2	39.5	79.0	75.1	58.5	63.3
Equity in noncorporate business	545.4	176.0	193.4	324.2	385.3	463.7	656.4	545.7
Financial assets	416.7	286.8	407.7	523.7	562.0	782.4	682.9	862.4
Safe assets	214.4	94.7	181.2	124.2	203.9	283.2	235.8	397.5
Deposits and MMMF shares	137.9	67.7	124.8	103.1	137.5	229.8	164.4	319.9
Bonds	122.4	66.0	92.7	83.1	148.6	148.3	132.3	224.1
Risky assets	255.3	283.2	288.6	491.6	471.4	536.3	588.0	641.5
Directly held corporate equity	264.2	246.1	228.5	441.4	435.4	436.3	486.3	536.4
Long-term mutual funds	51.0	57.5	133.9	130.0	146.4	274.0	265.7	308.5
Assets inside 401(k)	78.9	77.9	83.9	106.6	169.1	196.1	244.4	249.2
Liabilities	101.8	84.8	63.7	103.8	123.7	188.2	206.5	228.4
Home mortgages	90.5	81.8	59.3	94.2	120.2	174.4	197.3	215.8
Consumer credit	29.5	25.0	15.1	22.5	35.0	47.8	43.7	48.1
Personal income (NIPA; 1 year lag)	141.1	48.8	72.3	90.9	204.6	116.5	150.4	130.9

Note: Billions of dollars, levels outstanding.

Table 9A.2   Adjustments to FFA household net worth, 2010 annual

B.100 Households and nonprofit organizations: net worth	**$ 57,080,160**
Step 2. Subtract nonprofit assets	
Nonprofit organizations: real estate at market value	$ 1,888,508
Nonprofit organizations: equipment and software, current cost basis	$ 304,618
Equals	*$ 54,887,034*
Step 3. Add nonprofit liabilities	
Nonprofit organizations: municipal securities and loans, liability	$ 268,092
Nonprofit organizations: commercial mortgages, liability	$ 184,426
Nonprofit organizations: trade payables, liability	$ 268,745
Equals	*$ 55,608,297*
Step 4. Subtract non-SCF comparable assets	
Households and nonprofit organizations, total miscellaneous assets	$ 811,907
Equals	*$ 54,796,390*
Step 5. Add non-SCF comparable liabilities	
Households and nonprofit organizations, other loans and advances, liability	$ 135,816
Life insurance companies, deferred and unpaid life insurance premiums, asset	$ 22,560
Equals	*$ 54,954,766*
Step 6. Subtract off all pension fund assets	
Households and nonprofit organizations, pension fund reserves, asset	$ 12,332,064
Equals	*$ 42,622,702*
Step 7. Add DC pensions	
Private defined contribution pension funds, total financial assets	$ 3,574,161
Federal government retirement funds, total financial assets of held by Thrift Savings Plan	$ 246,937
Equals	**$ 46,443,800**

References

Antoniewicz, Rochelle L. 2000. "A Comparison of the Household Sector from the Flow of Funds Accounts and the Survey of Consumer Finances." Federal Reserve Board of Governors Survey of Consumer Finances Working Paper. http://www.federalreserve.gov/econresdata/scf/scf_workingpapers.htm.

Avery, Robert B., Gregory E. Elliehausen, and Arthur B. Kennickell. 1988. "Measuring Wealth with Survey Data: An Evaluation of the 1983 Survey of Consumer Finances." *Review of Income and Wealth* 34 (4): 339–69.

Avery, Robert B., and Arthur B. Kennickell. 1991. "Household Saving in the US" *Review of Income and Wealth* 37 (4): 409–32.

Bosworth, Barry. 2012. *The Decline in Saving: A Threat to America's Prosperity?* Washington, DC: Brookings Institution Press.

Bricker, Jesse, Brian Bucks, Arthur Kennickell, Traci Mach, and Kevin Moore. 2011. "Surveying the Aftermath of the Storm: Changes in Family Finances from 2007 to 2009." Finance and Economics Discussion Series 2011–17. Federal Reserve Board of Governors.

Bricker, Jesse, Arthur B. Kennickell, Kevin B. Moore, and John Sabelhaus. 2012. "Changes in US Family Finances from 2007 to 2010: Evidence from the Survey of Consumer Finances." *Federal Reserve Bulletin* 98 (2): 1–80.

Brown, Meta, Andrew Haughwout, Donghoon Lee, and Wilbert van der Klaauw. 2011. "Do We Know What We Owe? A Comparison of Borrower- and Lender-Reported Consumer Debt." Federal Reserve Bank of New York Staff Report no. 523.

Browning, Martin, and Annamaria Lusardi. 1996. "Household Saving: Micro Theories and Micro Facts." *Journal of Economic Literature* 34 (4): 1797–855.

Bucks, Brian, and Karen Pence. 2008. "Do Borrowers Know their Mortgage Terms?" *Journal of Urban Economics* 64 (2): 218–33.

Curtin, Richard T., Thomas Juster, and James N. Morgan. 1989. "Survey Estimates of Wealth: An Assessment of Quality." In *The Measurement of Saving, Investment, and Wealth*, edited by Robert E. Lipsey and Helen Stone Tice, 473–552. Chicago: University of Chicago Press.

De Nardi, Mariacristina, Eric French, and David Benson. 2012. "Consumption and the Great Recession." Federal Reserve Bank of Chicago, *Economic Perspectives* 1Q:1–17.

Dynan, Karen E. 2012. "Is A Household Debt Overhang Holding Back Consumption?" *Brookings Papers on Economic Activity* 44 (1): 299–362.

Furletti, Mark, and Christopher Ody. 2006. "Measuring US Credit Card Borrowing: An Analysis of the G.19's Estimate of Consumer Revolving Credit." Federal Reserve Bank of Philadelphia Payment Cards Center Discussion Paper. http://www.philadelphiafed.org/consumer-credit-and-payments/payment-cards-center/publications/discussion-papers/2006/DG192006April10.pdf.

Gale, William G., and Karen M. Pence. 2006. "Are Successive Generations Getting Wealthier, and if so, Why? Evidence from the 1990s." *Brookings Papers on Economic Activity* 2006 (1): 155–213.

Goodman, John R., and John B. Ittner. 1992. "The Accuracy of Home Owner's Estimates of House Value." *Journal of Housing Economics* 2:339–57.

Hubbard, R. Glenn, Jonathan Skinner, and Stephen P. Zeldes. 1994. "The Importance of Precautionary Motives in Explaining Individual and Aggregate Saving." *Carnegie-Rochester Conference Series on Public Policy* 40:59–125.

Johnson, Kathleen W. 2004. "Convenience or Necessity? Understanding the Recent Rise in Credit Card Debt." Finance and Economics Discussion Series 2004-47. Board of Governors of the Federal Reserve System.

Kennickell, Arthur B. 2011. "Tossed and Turned: Wealth Dynamics of US Households 2007–2009." Finance and Economics Discussion Series 2011-51. Board of Governors of the Federal Reserve System.

Lee, Donghoon, and Wilbert van der Klaauw. 2010. "An Introduction to the FRBNY Consumer Credit Panel." Federal Reserve Bank of New York Staff Report no. 479. http://www.newyorkfed.org/research/staff_reports/sr479.html.

Lettau, Martin, and Sydney C. Ludvigson. 2004. "Understanding Trend and Cycle in Asset Values: Reevaluating the Wealth Effect on Consumption." *American Economic Review* 94 (1): 276–99.

Maki, Dean M., and Michael G. Palumbo. 2001. "Disentangling the Wealth Effect: A Cohort Analysis of Household Saving in the 1990s." Finance and Economics Discussion Series 2001-21. Federal Reserve Board of Governors.

Petev, Ivaylo, Luigi Pistaferri, and Itay Saporta Eksten. 2011. "Consumption and the Great Recession: An Analysis of Trends, Perceptions, and Distributional Effects." Working Paper, Stanford University, August.

Sabelhaus, John, and Karen M. Pence. 1999. "Household Saving in the '90s: Evidence from Cross-Section Wealth Surveys." *Review of Income and Wealth* 45 (4): 435–53.

Wilson, John F., James L. Freund, Frederick O. Yohn, Jr., and Walther Lederer. 1989. "Measuring Household Saving: Recent Experience from the Flow-of-Funds Perspective." In *The Measurement of Saving, Investment, and Wealth*, edited by Robert E. Lipsey and Helen Stone Tice, 101–52. Chicago: University of Chicago Press.

Wolff, Edward N. 1998. "Recent Trends in the Size Distribution of Household Wealth." *Journal of Economic Perspectives* 12 (3): 131–50.

———. 2011. "Recent Trends in Household Wealth, 1983–2009: The Irresistible Rise of Household Debt." *Review of Economics and Institutions* 2(1).

Zinman, Jonathan. 2009. "Where Is the Missing Credit Card Debt? Clues and Implications." *Review of Income and Wealth* 55 (2): 249–65.

III

Integrated Economic Accounts

10

The Integrated Macroeconomic Accounts of the United States

Marco Cagetti, Elizabeth Ball Holmquist, Lisa Lynn,
Susan Hume McIntosh, and David Wasshausen

The integrated macroeconomic accounts (IMAs), produced jointly by the Bureau of Economic Analysis (BEA) and the Federal Reserve Board (FRB), present a sequence of accounts that relate income, saving, investment in real and financial assets, and asset revaluations to changes in net worth. In this chapter we first provide some background information on the IMAs and on their construction. Next, we discuss the usefulness of the IMAs, focusing for instance on the evolution of household net worth and its components, a set of series that has appeared frequently in discussions of the causes and effects of the recent financial crisis. We also discuss some of the challenges associated with integrating nonfinancial and financial data sources; that is, the current and capital accounts statistics from the BEA's National Income and Product Accounts (NIPAs) and the financial statistics from the FRB's financial accounts (FAs), previously called the Flow of Funds Accounts. In the final section, we discuss future plans for improving the IMAs, including a proposed framework and methodology for breaking the financial business

Marco Cagetti is senior economist in the Division of Research and Statistics at the Board of Governors of the Federal Reserve System. Elizabeth Ball Holmquist is a financial analyst in the Division of Research and Statistics at the Board of Governors of the Federal Reserve System. Lisa Lynn is an economist in the National Income and Wealth Division of the Bureau of Economic Analysis, US Department of Commerce. Susan Hume McIntosh is senior economist in the Division of Research and Statistics at the Board of Governors of the Federal Reserve System. David Wasshausen is chief of the Industry Sector Division of the Bureau of Economic Analysis, US Department of Commerce.

We would like to thank Joshua Gallin, Dale Jorgenson, Kurt Kunze, Brent Moulton, and Kimberly Zieschang for comments and suggestions. The views expressed herein are those of the authors and do not necessarily reflect the view of the Board of Governors, the Federal Reserve System, or the Bureau of Economic Analysis. For acknowledgments, sources of research support, and disclosure of the authors' material financial relationships, if any, please see http://www.nber.org/chapters/c12834.ack.

sector into three subsectors: (a) central bank, (b) insurance and pension funds, and (c) other financial business.

10.1   Background and Evolution

The integrated macroeconomic accounts (IMAs) were developed as part of an interagency effort to further harmonize the Bureau of Economic Analysis's (BEA) National Income and Product Accounts (NIPAs) and the Federal Reserve Board's (FRB) financial accounts (FAs). Work began on these accounts in 2002 and the first version of the tables was presented at the National Bureau of Economic Research (NBER) Conference on Research in Income and Wealth's "Architecture for the National Accounts" in April 2004, with annual data for 1985 to 2002.[1] A February 2007 *Survey of Current Business* article officially introduced the regular production of the IMAs.[2] The System of National Accounts (SNA 1993) was used as the organizing framework in an effort to bring these accounts into closer accordance with international guidelines. While the resultant set of IMAs are largely in accordance with the SNA, there remain differences, particularly with respect to the way sectors are defined. The IMAs use a consistent set of sectors throughout the entire sequence of accounts, and these sectors are primarily based on definitions used in either the NIPAs or FAs. In the SNA, institutions are grouped into five mutually exclusive sectors: (a) nonfinancial corporations, (b) financial corporations, (c) general government, (d) nonprofit institutions serving households (NPISH), and (e) households. In the IMAs, estimates are calculated and presented for the following seven, mutually exclusive sectors: (a) households and NPISH, (b) nonfinancial noncorporate business, (c) nonfinancial corporate business, (d) financial business, (e) federal government, (f) state and local government, and (g) rest of world. The primary difference is in the treatment of noncorporate business (which includes entities such as sole proprietorships, general partnerships, limited liability partnerships, and government enterprises), which, with the exception of government enterprises, are classified as either nonfinancial noncorporate business or financial business in the IMAs. Government enterprise activities are reflected in the government sectors within the IMAs. In contrast, in the SNA, limited liability companies, limited partnerships, and government enterprises are classified as "quasi-corporations" in the financial or nonfinancial corporate sectors, and general partnerships and sole proprietorships are classified in the household sector.

Most of the IMA series are derived from published NIPA and FA data. Current account and capital account statistics are based on NIPA data, while the financial account statistics are based on FA data. The other changes

---

1. See Teplin et al. (2006).
2. For more information, see Bond et al. (2007).

in volume, revaluation, and balance sheet accounts reflect a combination of both BEA and FA data. The BEA provides the FRB with unpublished data, where necessary, and the FRB is responsible for compiling the full set of integrated accounts. The IMAs are updated quarterly about seventy-five days after the end of the quarter and are published by both the BEA and FRB. The BEA-supplied statistics for the most recent quarter typically reflect revisions to the previous quarter, with more substantial historical revisions stemming from the NIPA annual revision introduced with each September IMA release. The FRB-supplied statistics are not constrained by a set revision cycle and thus are open to historical revisions with each quarterly update.

Since initial publication of the IMAs in 2007, there have been several improvements implemented into these accounts. One of the more important improvements was the introduction in June 2010 of quarterly IMA statistics, beginning with 1992. In June 2012, those quarterly statistics were carried back to 1960. Slightly less detail is available quarterly in the current account, primarily reflecting insufficient source data on gross flows of property income paid and received. Another recent improvement is the introduction of farmland into the real estate component of the balance sheets for both corporate and noncorporate nonfinancial businesses. Estimates for farmland were developed primarily using Economic Research Service statistics, published by the United States Department of Agriculture. Later in the chapter we discuss future plans for the IMAs.

10.2   Construction of the Accounts

The IMAs link saving, capital accumulation, investment in financial assets, and balance sheet positions within an integrated framework with consistent definitions, classifications, and accounting conventions. Each of the seven sectors underlying the total economy has a full complement of accounts: the current account (production and distribution of income accounts), and the accumulation accounts (capital, financial, other volume changes, and revaluation accounts). These accounts allow one to trace the factors leading to changes in the net worth position on the balance sheet of each sector. As an example, in section 10.3, we will discuss the evolution of household net worth and its composition, a set of statistics that helps us understand the causes and consequences of the financial crisis.

Figure 10.1 provides a diagram of the sequence of accounts presented in the IMAs. Broadly speaking, in the first account (current account), the IMAs record production and income. Subtracting consumption from income yields net saving. From the capital account we observe if capital formation (aka investment in "real" assets) is smaller than saving, the difference is lent to other sectors using financial instruments; otherwise, the difference must be borrowed. Net lending or borrowing, therefore, link the

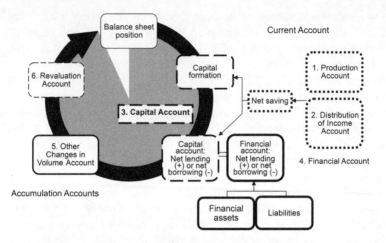

Fig. 10.1   Accumulation accounts/current account

"real" and the "financial" side of the economy. The next account, the financial account, records the lending and borrowing through the various financial instruments. Finally, the balance sheet position reflects real and financial investment flows, other changes in volume (fifth account), and holding gains/losses on assets (sixth account). Next, we will walk through the accounts using both figure 10.1 and estimates for the household and NPISH sector, which can be found in table 10A.1, found in appendix A.

The first account in the IMAs is the current account. Its first component (dotted lines) is the production account, labeled number 1 in figure 10.1, which shows the contribution made by each sector toward US production, or gross value added.[3] Consumption of fixed capital, or economic depreciation, is subtracted from gross value added to arrive at net value added. The current account also details the components of value added, including compensation and taxes paid, and net operating surplus[4] (lines 3–8 in appendix A). Sources of income (such as compensation received and net interest and net dividends received) by type are also presented in the current account (lines 10–19).

The second part of the current account, the distribution of income account (labeled 2 in figure 10.1, lines 21–28 in appendix A), shows the uses of income and how the income from current production is used to finance consumption and savings. Net saving (line 28), measured as the portion of

3. The GDP for the US economy can be calculated as the sum of gross value added for all sectors, plus the statistical discrepancy.
4. Net operating surplus reflects the income earned from the production of goods and services. It is a profits-like measure that is derived as gross output from current production minus related production costs (such as intermediate inputs, employee compensation, and taxes less subsidies).

current income that is set aside rather than spent on consumption or related purposes, is derived by subtracting consumption from disposable income.

Looking at the household and NPISH sector as an example, we see that gross value added for the sector in 2010 was $1.8 trillion (line 1). From current production, the sector earned a net income of $10.9 trillion (line 9), and, after income is adjusted for taxes, transfers, and social contributions/benefits, the sector's disposable income totaled $10.8 trillion (line 26). Subtracting $10.2 trillion of consumption (line 27), the sector's net saving amounted to $0.6 trillion (line 28).

Net saving then enters the capital account, the first in the sequence of accumulation accounts. The accumulation accounts describe the change in the sector balance sheet between its opening and closing position. There are four accumulation accounts: capital account, financial account, other changes in the volume of assets account, and revaluation account. The capital account, shown by the dashed lines and labeled number 3, records transactions linked to the net acquisition of nonfinancial assets and capital transfers involving the redistribution of wealth used for the purchase of capital. This account consists of net capital formation (gross fixed capital formation less consumption of fixed assets), net capital transfers, acquisition of nonproduced nonfinancial assets and change in private inventories (lines 29–38). Each of these estimates is derived from estimates in the NIPAs and the fixed-asset accounts published by the BEA. Net capital transfers include transactions such as disaster-related insurance benefits, estate and gift taxes, and financial stabilization payments made by the federal government. Nonproduced nonfinancial assets transactions include purchases of land, payments for drilling rights, electromagnetic spectrum proceeds, and miscellaneous international transactions. If net saving derived from the current account is smaller than capital accumulation, the sector is a net borrower, and if net saving is greater than capital accumulation, the sector is a net lender. This difference between net saving and capital accumulation is referred to as net lending (+) or net borrowing (−). As an example, in 2010, capital formation by the household and NPISH sector amounted to about $0.1 trillion. Since its saving was $0.6 trillion, the sector lent $0.5 trillion to the other sectors.

An alternate version of net lending/net borrowing (or NLNB) can be calculated from the financial account, shown in solid-lined boxes and labeled number 4 (in figure 10.1), by subtracting the net increase in liabilities (lines 70–80) from the net acquisition of financial assets (lines 40–69). In principle, the capital account and financial account measures of net lending/net borrowing should be the same, because saving that is not spent on purchases of fixed assets results in the acquisition of financial assets and borrowing that is used to finance the purchase of fixed assets results in the incurrence of financial liabilities. However, when compiling NLNB from the capital and financial accounts, the values for the two measures are almost never equal because of differences in source data, timing of recorded flows, and other statistical differences between data used to create the measures. To reconcile the two measures, the difference between NLNB derived from the two methods (that is, line 81 minus line 38) is included as a statistical discrepancy in the other changes in volume account.

Looking again at 2010, the household sector acquired $0.5 trillion of financial assets and decreased its liabilities by repaying about $0.2 trillion, resulting in a net lending of $0.8 trillion. Since the net lending obtained from the capital account amounted to about $0.6 trillion, there is a statistical discrepancy of about $0.2 trillion.

The other changes in volume account, labeled number 5, records the effect of exceptional events that cause either the value or volume of assets and liabilities to vary (lines 82–86). Included here are adjustments in classification and structure due to changes in data sources or calculations, disaster losses, nonproduced nonfinancial assets, and the statistical discrepancy described above. Disasters are generally defined as catastrophic events (such as hurricanes and earthquakes) with property losses exceeding 0.1 percent of GDP (which is currently about $15 billion). Nonproduced nonfinancial assets are included since they are not recorded on the balance sheet but are included in the capital account.

The last accumulation account is the revaluation account, labeled number 6, which records holding gains and losses stemming from changes in prices since the opening balance sheet position (lines 87–97). Typically, holding gains and losses account for most of the change in net worth on the balance sheet. One major difference between the SNA and the IMA tables is that debt securities (such as corporate bonds) are shown at book value rather than market value in the IMAs, and are therefore not shown in the revaluation account.[5]

The closing balance sheet position is equal to the opening balance sheet position plus the changes recorded in the accumulation accounts, which are shown on the circle in figure 10.1, and are equal to the change in net worth for the sector. In the IMAs, we have chosen to use NLNB as calculated from the capital account rather than the version calculated from the financial account, and, as mentioned above, the difference between the two measures (the statistical discrepancy) is recorded in the other volume changes account to be consistent with the balance sheet data.

Returning to our example, household sector net worth was $55.6 trillion at the end of 2009. In 2010, the sector saved $0.6 trillion (as measured by net savings in the capital account, line 28) and gained $2.6 trillion from changes in the prices of its assets (line 97). Net worth at the end of 2010 was $59.1 trillion, with other changes in volume adding $0.3 billion.

---

5. This convention was adopted early on at the beginning of the development of the FA. We are currently working to fill in this gap, or estimate this value, to conform with SNA guidelines.

One point of note is that, for the household and nonfinancial business sectors, the balance sheet shows FA estimates of the market value of real estate. These estimates are calculated using real estate price indices and net investment from the BEA. For the financial business and government sectors, only the current-cost net stock of structures is shown because there are no reliable estimates for the market value of real estate. All balance sheets for domestic sectors show the current-cost net stock of equipment and software. For those sectors where total real estate is reported, it may be tempting to impute a value for land as the difference between the value of real estate and current-cost net stock of structures; this practice is not recommended, however, because the two measures are estimated independently and rely on different source data. For example, for the nonfinancial corporate business sector, the difference between real estate and net stock of structures is slightly greater than zero in 2009, suggesting that the value of land owned by this sector in 2009 was negligible. Nevertheless, it is useful to analyze and question the relationship between real estate and structures in order to better understand the underlying source data and methods used to construct these statistics.

10.3   Uses of the IMAs

The recent financial crisis has vividly shown that analyzing the change in net worth and its composition is critical to understanding the health, risks, and prospects of an economic sector. Net worth is a broad measure of the wealth of a sector, often used in conjunction with other variables, such as income and interest rates, to study variables such as consumption and saving. The IMAs enable one to analyze net worth and its composition, clarifying how the current balance sheet position came about by distinguishing between saving, borrowing, holding gains or losses, and other changes in volume.

As an example, we can look at household and NPISH sectors in the IMAs. In the first half of the last decade, the household sector shifted from being a major lender to a major borrower (table 10.1, line 2), rivaled only as a borrower by the federal government sector (line 6). It was at this same time that the rest of the world sector (line 8) became the predominant lending sector.

At the same time, household net worth surged rapidly and the ratio of household net worth to disposable personal income reached record levels (figure 10.2). This increase was caused not by elevated saving, but by sizable capital gains both on housing wealth and on stock-market wealth (figure 10.3).

Indeed, the ratio of both housing wealth and stock market wealth to disposable personal income surged to historically unprecedented levels (figure 10.4). Not surprisingly, household debt also ballooned. The ratio of household debt to disposable personal income increased from around

Table 10.1   Net lending (+) or net borrowing (–) in the capital and financial accounts, by sector[a]

Sector		1970s	1980s	1990s	2000–2006	2007	2008	2009	2010	2011
1. All domestic sectors:	C	–16	–109	–160	–472	–704	–671	–455	–481	–453
	F	–17	–88	–10	–476	–473	–1678	–404	–646	–274
2. Households & nonprofits:	C	56	135	88	–168	–126	373	488	535	476
	F	78	209	146	–235	164	525	406	833	1037
3. Nonfin. noncorp. business:	C	–22	–38	–26	–49	–74	–53	14	6	–6
	F	–22	–37	–28	–101	–122	–53	14	6	–14
4. Nonfin. corp. business:	C	–21	–13	–26	–23	–94	–7	389	377	422
	F	–42	–82	8	26	–206	–943	563	151	272
5. Financial business:	C	5	–20	–2	72	–3	–47	275	157	125
	F	2	7	44	118	108	–267	46	–209	–146
6. Federal government:	C	–32	–166	–160	–215	–315	–756	–1446	–1462	–1357
	F	–33	–181	–169	–236	–344	–780	–1289	–1362	–1328
7. State & local govts.:	C	–2	–7	–34	–90	–93	–181	–175	–94	–113
	F	1	–4	11	–49	–72	–161	–144	–65	–95
8. Rest of the world:	C	–2	–74	117	559	716	674	378	480	484
	F	–3	58	112	569	618	737	246	254	393
9. Statistical discrepancy[b]	C	18	36	43	–86	–12	–2	77	1	–32

Source: Integrated macroeconomic accounts, June 7, 2012.

[a]Data in billions. Rows designated by "C" represent net lending or net borrowing calculated from the capital account; rows designated by "F" represent net lending or borrowing calculated from the financial account.

[b]Equals rest of the world capital account net lending (+) or net borrowing (–) (line 8) less all domestic sectors' capital account net lending (+) or net borrowing (–) (line 1).

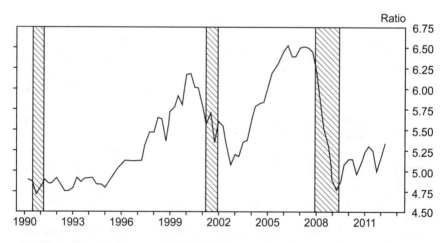

Fig. 10.2   Household net worth relative to disposable personal income
Source: Integrated macroeconomic accounts, June 7, 2012.
Note: Bars indicate NBER recession periods.

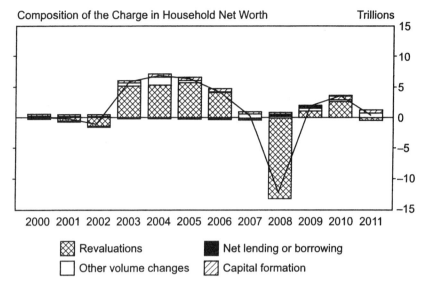

Fig. 10.3   Composition of the change in household net worth
Source: Integrated macroeconomic accounts, June 7, 2012.

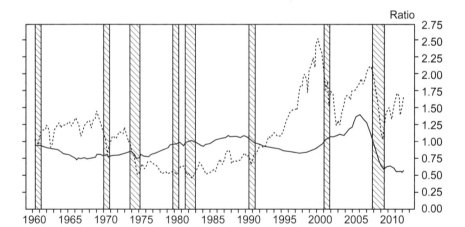

Fig. 10.4   Corporate and home equity relative to disposable personal income
Source: Flow of Funds Accounts of the United States, June 7, 2012.
[1]Includes directly held publicly traded and closely held equity shared and equity held indirectly through mutual funds; life insurance companies; private retirement funds; and local, state, and federal government retirement funds.
Note: Bars indicate NBER recession periods.

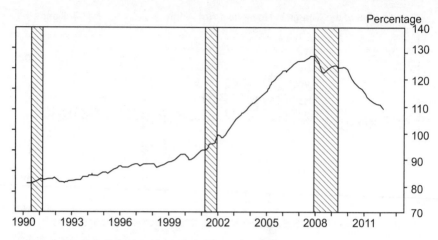

Fig. 10.5   Household debt relative to disposable personal income, quarterly
Source: Integrated macroeconomic accounts, June 7, 2012.
Note: Bars indicate NBER recession periods.

90 percent at the beginning of the decade to an all-time high of around 130 percent in the middle of 2007 (figure 10.5).

This ratio dropped to 111 percent by the end of 2011 as consumers borrowed less and as a significant amount of mortgage debt was written off. As can be seen in table 10.1, line 2, the household sector shifted back to being a major net lender in 2008.

Net borrowing by the federal government (table 10.1, line 6), on the other hand, ballooned to over $1.3 trillion in both 2009 and 2010. In 2009, the rest of the world sector (line 8) was a significant lender, along with the financial business sector (line 5). The nonfinancial corporate business sector (line 4), traditionally a net borrower, became a net lender in 2009, as capital expenditures remained relatively low and retained earnings elevated.

10.4   Challenges in Linking Current, Capital, and Financial Accounts

One innovative feature of the integrated accounts is the ability to compare net lending/net borrowing calculated from the capital account with the alternative measure calculated from the financial account. As discussed above, in the capital account measure, a sector's net lending or net borrowing is the difference between its net saving (disposable income less current spending) and its net investment (gross purchases of "physical" capital less depreciation on its existing capital stock). In the financial account measure, a sector's net lending/net borrowing is the difference between its net acquisition of financial assets and its net increase in liabilities. Thus, except for statistical discrepancies, the two measures of a sector's net lending/net borrowing should be the same.

Figure 10.6 compares the capital account total net lending or net borrowing for all domestic sectors (the black line) with the financial account measure (the dotted line). The two lines are very close to each other and hover around zero until about 1980. From that point forward, the United States becomes an increasingly larger net borrower vis-à-vis the rest of the world. The two measures of net lending/net borrowing remain fairly similar, although the financial account measure is more volatile, until around 2008, the year of the financial crisis, when the two lines diverge sharply. This divergence could be partly due to data sources subject to historical benchmark revisions, but is more likely due to data gaps in the financial accounts. These data gaps could reflect off-balance sheet data that have not been captured completely, such as derivatives, or transactions taking place at a level of business structure not currently included in any sector in the accounts, such as nonfinancial holding companies. Also, the treatment of intangibles in the capital and financial accounts could be inconsistent. These data gaps and differences were probably more significant during the financial crisis, and perhaps unsurprisingly, when you compare the two measures of net lending/net borrowing by sector, as shown in table 10.1, the greatest differences appear to be for the nonfinancial corporate business sector (line 4) and the financial business sector (line 5). In 2009, the two measures of total NLNB

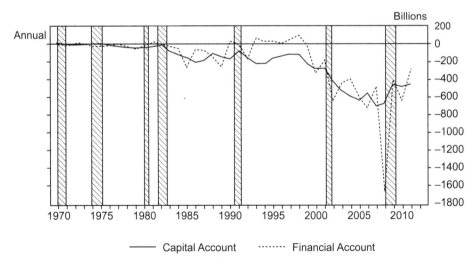

Fig. 10.6   Net lending (+) or net borrowing (–) in the capital and financial accounts
Source: Integrated macroeconomic accounts, June 7, 2012.
Note: Bars indicate NBER recession periods.

(figure 10.6) moved closer together as the economy showed some improvement and have maintained a similar pattern in the most recent years.

Additional issues in comparing the capital account and financial account measures of net lending/net borrowing by sector could be due to the different treatment of debt charge-offs, as well as company- versus establishment-based statistics.

In the financial accounts, debt charge-offs are a component of NLNB, rather than of other changes in volume accounts, as suggested by the SNA.[6] That is, if debt is charged off, net acquisition of assets falls and net lending decreases for the issuing sector. In other words, charge-offs are not distinguished from repayments. However in the NIPAs, charge-offs are not part of net lending/net borrowing as they do not directly change saving or investment. Before the most recent financial crisis, mortgage debt charge-offs for the financial sector were very small.[7] With the financial crisis, however, charge-off rates increased rapidly from a few basis points to more than two percent as many houses entered foreclosure.[8] Because the mortgage loans (an asset) are generally held by financial institutions and the corresponding mortgage debt is held by primarily by nonfinancial sectors, in particular households, charge-offs generate a discrepancy between the respective sectors' net lending and borrowing computed from the capital and financial accounts. Figure 10.7 shows a rough measure of charge-offs for both residential and commercial mortgages (the dashed line) exploding in 2008, which helps to explain the discrepancy in net lending/net borrowing beginning in 2008 (the distance between the solid and the dotted line).[9]

Finally, in the capital accounts, net lending/net borrowing reflects a mix of company- and establishment-based statistics, while net lending/borrowing from the financial accounts primarily reflects institutional-based reporting. The NIPA measures of profits and interest are derived primarily from IRS tabulations of business tax returns, which are reported on a consolidated basis. Therefore, financial activities of captive finance companies (a subsidiary whose purpose is to provide financing to customers buying the parent company's product) are not reflected in the profits of the financial sector. Unfortunately, this is not an easily remedied issue. The BEA is actively work-

6. This convention is due to lack of data on all types of loans. While data on charge-offs on loans at banks exists, there is currently no official measure of charge-offs on securitized loans, which comprise the majority of mortgage debt in the United States.

7. A precise series for charge-offs on debt held by financial institutions does not exist. In chart 6 we approximate the value of charge-offs on mortgage debt by applying the charge-off rate on mortgages held at banks to the total amount of outstanding mortgages. This is a rough approximation because the charge-off rate on mortgages held in pools could be different, and because we do not distinguish mortgages held by the financial sector from mortgages held by other sectors.

8. We thank Jim Kennedy and Maria Perozek for the analysis of the effects of charge-offs on the saving rate.

9. The charge-off measure is just a rough approximation based on the charge-off rates for mortgages held at banks.

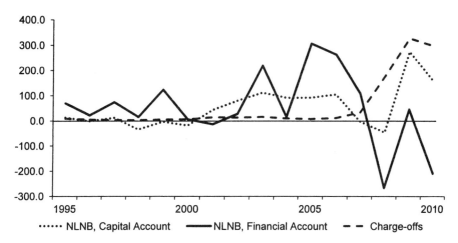

Fig. 10.7   Net lending/net borrowing, financial business
Source: Integrated macroeconomic accounts, June 7, 2012.

ing with IRS to identify and obtain additional information on the activities of subsidiaries, which should enable us to better understand the financial sector.[10]

10.5   Future Plans

10.5.1   Subsectoring Finance

Following the financial crisis that began in 2008, members of the G-20 established the G-20 Data Gaps Initiative in an attempt to improve global financial statistics, potentially helping policymakers and market participants identify and address stresses in the financial system before another crisis occurs. One of the conclusions drawn was that sectoral data matter, and emphasis was placed on producing (and publishing) subsector detail for the financial sector. Specifically, one of the recommendations was "to develop a strategy to promote the compilation and dissemination of the balance sheet approach (BSA), flow of funds, and sectoral data more generally." In February 2011, the IMF and OECD jointly organized a conference, "Strengthening Sectoral Position and Flow Data in the Macroeconomic Accounts." The following four financial subsectors, including their corresponding North American Industrial Classification System (NAICS) code, were proposed: (a) central bank (521), (b) other deposit-taking institutions (5221), (c) insur-

10. In the BEAs annual industry accounts (AIA), NIPA profits are converting from a company to an establishment basis primarily using employment data from the Economic Census. Obtaining additional information on subsidiaries from the IRS would potentially improve the AIA estimates as well.

ance and pension funds (524 + 525110), and (d) other financial business (remaining 52 and 55). The IMAs provide an excellent framework to address data gaps in the national accounts of a country and expanding the IMAs to include these additional tables should help analysts better evaluate the risk characteristics of different types of financial institutions.

While sufficient data exist to meet the subsectoring recommendations for the financial account, the current and capital accounts present a challenge. The BEA and FRB initially attempted to follow the recommended subsectoring in the IMAs; however, we eventually concluded that there were insufficient data in IRS tax return–based estimates to accurately identify "other deposit-taking institutions" from "other financial business." Specifically, the consolidated IRS tax return–based statistics for bank holding companies (NAICS 551111—mapped to "other financial business") include significant activity for subsidiaries classified as "other deposit-taking institutions" (NAICS 5221). To better understand the magnitude of activity of depository subsidiaries reported in IRS statistics as bank holding companies, the BEA received a sample of bank holding company subsidiary data from 2010 preliminary IRS statistics. Our sample suggested that for 2010, within corporate bank holding companies, approximately 40 percent of receipts, 60 percent of interest received, and 20 percent of dividends received were attributable to subsidiaries associated with "other depository taking institutions," rather than "other financial business."

As mentioned in section 10.4 above, the nature of the company-based statistics presents some challenges for us and we are actively researching ways to address this. An additional challenge we faced with accommodating the proposed subsectors is that the NIPA industry-based estimates do not always contain sufficient NAICS detail. For example, the subsector "insurance and pension funds" reflects the sum of NAICS 524 (insurance) and NAICS 525110 (pension funds), however separate estimates for NAICS 525110 do not exist in the NIPAs.

As a first step toward completing this financial subsectoring in the IMAs, we are proposing to combine "other deposit taking corporations" with "other financial business." Even with combining two of the four subsectors, a number of assumptions are needed in order to derive the remaining subsectors. Nevertheless, publishing these additional tables should help analysts better evaluate the risk characteristics of different types of financial institutions. It should be noted that, with the exception of property income flows associated with government pensions, IMA estimates for total financial business presented in the currently published tables are unaffected by this proposal. It should also be emphasized that estimates presented for the subsectors are extremely preliminary and subject to change. Emphasis instead should be placed on the framework and methodologies described herein. The following sections briefly describe how each of the subsectors will be constructed. Draft tables for the financial business subsectors can be found in appendix B.

Central Bank (Table 10B.2)

The central bank, for purposes of the IMAs, is essentially defined as the Federal Reserve. The Federal Reserve is separately recognized under NAICS 521 and underlying detail already exists for many of the IMA series in the current, capital, financial, and balance sheet accounts. The NIPA estimates for Federal Reserve (which underlie capital and current account data for this subsector) rely heavily on the Federal Reserve annual report as a primary data source, and include both the Federal Reserve Banks and the Federal Reserve Board. In this sector, gross value added is estimated from unpublished statistics from the BEAs annual industry accounts (AIAs). For this specific industry/subsector, there is no distinction between company versus establishment so using AIA (establishment-based) in lieu of an indirectly derived NIPA (mostly company-based) estimate is not problematic. Compensation estimates are derived from unpublished NIPA detail, which are consistent with the AIA estimates. There are several series within the current and capital accounts for which no data are available (such as other current transfers and reinvested earnings on FDI abroad), and in these cases we have assumed that the values are zero. The net operating surplus (NOS) is derived residually.

In the financial accounts, the central bank subsector is defined as the monetary authority; that is, the assets and liabilities of the Federal Reserve Banks and the Treasury monetary accounts that supply or absorb bank reserves.[11] For the financial accounts, the data come from the Federal Reserve statistical release H.4.1, Factors Affecting Reserve Balances. It is worth noting that the net lending/net borrowing series shown for the central bank is somewhat confusing because of the way central bank operations appear in the accounts (for instance, currency and deposits are a liability of the central bank). However, looking separately at the assets and liabilities, both in the financial accounts and in the balance sheet, can help to understand the behavior of the central bank. For example, the loans extended to financial institutions in 2008 and the operations related to the quantitative easing policies since the crisis are reflected in the sharp increase in the central bank's assets.

Insurance and Pension Funds (Table 10B.3)

The insurance and pension fund subsector is defined as the NAICS insurance industry (524) plus pension fund industry (NAICS 525110). Within the current and capital accounts, estimating the insurance portion of this subsector is fairly straightforward because NIPA estimates for this industry currently exist and, in many cases, are published. Unfortunately, that is not

---

11. The Federal Reserve System includes the twelve Federal Reserve Banks and the Board of Governors of the Federal Reserve System in Washington, DC. Essentially all of the accounts of the monetary authority sectors are held at the Federal Reserve Banks, not at the Board of Governors. Technically, the monetary authority sector in the financial accounts excludes the Board of Governors.

the case with pension funds, as very little information currently exists in the NIPAs for this industry. Fortunately, most of the current and capital account series for pension funds are fairly small, with the exception of interest and dividends, which flow through pension funds into the household sector. Accordingly, we have assumed these small series, with no source data, are zero for pension funds and therefore only the receipts and payments of property income associated with pension funds are reflected in this subsector. Because these transactions pass through this subsector, there is no impact on net lending/net borrowing. Estimates for these flows were derived using data from multiple sources, but rely most heavily on statistics published in the FAs (for pension asset compositions and interest rates), annual reports for federal government retirement funds, IRS Form 5500 data, and statistics published in the Census Bureau Survey of Public-Employee Retirement Systems.[12]

In this proposal, we are including property income associated with both defined benefit and defined contribution plans.[13] It is debatable whether or not property income associated with defined contribution plans should be reflected in this account at all, since the property income is considered to be owned directly by the household sector. Nevertheless, we thought it would be helpful to the users of these accounts to see the effect of both types of pension plans. Moreover, the financial accounts for this subsector, discussed next, reflect both defined benefit and defined contributions plans.

In the financial accounts, the insurance sector is based on reports filed to insurance authorities. Of note, it does not include most insurance holding companies. For pensions, the financial account also reflects both defined benefit and defined contribution plans.

Looking at table 10B.3 in the appendix, which shows preliminary estimates for the subsector, we can see that the industry's share of gross value added is approximately 1/3 of that of the total financial sector. Operating surplus (table 10B.3, line 10), which is a profits-like measure that excludes income from interest and dividends, rebounded for the subsector in 2010, and was almost twice 2008 levels. In general, both the financial and capital accounts indicate that this subsector has been a net lender to the economy (figure 10.8).

Other Financial Business (Including Other Deposit-Taking Corporations, Table 10B.4)

The other financial business subsector is calculated residually as total financial business (as shown in table 10B.4) less the insurance and pension

12. We thank Marshall Reinsdorf for helpful comments regarding the treatment of pensions in the National Income and Product Accounts. We also thank David Lenze, Dylan Rassier, and Benyam Tsehaye for providing estimates of pension-related dividends and interest.
13. Property income flows associated with government-defined contribution plans were not available and therefore not reflected in the accompanying tables.

subsector, and less the central bank subsector. This subsector implicitly includes estimates for credit intermediaries, security brokerages, investment pools, other deposit-taking corporations, and financial holding companies.

Preliminary estimates show that other financial business accounts for approximately 2/3 of production for the financial sector. Looking at preliminary net lending/net borrowing for the sector (figure 10.9), financial NLNB is much more volatile than the corresponding measure in the capital account. There has also been a discrepancy between capital and financial

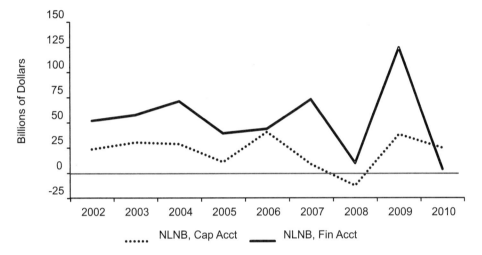

Fig. 10.8   Net lending/net borrowing, pension and insurance subsector

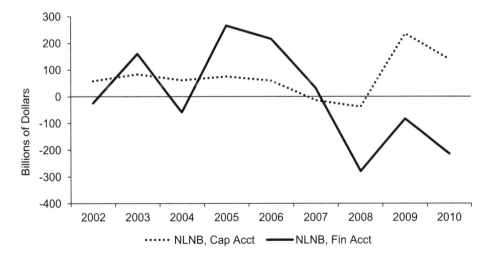

Fig. 10.9   Net lending/net borrowing, other financial business

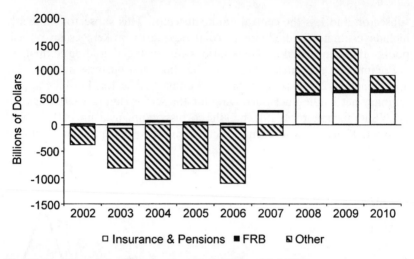

Fig. 10.10   Financial subsector net worth (in billions of dollars)

accounts since 2008, which can be in part explained by the treatment of charge-offs, as explained in section 10.4.

Brief Observations Relating to Proposed Financial Subsector Data

In interpreting the financial sector tables, it is important to highlight a few issues in the construction of net worth. As for all other sectors, net worth is the difference between assets and liabilities. The SNA guidelines suggest to treat the market value of the outstanding shares issued by a corporation as a liability for the sector. Therefore, other things equal, declines in stock prices will cause an increase in the net worth of the sector, which complicates the interpretation of the net worth measure for the financial sectors (which are mostly comprised by corporations), as well as for the nonfinancial corporate sector. As shown in figure 10.10, the large increases in net worth in 2007 and 2008 can be explained by the large decline in financial stock prices during the crisis, and should obviously not be interpreted as an increase in the value of these companies. Rather, one should exclude equity capital from possible balance-sheet based measure of firm value.

In addition, at the moment, our measure of net worth does not include the market value of real estate held by financial companies.[14] As a result, our financial balance sheets do not capture the large declines in commercial real estate during the crisis.

It is also interesting to point out a few facts about net lending/net bor-

14. The market value of real estate held by nonfinancial businesses is instead recorded in the nonfinancial corporate and noncorporate business accounts.

rowing of the financial sectors. Usually both the capital account and the financial account indicate that the pension and insurance subsector is a net lender for each year. There is a greater divergence in net lending/net borrowing trends for the other financial business subsector; in this subsector, NLNB for the financial account is much more volatile, with the lending and borrowing amounts much greater than in the capital account. As mentioned in sections above, conceptually the two measures should match, but disparities can arise due to differences in timing, source data, and other statistical differences. This subsector includes a wide variety of institutions with different risk exposures and cyclical behaviors, and different portfolio composition, which could help explain the larger volatility of NLNB in the financial accounts. Separating the various types of institutions within the subsectors will be helpful in understanding the behavior of the series and the discrepancy between financial and capital accounts. A comparison of net lending/net borrowing for the subsectors can be found below in figures 10.11 and 10.12.

10.5.2. Other Future Developments

A current drawback of the IMAs, as pointed out by Palumbo and Parker (2009) and by Eichner, Kohn, and Palumbo (2010), is that the accounts did not show the increased exposure of the financial business sector to house price risk because of the aggregation of the sector and of certain asset classes. As discussed earlier, the sector consolidation masked how lever-

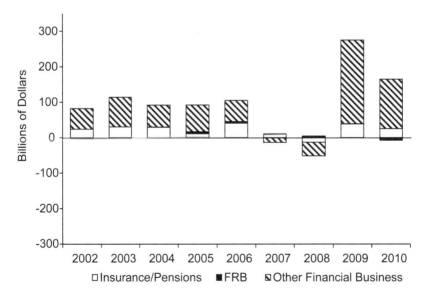

Fig. 10.11   Net lending/net borrowing—capital account

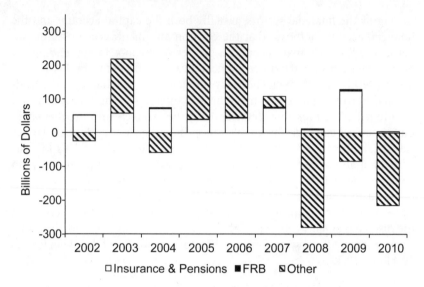

Fig. 10.12   Net lending/net borrowing—financial account

aged some of the financial subsectors had become. In addition, structured financial products and traditional corporate bonds and commercial paper, which are group together as "debt securities" in the IMA, have very different risk characteristics. To address this drawback, we are examining the feasibility of separating the holdings of structured products from traditional debt instruments.

In addition to presenting additional detail for the financial business sector, we are also investigating the possibility of presenting households separately from nonprofit institutions serving households. These two sectors have notably different characteristics from one another and being able to analyze them separately would be helpful.[15] We would also like to incorporate real estate values into the balance sheets for the financial and government sectors. Incorporating conservative estimates may be an improvement over assuming the value is zero.

In addition to these longer term projects, we believe there are a number of useful series and ratios (constructed from currently published IMA statistics) that could be explicitly added to the addenda of the IMAs. For example, in the household and nonprofit institutions serving households sector, the ratio of real estate to disposable income quickly reveals the housing "bubble"

---

15. Here, the primary challenge for the financial accounts is that most data for nonprofit institutions is obtained from tax return–based data, which does not allow us to precisely identify the different financial instruments required to make this split.

that peaked in the mid 2000s. Another useful ratio might be the value of corporate equities to disposable income for households and institutions, which peaked in 1999 and then fell rapidly. A useful series that could be added to the household and institutions sector is household net worth from the FRB's Survey of Consumer Finances (SCF). A quick comparison showed household net worth measured indirectly in the IMAs tracks very well the mean household net worth measured directly in the SCF—an important validation for both sets of estimates.[16] For the financial business sector, including selected estimates from the BEA's AIAs might also be useful for comparison purposes. Including these types of related statistics can provide an important validity check and serves to further integrate economic accounts.

The IMA have already proven to be valuable in studying the US economy. The Federal Reserve and BEA will continue to work together to improve the presentation and data availability of these accounts so that in the future policymakers will be better able to see shifts in the financial climate of the United States prior to business cycle expansions and contractions.

---

16. The SCF is a triennial interview survey of US families, sponsored by the Board of Governors of the Federal Reserve System with the cooperation of the US Department of the Treasury. For more information see: http://www.federalreserve.gov/Pubs/Bulletin/2012/articles /scf/scf.htm. For a comparison of the net worth estimates implied by the two data sets, see Alice Henriques and Joanne Hsu (chapter 9, this volume).

Appendix A

Table 10A.1   Households and nonprofit institutions serving households (billions of dollars)

			2003	2004	2005	2006	2007	2008	2009	2010
		Current account								
1	FA156902505	**Gross value added**	**1347.2**	**1423.8**	**1506.4**	**1602.8**	**1685.8**	**1805.7**	**1836.0**	**1838.4**
2	FA156300003	**Less: Consumption of fixed capital**	**200.5**	**222.2**	**245.1**	**268.1**	**285.5**	**294.6**	**292.5**	**295.2**
3	FA156902605	**Equals: Net value added**	**1,146.7**	**1,201.6**	**1,261.3**	**1,334.7**	**1,400.3**	**1,511.1**	**1,543.5**	**1,543.2**
4	FA156025005	Compensation paid by households and NPISHs	520.6	550.7	571.1	603.5	634.6	671.5	693.8	706.8
5	FA156020001	Wages and salaries	435.2	456.7	473.4	502.0	532.0	562.3	579.7	591.7
6	FA156401001	Employers' social contributions	85.4	94.0	97.8	101.5	102.6	109.2	114.1	115.1
7	FA156240101	Taxes on production and imports less subsidies	110.0	116.4	121.3	131.1	133.9	142.0	147.1	151.4
8	FA156402101	Operating surplus, net	516.1	534.4	568.9	600.2	631.9	697.6	702.6	685.0
9	FA156140005	**Net national income/Balance of primary incomes, net**	**8,652.0**	**9,149.5**	**9,655.5**	**10,366.8**	**10,895.1**	**11,320.8**	**10,553.0**	**10,910.9**
10	FA156402101	Operating surplus, net	516.1	534.4	568.9	600.2	631.9	697.6	702.6	685.0
11	FA156025105	Compensation of employees (received)	6,382.6	6,693.4	7,065.0	7,477.0	7,855.9	8,068.3	7,806.4	7,971.4
12	FA156020101	Wages and salaries	5,154.6	5,410.7	5,706.0	6,070.1	6,415.5	6,545.9	6,275.3	6,408.2
13	FA156401101	Employers' social contributions	1,228.0	1,282.7	1,359.1	1,406.9	1,440.4	1,522.5	1,531.1	1,563.1
14	FA156150105	Property income (received)	2,299.6	2,498.6	2,669.9	3,023.4	3,219.9	3,360.9	2,757.8	2,872.3
15	FA156130101	Interest	890.9	861.5	988.3	1,128.9	1,266.5	1,383.4	1,110.1	1,004.5
16	FA156120105	Distributed income of corporations	1,408.8	1,637.1	1,681.6	1,894.5	1,953.4	1,977.5	1,647.7	1,867.7
17	FA156121101	Dividends	423.1	548.3	555.0	702.2	791.9	783.4	598.8	717.7
18	FA156122101	Withdrawals from income of quasi-corporations[a]	985.7	1,088.8	1,126.6	1,192.3	1,161.5	1,194.1	1,049.0	1,150.0
19	FA156130001	Less: Uses of property income (interest paid)	546.4	576.9	648.3	733.8	812.6	806.0	713.8	617.8
20	FA156140005	**Net national income/Balance of primary incomes, net**	**8,652.0**	**9,149.5**	**9,655.5**	**10,366.8**	**10,895.1**	**11,320.8**	**10,553.0**	**10,910.9**
21	FA156220001	Less: Current taxes on income, wealth, etc. (paid)	1,000.3	1,047.8	1,208.6	1,352.4	1,488.7	1,435.7	1,141.4	1,193.9
22	FA156404105	Plus: Social benefits (received)	1,316.0	1,398.6	1,482.7	1,583.6	1,687.9	1,842.4	2,099.9	2,242.9
23	FA156600001	Less: Social contributions (paid)	778.9	827.3	872.7	921.8	959.5	987.3	964.1	986.8
24	FA156403101	Plus: Other current transfers (received)	25.7	16.9	25.8	21.4	30.5	36.8	38.2	38.3
25	FA156403001	Less: Other current transfers (paid)	105.7	116.1	131.0	138.7	150.6	154.2	161.9	173.1
26	FA156012095	**Equals: Disposable income, net**	**8,108.8**	**8,573.8**	**8,951.7**	**9,558.9**	**10,014.7**	**10,622.9**	**10,423.7**	**10,838.3**
27	FA156901001	Less: Final consumption expenditures	7,804.1	8,270.6	8,803.5	9,301.0	9,772.3	10,035.5	9,866.1	10,245.5
28	FA156006005	**Equals: Net saving**	**304.7**	**303.2**	**148.2**	**257.9**	**242.5**	**587.3**	**557.6**	**592.8**

Line	Code	Description								
29	**FA156006315**	**Net saving less capital transfers**	**291.5**	**301.9**	**170.1**	**241.1**	**239.4**	**595.9**	**604.2**	**635.3**
30	FA156006005	Net saving	304.7	303.2	148.2	257.9	242.5	587.3	557.6	592.8
31	FA155440005	Less: Capital transfers paid (net)	13.1	1.4	–21.9	16.8	3.0	–8.6	–46.6	–42.6
30	**FA155050905**	**Capital formation, net**	**377.8**	**459.5**	**526.7**	**499.3**	**365.1**	**223.4**	**115.9**	**99.9**
33	FA155019005	Gross fixed capital formation, excluding consumer durables	586.7	690.4	781.0	777.7	661.9	529.2	419.6	406.5
34	FA155012005	Residential	498.9	594.4	681.9	670.1	541.7	397.2	296.0	287.7
35	FA165013005	Nonresidential (nonprofit organizations)	87.8	95.9	99.1	107.5	120.2	132.0	123.6	118.8
36	FA156300003	Less: Consumption of fixed capital	200.5	222.2	245.1	268.1	285.5	294.6	292.5	295.2
37	FA155420003	Acquisition of nonproduced nonfinancial asstes	–8.5	–8.7	–9.2	–10.2	–11.3	–11.2	–11.2	–11.3
38	**FA155000905**	**Net lending (+) or borrowing (–), capital account (lines 29–32)**	**–86.2**	**–157.6**	**–356.6**	**–258.2**	**–125.7**	**372.6**	**488.3**	**535.4**

Line	Code	Description								
39	**FA155000905**	**Net lending (+) or borrowing (–), capital account (line 38)**	**–86.2**	**–157.6**	**–356.6**	**–258.2**	**–125.7**	**372.6**	**488.3**	**535.4**
40	**FA154090005**	**Net acquisition of financial assets**	**945.0**	**1222.8**	**803.2**	**793.2**	**1056.8**	**369.7**	**227.3**	**640.9**
41	**FA154000005**	**Currency and deposits**	**260.9**	**410.4**	**370.7**	**450.7**	**421.9**	**405.0**	**145.2**	**180.7**
42	FA153020005	Currency and transferable deposits	–31.0	–58.2	–114.2	–40.0	–74.6	224.4	24.0	–25.3
43	FA153030005	Time and savings deposits	289.8	463.2	482.5	485.5	481.1	204.2	127.6	201.7
44	FA153091003	Foreign deposits	2.2	5.4	2.4	5.2	15.4	–23.7	–6.4	4.3
45	FA313131003	Postal saving system deposits	0.0	0.0	0.0	0.0	0.0	0.0	0.0	0.0
46	**FA154022005**	**Debt securities**	**51.3**	**281.0**	**228.7**	**120.6**	**524.0**	**–22.2**	**–114.0**	**251.9**
47	FA163069103	Open market paper	–4.9	6.4	14.7	19.0	–10.2	–101.3	28.7	28.8
48	FA313161400	US savings bonds	8.9	0.6	0.7	–2.7	–6.0	–2.4	–2.8	–3.3
49	FA153061105	Treasury securities	11.0	17.1	–96.9	–81.2	–44.0	159.2	425.2	454.5
50	FA153061705	Agency- and GSE-backed securities[b]	135.1	83.7	110.8	–45.6	320.2	96.8	–566.7	–4.7
51	FA153062005	Municipal securities	25.4	121.0	77.3	42.0	44.1	41.8	129.3	58.1
52	FA153063005	Corporate and foreign bonds	–124.1	52.2	122.1	189.0	219.8	–216.3	–127.7	–281.5
53	**FA154035005**	**Loans**	**67.3**	**116.2**	**7.8**	**63.5**	**206.8**	**–110.2**	**–89.0**	**13.8**
54	FA154041005	Short-term	63.0	105.8	–0.3	80.8	219.2	–111.6	–79.4	25.1
55	FA153065005	Long-term (mortgages)	4.3	10.4	8.1	–17.2	–12.4	1.4	–9.7	–11.3
56	**FA153081015**	**Equity and investment fund shares**	**144.1**	**–28.3**	**–153.9**	**–187.8**	**–381.1**	**–145.3**	**106.1**	**–63.9**
57	FA153064105	Corporate equities	–101.8	–269.9	–368.3	–581.5	–845.9	–108.4	88.0	–132.6
58	FA153064205	Mutual fund shares	264.4	170.9	175.6	167.8	214.2	12.0	304.8	202.0
59	FA153034005	Money market mutual fund shares	–118.6	–53.1	33.2	165.2	232.2	235.1	–268.7	–183.4
60	FA152090205	Equity in noncorporate business	100.7	123.8	5.6	60.6	18.4	–284.0	–19.1	46.1
61	FA153094305	Equity investment under Public-Private Inv. Program[c]	0.0	0.0	0.0	0.0	0.0	0.0	1.2	4.0

(continued)

Table 10A.1   (continued)

	2003	2004	2005	2006	2007	2008	2009	2010
62 FA153052005 Insurance, pension, and standardized guarantee schemes	**420.5**	**443.4**	**349.8**	**346.1**	**285.2**	**242.5**	**178.9**	**258.4**
63 FA153052045 Net equity in life insurance and pension funds	364.1	391.0	291.7	308.7	219.1	187.4	159.0	217.9
64 FA153040005 Net equity in life insurance reserves	66.8	33.1	16.1	57.8	18.0	61.7	23.7	9.0
65 FA153050005 Net equity in pension fund reserves	297.3	357.9	275.7	250.9	201.1	125.7	135.4	208.9
66 FA153052035 Prepayments of premiums and reserves against claims	56.4	52.5	58.0	37.4	66.1	55.1	19.9	40.5
67 FA153076005 Net equity in reserves of property-casualty insurance companies	22.9	23.6	25.6	4.6	6.7	11.0	-5.1	3.2
68 FA543195005 Net equity in other life insurance company reserves	13.9	11.4	9.5	14.8	15.5	17.6	8.4	14.8
69 FA313195105 Net equity in retiree health-care funds	19.6	17.4	23.0	18.1	43.9	26.5	16.6	22.5
70 FA154190005 Net incurrence of liabilities	**1,033.8**	**1,147.9**	**1,152.3**	**1,223.0**	**892.8**	**-155.6**	**-178.4**	**-192.4**
71 FA163162003 Debt securities (municiapals)	**13.8**	**15.8**	**14.8**	**16.3**	**20.6**	**8.0**	**6.0**	**-2.3**
72 FA154135005 Loans	**1,014.2**	**1,114.0**	**1,123.5**	**1,192.6**	**856.6**	**-189.0**	**-195.4**	**-214.1**
73 FA154141005 Short-term	135.3	179.4	77.1	191.6	168.8	-129.8	-44.2	99.5
74 FA153166000 Consumer credit	105.9	117.2	100.4	115.2	141.4	20.1	-115.8	-30.6
75 FA153168005 Depository institution loans[e]	-3.4	-19.6	8.2	12.1	-9.2	4.6	32.9	52.4
76 FA153169005 Other loans and advances	-1.5	0.3	0.0	4.8	3.2	6.2	0.5	2.4
77 FA153167005 Security credit	34.3	81.5	-31.6	59.7	33.4	-160.7	38.1	75.2
78 FA153165005 Long-term (mortgages)	878.9	934.6	1,046.4	1,001.0	687.8	-59.2	-151.2	-313.6
79 FA543077003 Insurance, pension, and standardized guarantee schemes	**0.9**	**1.6**	**1.0**	**0.5**	**1.0**	**3.2**	**-4.9**	**2.7**
80 FA163170003 Other accounts payable (trade debt)	**4.8**	**16.5**	**13.0**	**13.6**	**14.6**	**22.2**	**16.0**	**21.4**
Addendum:								
81 FA155000005 Net lending (+) or borrowing (−), financial account (lines 40–70)	-88.8	75.0	-349.2	-429.8	163.9	525.3	405.7	833.3
Other changes in volume account								
82 FU158090185 Total other volume changes	**448.4**	**1,287.2**	**305.9**	**122.0**	**610.0**	**181.8**	**398.6**	**318.5**
83 FU155111005 Net investment in consumer durable goods	242.6	249.7	249.5	238.8	232.8	134.8	48.1	100.9
84 FU155404003 Disaster losses	0.0	12.0	50.4	0.0	0.0	8.3	0.0	0.0
85 FU158090085 Other volume changes	208.3	792.8	-1.3	54.8	87.7	-114.1	433.1	-80.2
86 FU157005045 Less: Statistical discrepancy (lines 38-[40-70])[d]	2.6	-232.5	-7.4	171.7	-289.6	-152.8	82.6	-297.8
Revaluation account								
87 FD152010705 Nonfinancial assets	**1,259.2**	**2,347.0**	**2,868.3**	**356.9**	**-1,920.4**	**-3,825.2**	**-1,216.4**	**-486.1**
88 FD155035725 Real estate	1,341.0	2,380.0	2,909.5	3,92.8	-1,868.3	-3,792.7	-1,171.8	-395.2
89 FD155111005 Consumer durable goods	-85.2	-37.6	-45.6	-43.2	-58.1	-36.3	-43.3	-90.7
90 FD165015205 Equipment and software	3.4	4.6	4.4	7.3	5.9	3.8	-1.2	-0.3

91 FD158080095	**Financial assets**	**3,923.3**	**3,004.6**	**2,917.5**	**3,703.7**	**1,588.8**	**-9,564.0**	**2,254.1**	**3,097.3**
92 FD153064105	Corporate equities	1,722.7	961.2	976.4	2,130.9	827.8	-3,763.9	1,567.1	1,314.2
93 FD153064205	Mutual fund shares	427.6	346.0	67.7	354.7	198.6	-1,276.1	513.3	246.4
94 FD152090205	Equity on noncorporate business	515.5	1,124.6	1,318.4	263.7	119.8	-1,327.4	-1,232.5	551.5
95 FD153094305	Equity investment under Public–Private Inv. Program	0.0	0.0	0.0	0.0	0.0	0.0	-0.3	-1.0
96 FD153052045	Insurance, pension, and standardized guarantee schemes	1,257.5	572.8	555.1	954.4	442.7	-3,196.6	1,406.4	986.2
97 FD158200705	**Changes in net worth due to nominal holding gains/losses**	**5,182.5**	**5,351.6**	**5,785.8**	**4,060.7**	**-331.6**	**-13,389.2**	**1,037.7**	**2,611.2**
	Changes in balance sheet account								
98 FR152090005	**Change in net worth (lines 32 + 38 + 82 + 97)**	**5,922.4**	**6,940.6**	**6,261.8**	**4,423.7**	**517.9**	**-12,611.5**	**2,040.5**	**3,565.0**
	Balance sheet account (end of period)								
99 FL152000005	**Total assets**	**57,844.9**	**65,953.7**	**73,366.8**	**78,997.5**	**80,410.8**	**67,648.6**	**69,467.2**	**72,852.6**
100 FL152010005	**Nonfinancial assets**	**21,853.6**	**24,891.6**	**28,477.9**	**29,579.9**	**28,254.0**	**24,787.4**	**23,740.2**	**23,448.2**
101 FL155035005	Real estate	17,981.0	20,789.3	24,156.3	25,043.0	23,523.6	19,937.1	18,874.5	18,557.0
102 FL155111005	Consumer durable goods	3,682.0	3,894.1	4,098.0	4,293.6	4,468.3	4,566.8	4,571.6	4,581.8
103 FL165015205	Equipment and software	190.6	208.1	223.7	243.2	262.0	283.6	294.1	309.4
104 FL154090005	**Financial assets**	**35,991.3**	**41,062.1**	**44,888.8**	**49,417.6**	**52,156.8**	**42,861.1**	**45,727.0**	**49,404.5**
105 FL154000005	**Currency and deposits**	**4,476.2**	**4,912.1**	**5,282.8**	**5,733.4**	**6,155.3**	**6,525.3**	**6,656.0**	**6,836.7**
106 FL153022005	Currency and transferable deposits	458.2	400.0	285.8	245.8	160.2	349.6	373.6	348.3
107 FL153091003	Foreign deposits	52.1	57.5	59.9	65.2	80.5	56.9	50.5	54.8
108 FL153030005	Time and savings deposits	3,965.9	4,454.6	4,937.1	5,422.4	5,914.6	6,118.8	6,231.9	6,433.6
109 FL313131003	Postal saving system deposits	0.0	0.0	0.0	0.0	0.0	0.0	0.0	0.0
110 FL154022005	**Debt securities**	**2,713.4**	**3,812.4**	**4,150.3**	**4,302.9**	**4,920.4**	**4,832.8**	**5,115.6**	**5,306.8**
111 FL163069103	Open market paper	77.3	83.7	98.4	117.5	107.3	6.0	34.6	63.4
112 FL313161400	US savings bonds	203.8	204.4	205.1	202.4	196.4	194.0	191.2	187.9
113 FL153061105	Treasury securities	204.2	288.2	265.6	197.2	68.3	62.6	624.3	1,019.1
114 FL153061705	Agency- and GSE-backet securities[b]	384.0	406.0	513.5	443.1	693.3	736.9	141.9	126.0
115 FL153062005	Municipal securities	703.7	1,561.8	1,639.1	1,681.4	1,725.4	1,767.2	1,896.5	1,954.6
116 FL153063005	Corporate and foreign bonds	1,140.4	1,268.3	1,428.6	1,661.4	2,129.8	2,066.2	2,227.0	1,955.7
117 FL154035005	**Loans**	**599.4**	**715.6**	**723.4**	**787.0**	**993.8**	**883.5**	**796.8**	**810.6**
118 FL154041005	Short-term	478.5	584.3	584.0	664.7	884.0	772.4	695.4	720.4
119 FL153065005	Long-term (mortgages)	120.9	131.3	139.5	122.2	109.8	111.2	101.5	90.2
120 FL153081015	**Equity and investment fund shares**	**16,968.9**	**19,372.5**	**21,581.0**	**24,142.5**	**24,907.5**	**18,394.9**	**19,348.7**	**21,395.8**
121 FL153064105	Corporate equities	6,784.2	7,475.5	8,083.5	9,632.9	9,614.8	5,742.5	7,397.6	8,579.2
122 FL153064205	Mutual fund shares	2,915.3	3,432.3	3,675.5	4,198.1	4,610.9	3,346.8	4,164.9	4,613.4
123 FL153034005	Money market fund shares	969.2	916.1	949.2	1,114.5	1,346.7	1,581.8	1,313.1	1,129.7
124 FL152090205	Equity in noncorporate business	6,300.2	7,548.6	8,872.6	9,197.0	9,335.2	7,723.8	6,472.1	7,069.7
125 FL153094305	Equity investment under Public–Private Inv. Program[c]	0.0	0.0	0.0	0.0	0.0	0.0	0.9	3.8

(continued)

Table 10A.1 (continued)

		2003	2004	2005	2006	2007	2008	2009	2010
126	FL153052005	**Insurance, pension, and standardized guarantee schemes**	11,233.4	12,249.6	13,151.3	14,451.8	15,179.7	12,224.6	13,810.0	15,054.6
127	FL153052045	Net equity in life insurance and pension funds	10,732.1	11,695.8	12,542.7	13,805.8	14,467.5	11,458.3	13,023.7	14,227.9
128	FL153040005	Net equity in life insurance reserves	1,013.2	1,060.4	1,082.6	1,055.2	1,076.8	1,049.8	1,109.2	1,137.2
129	FL153050005	Net equity in pension fund reserves	9,718.9	10,635.5	11,460.1	12,750.6	13,390.7	10,408.5	11,914.5	13,090.7
130	FL153052035	Prepayments of premiums and reserves against claims	501.3	553.8	608.7	646.1	712.2	766.3	786.2	826.7
131	FL153076005	Net equity in reserves of property-casualty insurance companies	266.8	290.4	316.0	320.5	327.3	337.3	332.2	335.4
132	FL543195005	Net equity in reserves of life insurance company reserves	199.5	211.0	217.3	232.1	247.6	265.2	273.6	288.4
133	FL313195105	Net equity in retiree health-care funds	35.0	52.4	75.4	93.5	137.3	163.8	180.4	202.9
134	FL152100005	**Total liabilities and net worth**	57,844.9	65,953.7	73,366.8	78,997.5	80,410.8	67,648.6	69,467.2	72,852.6
135	FL154190005	**Liabilities**	9,823.1	10,991.2	12,142.5	13,349.4	14,244.1	14,094.1	13,872.3	13,692.7
136	FL163162003	**Debt securities (municipals)**	177.7	198.9	213.7	230.1	250.7	258.7	264.6	262.3
137	FL154135005	**Loans**	9,467.7	10,596.5	11,720.1	12,896.6	13,755.7	13,571.7	13,332.8	13,131.5
138	FL154141005	Short-term	2,399.7	2,579.1	2,656.2	2,831.8	3,003.1	2,873.3	2,785.7	2,899.1
139	FL153166000	Consumer credit	2,102.9	2,220.1	2,320.6	2,384.6	2,528.5	2,548.6	2,438.5	2,411.6
140	FL153168005	Depository institution loans[e]	-4.4	-24.0	-15.8	31.3	22.1	26.7	10.4	73.2
141	FL153169005	Other loans and advances	118.7	119.0	119.0	123.8	127.0	133.2	133.7	136.1
142	FL153167005	Security credit	182.5	264.0	232.4	292.1	325.5	164.8	203.0	278.2
143	FL153165005	Long-term (mortgages)	7,068.0	8,017.4	9,063.9	10,064.8	10,752.6	10,698.4	10,547.2	10,232.4
144	FL543077003	**Insurance, pension, and standardized guarantee schemes**	20.9	22.5	22.4	22.8	23.9	27.0	22.1	24.7
145	FL163177003	**Other accounts payable (trade debt)**	156.8	173.3	186.3	199.9	214.5	236.7	252.7	274.1
146	FL152090005	**Net worth**	48,021.9	54,962.5	61,224.3	65,648.1	66,166.0	53,554.5	55,594.9	59,159.9

Source: SNA tables, June 7, 2012.

Notes: Quarterly figures are seasonally adjusted annual rates. NPISHs = nonprofit institutions serving households.

[a] Consists of rental income of tenant-occupied housing and proprietors' income. Quasi-corporations are unincorporated enterprises that function as if they were corporations; they primarily cover their operating costs through sales, and they keep a complete set of financial records.

[b] Government-sponsored enterprises (GSEs) consist of Federal Home Loan Banks, Fannie Mae, Freddie Mac, Federal Agricultural Mortgage Corporation, Farm Credit System, the Financing Corporation, and the Resolution Funding Corporation, and they included the Student Loan Marketing Association until it was fully privatized in the fourth quarter of 2004.

[c] Funds invested by financial institutions such as domestic hedge funds through the Public-Private Investment Program (PPIP).

[d] The statistical discrepancy is the difference between net lending or net borrowing derived in the capital account and the same concept derived in the financial account. The discrepancy reflects differences in source data, timing of recorded flows, and other statistical differences between the capital and financial accounts.

[e] Not elsewhere classified.

Appendix B

Table 10B.1   Financial business (billions of dollars)

	2002	2003	2004	2005	2006	2007	2008	2009	2010
	Current account								
1 Gross value added	**883.2**	**922.3**	**964.5**	**1,085.8**	**1,189.4**	**1,118.6**	**1,031.0**	**1,119.7**	**1,372.9**
2 Less: Consumption of fixed capital	**107.4**	**113.0**	**120.5**	**127.3**	**132.8**	**140.6**	**172.7**	**176.9**	**179.1**
3 Equals: Net value added	**775.8**	**809.3**	**844.1**	**958.5**	**1,056.7**	**978.1**	**858.3**	**942.8**	**1,193.8**
4 Compensation of employees (paid)	447.3	467.3	497.4	541.8	584.4	610.3	610.4	568.0	584.7
5 Wages and salaries	371.1	393.6	420.0	454.5	492.4	521.0	513.3	471.1	487.1
6 Employers' social contributions	76.3	73.7	77.4	87.3	92.0	89.2	97.1	96.8	97.6
7 Taxes on production and imports less subsidies	37.6	39.9	43.4	46.1	50.5	53.4	51.2	54.7	55.1
8 Operating surplus, net	290.9	302.1	303.3	370.6	421.8	314.4	196.7	320.2	554.0
9 Net national income/Balance of primary incomes, net	**212.7**	**231.8**	**252.0**	**271.7**	**274.5**	**200.6**	**42.3**	**260.0**	**314.8**
10 Operating surplus, net	290.9	302.1	303.3	370.6	421.8	314.4	196.7	320.2	554.0
11 Property income (received)	1,282.7	1,178.8	1,415.9	1,794.1	2,345.2	2,825.7	2,435.6	1,740.6	1,741.8
12 Interest	1,179.4	1,063.9	1,267.3	1,631.9	2,119.3	2,546.6	2,150.2	1,499.7	1,485.5
13 Distributed income of corporations (dividends)	89.2	93.9	118.5	159.2	184.3	231.5	236.1	189.2	190.3
14 Reinvested earnings on US direct investment abroad	14.1	20.9	30.1	3.0	41.6	47.6	49.3	51.7	66.0
15 Less: Uses of property income (paid)	1,582.1	1,479.6	1,756.2	2,222.9	2,887.2	3,375.0	2,973.4	2,191.5	2,177.3
16 Interest	1,341.3	1,232.5	1,450.7	1,872.1	2,464.3	2,909.2	2,562.9	1,776.6	1,697.3
17 Distributed income of corporations	240.5	244.5	296.2	342.8	410.0	455.7	403.4	412.5	463.8
18 Dividends	185.6	193.3	242.1	284.8	340.1	396.7	368.3	356.6	406.8
19 Withdrawals from income of quasi-corporations[a]	54.9	51.2	54.1	58.0	69.9	59.0	35.1	55.9	57.0
20 Reinvested earnings on foreign direct investment	0.3	2.5	9.3	8.0	12.9	10.1	7.1	2.4	16.2
21 Rents on land and natural resources	0.0	0.0	0.0	0.0	0.0	0.0	0.0	0.0	0.0
22 Net national income/Balance of primary incomes, net	**212.7**	**231.8**	**252.0**	**271.7**	**274.5**	**200.6**	**42.3**	**260.0**	**314.8**
23 Less: Current taxes on income, wealth, etc. (paid)	95.2	110.9	119.1	140.5	165.6	151.7	81.6	97.4	181.8
24 Less: Other current transfers (paid)	8.1	−13.2	−9.5	−16.6	−26.0	4.6	45.6	18.7	15.0
25 Equals: Disposable income, net	**109.3**	**134.1**	**142.5**	**147.7**	**134.8**	**44.3**	**−85.0**	**143.9**	**118.0**
26 Equals: Net saving	**109.3**	**134.1**	**142.5**	**147.7**	**134.8**	**44.3**	**−85.0**	**143.9**	**118.0**
	Capital account								
27 Net saving less capital transfers	109.3	134.1	126.3	120.0	134.8	44.3	−24.5	265.9	159.5
28 Net saving	109.3	134.1	142.5	147.7	134.8	44.3	−85.0	143.9	118.0
29 Less: Capital transfers paid (net)	0.0	0.0	16.2	27.7	0.0	0.0	−60.5	−121.9	−41.5
30 Capital formation, net	**29.0**	**22.3**	**34.6**	**28.0**	**29.9**	**46.9**	**22.2**	**−8.8**	**2.6**
31 Gross fixed capital formation (nonresidential)	136.4	135.4	155.1	155.3	162.7	187.5	195.0	168.1	181.7
32 Less: Consumption of fixed capital	107.4	113.0	120.5	127.3	132.8	140.6	172.7	176.9	179.1
33 Net lending (+) or borrowing (−), capital account (lines 27–30)	**80.3**	**111.7**	**91.7**	**92.0**	**104.9**	**−2.6**	**−46.7**	**274.6**	**156.9**

(*continued*)

Table 10B.1   (continued)

	2002	2003	2004	2005	2006	2007	2008	2009	2010
	Financial account								
34 **Net lending (+) or borrowing (−) (line 33)**	80.3	111.7	91.7	92.0	104.9	−2.6	−46.7	274.6	156.9
35 **Net acquisition of financial assets**	2,300.9	2,780.3	2,966.0	3,311.3	4,128.2	4,804.9	4,606.5	−1,592.3	−678.9
36 **Monetary gold**	0.0	0.0	0.0	0.0	0.0	0.0	0.0	0.0	0.0
37 **Currency and deposits**	−11.4	−42.3	33.9	−5.0	60.6	169.4	1,017.5	236.1	−141.2
38 **Debt securities**	886.6	1,037.0	463.3	615.3	1,119.3	1,112.5	1,451.2	942.0	733.8
39 SDR certificates	0.0	0.0	0.0	0.0	0.0	0.0	0.0	3.0	0.0
40 Open market paper	−130.2	−164.5	33.4	196.3	232.4	−94.8	34.2	−393.4	−127.0
41 Treasury securities	196.4	88.2	−52.6	48.4	92.1	108.0	436.0	440.6	461.4
42 Agency- and GSE-backed securities[b]	539.3	419.7	−168.8	−189.1	135.9	301.6	858.9	603.7	83.1
43 Municipal securities	55.5	101.3	87.0	112.6	123.4	180.1	51.7	15.6	29.4
44 Corporate and foreign bonds	201.2	567.7	523.4	407.2	499.8	584.3	7.1	210.5	221.2
45 Nonmarketable government securities	24.5	24.7	40.9	40.0	35.8	33.3	63.3	61.9	65.7
46 **Loans**	931.0	1,110.6	1,570.6	1,954.6	2,025.5	2,332.8	1,645.4	−2,795.2	−974.1
47 Short-term	35.5	121.3	362.0	547.6	633.5	1,264.4	1,556.7	−2,508.3	−471.7
48 Long-term	895.5	989.3	1,208.5	1,407.0	1,392.0	1,068.4	88.7	−286.8	−502.5
49 **Equity and investment fund shares**	385.4	341.7	663.2	512.3	518.2	998.7	608.5	−53.7	−40.8
50 Corporate equities	169.9	258.0	329.5	236.4	124.3	166.3	−8.9	51.6	62.1
51 Mutual fund shares	101.0	−2.6	97.1	52.2	102.6	117.2	24.7	101.4	72.4
52 Money market mutual fund shares	−14.0	−67.4	−104.6	35.4	60.9	333.8	303.9	−170.9	−158.1
53 Equity in government-sponsored enterprises[b]	1.9	2.5	2.4	2.0	0.0	8.3	−5.3	0.0	−3.2
54 US direct investment abroad	23.4	24.3	43.8	11.5	25.8	107.0	66.4	23.8	29.3
55 Stock in Federal Reserve Banks	1.0	0.5	3.1	1.6	1.8	3.1	2.6	4.6	0.9
56 Investment in subsidiaries	102.2	126.4	291.9	173.2	202.8	263.1	225.0	−64.1	−44.2
57 **Insurance, pension, and standardized guarantee schemes**	14.6	−17.3	−36.8	−2.3	4.9	47.9	47.3	10.6	5.2
58 **Other accounts receivable**	94.5	350.6	271.9	236.3	399.7	143.5	−163.3	67.9	−261.8
59 **Net incurrence of liabilities**	2,272.2	2,562.0	2,950.5	3,004.7	3,865.3	4,696.7	4,873.3	−1,637.9	−469.8
60 **Currency and deposits**	383.2	465.7	612.5	617.7	616.2	536.5	2,209.1	240.1	303.0
61 **Debt securities**	845.5	1,010.0	805.9	1,039.2	1,323.3	1,504.8	362.8	−1,095.8	−731.1
62 Agency- and GSE-backed securities[b]	546.7	586.2	115.8	80.4	328.2	905.7	768.7	−60.1	−46.9
63 Corporate bonds	398.8	487.3	668.5	744.6	798.8	710.6	−280.3	−587.6	−582.5
64 Commercial paper	−99.9	−63.5	21.7	214.2	196.3	−111.4	−125.6	−448.2	−101.7

#									
65	**Loans**	105.7	370.6	311.1	424.9	564.7	582.9	−1,063.9	−448.0
66	Short-term	94.5	361.7	285.6	410.8	558.1	578.2	−1,067.2	−448.2
67	Long-term	11.2	8.9	25.5	14.1	6.6	4.7	3.4	0.2
68	**Equity and investment fund shares**	358.9	256.2	651.7	699.9	933.2	1,454.2	258.4	99.2
69	Money market mutual fund shares	−16.7	−207.5	−136.5	127.0	305.3	720.9	−499.0	−502.9
70	Corporate equity issues	71.5	66.1	118.3	78.5	59.5	637.6	314.3	190.8
71	Mutual fund shares	181.1	288.6	298.2	260.2	336.8	31.0	490.5	389.3
72	Equity in government-sponsored enterprises[b]	2.0	3.2	2.5	1.9	0.2	−4.2	0.0	−2.7
73	Foreign direct investment in the United States	9.6	23.9	50.2	13.9	52.0	120.7	46.1	50.1
74	Equity in noncorporate business	0.6	−3.4	−4.2	−1.2	−6.8	11.5	−3.6	0.4
75	Investment by parent	109.7	84.9	320.1	218.1	184.4	233.0	−94.5	−26.6
76	Stock in Federal Reserve Banks	1.0	0.5	3.1	1.6	1.8	2.6	4.6	0.9
77	**Insurance, pension, and standardized guarantee schemes**	399.8	405.5	414.0	351.0	345.0	272.8	174.3	242.0
78	**Other accounts payable**	179.0	54.1	155.3	−128.0	82.9	342.2	−150.9	65.0
	Addendum:								
79	Net lending (+) or borrowing (−), financial account (lines 35–39)	28.7	218.3	15.6	306.6	263.0	108.2	45.6	−209.1

Other changes in volume account

#									
80	**Total other volume changes**	76.5	12.3	−60.9	154.4	32.5	−94.5	463.7	−353.3
81	Disaster losses	0.0	0.0	1.7	1.7	0.0	0.0	0.0	0.0
82	Other volume changes	128.1	−94.3	13.5	−61.9	−125.6	−205.3	692.7	12.7
83	Less: Statistical discrepancy (line 33−[35–59])[c]	51.7	−106.5	76.1	−214.6	−158.1	−110.8	229.1	366.0

Revaluation account

#									
84	**Nonfinancial assets**	32.8	40.0	88.4	101.9	98.9	57.3	−53.8	−4.2
85	Structures (nonresidential)	23.4	21.1	69.4	83.1	74.7	45.8	−50.3	1.4
86	Equipment and software	9.4	18.9	18.9	18.8	24.3	11.5	−3.4	−5.5
87	**Financial assets**	−1,603.6	2,145.5	1,202.1	1,004.2	1,931.8	931.6	2,645.5	1,780.3
88	Corporate equities	−1,469.4	1,862.9	1,045.5	712.8	1,616.6	719.5	2,191.2	1,458.9
89	Mutual fund shares	−162.6	252.6	106.0	260.8	279.5	166.3	441.9	279.9
90	US direct investment abroad	28.4	30.0	50.6	30.7	35.7	45.8	12.3	41.5
91	**Liabilities**	−1,911.4	2,774.7	1,507.7	1,203.9	2,499.5	−210.3	3,554.1	2,084.7
92	Corporate equity issues	−366.9	795.9	458.8	262.3	716.6	−984.4	443.4	517.2
93	Mutual fund shares	−678.1	727.2	483.8	352.4	682.6	396.0	1,035.8	583.7
94	Foreign direct investment in the United States	−15.1	8.4	4.0	9.4	22.5	−56.7	22.4	17.4
95	Equity in noncorporate business	−1.9	11.4	2.4	1.7	4.9	−0.6	6.3	1.3
96	Pension fund reserves	−849.5	1,232.0	558.7	548.9	1,039.6	439.1	1,370.7	967.2
97	Investment by parent	0.0	−0.1	0.0	29.0	33.2	−3.7	675.6	−2.0
98	**Changes in net worth due to nominal holding gains/losses**	340.6	−589.2	−217.3	−97.8	−468.7	1,199.2	−962.4	−308.6

(continued)

Table 10B.1   (continued)

	2002	2003	2004	2005	2006	2007	2008	2009	2010
	Changes in balance sheet account								
99 **Change in net worth (lines 30 + 33 + 80 + 98)**	526.4	−442.8	−151.9	176.7	−301.4	1,149.1	1,592.2	−232.9	−502.4
	Balance sheet account (end of period)								
100 **Total assets**	40,062.6	44,885.5	49,111.2	53,374.2	59,500.5	65,323.0	64,008.6	65,658.2	66,273.1
101 **Nonfinancial assets**[d]	1,147.9	1,194.1	1,296.9	1,404.4	1,511.0	1,591.7	1,678.2	1,615.7	1,614.1
102 Structures (nonresidential)	667.2	685.6	755.7	838.9	914.0	967.2	1,034.3	985.0	978.5
103 Equipment and software	480.7	508.6	541.2	565.4	597.0	624.5	643.9	630.7	635.6
104 **Financial assets**	38,914.7	43,691.4	47,814.3	51,969.9	57,989.5	63,731.3	62,330.4	64,042.5	64,659.0
105 Monetary gold	11.0	11.0	11.0	11.0	11.0	11.0	11.0	11.0	11.0
106 **Currency and deposits**	783.5	743.9	779.0	771.3	833.2	1,005.0	2,058.3	2,309.0	2,168.4
107 **Debt securities**	12,655.0	13,529.5	14,012.8	14,608.9	15,682.8	16,795.3	18,246.2	19,210.7	19,460.3
108 SDR certificates	2.2	2.2	2.2	2.2	2.2	2.2	2.2	5.2	5.2
109 Open market paper	950.0	785.6	818.9	1,015.2	1,244.3	1,149.5	1,183.4	790.0	663.0
110 Treasury securities	1,631.7	1,643.9	1,591.2	1,639.6	1,727.4	1,835.4	2,271.3	2,712.0	3,173.4
111 Agency- and GSE-backed securities[b]	4,312.4	4,567.6	4,418.8	4,229.7	4,363.7	4,665.5	5,524.2	6,182.4	5,802.7
112 Municipal securities	1,033.4	1,134.7	1,221.8	1,334.4	1,457.5	1,637.6	1,689.2	1,704.8	1,734.2
113 Corporate and foreign bonds	3,934.9	4,580.6	5,104.0	5,504.9	5,969.1	6,553.4	6,560.6	6,739.2	6,938.9
114 Nonmarketable government securities	790.3	815.0	855.9	882.9	918.7	952.0	1,015.3	1,077.2	1,142.9
115 **Loans**	13,328.0	14,482.8	16,068.2	18,022.8	20,029.2	22,351.6	23,996.6	21,228.9	20,290.0
116 Short-term	5,342.8	5,496.5	5,858.6	6,406.2	7,019.4	8,273.4	9,829.8	7,348.9	6,912.4
117 Long-term	7,985.2	8,986.2	10,209.6	11,616.6	13,009.8	14,078.2	14,166.9	13,880.1	13,377.6
118 **Equity and investment fund shares**	9,524.0	12,011.2	13,876.5	15,393.1	17,876.2	19,806.5	14,245.0	17,513.0	19,252.4
119 Corporate equities	5,974.2	8,095.0	9,470.1	10,419.2	12,160.1	13,045.9	7,820.5	10,063.4	11,584.4
120 Mutual fund shares	1,201.9	1,452.0	1,655.1	1,968.1	2,350.2	2,633.8	1,694.1	2,237.4	2,589.8
121 Money market fund shares	680.2	612.8	508.2	543.6	604.6	938.4	1,242.3	1,071.4	913.3
122 Equity in government-sponsored enterprises[b]	35.2	37.7	40.1	42.0	42.0	50.3	45.0	45.0	41.7
123 US direct investment abroad	255.1	309.4	403.8	446.0	507.4	660.2	737.4	773.5	844.3
124 Stock in Federal Reserve Banks	8.4	8.8	11.9	13.5	15.3	18.5	21.1	25.6	26.5
125 Investment in subsidiaries	1,369.0	1,495.4	1,787.3	1,960.6	2,196.5	2,459.6	2,684.6	3,296.6	3,252.4
126 **Insurance, pension, and standardized guarantee schemes**	319.5	387.7	397.6	405.5	562.1	627.1	522.5	618.2	672.5
127 **Other accounts receivable**	2,293.5	2,525.3	2,669.2	2,757.3	2,994.9	3,134.7	3,250.7	3,151.7	2,804.4
128 **Total liabilities and net worth**	40,062.6	44,885.5	49,111.2	53,374.2	59,500.5	65,323.0	64,008.6	65,658.2	66,273.1
129 **Liabilities**	40,425.3	45,691.1	50,068.6	54,155.0	60,582.6	65,256.1	62,349.4	64,231.9	65,349.2
130 **Currency and deposits**	6,373.9	6,839.1	7,477.1	8,095.4	8,712.3	9,248.2	11,420.9	11,654.5	11,954.1

131	**Debt securities**	9,312.8	10,158.1	10,978.9	11,963.6	13,272.1	14,906.8	15,269.3	14,498.9	13,259.8
132	Agency- and GSE-backed securities[b]	5,509.0	5,944.5	6,060.3	6,140.7	6,468.9	7,374.6	8,143.4	8,083.3	7,574.0
133	Corporate bonds	2,805.9	3,279.2	3,962.6	4,652.7	5,440.1	6,280.4	6,000.1	5,737.9	5,109.9
134	Commercial paper	997.9	934.4	956.0	1,170.2	1,363.2	1,251.8	1,125.8	677.6	575.9
135	**Loans**	2,434.0	2,804.6	3,115.7	3,540.6	4,102.1	4,685.0	4,614.9	3,682.7	3,211.1
136	Short-term	2,337.1	2,698.7	2,984.4	3,395.1	3,950.0	4,528.3	4,451.4	3,515.8	3,044.0
137	Long-term	97.0	105.9	131.4	145.5	152.1	156.7	163.5	166.9	167.1
138	**Equity and investment fund shares**	10,408.7	12,207.6	13,808.4	15,163.2	17,556.3	18,361.1	15,157.2	17,599.1	18,815.8
139	Money market fund shares	2,223.9	2,016.4	1,879.8	2,006.9	2,312.1	3,033.1	3,757.3	3,258.3	2,755.3
140	Corporate equity issues	2,852.0	3,713.9	4,291.1	4,631.9	5,408.0	4,602.2	2,875.4	3,633.2	4,341.1
141	Mutual fund shares	3,638.4	4,654.2	5,436.3	6,048.9	7,068.3	7,829.0	5,435.3	6,961.6	7,934.5
142	Equity in government-sponsored enterprises[b]	39.1	42.3	44.8	46.7	46.9	56.0	51.8	51.8	49.0
143	Foreign direct investment in the United States	243.5	275.7	329.9	353.2	427.8	380.4	343.5	411.9	479.5
144	Equity in noncorporate business	5.0	13.0	11.2	11.7	9.8	11.6	9.5	12.1	13.8
145	Investment by parent	1,398.6	1,483.4	1,803.4	2,050.4	2,268.1	2,430.5	2,663.5	3,244.5	3,215.9
146	Stock in Federal Reserve Banks	8.4	8.8	11.9	13.5	15.3	18.5	21.1	25.6	26.5
147	**Insurance, pension, and standardized guarantee schemes**	10,058.7	11,807.1	12,840.5	13,754.8	15,205.9	15,960.3	12,884.5	14,550.4	15,827.6
148	**Other accounts payable**	1,837.2	1,874.6	1,848.0	1,637.4	1,733.9	2,094.7	3,002.5	2,246.4	2,280.9
149	**Net worth**	−362.7	−805.5	−957.4	−780.7	−1,082.1	66.9	1,659.2	1,426.3	923.9

[a]Consists of rental income of tenant-occupied housing and proprietors' income. Quasi-corporations are unincorporated enterprises that function as if they were corporations; they primarily cover their operating costs through sales, and they keep a complete set of financial records.

[b]Government-sponsored enterprises (GSEs) consist of Federal Home Loan Banks, Fannie Mae, Freddie Mac, Federal Agricultural Mortgage Corporation, Farm Credit System, the Financing Corporation, and the Resolution Funding Corporation, and they included the Student Loan Marketing Association until it was fully privatized in the fourth quarter of 2004.

[c]The statistical discrepancy is the difference between net lending or net borrowing derived in the capital account and the same concept derived in the financial account. The discrepancy reflects differences in source data, timing of recorded flows, and other statistical differences between the capital and financial accounts.

[d]Excludes land. Includes corporate and noncorporate financial business.

Table 10B.2   Central bank (billions of dollars)

	2002	2003	2004	2005	2006	2007	2008	2009	2010
	Current account								
1 Gross value added	1.7	1.6	1.6	1.7	1.8	2.0	2.4	3.0	2.7
2 Less: Consumption of fixed capital	1.7	1.8	1.9	2.0	2.0	2.1	0.8	0.8	0.8
3 Equals: Net value added	0.0	-0.1	-0.3	-0.3	-0.2	-0.1	1.7	2.3	1.9
4 Compensation of employees (paid)	1.5	1.5	1.5	1.6	1.7	1.8	2.0	2.1	2.1
5 Wages and salaries	1.3	1.3	1.3	1.4	1.5	1.6	1.7	1.8	1.9
6 Employers' social contributions	0.2	0.2	0.2	0.2	0.2	0.2	0.2	0.2	0.2
7 Taxes on production and imports less subsidies	0.0	0.0	0.0	0.0	0.0	0.0	0.0	0.0	0.0
8 Operating surplus, net	-1.5	-1.6	-1.8	-1.8	-1.8	-1.9	-0.3	0.2	-0.2
9 Net national income/Balance of primary incomes, net	23.6	20.7	20.2	27.1	34.6	38.3	37.5	50.7	75.0
10 Operating surplus, net	-1.5	-1.6	-1.8	-1.8	-1.8	-1.9	-0.3	0.2	-0.2
11 Property income (received)	26.8	23.8	23.5	30.7	38.4	42.6	41.1	54.5	79.4
12 Interest	26.8	23.8	23.5	30.7	38.4	42.6	41.1	54.5	79.4
13 Distributed income of corporations (dividends)	0.0	0.0	0.0	0.0	0.0	0.0	0.0	0.0	0.0
14 Reinvested earnings on US direct investment abroad	0.0	0.0	0.0	0.0	0.0	0.0	0.0	0.0	0.0
15 Less: Uses of property income (paid)	1.7	1.5	1.5	1.8	1.9	2.5	3.3	4.0	4.2
16 Interest	1.2	1.0	0.9	1.0	1.1	1.5	2.1	2.6	2.6
17 Distributed income of corporations	0.5	0.5	0.6	0.8	0.9	1.0	1.2	1.4	1.6
18 Dividends	0.5	0.5	0.6	0.8	0.9	1.0	1.2	1.4	1.6
19 Withdrawals from income of quasi-corporations[a]	0.0	0.0	0.0	0.0	0.0	0.0	0.0	0.0	0.0
20 Reinvested earnings on foreign direct investment	0.0	0.0	0.0	0.0	0.0	0.0	0.0	0.0	0.0
21 Rents on land and natural resources	0.0	0.0	0.0	0.0	0.0	0.0	0.0	0.0	0.0
22 Net national income/Balance of primary incomes, net	23.6	20.7	20.2	27.1	34.6	38.3	37.5	50.7	75.0
23 Less: Current taxes on income, wealth, etc. (paid)	24.5	22.0	18.1	21.5	29.1	34.6	31.7	47.4	79.3
24 Less: Other current transfers (paid)	0.0	0.0	0.0	0.0	0.0	0.0	0.0	0.0	0.0
25 Equals: Disposable income, net	-0.9	-1.3	2.1	5.7	5.6	3.7	5.8	3.3	-4.3
26 Equals: Net saving	-0.9	-1.3	2.1	5.7	5.6	3.7	5.8	3.3	-4.3

Capital account

27 Net saving less capital transfers	**-0.9**	-1.3	**2.1**	5.7	**5.6**	3.7	**5.8**	3.3	**-5.3**
28 Net saving	-0.9	-1.3	2.1	5.7	5.6	3.7	5.8	3.3	-4.3
29 Less: Capital transfers paid (net)	0.0	0.0	0.0	0.0	0.0	0.0	0.0	0.0	1.0
30 **Capital formation, net**	**0.7**	**0.6**	**1.1**	**-0.1**	**0.8**	**0.8**	**-0.2**	**-0.1**	**-0.1**
31 Gross fixed capital formation (nonresidential)	2.3	2.4	3.1	1.9	2.8	2.9	0.6	0.7	0.7
32 Less: Consumption of fixed capital	1.7	1.8	1.9	2.0	2.0	2.1	0.8	0.8	0.8
33 **Net lending (+) or borrowing (−), capital account (lines 27–30)**	**-1.5**	**-1.9**	**1.0**	**5.8**	**4.8**	**2.9**	**6.0**	**3.4**	**-5.2**

Financial account

34 **Net lending (+) or borrowing (−) (line 33)**	**-1.5**	**-1.9**	**1.0**	**5.8**	**4.8**	**2.9**	**6.0**	**3.4**	**-5.2**
35 **Net acquisition of financial assets**	**70.7**	**43.2**	**44.4**	**37.4**	**29.6**	**43.1**	**1,319.3**	**-3.4**	**186.0**
36 **Monetary gold**	**0.0**	**0.0**	**0.0**	**0.0**	**0.0**	**0.0**	**0.0**	**0.0**	**0.0**
37 **Currency and deposits**	**2.3**	**0.4**	**2.5**	**0.4**	**0.8**	**1.3**	**-0.8**	**3.7**	**1.8**
38 **Debt securities**	**77.7**	**37.2**	**51.2**	**26.4**	**34.7**	**-38.3**	**-245.0**	**1,352.2**	**316.3**
39 SDR certificates	0.0	0.0	0.0	0.0	0.0	0.0	0.0	3.0	0.0
40 Bankers' acceptances	0.0	0.0	0.0	0.0	0.0	0.0	0.0	0.0	0.0
41 Treasury securities	77.7	37.3	51.2	26.4	34.7	-38.3	-264.7	300.7	244.9
42 Agency- and GSE-backed securities[b]	0.0	0.0	0.0	0.0	0.0	0.0	19.7	1,048.5	71.4
43 Loans (short-term)	-10.7	4.3	-10.8	13.8	-6.0	78.3	1,564.7	-1,434.1	-151.4
44 Equity and investment fund shares	0.0	0.0	0.0	0.0	0.0	0.0	0.0	25.1	1.3
45 Other accounts receivable	1.4	1.3	1.5	-3.2	0.1	1.8	0.5	49.6	18.0
46 **Net incurrence of liabilities**	**69.6**	**42.7**	**41.7**	**36.1**	**27.2**	**39.9**	**1,316.7**	**-8.0**	**185.1**
47 **Currency and deposits**	**47.4**	**38.0**	**32.3**	**33.6**	**24.8**	**23.1**	**1,270.2**	**-3.4**	**173.9**
48 **Loans (short-term)**	**21.1**	**4.6**	**5.1**	**-0.3**	**-0.9**	**14.4**	**44.4**	**-10.6**	**-18.0**
49 Equity and investment fund shares	1.0	0.5	3.1	1.6	1.8	3.1	2.6	4.6	0.9
50 Other accounts payable	0.1	-0.3	1.2	1.1	1.4	-0.7	-0.5	1.5	28.3
Addendum:									
51 Net lending (+) or borrowing (−), financial account (lines 35–46)	1.1	0.5	2.8	1.3	2.4	3.1	2.6	4.6	0.9

(continued)

Table 10B.2 (continued)

	2002	2003	2004	2005	2006	2007	2008	2009	2010
Other changes in volume account									
52 Total other volume changes	**1.9**	**1.7**	**0.1**	**-5.1**	**-3.6**	**-0.3**	**-3.8**	**0.8**	**6.1**
53 Other volume changes	-0.8	-0.7	-1.7	-0.6	-1.2	-0.5	-0.4	-0.4	0.0
54 Less: Statistical discrepancy (line 33–[35–46])^c	-2.6	-2.4	-1.8	4.5	2.4	-0.2	3.4	-1.2	-6.1
Revaluation account									
55 Nonfinancial assets	**0.0**	**0.0**	**1.0**	**1.0**	**1.0**	**0.0**	**1.0**	**0.0**	**0.0**
56 Structures (nonresidential)	0.0	0.0	1.0	1.0	1.0	0.0	0.0	0.0	0.0
57 Equipment and software	0.0	0.0	0.0	0.0	0.0	0.0	0.0	0.0	0.0
58 Changes in net worth due to nominal holding gains/losses	**0.0**	**0.0**	**1.0**	**1.0**	**1.0**	**0.0**	**1.0**	**0.0**	**0.0**
Changes in balance sheet account									
59 Change in net worth (lines 30 + 33 + 52 + 58)	**1.0**	**0.4**	**3.2**	**1.6**	**3.0**	**3.4**	**3.0**	**4.1**	**0.8**
Balance sheet account (end of period)									
60 Total assets	**762.4**	**805.5**	**850.4**	**888.1**	**918.2**	**961.6**	**2,281.3**	**2,277.4**	**2,463.3**
61 Nonfinancial assets^d	**8.7**	**8.6**	**9.1**	**9.4**	**9.9**	**10.3**	**10.6**	**10.2**	**10.1**
62 Structures (nonresidential)	5.2	5.4	5.9	6.6	7.1	7.6	8.1	7.6	7.5
63 Equipment and software	3.5	3.3	3.2	2.9	2.8	2.7	2.6	2.5	2.6
64 Financial assets	**753.6**	**796.8**	**841.3**	**878.7**	**908.2**	**951.3**	**2,270.6**	**2,267.2**	**2,453.2**
65 Monetary gold	**11.0**	**11.0**	**11.0**	**11.0**	**11.0**	**11.0**	**11.0**	**11.0**	**11.0**
66 Currency and deposits	**51.8**	**54.9**	**58.6**	**56.2**	**58.2**	**61.8**	**61.9**	**65.7**	**68.1**
67 Debt securities	**631.6**	**668.9**	**720.0**	**746.4**	**781.1**	**742.8**	**497.8**	**1,850.0**	**2,166.3**
68 SDR certificates	2.2	2.2	2.2	2.2	2.2	2.2	2.2	5.2	5.2
69 Bankers' acceptances	0.0	0.0	0.0	0.0	0.0	0.0	0.0	0.0	0.0
70 Treasury securities	629.4	666.7	717.8	744.2	778.9	740.6	475.9	776.6	1,021.5
71 Agency- and GSE-backed securities^b	0.0	0.0	0.0	0.0	0.0	0.0	19.7	1,068.3	1,139.6

72	Loans (short-term)	39.5	43.8	33.0	46.8	40.8	119.1	1,683.8	249.7	98.4
73	Equity and investment fund shares	0.0	0.0	0.0	0.0	0.0	0.0	0.0	25.1	26.4
74	Other accounts receivable	19.6	18.2	18.6	18.1	17.0	16.5	16.1	65.6	83.0
75	Total liabilities and net worth	762.4	805.5	850.4	888.1	918.2	961.6	2,281.3	2,277.4	2,463.3
76	Liabilities	745.3	788.0	829.6	865.7	892.9	932.8	2,249.6	2,241.6	2,426.7
77	Currency and deposits	716.0	754.0	786.3	819.9	844.8	867.9	2,138.1	2,134.6	2,308.6
78	Loans (short-term)	21.1	25.7	30.8	30.5	29.6	44.0	88.4	77.7	59.7
79	Equity and investment fund shares	8.4	8.8	11.9	13.5	15.3	18.5	21.1	25.6	26.5
80	Other accounts payable	-0.2	-0.6	0.6	1.8	3.2	2.5	2.1	3.6	31.9
81	Net worth	17.1	17.5	20.7	22.3	25.3	28.7	31.7	35.8	36.6

[a]Consists of rental income of tenant-occupied housing and proprietors' income. Quasi-corporations are unincorporated enterprises that function as if they were corporations; they primarily cover their operating costs through sales, and they keep a complete set of financial records.

[b]Government-sponsored enterprises (GSEs) consist of Federal Home Loan Banks, Fannie Mae, Freddie Mac, Federal Agricultural Mortgage Corporation, Farm Credit System, the Financing Corporation, and the Resolution Funding Corporation, and they included the Student Loan Marketing Association until it was fully privatized in the fourth quarter of 2004.

[c]The statistical discrepancy is the difference between net lending or net borrowing derived in the capital account and the same concept derived in the financial account. The discrepancy reflects differences in source data, timing of recorded flows, and other statistical differences between the capital and financial accounts.

[d]Excludes land. Includes corporate and noncorporate financial business.

Table 10B.3   Insurance and pension funds (billions of dollars)

	2002	2003	2004	2005	2006	2007	2008	2009	2010
	Current account								
1 Gross value added	271.5	283.8	310.8	317.3	365.6	369.3	355.1	368.9	455.5
2 Less: Consumption of fixed capital	17.1	17.9	19.2	20.2	20.8	21.8	31.6	32.4	32.9
3 Equals: Net value added	254.3	265.9	291.6	297.0	344.8	347.5	323.5	336.6	422.6
4 Compensation of employees (paid)	146.9	155.5	164.0	172.9	183.5	188.6	193.1	190.9	195.9
5 Wages and salaries	120.9	128.9	136.9	142.5	151.9	158.3	160.4	156.5	161.4
6 Employers' social contributions	26.0	26.6	27.1	30.4	31.6	30.3	32.7	34.4	34.6
7 Taxes on production and imports less subsidies	16.2	17.6	19.4	20.3	21.8	22.2	20.5	22.6	22.8
8 Operating surplus, net	91.2	92.8	108.2	103.8	139.5	136.7	109.9	123.0	203.9
9 Net national income/Balance of primary incomes, net	33.8	32.5	51.1	23.5	45.5	43.5	28.8	59.7	57.4
10 Operating surplus, net	91.2	92.8	108.2	103.8	139.5	136.7	109.9	123.0	203.9
11 Property income (received)	440.3	432.5	459.0	483.3	543.2	603.4	550.4	568.8	483.1
12 Interest	364.1	351.3	364.9	387.4	413.4	457.4	399.0	430.4	346.7
13 Distributed income of corporations (dividends)	69.7	70.1	80.8	95.0	114.9	131.4	137.8	126.5	119.5
14 Reinvested earnings on US direct investment abroad	6.5	11.0	13.2	0.9	15.0	14.7	13.5	11.9	16.9
15 Less: Uses of property income (paid)	497.6	492.7	516.1	563.7	637.2	696.6	631.5	632.1	629.6
16 Interest	398.4	391.8	404.1	433.8	486.3	530.1	467.1	487.4	478.4
17 Distributed income of corporations	99.1	99.2	105.5	125.1	143.1	160.1	160.3	143.2	142.3
18 Dividends	82.0	82.8	88.2	106.2	125.5	141.8	143.2	127.1	127.1
19 Withdrawals from income of quasi-corporations[a]	17.1	16.4	17.3	18.9	17.7	18.4	17.2	16.1	15.3
20 Reinvested earnings on foreign direct investment	0.2	1.8	6.5	4.8	7.7	6.4	4.1	1.5	8.8
21 Rents on land and natural resources	0.0	0.0	0.0	0.0	0.0	0.0	0.0	0.0	0.0
22 Net national income/Balance of primary incomes, net	33.8	32.5	51.1	23.5	45.5	43.5	28.8	59.7	57.4
23 Less: Current taxes on income, wealth, etc. (paid)	15.4	28.8	33.8	35.1	48.6	46.4	22.4	31.4	38.2
24 Less: Other current transfers (paid)	-5.8	-29.1	-25.0	-35.8	-44.2	-13.4	22.5	-4.3	-3.1
25 Equals: Disposable income, net	24.2	32.8	42.3	24.2	41.1	10.5	-16.1	32.6	22.3
26 Equals: Net saving	24.2	32.8	42.3	24.2	41.1	10.5	-16.1	32.6	22.3
	Capital account								
27 Net saving less capital transfers	24.2	32.9	31.7	10.8	41.1	10.5	-10.0	40.2	26.9
28 Net saving	24.2	32.8	42.3	24.2	41.1	10.5	-16.1	32.6	22.3
29 Less: Capital transfers paid (net)	0.0	-0.1	10.6	13.4	0.0	0.0	-6.1	-7.6	-4.6

30 **Capital formation, net**	**0.4**	**2.5**	**2.8**	**-0.1**	**0.3**	**1.6**	**2.7**	**1.9**	**1.8**
31 Gross fixed capital formation (nonresidential)	17.5	20.4	22.0	20.1	21.1	23.4	34.3	34.2	34.7
32 Less: Consumption of fixed capital	17.1	17.9	19.2	20.2	20.8	21.8	31.6	32.4	32.9
33 **Net lending (+) or borrowing (−), capital account (lines 27–30)**	**23.8**	**30.5**	**28.9**	**11.0**	**40.8**	**9.0**	**-12.8**	**38.3**	**25.1**

Financial account

34 **Net lending (+) or borrowing (−) (line 33)**	**23.8**	**30.5**	**28.9**	**11.0**	**40.8**	**9.0**	**-12.8**	**38.3**	**25.1**
35 **Net acquisition of financial assets**	**487.0**	**500.7**	**495.4**	**393.3**	**438.9**	**363.8**	**251.3**	**265.9**	**279.0**
36 **Currency and deposits**	**9.1**	**24.0**	**-4.4**	**-4.3**	**15.3**	**25.0**	**10.2**	**-23.5**	**10.1**
37 **Debt securities**	**248.2**	**365.4**	**305.0**	**281.6**	**302.7**	**217.1**	**149.7**	**372.2**	**290.5**
38 Commercial paper	7.4	−29.4	−17.4	3.6	12.7	0.8	0.1	−10.3	−20.9
39 Treasury securities	57.6	13.3	25.9	27.9	20.5	−20.6	74.0	211.4	127.8
40 Agency- and GSE-backed securities[b]	90.5	103.8	39.9	33.6	79.0	61.1	−0.5	−71.3	−28.9
41 Municipal securities	9.6	50.9	45.0	47.6	27.7	40.0	15.3	13.6	18.3
42 Corporate and foreign bonds	58.5	202.2	170.5	128.8	127.0	102.4	−2.5	167.0	128.5
43 Nonmarketable government securities	24.5	24.7	40.9	40.0	35.8	33.3	63.3	61.9	65.7
44 **Loans**	**8.0**	**6.6**	**8.0**	**18.7**	**31.1**	**35.6**	**52.6**	**-21.6**	**-7.9**
45 Short-term	0.2	−3.6	0.8	5.1	14.2	16.0	35.5	−7.2	−1.0
46 Long-term	7.8	10.2	7.2	13.5	16.8	19.6	17.1	−14.4	−7.0
47 **Equity and investment fund shares**	**213.7**	**97.7**	**196.1**	**83.8**	**42.2**	**37.7**	**-5.4**	**-55.5**	**17.9**
48 Corporate equities	83.0	92.5	83.2	19.1	−76.6	−107.5	−75.1	−153.1	−46.4
49 Mutual fund shares	99.5	3.0	99.0	54.9	98.8	113.6	23.3	87.3	78.1
50 Money market mutual fund shares	16.9	−2.9	2.4	−2.4	16.0	7.5	33.9	−8.1	−17.1
51 Equity in government-sponsored enterprises[b]	0.2	0.7	0.6	−0.1	0.0	0.6	1.0	−0.3	0.0
52 US direct investment abroad	14.1	4.4	10.9	12.2	3.9	23.4	11.5	18.8	3.4
53 **Insurance, pension, and standardized guarantee schemes**	**14.6**	**-17.3**	**-36.8**	**-2.3**	**-3.0**	**31.7**	**42.0**	**7.7**	**-3.0**
54 **Other accounts receivable**	**-6.5**	**24.3**	**27.5**	**15.9**	**50.6**	**16.7**	**2.2**	**-13.5**	**-28.5**
55 **Net incurrence of liabilities**	**435.0**	**442.8**	**424.0**	**353.9**	**395.0**	**290.5**	**241.4**	**141.3**	**275.1**
56 **Loans (short-term)**	**13.9**	**4.9**	**0.9**	**8.0**	**2.9**	**12.8**	**20.8**	**-8.8**	**-4.6**
57 **Equity and investment fund shares**	**15.1**	**1.8**	**-2.8**	**-0.9**	**11.7**	**-32.5**	**4.6**	**17.7**	**13.8**
58 Corporate equity issues	−0.3	0.2	−21.3	−10.8	−28.5	−43.9	−10.3	−6.2	−17.5
59 Foreign direct investment in the United States	11.4	−2.2	16.0	0.2	37.5	6.1	27.4	14.6	9.1
60 Investment by parent	4.0	3.8	2.5	9.7	2.7	5.3	−12.5	9.3	22.2
61 **Insurance, pension, and standardized guarantee schemes**	**399.8**	**405.5**	**414.0**	**351.0**	**345.0**	**294.6**	**272.8**	**174.3**	**242.0**
62 **Other accounts payable**	**6.2**	**30.6**	**12.0**	**-4.3**	**35.5**	**15.6**	**-56.8**	**-41.8**	**23.9**

Addendum:

63 Net lending (+) or borrowing (−), financial account (lines 35–55)	52.0	57.9	71.4	39.4	43.9	73.2	9.9	124.5	3.8

(continued)

Table 10B.3 (continued)

	2002	2003	2004	2005	2006	2007	2008	2009	2010
Other changes in volume account									
64 **Total other volume changes**	**57.8**	**7.9**	**36.8**	**5.8**	**-54.4**	**63.0**	**97.0**	**50.7**	**-30.3**
65 Disaster losses	0.0	0.0	0.2	0.4	0.0	0.0	0.1	0.0	0.0
66 Other volume changes	29.6	-19.6	-5.9	-23.0	-57.5	-1.3	74.2	-35.5	-9.0
67 Less: Statistical discrepancy (line 33-[35-55])^c	-28.2	-27.4	-42.5	-28.4	-3.1	-64.2	-22.7	-86.2	21.3
Revaluation account									
68 **Nonfinancial assets**	**0.8**	**1.5**	**67.7**	**-55.1**	**13.8**	**8.3**	**13.4**	**-9.5**	**-1.7**
69 Structures (nonresidential)	1.8	2.2	67.5	-55.2	12.5	8.9	12.3	-8.1	-0.3
70 Equipment and software	-0.9	-0.7	0.2	0.1	1.3	-0.6	1.1	-1.4	-1.4
71 **Financial assets**	**-873.7**	**1,305.4**	**611.4**	**586.7**	**1,101.4**	**426.4**	**-3,327.3**	**1,408.1**	**1,033.2**
72 Corporate equities	-733.8	1,053.1	510.8	323.3	825.9	263.6	-2,343.7	968.1	742.2
73 Mutual fund shares	-159.1	249.0	104.0	259.8	276.2	165.0	-953.1	430.2	275.2
74 US direct investment abroad	19.3	3.4	-3.4	3.6	-0.8	-2.2	-30.6	9.7	15.8
75 **Liabilities**	**-916.8**	**1,394.0**	**617.4**	**576.1**	**1,187.2**	**214.3**	**-3,555.6**	**1,440.8**	**1,024.1**
76 Corporate equity issues	-63.7	157.8	61.5	29.6	139.8	-192.8	-386.4	49.4	42.5
77 Foreign direct investment in the United States	-3.6	4.1	-2.8	-2.3	7.8	-32.0	-61.3	20.6	14.4
78 Pension fund reserves	-849.5	1,232.0	558.7	548.9	1,039.6	439.1	-3,107.9	1,370.7	967.2
79 Investment by parent	0.0	0.0	0.0	0.0	0.0	0.0	0.0	0.0	0.0
80 **Changes in net worth due to nominal holding gains/losses**	**44.0**	**-87.0**	**61.7**	**-44.5**	**-72.1**	**220.3**	**241.7**	**-42.2**	**7.4**
81 **Change in net worth (lines 30 + 33 + 64 + 80)**	**126.0**	**-46.2**	**130.2**	**-27.9**	**-85.4**	**293.8**	**328.7**	**48.7**	**4.0**
Balance sheet account (end of period)									
82 **Total assets**	**10,967.8**	**12,867.0**	**14,100.3**	**15,013.0**	**16,585.2**	**17,406.2**	**14,200.6**	**15,951.2**	**17,311.5**
83 **Nonfinancial assets**^d	**198.5**	**207.5**	**287.6**	**234.5**	**250.5**	**264.1**	**281.1**	**273.8**	**273.9**
84 Structures (nonresidential)	124.7	127.3	201.2	146.5	159.8	171.0	183.5	175.9	174.4
85 Equipment and software	73.8	80.2	86.4	88.0	90.6	93.0	97.7	97.8	99.4
86 **Financial assets**	**10,769.3**	**12,659.5**	**13,812.6**	**14,778.5**	**16,334.7**	**17,142.1**	**13,919.4**	**15,677.4**	**17,037.6**
87 **Currency and deposits**	**143.5**	**167.5**	**163.2**	**158.9**	**174.1**	**199.1**	**209.4**	**185.9**	**196.0**
88 **Debt securities**	**4,555.4**	**4,920.9**	**5,225.8**	**5,488.2**	**5,756.0**	**5,973.1**	**6,122.8**	**6,507.6**	**6,798.0**
89 Commercial paper	150.2	120.7	103.4	107.0	119.6	120.4	120.5	110.3	89.4
90 Treasury securities	474.0	487.2	513.1	541.1	561.6	541.1	615.0	826.4	954.2

91	Agency- and GSE-backed securities[b]	824.2	928.0	967.9	1,001.5	1,080.5	1,141.6	1,141.1	1,069.8	1,040.8
92	Municipal securities	203.7	254.7	299.7	347.3	375.1	415.1	430.4	444.0	462.3
93	Corporate and foreign bonds	2,113.1	2,315.3	2,485.8	2,608.4	2,700.5	2,802.9	2,800.5	2,980.0	3,108.5
94	Nonmarketable government securities	790.3	815.0	855.9	882.9	918.7	952.0	1,015.3	1,077.2	1,142.9
95	**Loans**	**450.5**	**457.1**	**465.1**	**483.8**	**514.8**	**550.4**	**603.0**	**568.8**	**560.9**
96	Short-term	167.0	163.4	164.3	169.4	183.6	199.6	235.1	215.3	214.3
97	Long-term	283.4	293.7	300.9	314.4	331.2	350.8	367.9	353.5	346.5
98	**Equity and investment fund shares**	**4,947.6**	**6,350.7**	**7,158.1**	**7,828.6**	**8,972.2**	**9,436.2**	**6,103.5**	**7,456.1**	**8,507.2**
99	Corporate equities	3,549.5	4,695.1	5,289.0	5,631.5	6,380.8	6,536.9	4,118.2	4,933.2	5,629.1
100	Mutual fund shares	1,178.8	1,430.8	1,633.8	1,948.5	2,323.6	2,602.2	1,672.5	2,190.0	2,543.3
101	Money market fund shares	127.6	124.7	127.1	124.7	140.7	148.1	182.0	173.9	156.8
102	Equity in government-sponsored enterprises[b]	0.5	1.1	1.7	1.6	1.6	2.2	3.2	2.9	2.9
103	US direct investment abroad	91.2	99.0	106.5	122.3	125.4	146.7	127.6	156.0	175.2
104	Insurance, pension, and standardized guarantee schemes	319.5	387.7	397.6	405.5	453.6	502.4	392.5	485.4	531.4
105	Other accounts receivable	352.7	375.7	402.8	413.5	464.0	480.9	488.3	473.7	444.2
106	**Total liabilities and net worth**	**10,967.8**	**12,867.0**	**14,100.3**	**15,013.0**	**16,585.2**	**17,406.2**	**14,200.6**	**15,951.2**	**17,311.5**
107	Liabilities	10,995.9	12,941.4	14,044.4	14,985.0	16,642.6	17,169.7	13,635.4	15,337.4	16,693.7
108	Loans (short-term)	20.0	24.8	25.7	33.7	36.6	49.4	70.2	61.4	56.8
109	**Equity and investment fund shares**	**790.3**	**954.1**	**1,010.0**	**1,036.4**	**1,195.7**	**938.4**	**495.4**	**583.1**	**653.9**
110	Corporate equity issues	657.8	815.8	856.1	874.8	986.1	749.4	352.7	396.0	420.9
111	Foreign direct investment in the United States	112.9	114.8	128.0	125.9	171.2	145.3	111.4	146.7	170.2
112	Investment by parent	19.6	23.4	25.9	35.6	38.3	43.7	31.2	40.5	62.7
113	**Insurance, pension, and standardized guarantee schemes**	**10,058.7**	**11,807.1**	**12,840.5**	**13,754.8**	**15,205.9**	**15,960.3**	**12,884.5**	**14,550.4**	**15,827.6**
114	Other accounts payable	126.8	155.3	168.1	160.0	204.4	221.6	185.4	142.6	155.4
115	**Net worth**	**-28.1**	**-74.3**	**55.9**	**28.0**	**-57.4**	**236.4**	**565.1**	**613.8**	**617.8**

[a] Consists of rental income of tenant-occupied housing and proprietors' income. Quasi-corporations are unincorporated enterprises that function as if they were corporations; they primarily cover their operating costs through sales, and they keep a complete set of financial records.

[b] Government-sponsored enterprises (GSEs) consist of Federal Home Loan Banks, Fannie Mae, Freddie Mac, Federal Agricultural Mortgage Corporation, Farm Credit System, the Financing Corporation, and the Resolution Funding Corporation, and they included the Student Loan Marketing Association until it was fully privatized in the fourth quarter of 2004.

[c] The statistical discrepancy is the difference between net lending or net borrowing derived in the capital account and the same concept derived in the financial account. The discrepancy reflects differences in source data, timing of recorded flows, and other statistical differences between the capital and financial accounts.

[d] Excludes land.   Includes corporate and noncorporate financial business.

Table 10B.4   Other financial business (billions of dollars)

	2002	2003	2004	2005	2006	2007	2008	2009	2010
	Current account								
1 Gross value added	**610.0**	**636.9**	**652.0**	**766.8**	**822.0**	**747.3**	**673.5**	**747.7**	**914.7**
2 Less: Consumption of fixed capital	**88.6**	**93.3**	**99.3**	**105.1**	**110.0**	**116.7**	**140.3**	**143.8**	**145.4**
3 Equals: Net value added	**521.4**	**543.6**	**552.7**	**661.7**	**712.0**	**630.6**	**533.2**	**604.0**	**769.3**
4 Compensation of employees (paid)	298.9	310.4	331.9	367.3	399.3	419.9	415.3	375.0	386.7
5 Wages and salaries	248.9	263.4	281.8	310.6	339.0	361.2	351.1	312.8	323.9
6 Employers' social contributions	50.1	46.9	50.1	56.7	60.2	58.7	64.2	62.1	62.8
7 Taxes on production and imports less subsidies	21.3	22.3	24.0	25.8	28.6	31.2	30.7	32.1	32.3
8 Operating surplus, net	201.2	210.9	196.9	268.6	284.2	179.6	87.1	197.0	350.3
9 Net national income/Balance of primary incomes, net	**155.2**	**178.6**	**180.7**	**221.1**	**194.4**	**118.8**	**-24.0**	**149.5**	**182.5**
10 Operating surplus, net	201.2	210.9	196.9	268.6	284.2	179.6	87.1	197.0	350.3
11 Property income (received)	865.2	772.1	983.0	1,329.6	1,811.4	2,229.7	1,895.4	1,163.0	1,228.0
12 Interest	838.1	738.4	928.4	1,263.4	1,715.4	2,096.6	1,761.4	1,060.5	1,108.2
13 Distributed income of corporations (dividends)	19.5	23.8	37.7	64.2	69.4	100.1	98.2	62.6	70.8
14 Reinvested earnings on US direct investment abroad	7.6	9.9	16.9	2.1	26.6	32.9	35.8	39.8	49.1
15 Less: Uses of property income (paid)	1,132.3	1,034.9	1,288.2	1,707.1	2,295.9	2,725.9	2,390.0	1,601.1	1,592.2
16 Interest	991.3	889.4	1,095.3	1,486.9	2,024.8	2,427.7	2,145.1	1,332.3	1,264.9
17 Distributed income of corporations	140.9	144.8	190.1	217.0	266.0	294.6	241.9	267.9	319.9
18 Dividends	103.0	110.1	153.3	177.9	213.7	254.0	223.9	228.1	278.1
19 Withdrawals from income of quasi-corporations[a]	37.8	34.8	36.8	39.1	52.2	40.6	17.9	39.8	41.7
20 Reinvested earnings on foreign direct investment	0.1	0.7	2.8	3.2	5.2	3.7	3.0	0.9	7.4
21 Rents on land and natural resources	0.0	0.0	0.0	0.0	0.0	0.0	0.0	0.0	0.0
22 Net national income/Balance of primary incomes, net	**155.2**	**178.6**	**180.7**	**221.1**	**194.4**	**118.8**	**-24.0**	**149.5**	**182.5**
23 Less: Current taxes on income, wealth, etc. (paid)	55.3	60.1	67.2	84.0	87.9	70.7	27.5	18.6	64.3
24 Less: Other current transfers (paid)	13.9	15.9	15.5	19.2	18.2	18.0	23.1	23.0	18.1
25 Equals: Disposable income, net	**86.1**	**102.6**	**98.0**	**117.9**	**88.2**	**30.0**	**-74.6**	**108.0**	**100.0**
26 Equals: Net saving	**86.1**	**102.6**	**98.0**	**117.9**	**88.2**	**30.0**	**-74.6**	**108.0**	**100.0**

				Capital account					
27	Net saving less capital transfers	**86.1**	**102.5**	**92.4**	**103.6**	**88.2**	**30.0**	**−20.2**	**222.3**	**137.9**
28	Net saving	86.1	102.6	98.0	117.9	88.2	30.0	−74.6	108.0	100.0
29	Less: Capital transfers paid (net)	0.0	0.1	5.6	14.3	0.0	0.0	−54.4	−114.3	−37.9
30	**Capital formation, net**	**27.9**	**19.3**	**30.7**	**28.2**	**28.9**	**44.5**	**19.8**	**−10.6**	**0.9**
31	Gross fixed capital formation (nonresidential)	116.6	112.6	130.0	133.3	138.9	161.3	160.1	133.2	146.3
32	Less: Consumption of fixed capital	88.6	93.3	99.3	105.1	110.0	116.7	140.3	143.8	145.4
33	**Net lending (+) or borrowing (−), capital account (lines 27–30)**	**58.1**	**83.2**	**61.7**	**75.3**	**59.4**	**−14.5**	**−39.9**	**232.9**	**137.0**
					Financial account					
34	**Net lending (+) or borrowing (−) (line 33)**	**58.1**	**83.2**	**61.7**	**75.3**	**59.4**	**−14.5**	**−39.9**	**232.9**	**137.0**
35	**Net acquisition of financial assets**	**1,743.2**	**2,236.4**	**2,426.2**	**2,880.6**	**3,659.7**	**4,398.0**	**3,035.9**	**−1,854.8**	**−1,143.9**
36	**Currency and deposits**	**−22.8**	**−66.7**	**35.8**	**−1.1**	**44.5**	**143.1**	**1,008.1**	**255.9**	**−153.1**
37	**Debt securities**	**560.7**	**634.4**	**107.1**	**307.3**	**781.9**	**933.7**	**1,546.5**	**−782.4**	**127.0**
38	Commercial paper	−137.6	−135.1	50.8	192.7	219.7	−95.6	34.1	−383.1	−106.1
39	Treasury securities	61.1	37.6	−129.7	−5.9	36.9	166.9	626.7	−71.5	88.7
40	Agency- and GSE-backed securities[b]	448.8	315.9	−208.7	−222.7	56.9	240.5	839.7	−373.5	40.6
41	Municipal securities	45.9	50.4	42.0	65.0	95.7	140.1	36.4	2.0	11.1
42	Corporate and foreign bonds	142.7	365.5	352.9	278.4	372.8	481.9	9.6	43.5	92.7
43	**Loans**	**933.7**	**1,099.7**	**1,573.4**	**1,922.1**	**2,000.4**	**2,218.9**	**28.1**	**−1,339.5**	**−814.8**
44	Short-term	46.0	120.6	372.0	528.7	625.3	1,170.1	−43.5	−1,067.0	−319.3
45	Long-term	887.7	979.1	1,201.3	1,393.5	1,375.2	1,048.8	71.6	−272.4	−495.5
46	**Equity and investment fund shares**	**171.7**	**244.0**	**467.1**	**428.5**	**476.0**	**961.0**	**613.9**	**−23.3**	**−60.0**
47	Corporate equities	86.9	165.5	246.3	217.3	200.9	273.8	66.2	179.6	107.2
48	Mutual fund shares	1.5	−5.6	−1.9	−2.7	3.8	3.6	1.4	14.1	−5.7
49	Money market mutual fund shares	−30.9	−64.5	−107.0	37.8	44.9	326.3	270.0	−162.8	−141.0
50	Equity in government-sponsored enterprises[b]	1.7	1.8	1.8	2.1	0.0	7.7	−6.3	0.3	−3.2
51	US direct investment abroad	9.3	19.9	32.9	−0.7	21.9	83.6	54.9	5.0	25.9
52	Stock in Federal Reserve Banks	1.0	0.5	3.1	1.6	1.8	3.1	2.6	4.6	0.9
53	Investment in subsidiaries	102.2	126.4	291.9	173.2	202.8	263.1	225.0	−64.1	−44.2
54	**Insurance, pension, and standardized guarantee schemes**	**0.0**	**0.0**	**0.0**	**0.0**	**0.0**	**16.2**	**5.3**	**2.9**	**8.2**
55	Other accounts receivable	99.6	325.0	242.9	223.6	349.0	125.0	−166.0	31.8	−251.3

(continued)

Table 10B.4 (continued)

	2002	2003	2004	2005	2006	2007	2008	2009	2010
56 **Net incurrence of liabilities**	**1,767.6**	**2,076.5**	**2,484.8**	**2,614.7**	**3,443.1**	**4,366.3**	**3,315.2**	**−1,771.2**	**−930.0**
57 **Currency and deposits**	**335.8**	**427.7**	**580.2**	**584.1**	**591.4**	**513.4**	**938.9**	**243.5**	**129.1**
58 **Debt securities**	**845.5**	**1,010.0**	**805.9**	**1,039.2**	**1,323.3**	**1,504.8**	**362.8**	**−1,095.8**	**−731.1**
59 Agency- and GSE-backed securities[b]	546.7	586.2	115.8	80.4	328.2	905.7	768.7	−60.1	−46.9
60 Corporate bonds	398.8	487.3	668.5	744.6	798.8	710.6	−280.3	−587.6	−582.5
61 Commercial paper	−99.9	−63.5	21.7	214.2	196.3	−111.4	−125.6	−448.2	−101.7
62 **Loans**	**70.7**	**361.1**	**305.1**	**417.2**	**562.7**	**555.7**	**−135.3**	**−1,044.5**	**−425.4**
63 Short-term	59.5	352.2	279.6	403.1	556.1	551.0	−142.0	−1,047.8	−425.6
64 Long-term	11.2	8.9	25.5	14.1	6.6	4.7	6.8	3.4	0.2
65 **Equity and investment fund shares**	**342.8**	**253.9**	**651.4**	**699.2**	**919.7**	**1,483.6**	**1,749.2**	**236.1**	**84.5**
66 Money market mutual fund shares	−16.7	−207.5	−136.5	127.0	305.3	720.9	724.2	−499.0	−502.9
67 Corporate equity issues	71.8	65.9	139.6	89.3	88.0	222.5	647.9	320.5	208.3
68 Mutual fund shares	181.1	288.6	298.2	260.2	336.8	364.7	31.0	490.5	389.3
69 Equity in government-sponsored enterprises[b]	2.0	3.2	2.5	1.9	0.2	9.1	−4.2	0.0	−2.7
70 Foreign direct investment in the United States	−1.8	26.1	34.2	13.7	14.5	3.2	93.3	31.5	41.0
71 Equity in noncorporate business	0.6	−3.4	−4.2	−1.2	−6.8	2.4	11.5	−3.6	0.4
72 Investment by parent	105.7	81.1	317.6	208.4	181.7	160.8	245.5	−103.8	−48.8
73 **Other accounts payable**	**172.7**	**23.8**	**142.1**	**−124.8**	**46.0**	**308.7**	**399.5**	**−110.6**	**12.8**
Addendum:									
74 Net lending (+) or borrowing (−), financial account (lines 35–56)	−24.4	159.9	−58.6	265.9	216.7	31.9	−279.3	−83.5	−213.8
Other changes in volume account									
75 **Total other volume changes**	**16.8**	**2.7**	**−97.8**	**153.7**	**90.5**	**−157.1**	**−439.5**	**412.2**	**−329.1**
76 Disaster losses	0.0	0.0	1.5	1.3	0.0	0.0	0.5	0.0	0.0
77 Other volume changes	99.3	−74.0	21.1	−38.3	−67.0	−203.5	−200.7	728.6	21.7
78 Less: Statistical discrepancy (line 33–[35–56])[c]	82.5	−76.7	120.3	−190.6	−157.3	−46.4	239.4	316.4	350.8
Revaluation account									
79 **Nonfinancial assets**	**32.0**	**38.5**	**19.7**	**156.0**	**84.1**	**49.0**	**50.4**	**−44.3**	**−2.5**
80 Structures (nonresidential)	21.6	18.9	0.9	137.3	61.2	36.9	47.0	−42.2	1.7
81 Equipment and software	10.3	19.6	18.7	18.7	23.0	12.1	4.5	−2.0	−4.1
82 **Financial assets**	**−729.9**	**840.1**	**590.7**	**417.5**	**830.4**	**505.2**	**−2,842.7**	**1,237.4**	**747.1**
83 Corporate equities	−735.6	809.8	534.7	389.5	790.7	455.9	−2,872.7	1,223.1	716.7
84 Mutual fund shares	−3.5	3.6	2.0	1.0	3.3	1.3	−11.3	11.7	4.7
85 US direct investment abroad	9.1	26.6	54.0	27.1	36.5	48.0	41.4	2.6	25.7

86	**Liabilities**	**−994.6**	**1,380.7**	**890.3**	**627.8**	**1,312.3**	**−424.6**	**−4,512.6**	**2,113.3**	**1,060.6**
87	Corporate equity issues	−303.2	638.1	397.3	232.7	576.8	−791.6	−1,978.0	394.0	474.7
88	Mutual fund shares	−678.1	727.2	483.8	352.4	682.6	396.0	−2,424.7	1,035.8	583.7
89	Foreign direct investment in the United States	−11.5	4.3	6.8	11.7	14.7	−24.7	−96.3	1.8	3.0
90	Equity in noncorporate business	−1.9	11.4	2.4	1.7	4.9	−0.6	−13.6	6.3	1.3
91	Investment by parent	0.0	−0.1	0.0	29.0	33.2	−3.7	0.0	675.6	−2.0
92	**Changes in net worth due to nominal holding gains/losses**	296.6	−502.2	−280.0	−54.3	−397.6	978.9	1,720.3	−920.2	−316.0
	Changes in balance sheet account									
93	**Change in net worth (lines 30 + 33 + 75 + 92)**	399.4	−397.0	−285.3	203.0	−219.0	851.9	1,260.5	−285.7	−507.2
	Balance sheet account (end of period)									
94	**Total assets**	**28,332.4**	**31,213.0**	**34,160.5**	**37,473.1**	**41,997.1**	**46,955.2**	**47,526.7**	**47,429.6**	**46,498.3**
95	**Nonfinancial assets**[d]	**940.7**	**978.0**	**1,000.2**	**1,160.5**	**1,250.6**	**1,317.3**	**1,386.5**	**1,331.7**	**1,330.1**
96	Structures (nonresidential)	537.3	552.9	548.6	685.8	747.1	788.6	842.7	801.5	796.6
97	Equipment and software	403.4	425.1	451.6	474.5	503.6	528.8	543.6	530.4	533.6
98	**Financial assets**	**27,391.8**	**30,235.1**	**33,160.4**	**36,312.7**	**40,746.6**	**45,637.9**	**46,140.4**	**46,097.9**	**45,168.2**
99	**Currency and deposits**	**588.2**	**521.5**	**557.2**	**556.2**	**600.9**	**744.1**	**1,787.0**	**2,057.4**	**1,904.3**
100	**Debt securities**	**7,468.0**	**7,939.7**	**8,067.0**	**8,374.3**	**9,145.7**	**10,079.4**	**11,625.6**	**10,853.1**	**10,496.0**
101	Commercial market paper	799.8	664.9	715.5	908.2	1,124.7	1,029.1	1,062.9	679.7	573.6
102	Treasury securities	528.3	490.0	360.3	354.3	386.9	553.7	1,180.4	1,109.0	1,197.7
103	Agency- and GSE-backed securities[b]	3,488.2	3,639.6	3,450.9	3,228.2	3,283.2	3,523.7	4,363.4	4,044.3	3,622.3
104	Municipal securities	829.7	880.0	922.1	987.1	1,082.4	1,222.5	1,258.8	1,260.8	1,271.9
105	Corporate and foreign bonds	1,821.8	2,265.3	2,618.2	2,896.5	3,268.6	3,750.5	3,760.1	3,759.2	3,830.4
106	**Loans**	**12,838.0**	**13,981.9**	**15,570.1**	**17,492.2**	**19,473.6**	**21,682.1**	**21,709.8**	**20,410.4**	**19,630.7**
107	Short-term	5,136.3	5,289.3	5,661.3	6,190.0	6,795.0	7,954.7	7,910.9	6,883.9	6,599.7
108	Long-term	7,701.8	8,692.5	9,908.7	11,302.2	12,678.6	13,727.4	13,799.0	13,526.6	13,031.1
109	**Equity and investment fund shares**	**4,576.4**	**5,660.5**	**6,718.4**	**7,564.5**	**8,904.0**	**10,370.3**	**8,141.5**	**10,031.8**	**10,718.8**
110	Corporate equities	2,424.7	3,399.9	4,181.1	4,787.7	5,779.3	6,509.0	3,702.3	5,105.1	5,928.9
111	Mutual fund shares	23.1	21.2	21.3	19.6	26.6	31.6	21.6	47.4	46.5
112	Money market fund shares	552.6	488.1	381.1	418.9	463.9	790.2	1,060.3	897.5	−756.5
113	Equity in government-sponsored enterprises[b]	34.7	36.6	38.4	40.4	40.4	48.1	41.8	42.1	38.8
114	US direct investment abroad	163.9	210.4	297.3	323.7	382.0	513.5	609.8	617.5	669.1
115	Stock in Federal Reserve Banks	8.4	8.8	11.9	13.5	15.3	18.5	21.1	25.6	26.5
116	Investment in subsidiaries	1,369.0	1,495.4	1,787.3	1,960.6	2,196.5	2,459.6	2,684.6	3,296.6	3,252.4
117	**Insurance, pension, and standardized guarantee schemes**	**0.0**	**0.0**	**0.0**	**0.0**	**108.5**	**124.7**	**130.0**	**132.8**	**141.1**
118	**Other accounts receivable**	**1,921.2**	**2,131.4**	**2,247.8**	**2,325.7**	**2,513.9**	**2,637.3**	**2,746.3**	**2,612.4**	**2,277.2**

(continued)

Table 10B.4   (continued)

	2002	2003	2004	2005	2006	2007	2008	2009	2010
119 Total liabilities and net worth	28,332.4	31,213.0	34,160.5	37,473.1	41,997.1	46,955.2	47,526.7	47,429.6	46,498.3
120 Liabilities	28,684.1	31,961.7	35,194.6	38,304.3	43,047.1	47,153.6	46,464.4	46,652.9	46,228.8
121 Currency and deposits	5,657.9	6,085.1	6,690.8	7,275.5	7,867.5	8,380.3	9,282.8	9,519.9	9,645.5
122 Debt securities	9,312.8	10,158.1	10,978.9	11,963.6	13,272.1	14,906.8	15,269.3	14,498.9	13,259.8
123 Agency- and GSE-backed securities[b]	5,509.0	5,944.5	6,060.3	6,140.7	6,468.9	7,374.6	8,143.4	8,083.3	7,574.0
124 Corporate bonds	2,805.9	3,279.2	3,962.6	4,652.7	5,440.1	6,280.4	6,000.1	5,737.9	5,109.9
125 Commercial paper	997.9	934.4	956.0	1,170.2	1,363.2	1,251.8	1,125.8	677.6	575.9
126 Loans	2,392.9	2,754.1	3,059.2	3,476.4	4,035.9	4,591.6	4,456.3	3,543.6	3,094.6
127 Short-term	2,296.0	2,648.2	2,927.9	3,330.9	3,883.8	4,434.9	4,292.8	3,376.7	2,927.5
128 Long-term	97.0	105.9	131.4	145.5	152.1	156.7	163.5	166.9	167.1
129 Equity and investment fund shares	9,610.0	11,244.7	12,786.5	14,113.3	16,345.3	17,404.2	14,640.7	16,990.4	18,135.4
130 Money market fund shares	2,223.9	2,016.4	1,879.8	2,006.9	2,312.1	3,033.1	3,757.3	3,258.3	2,755.3
131 Corporate equity issues	2,194.2	2,898.1	3,435.0	3,757.1	4,421.9	3,852.8	2,522.7	3,237.2	3,920.2
132 Mutual fund shares	3,638.4	4,654.2	5,436.3	6,048.9	7,068.3	7,829.0	5,435.3	6,961.6	7,934.5
133 Equity in government-sponsored enterprises[b]	39.1	42.3	44.8	46.7	46.9	56.0	51.8	51.8	49.0
134 Foreign direct investment in the United States	130.6	160.9	201.9	227.3	256.6	235.1	232.1	265.2	309.3
135 Equity in noncorporate business	5.0	13.0	11.2	11.7	9.8	11.6	9.5	12.1	13.8
136 Investment by parent	1,379.0	1,460.0	1,777.5	2,014.8	2,229.8	2,386.8	2,632.3	3,204.0	3,153.2
137 Other accounts payable	1,710.6	1,719.9	1,679.3	1,475.6	1,526.3	1,870.6	2,815.0	2,100.2	2,093.6
138 Net worth	−351.7	−748.1	−1,034.0	−831.0	−1,050.0	−198.2	1,062.4	776.7	269.5

[a]Consists of rental income of tenant-occupied housing and proprietors' income. Quasi-corporations are unincorporated enterprises that function as if they were corporations; they primarily cover their operating costs through sales, and they keep a complete set of financial records.

[b]Government-sponsored enterprises (GSEs) consist of Federal Home Loan Banks, Fannie Mae, Freddie Mac, Federal Agricultural Mortgage Corporation, Farm Credit System, the Financing Corporation, and the Resolution Funding Corporation, and they included the Student Loan Marketing Association until it was fully privatized in the fourth quarter of 2004.

[c]The statistical discrepancy is the difference between net lending or net borrowing derived in the capital account and the same concept derived in the financial account. The discrepancy reflects differences in source data, timing of recorded flows, and other statistical differences between the capital and financial accounts.

[d]Excludes land.   Includes corporate and noncorporate financial business.

References

Bond, Charlotte Anne, Teran Martin, Susan Hume McIntosh, and Charles Ian Mead. 2007. "Integrated Macroeconomic Accounts for the United States." Bureau of Economic Analysis, Department of Commerce. *Survey of Current Business*, February:14–31.

Eichner, Matthew J., Donald L. Kohn, and Michael G. Palumbo. 2010. "Financial Statistics for the United States and the Crisis: What Did They Get Right, What Did They Miss, and How Should They Change?" Finance and Economics Discussion Series Paper no. 2010-20. Washington, DC: Federal Reserve Board.

European Commission, International Monetary Fund, Organisation for Economic Co-operation and Development, United Nations, and World Bank. 2009. System of National Accounts 2008. New York.

Palumbo, Michael G., and Jonathan A. Parker. 2009. "The Integrated Financial and Real System of National Accounts for the United States: Does It Presage the Financial Crisis?" *American Economic Review* 99 (2): 80–6.

Teplin, Albert M., Rochelle Antoniewicz, Susan Hume McIntosh, Michael G. Palumbo, Genevieve Solomon, Charles Ian Meade, Karin Moses, and Brent Moulton. 2006. "Integrated Macroeconomic Accounts for the United States: Draft SNA-USA." In *A New Architecture for the US National Accounts*, edited by Dale W. Jorgenson, J. Steven Landefeld, and William D. Nordhaus, 471–540. Chicago: University of Chicago Press.

11

A Prototype BEA/BLS Industry-Level Production Account for the United States

Susan Fleck, Steven Rosenthal, Matthew Russell, Erich H. Strassner, and Lisa Usher

In recent years, structural changes at the industry level in the United States and their implications for competitiveness have emerged as important economic issues. The most recent business cycle and subsequent recovery, in particular, led to heightened interest in understanding the sources of economic growth, including output, input, and multifactor productivity (MFP) growth across all industries in the US economy.

Gross domestic product (GDP) by industry statistics provide detailed

Susan Fleck was chief of the Division of Major Sector Productivity, Office of Productivity and Technology, Bureau of Labor Statistics, US Department of Labor at the time this project was carried out. She is now with the Citizenship and Immigration Service, US Department of Homeland Security. Steven Rosenthal is an economist at the Bureau of Labor Statistics, US Department of Labor. Matthew Russell is an economist in the Industry Economic Accounts Directorate at the Bureau of Economic Analysis, US Department of Commerce. Erich H. Strassner is chief of the Industry Applications Division in the Industry Economic Accounts Directorate at the Bureau of Economic Analysis, US Department of Commerce. Lisa Usher is chief of the Division of Industry Productivity Studies at the Bureau of Labor Statistics, US Department of Labor.

We thank William Jolliff, Sarah Osborne, and Peter Kuhbach of the Bureau of Economic Analysis and Kevin Delaney, Mark Dumas, Bhavani Khandrika, and Randall Kinoshita of the Bureau of Labor Statistics for substantial contributions to the development of this prototype account. Carol E. Moylan of the BEA and John Ruser of the BLS provided valuable guidance to this project. We are also grateful to Dale Jorgenson of Harvard University and the BEA's Advisory Committee, Mun Ho of the Institute of Quantitative Social Science at Harvard University, and Jon Samuels of the BEA for their advice and consultation throughout this project, and also for sharing underlying data sets from their work, which proved to be of great benefit in developing this account. We also appreciate the helpful comments we received at the Second World KLEMS conference held at Harvard University on August 9–10, 2012. The views expressed in this chapter are solely those of the authors and are not necessarily those of the Bureau of Economic Analysis, US Department of Commerce, and the Bureau of Labor Statistics, US Department of Labor. For acknowledgments, sources of research support, and disclosure of the authors' material financial relationships, if any, please see http://www.nber.org/chapters/c13005.ack.

information on the industry sources of aggregate value-added growth, but do not include estimates of the contributions of capital and labor inputs and MFP to economic growth. MFP measures the output per unit of capital, labor, and intermediate inputs, and is an important component of growth in GDP. MFP growth is calculated as the growth that cannot be explained by changes in the combined contribution of these factor inputs. The official MFP measures provide information on components of economic growth in the market economy; but, they do not report detailed information on the nonmarket economy. While these two sets of statistics share a common economic accounting framework, in the United States they are prepared by two separate agencies. The GDP statistics are published by the Bureau of Economic Analysis (BEA), US Department of Commerce and MFP and labor productivity statistics are published by the Bureau of Labor Statistics (BLS), US Department of Labor. Differences in concepts and methods used by each agency persist due to the different nature of each program, but each statistical program depends on the other to prepare its measures.

This chapter builds on the GDP by industry statistics produced by the BEA and the capital and labor statistics produced by the BLS to assemble an industry-level production account for the United States that is consistent with GDP.[1] The key feature of this internally consistent prototype account is to provide values, prices, and quantities of outputs and inputs used in the industry-production process. This set of accounts allows one to decompose the industry contributions of inputs and MFP to the sources of GDP growth at the aggregate level.

Productivity statistics integrated with national economic accounts' GDP statistics have long been sought to provide a rich source of information for policymakers, business analysts, and economists. The usefulness of such integrated analysis on the sources of growth within the framework of the US National Income and Product Accounts (NIPAs) was first presented by Jorgenson and Landefeld (2006) in *A New Architecture for the US National Accounts*. In 2008, the Advisory Committee on Measuring Innovation in the 21st Century Economy to the US Secretary of Commerce endorsed the development of official industry-level production account statistics for the United States. Specifically, the committee recommended that the government

develop annual, industry-level measures of total factor productivity by restructuring the NIPAs to create a more complete and consistent set of accounts integrated with data from other statistical agencies to allow for consistent estimation of the contributions of innovation to economic growth.[2]

1. The complete data set is available on the BEA's website at https://www.bea.gov/industry/index.htm#integrated, and on the BLS website at www.bls.gov/mfp.
2. Advisory Committee on Measuring Innovation in the 21st Century Economy (2008, 5).

Integrated GDP, GDP by industry, and productivity statistics consistent with the framework of national economic accounts have been developing at an accelerating rate within the international community and have garnered significant attention in recent years. Jorgenson (2012) describes the establishment and evolution of the World KLEMS Initiative, whose goal is to develop capital (K), labor (L), energy (E), materials (M), and services (S) data sets for countries around the world, with the objective to provide a new framework for analyzing the sources of economic growth at the industry level.[3] This new framework builds on recent developments in the United Nations' *System of National Accounts 2008*, which now recommends the incorporation of labor composition in measuring labor input and the prices and quantities of capital services in measuring capital input.[4] In addition, Schreyer (2009) outlines the role of capital services in capital measurement and provides recommendations on methods used to construct the prices and quantities of capital services for those Organisation of Economic and Co-operation and Development (OECD) countries that do not measure MFP. Official industry-level production account statistics are published on a regular basis in Australia, Canada, Denmark, Finland, Italy, the Netherlands, and Sweden.

This BEA/BLS effort is the latest in a series of collaborations that was formalized in 2002 between the BEA and the BLS to better harmonize and reconcile GDP, GDP by industry, and productivity statistics. Early work involved reconciling price differences between the two agency's measures of industry output to improve industry comparisons. Fraumeni, Harper, Powers, and Yuskavage (FHPY) (2006) detailed the agency collaborations toward reconciling output measures where common data sources were used; the authors also developed a conceptual framework and illustrative production account for the nonfarm business sector. An important step undertaken by the BEA around this time involved integrating the national accounts' GDP statistics with the annual GDP by industry and input-output statistics (Moyer et al. 2004; Lawson et al. 2006). Subsequently, Strassner, Medeiros, and Smith (2005) of the BEA produced detailed KLEMS (estimates of inputs within the framework of the integrated industry accounts. Harper et al. (2009) first implemented an integrated production account for the private business sector as outlined by FHPY (2006), made recommendations of how to expand the production account to cover the total economy, and presented alternative rental prices to improve the measurement of capital

---

3. Jorgenson (2012) includes a summary of results from Jorgenson, Ho, and Samuels (2012) covering the period 1947–2010 that uses the same industry classification system as that used to produce the BEA/BLS prototype. The work of Jorgenson, Ho, and Samuels was financed by a grant to Harvard University, which also financed the First and Second World KLEMS conferences.

4. Chapters 19 and 20 of *System of National Accounts 2008* provide the relevant details on the measurement of labor composition and capital services.

services for the nonmarket economy.[5] Most recently, Harper et al. (2010) of the BLS integrated both the BLS and the BEA KLEMS statistics to publish BLS nonmanufacturing MFP measures.[6]

This chapter builds on these previous efforts by developing a prototype BEA/BLS industry-level production account for the United States for the period 1998 to 2010 on a 2002 North American Industry Classification (NAICS) basis. The account incorporates gross output, value added, and intermediate inputs—including energy, materials, and purchased services—statistics by industry from the BEA, and labor and capital input measures by industry from the BLS. The BEA and BLS data are both consistent with the industry accounts statistics as of December 2011. The BLS labor and capital measures reflect adjustments that were made to published BLS data where necessary to provide consistency in concepts and coverage for this prototype account.[7]

We present contributions of KLEMS inputs and MFP to gross output growth at roughly the three-digit NAICS level of industry detail based on a gross-output production accounting framework.[8] The gross output concept differs from the sectoral concept used by the BLS in its industry-level MFP statistics. The sectoral approach excludes intermediate production and purchases that come from within the industry (i.e., intraindustry transactions) from both output and inputs. This is the primary conceptual difference between the MFP measures presented here and the official BLS productivity statistics.[9] Both approaches are discussed in Schreyer (2001).

The starting point for this prototype production account is the fundamental economic accounting identity that under the zero profit assumption, the value of gross output equals the value of payments for KLEMS inputs to production, including intraindustry transactions.[10] The complete

5. This analysis laid the groundwork for the BLS to produce total economy measures of output per unit of input that included the coverage of nonmarket production by government and nonprofit institutions. The study also developed cross-agency understanding of the methodological differences between BLS private business measures and BEA GDP. Improved data tables with these measures are now updated on a periodic basis by both agencies. "Summary Integrated Production Account Tables" (April 21, 2011) are available at http://bea.gov/national /integrated_prod.htm. "1987–2010 Total Economy Production Account Tables" are available at http://www.bls.gov/mfp/mprdload.htm.

6. This article also presented Domar percentage-point contributions of these industries and sectors to private business multifactor productivity growth.

7. The BLS regularly publishes labor and capital measures that are consistent with NIPA industry-level definitions, but with differences in coverage and concepts that will be discussed later in this chapter For this account, we incorporate data across all legal forms of organization at the industry level to ensure consistency with GDP.

8. Jorgenson, Gollop, and Fraumeni (1987) and Jorgenson, Ho, and Stiroh (2005) rely on gross output measures.

9. The National Academy of Sciences (1979) (Rees) Panel to Review Productivity Statistics recommended a sectoral framework for measuring productivity. Aggregating industry-level sectoral output to the total economy produces value-added output. The sectoral framework provides a unifying rationale of output measurement from detailed industry to major sectors.

10. Intraindustry purchases can be a relatively important source of production for certain industries; for example, the semiconductor industry relies heavily on intraindustry transactions to produce microprocessor chips.

set of accounts that we present in this chapter decomposes changes in these values over time into changes in prices and changes in quantities, thus permitting an index number estimate of MFP growth by industry. This study also includes estimates of the Domar-weighted contributions of industry MFP to economy-wide MFP. We also include illustrative results of a labor composition adjustment to BLS labor hours for purposes of understanding its impact on estimating the contribution of labor input and MFP by industry.[11] This adjustment for labor composition reflects the heterogeneity of each industry's workforce and yields a symmetric treatment of labor and capital services in this prototype production account.

The initial results of the prototype account show the following:

- In 1998 to 2010, capital accounted for about 60 percent of US economic growth, labor accounted for about 10 percent, and MFP accounted for about 30 percent of growth.
- In forty-eight out of sixty-three industries, at least one KLEMS input to production was a more important source of real gross output growth than was MFP.

The remainder of the chapter proceeds in five sections. We provide a first look at prototype industry-level results. We present BLS MFP measures and compare them with the industry production account results. We describe the methodology for this prototype industry-level account, including a description of how the various data sets are compiled. We discuss some of the conceptual and estimation challenges that require resolution before this account can be released on a regular basis. Lastly, we conclude with comments on possible future work and next steps in this important collaboration.

11.1   A First Look at Prototype Results

This prototype BEA/BLS industry-level production account can be used to trace the sources of US economic growth across all goods- and services-producing industries in the US economy. This new production account presents the contributions of both value-added and intermediate input factors of production and the contribution of MFP to US real gross output growth, at roughly the three-digit NAICS industry level as published in the US industry economic accounts. This section highlights the sources of US economic growth over the period 1998 to 2010, including MFP trends during this period at the industry level, and also details the contributions of each industry's MFP to economy-wide MFP.

---

11. Domar weights consist of a ratio of current dollar gross output divided by aggregate value added. These weights are unique in that they sum to more than one, reflecting the fact that an increase in an industry's productivity has a direct effect on the industry's output as well a secondary effect through the output of one industry delivered to another as intermediate inputs.

Table 11.1   Aggregate factor contributions to GDP growth, 1998–2010

All industry value-added growth	1.90
Aggregate labor contribution	0.20
College graduate	0.46
No college degree	-0.25
Aggregate capital contribution	1.15
Aggregate MFP growth	0.56

Note: Growth is expressed as the difference in natural logs. Individual components may not sum to totals due to rounding.

11.1.1   Sources of US Output Growth, 1998 to 2010

With the development of a prototype industry-level production account spanning all industries integrated within an input-output framework, useful information can be generated by tracing the sources of output growth across each industry's KLEMS inputs—both its primary, value-added inputs, and its secondary, intermediate inputs—and to MFP. Table 11.1 presents the sources of aggregate value-added growth for the United States that are attributable to the primary, value-added inputs of capital and labor, and to MFP.[12]

Table 11.2 extends the analysis by showing the contributions of all KLEMS inputs and MFP to gross output growth for selected industries, ranked by the largest positive contributions of intermediate inputs, capital, and labor. The contributions from at least one of the primary, value-added inputs of capital and labor, or secondary, intermediate inputs of energy, materials, and purchased services were greater than MFP growth in more than 75 percent of the sixty-three industries included in this account.

In the three industries with the largest percent changes in gross output—positive or negative—support activities for mining; securities, commodity contracts, and investments; and information and data processing services—intermediate input contributions were the largest contributor to the percent changes in gross output, reflecting their relative weight as a well as recent trends in the sourcing of production. In six of the top ten industries with the strongest output growth, intermediate inputs were the most significant factor. Conversely, in all but one of the ten industries that showed the largest output decline, negative intermediate input contributions were the largest contributors (table 11A.3).

Among capital-intensive industries, rental and leasing and information and data processing services were the industries with the largest capital contributions to output growth. For rental and leasing, capital contributed 2.89 percentage points to real output growth of 1.7 percent. For information and data processing services, capital contributed 1.76 percentage points to real output growth of 7.8 percent.

---

12. Rates of change and contributions in all tables in this chapter reflect annual rates over the period indicated.

Table 11.2   Largest factor input contributions to output growth, 1998–2010 (percentage point)

Description	Capital	Labor	Intermediate	Energy	Material	Service	MFP	Output
Largest intermediate contributions								
Support activities for mining	0.13	0.78	6.26	0.27	2.98	3.01	1.70	8.86
Securities, commodity contracts, investments	-0.39	0.85	5.36	-0.02	0.10	5.28	2.52	8.33
Information and data processing services	1.76	0.34	3.93	0.03	0.60	3.31	1.77	7.81
Federal government	0.10	0.36	2.23	0.04	0.26	1.92	0.22	2.90
Federal Reserve banks, credit intermediation, and related activities	1.38	0.12	1.93	0.00	0.03	1.90	0.67	4.10
Largest capital contributions								
Rental and leasing services and lessors of intangible assets	2.89	-0.11	0.22	-0.02	0.00	0.24	-1.31	1.69
Information and data processing services	1.76	0.34	3.93	0.03	0.60	3.31	1.77	7.81
Legal services	1.68	0.39	-0.33	-0.01	-0.05	-0.27	-1.80	-0.06
Broadcasting and telecommunication	1.66	-0.36	1.35	-0.01	0.28	1.08	1.79	4.44
Publishing	1.62	-0.41	1.05	-0.02	-0.09	1.16	0.16	2.43
Largest labor contributions								
Computer systems design and related services	-0.13	2.30	1.54	-0.01	0.28	1.26	2.52	6.23
Educational services	0.21	1.67	0.96	0.03	0.16	0.77	-1.19	1.65
Ambulatory health-care services	0.29	1.60	0.85	0.00	0.11	0.73	0.53	3.27
Warehousing and storage	0.39	1.52	1.67	0.11	0.20	1.37	0.27	3.86
Management of companies and enterprises	1.19	1.44	1.01	0.00	0.20	0.81	-2.54	1.11

Similarly, several labor-intensive industries had the highest labor contribution to output growth (see table 11.2 and table 11A.3 in the appendix). Computer systems design and related services, education services, and ambulatory health-care services were among the industries with the largest labor contributions to output growth.

In the top ten industries ranked by size of workforce for 2010, the sources of output growth were mixed (table 11.3). Among the largest industries ranked by size of employment, labor was the greatest input contribution for state and local government at 0.83 percentage points, and in ambulatory health-care services at 1.60 percentage points. Among these ten industries, wholesale trade and retail trade were the industries that showed the greatest capital contributions as the largest contributor to output growth.[13] The intermediate inputs contribution was the largest contributor to output growth in federal government at 2.23 percentage points, led by the contribution of purchased-services inputs. In food services and drinking places, the intermediate input contribution of 0.74 percentage points was also led by purchased-services inputs. In hospitals and nursing and residential care facilities, the intermediate inputs contribution of 1.70 percentage points was also the most significant contributor to output growth, with, once again, purchased-services inputs accounting for the largest contribution. MFP growth or declines were the largest contributors to output growth or declines in administrative and support services at 1.22 percentage points, other services at –1.33 percentage points, and construction at –1.33 percentage points for these selected industries.

Labor Composition

In this prototype, we decompose the labor contributions to output growth into demographic characteristics that account for the contributions of the college-educated workforce and those workers that did not attend college. This adjustment to labor input allows for the contribution of labor to reflect changes in the composition of the skill level of the labor force over time, in addition to the number of hours worked by industry.

In over 80 percent of the industries measured, the contributions from the college workforce were higher than those that did not attend college, reflecting the industries' shift in demand toward college-educated workers (see table 11A.4 in the appendix). The median contribution of workers with a college education was 0.07 percentage points while the non-college-educated workers' subtracted 0.19 percentage points from economy-wide output growth over the period 1998 to 2010.

Ranking the industries by college-educated labor contributions shows that

---

13. Wholesale and retail trade output measures reflect the gross margin output concept, which subtracts the costs of goods sold from its sales and inventories, and therefore also excludes them from its input costs.

Table 11.3 Contributions to output growth from ten largest employment industries, 1998–2010 (percentage point)

2010 Employment (in thousands)	Description	Capital	Labor	Intermediates	Energy	Material	Service	MFP	Output
19,541	State and local government	0.19	0.83	0.68	0.01	0.12	0.55	-0.40	1.30
14,743	Retail trade	0.99	-0.08	0.83	-0.03	0.27	0.59	0.31	2.05
9,506	Food services and drinking places	-0.04	0.47	0.74	0.01	0.00	0.72	0.45	1.63
7,818	Hospitals and nursing and residential care facilities	0.27	0.96	1.70	0.02	0.11	1.57	-0.13	2.79
7,150	Administrative and support services	0.81	-0.22	-0.08	0.00	0.04	-0.11	1.22	1.72
6,743	Other services, except government	0.41	0.22	0.44	-0.02	-0.18	0.65	-1.33	-0.26
6,024	Ambulatory health-care services	0.29	1.60	0.85	0.00	0.11	0.73	0.53	3.27
5,767	Construction	0.34	-0.30	-1.12	-0.03	-0.93	-0.16	-1.33	-2.41
5,520	Wholesale trade	0.92	-0.17	1.21	0.00	0.28	0.93	0.76	2.71
5,425	Federal government	0.10	0.36	2.23	0.04	0.26	1.92	0.22	2.90

Table 11.4   Labor contribution, 1998–2010 (percentage point)

Description	College labor	No college labor	Labor composition
No college largest contributions			
Warehousing and storage	0.26	1.27	1.52
Social assistance	0.36	0.70	1.07
Ambulatory health-care services	1.07	0.53	1.60
College largest contributions			
Management of companies and enterprises	2.42	–0.88	1.44
Computer systems design and related services	2.10	0.20	2.30
Educational services	1.52	0.16	1.67

Note: Component input contributions may not sum to total labor contributions due to rounding.

computer systems design and related services, management of companies and enterprises, and education services have the largest labor contributions to output growth (table 11.4).

Warehousing and storage, social assistance, and administrative and support services had the highest labor contributions of non-college-educated labor to output growth.

MFP Growth Trends at the Industry Level

"High-tech" industries showed some of the strongest MFP growth over the period 1998 to 2010 (table 11.5). Computer and electronic product manufacturing, information and data processing services, computer systems design and related services, and broadcasting and telecommunications were among the industries with the largest MFP growth. These information-communications-technology-producing industries were among the top ten industries with MFP growth.

From 1998 to 2010, computer and electronic products manufacturing led MFP growth at an average annual rate of 9.6 percent (See table 11A.2 in the appendix). This MFP growth was driven by rising output at a 5.5 percent average annual rate, and falling intermediate inputs at a 6.6 percent average annual rate. Computer systems design and related services MFP grew 2.5 percent at an average annual rate, driven by strong output growth. Oil and gas extraction showed the largest MFP decline during the period, falling at an average annual rate of 2.7 percent, driven by intermediate inputs growth of 2.2 percent. Management of companies and enterprises and legal services were also among the industries with the largest average annual declines in MFP, decreasing 2.5 percent and 1.8 percent at average annual rates, respectively.

Contributions to Economy-Wide MFP

From 1998 to 2010, economy-wide MFP grew at an average annual rate of 0.56 percent. Both goods-producing industries and services-producing industries had positive contributions to aggregate MFP growth through

Table 11.5   Multifactor productivity growth for selected industries (percent change)

Description	1998–2000	2000–2007	2007–2010	1998–2010
Computer and electronic product manufacturing	12.2	8.5	10.7	9.6
Computer systems design and related services	−0.5	3.1	3.2	2.5
Broadcasting and telecommunication	−0.1	2.8	0.6	1.8
Information and data processing services	−13.0	6.4	0.8	1.8
Oil and gas extraction	−12.8	−1.0	0.1	−2.7
Management of companies and enterprises	−0.3	−2.6	−3.8	−2.5
Legal services	0.2	−2.1	−2.4	−1.8
Securities, commodity contracts, investments	5.3	1.0	4.2	2.5
Apparel and leather and allied products	1.2	1.3	11.8	3.9
Construction	−0.6	−2.2	0.2	−1.3

the period 1998 to 2010. Services-producing industries contributed about 0.23 percentage points to the economy-wide MFP while goods-producing industries contributed 0.33 percentage points.

From 2000 to 2007, economy-wide MFP increased at an average annual rate of 0.61 percent, while MFP increased at an average annual rate of 0.17 percent from 2007 to 2010. The goods-producing sector accounted for more of the increase in MFP, adding 0.14 percentage points of the 0.17 percentage point increase from 2007 to 2010.

Goods-Producing Sector Contributions to Economy-Wide MFP[14]

From 1998 to 2010, computer and electronic products manufacturing contributed 0.33 percentage points to economy-wide MFP, significantly more than any other industry (table 11.6). The farms industry was a distant second within the goods-producing sector, contributing 0.04 percentage points to the increase in economy-wide MFP. Miscellaneous manufacturing was also among the leading contributors, adding 0.02 percentage points to economy-wide MFP.

The contribution of computer and electronic products manufacturing to economy-wide MFP growth experienced a leveling off in recent years. Over the period studied, the contributions from computer and electronic products manufacturing were the greatest in the 1998 to 2000 period, 0.60 percentage points; in the more recent period of 2007 to 2010, the contribution was 0.28 percentage points. This trend is consistent with BLS estimates of the contributions of three-digit manufacturing industries to private nonfarm business MFP.[15] The trend also confirms the accepted story of an IT-induced productivity speed-up in the last half of the 1990s.

14. In the US industry economic accounts, the goods-producing sector consists of agriculture, forestry, fishing, and hunting; mining; construction; and manufacturing.
15. See http://www.bls.gov/mfp/mfgcon.pdf, Bureau of Labor Statistics (2012).

Table 11.6   Contributions to multifactor productivity growth from selected goods-producing industries (percentage point)

Description	1998–2000	2000–2007	2007–2010	1998–2010
Computer and electronic products	0.600	0.274	0.278	0.329
Farms	0.063	0.012	0.085	0.039
Miscellaneous manufacturing	0.034	0.019	0.024	0.023
Machinery	−0.028	0.028	0.038	0.021
Nonmetallic mineral products	−0.015	−0.006	−0.005	−0.007
Utilities	0.111	−0.023	−0.061	−0.010
Oil and gas extraction	−0.123	−0.015	0.010	−0.027
Construction	−0.059	−0.210	0.014	−0.129
Total goods	0.773	0.279	0.144	0.328

Table 11.7   Contributions to multifactor productivity growth from selected services-producing industries (percentage point)

Description	1998–2000	2000–2007	2007–2010	1998–2010
Securities, commodity contracts, and investments	0.167	0.033	0.145	0.084
Broadcasting and telecommunications	−0.004	0.129	0.026	0.081
Wholesale trade	0.179	0.111	−0.114	0.066
Administrative and support services	−0.012	0.061	0.057	0.048
Federal Reserve banks, credit intermediation, and related activities	0.020	−0.006	0.171	0.043
Computer systems design and related services	−0.008	0.048	0.057	0.041
Information and data processing services	−0.094	0.057	0.007	0.019
Publishing industries (includes software)	−0.115	0.041	−0.009	0.002
Real estate	0.193	−0.018	−0.235	−0.037
State and local	−0.059	−0.064	−0.029	−0.055
Other services, except government	−0.021	−0.065	−0.059	−0.056
Management of companies and enterprises	−0.008	−0.068	−0.104	−0.067
Total service	0.155	0.335	0.028	0.228

Services-Producing Sector Contributions to Economy-Wide MFP[16]

From 1998 to 2010, the securities, commodity contracts, and investments and broadcasting and telecommunications industries were among the top contributors to economy-wide MFP growth with securities, commodity contracts, and investments contributing the most, 0.08 percentage points (table 11.7).

During the 2000 to 2007 subperiod, all services-producing, sector-related,

16. In the US industry economic accounts, the services-producing sector consists of utilities; wholesale trade; retail trade; transportation and warehousing; information; finance, insurance, real estate, rental, and leasing; professional and business services; educational services, health care, and social assistance; arts, entertainment, recreation, accommodation, and food services; and other services, except government.

information-communications-technology-producing industries added to economy-wide MFP growth, including publishing (which includes software publishing), broadcasting and telecommunications, information and data processing services, and computer systems design and related services. Wholesale trade was also among the largest contributors to MFP growth, contributing 0.11 percentage points to economy-wide MFP growth during this period.

From 2007 to 2010, Federal Reserve Banks, credit intermediation, and related activities led the increase in aggregate MFP, adding 0.17 percentage points to MFP growth. Credit intermediation and related activities and securities, commodity contracts, and investments were also among the largest contributors to the increase in MFP over this period, increasing aggregate MFP growth by 0.14 percentage points. These positive contributions were partly offset by negative contributions by the real estate industry, which subtracted 0.23 percentage points.

11.2   BLS MFP and Industry Contributions to BLS MFP—A Comparison

The output measures used in the BLS MFP measures are constructed to be as consistent as possible with the BLS major sector labor productivity measures (except that the MFP measures exclude government enterprises). This consistency allows BLS MFP data to help explain the sources of growth in the official labor productivity series. In a model where capital and labor are the measured inputs, sources of labor productivity growth include increases in capital intensity (i.e., capital deepening) and improvements in the skills of the labor force (i.e., labor composition). Additional sources of labor productivity are attributed to MFP, which may reflect changes in a variety of factors that are not included as measured inputs, including technology change, economies of scale, and improvements in management techniques or organization of production, among other factors.

For BLS official estimates of private business and private nonfarm business MFP, the relationship of aggregate multifactor productivity to aggregate labor productivity is given by the following equation:

$$d(\ln Y - \ln L) = d \ln A + w_k[d(\ln K - \ln L)] + w_l[d \ln LC],$$

where

Y = output,
L = labor,
K = capital,
LC = labor composition,
d denotes the derivative with respect to time, and
w_i denotes the cost share weight of input i, $(i = k, l)$.

This equation shows that labor productivity growth is decomposed into the contribution of MFP growth, the contribution resulting from K/L substitution (capital deepening) and the contribution of the labor composition effect. This relationship between MFP and labor productivity ties the private business and private nonfarm business MFP measures to the official published estimates of business and nonfarm business labor productivity, with the caveat that government enterprises is excluded.

Furthermore, the BLS industry contributions roughly sum to the official published estimates of private business and private nonfarm business MFP. When compared to the industry-level Domar contributions to economy-wide MFP for the industry production account measures presented in this chapter, the industry-level Domar contributions to private business sector MFP are comparable in magnitude and order. Table 11.8 shows BLS MFP growth for selected industries. For tables 11.9 and 11.10, the Domar-weighting scheme is applied based on the relative importance of each industry to total private business MFP.

Table 11.8   BLS multifactor productivity growth for selected industries

Description	1998–2000	2000–2007	2007–2010	1998–2010
Computer and electronic products	14.1	9.9	11.7	11.0
Computer systems design and related services	–1.1	3.1	3.3	2.4
Broadcasting and telecommunications	0.4	3.3	0.5	2.1
Information and data processing services	–15.3	5.6	1.1	0.7
Oil and gas extraction	–9.3	–0.6	–0.2	–2.0
Management of companies and enterprises	0.6	–1.1	–2.5	–1.2
Legal services	1.3	–0.1	–1.0	–0.1
Securities, commodity contracts, and investments	8.6	2.0	2.5	3.2
Apparel and leather and applied products	2.6	4.2	2.6	3.6
Construction	–0.2	–2.0	0.7	–1.0

Table 11.9   Contributions to private business multifactor productivity growth from selected goods-producing industries

Description	1998–2000	2000–2007	2007–2010	1998–2010
Computer and electronic products	0.81	0.35	0.34	0.43
Farm	0.11	0.02	0.14	0.06
Miscellaneous manufacturing	0.05	0.03	0.05	0.04
Machinery	–0.05	0.05	0.09	0.04
Nonmetallic mineral products	–0.02	–0.01	0.00	–0.01
Utilities	–0.22	0.10	0.08	0.04
Oil and extraction	–0.13	–0.02	–0.03	–0.04
Construction	-0.02	–0.25	0.07	–0.13
Private business MFP	1.79	1.44	0.45	1.25

Table 11.10   **Contributions to private business multifactor productivity growth from selected services-producing industries**

Description	1998–2000	2000–2007	2007–2010	1998–2010
Securities, commodity contracts, and investments	0.38	0.08	0.16	0.15
Broadcasting and telecommunications	0.02	0.19	0.03	0.12
Wholesale trade	0.19	0.19	–0.12	0.11
Administrative and support services	0.01	0.07	0.04	0.05
Federal Reserve banks, credit intermediation, and related activities	0.09	–0.01	0.24	0.07
Computer systems design and related services	–0.02	0.06	0.08	0.05
Information and data processing services	–0.16	0.08	0.01	0.02
Publishing industries (includes software)	–0.11	0.08	–0.01	0.03
Real estate	0.18	0.06	–0.31	–0.01
Other service, except government	0.04	–0.05	–0.04	–0.03
Management of companies and enterprises	0.02	–0.04	–0.10	–0.05
Private business MFP	1.79	1.44	0.45	1.25

BLS MFP Growth Rates for Selected Industries. Table 11.8 shows that the BLS MFP growth rates for selected industries are similar to the industry production account MFP growth rates. One exception is the 2007 to 2010 MFP growth rate for apparel and leather and applied products. Computer and electronic products similarly show the largest MFP growth of these industries, an average annual rate of 11.0 percent for the 1998 to 2010 period.

Goods-Producing Sector Contributions to BLS Private Business MFP. For the 1998 to 2010 period, the industry contributions to BLS private business MFP show similar results to the industry production account contributions. As expected, computer and electronic products dominate the contributions to private business MFP, 0.43 percentage points, approximately a third of the total MFP growth rate for the 1998 to 2010 period.

Services-Producing Sector Contributions to BLS Private Business MFP. As in the industry production account measures, securities, commodity contracts and investments, broadcasting and telecommunications, and wholesale trade show the highest contributions to private business multifactor productivity growth.

Largest Differences between BLS MFP and BEA/BLS Industry-Level Production Account MFP. Table 11.11 shows the largest positive differences between BLS MFP and the industry-level production account MFP. Table 11.12 highlights the difference between BLS sectoral output and BEA gross output measures for those industries. In its sectoral approach, the BLS excludes intraindustry transactions—that is, sales between establishments

Table 11.11   Seven largest positive differences in annual percent change in MFP measure by industry, 1998–2010 (BLS MFP less BEA MFP)

Description	1998–2010
Air transportation	2.5
Legal services	1.7
Utilities	1.4
Computer and electronic products	1.4
Management of companies and enterprises	1.3
Educational services	0.9
Insurance carriers and related activities	0.8

Table 11.12   Differences in output measures

Description	BLS sectoral output (1998–2010)	BEA gross output (1998–2010)	Difference
Air transportation	1.8	–0.3	2.1
Legal services	0.1	–0.1	0.2
Utilities	–0.1	–1.4	1.3
Computer and electronic product manufacturing	3.9	5.5	–1.6
Management of companies and enterprises	1.5	1.1	0.4
Educational services	2.6	1.7	0.9
Insurance carriers and related activities	3.1	1.6	1.5

within the same industry—from both output and intermediate purchases. For half of the measures, the conceptual difference between the output measures explains most of the difference in MFP growth. A major exception is computer and electronic products. The difference for this sector is primarily due to differences in the way intermediate inputs are calculated.

Table 11.13 shows the largest negative differences between BLS and the production accounts MFP. Table 11.14 shows the differences between sectoral output and gross output measures. Some of the differences in MFP between the industries are due to the difference in output measures. The rest are attributable to differences in intermediate inputs.

11.3   Methodology

This section provides a brief overview of the conceptual framework and estimation methods used to prepare the prototype BEA/BLS industry-level production account. We provide a description of the gross-output growth accounting framework, discuss the estimation methods used to prepare our results, and summarize the source data methods used by the BEA and BLS to produce the gross output, value added, intermediate inputs, capital input,

Table 11.13   **Seven largest negative differences in annual percent change in MFP measure by industry, 1998–2010 (BLS MFP less BEA MFP)**

Description	1998–2010
Funds, trusts, and other financial vehicles	−1.6
Information and data processing services	−1.1
Petroleum and coal products	−0.6
Accommodation	−0.6
Textile mills and textile product mills	−0.5
Mining, except oil and gas	−0.4
Apparel and leather and applied products	−0.3

Table 11.14   **Differences in output measures**

Description	Sectoral output (1998–2010)	Gross output (1998–2010)	Difference
Funds, trusts, and other financial vehicles	2.6	2.6	0.0
Information and data processing services	8.3	7.8	0.5
Petroleum and coal products	0.7	1.4	−0.7
Accommodation	1.3	2.6	−1.3
Textile mills and textile product mills	−5.5	−5.9	0.4
Mining, except oil and gas	−1.2	−1.2	0.0
Apparel and leather and applied products	−12.8	−12.3	−0.5

and labor input used in this account, including adjustments we made to achieve better integration of these data sets.

11.3.1   Conceptual Overview of Measurement

For the prototype BEA/BLS production account framework, we assume the following type of production function relating gross output of an industry to three factor inputs using the gross output production function model: $Q = F(K, L, II, t)$ where Q stands for gross output, K stands for capital, L stands for labor, II stands for the intermediate inputs, and t stands for time.[17]

Under the assumption of constant returns to scale, perfect competition, and factors being paid their marginal product, the gross-output growth model can be rearranged in terms of MFP growth computed in the following, simplified way:

$$(1) \quad \frac{d\ln Q}{dt} = \left(\frac{\partial \ln Q}{\partial \ln K} \frac{d\ln K}{dt} \right) + \left(\frac{\partial \ln Q}{\partial \ln II} \frac{d\ln II}{dt} \right) + \left(\frac{\partial \ln Q}{\partial \ln L} \frac{d\ln L}{dt} \right) + \left(\frac{\partial \ln Q}{\partial t} \right)$$

17. For simplicity, we express total intermediate inputs instead of the separate cost components of energy, materials, and purchased services. This model is also used by the BLS for its published measures for industry-level MFP, with the exception that Q is sectoral output and II reflects the subtraction of intraindustry inputs from intermediate inputs.

$$(2)\left(\frac{\partial \ln Q}{\partial t}\right) = \frac{d \ln Q}{dt} - \left(\frac{\partial \ln Q}{\partial \ln K}\frac{d \ln K}{dt}\right) - \left(\frac{\partial \ln Q}{\partial \ln II}\frac{d \ln II}{dt}\right) - \left(\frac{\partial \ln Q}{\partial \ln L}\frac{d \ln L}{dt}\right).$$

With these assumptions, the unknown elasticities can be replaced with the observable factor share, v_i, for each input. Shown below is the factor share for capital input:

$$(3)\qquad \frac{\partial \ln Q}{\partial \ln K} = \frac{P_K K = Capital\ Compensation}{(P_K K + P_L L + P_{II} II) = Total\ Input\ Cost} = v_K,$$

where P_K is the price of capital, P_L is the price of labor, and P_{II} is the price of intermediate inputs. The assumption of constant returns to scale ensures that the factor shares sum to one.

$$(4)\qquad \frac{P_K K}{(P_K K + P_L L + P_{II} II)} = v_K \text{ where } v_K + v_L + v_{II} = 1$$

$$\frac{P_L L}{(P_K K + P_L L + P_{II} II)} = v_L$$

$$\frac{P_{II} II}{(P_K K + P_L L + P_{II} II)} = v_{II}.$$

In discrete time, the input weights are two-year averages of the cost shares for each input in years t and t-1, where $\widetilde{v_K} = (1/2)v_{K,t} + (1/2)v_{K,t-1}$. MFP growth can be rewritten in the following way, relating MFP growth for an industry as the residual of the difference in the growth in output and the growth in the combined inputs:

$$(5)\qquad \text{MFP growth} = \Delta \ln Q - \widetilde{v_K}\Delta \ln(K) - \widetilde{v_L}\Delta \ln(L) - \widetilde{v_{II}}\Delta \ln(II).$$

There are no assumptions restricting individual industries in this analysis of MFP; each industry faces the above production function individually and without regard to any other industry.

11.3.2   Estimation Methods—Aggregation

The MFP index is computed by dividing an index of real gross output by an index of combined inputs. A combined real input measure is computed within a Tornqvist index number formula that aggregates real intermediate inputs by industry for energy, materials, and purchased services with the labor and capital input using average cost shares.[18]

The current-dollar cost shares of the three main input components are generated using published and computed data sets. The current dollar intermediate inputs measure is a sum of the current dollar energy, material, and purchased-services expenditures of an industry from the BEA annual

18. The BEA's national and industry accounts use Fisher-ideal indexes to express official chain-type price and quantity indexes. This study follows the productivity literature and uses the Tornqvist index for aggregation.

industry accounts. The current dollar labor component is a measure of the compensation of workers in that industry. The BEA-published labor compensation figures are supplemented to include the self-employed compensation estimate that is detailed in the labor input section using the assumption that self-employed workers receive similar wages to the payrolled employees. Lastly, nominal capital compensation is computed as a residual of the value of gross output less the sum of labor compensation and intermediate input expenditures.[19]

The intermediate inputs average share is an industry's current-dollar expenditure on energy, materials, and services divided by the value of gross-output production averaged over two periods. The average share for the remaining inputs is computed in a similar fashion. The KLEMS measures are Tornqvist aggregated using the average cost shares and the quantity indexes of each input.

11.3.3 Estimation Methods—Gross Output, Value Added, and Intermediate Inputs

The BEA industry accounts provide a time series of nominal and real gross output, intermediate inputs, and value added for industries defined according to the 2002 NAICS (Mayerhauser and Strassner 2010). These accounts are integrated conceptually and statistically with final expenditures and GDP from the NIPAs, and are prepared within a balanced input-output framework that allows for integrated analysis of industry output, inputs, employment, and final demand. In 2005, these accounts were expanded to provide additional information on the composition of intermediate inputs by industry, which made these accounts more useful to observe changes in spending related to energy, materials, and purchased services (Strassner, Medeiros, and Smith 2005).

The industry accounts methodology can be summarized in four broad steps:[20]

1. Prepare annual make tables. The make table shows the production of both primary and secondary commodities (goods and services) by industries.

2. Prepare initial annual use tables. The use table shows the consumption of commodities by industries (intermediate inputs) and by final demand, as well as the contribution of value added by industry.

3. Balance the use table.

4. Prepare price and quantity indexes for gross output, intermediate inputs, and value added.

---

19. This is a common assumption in productivity literature and ensures that the factor shares sum to unity.

20. See Mayerhauser and Strassner (2010) for the most complete description of the industry accounts methodology.

On an annual basis, a wide array of source data as described in Gilmore et al. (2011) is used to update the annual time series. Nominal value added by industry estimates are available for the compensation of employees and taxes on production and imports less subsidies. The gross operating surplus component of value added by industry is derived from gross domestic income data adjusted to an establishment basis. Annual survey data available from the Census Bureau are used in updating industry and commodity gross output as well as for intermediate inputs by industry and the cost categories of energy, materials, and purchased services. Lastly, annual data are also used from the NIPAs and the BEA international transactions accounts for updating estimates of final expenditures to assure an integrated framework.

The balancing process ensures two simultaneous conditions. First, that each industry's output equals its intermediate inputs plus its value-added components, and second, that the sum of intermediate and final uses for each commodity is equal to its gross output. The use table is balanced with a biproportional scaling procedure that sequentially adjusts the rows and columns to meet these two conditions and other predetermined controls, including NIPA final expenditure category values including total GDP, industry compensation, and commodity and industry gross output totals from the make table.[21] Intermediate inputs, gross operating surplus, and the commodity composition of final uses are subject to adjustment during the balancing process.

Price-adjusted measures of GDP by industry are prepared using double deflation using a Fisher-ideal index number formula, which allows gross output and intermediate inputs to be deflated separately and real value added computed as the residual. Price and quantity indexes for gross output by industry are derived by deflating the commodities produced by an industry as part of its gross output. Price and quantity indexes for intermediate inputs are derived by deflating the commodities that are consumed by an industry as intermediate inputs. The domestic and imported portions of intermediate inputs are deflated separately to account for the commodities purchased as inputs from domestic and from foreign sources.[22] Intermediate inputs at a detailed product level are disaggregated to obtain the domestic and imported portions of intermediate inputs included in each KLEMS input-cost category. For each detailed commodity used by an industry, the portion attributable to imports is calculated as the economy-wide ratio of

21. The use table balancing incorporates over 350 final expenditure category "controls" as published in the NIPAs.

22. Intermediate inputs at a detailed product level are disaggregated to obtain the domestic and imported portions of intermediate inputs included in each KLEMS category using the so-called import comparability, or proportionality, assumption. For each detailed commodity used by an industry, the portion attributable to imports is calculated as the economy-wide ratio of commodity imports to the total domestic supply of the commodity.

commodity imports to the total domestic supply of the commodity.[23] Real value added is computed as the difference between real output and real intermediate inputs within a Fisher-ideal index-number formula.

11.3.4   Estimation Methods—Capital Input

Capital inputs for the MFP measures are computed in accordance with a service flow concept for physical capital assets—equipment, structures, inventories, and land. Capital inputs for major sectors are determined in three main steps: (a) a very detailed array of capital stocks is developed for various asset types in various industries; (b) asset-type capital stocks are aggregated for each industry to measure capital input for the industry; and (c) industry capital inputs are aggregated to measure sectoral level capital input.

Financial assets are excluded from capital services measures. The aggregate capital services measures are obtained by Tornqvist aggregation of the capital stocks for each asset type within each of sixty-five NAICS industry groupings using estimated rental prices for each asset type. Each rental price reflects the nominal rate of return to all assets within the industry and rates of economic depreciation and revaluation for the specific asset; rental prices are adjusted for the effects of taxes. Current-dollar capital costs can be defined as each asset's rental price multiplied by its constant-dollar stock, adjusting for capital composition effects.

11.3.5   Asset Detail

The asset detail consists of eighty-six asset types for fixed business equipment and software, structures, inventories, and land. The BLS measures of capital stocks for equipment and structures are prepared using NIPA data on real gross investment. Real stocks are constructed as vintage aggregates of historical investments (in real terms) in accordance with an "efficiency" or service flow concept (as distinct from a price or value concept). The efficiency of each asset is assumed to deteriorate only gradually during the early years of an asset's service life and then more quickly in its later life. These "age/efficiency" schedules are based, to the extent possible, on empirical evidence of capital deterioration. Inventory stocks are developed using data from the NIPA and IRS. The BLS measures farm and nonfarm nonmanufacturing final inventories and manufacturing inventories by stage of processing: finished goods, work in process, and materials and supplies. Farm land input is based on data from the Economic Research Service of the US Department of Agriculture. A benchmark for nonfarm land is estimated by applying a

---

23. For example, if imports represent 35 percent of the domestic supply of semiconductors, then the estimates in the import-use table assume that imports comprise 35 percent of the value of semiconductors in each industry that uses semiconductors.

land-structure ratio based on unpublished estimates by the BLS to the value of structures.

Among equipment, the BLS provides additional detail on information processing equipment and software (IPES). The IPES is composed of four broad classes of assets: computers and related equipment, software, communications equipment, and other IPES equipment. Computers and related equipment includes mainframe computers, personal computers, printers, terminals, tape drives, storage devices, and integrated systems. Software is comprised of prepackaged, custom, and own-account software. Communications equipment is not further differentiated. Other IPES includes medical equipment and related instruments, electromedical instruments, nonmedical instruments, photocopying and related equipment, and office and accounting machinery. Structures include nonresidential structures and residential capital that are rented out by profit-making firms or persons.

11.3.6   Capital Stocks

A central concept in the production of BLS capital measures is that of the "productive" capital stock, or the stock measured in efficiency units. Conceptually, the productive stock represents the amount of new investment required to produce the same capital *services* actually produced by existing assets of all vintages. Thus, total current services from assets of all vintages are proportional to the productive stock. It is this measure of capital stock that is directly associated with productivity. The measurement of the productive stock involves vintage aggregation, which requires historical data on real investment and an "age/efficiency" function that describes the pattern of services that capital goods supply as they age.

The BLS computes each type of stock by the perpetual inventory method. The stock at the end of a period is equal to a weighted sum of all past investment, where the weights are the asset's efficiency (defined below) as of a given age.

Mathematically, the productive stock K_t, at the end of the period t is given by:

$$K_t = \sum_{\tau=t}^{\infty} S_{\tau-t} I_{2t-\tau,}$$

where I_t is investment in period t and s_t is the efficiency function.

The efficiency function is a schedule that indicates the quantity of services provided by an asset of a given age, relative to a new asset of the same type. This function is generally assigned a value of 1.00 when the asset is new and declines as the asset ages, eventually approaching or reaching zero. Consequently, investments in the more distant past contribute less to current output.

The mathematical form BLS uses for the age/efficiency relationship is the hyperbolic function:

$$s_t = \frac{(L - t)}{(L - \beta_t)} \text{ where } 0 < t < L,$$

$$s_t = 0 \qquad t > L,$$

where

s_t is the relative efficiency of a t-year-old asset,
L is the service life,
t is the age of the asset, and
β is the parameter allowing the shape of the curve to vary.

The BLS uses an efficiency function that declines initially at one-half the straight-line depreciation rate for equipment ($\beta = 0.5$) and at one-fourth the straight-line rate for structures ($\beta = 0.75$).

11.3.7 Rental Prices

The "implicit rental price" of capital is based on the neoclassical principle that inputs should be aggregated using weights that reflect their marginal products. The assumption used to formulate the rental price expression is that the purchase price of a capital asset equals the discounted value of the stream of services (and, hence, implicitly the rents) that the asset will provide.
Rental prices are calculated for each asset as:

$$C_t = \left(\frac{(1 - u_t z_t - e_t)(p_t r_t + p_t d_t - \Delta p_t)}{(1 - u_t)} \right) + p_t x_t,$$

where

u_t is the corporate income tax rate,
z_t is the present value of \$1 of tax depreciation allowances,
e_t is the effective rate of the investment tax credit,
r_t is the nominal rate of return on capital,
d_t is the average rate of economic depreciation,
p_t is the deflator for new capital goods,
Δp_t is the revaluation of assets due to inflation in new goods prices, and
x_t is the rate of property taxation on wealth.

The following equation is used to derive the implicit internal rate of return, r_t, by substituting c_t from the above equation in the product $c_t K_t$:

$$r_t = \left(\frac{[Y_t - K_t p_t x_t - K_t(p_t d_t - \Delta p_t)(1 - u_t z_t - e_t)]/(1 - u_t)}{[K_t p_t (1 - u_t z_t - e_t)]/(1 - u_t)} \right),$$

where

Y_t is capital income and
K_t is productive capital stock.

After determining the internal rate of return in each industry, rental prices are computed separately for each type of asset within each industry.[24]

11.3.8   Government, Nonprofit, and Owner-Occupied Capital

For the purposes of the industry production account, the BLS prepared capital measures that are conceptually consistent with the total economy production accounts as described in Harper et al. (2009). These measures are not consistent with BLS major sector published measures, which exclude government, household and nonprofit institutions, and owner-occupied housing capital.

For the industry production account, the addition of government, household and nonprofit institutions, and owner-occupied housing capital measures require detailed capital stock for each so that a rental price can be calculated. Industry-specific rates of return are used in generating rental prices for nonprofit and owner-occupied housing. For government (federal, state, and local), rental prices are based on a weighted average of the rates of return and capital gains for the private business industries to calculate capital income, capital stock, and capital input. A detailed breakdown of capital data for the government stock, owner-occupied housing, and nonprofits was collected from the BEA NIPA tables in order to generate rental prices on those assets.

11.3.9   Estimation Methods—Labor Input

Labor Hours

The labor hours reflect annual hours worked. Hours are measured separately for different categories of workers in each industry and are then summed. Hours for each industry and class of worker are calculated as the product of employment, average weekly hours, and fifty-two weeks per year. They are also adjusted to reflect hours at work. The measures generally reflect the data and methods underlying the hours used in the BLS industry productivity and cost measures, but have been adjusted where necessary to improve consistency with the BEA industry accounts. Hours for NIPA industries were aggregated from estimates for more detailed industries.

The primary source of hours and employment data is the BLS Current Employment Statistics (CES) program. The CES data are based on payroll records from a sample of establishments in which the probability of sample selection is related to the establishment size. Data on employment and hours are collected monthly; the reference period for these data is the payroll period including the 12th of the month. Jobs rather than persons are counted in the CES, so that multiple jobholders are counted more than

---

24. It is worth noting that Jorgenson, Ho, and Stiroh (2005) estimate capital services prices that take into account tax differences across legal forms of organization.

once. Average weekly hours for production and nonsupervisory workers are obtained directly from the CES, while those for nonproduction and supervisory workers are derived using data from the Current Population Survey (CPS) in conjunction with the CES data.[25]

To adjust from hours paid to hours worked, ratios of hours at work to hours paid, developed from information on employer leave practices in the BLS National Compensation Survey (NCS), are used to adjust the CES paid hours (which includes paid holidays, sick leave, and vacation time) to an hours-worked basis. The BLS Hours at Work Survey provided the ratios for years prior to 2000.

To include the self-employed, data from the Current Population Survey (CPS) are used to estimate the number of self-employed workers (partners and proprietors) and their hours. The CPS, a monthly survey of households, counts persons employed, not jobs. Information about primary and secondary jobs for each person is identified and processed separately in order to accurately assign employment and hours estimates to the proper industry and worker category. The CPS-based hours of the self-employed reflect hours worked.

To include employment and hours in other sectors not covered by CES data, other source data are used. Estimates of employment and hours for industries in the farm sector are based on data from the US Department of Agriculture. Measures for industries in the nonfarm agriculture sector are based primarily on data from the CPS, together with data from the BLS Quarterly Census of Employment and Wages (QCEW). For mining industries, estimates of nonproduction worker hours are derived from data collected by the Mine Safety and Health Administration. Employment data for the postal service industry are from the CES survey, but estimates of hours for this industry are from the US Postal Service.

Labor Composition

Accounting for labor composition—that is, adjusting labor input of total hours by industry to reflect differences in time and skill—has become an important component of productivity measurement. The importance of this work has been described by Jorgenson, Gollop, and Fraumeni (1987) and by the BLS (1993), among others. Just as a key component of including heterogeneous types of assets for capital allows for the measurement of not just the increases in investment, but also the shift in investment to asset types with a higher marginal product, similarly, including a labor input measure that captures demographic characteristic improves the MFP measure by not

---

25. "Construction of Average Weekly Hours for Supervisory and Nonproduction Wage and Salary Workers in Detailed Industries," available at http://www.bls.gov/lpc/iprswawhtechnote .pdf.

just capturing an increase in hours worked, but also industry shifts toward higher-skilled workers.

Consequently, we have incorporated labor composition indexes in the quantity measures of labor input in this prototype, integrated account. These measures account for the heterogeneity of the workforce across sex, employment class, age, and education. This approach in measuring labor input is currently used by the BLS in official private business and private nonfarm business productivity, and is being investigated at the industry level.

A labor composition index was generated using the comprehensive set of hours' measures from BLS and labor matrices of demographic characteristics provided by Dale Jorgenson Associates (DJA) consistent with data used in Jorgenson, Ho, and Samuels (2012). The 192 unique demographic categories are divided by gender, class of worker, age (eight categories), and education (six categories).

Using the DJA labor matrices, a set of compensation shares were generated for payrolled workers. These shares were multiplied by the published BEA labor compensation figures to produce a sixty-three-industry set of ninety-six unique demographic categories of compensation for payrolled workers. Similarly, a set of hours' shares were generated and applied to the BLS payrolled worker hours to allocate payrolled hours by industry by ninety-six demographic categories.[26] The payrolled compensation data are consistent with published BEA data and the self-employed compensation estimates are based on the assumption that payrolled employees of a given demographic characteristic will receive similar compensation per hour of work as the self-employed workers.

11.4   Conceptual and Measurement Challenges

While this prototype industry-level production account represents an important step in integrating the national accounts with MFP statistics, concerns and challenges remain. Differences arise, in part, because of the different goals of each agency. The BEA's mission is to promote a better understanding of the US economy by providing the most timely, relevant, and accurate economic accounts, which has led to the development of a set of accounts that provides complete and consistent coverage of the domestic output of the entire economy. The BLS mission has been to provide maximum reliability in its productivity measures using economic concepts

---

26. While detailed data exist for self-employed income from the national accounts, a labor compensation measure for the self-employed does not exist mainly for reasons of conceptual problems. A common assumption in the productivity literature and one adopted by this study is to assume that the payrolled compensation per hour is the same as the self-employed compensation per hour. The BEA adjusted this assumption in two cases where anecdotal evidence suggested that this assumption may not be valid and the results from the model suggested a change; those two industries were NAICS 624–Social Assistance and NAICS Performing Arts, Spectator Sports, Museums, and Related Activities.

and methods that are most appropriate for measuring productivity, and to ensure consistency between its official labor productivity series and multifactor productivity series. As a result, some of the data presented here reflect differences in concepts and coverage from the official BLS productivity data. Some challenges remain, including:

The use of a gross-output concept for measuring MFP in the industry-level production account contrasts with the sectoral industry output approach used in the official productivity measures produced by the BLS. The BLS adjusts output and intermediate inputs to exclude the double-counting that occurs when sales between firms in the same industry or sector are included. Double counting occurs both in the output measure and in the purchased intermediates used to produce that output, and therefore is added identically to both the numerator and denominator of the productivity ratio. Inputs of materials produced and consumed in the same sector are already represented by the inputs used to make them. Counting both the intrasector transaction and the inputs that they embody gives an overstated importance to these inputs relative to other inputs. Additionally, adding the same transactions to both the numerator and denominator of the productivity equation causes productivity change to be dampened.

The production accounts and MFP measures presented here reflect output consistent with GDP for the total economy. These accounts are in keeping with the BEA goal to measure total domestic production. Official BLS productivity measures exclude certain activities because reliable data are lacking to construct output estimates independently of input costs. Estimates for real gross products of general government, private households, and nonprofit institutions are largely based on labor compensation. Owner-occupied housing and rental value of nonprofit equipment and buildings have no adequate measures for corresponding labor inputs. Government enterprises are excluded because subsidies account for a substantial portion of capital income. Therefore, there is no adequate measure of government enterprise capital income in GDP.

Because of these issues, the BLS constructs private business and private nonfarm business MFP measures that exclude from GDP general government, government enterprises, private households, nonprofit institutions, and the rental value of owner-occupied dwellings. The private business sector accounted for approximately 74 percent of gross domestic product in 2010. In the more aggregate sectors, private business and private nonfarm business, the delivery of goods to final users closely corresponds to value-added output. In these measures, output, consisting of only goods and services sold to final consumers, is measured net of price changes and interindustry transactions and the input measure is an aggregate of labor input and capital service flows.

For its total economy production account measures, the BLS replaces the capital consumption allowances that are included in GDP with its own measures of nominal capital services of government and nonprofit assets, therefore altering GDP to account for a more complete estimate of capital services input. This adjustment to GDP is based on recommendations in the Harper et al. (2008) paper on BLS-BEA integrated GDP-productivity accounts.

This prototype confirms a long-standing challenge related to the presence of negative MFP growth within the nonmanufacturing sector, implying the likelihood that some mismeasurement of outputs and/or inputs remains.[27] Long-term declining productivity in such industries as construction, management of companies, rental and leasing services, legal services and other services is counterintuitive and raises questions about the accuracy of the data. Challenges remain in accurately measuring the output of many industries. These results suggest further work by the BEA and BLS to reconcile output differences, as well as work with the US Census Bureau to continue to improve services-sector measurement, including the expansion of business expense data reported on the annual business expenses and services annual surveys, which would be used to improve the measurement of intermediate inputs by industry.

For many of the industries presented here the MFP trends are similar to those published by the BLS, but for some industries these trends differ. Reconciling the reasons for these differences will be part of the ongoing collaborative work of the two agencies.

11.5   Conclusion and Possible Next Steps

This chapter provides an important down payment on an integrated, industry-level production account for the United States. It builds on a long-standing history of collaboration between the BEA and BLS and illustrates the importance of understanding the sources of economic growth, including KLEMS inputs and MFP growth, within an integrated national economic accounts framework, as first described by Jorgenson and Landefeld (2006).

However, much work remains before a BEA/BLS industry-level production account will be released on a regular basis. Challenges to a regular release include an increasingly tough US budgetary resource environment for introducing new initiatives in addition to methodology considerations seeking resolution in future work.

This prototype was prepared absent any new resources at the BEA or BLS, which poses a practical challenge for continuing this initiative in future years. Within the BEA, there are many near-term initiatives to improve the

27. Harper et al. (2010) provide a clear exposition of both the so-called "productivity paradox" of negative multifactor productivity growth as well as some of the improvements that have occurred in services-sector measurement.

accuracy, relevance, and timeliness of its national and industry accounts. For example, Strassner and Wasshausen (2012) recently described the BEA's work on a fiscal year 2013 budget initiative to produce US quarterly GDP by industry on a near "real-time" basis, which currently is also unfunded. Within the BLS, resource constraints and other important initiatives pose a challenge to expanding work in the productivity program. For example, the BLS is also working on developing a prototype for calculating quarterly MFP.

Future work on an integrated, industry-level production account will build on this effort and the upcoming release of the 2013 comprehensive revision of the industry accounts. The 2013 comprehensive revision will include the publication of the 2007 benchmark input-output accounts on a 2007 NAICS basis, fully integrated with the time series of annual industry accounts and NIPAs.[28] This release will mark the completion of "full integration" of the industry accounts with the NIPAs, first described by Lawson et al. (2006). The enhanced integration will allow for a higher degree of consistency among the NIPAs, the benchmark input-output accounts, and the annual industry accounts.

Further work to incorporate a labor composition adjustment at the industry level remains a research item on both the BEA and BLS research agendas. This project makes use of the DJA labor matrices used in similar studies such as that by Jorgenson, Ho, and Samuels (2012). The illustrative adjustments incorporated into this account are based on a good approximation, but further work remains in this area. The BLS is close to finalizing a methodology to incorporate industry labor composition measures into its official major sector manufacturing and NIPA-level industry MFP measures.

This initiative to produce an integrated, industry-level production account, despite budgetary considerations, remains one of the BEA's flagship projects (Moyer 2009). Toward this goal, the BEA has been working to produce an internally consistent industry-level production account, consistent with GDP, that incorporates capital measures based on a set of assumptions that are consistent with the BEA's fixed assets account. Using the assumption that the age-efficiency profile is defined by a constant geometric rate along with similar tax factors as was used in the BLS measure, an alternate capital measure was computed and below is an illustrative example of some of the results that were generated. The age-efficiency assumption implies a geometric pattern in the acquisition price of capital goods as well as a geometric

---

28. Traditionally, the benchmark input-output accounts have been released before the comprehensive revision of the NIPAs, and as a consequence, they have not been fully consistent with the NIPAs and with the annual industry accounts. With this comprehensive revision, the benchmark I-O accounts will be released after the NIPA comprehensive revision, and will be updated to reflect future revisions of the NIPAs and the industry accounts, creating—for the first time—a times series of benchmark input-output accounts for the United States.

Table 11.15   **Preliminary capital input growth rates versus BLS capital input (percent growth)**

	1998–2010		2000–2007		2007–2010		2009–2010	
Description	BEA	BLS	BEA	BLS	BEA	BLS	BEA	BLS
Apparel and leather and allied products	–2.1	–2.2	–2.4	–2.8	–5.0	–3.9	–5.9	–3.8
Furniture and related products	1.1	1.4	1.6	1.5	–3.9	–2.3	–4.3	–3.3
Miscellaneous professional, scientific, and technical	9.0	8.4	8.8	8.6	3.9	3.8	3.1	2.7

rate of economic depreciation, which is consistent with BEA measures of private investment in equipment and software in the NIPAs and in the fixed assets account. Since the age-price profile is geometric, the age efficiency profile must also follow the same geometric pattern.[29]

Table 11.15 presents results for two manufacturing industries and one service sector industry where the rates of capital input growth are similar. Despite the differing assumptions with respect to the capital input model, the two measures are remarkably similar in the time periods evaluated. Since official BLS statistics are available through 2010 and the underlying NIPA data are also available through 2010, growth rates incorporate one extra year of data in this comparison. The MFP produced likely would have yielded similar results as well since the capital input measures would not have differed by much.

29. Jorgenson, Ho, Stiroh (2005, 152).

Appendix

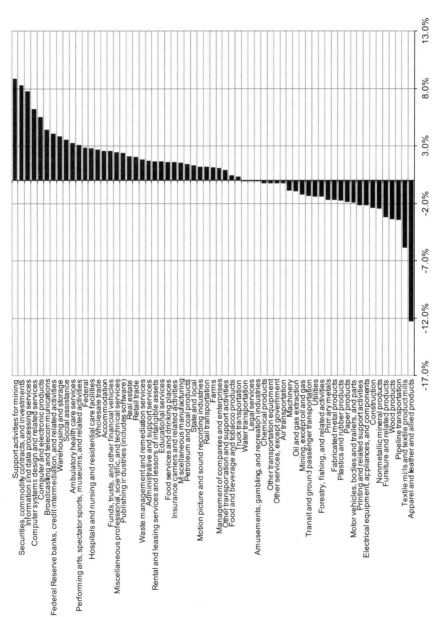

Fig. 11A.1   Output growth, 1998–2010

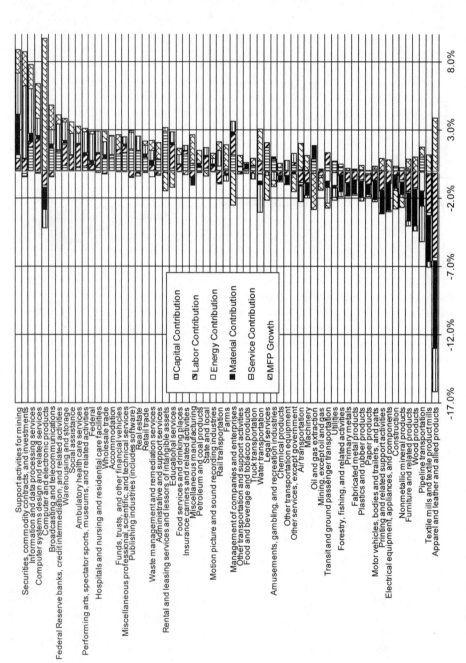

Fig. 11A.2 Output growth by component contribution, 1998–2010

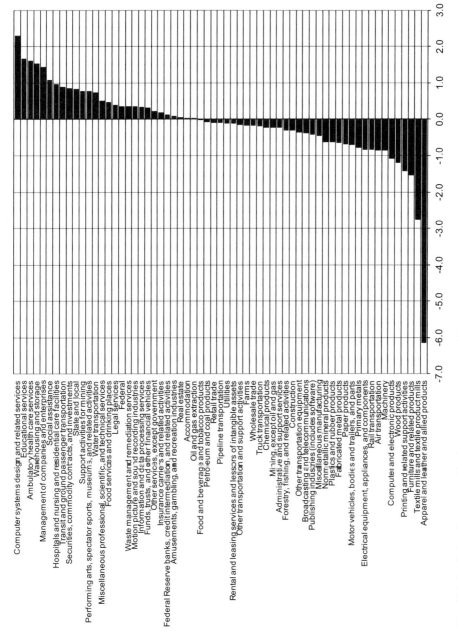

Fig. 11A.3   Labor input contribution to output growth, 1998–2010 (percentage point)

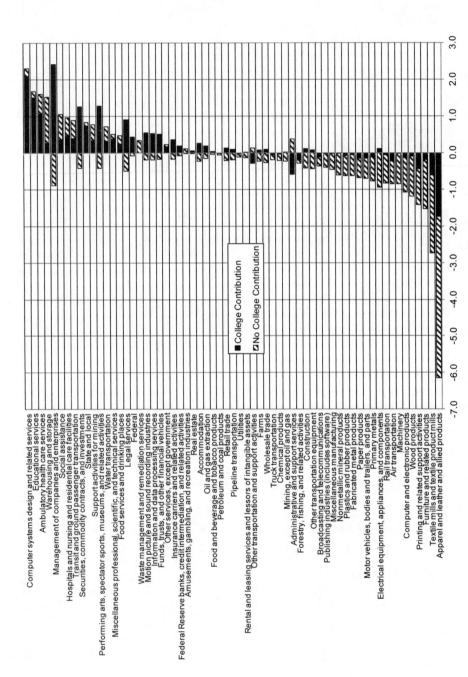

Fig. 11A.4 Labor input contribution to output growth by education, 1998–2010 (percentage point)

356

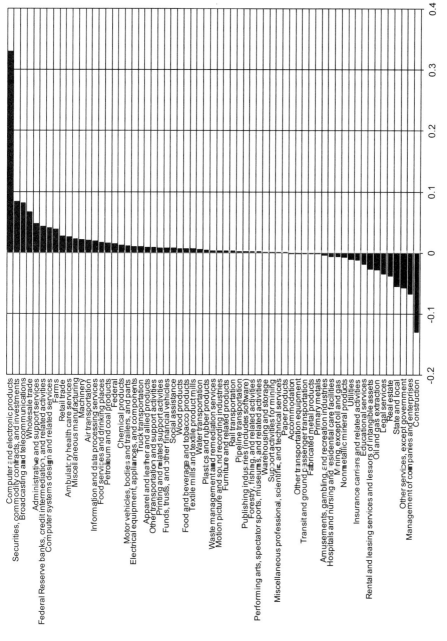

Fig. 11A.5   Contributions to aggregate MFP growth, 1998–2010

357

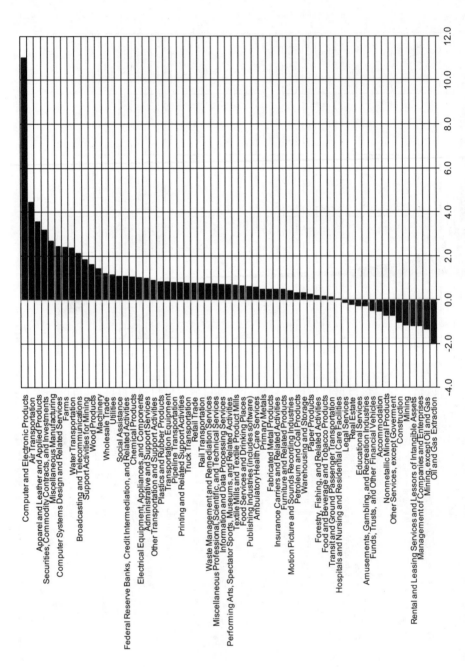

Fig. 11A.6 BLS multifactor productivity growth, 1998–2010

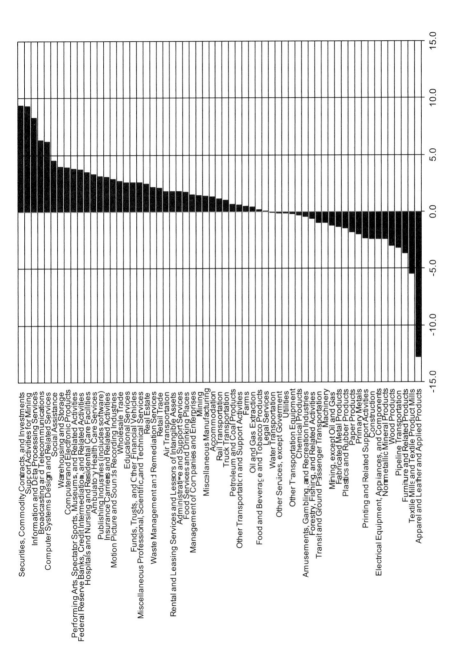

Fig. 11A.7 BLS sectoral output growth, 1998–2010

Table 11A.1   Contributions to aggregate multifactor productivity growth (percentage point)

Description	1998–2000	2000–2007	2007–2010	1998–2010
Farms	0.063	0.012	0.085	0.039
Forestry, fishing, and related activities	0.008	0.008	–0.014	0.002
Oil and gas extraction	–0.123	–0.015	0.010	–0.027
Mining, except oil and gas	0.018	–0.014	–0.002	–0.006
Support activities for mining	0.033	–0.010	0.007	0.001
Utilities	0.111	–0.023	–0.061	–0.010
Construction	–0.059	–0.210	0.014	–0.129
Food and beverage and tobacco products	0.021	0.018	–0.029	0.006
Textile mills and textile product mills	0.008	0.006	0.007	0.006
Apparel and leather and allied products	0.009	0.005	0.016	0.009
Wood products	0.002	0.008	0.009	0.007
Paper products	0.005	0.006	–0.015	0.000
Printing and related support activities	0.005	0.011	0.004	0.008
Petroleum and coal products	–0.013	0.022	0.018	0.015
Chemical products	0.026	0.054	–0.093	0.013
Plastics and rubber products	0.009	0.006	–0.003	0.004
Nonmetallic mineral products	–0.015	–0.006	–0.005	–0.007
Primary metals	0.008	–0.008	0.007	–0.002
Fabricated metal products	0.013	0.008	–0.031	–0.001
Machinery	–0.028	0.028	0.038	0.021
Computer and electronic products	0.600	0.274	0.278	0.329
Electrical equipment, appliances, and components	0.037	0.007	–0.003	0.010
Motor vehicles, bodies and trailers, and parts	–0.024	0.057	–0.070	0.012
Other transportation equipment	0.023	0.014	–0.050	–0.001
Furniture and related products	0.002	0.003	0.003	0.003
Miscellaneous manufacturing	0.034	0.019	0.024	0.023
Wholesale trade	0.179	0.111	–0.114	0.066
Retail trade	–0.021	0.013	0.091	0.027
Air transportation	0.031	0.031	–0.013	0.020
Rail transportation	0.015	0.001	–0.002	0.003
Water transportation	–0.002	0.008	0.005	0.005
Truck transportation	0.024	0.009	0.003	0.010
Transit and ground passenger transportation	0.003	–0.001	–0.003	–0.001
Pipeline transportation	0.017	0.001	–0.003	0.003
Other transportation and support activities	0.005	0.021	–0.018	0.008
Warehousing and storage	–0.006	0.003	0.003	0.001
Publishing industries (includes software)	–0.115	0.041	–0.009	0.002
Motion picture and sound recording industries	–0.036	0.020	–0.011	0.003
Broadcasting and telecommunications	–0.004	0.129	0.026	0.081
Information and data processing services	–0.094	0.057	0.007	0.019
Federal Reserve banks, credit intermediation, and related activities	0.020	–0.006	0.171	0.043
Securities, commodity contracts, and investments	0.167	0.033	0.145	0.084
Insurance carriers and related activities	0.049	–0.024	–0.024	–0.012
Funds, trusts, and other financial vehicles	–0.006	0.010	0.013	0.008
Real estate	0.193	–0.018	–0.235	–0.037
Rental and leasing services and lessors of intangible assets	–0.148	–0.020	0.042	–0.026
Legal services	0.004	–0.041	–0.045	–0.035

Table 11A.1 (continued)

Description	1998–2000	2000–2007	2007–2010	1998–2010
Miscellaneous professional, scientific, and technical services	−0.099	0.008	0.048	0.000
Computer systems design and related services	−0.008	0.048	0.057	0.041
Management of companies and enterprises	−0.008	−0.068	−0.104	−0.067
Administrative and support services	−0.012	0.061	0.057	0.048
Waste management and remediation services	0.007	0.003	0.003	0.004
Educational services	−0.012	−0.018	−0.021	−0.018
Ambulatory health-care services	0.089	−0.001	0.046	0.026
Hospitals and nursing and residential care facilities	−0.018	−0.016	0.027	−0.005
Social assistance	0.000	0.012	0.004	0.008
Performing arts, spectator sports, museums, and related activities	0.011	−0.004	0.010	0.002
Amusements, gambling, and recreation industries	0.002	−0.003	−0.009	−0.004
Accommodation	−0.001	0.008	−0.019	0.000
Food services and drinking places	0.064	0.026	−0.037	0.017
Other services, except government	−0.021	−0.065	−0.059	−0.056
Federal	−0.051	0.028	0.027	0.015
State and local	−0.059	−0.064	−0.029	−0.055
Sum	0.928	0.614	0.171	0.556

Table 11A.2   **Multifactor productivity growth (percent growth)**

Description	1998–2000	2000–2007	2007–2010	1998–2010
Farms	3.0	0.6	3.7	1.8
Forestry, fishing, and related activities	1.8	2.0	−4.9	0.2
Oil and gas extraction	−12.8	−1.0	0.1	−2.7
Mining, except oil and gas	3.2	−2.4	−0.1	−0.9
Support activities for mining	13.2	−1.3	1.0	1.7
Utilities	3.4	−0.5	−2.1	−0.2
Construction	−0.6	−2.2	0.2	−1.3
Food and beverage and tobacco products	0.4	0.4	−0.6	0.1
Textile mills and textile product mills	0.8	1.0	1.8	1.2
Apparel and leather and allied products	1.2	1.3	11.8	3.9
Wood products	0.2	0.9	1.7	1.0
Paper products	0.3	0.5	−1.2	0.0
Printing and related support activities	0.5	1.2	0.6	0.9
Petroleum and coal products	−1.0	1.6	0.6	0.9
Chemical products	0.6	1.2	−1.9	0.3
Plastics and rubber products	0.5	0.4	−0.1	0.3
Nonmetallic mineral products	−1.5	−0.6	−0.4	−0.7
Primary metals	0.4	−0.3	0.3	0.0
Fabricated metal products	0.5	0.4	−1.2	0.0
Machinery	−0.9	1.3	2.0	1.1
Computer and electronic products	12.2	8.5	10.7	9.6
Electrical equipment, appliances, and components	3.0	0.8	−0.6	0.8

(continued)

Table 11A.2 (continued)

Description	1998–2000	2000–2007	2007–2010	1998–2010
Motor vehicles, bodies and trailers, and parts	−0.5	1.4	−2.2	0.2
Other transportation equipment	1.1	0.9	−2.9	0.0
Furniture and related products	0.2	0.5	1.5	0.7
Miscellaneous manufacturing	2.9	1.7	2.3	2.1
Wholesale trade	2.0	1.3	−1.4	0.8
Retail trade	−0.2	0.1	1.1	0.3
Air transportation	2.4	3.2	−1.3	1.9
Rail transportation	3.4	0.3	−0.4	0.6
Water transportation	−0.6	3.3	2.0	2.3
Truck transportation	1.2	0.4	0.3	0.5
Transit and ground passenger transportation	1.0	−0.3	−1.4	−0.4
Pipeline transportation	6.6	0.1	−2.0	0.7
Other transportation and support activities	0.4	2.0	−1.8	0.8
Warehousing and storage	−2.0	0.8	0.6	0.3
Publishing industries (includes software)	−4.5	1.7	−0.4	0.2
Motion picture and sound recording industries	−4.7	2.6	−1.5	0.4
Broadcasting and telecommunications	−0.1	2.8	0.6	1.8
Information and data processing services	−13.0	6.4	0.8	1.8
Federal Reserve banks, credit intermediation, and related activities	0.4	0.0	2.4	0.7
Securities, commodity contracts, and investments	5.3	1.0	4.2	2.5
Insurance carriers and related activities	1.1	−0.6	−0.4	−0.3
Funds, trusts, and other financial vehicles	−0.6	1.3	1.6	1.1
Real estate	1.3	−0.1	−1.5	−0.2
Rental and leasing services and lessors of intangible assets	−7.4	−1.1	2.2	−1.3
Legal services	0.2	−2.1	−2.4	−1.8
Miscellaneous professional, scientific, and technical services	−1.6	0.1	0.7	0.0
Computer systems design and related services	−0.5	3.1	3.2	2.5
Management of companies and enterprises	−0.3	−2.6	−3.8	−2.5
Administrative and support services	−0.3	1.6	1.4	1.2
Waste management and remediation services	1.2	0.7	0.5	0.7
Educational services	−0.9	−1.3	−1.3	−1.2
Ambulatory health-care services	1.9	0.0	0.9	0.5
Hospitals and nursing and residential care facilities	−0.4	−0.3	0.5	−0.1
Social assistance	0.1	1.2	0.4	0.8
Performing arts, spectator sports, museums, and related activities	1.5	−0.4	1.0	0.3
Amusements, gambling, and recreation industries	0.2	−0.3	−1.4	−0.5
Accommodation	−0.1	0.6	−1.1	0.1
Food services and drinking places	1.8	0.7	−1.0	0.5
Other services, except government	−0.5	−1.5	−1.5	−1.3
Federal	−0.8	0.4	0.4	0.2
State and local	−0.5	−0.5	−0.2	−0.4

Table 11A.3   Contributions to output growth, 1998–2010 (percentage point)

Description	Output	Capital	Labor	Energy	Material	Service	MFP
Farms	1.16	0.03	−0.17	0.11	−0.17	−0.43	1.78
Forestry, fishing, and related activities	−1.41	0.27	−0.29	−0.05	−1.21	−0.33	0.21
Oil and gas extraction	−0.95	0.68	0.03	0.16	1.02	−0.17	−2.67
Mining, except oil and gas	−1.21	−0.08	−0.22	−0.03	0.18	−0.14	−0.93
Support activities for mining	8.86	0.13	0.78	0.27	2.98	3.01	1.70
Utilities	−1.40	0.69	−0.11	−0.92	−0.21	−0.67	−0.23
Construction	−2.41	0.34	−0.30	−0.03	−0.93	−0.16	−1.33
Food and beverage and tobacco products	0.42	0.12	−0.01	0.02	0.34	−0.17	0.12
Textile mills and textile product mills	−5.87	−0.29	−2.74	−0.19	−3.40	−0.42	1.17
Apparel and leather and allied products	−12.26	−0.18	−6.14	−0.26	−6.39	−3.20	3.89
Wood products	−3.39	0.01	−1.20	−0.14	−2.68	−0.38	1.00
Paper products	−1.85	−0.28	−0.68	−0.06	−0.69	−0.18	0.04
Printing and related support activities	−2.15	0.01	−1.42	−0.06	−1.59	−0.02	0.92
Petroleum and coal products	1.43	0.31	−0.07	0.01	0.24	−0.06	0.93
Chemical products	−0.23	0.23	−0.22	−0.11	−0.39	−0.07	0.33
Plastics and rubber products	−1.76	0.11	−0.62	−0.12	−1.21	−0.23	0.31
Nonmetallic mineral products	−2.43	0.22	−0.61	−0.17	−0.92	−0.21	−0.73
Primary metals	−1.66	−0.10	−0.77	0.05	−0.92	0.13	−0.04
Fabricated metal products	−1.70	0.07	−0.63	−0.08	−0.95	−0.12	0.03
Machinery	−0.89	0.02	−0.85	−0.04	−0.87	−0.25	1.09
Computer and electronic products	5.52	0.05	−1.08	−0.11	−1.65	−1.35	9.64
Electrical equipment, appliances, and components	−2.17	−0.02	−0.82	−0.06	−1.97	−0.12	0.83
Motor vehicles, bodies and trailers, and parts	−1.94	0.14	−0.70	−0.02	−1.36	−0.18	0.18
Other transportation equipment	−0.24	0.04	−0.35	−0.01	−0.59	0.71	−0.03
Furniture and related products	−3.17	0.15	−1.53	−0.08	−2.02	−0.38	0.69
Miscellaneous manufacturing	1.54	0.40	−0.45	−0.03	−0.60	0.17	2.05
Wholesale trade	2.71	0.92	−0.17	0.00	0.28	0.93	0.76
Retail trade	2.05	0.99	−0.08	−0.03	0.27	0.59	0.31
Air transportation	−0.27	0.09	0.84	−0.16	−0.12	−1.15	1.91
Rail transportation	1.17	0.05	−0.83	0.32	−0.13	1.12	0.65
Water transportation	−0.01	−0.22	0.72	−0.52	−0.27	−2.06	2.32
Truck transportation	0.34	0.35	−0.19	0.03	0.01	−0.38	0.53
Transit and ground passenger transportation	−1.35	0.48	0.88	−0.76	−0.44	−1.14	−0.36
Pipeline transportation	−3.44	1.05	−0.09	−1.37	−1.12	−2.60	0.70
Other transportation and support activities	0.92	−0.05	−0.15	0.28	0.00	0.06	0.80
Warehousing and storage	3.86	0.39	1.52	0.11	0.20	1.37	0.27
Publishing industries (includes software)	2.43	1.62	−0.41	−0.02	−0.09	1.16	0.16
Motion picture and sound recording industries	1.20	−0.08	0.34	0.00	0.16	0.39	0.38

(continued)

363

Table 11A.3 (continued)

Description	Output	Capital	Labor	Energy	Material	Service	MFP
Broadcasting and telecommunications	4.44	1.66	–0.36	–0.01	0.28	1.08	1.79
Information and data processing services	7.81	1.76	0.34	0.03	0.60	3.31	1.77
Federal Reserve banks, credit intermediation, and related activities	4.10	1.38	0.12	0.00	0.03	1.90	0.67
Securities, commodity contracts, and investments	8.33	–0.39	0.85	–0.02	0.10	5.28	2.52
Insurance carriers and related activities	1.59	1.24	0.18	0.00	0.05	0.41	–0.29
Funds, trusts, and other financial vehicles	2.57	1.22	0.32	–0.01	–0.01	–0.04	1.08
Real estate	2.14	1.44	0.05	–0.06	–0.11	1.04	–0.22
Rental and leasing services and lessors of intangible assets	1.69	2.89	–0.11	–0.02	0.00	0.24	–1.31
Legal services	–0.06	1.68	0.39	–0.01	–0.05	–0.27	–1.80
Miscellaneous professional, scientific, and technical services	2.47	1.32	0.51	–0.01	0.14	0.53	0.00
Computer systems design and related services	6.23	–0.13	2.30	–0.01	0.28	1.26	2.52
Management of companies and enterprises	1.11	1.19	1.44	0.00	0.20	0.81	–2.54
Administrative and support services	1.72	0.81	–0.22	0.00	0.04	–0.11	1.22
Waste management and remediation services	1.83	0.05	0.35	–0.43	0.39	0.72	0.73
Educational services	1.65	0.21	1.67	0.03	0.16	0.77	–1.19
Ambulatory health-care services	3.27	0.29	1.60	0.00	0.11	0.73	0.53
Hospitals and nursing and residential care facilities	2.79	0.27	0.96	0.02	0.11	1.57	–0.13
Social assistance	3.60	0.08	1.07	0.02	0.03	1.55	0.85
Performing arts, spectator sports, museums, and related activities	3.09	0.37	0.77	0.03	0.15	1.51	0.26
Amusements, gambling, and recreation industries	–0.10	0.76	0.08	–0.09	0.20	–0.59	–0.46
Accommodation	2.60	0.97	0.03	0.11	0.07	1.36	0.05
Food services and drinking places	1.63	–0.04	0.47	0.01	0.00	0.72	0.45
Other services, except government	–0.26	0.41	0.22	–0.02	–0.18	0.65	–1.33
Federal	2.90	0.10	0.36	0.04	0.26	1.92	0.22
State and local	1.30	0.19	0.83	0.01	0.12	0.55	–0.40

Table 11A.4   **Labor contribution, 1998–2010 (percentage point)**

Description	College labor contribution	No college labor contribution	Labor composition contribution
Farms	0.07	−0.23	−0.17
Forestry, fishing, and related activities	−0.19	−0.09	−0.29
Oil and gas extraction	0.20	−0.16	0.03
Mining, except oil and gas	0.01	−0.23	−0.22
Support activities for mining	0.33	0.45	0.78
Utilities	−0.02	−0.09	−0.11
Construction	0.12	−0.42	−0.30
Food and beverage and tobacco products	0.03	−0.04	−0.01
Textile mills and textile product mills	−0.61	−2.14	−2.74
Apparel and leather and allied products	−1.74	−4.39	−6.14
Wood products	−0.09	−1.10	−1.20
Paper products	−0.15	−0.53	−0.68
Printing and related support activities	−0.43	−0.98	−1.42
Petroleum and coal products	−0.02	−0.05	−0.07
Chemical products	−0.03	−0.18	−0.22
Plastics and rubber products	−0.09	−0.54	−0.62
Nonmetallic mineral products	−0.03	−0.59	−0.61
Primary metals	−0.11	−0.67	−0.77
Fabricated metal products	−0.06	−0.56	−0.63
Machinery	−0.03	−0.82	−0.85
Computer and electronic products	−0.14	−0.93	−1.08
Electrical equipment, appliances, and components	0.12	−0.94	−0.82
Motor vehicles, bodies and trailers, and parts	−0.16	−0.54	−0.70
Other transportation equipment	0.08	−0.43	−0.35
Furniture and related products	−0.18	−1.35	−1.53
Miscellaneous manufacturing	−0.01	−0.43	−0.45
Wholesale trade	0.09	−0.26	−0.17
Retail trade	0.13	−0.21	−0.08
Air transportation	−0.23	−0.61	−0.84
Rail transportation	−0.05	−0.78	−0.83
Water transportation	0.33	0.39	0.72
Truck transportation	−0.05	−0.14	−0.19
Transit and ground passenger transportation	0.40	0.48	0.88
Pipeline transportation	0.09	−0.19	−0.09
Other transportation and support activities	−0.28	0.12	−0.15
Warehousing and storage	0.26	1.27	1.52
Publishing industries (includes software)	−0.03	−0.38	−0.41
Motion picture and sound recording industries	0.55	−0.20	0.34
Broadcasting and telecommunications	−0.12	−0.24	−0.36
Information and data processing services	0.53	−0.19	0.34
Federal Reserve banks, credit intermediation, and related activities	0.19	−0.07	0.12
Securities, commodity contracts, and investments	1.26	−0.41	0.85
Insurance carriers and related activities	0.36	−0.18	0.18
Funds, trusts, and other financial vehicles	0.50	−0.18	0.32
Real estate	0.06	−0.01	0.05

(continued)

365

Table 11A.4 (continued)

Description	College labor contribution	No college labor contribution	Labor composition contribution
Rental and leasing services and lessors of intangible assets	0.02	–0.13	–0.11
Legal services	0.90	–0.50	0.39
Miscellaneous professional, scientific, and technical services	0.37	0.14	0.51
Computer systems design and related services	2.10	0.20	2.30
Management of companies and enterprises	2.42	0.88	1.44
Administrative and support services	–0.59	0.37	–0.22
Waste management and remediation services	0.00	0.34	0.35
Educational services	1.52	0.16	1.67
Ambulatory health-care services	1.07	0.53	1.60
Hospitals and nursing and residential care facilities	0.47	0.48	0.96
Social assistance	0.36	0.70	1.07
Performing arts, spectator sports, museums, and related activities	1.28	–0.41	0.77
Amusements, gambling, and recreation industries	–0.02	0.11	0.08
Accommodation	0.26	–0.22	0.03
Food services and drinking places	0.24	0.23	0.47
Other services, except government	0.17	0.06	0.22
Federal	0.43	–0.08	0.36
State and local	0.74	0.09	0.83

Table 11A.5   Aggregate multifactor productivity growth, sorted by contribution, 1998–2010

Description	2009 value added share	Domar weight	MFP growth	Contribution to aggregate MFP
Computer and electronic products	1.5	0.035	9.6	0.329
Securities, commodity contracts, and investments	1.2	0.033	2.5	0.084
Broadcasting and telecommunications	2.4	0.047	1.8	0.081
Wholesale trade	5.5	0.084	0.8	0.066
Administrative and support services	2.6	0.040	1.2	0.048
Federal Reserve banks, credit intermediation, and related activities	3.8	0.064	0.7	0.043
Computer systems design and related services	1.2	0.016	2.5	0.041
Farms	0.8	0.021	1.8	0.039
Retail trade	6.0	0.096	0.3	0.027
Ambulatory health-care services	3.6	0.050	0.5	0.026
Miscellaneous manufacturing	0.6	0.011	2.1	0.023
Machinery	0.8	0.024	1.1	0.021
Air transportation	0.4	0.011	1.9	0.020
Information and data processing services	0.6	0.009	1.8	0.019
Food services and drinking places	2.1	0.037	0.5	0.017
Petroleum and coal products	0.7	0.030	0.9	0.015
Federal	4.4	0.068	0.2	0.015
Chemical products	1.7	0.044	0.3	0.013
Motor vehicles, bodies and trailers, and parts	0.2	0.039	0.2	0.012
Electrical equipment, appliances, and components	0.4	0.010	0.8	0.010

Table 11A.5   (continued)

Description	2009 value added share	Domar weight	MFP growth	Contribution to aggregate MFP
Truck transportation	0.8	0.019	0.5	0.010
Apparel and leather and allied products	0.1	0.004	3.9	0.009
Other transportation and support activities	0.7	0.010	0.8	0.008
Printing and related support activities	0.2	0.009	0.9	0.008
Funds, trusts, and other financial vehicles	0.2	0.008	1.1	0.008
Social assistance	0.6	0.009	0.8	0.008
Wood products	0.1	0.008	1.0	0.007
Food and beverage and tobacco products	1.6	0.054	0.1	0.006
Textile mills and textile product mills	0.1	0.006	1.2	0.006
Water transportation	0.1	0.003	2.3	0.005
Plastics and rubber products	0.5	0.015	0.3	0.004
Waste management and remediation services	0.3	0.005	0.7	0.004
Motion picture and sound recording industries	0.4	0.007	0.4	0.003
Furniture and related products	0.2	0.006	0.7	0.003
Rail transportation	0.2	0.005	0.6	0.003
Pipeline transportation	0.1	0.002	0.7	0.003
Publishing industries (includes software)	1.0	0.023	0.2	0.002
Forestry, fishing, and related activities	0.2	0.004	0.2	0.002
Performing arts, spectator sports, museums, and related activities	0.5	0.008	0.3	0.002
Warehousing and storage	0.3	0.004	0.3	0.001
Support activities for mining	0.3	0.006	1.7	0.001
Miscellaneous professional, scientific, and technical services	4.7	0.066	0.0	0.000
Paper products	0.4	0.014	0.0	0.000
Accommodation	0.7	0.015	0.1	0.000
Other transportation equipment	0.6	0.017	0.0	−0.001
Transit and ground passenger transportation	0.2	0.002	−0.4	−0.001
Fabricated metal products	0.8	0.023	0.0	−0.001
Primary metals	0.3	0.016	0.0	−0.002
Amusements, gambling, and recreation industries	0.4	0.007	−0.5	−0.004
Hospitals and nursing and residential care facilities	3.3	0.049	−0.1	−0.005
Mining, except oil and gas	0.3	0.005	−0.9	−0.006
Nonmetallic mineral products	0.2	0.009	−0.7	−0.007
Utilities	1.9	0.031	−0.2	−0.010
Insurance carriers and related activities	2.7	0.045	−0.3	−0.012
Educational services	1.1	0.015	−1.2	−0.018
Rental and leasing services and lessors of intangible assets	1.3	0.020	−1.3	−0.026
Oil and gas extraction	0.9	0.014	−2.7	−0.027
Legal services	1.5	0.019	−1.8	−0.035
Real estate	12.0	0.161	−0.2	−0.037
State and local	9.4	0.138	−0.4	−0.055
Other services, except government	2.4	0.042	−1.3	−0.056
Management of companies and enterprises	1.8	0.026	−2.5	−0.067
Construction	3.9	0.091	−1.3	−0.129
Sum	100.0	1.8		0.556

Notes: Value-added share is the share of industry value added to GDP. Domar weights are calculated as a ratio of gross output of an industry to GDP. Aggregate MFP growth calculated as the sum of industry percentage point contributions to aggregate MFP.

Table 11A.6   Contributions to BLS aggregate multifactor productivity growth (percentage point)

Description	1998–2000	2000–2007	2007–2010	1998–2010
Farms	0.11	0.02	0.14	0.06
Forestry, fishing, and related activities	0.01	0.01	−0.02	0.00
Oil and gas extraction	−0.13	−0.02	−0.03	−0.04
Mining, except oil and gas	0.01	−0.02	0.00	−0.01
Support activities for mining	0.05	−0.01	0.01	0.00
Utilities	−0.22	0.10	0.08	0.04
Construction	−0.02	−0.25	0.07	−0.13
Food and beverage and tobacco products	−0.01	0.04	−0.05	0.01
Textile mills and textile product mills	0.01	0.01	−0.01	0.01
Apparel and leather and allied products	0.02	0.01	0.01	0.01
Wood products	0.02	0.01	−0.02	0.00
Paper products	0.00	0.01	0.00	0.01
Printing and related support activities	−0.04	−0.03	0.18	0.02
Petroleum and coal products	0.05	0.10	−0.05	0.05
Chemical products	0.02	0.01	0.02	0.01
Plastics and rubber products	0.01	0.01	0.02	0.01
Nonmetallic mineral products	−0.02	−0.01	0.00	−0.01
Primary metals	0.03	−0.01	0.02	0.00
Fabricated metal products	0.02	0.02	0.01	0.01
Machinery	−0.05	0.05	0.09	0.04
Computer and electronic products	0.81	0.35	0.34	0.43
Electrical equipment, appliances, and components	0.05	0.02	−0.01	0.02
Other transportation equipment	0.02	0.10	−0.01	0.06
Furniture and related products	0.00	0.01	−0.01	0.00
Miscellaneous manufacturing	0.05	0.03	0.05	0.04
Wholesale trade	0.19	0.19	−0.12	0.11
Retail trade	0.02	0.07	0.18	0.09
Air transportation	0.07	0.05	0.02	0.05
Rail transportation	0.02	0.00	0.00	0.00
Water transportation	0.00	0.01	0.01	0.01
Truck transportation	0.04	0.02	0.02	0.02
Transit and ground passenger transportation	0.01	0.00	0.00	0.00
Pipeline transportation	0.02	0.00	0.00	0.01
Other transportation and support activities	0.01	0.03	−0.02	0.01
Warehousing and storage	−0.01	0.00	0.01	0.00
Publishing industries	−0.11	0.08	−0.01	0.03
Motion picture and sound recording industries	−0.05	0.03	−0.01	0.01
Broadcasting and telecommunications	0.02	0.19	0.03	0.12
Information and data processing services	−0.16	0.08	0.01	0.02
Federal Reserve banks, credit intermediation, and related activities	0.09	−0.01	0.24	0.07
Securities, commodity contracts, and investments	0.38	0.08	0.16	0.15
Insurance carriers and related activities	0.14	−0.02	0.03	0.02
Funds, trusts, and other financial vehicles	0.02	−0.01	0.00	0.00
Real estate	0.18	0.06	−0.31	−0.01
Rental and leasing services and lessors of intangible assets	−0.18	−0.02	0.06	−0.03
Legal services	0.03	0.00	−0.02	0.00

Table 11A.6   (continued)

Description	1998–2000	2000–2007	2007–2010	1998–2010
Computer systems design and related services	–0.02	0.06	0.08	0.05
Miscellaneous professional, scientific, and technical services	–0.07	0.04	0.22	0.07
Management of companies and enterprises	0.02	–0.04	–0.10	–0.05
Administrative and support services	0.01	0.07	0.04	0.05
Waste management and remediation services	0.01	0.00	0.00	0.00
Educational services	0.01	–0.01	0.00	0.00
Ambulatory health-care services	0.07	0.02	0.05	0.03
Hospitals and nursing and residential care facilities	0.00	–0.01	0.03	0.00
Social assistance	0.00	0.01	0.01	0.01
Performing arts, spectator sports, museums, and related activities	0.02	0.00	0.01	0.00
Amusements, gambling, and recreation industries	0.01	0.00	–0.01	0.00
Accommodation	0.03	–0.01	–0.03	–0.01
Food services and drinking places	0.05	0.03	–0.01	0.02
Other services, except government	0.04	–0.05	–0.04	–0.03
Total NMF Contributions	**0.59**	**0.72**	**0.63**	**0.68**
Total MFG Contribution	**0.93**	**0.72**	**0.49**	**0.70**
Private Business MFP	**1.79**	**1.44**	**0.45**	**1.25**

Table 11A.7   **BLS multifactor productivity growth (percent growth-BLS data)**

Description	1998–2000	2000–2007	2007–2010	1998–2010
Farms	4.1	0.7	5.1	2.4
Forestry, fishing, and related activities	1.6	2.6	–6.0	0.2
Oil and gas extraction	–9.3	–0.6	–0.2	–2.0
Mining, except oil and gas	1.3	–2.5	–0.5	–1.3
Support activities for mining	14.3	–1.2	1.1	1.8
Utilities	–6.2	2.9	2.3	1.2
Construction	–0.2	–2.0	0.7	–1.0
Food and beverage and tobacco products	–0.1	0.7	–0.8	0.2
Textile mills and textile product mills	0.9	1.6	–1.7	0.7
Apparel and leather and allied products	2.6	4.2	2.6	3.6
Wood products	0.8	1.0	3.6	1.6
Paper products	0.7	0.7	–1.2	0.3
Printing and related support activities	0.1	1.3	0.0	0.8
Petroleum and coal products	–2.8	0.4	2.3	0.3
Chemical products	1.0	1.9	–0.9	1.0
Plastics and rubber products	0.7	0.6	1.5	0.8
Nonmetallic mineral products	–1.7	–0.7	–0.1	–0.7
Primary metals	1.9	–0.4	1.7	0.5
Fabricated metal products	0.6	0.6	0.1	0.5
Machinery	–1.4	1.6	2.9	1.4

(continued)

Table 11A.7   (continued)

Description	1998–2000	2000–2007	2007–2010	1998–2010
Computer and electronic products	14.1	9.9	11.7	11.0
Electrical equipment, appliances, and				
components	3.6	1.4	–1.6	1.0
Other transportation equipment	0.3	1.7	–0.9	0.8
Furniture and related products	0.4	1.1	–0.9	0.5
Miscellaneous manufacturing	3.2	2.0	4.1	2.7
Wholesale trade	2.0	2.1	–1.4	1.2
Retail trade	0.2	0.6	1.6	0.8
Air transportation	5.4	5.3	1.8	4.5
Rail transportation	3.4	0.4	–0.2	0.7
Water transportation	–0.7	3.4	2.0	2.4
Truck transportation	1.7	0.6	0.6	0.8
Transit and ground passenger transportation	3.3	–0.2	–1.1	0.1
Pipeline transportation	7.2	0.2	–1.9	0.8
Other transportation and support activities	0.8	2.0	–1.6	0.9
Warehousing and storage	–1.8	0.6	1.0	0.3
Publishing industries	–4.1	2.4	–0.4	0.6
Motion picture and sound recording industries	–7.5	3.7	–1.7	0.4
Broadcasting and telecommunications	0.4	3.3	0.5	2.1
Information and data processing services	–15.3	5.6	1.1	0.7
Federal Reserve banks, credit intermediation,				
and related activities	1.6	0.0	3.3	1.1
Securities, commodity contracts, and investments	8.6	2.0	2.5	3.2
Insurance carriers and related activities	4.7	–1.0	1.1	0.5
Funds, trusts, and other financial vehicles	1.3	–0.7	–1.2	–0.5
Real estate	2.1	0.6	–3.6	–0.2
Rental and leasing services and lessors of				
intangible assets	–7.0	–1.0	2.4	–1.2
Legal services	1.3	–0.1	–1.0	–0.1
Computer systems design and related services	–1.1	3.1	3.3	2.4
Miscellaneous professional, scientific, and				
technical services	–0.9	0.5	2.4	0.7
Management of companies and enterprises	0.6	–1.1	–2.5	–1.2
Administrative and support services	0.1	1.3	0.9	1.0
Waste management and remediation services	1.4	0.7	0.5	0.7
Educational services	0.9	–0.8	0.1	–0.3
Ambulatory health-care services	1.2	0.3	0.8	0.6
Hospitals and nursing and residential care				
facilities	–0.1	–0.3	0.7	0.0
Social assistance	0.0	1.4	1.0	1.1
Performing arts, spectator sports, museums, and				
related activities	3.1	0.1	0.5	0.7
Amusements, gambling, and recreation industries	1.3	–0.5	–0.8	–0.3
Accommodation	1.7	–0.7	–1.7	–0.5
Food services and drinking places	1.5	0.8	–0.2	0.6
Other services, except government	0.8	–1.0	–1.0	–0.7

References

Advisory Committee on Measuring Innovation in the 21st Century Economy. 2008. "Innovation Measurement: Tracking the State of Innovation in the American Economy." January. Washington, DC: US Department of Commerce.

Bureau of Labor Statistics. 1993. *Labor Composition and US Productivity Growth, 1948–1990.* Washington, DC: US Government Printing Office.

———. 2012. "Multifactor Productivity Trends in Manufacturing, 2010." June 26. www.bls.gov/news.release/pdf/prod5.pdf.

Fraumeni, Barbara M., Michael J. Harper, Susan G. Powers, and Robert E. Yuskavage. 2006. "An Integrated BEA/BLS Production Account: A First Step and Theoretical Considerations." In *A New Architecture for the US National Accounts*, edited by Dale W. Jorgenson, J. Steven Landefeld, and William D. Nordhaus, 355–438. Chicago: University of Chicago Press.

Gilmore, Teresa L., Amanda S. Lyndaker, Sarah J. Pack, and Simon N. Randrianrarivelo. 2011. "Annual Industry Accounts: Revised Statistics for 2003–2010." *Survey of Current Business* 91 (December): 15–27.

Harper, Michael, Bhavani Khandrika, Randal Kinoshita, and Steven Rosenthal. 2010. "Nonmanufacturing Industry Contributions to Multifactor Productivity, 1987–2006." *Monthly Labor Review* 133 (June): 16–31.

Harper, Michael, Brent Moulton, Steven Rosenthal, and Dave Wasshausen. 2009. "Integrated GDP-Productivity Accounts." *American Economic Review* 99 (2): 74–9.

Jorgenson, Dale W. 2012. "The World KLEMS Initiative." *International Productivity Monitor* (November):5–19.

Jorgenson, Dale W., Frank Gollop, and Barbara Fraumeni. 1987. *Productivity and US Economic Growth.* Cambridge, MA: Harvard University Press.

Jorgenson, Dale W., Mun S. Ho, and Jon Samuels. 2012. "A Prototype Industry-Level Production Account for the United States, 1947–2010." Paper for the 2nd World KLEMS Conference, Harvard University, Cambridge, Massachusetts, August 9–10.

Jorgenson, Dale W., Mun S. Ho, and Kevin Stiroh. 2005. *Productivity, Information Technology and the American Growth Resurgence, Vol. 3.* Cambridge, MA: The MIT Press.

Jorgenson, Dale W., and J. Steven Landefeld. 2006. "Blueprint for Expanded and Integrated US Accounts: Review, Assessment, and Next Steps." In *A New Architecture for the US National Accounts*, edited by Dale W. Jorgenson, J. Steven Landefeld, and William D. Nordhaus, 13–112. Chicago: University of Chicago Press.

Lawson, Ann M., Brian C. Moyer, Sumiye Okubo, and Mark A. Planting. 2006. "Integrating Industry and National Economic Accounts: First Steps and Future Improvements." In *A New Architecture for the US National Accounts*, edited by Dale W. Jorgenson, J. Steven Landefeld, and William D. Nordhaus, 215–61. Chicago: University of Chicago Press.

Mayerhauser, Nicole M., and Erich H. Strassner. 2010. "Preview of the Comprehensive Revision of the Annual Industry Accounts: Changes in Definitions, Classifications, and Statistical Methods." *Survey of Current Business* 90 (March): 21–34.

Moyer, Brian C. 2009. "Future Directions for the Industry Accounts." *Survey of Current Business* 89 (June): 29–32.

Moyer, Brian C., Mark A. Planting, Mahnaz Fahim-Nader, and Sherlene K. S. Lum. 2004. "Preview of the Comprehensive Revision of the Annual Industry Accounts:

Integrating the Annual Input-Output Accounts and the Gross-Domestic-Product-by-Industry Accounts." *Survey of Current Business* 84 (March): 38–51.

National Academy of Sciences. 1979. *Measurement and Interpretation of Productivity*. Washington, DC: National Research Council.

Schreyer, Paul. 2001. *Productivity Manual: A Guide to the Measurement of Industry-Level and Aggregate Productivity Growth*. Paris: Organisation for Economic Co-operation and Development.

———. 2009. *OECD Manual: Measuring Capital*. Paris: Organisation for Economic Co-operation and Development.

Strassner, Erich H., Gabriel W. Medeiros, and George M. Smith. 2005. "Annual Industry Accounts: Introducing KLEMS Input Estimates for 1997–2003." *Survey of Current Business* 85 (September): 31–65.

Strassner, Erich H., and David B. Wasshausen. 2012. "Prototype Quarterly Statistics on US Gross Domestic Product by Industry, 2007–2011." *Survey of Current Business* 92 (June): 49–65.

United Nations, Commission of the European Communities, International Monetary Fund, Organisation for Economic Co-operation and Development, and World Bank. 2009. *System of National Accounts 2008*. New York: United Nations.

Toward the Development of Sectoral Financial Positions and Flows in a From-Whom-to-Whom Framework

Manik Shrestha

12.1 Introduction

In the wake of the 2008 financial and economic crisis, the G-20 economies asked the Financial Stability Board (FSB) and the International Monetary Fund (IMF) to identify data gaps shedding light on economic and financial vulnerabilities, and make recommendations whose implementation by countries would close those gaps. The FSB and IMF came up with twenty recommendations covering a wide range of economic and financial statistics. The IMF and the FSB undertook extensive consultations with users and compilers of economic and financial statistics[1] and produced a set of recommendations structured around four themes: buildup of risks in the financial sector, cross-border financial linkages, vulnerability of domestic economies to shocks, and improving communication of official statistics.[2] These data initiatives are known as the G-20 Data Gaps Initiative[3] (DGI) that has been

Manik Shrestha is lead statistical methodologist in the Statistics Department of the International Monetary Fund.

I would like to thank Segismundo Fassler and Reimund Mink for their collaboration with me to prepare an IMF working paper (WP/12/57) titled "An Integrated Framework for Financial Positions and Flows on a From-Whom-to-Whom Basis: Concepts, Current Status, and Prospects" (see Shrestha, Mink, and Fassler 2012). This chapter is a sequel to this IMF working paper. The views expressed here are those of the author and should not be attributed to the IMF, its executive board, or its management. For acknowledgments, sources of research support, and disclosure of the author's material financial relationships, if any, please see http://www.nber.org/chapters/c12835.ack.

1. For instance, the senior officials conference of July 2009, the papers for which are available at http://www.imf.org/external/np/seminars/eng/2009/usersconf/index.htm. Information on subsequent global conferences is available at http://www.imf.org/external/data.htm.

2. For a brief description of current status and policy relevance of these data initiatives, see Heath (2013).

3. See http://www.imf.org/external/np/g20/pdf/102909.pdf and www.imf.org/external/data.htm#add.

endorsed by the G-20 finance ministers and central bank governors[4] and the IMF's International Monetary and Financial Committee. To coordinate the work among the international agencies, the IMF set up the Inter-Agency Group on Economic and Financial Statistics (IAG).[5]

Recommendation 15 of the DGI calls for developing "a strategy to promote the compilation and dissemination of the balance sheet approach, flow of funds, and sectoral data more generally, starting with the G-20 economies." The objective of Recommendation 15 is to expand the dissemination and reporting of internationally comparable and detailed full sequence of national accounts by institutional sectors on an annual and quarterly basis by both G-20 economies as well as non-G-20 advanced and emerging market economies. This expansion would involve improving the compilation of sectoral national accounts in terms of details (subsectors and asset details), closing data gaps, and developing financial positions and flows on a *from-whom-to-whom* basis. This chapter emphasizes the development of integrated macroeconomic accounts that relate income, current expenditures, disposable income, saving, investment in nonfinancial assets and financial assets, revaluation and other changes in assets and liabilities, changes in net worth, and balance sheets. The chapter, however, focuses on the implementation of sectoral financial positions and flows on a from-whom-to-whom basis.

The functioning of economic and financial systems involves interactions/ exchanges and debtor/creditor relationships among all economic entities that may have different motivations and functions, engage in different activities, and have different behaviors. With the increasing role of domestic and international markets, which are becoming more complex, sophisticated, and integrated as well as innovating new products and services, the nature and intensity of interrelationships and linkages among and within groups of entities (subsectors) and among and within the various functions (for example, production, consumption, capital accumulation, and financial investment) are also going through drastic transformations. It is, therefore, imperative to understand not only the characteristics of a subsector or a function, but also the interlinkages among the subsectors and functions. The analytic and policy responses related to a subsector or a function should take into account the intended and unintended implications on other subsectors and functions. Only an integrated statistical framework that presents

4. The Communiqué of Finance Ministers and Central Bank Governors of the G-20, Mexico City, Mexico, November 4–5, 2012, states that "Recognizing the need for adequate statistical resources, we endorse the progress report of the FSB and the IMF on closing information gaps, and in particular look forward to the implementation of the data reporting templates for global systemically important financial institutions." http://www.g20mexico.org.

5. The members of the IAG are the Bank for International Settlements (BIS), the European Central Bank (ECB), Eurostat, the IMF (Chair), the Organisation for Economic Co-operation and Development (OECD), the United Nations Statistics Division (UNSD), and the World Bank. This work is undertaken in consultation with the FSB.

macroeconomic statistics for all sectors and subsectors in a consistent way can meet the analytic and policy needs for information arising from highly interconnected economic and financial systems.

Academics, analysts, and policymakers have given increasing attention to the balance sheets and wealth of the economic sectors because financial and economic crises are characterized by abrupt revaluations or other changes in the capital positions of key sectors of the economy. The data of interest thus comprise not only the balance sheets but also the accumulation accounts for each economic sector within an economy, showing the level as well as the change in sectoral balance sheet positions broken down into three of the principal types of flows in the System of National Accounts (SNA): changes in position arising from transactions, revaluations, and other changes in the volume of assets. Although sectoral balance sheets and accumulation accounts, integrated with sectoral current accounts showing production, income and current expenditure flows, are envisaged in the present and two previous national accounting standards, their implementation has been uneven even among the advanced economies.

The global crisis of 2008 highlighted particularly the need to understand financial interconnectedness among the various sectors of an economy and between them and their counterparties in the rest of the world. This kind of analysis has been most seriously hampered by the lack of adequate data among the G-20 economies. Although some recent improvements in the development of statistical methodologies and data availability have supported the compilation of partial financial balance sheet and accumulation account data on a from-whom-to-whom basis, a fully integrated approach for sectoral financial positions and flows within the macroeconomic statistics framework is yet to be achieved. Thus, Recommendation 15 also implies, through its reference to compiling "flow of funds" statistics, compilation of breakdowns of the financial positions and flows of each economic sector by its counterparty sectors. Data sets providing this kind of information are said to provide "from-whom-to-whom" financial statistics, also known as "three-dimensional approach for presenting financial statistics that provide both debtor and creditor information for each financial instrument."

The SNA provides an integrated framework for developing sectoral financial positions and flows on a from-whom-to-whom basis because its underlying principles ensure that the linkages of the economic and financial actions of an economy are captured.[6] However, the SNA's standard presentation is not explicitly designed to show the intersectoral linkages, as traditionally it has focused primarily on answering "who does what," but not "who does what with whom." As the SNA is the internationally

---

6. In 2008 the United Nations Statistical Commission approved the *System of National Accounts 2008* (*2008 SNA*). The final version of the 2008 SNA was released by the UN in September 2009 on its external website at http://unstats.un.org/unsd/nationalaccount/sna2008.asp.

accepted methodology for the compilation of the national accounts, the lack of prominence it gives to the from-whom-to-whom principle for data compilation and presentation may be one of the reasons why these statistics are not more widely available.

Promoting the implementation of the SNA sectoral accounts with from-whom-to-whom intersectoral relationships for financial positions and flows is thus an important step in filling one of the most significant data gaps identified during the 2008 global crisis. The integrated framework on a from-whom-to-whom basis allows answering questions like "Who is financing whom, in what amount, and with which type of financial instrument?" A key lesson from the 2008 global crisis is that understanding the balance sheet strength of an entity or a subsector alone is not sufficient. It is also important to understand risks, vulnerabilities, and spillover effects arising from the financial interconnection. Regarding the allocation of income, it also permits tracing who is paying/receiving income (e.g., interest) to/from whom. The from-whom-to-whom compilation approach also enhances the quality and consistency of data by providing a systematic tool for cross-checking, data validation, and balancing opportunities as well as filling data gaps.

Countries are at different stages of implementation of the sectoral accounts and balance sheets. Designing and implementing changes to or initiating new data collection systems are costly and priorities must therefore be established among the various potential improvements. Implementation of sectoral financial positions and flows on a from-whom-to-whom basis is considered to be the most challenging in terms of resource requirements and data collection. Further, more detailed data on a counterparty basis implies a need to address the issue of confidentiality, especially for small economies or highly specialized economies.

The flexibility provided by the SNA in terms of the level of detail of data compilation and presentation should also allow the use of this framework to comply with the requirements of other analytical tools for the assessment of financial vulnerabilities and risks. One such tool is the IMF's balance sheet approach (BSA) that provides a breakdown of counterparty positions in financial assets and liabilities by maturity and currency (domestic and foreign).

Following this introduction, section 12.2 of this chapter elaborates how the SNA can provide an integrated framework for compiling sectoral financial positions and flows on a from-whom-to-whom basis and ensure consistency among the different domains of the macroeconomic accounts. Section 12.3 describes developments in accounting on a from-whom-to-whom basis. Section 12.4 discusses the initiatives at the international and country levels for the implementation of the integrated sectoral national accounts and balance sheets. Section 12.5 contains some preliminary thoughts on implementing the three-dimensional approach for compiling data on sectoral financial positions and flows, and section 12.6 provides some concluding remarks.

12.2 The SNA Integrated Accounts

12.2.1 Depicting the Economy: Relationships between Economic Agents
through Economic and Financial Flows and Financial Positions

Understanding the functioning of an economy requires a comprehensive
picture of the economic actions covering all aspects of the economic and
financial activities. The main economic activities take place in the spheres
of production, income distribution and use, and accumulation. On a sche-
matic form the economic cycle can be described as follows: the economic
agents interact in the production of goods and services, the income generated in production is distributed among the participants in this process
between capital and labor contributions, a redistribution of income among
the economic agents is made through current transfers, income is used for
consumption or saving, and savings plus net capital transfers received provide own sources for financing investment ("real" and financial). If own
financing resources are lower than the funds needed for real investment,
the deficit of funds is filled by incurring financial liabilities and/or disposing of financial assets (net borrowing). Correspondingly, if own financing
resources exceed the funds needed for real investment, the surplus is reflected
in acquisitions of additional financial assets and/or the extinguishing of
liabilities (net lending).

Economic entities with a surplus of funds will acquire financial assets or
extinguish their liabilities or both. Entities with a deficit of financing will
incur liabilities or be obliged to dispose financial assets to fill the financing
gap. In other words, economic actions taken place in the "real" sphere of
the economy have consequences in the "financial" sphere. A debtor/creditor
relationship is established between entities with a financing gap (borrowers)
and those with excess funds (the creditors). In the recent periods, the debtor/
creditor relationships created within the financial markets for speculative
purposes have grown substantially and become more complex.

The SNA provides an integrated statistical framework for presenting relationships between economic flows in the real and the financial spheres of the
economy as well as the debtor/creditor relationships. The quadruple-entry
consistency imposed on the data, while ensuring conceptual consistency,
creates practical challenges for compilers due to inevitable data gaps and
differences (both conceptual and other; for example, coverage, details, frequency, and timeliness) among data sources and between micro- and macro-
accounting. Particularly with respect to the data consistency between real
and financial transactions (net lending/borrowing derived from nonfinancial
transactions with that derived from financial transactions), country practices show the strength of the statistical framework for developing vertical
(for example, the relationship between real and financial transactions for a
subsector) and horizontal (for example, claims of all holders of a debt secu-

rity on its issuers) consistency methods to enhance data quality. Achievements in the adoption of uniform business accounting standards and public sector accounting standards as well as the consistency between these two will contribute to the consistency of the macroaccounts. Still, it should be kept in mind that accounting standards are geared toward individual units and therefore not necessarily assure interunit consistency. Close collaboration among the various data collection systems is being emphasized more to ensure data consistency. Data consistency should, therefore, be addressed at all stages of data collection and compilation. It should be recognized that it may not be possible to resolve some discrepancies within a given statistical infrastructure. In such a case, the discrepancies should be shown explicitly, causes for them should be explained, their development should be closely monitored, and plans for possible resolution should be adopted.

The SNA follows the residence approach to record flows and positions of institutional units, grouped into sectors and subsectors, resident in an economy between them and with nonresidents. It may not be able to provide for full risk-based measures for macroprudential analysis and for financial stability purposes particularly when cross-border operations (through branches and subsidiaries) controlled by home country entities grow in significance.

In the wake of the 2008 global crisis a need has been identified for the development of statistics on a worldwide-group-consolidated basis—showing also the cross-border financial activities of corporate groups including potentially intragroup flows and positions as formulated in Recommendation 13 of the G-20 report mentioned earlier.[7] Large groups of financial or nonfinancial corporations or conglomerates exist whereby a parent corporation controls several subsidiaries, some of which may control subsidiaries of their own, and so on. Therefore, the concept of a corporate group deviates from the grouping or aggregating of institutional units to an institutional sector as the corporate group concept puts together institutional units based on the concept of control. Such an approach complements the macroeconomic analysis based on the SNA approach.

12.2.2   What the SNA Offers to Ensure the Integrated Framework

The SNA offers the following attributes to ensure that it provides an integrated framework for capturing and presenting macroeconomic statistics on a residency basis:

1. The SNA includes all resident institutional units grouped into subsectors and sectors and nonresident institutional units grouped into the rest of the world.

---

7. See the FSB/IMF reports on the G-20 Data Gaps Initiative mentioned in footnote 3.

2. The SNA includes all economic flows and stocks of resident institutional (sub)sectors and between residents and nonresidents.

3. The SNA applies a consistent set of accounting principles, concepts, and classifications.

4. The SNA uses uniform accounting structures for all resident institutional units grouped into subsectors and sectors and for the rest of the world.

A brief description of each of these attributes is given below.

Institutional Units and Sectors and Subsectors

Institutional units, according to the SNA, are the economic units that can engage in transactions and can own assets and incur liabilities on their own behalf. Institutional units are grouped together into institutional sectors, based on their functions, behavior, and objectives. The SNA distinguishes five main institutional sectors (nonfinancial corporations, financial corporations, general government, households, and nonprofit institutions serving households). It also provides for a hierarchical classification for further dividing the sectors into subsectors.

However, it should be kept in mind that if data on detailed institutional sectors are to be compiled for financial positions and flows on a from-whom-to-whom basis, the breakdown of the data by sector and subsector is an important feature for analyzing creditor/debtor relationships. A further breakdown of the main SNA institutional sectors may therefore be necessary. The further subsectoral breakdowns of the financial corporations may be of importance given that they are at the center of the analysis of financial risks, vulnerabilities, and spillovers arising from their role in financial intermediation, the size of their assets holdings and liabilities, and the variety of financial instruments in their portfolios. For the financial corporations sector, the 2008 SNA recommends nine subsectors (central bank, deposit-taking corporations other than central bank, money market funds [MMF], non-MMF investment funds, other financial corporations except insurance and pension funds, financial auxiliaries, captive financial institutions and money lenders, insurance corporations, and pension funds). Any corporate sector or subsector can be further classified into public, foreign controlled, and national private enterprises. The general government may be further divided into central, state, and local governments and social security can be identified separately for the general government as a whole or at each level of government. The implementation of the DGI for sectoral national accounts emphasizes more detailed sectoral breakdowns, particularly for subsectors of financial corporations (given the increased role of nonbank financial institutions) and separate reporting of public sector nonfinancial and financial sectors.

Economic Flows and Stocks

The SNA uses a set of economic flows and stocks for describing the economic and financial activities of resident economic entities and of the rest of the world.

Economic flows are classified into transactions and other economic flows. Transactions cover economic actions between two economic entities by mutual agreement. The SNA also considers some economic actions undertaken within an economic unit as a transaction (e.g., an increase in inventories of own-produced output by a producer unit).

Economic flows that are not a result of transactions are called "other economic flows" in the SNA terminology. These flows are of two types: other changes in the volume of assets and liabilities, and revaluations. Other changes in the volume of assets and liabilities reflect changes affecting the wealth of an economic entity as a result of the appearance or disappearance of assets/liabilities (for example, losses from natural disasters or write off of a debt by the creditor). Revaluations (also known as holding gains and losses) reflect changes in the value of assets and liabilities due to changes in their prices, including exchange rates.

The balance sheet records stocks of nonfinancial assets and financial assets and liability positions. The stocks/positions are changed through transactions and other economic flows. Although the SNA recommends a standard classification of financial assets and liabilities for flows and positions that provides the basis for the comparison of data across countries, it also recognizes that further breakdowns of assets and liabilities may be required to meet specific analytical needs and country-specific circumstances. In particular, remaining maturity and currency breakdowns have become more important for analyzing maturity and currency mismatches.

Accounting Principles

Accounting principles determine the bookkeeping conventions and entries, time of recording, and valuation.

Double and Quadruple Entry Accounting. As in business accounting, entries for an entity follow the double entry principle to register a transaction. Thus, for the entity undertaking the action there should be one entry as a debit and one as a credit for exactly the same value, ensuring vertical consistency of all transactions for this entity. It follows that when there is a transaction between two institutional units the double entry accounting principle implies that four entries are required in the accounts (two for each institutional unit carrying out the transaction) leading to a quadruple entry system. The quadruple entry accounting ensures vertical consistency (debits and credits for all transactions for an institutional unit are equal), horizontal consistency (debit entries of a transaction type for all entities are equal to the credit entries of that transaction type for all counterpart entities), and consistency in the counterparty relationship.

The quadruple entry accounting provides the underlying basis for developing data on a from-whom-to-whom basis.[8] However, the SNA accounting structure (as described below) is not built to make explicit the relationship between two parties in a transaction as it aggregates (for each sector or the economy as a whole) all transactions of the same kind without distinguishing with whom these transactions take place.[9]

Time of Recording. One implication of the quadruple entry accounting principle is that entries related to a transaction and other economic flow should be recorded at the same time in the various accounts of the system for all counterparties involved. The SNA uses the accrual principle of accounting; that is, transactions between institutional units are to be recorded when claims and obligations arise, are transferred, transformed, or extinguished.

Valuation. The quadruple entry principle also implies that entries for a transaction as well as financial positions should be recorded at the same value for the counterparties involved. Thus, a financial asset and its counterpart liability are recorded for the same amount in the debtor and the creditor accounts. Transactions are recorded at the current market prices at the time the transaction takes place and positions are recorded at the point of time the balance sheet refers to.

Concepts and Classifications

The SNA concepts and definitions are drawn from economic theories and are applied consistently throughout the system. The SNA integrated accounts (transactions, other economic flows, and balance sheets) are built on the systematic classification of the following three pillars: (a) institutional units and (sub)sectors, (b) transactions and other flows, and (c) assets and liabilities. The SNA uses concepts of economic territory, production boundary, and asset boundary to define the scope of resident entities, transactions, other economic flows, nonfinancial assets, and financial assets and liabilities.

---

8. The principle of quadruple entry also allows the recording of transactions involving more than two parties. Cases in example are the trade of securities or other negotiable financial instruments on secondary markets and the assumption of guaranteed debt by the guarantor. In both cases three parties are involved—the two transactors as creditors and the debtor in the first case, and the guarantor, the original debtor, and the creditor in the second case.

9. Financial transactions between resident units are balanced by definition; that is, total (net) acquisition of assets is equal to total (net) incurrence of liabilities, therefore for the economy net acquisition of financial assets minus net incurrence of liabilities represent the net lending to (borrowing from) the rest of the world. Transactions between residents and nonresidents are shown in the accounts of the rest of the world, which records the financial transactions at a consolidated level of financial assets and liabilities without a breakdown by creditor sector or debtor sector.

Accounting Structure

The accounting structure of the SNA is used to organize and present data on transactions, other economic flows, and stocks of assets and liabilities for the sectors and subsectors of an economy and the rest of the world.

The sequence of accounts on current transactions records consistently the production and generation, distribution and use of income, with savings as a balancing item. The sequence of current accounts is followed by the accumulation accounts. While all changes in assets, liabilities, and net worth are included in the accumulation accounts, the corresponding positions are shown in the balance sheet. The balance sheet comprises three elements: (a) nonfinancial assets (b) financial asset and liability positions, and (c) net worth as the balancing item between assets and liabilities. Drawing up a balance sheet makes it possible to focus on the net worth of a sector or subsector of an economy and how it changes over time. Accordingly, the change in net worth is composed of saving, net capital transfers receivable, holding gains less holding losses, and other (net) changes in the volume of assets or liabilities. Table 12.1 shows how transactions, other flows, and positions are presented in the SNA.

Flows and positions as presented in the SNA are somewhat incomplete as they cover only the flow accounts and balance sheets by (sub)sector without

Table 12.1   **Flows and stocks/positions as presented in the SNA**

		Transactions	Other flows	Stocks/positions
Current account		Production of goods and services, generation, distribution, redistribution, and use of income		
Accumulation accounts	Capital account	Net acquisition of nonfinancial assets, saving and capital transfers		
	Financial account	Net acquisition of financial assets and net incurrence of liabilities		
	Revaluation account		Revaluation of assets and liabilities	
	Other changes in the volume of assets account		Other changes in volume of assets and liabilities	
Balance sheet				Nonfinancial assets. financial assets and liabilities, and net worth as a balancing item

detailed data by counterparty (sub)sector. That is, although they show which institutional sectors are acquiring assets, and what financial assets they are transacting in, they do not identify the sectors that incur the corresponding liabilities. Similarly, while they enable net borrowing sectors to be identified, and show how they borrow, the accounts do not show which sectors took up and hold the financial instruments. For a full understanding of financial positions and flows, it is important to know not just what types of liabilities a sector uses to finance its economic and financial activities, but also which sectors are providing the financing. In addition, it is often necessary to analyze financial transactions between subsectors of a sector, particularly for financial corporations and general government.

Chapter 27 of the 2008 SNA provides some inputs to an integrated framework of financial positions and flows on a from-whom-to-whom basis. It describes that detailed flow of funds accounts are based on three-dimensional tables. Such a table records transactions or financial asset and liability positions cross classified by type of asset, creditor sector, and debtor sector.

12.2.3 The SNA and the From-Whom-to-Whom Approach for Financial Positions and Flows

While the SNA's main accounting structure shows the accounts for each institutional (sub)sector without counterparty details, it provides the conceptual framework to present financial positions and flows in a from-whom-to-whom framework.[10] The main reason why the SNA is not overly explicit on a from-whom-to-whom presentation of financial statistics is the reporting burden it poses on compilers, in particular for securities and other negotiable financial instruments. However, the 2008 global crisis revealed the importance of understanding spillover effects on balance sheet vulnerabilities arising from financial linkages between sectors and with the rest of the world.

The *Handbook on Securities Statistics* (prepared by the Bank for International Settlements [BIS], European Central Bank [ECB], and IMF), in particular its part 2 on debt securities holdings, covers the conceptual framework for positions and flows as outlined in the SNA but also extends this approach by reflecting the from-whom-to-whom relationships.[11] It presents the relationships between the resident sectors as creditors and residents and nonresidents as debtors, and between nonresidents as creditors and residents as debtors of financial instruments.

From a statistical point of view, the construction of the accounts on a from-whom-to-whom basis is an important compilation tool for enhancing

---

10. See chapter 27 of the 2008 SNA on the *Links to Monetary Statistics and the Flow of Funds*.
11. See Bank for International Settlements, European Central Bank and International Monetary Fund *Handbook on Securities Statistics*, part 1 (debt securities issues), part 2 (debt securities holdings), and part 3 (equity securities). http://www.imf.org/external/np/sta/wgsd/hbook.htm.

the quality and consistency of the data. The fully integrated sectoral national accounts, balance sheets, and flow of funds would improve the integration of scattered information and highlight the inconsistencies between the data sets of the various macroeconomic domains as it ensures a holistic approach to all the sectors of an economy and rest of the world. The sectoral national accounts will provide an integration framework for macroeconomic data on external, fiscal, and financial sectors with those of the rest of the economy. At the country level, this will facilitate the coordination of work on different macroeconomic statistics domains and promote their consistency at the data collection and compilation stages, thus eliminating or significantly reducing inconsistency of disseminated data.

12.2.4   Application of the SNA Framework for Presenting Intersectoral Linkages

The SNA has not given a primary emphasis to the compilation of the accounts on a from-whom-to-whom basis. However, its underlying principles and framework allow for compiling such accounts. Moreover, the SNA itself provides, albeit on a secondary plan, some references to the compilation of the accounts on a three dimensional basis; that is, including the from-whom-to-whom information. In the case of the financial positions and flows it calls this presentation "detailed flows of funds." From-whom-to-whom accounts permit tracing the debtor/creditor relationships between institutional sectors; that is, they can be used to show transactions, revaluations, other changes in financial assets and liabilities, and balance sheet positions cross classified by debtor sector and creditor sector.

Table 12.2 shows the integrated framework of accounts on a from-whom-to-whom basis by institutional sector and the rest of the world in a matrix format. For an economy, it shows transactions for a financial instrument acquired by residents (grouped into sectors) and nonresidents vis-à-vis institutional units as debtors, broken down by residents (again grouped into sectors) and nonresidents. Similar accounts for each financial instrument can be prepared for financial positions, revaluation, and other volume changes.

For residents, the presentation of nonconsolidated data is recommended. This means that intrasectoral positions, transactions, revaluations, and other changes in the volume of assets and liabilities are not eliminated (cells shaded medium gray). The financial assets of nonresidents issued by nonresidents are not covered (black cell). These are not relevant from a national economy's perspective. For economies that are open to capital flows, information on counterparty economies and nonresident sectors becomes highly desirable.

The from-whom-to-whom financial account of an institutional sector or of the rest of the world is an extension of the nonconsolidated financial account (matching debtor and creditor sectors). Similarly, the from-whom-to-whom financial balance sheet of a sector or of the rest of the world is an

Table 12.2   From-whom-to-whom transactions between five resident sectors and the rest of the world for one financial instrument, nonconsolidated

Creditor by residency and by resident sector / Debtor by residency and by resident sector	Residents					Nonresidents	All creditors
	Nonfinancial corporations	Financial corporations	General government	Households	Nonprofit institutions serving households		
Residents — Nonfinancial corporations							
Residents — Financial corporations							
Residents — General government							
Residents — Households							
Residents — Nonprofit institutions Serving households							
Nonresidents							
All debtors							

extension of the nonconsolidated financial balance sheet (again matching debtor and creditor sectors). Deriving the from-whom-to-whom financial account and balance sheet makes it also possible to draw up from-whom-to-whom revaluation accounts and other changes in the volume of assets and liabilities by (sub)sector. The information on revaluations has substantive analytical value, as it allows quantifying the effects of asset price movements for a specific financial instrument by sector vis-à-vis other sectors as well as its effects on the net worth. Implementation of a complete set of sectoral financial positions and flows is challenging and may have to be prioritized in stages. Appendix C describes a possible sequencing of presentation formats from simple to more advanced counterparty details for sectoral financial positions and flows.

12.3   Developments in Accounting on a From-Whom-to-Whom Basis

12.3.1   Experiences in the Compilation and Use of Flow of Funds

Although official statistics for some countries, mainly advanced economies, disseminate data on financial positions and flows by institutional sectors, for the large majority of cases, information on a from-whom-to-whom basis is lacking. A review of data availability in G-20 economies recently conducted by the IMF's Statistics Department reveals that Australia disseminates financial transactions and positions with a breakdown by counterparties within an integrated framework. A few G-20 economies (Japan, the United States, and Canada) disseminate financial accounts and financial balance sheets with significant details for instruments and subsectors that make it possible to identify the debtor/creditor relationships in many cases, while some (France, Italy, Korea, and the United Kingdom) publish these data with some counterparty details.[12]

The Euro area accounts also show some detailed from-whom-to-whom data for loans and deposits. This also applies for the quarterly sectoral accounts compiled by many European countries (e.g., Austria, France, Germany, Italy, Portugal, Spain, and the United Kingdom). Some European countries (for example, Austria and Spain) publish full sectoral financial positions and transactions on a from-whom-to-whom basis.

Among the G-20 emerging market economies, some partial information (sectors and instruments) on the flow of funds (financial flows) on a from-whom-to-whom basis is available for only a couple of countries. However, in many cases, partial information on financial positions and flows by sector and corresponding counterparty exists for financial institutions.

Some clarification of the term "flow of funds" would be useful. It is evi-

---

12. See Dawson (1996) for detailed elaboration of the compilation and use of US flow of funds.

dent that the term "flow of funds" is used with different meanings among the data compilers and users. Sometimes the term is used to describe the financial transactions only, while in other cases flow of funds refer to both financial transactions and positions. Many countries use this term to compile data on resources and uses of funds for sectors of an economy. For example, Indonesia, Mexico, and South Africa, which compile the financial account by institutional sector, refer to these sectoral financial accounts as flow of funds. The United States refers to both the sectoral financial accounts and the balance sheets as the flow of funds accounts. Many countries (e.g., European countries) adhere strictly to the SNA terminology. In some instances, the flows in the flow of funds are derived as the difference between opening and closings positions, and thus, also include other economic flows (revaluations and changes in the volumes of assets and liabilities). In these cases, it would be conceptually wrong to use them for explaining net lending and borrowing.

A broad implementation of the from-whom-to-whom framework for financial positions and flows within an integrated framework of macroeconomic accounts has not yet been materialized. However, G-20 advanced economies seem to be in a good position to lead the development of these statistics by further extending the financial accounts and balance sheets already compiled and disseminated based on the SNA/European system of accounts (ESA) methodology. Reaching an agreement on harmonized terminology among countries is also necessary so as to avoid confusion.

12.3.2   The Balance Sheet Approach

The balance sheet approach (BSA) is an analytical framework for ascertaining how balance sheet weaknesses contribute to the origin and propagation of financial crisis.[13] In addition to the traditional analysis of flows, the BSA focuses on the examination of stocks of assets and liabilities in a country's sectoral balance sheets. It starts with an analysis of sectoral vulnerabilities. Weaknesses of one sector can spill over to other sectors and can have an impact on the whole economy since financial difficulties of a debtor represent difficulties for its creditors. This approach of analyzing the origins and propagation of financial crisis has gained momentum since the financial crisis of the 1990s. In fact, the IMF has been involved in the development of data sources and using the BSA in its surveillance work. Table 12.3 shows a simplified version of the BSA matrix. As the liabilities in the BSA matrix are consolidated sectoral data, the matrix's diagonal (shaded boxes) of intrasectoral holdings remains empty.

In assessing balance sheet risks, the BSA framework considers four types of balance sheet mismatches that can trigger a financial crisis. These mismatches are (a) currency mismatches (liabilities in foreign currency and

---

13. See Allen et al. (2002) and Mathisen and Pellechio (2006).

Table 12.3   A simplified BSA presentation of intersectoral positions of financial assets and liabilities

Holder of the liability (creditor)	Government sector (incl. central bank)	Financial sector	Nonfinancial Sector	Rest of the world	Total
Issuer of the liability (debtor)					
Government sector (incl. central bank)					
Domestic currency					
Total other liabilities					
short term					
in foreign currency					
in domestic currency					
medium and long term					
in foreign currency					
in domestic currency					
Financial sector					
Total liabilities					
deposits and other short term					
in foreign currency					
in domestic currency					
medium and long term					
in foreign currency					
in domestic currency					
Equity (capital)					
Nonfinancial sector					
Total liabilities					
short term					
in foreign currency					
in domestic currency					
medium and long term					
in foreign currency					
in domestic currency					
Equity (capital)					
Rest of the world					
Total liabilities (all in foreign currency)					
currency and short term					
medium and long term					
Equity					

Source: Allen et al. (2002)

assets in domestic currency or vice versa—capital losses and default risk from devaluation or appreciation of exchange rate); (b) maturity mismatches (assets are long term and liabilities are short term causing risk of defaults associated with difficulties on debt rollover and increase in short-term interest rates); (c) capital structure mismatches (excessive reliance in debt instead of equity); and (d) solvency risk (assets not enough to cover liabilities).

The BSA refers to the SNA balance sheets but is limited to analyzing only positions (stocks) of financial assets and liabilities. It shows, for each financial instrument included, the sector incurring the liability (the debtor) and the sector acquiring the counterpart asset (the creditor). In other words, it corresponds to the "detailed flow of funds" in the SNA. The main source data for the compilation of the BSA are the Standardized Report Forms (SRFs) for monetary statistics reported monthly to the IMF's Statistics Department (STA). As of the end of 2012, thirty-one countries report data for all the subsectors of financial corporations (central banks, other depository corporations [ODCs] and other financial corporations [OFCs]). Reports covering only the central banks and the ODCs are received from 102 countries (including the countries in the Euro area). Other data sources for completing a BSA include the international investment position (IIP), the Coordinated Portfolio Investment Survey (CPIS), the Quarterly External Debt Statistics (QEDS), the Joint External Debt Hub (JEDH), and BIS's international banking statistics.

The sector breakdown of the BSA matrices consist of the central government, state and local government, financial sector and its subsectors, the nonfinancial corporations (public and other), other resident sectors, and the rest of the world. The currency denominations and the maturity (original) breakdowns of assets and liabilities play an important role in the classification of assets and liabilities in the BSA. The classification of financial instruments by category follows the SNA but new breakdowns by subcategory are recommended, data availability of which are not always ensured.

Compilation of the BSA

The BSA matrices are compiled monthly for a selected number of countries based solely on the monetary statistics, although users can extend the coverage of the BSA using additional source data, usually available on a lower frequency. The main source data are the SRF reports received electronically by the IMF. Three different SRF reports are used to collect data, respectively, from (a) the central banks, (b) ODCs, and (c) OFCs. Data on financial assets and liabilities are collected for the main categories of financial instruments used in the SNA with a breakdown by currency (national and foreign currency) and sector. The standard sectors considered are the central bank, ODCs, OFCs, central government, state and local government, nonfinancial corporations (separate data for public and other nonfinancial corporations), other resident sectors (households and nonprofit institutions serving households), and nonresidents (rest of the world). These data provide satisfactory creditor/ debtor positions between the financial corporations subsectors and other sectors of the economy and the rest of the world.

In the monthly data, positions between government subsectors and the other resident sectors of the economy are incomplete because the creditor and debtor positions between general government, the nonfinancial corporations, and other resident sectors are not available on a monthly basis. The positions between general government and the rest of the world can be extracted from the IIP, the QEDS, and the CPIS, which are available at a lower frequency.

Data on positions between the nonfinancial corporations and other sectors of the economy are also incomplete, as data on the positions held by this sector against general government and other resident sectors are usually not available. Stocks of liabilities of the nonfinancial sector held as financial assets by the rest of the world are available from the IIP, the QEDS, and the JEDH, while data on their holding of financial assets against the rest of the world are available from the IIP and the CPIS.

12.3.3   The Coordinated Portfolio Investment Survey (CPIS)

The purpose of the CPIS is to collect information on the stock of cross-border holdings of portfolio investment in securities (equity securities, and short- and long-term debt securities).[14] The CPIS has been conducted annually since 2001 and collects data from about seventy-six countries on their year-end portfolio investment positions on the targeted financial instruments with a breakdown by country of issuer. The coverage of the CPIS corresponds to the coverage of the portfolio investment in the IIP. The concepts and principles underlying the CPIS are those contained in the sixth edition of the *Balance of Payments and International Investment Position Manual (BPM6)*.[15]

The data collected permit the presentation at the level of each financial instrument on a from-whom-to-whom basis showing the countries that hold the assets vis-à-vis the issuer countries. The results of the survey show increases in the value of cross-border portfolio investment in most years.

The CPIS contains a number of encouraged items that are not reported by some countries. In particular, the CPIS contains several detailed splits of data, including on the domestic sector of holder of securities, and on the currency composition of the securities held. Thus, the CPIS identifies securities held by resident sectors with a breakdown of the resident holding sectors: monetary authorities, banks, other financial institutions (insurance corpora-

14. For the CPIS Guide, data, and metadata, please visit the IMF website at http://www.imf .org/external/np/sta/pi/cpis.htm.
15. See International Monetary Fund (2009).

tions and pension funds, investment funds, and others), general government, and nonfinancial sector (nonfinancial corporations, households, and other). Data on portfolio investment liabilities by economy of nonresident holder are also reported.

In response to requests from data users, a number of enhancements to the CPIS are expected to be implemented starting with data for 2013. Such enhancements are expected to include increased frequency (i.e., semiannual CPIS data collections), timeliness (i.e., acceleration in the collection and redissemination of data), and scope. The increased scope covers collection of information, on a voluntary basis, on the sector of the issuer of securities; on short or negative positions; and data, on a from-whom-to-whom basis, on the domestic sector of holder vis-à-vis the sector of issuer for the twenty-five economies that are considered by the IMF to have systemically important financial sectors.[16]

12.3.4   Coordinated Direct Investment Survey (CDIS)

The IMF conducted a CDIS for the first time in 2009 and has been conducting the survey annually since then.[17] Preliminary estimates of positions for a given year are released before end-December of the following year, and revised data are usually released six months later. Participation in the CDIS is voluntary and over ninety economies currently participate in the survey.

The purpose of the CDIS is to improve the quality of direct investment position statistics in the IIP and by immediate counterpart economy. Specifically, the objectives of the CDIS are to collect comprehensive and harmonized data, with geographic detail of counterpart country, on direct investment positions. The concepts, coverage, valuation, and classification of data collected in the CDIS are consistent with the *BPM6* and the fourth edition of the *OECD Benchmark Definition of Foreign Direct Investment*.

The CDIS database presents detailed data on "inward" direct investment position (i.e., direct investment into the reporting economy) cross classified by economy of immediate investor, and data on "outward" direct investment position (i.e., direct investment abroad by the reporting economy) cross classified by economy of immediate investment. All participants in the CDIS provide data on their inward direct investment and most participants also provide data on their outward direct investment. The CDIS database is available publicly and contains breakdowns of direct investment position data

16. The IMF has made it mandatory for twenty-five jurisdictions with systemically important financial sectors to undergo financial stability assessments under the Financial Sector Assessment Program (FSAP) every five years. (http://www.imf.org/external/np/sec/pr/2010/pr10357 .htm). These jurisdictions are Australia, Austria, Belgium, Brazil, Canada, China, France, Germany, Hong Kong SAR, India, Ireland, Italy, Japan, Luxembourg, Mexico, The Netherlands, Russian Federation, Singapore, South Korea, Spain, Sweden, Switzerland, Turkey, United Kingdom, and the United States.

17. For CDIS Guide, data, and metadata, please visit the IMF website at http://www.imf .org/external/np/sta/cdis/index.htm.

including, in most instances, separate data on equity and debt positions, as well as tables that present "mirror" data (i.e., data on direct investment positions obtained from counterpart economies participating in the CDIS).

12.3.5   BIS International Banking Statistics

The BIS compiles quarterly data on gross balance sheet positions of banks in major banking centers against entities (banks and nonbanks) located in other countries worldwide.[18] The statistics cover separate data on cross-border claims and liabilities in all currencies, and claims and liabilities vis-à-vis residents in foreign currency.[19]

Data are based on the residency and nonconsolidated concepts, consistently with the balance of payments and IIP statistics. There is, however, a deviation from these statistics in that the locational statistics also include banks' foreign currency positions vis-à-vis residents.

The locational international banking statistics provide information on international claims and liabilities for more than forty of the most important banking centers by country of residence of the counterparties, by major individual currencies, and sectors (only banks and nonbanks). Financial assets and liabilities are presented for three aggregated categories: (a) loans and deposits, (b) holdings and own issues of debt securities, and (c) other assets and liabilities. The latter two categories mainly cover portfolio and direct investment.

The statistics, aggregated at the country/financial center level, are reported by central banks and monetary authorities in the countries and financial centers that conduct large volumes of international lending and borrowing or deposit taking. The statistics provide a measure of the role of banks in intermediating international capital flows, a measure of the external debt owed to banks as reported from the creditor side, and a measure of the importance of financial centers and offshore banking activity.

The BIS and member central banks are strengthening the international banking statistics with more granular sectoral, instrument, and other breakdowns, with instruments and sectors consistent with national accounts defi-

---

18. For the locational international banking statistics guide and data, please visit the BIS website at http://www.bis.org/statistics/bankstats.htm.

19. The BIS also collects and publishes consolidated banking statistics on banks' on-balance sheet financial claims on the rest of the world. The quarterly data cover contractual lending by the head office and all its branches and subsidiaries on a worldwide consolidated basis, that is, net of interoffice accounts. Total claims are broken down by remaining maturity, sector (banks, nonbank private sector, and public sector), as well as vis-à-vis country. Two sets of statistics are compiled. The first set collects data on an immediate borrower basis, that is, claims are attributed to the country where the original risk lies. The second set collects data on an ultimate risk basis; that is, claims are attributed to the country where the final risk lies. Currently, central banks in thirty countries report their aggregate national consolidated data to the BIS, which uses them as the basis for calculating and publishing global data. For more information, please visit the BIS website at http://www.bis.org/statistics/consstats.htm.

nitions. The enhancements are expected to be reflected in the BIS data over the coming few years, and, inter alia, should support efforts to better monitor maturity and currency mismatches among international banks.

12.3.6   Security-by-Security Statistics

Globalization, financial innovation, and dynamic changes in the structures, interconnectedness, and responses of financial markets have led to a higher demand for more detailed, timely, and harmonized securities statistics that make it possible for users and policymakers to respond quickly to, or even anticipate, financial market developments. These requirements may increasingly be met by moving gradually to innovative statistical compilation systems that are based on collection of highly granular data at individual security level. The underlying idea is that such data can be arranged and aggregated by statistics compilers in a highly flexible manner to meet changing needs in statistical indicators, rather than relying on systems that use processed and aggregated data and, thus, are not flexible enough for deriving, as needs arise, indicators that the underlying data system is capable to produce. Modern information technology provides a sufficient technical support for handling large microdatabases.

Securities statistics are particularly suited to this approach as the majority of securities have a unique identifier and many of the analytically relevant information on securities issues and holdings may be obtained from commercial sources. Such data complemented with additional direct and indirect data sources can be aggregated and consolidated within a reference securities database. The development of a single reference securities database in the European System of Central Banks—the Centralized Securities Database (CSDB)—is the cornerstone of the transition to security-by-security-based securities statistics in Europe. The development of the CSDB is described below under the subsection on Euro area accounts.

More importantly, strengthening of securities statistics is relevant to the improvement of many domains of macroeconomic statistics. Not surprisingly, many countries have started to develop a security-by-security database, which is an important pillar for developing sectoral financial positions and flows in a from-whom-to-whom framework. The focus of the international community has been on providing clear international methodological guidance on compiling securities data, through the *Handbook on Securities Statistics* and on making data more readily available through the BIS.[20] It has strengthened the collection and dissemination of securities data. The number of central banks reporting data has risen to about sixty, including virtually all G-20 members, as of the end of 2012.[21]

---

20. *Handbook on Securities Statistics*, (www.imf.org/external/np/sta/wgsd/index.htm).
21. Data are available at the BIS website http://www.bis.org/statistics/secstats.htm.

12.3.7   Euro Area Accounts on a From-Whom-to-Whom Basis

The ECB has been publishing, since June 2007, the quarterly integrated Euro area accounts for institutional sectors (the Euro area accounts or EAA). These data are produced in collaboration with the national central banks, Eurostat and the national statistical institutes, and start in the first quarter of 1999. The data become available approximately four months after the end of the reference quarter. The Euro area accounts provide consistent and comprehensive information on macroeconomic developments, both for the economy as a whole and by institutional sectors (nonfinancial corporations, financial corporations, government, and households). They encompass integrated nonfinancial and financial accounts, including balance sheets.

In addition, the ECB prepares and makes analytical use of financial positions and flows on a from-whom-to-whom basis (by debtor/creditor) for euro area aggregates. The development and use of the financial data on a from-whom-to-whom framework are limited, but are expanding as efforts are being made at the country and regional levels to improve such statistics. Four main areas of such data framework developed and used by the ECB are noteworthy. They are (a) deposits and loans on a from-whom-to-whom basis, (b) monetary aggregates and their counterparties, (c) general government debt, and (d) securities issues and holdings. A brief description these initiatives are given below.[22]

Deposits and Loans on a From-Whom-to-Whom Basis

The ECB compiles, only at the Euro-area level, outstanding amounts and transactions for deposits, short-term loans and long-term loans by counterpart sector. Cross-sectional tables provide an overview of the activities between the various sectors of the Euro-area economy in the latest available period, whereas the time series show detail from a time perspective. These data are available on a quarterly basis at the ECB's website.

Monitoring Monetary Transmission Processes by
Integrating Money in a From-Whom-to-Whom Framework

The integration of monetary aggregates and its counterparts in a from-whom-to-whom framework is derived from the consolidated financial transactions and balance sheets of the resident money-issuing sector vis-à-vis the resident money-holding sectors. An initial set of source data available are the balance sheets of monetary financial institutions (MFI) from which monetary aggregates and the main counterparts to broad money are to be calculated. These balance sheet statistics comprise often rather

---

22. See ECB, *Monthly Bulletin*, various issues and statistical section for more information.

detailed breakdowns of various financial instruments, such as deposits, loans, and debt securities by maturity and counterpart sector. Balance of payment statistics and statistics on securities issuance by general government and by financial and nonfinancial corporations complement this data set.

The corresponding financial accounts and balance sheets derived from these source data, with a breakdown of the financial corporations sector, of the financial asset and liability categories, and of the counterparts, allow the identification of broad money. A simple example of integrating money and credit in a from-whom-to-whom framework is presented in appendix A.

The *money-issuing sector* is assumed to consist of the central bank, resident deposit-taking corporations, and resident money market funds, together comprising the MFI subsector. Money holders are the remaining resident sectors, including the remaining subsectors in the financial corporations sector and all subsectors of general government. (This is a simplification—in reality, central government may have monetary liabilities, and its holdings of monetary instruments issued by MFIs may be excluded from the monetary aggregates.) Holdings of money by the money-issuing sector itself are consolidated. The rest of the world sector is assumed to be money neutral; that is, neither the liabilities of nonresidents, nor nonresidents' holdings of money issued by resident money issuers, are counted in money.

Monetary variables are considered to comprise (a) currency (issued by the central bank); (b) transferable deposits held with MFIs; (c) deposits redeemable at a period of notice of up to and including three months (i.e., short-term savings deposits) held with MFIs; (d) deposits with an agreed maturity of up to and including two years (i.e., short-term time deposits) held with MFIs; and (e) repurchase agreements, money market fund shares or units, and debt securities with an original maturity of up to and including two years issued by MFIs. These monetary variables may also cover structured securities and structured deposits. Depending on the coverage, various *monetary aggregates* may be derived.

Monitoring Government Debt in a From-Whom-to-Whom Framework

Data on general government gross debt are used to monitor fiscal developments within the Euro area. General government gross debt or Maastricht debt excludes, as gross consolidated debt, any government debt held as a financial asset by government units. It comprises the financial instruments currency and deposits, debt securities, and loans.

Maastricht debt provides debt data with a breakdown by holder or creditor. They are split into debt held by residents of an economy within the Euro area or within the European Union and by nonresident holders. Holdings of debt by residents are calculated as the sum of the debt held by the central bank, other monetary financial institutions, other financial institutions, and other residents. In addition to their breakdown by instrument and holder, debt is also presented by original and residual maturities and by currency of denomination.

Monitoring Securities Issues and Holdings
in a From-Whom-to-Whom Framework

The from-whom-to-whom framework allows for a detailed presentation of financing and financial investment via securities, which the ECB uses for a number of purposes, especially in the context of monetary policy and financial stability analysis. It sheds light on the sectoral compositions of assets and liabilities, and on potential strengths and vulnerabilities in portfolios.

The complexity of from-whom-to-whom tables for securities is determined by the detail of the breakdowns chosen for securities (by subcategory) and for the creditors and debtors (by residency, sector, and subsector). Combining these breakdowns leads to a rather large number of from-whom-to-whom relationships, especially as the data may need to be presented for both positions and flows. Accordingly, a selection by security subcategory, sector, and subsector is essential.

At the ECB, a centralized security-by-security database (CSDB) has been set up by the European System of Central Banks (ESCB) to further improve the quality of position and flow data on securities. The CSDB is a microdatabase that stores information on individual securities, from which statistics can be compiled flexibly to serve diverse needs. The CSDB covers various categories of financial instruments, such as debt securities, equity securities, and investment fund shares or units. Information stored on an instrument is broken down into attributes that describe selected characteristics of the instrument. The selection of attributes may vary depending on the purpose of the database. Attributes useful for statistical applications include the international securities identification number (ISIN), name of the issuer, residence of the issuer, the sector and subsector of issuer, issue date, redemption date, the type of security, the currency of denomination, the issue price, the redemption price, the outstanding amount or the market capitalization, and the coupon payments and dates.

The production of statistics from the CSDB can be presented as a three-stage process. First, it involves inputs by collecting and purchasing data on individual securities from a range of sources, such as central banks, government agencies, commercial data providers and securities exchanges (in their capacity as custodians). Second, it covers data quality management. The individual security data collected from different sources are received into the database, merged, and stored. Checks for completeness, plausibility, and consistency are then performed, and where errors are detected, observations are corrected. Third, it involves the storing of individual security data according to various classification criteria.

There is a project ongoing to link the CSDB dealing with securities issues statistics to securities holdings statistics for resident holders grouped by sector and subsector, as well as for nonresident holders. For this purpose, information provided by respondents (as holders or custodians) is linked at the individual security level to the data stored in the CSDB. The link is often made using the ISIN, but also referring to information on the debt securities holders and holdings: (a) the holder by residency and institutional sector and subsector and also by large and complex financial or nonfinancial group; and (b) the amount of holdings in currency.

Current reporting schemes on securities holdings are mainly based on two groups of agents having access to such type of information: (a) custodians (as well as centralized securities depositories); and (b) direct reporters. In most cases, data are collected from custodians on a security-by-security basis. This also refers to the collection of data on the securities holdings of residents from nonresident custodians to allow the breakdown of holdings by the residency of the issuer to be derived. Direct reporters provide security-by-security data on their holdings with various breakdowns: by type of instrument, maturity, residence of issuer, and so forth.

Establishing an integrated compilation framework for securities issues and securities holdings statistics, which provides timely and high-frequency data with breakdowns by type of financial instrument, currency denomination, maturity, issuing country, and sector or subsector is rather demanding and cost intensive. Accordingly, the ESCB has agreed that it will still take a few years to use it for the regular production of securities statistics, starting with financial balance sheet data.

12.4   Implementation of the Sectoral Accounts, Balance Sheets, and Flow of Funds

For residency-based macroeconomic statistics, the SNA serves as the integrated statistical framework for producing a consistent set of macroeconomic and financial statistics, including sectoral financial positions and flows on a from-whom-to-whom basis. This section, therefore, discusses the implementation of the broader sectoral accounts and balance sheets within the SNA framework.

Although the SNA, with its latest 2008 version, provides the statistical framework for compiling integrated sectoral accounts, balance sheets, and flow of funds, the framework has not been fully utilized in practice to compile and disseminate these accounts in a fully integrated and comprehensive way. Past efforts in statistical development made good progress in certain domains of macroeconomic statistics. Significant amounts of information is available in some specific areas. For example, detailed monetary and financial statistics are available for depository financial corporations. Other balance sheet data where progress has been made include external debt, international reserves, international investment positions, and coordinated cross-border portfolio and direct investment. Detailed financial information may be available for the government sector and subsectors (particularly for many OECD countries), and initiatives have been taken to better cover financial balance sheets of the household sector and nonbank financial institutions. However, serious data gaps exist for specific sectors such as the nonfinancial corporations or for specific areas such as the stocks and flows of nonfinancial assets, particularly the nonproduced nonfinancial assets. A status on the availability of sectoral balance sheets and accumulations accounts in the G-20 economies as of the end of 2012 is presented in appendix B.

One important aspect that hampered analytical work and policy evaluation at the regional and multilateral levels at the wake of the 2008 global crisis was the lack of international comparability of disseminated sectoral national accounts. Not only the implementation of the SNA by countries was uneven in terms of the scope of the accounts disseminated, but also classifications used to disseminate national data differ across countries. As a result, international comparability could be ascertained only at a higher level of aggregation, reducing the usefulness of these data. It should be noted that Eurostat and ECB made substantial contribution to the harmonization of sectoral accounts within the European Union. However, the 2008 global crisis revealed that stronger and well-coordinated international efforts are needed to ensure the development and dissemination of internationally comparable sectoral accounts, balance sheets, and flow of funds.

With the objective of seeking consensus on the strategy for expanding the scope of internationally comparable sectoral accounts and balance sheets, the IMF and OECD, in collaboration with other members of the IAG, organized a conference, "Strengthening Sectoral Position and Flow Data in the Macroeconomic Accounts," from February 28 to March 2, 2011, at IMF Headquarters.[23] The conference (a) provided guidance toward a minimum and encouraged set of internationally comparable sectoral accounts and balance sheets; (b) discussed priorities, time frame, and way forward; (c) reached common understanding on the international collaboration for data collection and dissemination by international organizations; and (d) deliberated on the outreach, training, and technical assistance programs for supporting the implementation.

An important milestone in taking forward the work on implementing sectoral accounts and balance sheets is the development of templates for a minimum and encouraged set of internationally comparable sectoral accounts and balance sheets arrived at through a global consultative process led by the IMF. The process went through the various stages as follows:

- In early 2010, the IMF assessed the overall availability and current practices in the dissemination of sectoral accounts and balance sheets in G-20 economies and non-G-20 advanced economies.

23. The papers presented at the conference and the summary report are available at http://www.imf.org/external/np/seminars/eng/2011/sta/index.htm.

- A joint IMF-OECD conference provided guidance toward the development of the templates.
- An IAG working group, in consultation with various stakeholders, including several countries, finalized the templates in May 2012. The templates are available from the IMF's website (http://www.imf.org /external/np/sta/templates/sectacct/index.htm) and from the SNA website (http://unstats.un.org/unsd/nationalaccount/imp.asp) hosted by the United Nations Statistics Division (UNSD).
- In addition, the templates, at various stages of development, were discussed at the conference of G-20 senior officials on the G-20 Data Gaps Initiative at the IMF Headquarters in Washington, DC, from March 30 to 31, 2011; at the joint session of the OECD Working Party on Financial Statistics and the OECD Working Party on National Accounts in Paris from October 24 to 28, 2011; and at the meeting of the Advisory Expert Group on National Accounts in New York from April 21 to 23, 2012.

The templates set the scope of sectoral accounts and balance sheets and provide a basis for internationally coordinated efforts toward producing and disseminating internationally comparable sectoral accounts. The templates include guidance for classifications in four building blocks: (a) minimum and encouraged sector and subsector breakdowns; (b) transactions breakdowns in nonfinancial (current and capital) accounts; (c) classification of financial instruments (including debt on remaining maturity and currency composition); and (d) classification of nonfinancial assets. While the nonfinancial accounts and the stocks and transactions of financial assets and liabilities are to be compiled on a quarterly basis (with a quarterly timeliness), the stocks of nonfinancial assets are to be compiled on an annual basis (with nine-month timeliness). Appendix D shows the framework for minimum and encouraged classifications for the templates for quarterly current and capital accounts (appendix table 12D.1), for quarterly stocks and transactions of financial assets and liabilities (appendix table 12D.2), and for annual stocks of nonfinancial assets (appendix table 12D.3).

The relevant international organizations started to follow up on these recommendations in a coordinated fashion. As far as possible, the work on sectoral accounts is integrated with the implementation of the 2008 SNA. As part of the 2008 SNA implementation, important issues are discussed and guidance is provided by the Intersecretariat Working Group on National Accounts (ISWGNA) and its Advisory Expert Group on National Accounts.[24] It is anticipated that G-20 economies would compile statistics according to these templates as part of their broader plans for implementing the 2008 SNA. An economy may aim for greater detail than the minimum

---

24. The deliberations of the ISWGNA and AEG on the 2008 SNA implementation can be found at the United Nations Statistics Division's website (http://unstats.un.org/unsd/national account/iswgna.asp).

requirements established in the templates, including flow of funds (both financial positions and flows) on a from-whom-to-whom basis, depending on analytical and policy requirements.

To support the compilation of sectoral accounts and balance sheets, the IMF has initiated a series of bilateral consultations with G-20 and some non-G-20 countries and started to organize seminars for IMF member countries. Similarly, OECD, ECB, and Eurostat have intensified their outreach and consultations with their member states. Further, under the auspices of the IAG, currently available sectoral accounts data for the G-20 economies, primarily sourced from the OECD, and Eurostat and European Central Bank within Europe, are available on the Principal Global Indicators website.[25]

It should be noted that countries are at different stages of development of integrated sectoral accounts, and hence, the implementation will have different implications in terms of resources and institutional setup in different countries. Designing and implementing changes to or initiating new data collection systems are costly and priorities must therefore be established among the various potential improvements. A thorough assessment of the feasibility and resource requirements for implementing each element of the templates should be conducted. Country experiences show that the development of integrated sectoral accounts requires an active and close coordination among the various data producing agencies. Ultimately, requirements for analytical and policy purposes should guide the priorities for sectoral accounts, balance sheets, and flow of funds. For example, timeliness of sectoral accounts is highly important.

The priorities should be time bound as time frame determines the scope of data development that is feasible within a given resource constraint. There is an understanding among the stakeholders (international agencies and countries) that the initial stage of the sectoral accounts project should be implemented by 2014. Many countries (mostly advanced economies) are working toward implementing the 2008 SNA by 2014.[26] This is a good opportunity to incorporate proposals arising from the DGI work on sectoral accounts into the 2008 SNA implementation plans of countries.

Based on country experiences and the discussion at the IMF-OECD conference, some guidance on the priorities for strengthening sectoral accounts is evident. Initial focus should be given to the minimum set of internationally comparable sectoral accounts and balance sheets. Countries should then work on expanding the breakdowns for sectors (particularly for financial sector), financial instruments, and nonfinancial assets. Finally, the compilation of financial positions and flows on a from-whom-to-whom basis should be given priority in the medium term (probably after the initial stage mentioned in the previous paragraph). Such prioritization will allow countries

---

25. http://www.principalglobalindicators.org/default.aspx.
26. Australia, Canada, and the United States implemented and disseminated national accounts statistics according to the 2008 SNA in 2009, 2012, and 2013, respectively.

with different levels of development in the sectoral accounts to make progress. While the minimum set will serve as a benchmark for countries with no or partial sectoral accounts, countries with sufficient sectoral accounts can move toward implementing the fully integrated sectoral accounts and the compilation of financial positions and flows on a from-whom-to-whom basis.

It was recognized that for countries that do not yet compile sectoral accounts, the development of such statistics will require addressing large data gaps in their existing statistical systems. There is a need to study carefully the requirements, resource implications, institutional issues, reporting burden, and confidentiality issues before designing necessary surveys to collect data. Countries should evaluate what can be achieved by integrating and using available statistics. For countries that do not yet compile sectoral accounts, there is an advantage in making a quick start with sectors for which a significant amount of data is or may be made available (most likely, financial corporations and general government).

Appropriate funding for outreach, technical assistance, and training will be needed to support activities at the country and international levels. International organizations and donors will need to draw on their resources to adequately finance these activities. A two-track approach is needed to assist countries depending on whether a country has an advanced or good statistical system (most of the advanced economies) or it has a less developed statistical system (most of the emerging market economies). While outreach programs (workshops to discuss compilation issues) might be sufficient to assist the first group of countries, technical assistance and training programs will be needed to assist the second group of countries to implement the sectoral accounts initiative. International cooperation and some division of responsibilities among the international agencies might be necessary.

One important aspect of the sectoral accounts initiative is to enhance collaboration among the international organizations for collecting, sharing, and disseminating sectoral accounts. The main principle is that a country should be required to complete the templates for a given reference period or date and submit data to only one international organization. This will reduce burdens on countries and will avoid dissemination of conflicting data (for example, due to different vintages of data or timeliness of data capture) by international organizations.

12.5 Applying the From-Whom-to-Whom Framework for Financial Positions and Flows

12.5.1 Collecting and Compiling Data on a From-Whom-to-Whom Basis

A set of accounts that show by sector and type of financial instrument the transactions, other economic flows, and the positions of financial assets and liabilities vis-à-vis the counterpart sector, whether resident or cross border, reflect more accurately the reality of the interconnected domestic and global economy and provide more useful information for opportunely dealing with the financial positions and flows that can originate in a crisis.

Especially in the context of requirements related to multilateral surveillance, financial stability, and policy coordination, sectoral accounts on a from-whom-to-whom basis are a powerful tool to provide comparable data for G-20 as well as other economies. Such indicators reflecting imbalances may cover data on the current account derived consistently from the rest of the world, data on deficit and debt derived from general government, or data on private savings, and debt derived from the nonfinancial corporations and household sector accounts. Especially important is the ability to analyze sectoral imbalances in connection with sectoral real and financial linkages.

Transactions on a from-whom-to-whom basis permit understanding of how surpluses by one sector are allocated among different financial instruments and sectors and cross border, or how sectors with deficits meet their financial needs in terms of financial instruments used and sectors providing it, including the rest of the world. They also reflect the increasing activities in the financial markets for the sake of financial returns and speculative gains. No less important is identifying changes in balance sheets that result from revaluations and other changes like mergers and acquisitions. The greater subsector details proposed for the financial sector will augment the ability to understand and monitor relationships and dynamics between banks and nonbanks. The framework also allows to assess the effects of asset prices on sectoral net worth and to identify sectors that are affected by changes in prices of a certain asset class.

The compilation of the SNA accounts for financial positions and flows on a from-whom-to-whom basis will fill some important data gaps in the currently available macroeconomic statistics. This, however, requires further investments in new data collection systems as described above for securities databases. As discussed in the previous section, the collection of more detailed data from markets and institutional sectors has to be weighed against the response burden to the statistical units, confidentiality constraints, and the cost of collecting and processing the additional source data. As a result, compromises need to be established in the level of aggregation of the data to be collected as well as of the data sources to be used.

Without discussing specific issues in detail, some main areas that need to be addressed, while designing work plans for developing integrated sectoral accounts (including sectoral financial positions and flows on a from-whom-to-whom basis), should include the following: (a) allocation of responsibilities, (b) resources (staffing, financing, and information technology), (c) coordination and cooperation, (d) data and metadata dissemination, and (e) data transmission to international organizations. At the planning stage for the implementation of the work, countries should also have consultations with prospective users of the data.

The compilation of the integrated financial positions and flows on a from-whom-to-whom-basis has implications for the internal allocation of responsibilities within each country. The division of work among different institutions depends on a country's specific institutional arrangements for the compilation of the integrated national accounts statistics. Different agencies may be involved, each responsible for a specific part of the accounts in close interaction, thus ensuring full coverage and assuring consistency. Roles, responsibilities, and coordination mechanisms must be ensured through explicit and formal mechanisms.

Compilation of the financial positions and flows on a from-whom-to whom-basis will require more resources even for those countries that already produce financial account and balance sheets. There is additional work in data collection and processing, and the verification and validation of the data to ensure consistency across sectors on debtor/creditor positions by type of financial instrument requires close working relations among all agencies involved at different stages of compilation. Agreements have to be reached on a timetable for interagency submission of data and for releasing the final products, including the transmission of the information to international organizations.

The work on integrated sectoral accounts and balance sheets will facilitate the coordination of work on different macroeconomic statistics domains and promote their consistency at the level of data collection and compilation. This work could bring efficiencies. Such an approach will have implications for each agency's work as future work on various macroeconomic statistics domains will need to be coordinated. The sectoral accounts and balance sheets may, in fact, be used as the main framework for conducting the work on cross-sectoral data consistency on a more systematic and regular basis.

12.5.2   Phases in Implementing the From-Whom-to-Whom Data

As a condition for assuring international comparability, the accounts on financial positions and flows should be compiled and disseminated using the minimum and encouraged set of categories of assets/liabilities and institutional sectors as agreed on for the templates. Depending on their own analytical needs and data availability, countries may compile the data at more disaggregated levels reflecting their own institutional settings or for particular financial instruments.

Considering the difficulties that countries are likely to face in compiling exhaustive accounts, implementation could occur in phases. First, the accounts for the main institutional sectors by financial instrument category are likely to be implemented. With the development of data sources a further breakdown of the financial corporations' accounts by subsector may follow. In a further phase, from-whom-to-whom data may be collected and compiled for selected financial instruments, such as loans, deposits, or insurance and pension entitlements. Most challenging will be to provide such detailed data for securities and other negotiable financial instruments due to secondary market transactions. Due to data confidentiality, the collection of sectoral financial positions and flows on a from-whom-to-whom basis may be sometimes more problematic than simply collecting data on assets and liabilities without counterparty details, particularly when higher level of details is requested.

Not every country may need to follow the same path for developing sectoral financial positions and flows. There is no single sequence of stages that may be applicable in all cases. Country experiences suggest that the following phases may provide some guidelines:

traditional financial transactions and positions by main sectors; further details for financial corporations by subsectors and for general government, other economic flows may also be considered;

from-whom-to-whom financial positions and flows for subsectors of financial corporations and possibly general government;

from-whom-to-whom financial positions and flows for specific instruments (loans, deposits, some important negotiable instruments); and

fully integrated financial positions and flows on a from-whom-to-whom basis by sectors (subsectors)—starting from aggregated subsector and instrument details toward more disaggregated subsector and instrument details.

Technical assistance and training will be required particularly for those countries that have not yet implemented complete sectoral accounts. Training may adopt a regional format, thus maximizing the benefits of the resources used. Given existing resource constraints for technical assistance, an implementation based on selected pilot countries may be necessary. Existing international forums (such as the ISWGNA, OECD working parties on financial accounts and national accounts, and activities of the ECB and Eurostat) will be used to provide methodological support in the implementation of sectoral accounts and balance sheets. The IMF has held bilateral discussions with the Russian Federation, South Africa, Indonesia, and Thailand during 2011 and 2012 and is expanding the coverage of countries in the years to come. These countries have designed work programs to develop and disseminate sectoral accounts and balance sheets (Russian Federation by 2016, South Africa by 2014, Indonesia by 2015, and Thailand by 2014). Although the goal by these dates is to disseminate traditional sectoral accounts and balance sheets (without from-whom-to-whom details), the compilation system for developing the quarterly sectoral financial positions and flows is built, in principle, using the from-whom-to-whom framework. This will allow countries to publish partial from-whom-to-whom financial positions and flows and will set the stage for development of quarterly financial positions and flows on a from-whom-to-whom basis in the medium term.

As a first step, the presentation of sectoral financial positions and flows can follow simplified tables showing creditors' flows and positions by residency of debtors and by financial instruments (and a similar table for debtors' financial positions and flows). At a later stage, tables showing from-whom-to-whom data can be compiled. Appendix tables 12C.1 and 12C.2 in appendix C provide some guidance for applying such an approach.

12.6   Concluding Remarks

This chapter sets the background for promoting internationally coordinated efforts for compiling and disseminating data on sectoral financial positions and flows on a from-whom-to-whom basis within the integrated macroeconomic statistics framework, such as the SNA. The compilation of these data would fill a serious data gap as revealed by the global crisis of 2008: information shedding light on the financial interconnectedness among the various sectors of an economy and between them and their counterparties in the rest of the world.

The chapter elaborates the main attributes of the integrated macroeconomic accounts of the 2008 SNA, which allows it to serve as the framework for compiling sectoral accounts and balance sheets, including sectoral financial positions and flows on a from-whom-to-whom-basis. In particular, the SNA integrated framework ensures four consistency rules as follows: (a) vertical consistency (total of all debit entries and that of all credit entries of an institutional unit [sector] are equal); (b) horizontal consistency (debit entries of a transaction type for all units are equal to the credit entries of that transaction type for all units); (c) counterpart consistency (an entry arising from an exchange has a counterpart entry of the same value and at the same time in the account of the counterparty); and (d) stock-flow consistency (changes between opening and closing stocks are fully accounted in transactions, other volume changes, and revaluations). The core accounting structure of the 2008 SNA for financial positions and flows focuses on showing *who does what* rather than *who does what with whom.* This chapter recommends that prominence be given in the SNA to the from-whom-to-whom basis as the main underlying principle for compiling and disseminating sectoral financial positions and flows.

The advantage of using sectoral accounts and balance sheets that are compiled within the integrated SNA framework, contrary to using fragmentary data from different sources, is that such framework ensures data consistency for all entities and for all economic flows and positions, and thus allows for a systematic understanding of the relationships between economic flows in the real and the financial spheres, financial interconnectedness, and linkages among the various economic functions (e.g., between production, consumption, savings, and accumulation).

However, the 2008 global crisis revealed that stronger and well-coordinated international efforts are needed to ensure the development and dissemination of internationally comparable sectoral accounts, balance sheets, and flow of funds. An important milestone in taking forward the work on implementing sectoral accounts and balance sheets is the development of templates for a minimum and encouraged set of internationally comparable sectoral accounts and balance sheets. The templates provide guidance for developing plans for implementation, benchmarks for monitoring progress, and a yardstick for ensuring international comparability. Existing international forums will need to be used more effectively to provide methodological support in the implementation of sectoral accounts and balance sheets. Appropriate funding for outreach, technical assistance, and training will be needed to support activities at the country and international levels.

The current situation on the availability of data on financial positions and flows on a from-whom-to-whom basis is at an early stage. Given the importance to fill these data gaps, compiling and disseminating the accounts on sectoral financial positions and flows using the templates is a condition for achieving international comparability.

The chapter highlights some main areas that need to be addressed when designing work plans and setting up priorities for developing integrated sectoral accounts and balance sheets. Many advanced economies and several emerging market economies are already in the process of enhancing or developing the accounts in accordance with the agreed templates and in the context of their plans for the implementation of the 2008 SNA. Lessons learned from this exercise would be useful not only for other countries that will develop sectoral accounts in the future, but also to identify best practices to enhance the quality of data being compiled now.

The fully integrated SNA sectoral accounts and balance sheets would also improve the integration of scattered information and highlight the inconsistencies between the data sets of the various macroeconomic domains as it ensures a holistic approach to all sectors of an economy and rest of the world. The sectoral accounts will provide an integration framework for macroeconomic data on external, fiscal, and financial sectors with those of the rest of the economy. At the country level, this will facilitate the coordination of work on different macroeconomic statistics domains and promote their consistency at the data collection and compilation stages, thus eliminating or significantly reducing inconsistency of disseminated data.

The ongoing international initiative to improve collaboration among the international organizations for collecting, sharing, and disseminating sectoral accounts and balance sheets is commendable. This initiative should be given priority so that a mechanism is in place before many of the advanced economies and a few emerging market economies start producing these data in 2014. This will not only reduce burdens on countries, but enhance the usefulness of data for users and avoid confusions as all sources will be disseminating the same set of data on sectoral accounts and balance sheets.

Appendix A
Integrating Money and Credit in a From-Whom-to-Whom Framework

There are practical challenges that may have to be tackled when integrating money into the framework for financial positions and flows on a from-whom-to-whom basis. The definitions of money and of money-issuing, money-holding, and money-neutral sectors are not necessarily based on the classification of financial assets and institutional sectors described in section 12.3. Maturity thresholds, valuation methods, and recording principles for accrued interest in monetary statistics generally coincide with those recommended for use in the SNA.

Appendix table 12A.1 shows in *italics* the money holders' financial transactions in assets, which represent monetary claims on the money-issuing sector (resident MFIs). The outstanding money stock may be identified in a similar way in the financial balance sheet.

In appendix table 12A.2, credit as the counterpart to money is shown. The credit counterpart reveals how the change in money is related to lending by money issuers (MFIs) to other residents in all forms, including by the acquisition of securities issued by MFIs. This counterpart comprises part of the assets of the money-issuing sector.

Another part of the assets of the money-issuing sector, net of liabilities to nonresidents, constitutes the external counterpart, the net external assets of the money-issuing sector (in balance sheet terms), or changes in them (corresponding to transactions in the financial account).

The transactions and positions of the rest of the world correspond (after some rearrangements) to the balance of payments and IIP. Net external assets of MFIs, summarizing the money-issuing sector's transactions with the rest of the world, link to money through the MFI accounting framework. The balance of payments identity may then be exploited to show how the money-holding sectors' transactions with the rest of world relate to changes in money, since the money issuers' balance of payments transactions must equal all other resident sectors' balance of payments transactions with reverse sign (for this purpose it is desirable that errors and omissions in the balance of payments have been eliminated when compiling the sector accounts and balance sheets; otherwise, they may be attributed to the money-holding sectors).

Table 12A.1   Money in the framework for financial transactions on a from-whom-to-whom basis

| | | Creditor | | | | | |
| | | Financial Corporations | | | | | |
Type of claim and debtor (MFI)	Nonfinancial corporations	MFIs[a]	Other financial corporations	General government	Households and NPISH	Money-holders (total)	Rest of the world
Currency and deposits							
—short term[b]	*50*	60	*5*	*10*	*150*	*215*	60
—long term	10	20	0	0	30		10
Debt securities							
—short term[c]	*10*	30	*5*	*5*	*20*	*40*	30
—long term	5	10	0	0	10		10
Money market fund shares or units	*5*	5	*2*	*0*	*20*	*27*	0
Equity and remaining investment fund shares	0	5	5	0	5		2
Financial derivatives and employee stock options	2	10	10	0	0		10
Other accounts receivable/payable	1	2	2	0	0		2
Money	**65**		**12**	**15**	**190**	**282**	
Domestic nonmonetary liabilities (total)	18		17	0	45	80	
External liabilities of MFIs (total)							124

[a]MFIs cover the central bank, deposit-taking corporations, and money market funds.

[b]Short-term deposits cover transferable deposits, deposits redeemable at a period of notice of up to and including three months (i.e., short-term savings deposits), and deposits with an agreed maturity of up to and including two years (i.e., short-term time deposits) held with MFIs.

[c]Short-term debt securities cover debt securities with an original maturity of up to and including two years issued by MFIs.

Table 12A.2   Credit as the Counterpart to money in the framework for financial transactions on a from-whom-to-whom basis

Type of claim and creditor (MFI)	Debtor						
		Financial corporations					
	Nonfinancial corporations	MFIs[a]	Other financial corporations	General government	Households and NPISH	Money-holders (total)	Rest of the world
Currency and deposits		80					30
Debt securities	60	40	10	40		110	60
Loans	60		6	20	120	206	45
Money market fund shares or units		5					0
Equity	5	5				5	
Remaining investment fund shares or units			10			10	5
Insurance, pension, and standardized guarantee schemes			3	0		3	0
Financial derivatives and employee stock options	2	10	0	0	0	2	5
Other accounts receivable/payable	0	2	0	0	0	0	5
Domestic credit (total)	127		29	60	120	336	
External assets (total)							150
Net external assets (external counterpart)							26 (= 150 − 124)

[a] MFIs cover the central bank, deposit-taking corporations, and money market funds.

Appendix B

A Status of Availability of Sectoral Balance Sheets and Accumulation Accounts in G-20 Economies

As a first step of a program to strengthen the development and dissemination of sectoral accounts and balance sheets, the IMF Statistics Department has conducted a review of the availability of sectoral balance sheets and accumulation accounts disseminated by the G-20 economies. For each country the review examined the scope and details of the data officially disseminated and made available to the general public through the countries' statistical institutions (national statistical offices, central banks, and ministries of finance) or through OECD, ECB, and Eurostat. The review was focused on the existence of sectoral accounts within the framework of SNA. Information was gathered for stocks, transactions, and other flows of nonfinancial assets and stocks, transactions and other flows of financial assets and liabilities, using the classification of assets and liabilities as well as the classification of institutional sectors as established in the 2008 SNA at the first-digit level (and second digit in some cases) of the corresponding classifications. Note was taken when additional details were available, but without a thorough review of the details published by each country. Other main data characteristics (such as data frequency, timeliness, dissemination formats, and time series) were also reviewed. The IMF review of data availability was conducted during late 2010 and was presented at the IMF-OECD conference in early 2011.[27] This appendix presents the updated status on the availability of sectoral balance sheets and accumulations accounts in the G-20 economies as of the end of 2012.

Progress in the availability of the sectoral balance sheets and accumulation accounts in the G-20 economies since the IMF review has been incorporated and presented in the appendix tables 12B.2 and 12B.3. This exercise does not provide an assessment of the quality and accuracy of data. It should also be noted that this assessment is conducted to provide a broad indication of data gaps for the G-20 economies with respect to sectoral balance sheets and accumulation accounts, and therefore, the assessment for a country may not be comprehensive and fully accurate.

Appendix table 12B.1 shows the classification of assets and liabilities that was used in reviewing the availability of data on sectoral balance sheets and accumulation accounts. The main SNA breakdown of institutional sectors in appendix table 12B.2 and 12B.3 refers to (a) financial corporations, (b) nonfinancial corporations, (c) general governments, (d) households and nonprofit institutions serving households, and (e) the rest of the world. The

27. Shrestha (2011).

Table 12B.1   Classification of assets and liabilities used in the review of data availability

Nonfinancial assets	Financial instruments
Fixed assets	Monetary gold and SDRs
Dwellings	Currency
Inventories	Transferable deposits
Valuables	Transferable deposits with nonresidents
Nonproduced assets	Other deposits
Natural resources	Other deposits with nonresidents
Contracts, leases and licenses	Debt securities
	Debt securities short term
	Debt securities short term with residents
	Debt securities short term with nonresidents
	Debt securities long term
	Debt securities long term with residents
	Debt securities long term with nonresidents
	Loans
	Loans short term
	Loans short term with residents
	Loans short term with nonresidents
	Loans long term
	Loans long term with residents
	Loans long term with residents—mortgages
	Loans long term with nonresidents
	Equity and investment fund shares
	Investment fund shares
	Insurance, pension, and standardized guarantee schemes
	Financial derivatives and employee stock options
	Other accounts receivable/payable

main SNA financial instrument breakdown used in appendix table 12B.2 comprise (a) monetary gold and SDRs, (b) currency and deposits, (c) debt securities, (d) loans, (e) equity and investment fund shares, (f) insurance, pension, and standardized guarantee schemes, and (g) other accounts receivable/payable. The main SNA breakdown of nonfinancial assets in appendix table 12B.3 includes (a) fixed assets, (b) inventories, (c) valuables, and (d) nonproduced assets.

Table 12B.2 Availability of data on financial assets and liabilities in G20 economies

	Balance sheets					Transactions					
	Total economy	SNA main institutional sectors	SNA main instruments	Frequency	Additional sectoral (S) or instrument (I) breakdowns	Total economy	SNA main institutional sectors	SNA main instruments	Frequency	Other volume changes sectors—(S) instrument—(I)	Revaluations sectors—(S) instruments—(I)
Advanced economies											
Australia	Yes	All sectors	All instruments	Quarterly	For some (S) & some (I)	Yes	All sectors	All instruments	Quarterly	By (I)	By (I)
Canada	Yes	All sectors	All instruments	Quarterly	For some (S) & some (I)	Yes	All sectors	All instruments	Quarterly	No	No
France	Yes	All sectors	All instruments	Quarterly	For some (I)	Yes	All sectors	All instruments	Quarterly	By (S) & (I)	By (S) & (I)
Germany	Yes	All sectors	All instruments	Quarterly	For some (S) & some (I)	Yes	All sectors	All instruments	Quarterly	No	No
Italy	Yes	All sectors	All instruments	Quarterly	For some (S) & some (I)	Yes	All sectors	All instruments	Quarterly	No	No
Japan	Yes	All sectors	All instruments	Quarterly	For some (S)	Yes	All sectors	All instruments	Quarterly	B (I)	B (I)
Korea	Yes	All sectors	All instruments	Annual (Q partial)	For some (S) & some (I)	Yes	All sectors	All instruments	Annual (Q partial)	No	No
United Kingdom	Yes	All sectors	All instruments	Quarterly	For most (I)	Yes	All sectors	All instruments	Quarterly	No	No
United States	Yes	All sectors	All instruments	Quarterly	For some (I)	Yes	All sectors	All instruments	Quarterly	By (S)	By (S)
Emerging market economies											
Argentina	No	No	No	No	No	No	No	No	No	No	No
Brazil	Yes	Yes	Yes	Annual	No	No	Yes	All instruments	Annual	No	No
China	No	No	No	No	No	Yes	All sectors	Partial	Annual	No	No
India	No	No	No	No	No	Yes	Different classification	Partial	Annual	No	No
Indonesia	No	No	No	No	No	Yes	Different classification	Partial	Quarterly	No	No
Mexico	Yes	All sectors	All instruments	Annual	For (S)	Yes	All sectors	All instruments	Annual (Q for total economy)	By (S)	By (S)
Russia	No	No	No	No	No	No	No	No	No	No	No
Saudi Arabia	No	No	No	No	No	No	No	No	No	No	No
South Africa	No	Some (S)	No	Annual	No	Yes	All sectors	All instruments	Quarterly	No	No
Turkey	No	No	No	No	No	No	No	No	No	No	No

Table 12B.3   Availability of data on nonfinancial assets in G-20 economies

	Balance sheets					Transactions					
	Total economy	SNA main institutional sectors	SNA main assets	Frequency	Additional sectoral (S) or assets (A) breakdowns	Total Economy	SNA main institutional sectors	SNA main assets	Frequency	Other volume changes sectors—(S) assets—(A)	Revaluations sectors—(S) assets—(A)
Advanced Economies											
Australia	Yes	All sectors	Exc. Valuables	Quarterly	For all (A), exc. Valuables	Yes	All sectors	Exc. valuables	Quarterly	Some (A)	Some (A)
Canada	Yes	All sectors	Exc. Valuables	Quarterly	For most (S) & (A)	Yes	All sectors	Exc. valuables	Quarterly	No	No
France	Yes	All sectors	All assets	Annual	For some (A)	Yes	All sectors	All assets	Quarterly	By (S)&(A)	By (S)&(A)
Germany	Yes	All sectors	Partial	Annual	For some (A)	Yes	All sectors	All assets	Quarterly	No	No
Italy	Yes	No	Only fixed assets	Annual	For fixed assets	Yes	No	Fixed assets	Quarterly	No	No
Japan	Yes	All sectors	Exc. valuables	Annual	For some (A)	Yes	All sectors	All assets	Quarterly	By (A)	By (A)
Korea	Yes	All sectors	Fixed assets	Annual	For some (A)	Yes	No	Partial	Quarterly	No	No
United Kingdom	Yes	All sectors	Exc. natural res	Annual	For some (A)	Yes	All sectors	Exc. natural res	Quarterly	No	No
United States	Yes	All sectors	Exc. valuables	Quarterly	For some (A)	Yes	All sectors	Exc. valuables	Quarterly	By (S)	By (S)
Emerging market economies											
Argentina	Yes	No	Partial	Annual	For some (A)	Yes	No	Partial	Quarterly	No	No
Brazil	No	No	No	No	No	Yes	All sectors	Exc. valuables	Annual (Q partial)	No	No
China	No	No	No	No	No	Yes	All sectors	Exc. valuables	Annual	No	No
India	Yes	Different classification	Partial	Annual	No	Yes	Different classification	Partial	Annual (Q produced assets)	No	No
Indonesia	No	No	No	No	No	Yes	Different classification	Partial	Quarterly	No	No
Mexico	Yes	Yes	Partial	Annual	For (S)	Yes	All sectors	All assets	Annual (Q produced assets)	For (S)	For (S)
Russia	No	No	No	No	No	Yes	No	Partial	Quarterly	No	No
Saudi Arabia	No	No	No	No	No	Yes	No	Fixed assets	Annual	No	No
South Africa	Yes	No	Partial	Annual	No	Yes	Yes	Partial	Annual	No	No
Turkey	No	No	No	No	No	Yes	No	Fixed assets	Quarterly	No	No

Appendix C
Presentation of Sectoral Financial Positions and Flows

As a first step, tables may be designed to follow the residence of creditor approach. Such tables show institutional sectors as creditors that hold financial instruments. The holdings are part of the balance sheet (asset portfolio) of this sector, whereas transactions in financial instruments are part of the sector's financial account. The holdings of financial instruments by resident sectors are shown (with a breakdown by the residency of debtors but without a breakdown of the resident sector of debtors), and the financial instruments issued by residents and acquired by nonresidents are also shown. Appendix table 12C.1 reflects this approach and shows the financial instrument categories according to the 2008 SNA.

Some amendments to this table may be made by splitting the financial corporation sector into some subsectors, such as depository corporations, insurance corporations and pension funds, and other financial corporations. A breakdown of some financial instrument categories, such as deposits, loans, or debt securities by original maturity may also be feasible at this stage.

The tables on the from-whom-to-whom basis show positions and flows for financial instruments acquired by resident sectors and by nonresidents, with a breakdown by institutional sector for resident debtors (the cells of appendix table 12C.2 shaded light gray). Furthermore, acquisitions by nonresidents of financial instruments issued by residents are shown (penultimate column marked nonresidents) and also financial instruments issued by nonresidents and acquired by resident sectors (penultimate row marked nonresidents). However, acquisitions by nonresidents of financial instruments issued by nonresidents are not covered (black cells).

For residents, the presentation of nonconsolidated data on the holdings and acquisitions of financial instruments is recommended, covering intrasectoral positions and flows (diagonal cells of appendix table 12C.2 shaded in dark gray).

The collection and compilation of such from-whom-to-whom data has to follow a step-by-step approach based on the availability of corresponding source data. A first step is usually to integrate such data from monetary statistics, balance of payments, or government finance statistics providing usually detailed data on nonnegotiable financial instruments, such as deposits, loans, trade credit, or insurance and pension entitlements.

In a further step, from-whom-to-whom data may be derived by sector and subsector for securities based on detailed source data taken from financial statements and from securities databases. When developing data sources and a compilation system for sectoral financial positions and flows, it is important to design them with a view to supporting the broader objective of the compilation of integrated sectoral financial positions and flows on a from-whom-to-whom basis.

Table 12C.1   Financial instruments classified by creditor sector and residency of debtor

Debtor by residency and by financial instrument category		Creditor							
		Residents					Nonresidents	All creditors
		Nonfinancial corporations	Financial corporations	General government	Households and nonprofit institutions serving households	All residents		
Residents	Monetary gold and SDRs							
	Currency and deposits							
	Debt securities							
	Loans							
	Equity and investment fund shares or units							
	Insurance, pension, and standardized guarantee schemes							
	Financial derivatives and employee stock options							
	Other accounts receivable/payable							
Nonresidents	Monetary gold and SDRs							
	Currency and deposits							
	Debt securities							
	Loans							
	Equity and investment fund shares or units							
	Insurance, pension, and standardized guarantee schemes							
	Financial derivatives and employee stock options							
	Other accounts receivable/ payable							
All debtors	Monetary gold and SDRs							
	Currency and deposits							
	Debt securities							
	Loans							
	Equity and investment fund shares or units							
	Insurance, pension, and standardized guarantee schemes							
	Financial derivatives and employee stock options							
	Other accounts receivable/payable							

Note: A similar table may be compiled showing financial instruments classified by debtor sector and residency of creditor.

Table 12C.2   Acquisitions of financial instruments in a from-whom-to-whom framework by residency/resident sector of creditor and by residency/resident sector of debtor

Debtor by residency and resident sector and by financial instrument		Creditor by residency and resident sector					
		Residents				Non residents	All creditors
		Nonfinancial corporations	Financial corporations and subsectors	General government	Households and nonprofit institutions serving households		
Residents	Nonfinancial corporations	Monetary gold and SDRs					
		Currency and deposits					
		Debt securities					
		Loans					
		Equity and investment fund shares or units					
		Insurance, pension, and standardized guarantee schemes					
		Financial derivatives and employee stock options					
		Other accounts receivable/ payable					
	Financial corporations and subsectors	Monetary gold and SDRs					
		Currency and deposits					
		...					
	General government	Monetary gold and SDRs					
		Currency and deposits					
		...					
	Households and nonprofit institutions serving households	Monetary gold and SDRs					
		Currency and deposits					
		...					
Nonresidents		Monetary gold and SDRs					
		Currency and deposits					
		...					
All debtors		Monetary gold and SDRs					
		Currency and deposits					
		...					

Appendix D

Templates for Internationally Comparable Sectoral Accounts and Balance Sheets

Table 12D.1   Current and capital accounts: Sectors and transactions (quarterly, with timeliness of one quarter)

		Total economy	Nonfinancial corporations		Financial corporations					General government	Households and NPISHs	Rest of the world
				Of which: Public nonfinancial corporations	Monetary financial institutions	Insurance corporations and pension funds	Other financial corporations	Of which: Public financial corporations				
		S1	S11	S11001	S12					S13	S14 + S15	S2
					S121 + S122 + S123	S128 + S129	S124 + S125 + S1265 + S127	S12001				
P.6 (for S2)	Exports of goods and services											
P.7 (for S2)	Imports of goods and services											
B.1g	Value added, gross/gross domestic product											
D.1	Compensation of employees											
B.2g + B.3g	Operating surplus, gross and mixed income, gross											
D.2	Taxes on production and imports											
	Of which:											
D.21 (for S1)	Taxes on products											
D.29	Other taxes on production											
D.3	Subsidies											
	Of which:											
D.31 (for S1)	Subsidies on products											
D.39	Other subsidies on production											

(continued)

Table 12D.1   (continued)

			Total economy	Nonfinancial corporations	Of which: Public nonfinancial corporations	Financial corporations	Monetary financial institutions	Insurance corporations and pension funds	Other financial corporations	Of which: Public financial corporations	General government	Households and NPISHs	Rest of the world
			S1	S11	S11001	S12	S121 + S122 + S123	S128 + S129	S124 + S125 + S1265 + S127	S12001	S13	S14 + S15	S2
D.4	Property income												
	Of which:												
	D.41	Interest											
	D.4N	Property income other than interest											
D.41g	Total interest before FISIM allocation												
B.5g	Balance of primary incomes, gross/ national income, gross												
D.5	Current taxes on income, wealth, etc												
D.61	Net social contributions												
D.62	Social benefits other than social transfers in kind												
D.63	Social transfers in kind												
D.7	Other current transfers												
	Of which:												
	D.71	Net non-life insurance premiums											
	D.72	Non-life insurance claims											
	D.7N	Other current transfers, not elsewhere specified											
B.6g	Disposable income, gross												

Code	Description					
D.8	Adjustment for the change in pension entitlements					
P.3	Final consumption expenditure					
	Of which:					
P.31		Individual consumption expenditure				
P.32		Collective consumption expenditure				
B.8g	Saving, gross					
D.9	Capital transfers					
	Of which:					
D.91		Capital taxes				
D.9N		Investment grants and other capital transfers				
P.5g	Gross capital formation					
	Of which:					
P.51g		Gross fixed capital formation				
P.52+P.53		Changes in inventories and acquisition less disposals of valuables				
P.51c	Consumption of fixed capital					
NP	Acquisitions less disposals of nonproduced assets					
B.9	Net lending (+)/Net borrowing (−)					

Note: All but shaded areas are minimum; shaded area is encouraged.

Table 12D.2   Financial stocks and flows: Sectors and instruments (quarterly, with timeliness of one quarter)

	Total economy	Nonfinancial corporations		Financial corporations														General government		Households and NPISHs			Rest of the world
		Total	Of which: Public nonfinancial corporations	Total	Monetary financial institutions				Insurance corp. and pension funds			Other financial corporations					Of which: Public financial corporations	Total	Of which: Social Security funds	Total	Households	NPISHs	
					Total	Central bank	Other deposit-taking corporations	Money market funds	Total	Insurance corporations	Pension funds	Total	Non-MMF investment funds	Other financial intermediaries except insurance corporations and pension funds	Financial auxiliaries	Captive financial institutions and money lenders							
	S1	S11	S11001	S12	S121 + S122 + S123	S121	S122	S123	S128 + S129	S128	S129	S124 + S125 + S126 + S127	S124	S125	S126	S127	S12001	S13	S1314	S14 + S15	S14	S15	S2
F1 Monetary gold and SDRs																							
F11 Monetary gold																							
F12 SDRs																							
F2 Currency and deposits																							
Of which: Domestic currency																							
F21 Currency																							
F22 Transferable deposits																							
F221 Interbank positions																							
F229 Other transferable deposits																							
F29 Other deposits																							
F3 Debt securities																							
Of which: Domestic currency																							
F31 short term																							
F32 long term																							
With remaining maturity of one year and less																							

	With remaining maturity of more than a year
F4	Loans
	Of which: Domestic currency
	F41 short term
	F42 long term
	With remaining maturity of one year and less
	With remaining maturity of more than a year
F5	Equity and investment fund shares
	F51 Equity
	F511 Listed shares
	F512 Unlisted shares
	F519 Other equity
	F52 Investment fund shares/units
	F521 Money market fund shares/units
	F522 Non-MMF investment fund shares/units
F6	Insurance, pension and standardized guarantee schemes
	F61 Non-life insurance technical reserves
	F62 Life insurance and annuity entitlements
	F63 + F64 + F65 Retirement entitlements

(continued)

	Total economy	Nonfinancial corporations		Financial corporations															General government		Households and NPISHs			Rest of the world
		Total	Of which: Public nonfinancial corporations	Total	Monetary financial institutions				Insurance corp. and pension funds			Other financial corporations						Of which: Public financial corporations	Total	Of which: Social Security funds	Total	Households	NPISHs	
					Total	Central bank	Other deposit-taking corporations	Money market funds	Total	Insurance corporations	Pension funds	Total	Non-MMF investment funds	Other financial intermediaries except insurance corporations and pension funds	Financial auxiliaries	Captive financial institutions and money lenders								
	S1	S11	S1100I	S12	S121 + S122 + S123	S121	S122	S123	S128 + S129	S128	S129	S124 + S125 + S126 + S127	S124	S125	S126	S127	S12O0I	S13	S1314	S14 + S15	S14	S15	S2
F63 Pension entitlements																							
F64 Claim of pension fund on pension managers																							
F65 Entitlements to nonpension benefits																							
F66 Provisions for calls under standardized guarantees																							
F7 Financial derivatives and employee stock options																							
F71 Financial derivatives																							
F711 Options																							
F712 Forwards																							
F72 Employee stock options																							
F8 Other accounts receivable/payable																							
Of which: Domestic currency																							
F81 Trade credits and advances																							
F89 Other accounts receivable/payable																							

Note: All but shaded areas are minimum; shaded area is encouraged.

Table 12D.3   Stocks of nonfinancial assets: Sectors and asset types (annual, with timeliness of nine months)

	Total economy	Nonfinancial corporations	Of which: Public nonfinancial corporations	Financial corporations	Monetary financial institutions	Insurance corporations and pension funds	Other financial corporations	Of which: Public financial corporations	General government	Households and NPISHs	Rest of the world
	S1	S11	S11001	S12	S121 + S122 + S123	S128 + S129	S124 + S125 + S1265 + S127	S12001	S13	S14 + S15	S2
AN1 Produced nonfinancial assets											
AN11 Fixed assets of which,											
AN111 Dwellings											
AN112 Other buildings and structures											
AN12 Inventories											
AN13 Valuables											
AN2 Nonproduced, nonfinancial assets											
AN21 Natural resources of which,											
AN211 Land of which,											
AN. 2111 Land underlying buildings and structures											
AN212 Mineral and energy reserves											
AN22 Contracts, leases, and licenses											
AN23 Goodwill and marketing assets											

Note: All but shaded areas are minimum; shaded area is encouraged.

References

Allen, M., C. Rosenberg, C. Keller, B. Setser, and Nouriel Roubini. 2002. "A Balance Sheet Approach to Financial Crisis." IMF Working Paper no. WP/02/210. http://www.imf.org/external/pubs/cat/longres.aspx?sk=16167.0.

Bank for International Settlements, International Monetary Fund, and European Central Bank. Various Years. *Handbook on Securities Statistics*, Part 1, Part 2, and Part 3. http://www.imf.org/external/np/sta/wgsd/hbook.htm.

Bank for International Settlements. *Locational International Banking Statistics Guide and Data*. http://www.bis.org/statistics/bankstats.htm.

Dawson, John C., ed. 1996. *Flow of Funds Analysis, A Handbook for Practitioners,* Armonk and London.

European Central Bank. 2012. *Handbook on Quarterly Financial Accounts for the Euro Area: Sources and Methods.* http://www.ecb.int/stats/acc/html/index.en.html.

European Central Bank. 2010. *ECB Monthly Bulletin—Euro Area Statistics Methodological Notes: Chapter 3 Euro Area Accounts.* http://www.ecb.int/stats/acc/html/index.en.html.

European Central Bank. 2004. "Properties and Use of General Government Quarterly Accounts." *Monthly Bulletin* August: 65–77.

European Central Bank. 2006. "Sectoral Money Holding: Determinants and Recent Developments." *Monthly Bulletin* August.

European Central Bank. 2006. *Integrated Financial and Non-Financial Accounts for the Institutional Sectors in the Euro Area.* Frankfurt am Main: European Central Bank. October.

European Council. 1996. *European System of Accounts (ESA95).* Brussels.

Eurostat. 2012. European System of Accounts (ESA2010), draft version.

Financial Stability Board and International Monetary Fund. 2009. *The Financial Crisis and Information Gaps—Report to the G-20 Finance Ministers and Central Bank Governors.* Washington, D.C. http://www.imf.org/external/np/g20/pdf/102909.pdf.

Financial Stability Board and International Monetary Fund. 2011. *The Financial Crisis and Information Gaps—Implementation Progress Report.* Washington, D.C. http://www.imf.org/external/np/g20/pdf/063011.pdf.

Heath, R. 2013. "Why are the G-20 Data Gaps Initiative and the SDDS Plus Relevant for Financial Stability Analysis?"IMF Working Paper no. WP/13/6. http://www.imf.org/external/pubs/cat/longres.aspx?sk=40227.0.

International Monetary Fund. 2009. *Balance of Payments and International Investment Position Manual,* Sixth Edition (BPM6). Washington, D.C.

International Monetary Fund. 2000. *Monetary and Financial Statistics Manual.* Washington, D.C.

International Monetary Fund. 2001. *Government Finance Statistics Manual,* Washington, D.C.

International Monetary Fund. *CDIS Guide, Data, Metadata.* Washington, D.C. http://www.imf.org/external/np/sta/pi/ cdis/index.htm.

International Monetary Fund. *CPIS Guide, Data, Metadata.* Washington, D.C. http://www.imf.org/external/np/sta/pi/ cpis.htm.

Mathisen, J., and A. Pellechio. 2006. "Using the Balance Sheet Approach in Surveillance: Framework and Data Sources and Availability."IMF Working Paper no. WP/06/100. http://www.imf.org/external/pubs/cat/ longres.aspx?sk=19800.0.

Shrestha, M. 2011. "A Status on the Availability of Sectoral Balance Sheets and Accumulation Accounts in G20 Economies." Paper presented at the IMF-OECD Conference on Strengthening Sectoral Position and Flow Data in the Macro-

economic Accounts, Washington, DC, February 28–March 2. http://www.imf.org
/external/np/seminars/eng/2011/sta/index.htm.

Shrestha, M., R. Mink, and S. Fassler. 2012. "An Integrated Framework for Financial Positions and Flows on a From-Whom-to-Whom Basis: Concepts, Current
Status, and Prospects." IMF Working Paper no. (WP/12/57). http://www.imf.org
/external/pubs/cat/longres.aspx?sk=25743.0.

United Nations, Eurostat, International Monetary Fund, Organisation for Economic Co-operation and Development and World Bank. 1993. *System of National
Accounts 1993*, Series F, No. 2, Rev. 4. New York: United Nations.

United Nations, European Commission, International Monetary Fund, Organisation for Economic Co-operation and Development and World Bank. 2009. *System
of National Accounts 2008*, Series F, No. 2, Rev. 5. New York: United Nations.

IV

**Measuring Sustainability:
The Environment, Human Capital,
Health, and Innovation**

Toward the Measurement of Net Economic Welfare
Air Pollution Damage in the US National Accounts— 2002, 2005, 2008

Nicholas Z. Muller

13.1 Introduction

Environmental accounting expands the accounting boundaries established in the conventional National Income and Product Accounts (NIPAs) by measuring the value of natural resources and environmental damage. The goal is to gain a more complete picture of national wealth and welfare. Prior research has developed static environmental accounts (Ho and Jorgensen 2007; Muller, Mendelsohn, and Nordhaus 2011). Static environmental accounts constitute an important step toward a fully integrated system of accounts because they provide a glimpse of what the NIPAs overlook: the value that various nonmarket goods and services contribute to national welfare at a given point in time.

This chapter argues that environmental accounts should follow the historic progression of the national accounts from annual measures expressed in current dollars to indices tracking changes expressed in real terms. The development and implementation of the NIPAs in the 1930s began with a focus on measurement of current dollar estimates of national income. Ultimately, in recognition that the NIPAs' primary value is not as an absolute but rather a relative measurement, price deflators were introduced to the NIPAs in 1951 (USBEA 2011). Now, changes in gross domestic product (GDP) are the primary focus, not levels. Similarly, dynamic augmented accounts comprise an improvement over static measurement. In particular, time series environmental accounting provides insights in three areas: changes in gross

Nicholas Z. Muller is assistant professor of economics at Middlebury College and a faculty research fellow of the National Bureau of Economic Research.

For acknowledgments, sources of research support, and disclosure of the author's material financial relationships, if any, please see http://www.nber.org/chapters/c12839.ack.

pollution damage and resource stocks, changes in resource consumption and pollution intensity, and differences in rates of growth with and without augmentation. Including these measures into augmented accounts is a critical step in closing the gap between the current market-based measures of output and a more complete picture of national economic welfare.[1]

This analysis conducts times series environmental accounting by applying the methods developed in Muller, Mendelsohn, and Nordhaus (2011) to measure the gross external damage (GED) due to air pollution emissions in the United States (US) economy in 2002, 2005, and 2008. Intuition suggests, and prior research confirms, that including the GED into the accounts in any one time period will shrink conventional, static measures of output such as GDP or value added (VA). After all, the GED is comprised of external costs neither reflected in market prices nor included in the NIPAs. Air pollution (and other types) is a residual of the production process and the atmosphere acts as a repository for waste disposal. When well-defined property rights exist for waste disposal (as in the case of a landfill), firms are charged per unit disposal. In the case of air pollution, firms often consume this valuable input free of charge; the role of environmental accounting, then, is to include the cost of consuming this scarce input into the NIPAs. To this end, this chapter computes environmentally adjusted value added (EVA), which is the value-added analogue to Bartelmus's (2009) environmentally adjusted gross output (EDP). EVA is defined as VA less GED.

While including GED into the NIPAs in any one time period will reduce measures of output, folding GED into the accounts over time can affect conventional measures of growth in either direction. Whether GED attenuates or augments conventional measures of growth depends on the relative rates and direction of change in market production and the GED. Three cases are both important and illustrative. First, an economy with VA growth less than its GED growth would have EVA changing at rates less than VA. In this case, augmented accounts ratchet back estimates of growth. Second, if the GED and the VA are changing at the same rate, growth rates for the VA and the EVA are equal. And, third, EVA growth may exceed VA growth if the GED grows more slowly than the VA (or if the GED contracts); this would cause the augmented EVA measure to enhance estimated rates of growth because the benefits of reduced GED act as a source of growth in the EVA measure. This chapter reports levels and rates of change of the VA and the EVA for each sector and the entire US economy over the period 2002 to 2008.

The value of relative measurement also holds for the nonmarket accounts. Although a paucity of data, measurement difficulties, and the codified structure of the current, market-oriented NIPAs make even annual, one-shot

1. Here, and in the title, net economic welfare is meant in the sense of Nordhaus and Tobin (1972): it is a proposed measure of national income and production that values many external costs overlooked by the NIPAs. One among these is air pollution damage, which is the exclusive focus of the chapter.

estimates of nonmarket accounts significant achievements, most meaningful are elicitations of rates of change in the value of goods and services outside the purview of the standard accounts. Prior work in the current context (measuring the damages from environmental pollution) developed annual estimates of the air pollution externality (Ho and Jorgensen 2007; Muller, Mendelsohn, and Nordhaus 2011).

Environmental accounts in multiple time periods may detect structural changes in economic activity: either in the form of sectoral composition of an economy or in terms of the pollution intensity of production in the extant sectoral mix. This latter point, changes in pollution intensity, highlights an additional benefit of measuring the GED across time. It is often the case that changes in pollution intensity arise due to regulation. Insofar as this is the case, the GED can provide an important way to measure the benefits of environmental policies. As regulated firms purchase, install, and operate pollution control devices, these capital and operating and maintenance costs are entered into the (existing) NIPAs as a cost of doing business.[2] Regulated industry's VA declines as a function of these expenditures, ceteris peribus. Abatement expenditures are often conventionally viewed as a drag on growth for firms, industries, and sectors that make such expenditures. The NIPAs capture returns to these expenditures either through the transfer to firms that produce and market abatement technology, or through any improvements to the production of market goods and services due to the reduced pollution flow. However, the NIPAs, by definition, miss nonmarket benefits that may arise from their use. This happens to be quite important for the case of air pollution since the vast majority of the GED is comprised of impacts to human health, which are not measured or reflected in market transactions. This highlights the importance of the augmented EVA measure. The EVA encompasses an important missing (from VA) measure of the benefit of these investments in environmental quality. Namely, the corresponding reduction to the GED that is comprised almost entirely of reduced mortality risk and incidence rates of chronic illness (both examples of nonmarket benefits). The EVA accounts for this source of growth.

Measuring the damages of air pollution necessitates having information on quantities of emissions *and* the marginal value of such emissions. In a modern, developed economy, such as the United States or countries in the European Union, measurements of pollution *quantities* have been established since the implementation of environmental policies. The primary challenge then to conducting or implementing environmental accounts for pollution is valuing emissions. With quantities of emissions reported by the US Environmental Protection Agency (USEPA), the GED is tabulated using the source- and pollutant-specific marginal damages produced by an

---

2. Fixed capital costs enter the NIPAs through measures of consumption of fixed capital (CFC). This analysis reports market VA net of CFC as reported by the USBEA (USBEA 2011).

integrated assessment model, the AP2 model (Muller and Mendelsohn 2007, 2009; Muller, Mendelsohn, and Nordhaus 2011; Muller 2011, 2012; NAS NRC 2009). The AP2 model encompasses emissions of and estimates marginal damages for: ammonia (NH_3), nitrogen oxides (NO_x), fine particulate matter ($PM_{2.5}$), sulfur dioxide (SO_2), and volatile organic compounds (VOCs). An important feature of AP2 is that it estimates marginal damages for specific source locations. This spatially tailored approach allows for heterogeneity in the marginal values.

The methodology embedded in the AP2 model uses assumptions that tend to be viewed as standard in the literature that measures the damages from air pollution. Critical among these assumptions are the dose-response parameter that links mortality rates to exposures to fine particulate matter, and the value attributed to small changes to mortality risks. The dose-response relationship from Pope et al. (2002) is employed by AP2, and the value of a statistical life (VSL) methodology is used to value mortality risks (Viscusi and Aldy 2003). The VSL employed herein is approximately $6 million ($2005). The marginal damages produced by AP2 are multiplied times reported emissions in order to tabulate total damages. This approach is congruent with how the NIPAs are calculated (Nordhaus 2006).

Computationally, the degree to which valuation is a difficult task depends on three factors. First is the extent of mixing of the pollutant; a well-mixed pollutant's impact does not vary according to location of emissions. Measuring such a pollutant's impact is relatively straightforward since value estimates do not vary by source. Second is the nature of impacts: market versus nonmarket effects. Impacts in markets have well-defined prices. Nonmarket effects require imputation. And third is the time horizon of impacts: effects may occur relatively soon after emissions or they may span many years. If pollutants persist in the environment, the issue of discounting arises. How do these parameters relate to the pollutants encompassed by the GED?

First, these pollutants are not well mixed; this suggests that source-specific marginal damages for emissions should be used. Evidence of the degree of heterogeneity in the marginal damages is provided by Muller and Mendelsohn (2009) and Fann, Fulcher, and Hubbell (2009). Second, the majority of adverse impacts from these pollutants involve increased mortality risks. Valuation of mortality risk is both difficult and contentious. Third, the impacts of the pollutants encompassed by the GED tend to occur within a year of emission. As a result, issues related to discounting do not arise.

The valuation of environmental damage, and in particular premature mortality effects, has received a mixed welcome in the environmental accounting literature. On one hand, Nordhaus and Kokkelenberg (1999) argue that valuation of environmental damage is essential to environmental accounting. On the other hand, the System of Environmental-Economic

Accounting (SEEA) (all versions) effectively exclude welfare-based valuation of environmental damage due to its controversial nature. While it is true that valuing nonmarket services (such as human health status) is uncertain and controversial, simply measuring tonnage of the pollutants encompassed by GED may in fact be misleading. Consider that pollution emissions may increase or decrease differently across space due to regulation or the distribution of industrial production. If, for example, emissions decrease in especially high damage areas, while low damage emissions increase significantly, it is *possible* for physical accounts and the GED to move in different directions. Which tack is preferred? In the simplest sense, the spatial variation in impacts per ton of emissions is driven by population density; emissions in cities cause more harm than emissions in rural areas. Although the value-based GED relies on methods that are uncertain, it is based on an approach to damage measurement that *picks up this spatial pattern*. In contrast, physical accounts overlook this by treating all tons equally, which is clearly a mistake.

In order to make meaningful comparisons of EVA and GED across years the paper deflates the marginal damages. Three approaches to deflation are used. First, the marginal damages are held fixed at 2005 levels for 2002 and 2008. This means that the only factors changing are emissions in 2002 and 2008. The second deflation strategy applies the sector-specific deflators reported by the United States Bureau of Economic Analysis (USBEA) for market prices. In this case both the market VA and the nonmarket GED are deflated in the same manner. The third deflation tactic uses the Fisher pollution price index numbers reported in Muller (2013). These are pollutant- and year-specific Fisher index numbers computed using the marginal damages across the United States in each year of this analysis. These are reported in table 13A.2 of the appendix.

The literature that focuses on environmental accounting is large and well developed. Arguments regarding augmenting the NIPAs appear in articles as far back as the late 1960s (Ayres and Kneese 1969; Leontief 1970; Nordhaus and Tobin 1972). More recent research in this area includes: Nordhaus and Kokkelenberg (1999); Bartelmus (1998, 2009); Vardon et al. (2007); Gundimeda et al. (2007); and Muller, Mendelsohn, and Nordhaus (2011).

The work of Bartelmus (2009) is probably most similar to the current analysis. There are three dimensions to the correspondence between Bartelmus' work and the current chapter. First, it develops and estimates an adjusted measure of economic output (EDP). Second, it applies this methodology empirically. And third, the study encompasses multiple data years. However, important distinctions include the present study's use of an integrated assessment model to value pollution according to source type and location. Further, the GED is expressed in real terms whereas Bartelmus reports EDP in current dollars. Finally, the EDP are computed globally and decomposed by region, while the GED are tabulated for the United States and decomposed by sector in the present chapter.

There are numerous reports available at the SEEA program's website that explore aspects of environmental accounting that overlap with the focus of the current chapter (United Nations 2011). For example, Murty and Gulati (2006) explore *firm-level* environmental accounting for air pollution impacts in India; the authors estimate shadow prices for local air pollutants emitted from thermal power plants in a few locations in India. Also on the SEEA website, there are many reports that focus on relatively current environmental accounting efforts throughout the world. Important examples that connect to the current chapter include reports on the mass of emissions of air pollutants, environmental tax revenue, and abatement expenditures.

This chapter builds on the prior work of Muller, Mendelsohn, and Nordhaus (2011), which measured both sector and industry GED and VA. The current analysis does not drill down below the sector level of aggregation because of limitations in the data. While GED can be computed at the industry level in all three data years, the USBEA reports measures of output at the six-digit level of detail in five-year increments that do not line up with the USEPA air pollution emission reporting system. While there exists considerable heterogeneity in emission intensity within a sector, this analysis cannot relate GED to VA for specific industries because of this data constraint.

The methodology used to estimate the marginal damages that are ultimately used in this chapter to compute the GED is linked to a literature on the measurement and valuation of air pollution damages. Important papers in this literature include: Mendelsohn (1980), Burtraw et al. (1998), Banzhaf, Burtraw, and Palmer (2004), Tong et al. (2006), Muller and Mendelsohn (2007, 2009), and Fann, Fulcher, and Hubbell (2009).

The empirical results indicate that the GED decreases dramatically from 2002 to 2008. Using the Fisher pollution index, real GED is estimated to be $480 billion in 2002, $430 billion in 2005, and $350 billion in 2008. On an annualized basis, the GED decreases by approximately 4 percent from 2002 to 2005 and then the GED declines by nearly 6 percent from 2005 to 2008. Much of this decline stems from reductions in the GED attributable to the agriculture, utility, manufacturing, and transportation sectors. In 2002 the total nominal GED/VA is approximately 0.054, and in 2008 the GED/VA is 0.030.

The GED/VA index shows considerable variation within sectors between 2002 and 2008. The utility sector shows a GED/VA of 0.96 in 2002. In 2008, the utility GED/VA drops to less than 0.50. Similarly, the agriculture and forestry sector begins in 2002 with a GED/VA of 0.90 and this index declines to less than 0.30 in 2008. The manufacturing sector begins in 2002 with a GED/VA of 0.056 and in 2008 the manufacturing GED/VA is estimated to be 0.032. This is not to suggest that the level of the manufacturing GED remains necessarily fixed; in 2002 the manufacturing GED was \$72 billion while in 2008 the GED for this sector was \$46 billion.

The chapter argues that two general factors drive the changes in the GED from 2002 to 2008. First, the macroeconomic conditions varied over this time period; the US economy was emerging from a recession in 2002 largely brought on by the correction in the technology sector. In 2008, by contrast, the economy was on the precipice of the Great Recession. Many sectors were experiencing outright contraction in output (or at least reduced growth) at this time. This had implications in terms of the GED as air pollution emissions were reduced along with gross output. An example of this is evident in the manufacturing sector. Annualized growth in VA was about 5 percent between 2002 and 2005. From 2005 to 2008, VA increased by just 0.5 percent, per annum. Insofar as emissions are positively correlated with output, such a slowdown is bound to yield fewer total emissions.

The second factor affecting the GED change between 2002 and 2008 is the regulatory environment. Regulatory constraints may affect gross output (or VA) through compliance costs. Such rules, by definition, impact the GED through binding emission limits. For example, utilities (especially coal-fired power plants) dramatically reduced their emission of SO_2 and NO_x between 2002 and 2008 specifically because of regulatory constraints. To an extent, the chapter is able to tease out these impacts in the calculation of GED. Further, sulfur content rules for diesel fuel used in highway vehicles as well as locomotives and marine vessels implemented in 2007 had noticeable impacts on the GED for the transportation sector. While disentangling these two factors (gross output and regulation) is difficult for many sectors, where feasible the chapter attempts to parse the effects of these two factors on GED and GED/VA.

Finally, the chapter provides evidence of a significant divergence between standard measures of economic growth and performance (such as VA) and the augmented EVA measure. In particular, the economy-wide EVA grows at greater annual rates from 2002 to 2005 and from 2005 to 2008 than VA. Between 2002 and 2005, the EVA grew at an annual rate of 3.07 percent while conventionally measured VA grew at 2.76 percent. Thus, incorporating the GED into this measure of growth alters (increases) the ex post estimate of growth by 0.3 percent. From 2005 to 2008, VA grew at an annual rate of 1.18 percent and the EVA grew at 1.47 percent per year. The divergence between the rates of growth in VA and EVA was just under 0.3 percent from 2005 to 2008. While including the GED into the NIPAs reduces the level of VA, in the US economy between 2002 and 2008, including the GED *increases* estimates of growth since the GED decreased over this time period.

The remainder of this chapter is organized as follows. Section 13.2 presents the accounting framework and tackles issues of deflation of the pollution shadow prices. Section 13.3 explores the empirical model used to estimate pollution shadow prices. Section 13.4 presents results, and 13.5 concludes.

13.2   Accounting Framework

The nominal GED is tabulated by multiplying the emissions produced by source (j) of pollutant (s), in sector (i), at time (t), denoted (E_{jsit}), by the estimated shadow price of emissions, MD_{jst} matched by source (j), pollutant (s) and time period (t). The MD_{jst} serves as an imputed price, or shadow price, for the E_{jsit}.

(1)
$$GED_{jsit} = MD_{jst} \times E_{jsit}.$$

Note that the shadow price is, in effect, the marginal damage of an emission expressed in monetary terms. The empirical estimation of the MD_{jst} is discussed below. Figure 13.1 provides a diagrammatic treatment of the GED calculation. Tonnage abated increases from left to right, with a current (arbitrary) level of abatement at (a). Tonnage emitted therefore increases from right to left; the corresponding emission level is given by the distance (d–a). GED is computed using the NIPA convention in which all tonnage is valued at the marginal value (Nordhaus 2006). The GED is given by abcd. Note that the GED tabulation has no bearing on microeconomic considerations of allocative efficiency.

The GED_{jsit} are then aggregated up to the industry and sector level by

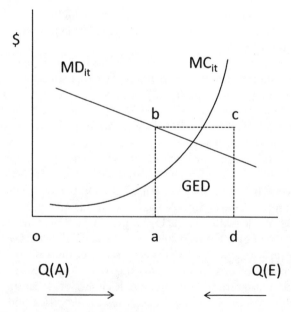

Fig. 13.1   Gross external damage graphical depiction

summing across all pollutants emitted by a source and across all sources within a sector as shown in equation (2).

$$(2) \qquad GED_{it} = \sum_{s}^{S} \sum_{j}^{N} GED_{jsit} \, .$$

Then, for sector (i), the EVA is tabulated by subtracting the GED_{it} and consumption of fixed capital (CFC_{it}) from the reported value added (VA_{it}).

$$(3) \qquad EVA_{it} = VA_{it} - GED_{it} - CFC_{it}.$$

Annual rates of change for VA, GED, and the EVA are computed using the following compound interest formula, which uses economy-wide GED in periods (t) and ($t + n$) as an example:

$$(4) \qquad \Delta GED_{t,t+n} = \left(\frac{GED_{t+n}}{GED_t} \right)^{1/n} - 1.$$

In this chapter, GED is related to VA (rather than gross output) because the accounting exercise conducted herein zeroes in on damages at each stage of production as opposed to the cumulative emissions in the supply chain. Hence, the appropriate measure of pollution intensity is GED relative to VA. If the GED encompassed cumulative damages at each stage of production, the correct intensity metric would compare GED to gross output (GO). For example, the GED recorded for the manufacture of steel only reflects emissions from the actual manufacturing of steel. The GED to GO approach would tabulate the emissions over the entire supply chain inclusive of the discharges and resulting GED emanating from the production inputs to steel manufacturing: coal mining and transport, iron ore mining and transport, production and delivery of electricity, and so on. This tack, while not pursued in the present analysis, may produce interesting insights into the share of GED associated with final consumption or production of a good relative to the embedded GED in the supply chain.

The EVA computed in this chapter is limited in scope to deducting the GED from air pollution. This omits other (potentially) important types of environmental damage: water pollution, toxins in soils, and greenhouse gases. Further, the chapter does not tabulate positive externalities produced by industries such as forestry, landscaping, or education, for example.

13.2.1 Deflation and Real Values

Since the empirical analysis spans multiple years, nominal versus real reporting is an important consideration. The chapter reports real GED, VA, and hence, EVA. The tabulation of real VA relies on the USBEA data and deflators (USBEA, 2011). (VA is reported in real 2005 US dollars.) The VA is expressed in real terms using sector-specific chain-type price indices (USBEA 2011) to deflate each sector's VA. As shown in equation (3), CFC is subtracted from VA as well.

Recall that GED is computed by multiplying source- and pollutant-specific marginal damages, or shadow prices, times reported emissions as in equation (1). Exploring nominal versus real GED rests on whether and how the shadow prices change through time. Muller (2013) documents changes in the shadow prices for 2002, 2005, and 2008. Two factors dictate changes in the marginal impacts of these pollutants: emission levels and proximal population densities.[3] The critical point for the current analysis is that the shadow prices *do in fact* change between 2002 and 2008 (see Muller 2013). In order to draw comparative inferences on the GED across time periods some attempt at deflating the shadow prices is critical.

The computation of the real GED uses three deflation approaches. First, the shadow prices estimated for the year 2005 are applied to value emissions from all three data years. By holding prices fixed, this tactic isolates changes in the GED due to emission (quantity) changes. The drawback is that changes in *relative* prices are not captured.

$$(5) \qquad GED_{it} = \sum_{s}^{S} \sum_{j}^{N} (MD_{js}^{05} \times E_{jits}),$$

where: MD_{js}^{05} = marginal damage source (j), pollutant (s), year 2005.

Second, pollution shadow price index numbers (estimated in Muller 2013) are used as price deflators to express the GED in real terms. These price indices are reported for each pollutant and for each year, with the year 2005 taken as the base year. The indices are tabulated using the Fisher (or ideal) index number formula (see Muller 2013) and they are reported in the appendix to this chapter.

$$(6) \qquad GED_{it} = \sum_{s}^{S} \sum_{j}^{N} ((P_{fst}^{-1} MD_{jts}) \times E_{jits}),$$

where: P_{fst} = Fisher-type price index for pollutant (s), time (t), relative to year 2005. This approach is the default deflator used throughout the analysis. The effect of the alternative deflators on the GED is tested in a sensitivity analysis.

Third, the USBEA's sector-specific GDP deflators (USBEA 2011) are used to express the GED in real terms. This approach assumes that the rate of change is the same for both market prices and the pollution shadow prices.

$$(7) \qquad GED_{it} = \sum_{s}^{S} \sum_{j}^{N} ((P_{dts}^{-1} MD_{jts}) \times E_{jits}),$$

3. Muller and Mendelsohn (2009) conduct a series of experiments that estimate the marginal damage *function* for specific sources. These suggest that the marginal damage function is flat: total damages are linear in emissions. However, pertinent to welfare analysis in regard to the current computation of GED is whether the marginal damages change if, for example, all sources in a given sector nonmarginally change their output. Such experimentation, while clearly interesting, is beyond the scope of the present analysis.

where: P_{dts} = GDP deflator for time (t), sector (s), relative to year 2005.

The use of GDP deflators does not allow for different rates of appreciation (depreciation) across pollutants. Note that the GDP deflators are always used to compute real market VA.

13.3 Empirical Model

The chapter uses the AP2 model, which is derived from the Air Pollution Emission Experiments and Policy Analysis Model (APEEP), which has been used in numerous prior applications (Muller and Mendelsohn 2007, 2009; Muller, Mendelsohn, and Nordhaus 2011; Henry, Muller, and Mendelsohn 2011; NAS NRC 2009). The AP2 is an integrated assessment model that links emissions to concentrations, exposures, physical impacts, and monetary damages for emissions of five common air pollutants: ammonia (NH_3), fine particulate matter ($PM_{2.5}$), sulfur dioxide (SO_2), nitrogen oxides (NO_x), and volatile organic compounds (VOC).

The model employs the USEPA's national emissions inventories for 2002, 2005, and 2008 (USEPA 2006, 2008, 2011). The inventories report emissions for point sources, which are coded according location, specifications (including properties of the smokestack), and by the North American Industry Classification System (NAICS) codes. The inventories also report emissions from nonpoint stationary and mobile sources. The nonpoint sources encompass all emissions sources without a monitored smokestack or release point. Examples of this type of source include (but are not limited to) homes, dry cleaners, and retail gasoline refueling stations. Sources of this type are matched to the corresponding NAICS code through source descriptions provided by the USEPA. Many sources cannot be linked to a NAICS code and are thus dropped from the analysis. Mobile sources include sources from on- and off-road vehicles of many different weight classes as well as railroads, airplanes, and vessels. This source category includes tractors, mining equipment, and other mobile sources that are used for commercial and industrial purposes. As with the nonpoint sources, only those source types that are able to be linked with a particular NAICS code are included in the analysis.

Beginning with these baseline emissions data, the model predicts corresponding ambient concentrations of $PM_{2.5}$, tropospheric ozone (O_3), SO_2, and NO_2 in every county in the coterminous United States. The predicted concentrations are used to estimate exposures in each county. These include human exposure, crop and timber exposure, and man-made materials exposure for substances that are sensitive to SO_2 exposure.

Peer-reviewed dose-response functional relationships are used to translate exposures into physical effects. Paramount among the dose-response functions in the model are those that govern the link between human mortality rates and exposures to O_3 and $PM_{2.5}$. (That is, premature mortality effects comprise 90 percent of total damages.) The model employs the findings from Bell et al. (2004) for the O_3-mortality link and from Pope et al. (2002) for the $PM_{2.5}$-mortality relationship.

The final stage in the AP2 model applies monetary values to the various physical effects due to air pollution exposure. For crops and timber this reduces to applying current market prices for these commodities to the predicted yield change in a given year. For impacts on human health, valuation relies on estimates of the willingness to pay to avoid either additional cases or additional mortality risks. For mortality risks, the study uses the VSL methodology (see Viscusi and Aldy 2003). This approach, which is widely applied by practitioners and academics (USEPA 1999), uses results from either (or both) revealed preference or stated preference studies to ascertain society's willingness to pay to avoid small increases to baseline risk levels. This study employs a VSL of approximately $6 million ($2005), which is the VSL used by the USEPA in their analysis of the benefits and costs of the Clean Air Act (USEPA 1999). The VSL is applied uniformly to populations of all ages. For valuation of chronic illnesses, the AP2 model uses results from studies that ask survey respondents how much they would be willing to pay to avoid a case of illness (either chronic bronchitis or chronic asthma).

The AP2 model is used to estimate the marginal damage ($/ton) for emissions of each of the five pollutants tracked by the model at the nearly 10,000 sources covered by the model. This entails the following algorithm, which was developed in Muller and Mendelsohn (2007, 2009), and subsequently applied in Muller, Mendelsohn, and Nordhaus (2011). AP2 begins by estimating baseline damages; baseline emissions (reported by USEPA) are processed through the model to compute baseline monetary damages for a given year. Then, one ton of one pollutant (perhaps NO_x) is added to baseline emissions from a specific source (perhaps a power plant in western Pennsylvania). The model is run again to compute the subsequent change in concentrations, exposures, physical effects, and monetary damages, all relative to the baseline case. The difference in damages between the add-one-ton case and the baseline comprises the marginal damage. The change in damages is strictly attributable to the additional ton (of NO_x in this hypothetical example) because everything else in the model has been held fixed by the researcher. The algorithm is then repeated for every source and every pollutant in the model for a total of 50,000 iterations. Note that after each experiment, emissions are reset to the baseline level.

13.4   Results

Table 13.1 displays the real GED by sector for 2002, 2005, and 2008. The GED shown in this table employs the Fisher pollution price indices to deflate the pollution shadow prices. Throughout the analysis the market

Table 13.1 Sector real GED ($ billion, 2005 prices)

2002		2005		2008	
Sector	GED	Sector	GED	Sector	GED
Utilities	160.38	Utilities	145.06	Utilities	108.00
Ag./forestry	83.94	Ag./forestry	78.50	Ag./forestry	64.80
Manufacturing	72.04	Transportation and warehousing	63.83	Manufacturing	46.08
Transportation and warehousing	61.72	Manufacturing	57.36	Transportation and warehousing	38.99
Construction	34.70	Construction	21.91	Construction	26.50
Admin. and waste mgmt. services	27.80	Admin. and waste mgmt. services	19.33	Admin. and waste mgmt. services	30.58
Accommodation and food services	10.61	Mining	13.96	Accommodation and food services	12.57
Mining	7.83	Accommodation and food services	10.51	Mining	9.21
Arts, ent., and rec.	5.95	Arts, ent., and rec.	6.63	Arts, ent., and rec.	5.81
Retail trade	4.49	Retail trade	4.69	Retail trade	3.74
Wholesale trade	3.17	Other services (except public administration)	2.35	Other services (except public administration)	1.31
Other services (except public administration)	2.61	Wholesale trade	1.65	Educational services	1.08
Health care and social assistance	1.66	Educational services	1.08	Wholesale trade	0.95
Educational services	0.85	Health care and social assistance	0.38	Finance and insurance	0.34
Real estate	0.12	Professional, scientific, and technical services	0.12	Health care and social assistance	0.27
Professional, scientific, and technical services	0.11	Real estate	0.11	Real estate	0.19
Information	0.05	Information	0.07	Professional, scientific, and technical services	0.09
Finance and insurance	0.00	Finance and insurance	0.01	Information	0.06
Management of companies and enterprises	0.00	Management of companies and enterprises	0.00	Management of companies and enterprises	0.00
Total	478.0		427.6		350.6

[a]GED deflated using Fisher pollution price indices; VA deflated using USBEA sector-specific price indices.

VA is deflated using the USBEA sector-specific deflators. The sectors are ranked according to the magnitude of the GED. In each of the three data years covered in the analysis, the rank ordering of sectors by GED remains remarkably similar. Utilities, agriculture, manufacturing, transportation, and construction generate the greatest GED for each year. Another clear and important pattern is that, for many industries, the GED decreases modestly from 2002 to 2005, and then decreases significantly from 2005 to 2008. For example, the utility GED begins at $160 billion in 2002, drops to $145 billion in 2005, and then drops to $108 billion in 2008. The agriculture and forestry sector is another clear example of the pattern. In 2002, GED from agriculture is estimated to be $84 billion. In 2005 agriculture GED decreases marginally to $79 billion. Then, in 2008, the GED for this sector falls to $65 billion. The transportation sector also exhibits this trend; the GED in 2002, 2005, and 2008 is estimated to be $62 billion, $64 billion, and $40 billion, respectively. The economy-wide GED also follows this pattern; in 2002 total GED was $480 billion, in 2005 GED decreased to $430 billion, and then in 2008 the GED declined to $350 billion. Note that the bottom five sectors in table 13.1 contribute less than 1 percent of the economy-wide GED in each year.

The GED for the manufacturing sector decreases more steadily over the time period covered by this analysis. Manufacturing GED in 2002 is estimated to be $72 billion. In 2005, the GED from this sector falls to $57 billion. Finally, in 2008, the manufacturing GED decreases to $46 billion.

Table 13.2 displays the nominal GED/VA ratio for all sectors in 2002, 2005, and 2008. For the utility sector, the GED/VA ratio begins in 2002 at 0.96. This declines to 0.71 in 2005 and then drops to 0.49 in 2008. These results indicate that the utility sector became much *less* pollution intensive between 2002 and 2008. In 2002, the total air pollution damage was nearly equivalent to reported VA in nominal terms. This implies the EVA for this sector was nearly zero in 2002.

In 2002, the agriculture sector shows a GED/VA of 0.90. This declines to 0.62 in 2005 and 0.25 in 2008. Much like the utility sector, agriculture EVA is quite close to zero in 2002. The transportation sector also shows a significant decrease in its GED/VA ratio; in 2002 the GED/VA is 0.22 for this sector. In 2005, the ratio drops to 0.17. However, in 2008, the ratio drops to roughly 0.13. The construction and manufacturing sectors show much less variation in the GED/VA ratios between 2002 and 2008. Between 2002 and 2008, the construction GED/VA ranges between 0.074 and 0.036. The manufacturing GED/VA is within the range of 0.056 and 0.032. The economy-wide GED/VA ratio also shows limited variation. The GED/VA ratio is estimated to be 0.054 in 2002, 0.039 in 2005, and 0.030 in 2008. Although the real GED declines precipitously from 2005 to 2008 (as reported in table 13.1), the nominal GED/VA does not show such a significant drop. A large share of total output in the US economy is contributed by sectors that have very

Table 13.2   **Nominal measure of pollution intensity: Sector GED/VA**

	GED/VA		
Sector	2002	2005	2008
Agriculture/forestry	0.903	0.621	0.253
Mining	0.079	0.076	0.062
Utilities	0.965	0.710	0.493
Construction	0.075	0.036	0.059
Manufacturing	0.056	0.037	0.032
Wholesale trade	0.005	0.002	0.001
Retail trade	0.006	0.006	0.005
Transportation and warehousing	0.228	0.176	0.134
Information	0.000	0.000	0.000
Finance and insurance	0.000	0.000	0.000
Real estate	0.000	0.000	0.000
Professional, scientific, and technical services	0.000	0.000	0.000
Management of companies and enterprises	0.000	0.000	0.000
Admin. and waste management	0.095	0.052	0.036
Educational services	0.009	0.009	0.008
Health care and social assistance	0.003	0.000	0.000
Arts, entertainment, and recreation	0.061	0.056	0.048
Accommodation and food services	0.037	0.029	0.032
Other services (except public administration)	0.009	0.008	0.004
Economy	0.055	0.039	0.030

[a]All values expressed in nominal terms.

low GED/VA scores. For many of these low-pollution sectors, GED and GED/VA did not change appreciably between 2002 and 2008. Therefore, although some sectors show precipitous declines in both pollution damage *and* pollution intensity, the overall change in GED/VA is attenuated by the low-GED and high-VA sectors including finance, real estate, and professional services.

The top-left panel of figure 13.2 shows the economy-wide VA and EVA measures between 2002 and 2008.[4] This figure indicates that the gap between VA and EVA, which is the GED, has decreased, albeit slightly between 2002 and 2008. The narrowing of the difference between VA and EVA is especially evident after 2005. The bottom-left panel of figure 13.2 focuses on the manufacturing sector. The overall pattern is quite similar to that for the total economy. The difference between the VA and the EVA attenuates between 2002 and 2008 as the GED declines. However, the trends in VA (and EVA) show some important differences with respect to the total economy. First,

4. The GED/VA is interpolated for the years 2003, 2004, 2006, and 2007 by projecting the annualized GED growth from 2002 to 2005 and from 2005 to 2008. These interpolated values are then matched to reported VA for the years without emissions data.

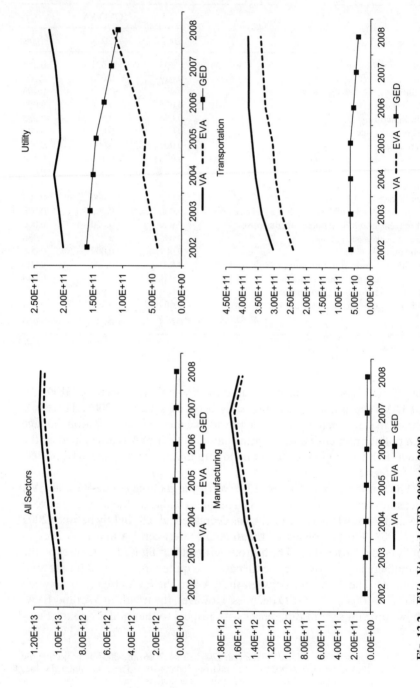

Fig. 13.2   EVA, VA, and GED, 2002 to 2008

Note: GED deflated using Fisher pollution price indices; VA deflated using sector-specific price indices. Vertical axis ($).

more modest rates of growth are evident between 2002 and 2003 as the manufacturing sector emerged from the recession following the technology sector correction. And second, manufacturing output falls after 2007 as the economy was headed into the Great Recession. The EVA basically tracks these changes, with the notable exception that the manufacturing GED shrinks appreciably after 2007.

The top-right panel of figure 13.2 shows the VA and the EVA for the utility sector. Note that in 2002, EVA is dramatically smaller in magnitude than market VA. That is, GED comprises a large share of the reported VA for this sector. Although VA is basically constant between 2002 and 2008 for this sector, EVA clearly grows over this time period. This pattern manifests because the GED is shrinking at a rate greater than market VA is increasing. This difference in growth rates is especially evident after 2005. Recall from table 13.1 that real GED decreased from $145 billion in 2005 to $108 billion in 2008. This is a gross decrease of 25 percent in real terms.

The bottom-right panel of figure 13.2 displays the VA and the EVA for the transportation sector. Like utilities, although less dramatically, the gap between the market VA and EVA decreases between 2002 and 2008. The decrease in GED is most evident after 2005, which reinforces one of the main findings from table 13.1; namely, that for many sectors, GED decreases modestly from 2002 to 2005 and then GED falls more significantly from 2005 and 2008.

Table 13.3 displays the annualized rates of change in the VA and the EVA for all sectors, between 2002 and 2005, and 2005 and 2008. Beginning with the 2002 to 2005 changes, the total economy real VA grew at an annual rate of 2.76 percent. The EVA grew by an estimated 3.07 percent. Including the GED into the NIPAs *increases* the estimated annual growth rate of the economy over this time period by 0.31 percent. This result stems from that fact that GED decreased more rapidly than VA grew over this time period. Hence, EVA and VA converged. In both 2002 and 2005 EVA is smaller than VA because a previously unmeasured cost is deducted from VA. Despite this, because the rate of change in these uninternalized costs (the GED) is sharply negative, corrected VA (the EVA) is estimated to have grown more quickly than VA.

Particularly sharp differences in rates of VA and EVA growth are found for agriculture, utilities, and transportation. The EVA is estimated to have increased at a rate of over 30 percent for the agriculture sector. Market VA increased at 6.8 percent. For the utility sector, EVA grew at 15 percent per year, while VA grew at just under 1 percent. For the transportation sector, EVA expanded at a rate of 8.2 percent and market VA increased by just under 7 percent per year.

Table 13.3 indicates that some sectors such as real estate, management, and professional services have almost no difference between the rates of VA

Table 13.3   Annualized rates of growth in EVA and market VA

	2005–2002		2008–2005	
Sector	Δ EVA[a,b,c] (%)	Δ VA (%)	Δ EVA (%)	Δ VA (%)
Agriculture/forestry	34.58	6.85	9.77	0.46
Mining	−11.85	−10.43	3.31	2.25
Utilities	15.25	0.87	24.42	2.83
Construction	0.38	−0.34	−5.60	−5.10
Manufacturing	5.51	4.90	0.77	0.50
Wholesale trade	4.26	4.16	2.45	2.41
Retail trade	1.43	1.43	−1.12	−1.15
Transportation and warehousing	8.26	6.86	4.94	1.96
Information	7.29	7.29	3.59	3.59
Finance and insurance	2.93	2.93	−2.51	−2.50
Real estate and rental and leasing	2.11	2.11	3.41	3.41
Professional, scientific, and technical services	3.79	3.79	4.42	4.42
Management of companies and enterprises	−1.01	−1.01	0.50	0.50
Admin. and waste management	7.85	6.38	1.46	2.36
Educational services	0.08	0.15	1.44	1.43
Health care and social assistance	3.06	3.00	3.44	3.44
Arts, entertainment, and recreation	1.94	2.03	1.06	0.78
Accommodation and food services	3.51	3.39	−0.30	−0.10
Other services (except public administration)	−0.78	−0.80	−0.77	−0.88
Economy	3.07	2.76	1.47	1.18

[a]EVA: (VA–GED)

[b]Annual rate of change = 100 x $((EVA_{2008}/EVA_{2005})^{(1/3)} - 1)$.

[c]GED deflated using Fisher pollution price indices; VA deflated using sector-specific GDP deflators.

and EVA growth. This should be expected given that these sectors produce almost no GED. For these cases, augmented accounts that focus on environmental damage really make no difference since most of their activities and, hence, the value of their production, lies within the bounds of the conventional NIPAs.

From 2005 to 2008, the total economy EVA is estimated to have increased by 1.47 percent per year, while market VA expanded by 1.18 percent. Again, including the GED into the NIPAs augments the estimated annual growth rate of the economy over this time period by 0.29 percent. Bringing GED into the EVA increases rates of growth for the same reason as in the 2002 to 2005 period; EVA reflects an additional cost which, while decreasing VA in each time period, enhances rates of growth because GED fell more rapidly than market VA grew.

Much like the 2002 to 2005 time period, between 2005 and 2008, the greatest divergence in growth rates between EVA and VA occurred in pollution-intensive sectors. For example, utility EVA is estimated to have grown by

24 percent per year, while market VA for this sector increased by a more modest 2.8 percent. The agriculture sector EVA grew by over 9 percent while the market VA increased by less than 1 percent. Similarly, the growth rates for EVA and VA in the transportation sector were 5 percent and 2 percent, respectively. Hence, one important point that emerges from table 13.3 is: including estimates of the GED for pollution intensive sectors can make a substantial difference in measures of output.

Not all sectors in table 13.3 show rates of change in EVA that are larger than VA. For example, table 13.3 shows that conditions in the construction sector were very different from the sectors highlighted in the discussion above. Between 2002 and 2005, the construction EVA grew at a rate of 0.4 percent and the VA for this sector contracted at 0.3 percent. Including the GED into the EVA *changes the sign of* the rate of change in output. Indeed, table 13.1 indicates that the GED declined for this sector between 2002 and 2005. However, between 2005 and 2008 the EVA decreased by 5.6 percent annually while the VA decreased by 5.1 percent per year. In this case, EVA amplifies the contraction in the construction sector; although market output in this area of the economy was contracting, the GED increased. The result is that the augmented EVA suggests an even greater rate of contraction that does the market VA.

The Great Recession was likely a major factor in driving this result. Specifically, it is well known that an oversupply of housing played a key role in the recession and that the consequences of this aspect of the recession (the correction in the housing market) were, in part, borne by the construction sector. Hence, the construction VA contracted rapidly after 2007, and the greater *negative* growth of the EVA suggests that VA was clearly contracting more rapidly than the GED over this time period.

The evidence reported in table 13.3 suggests that the reduction in social cost associated with air pollution emissions is a valuable component of production, one that contributes approximately 0.3 percentage points of growth on an annual basis between 2002 and 2008. Reporting measures of growth that fail to reflect the GED *underestimates* growth over this time period. These subtle differences in growth rates are reflected in figure 13.2, which maps the VA and the EVA for the entire economy between 2002 and 2008. Although the VA and the EVA roughly parallel one another, a slight convergence of VA and EVA is clear after 2007 as the Great Recession takes hold. The EVA and the VA converge precisely because the GED shrinks in absolute terms and relative to VA as shown in tables 13.1 and 13.2.

An accounting framework that recognizes the GED, the air pollution externality, reduces the level of VA. The EVA is smaller than the VA because the EVA is a measurement that is net of the GED. There is a previously unmeasured cost which, when included in the accounts, decreases the VA. That much is straightforward and clear. More interesting is the implication of including the GED into the accounts for measures of *growth*. Between

2002 and 2008, although the level of VA declines when GED are included to report EVA, the rate of growth increases. One way to characterize this difference is through the GED/VA index; throughout the time period covered in this analysis, GED/VA shrinks. By construction of the index this means that the GED is falling *relative to the VA*. Therefore, EVA is growing relative to VA. And, the difference between the EVA measure and market VA boils down to the inclusion (in the EVA) of the value in *reductions* to the GED, which conventionally measured VA omits.

This is an important augmentation to standard measures of growth. As regulated firms purchase, install, and operate pollution control devices, these capital and operating and maintenance costs are entered into the (existing) NIPAs as a cost of doing business either through consumption of fixed capital or operating and maintenance costs.[5] All else equal, regulated industry's VA declines as a function of these expenditures. Abatement costs act as a drag on growth for firms, industries, and sectors that make the expenditure. The NIPAs capture returns to these expenditures in two possible ways. First, through the transfer to firms that produce and/or market abatement technology, and second, through any improvements to the production of market goods and services due to the reduced pollution flow.[6] However, the NIPAs, by definition, miss nonmarket benefits. This happens to be quite important for the case of air pollution since the vast majority of the GED is comprised of impacts to human health that are not measured or reflected in market transactions. This highlights the importance of the augmented EVA measure. The EVA encompasses an important missing (from VA) measure of the benefit of these investments in environmental quality. Namely, the corresponding reduction to the GED, which is comprised almost entirely of reduced mortality risk and incidence rates of chronic illness (both examples of nonmarket benefits). The EVA accounts for this source of growth, and the empirical results in table 13.3, indicate that this makes an appreciable difference in ex post growth estimates relative to conventional measures. This measure of growth suggests that the return to society's investments in cleaner air have indeed produced a return of significant magnitude even on the scale of economy-wide VA.[7]

Although this analysis cannot relate GED to VA for industries within a

5. Note that the same argument can be made for a firm that purchases inputs that embody or contain less pollution or the capacity to yield less pollution when used for production. In either case (purchase abatement technology or clean inputs) a firm is making additional expenditures in order to comply with some regulator constraint.

6. This is the classic example of externality; a firm produces an output via processes that generate smoke that is dispersed from a smokestack. Downwind, a laundry service (for example) has its output reduced because the clean laundry is soiled by the smoke. Thus, curtailing the smoke yields an increase in production for the laundry service.

7. Clearly other estimates of the return to society's investments in environmental quality (and especially, clean air) exist. For example, the USEPA conducts regular cost benefit analyses of the entire Clean Air Act. The resulting tabulations from their reports, however, are not reflected in or related to the NIPAs, which is the goal of this study.

Table 13.4   **Industry decomposition of GED change: Utility, manufacturing, and transportation sectors**

Sector	Industry	2005 – 2002	2008 – 2005
Utility	Coal-fired power generation	−4.78[a] (−4)[b]	−34.80 (−26.4)
	Natural gas-fired power generation	−1.44 (−38)	4.05 (169)
	Oil-fired power generation	0.52 (14)	−2.23 (−52)
Transportation	Marine transport	9.95 (54)	−14.70 (−51.8)
	Truck transport	−4.20 (−16)	−5.37 (−24)
	Railroad transport	1.54 (24)	−4.15 (−52)
	Airport	−3.77 (−93)	−0.14 (−47)
Manufacturing	Petroleum refineries	4.50 (38)	−9.61 (−59)
	Cement mfg.	1.07 (53)	−4.11 (−70)
	Iron and steel mills	2.05 (45)	−1.95 (−34)

[a]Change in GED ($ billion).
[b]Percent change from GED in previous period.

sector, table 13.4 decomposes the gross GED changes between 2002 and 2005, and 2005 and 2008 for industries in the following sectors: utilities, transportation, and manufacturing. Between 2005 and 2002 the GED associated with coal-fired electric power generation decreased by about $5 billion. This comprises just a 4 percent reduction in damages. The GED due to natural gas-fired power production decreased by $1.4 billion. Although this is a small change in absolute terms, it amounts to a 38 percent drop in the GED. The GED from oil-fired power generation climbed by $500 million. From 2005 to 2008, the GED from coal-fired power decreased by $35 billion, which comprises a reduction of over 25 percent from 2005. In contrast, the GED due to natural gas-powered electric production increased by $4.0 billion; this is nearly a three-fold increase in the GED from this industry from 2005. Oil-fired power generation declined in 2008 by $2.2 billion. This amounts to a 52 percent drop from 2005.

Much of the change in the GED for coal-fired power generation is due to regulatory constraints. Both the Acid Rain Program (ARP) and the NO_x Budget program (NBP) limit aggregate emissions from most coal-fired capacity in the United States. Between 2002 and 2005 aggregate SO_2 emissions increased slightly program-wide; emissions increased by 26,000 tons (a 0.3 percent change) between 2002 and 2005 (USEPA CAMD 2012a). Over the same time period, NO_x emissions decreased by approximately 840,000 tons for facilities governed by the NBP. The result was a 4 percent decrease in the coal-fired power GED.[8] In contrast, between 2005 and 2008, emis-

8. The total GED for oil, gas, and coal-fired plants does not equate to the reported utility total in table 13.1. The difference stems from electric power generation sources that do not use either of these three primary fuels and from nonpower generation sources. These include power distribution, steam and air conditioning supply, and sewage treatment, among others.

sions of SO_2 decreased by 2.61 million tons (25 percent decrease) while NO_x emissions decreased by 640,000 tons (18 percent change) (USEPA CAMD 2012a). The GED correspondingly declines by one-quarter for coal-fired power plants.

In 2005, the USEPA issued the Clean Air Interstate Rule (CAIR). This was to serve as the replacement to both the NBP and the ARP and it proposed significant reductions to the annual emissions limits in place for the extant trading programs (USEPA 2012b). Because of the stringency of the proposed CAIR, many regulated generators bought and held large quantities of NO_x and especially SO_2 permits to ensure compliance with the proposed CAIR caps. Concurrently, some regulated firms invested heavily in pollution control equipment to achieve long-term compliance. Many of these capital intensive investments came on line after 2005; the ensuing emission reductions are evident in the reduced emission reported by USEPA and in the reduced GED in tables 13.1 and 13.4.

For coal-fired generators, power production over the time periods considered in this study was only weakly correlated with both emissions and the GED. The US Department of Energy reports that between 2002 and 2005, coal-fired capacity net generation increased by just 1 percent from 1.91 MMWH to 1.99 MMWH. The GED decreased by 4 percent over this period. From 2005 to 2008, net generation from coal capacity decreased from 1.99 MMWH to 1.97 MMWH. This comprises a 1.17 percent reduction in net power output from coal, yet the GED dropped by over 25 percent over the same time frame. By deduction, increased use of abatement technology at coal-fired power generators is likely the primary cause for the reduction in the GED in this industry.

Table 13A.3 in the appendix reports the changes in the GED for electric power generation using the 2005 shadow prices deflation method. The thrust of this table is to isolate the impact of emission changes. Beginning with coal-fired facilities, the GED change from 2002 to 2005 computed using 2005-fixed shadow prices is –$2.46 billion. Recall from table 13.4 that the GED change for coal-fired power plants was reported to be –$4.78 billion (using the Fisher deflators). An important distinction between the two deflation methods is that the Fisher indices allow *relative prices to change* while deflating the price level, whereas the fixed 2005 shadow prices holds both the level and the relative prices fixed. The fact that GED in 2002 is less when using 2005 fixed shadow prices implies that relative prices changed between 2002 and 2005. This change suggests that more emissions occurred in 2002 at plants that had higher shadow prices than in 2005.

For natural gas facilities, appendix table 13A.3 shows that GED in 2002, computed using the 2005 marginal damages, are smaller than the GED computed using the Fisher indices. Deflation using the Fisher indices adjusts the mean shadow prices level. The remaining gap in the GED change is due to differences in the relative prices. Like the case of coal, the higher GED computed using the Fisher pollution indices suggests more emissions were produced in 2002 by facilities with higher shadow prices than in 2005. For oil-fired plants, the change in GED from 2002 to 2005 is greater when using the 2005 marginal damages than the marginal damages deflated with the Fisher indices. This implies that emissions tended to occur in higher-damage locations in 2005. This stands in contrast to both coal- and gas-fired facilities. For the GED computed in 2008, the use of 2005 marginal damages has a very small effect on the plants of all three fuel types.

Table 13.4 also decomposes the GED from the transportation and manufacturing sectors. Beginning with transportation, commercial marine vessels produced about $10 billion more GED in 2005 than in 2002. In 2008, damages from this industry dropped by over $14 billion. For truck transportation, the GED declined in both periods: by $4 billion and $5 billion between 2002 and 2005, and 2005 and 2008, respectively. This pattern also holds for air transportation. (For this industry emissions are only tracked for evaporation of fuels and airport support vehicles, not airplanes in route.) Railroad transportation GED increased from 2002 to 2005 by about 24 percent and then the GED from this industry declined by 52 percent from 2005 to 2008.

The sharp decline in GED from the marine vessels, railroads, and trucks within transportation is evidence of a change in regulatory constraints between 2005 and 2008. Specifically, reductions in sulfur content of diesel fuels for use in vehicles operated on roadways took effect in 2006. This program, which was phased in between 2007 and 2010, is estimated to have reduced SO_2 emissions from diesel-powered vehicles by as much as 90 percent (USEPA 2012c). In addition to highway vehicles, the sulfur content of fuels used in locomotives and marine vessels was also lowered in 2007; like the policy for highway vehicles, this fuel standard is phased in over several years (USEPA 2012d). Although it is beyond the scope of this chapter to precisely parse the effect on GED of these regulatory standards, it is likely that their (partial) implementation contributed significantly to the decline in GED in the transportation sector.

Table 13.4 also breaks down the GED from the manufacturing sector. Petroleum refineries produced GED in 2005 that was about $5 billion more than the GED in 2002. Damages declined by nearly $10 billion in 2008. Cement manufacturers produced an increase in GED in 2005 of $1 billion, and $4 billion less GED in 2008 than in 2005. Iron and steel mills follow the same pattern; damages increase by 45 percent moving from 2002 to 2005, then the GED drops by 35 percent. These three high-damage industries show a pattern that is broadly indicative of the GED in the manufacturing sector as a whole; the GED decreases precipitously as the Great Recession begins to take hold in the later years of the sample.

Table 13.5 displays the results from the experiments that test the impact of different deflation techniques through the pollution shadow prices on the GED. Since year 2005 GED comprise the base year (and therefore GED in

Table 13.5   **Alternative deflation of pollution shadow prices and resulting GED**

	Deflator			
Sector	Nominal	GDP defl.	Fisher	2005 prices
		2002		
Economy	506.1	408.8	478.0[a]	472.8
Agriculture	84.7	68.4	83.9	78.1
Utility	173.4	140.1	160.4	157.0
Manufacturing	76.2	61.6	72.0	73.3
Construction	36.7	29.6	34.7	34.5
Transportation	67.8	54.8	61.7	63.9
		2008		
Economy	369.7	320.0	350.6	348.2
Agriculture	40.2	32.5	64.8	62.8
Utility	126.0	101.8	108.0	108.0
Manufacturing	51.3	41.5	46.1	46.4
Construction	36.0	29.1	26.5	26.2
Transportation	54.5	44.1	39.0	39.3

[a]GED ($, billion).

that year is unaffected by deflation), table 13.5 only reports GED for the years 2002 and 2008. The Fisher price indices are the default case; the 2005 shadow prices employ year 2005 marginal damages for both 2002 and 2008, and the GDP deflator applies the USBEA sector-specific GDP deflators that differ in magnitude for 2002 and 2008. Table 13.5 also reports nominal GED for purposes of comparison with the real values.

In the default case, economy-wide GED is estimated to be $480 billion in 2002 and $350 billion in 2008. Using the fixed-year 2005 shadow prices decreases the GED in 2002 to $473 billion. This comprises just a 1 percent difference relative to the Fisher deflators. The estimated GED in 2008 using 2005 prices is slightly lower than the GED estimated using the Fisher index at $348 billion. Economy-wide GED is estimated to be $409 billion in 2002 using the market deflator. Note that this approach pegs changes in the pollution shadow prices to changes in prices for market goods and services. For 2008, the total economy GED estimated when using the GDP deflator is about 10 percent smaller than when the other two deflators are used.

Table 13.5 also reports the different GED estimates for the five heaviest polluting sectors. Two patterns are evident. For all sectors, the GED in 2002 is estimated to be smallest when using the GDP deflator. The relative rankings in GED for 2008 across the different deflators does not show a clear pattern for the five sectors covered in table 13.5.

It is important for policymakers and national statisticians to recognize that the GED estimates are uncertain. This may stem from three sources:

parameter uncertainty, data uncertainty, and model uncertainty (Muller 2011). Table 13A.4 in the appendix focuses on parameter uncertainty in the area of mortality damages since this endpoint comprises the largest share of total damage. Specifically, table 13A.4 in the appendix shows that using the $PM_{2.5}$ mortality dose-response function reported in Roman et al. (2009) increases economy-wide GED by nearly two-thirds for each data year. In contrast, using a \$2 million VSL (rather than the default value of \$6 million) reduces total GED by nearly two-thirds. Hence, the GED estimates are, in fact, quite sensitive to parameter choices made by the researcher. The effect of these (and other) alternative model parameters on the GED/VA as well as on the EVA growth rates is left to future study.

13.5   Conclusion

This analysis uses the methodology developed and reported in Muller, Mendelsohn, and Nordhaus (2011) to compute the gross external damages (GED) from air pollution in the US economy for 2002, 2005, 2008. The time series measurement of the GED, the GED/VA, and the EVA (VA—GED) is an important extension to the annual measure of GED and GED/VA reported in Muller, Mendelsohn, and Nordhaus (2011). The NIPAs' primary value lies in relative measurement of indices such as GDP or VA over time. Similarly, while static nonmarket accounts are very important, the estimation of the air pollution damage indices over multiple years provides researchers and policymakers with insights in three areas: changes in gross pollution damage, changes in pollution intensity, and differences in rates of growth with and without augmentation.

The empirical results indicate that the GED changes dramatically from 2002 to 2008; the GED decreased annually by about 4 percent from 2002 to 2005 and by about 6 percent from 2005 to 2008. Much of the steep decline from 2005 to 2008 stems from reductions in the GED attributable to the agriculture, utility, manufacturing, and transportation sectors. The GED/VA, economy-wide, between 2002 and 2008 does not vary as much. In 2002 the nominal GED/VA is approximately 0.054, and in 2008 the GED/VA is 0.03. The small change in the GED/VA coupled with dramatic reductions in the GED is evidence of the recession-driven reduction in output observed in 2008. That is, as output slowed (and dropped in some sectors) in 2008 due to the recession, GED did too. The economy-wide GED intensity decreased by a relatively small amount.

Although the economy-wide nominal GED/VA index was relatively constant, the GED/VA shows considerable variation within sectors between 2002 and 2008. The utility sector's GED/VA is 0.96 in 2002. In 2008, the GED/VA drops to 0.49. Similarly, the agriculture and forestry sector has a GED/VA of over 0.85 in 2002 and this index declines to less than 0.30 in

2008. However, some sectors have less variation in levels of the GED/VA; the manufacturing sector begins in 2002 with a GED/VA of 0.056 and in 2008 the manufacturing GED/VA is estimated to be 0.032. This is not to suggest that the level of the manufacturing GED remains necessarily fixed. In 2002 the manufacturing GED was $72 billion while in 2008 the GED for this sector was $46 billion. Clearly the level of damage has changed for this sector. However, the air pollution damage intensity, relative to VA, has not changed by such a large degree. This is more evidence of the impact of the recession in the US economy in 2008. Specifically, manufacturing output declined in the latter years of this time period and GED did too. This is in contrast to a sector such as utilities in which VA grew while GED dropped precipitously. The difference is that the utility sector composition was changing with greater use of cleaner inputs such as natural gas as well as more widespread employment of air pollution abatement technology, especially at coal-fired power stations.

The chapter also reports that the EVA (VA-GED) grew at greater annual rates between both 2002 and 2005, and 2005 and 2008, than VA. Between 2002 and 2005, the EVA grew at an annual rate of 3.07 percent while VA grew at 2.76 percent. Incorporating the GED increases the ex post estimate of growth by 0.31 percent. From 2005 to 2008, VA grew at an annual rate of 1.18 percent and the EVA grew at 1.47 percent per year. Including GED in the accounts again yields a divergence between the rates of growth of 0.3 percent from 2005 to 2008. While including the GED into the NIPAs reduces the level of VA, in the US economy between 2002 and 2008, including the GED *increases* estimates of growth since the GED decreased over this time period.

While the chapter finds that in the US economy over the period from 2002 to 2008 the augmented measure of growth and performance (the EVA) suggests higher rates of growth, it is certainly feasible or possible for the EVA and VA annual rates of change to relate differently in other economies (in different stages of development) or in the US economy in other time periods. For example, an economy with VA growth less than its GED growth would have EVA changing at rates less than VA. This case describes an economy with rates of pollution intensity growth greater than absolute growth. An example might include a developing economy that is just beginning to modernize; one that features considerable resource extraction and heavy manufacturing. In this setting standard measures of growth *overestimate* actual growth.

The case of the US economy from 2002 to 2008 exemplifies EVA growth, which exceeds VA growth. In this setting, the GED decreases. Contracting GED with (even modest) VA growth yields higher EVA growth rates relative to VA. Two broad reasons for this pattern include VA growth in sectors that are not pollution intensive (finance, real estate, or professional services, for example), or a reduction in pollution intensity in sectors which, traditionally, have produced copious amounts of GED (utilities, agriculture, and transportation, for example). Both are evident in the United States between 2002 and 2008.

This chapter suggests research on a number of fronts. First, as more emissions data becomes available from the USEPA, the scope of the analysis could be extended. Particularly interesting in this area are extensions to 1999 and 2011. The former includes emissions from just prior to the implementation of Phase II in the Clean Air Act's Acid Rain Program, which featured a dramatic tightening of SO_2 emission caps for electric power producers. Tabulating GED/VA and EVA between 1999 and 2002 is likely to provide insights regarding alternative measures of the social value of that regulatory program. Extending the analysis to 2011 would also be of interest because of the opportunity to compare the pollution indices with 2008. In 2011, the US economy was growing slowly as it emerged from a significant recession; its structure was altered by the housing and financial market collapse, which likely had impacts on demand for transportation and utility services.

Appendix

Table 13A.1   Sector GED/VA[a]

2002		2005		2008	
Sector	GED/VA	Sector	GED/VA	Sector	GED/VA
Ag./forestry[a]	0.805	Utilities	0.705	Utilities	0.482
Utilities	0.800	Ag./forestry	0.618	Ag./forestry	0.479
Transportation and Warehousing	0.204	Transportation and warehousing	0.173	Transportation and warehousing	0.099
Admin. and waste mgmt. services	0.090	Mining	0.073	Admin. and waste mgmt. services	0.055
Construction	0.056	Arts, ent., and rec.	0.056	Construction	0.051
Arts, ent., and rec.	0.053	Admin. and waste mgmt. services	0.052	Arts, ent., and rec.	0.048
Manufacturing	0.053	Manufacturing	0.037	Mining	0.045
Accommodation and food services	0.032	Construction	0.036	Accommodation and food services	0.034
Mining	0.029	Accommodation and food services	0.029	Manufacturing	0.029
Other services (except public administration)	0.008	Educational services	0.009	Educational services	0.009
Educational services	0.007	Other services (except public administration)	0.008	Retail trade	0.005
Retail trade	0.006	Retail trade	0.006	Other services (except public administration)	0.004
Wholesale trade	0.005	Wholesale trade	0.002	Wholesale trade	0.001
Health care and social assistance	0.002	Health care and social assistance	0.000	Finance and insurance	0.000
Professional, scientific, and technical services	0.000	Professional, scientific, and technical services	0.000	Health care and social assistance	0.000
Information	0.000	Information	0.000	Real estate	0.000
Real estate	0.000	Real estate	0.000	Information	0.000
Finance and insurance	0.000	Finance and insurance	0.000	Professional, scientific, and technical services	0.000
Management of companies and enterprises	0.000	Management of companies and enterprises	0.000	Management of companies and enterprises	0.000
Economy	0.048		0.040		0.030

[a]GED deflated using Fisher pollution price indices; VA deflated using sector-specific price indices.

Table 13A.2   **Fisher index numbers for pollution shadow prices**

Pollutant	2002/2005 Fisher price index	2008/2005 Fisher price index
NH_3	1.001 (0.032)	0.500 (0.056)
$PM_{2.5}$	1.060 (0.001)	1.028 (0.004)
NO_x	1.190 (0.030)	1.884 (0.124)
SO_2	1.062 (0.002)	1.116 (0.008)
VOC	1.087 (0.002)	1.061 (0.009)
GDP deflator	92.196	108.582

Source: Muller (2013).

Note: All index numbers computed with 2005 as base year. Values in parentheses are bootstrap standard errors.

Table 13A.3   **GED from electric power generation using 2005 shadow prices**

Sector	Industry	2005-2002	2008-2005
Utility	Coal-fired power generation	−2.46[a] (−2)[b]	−34.4 (−26)
	Natural gas-fired power generation	−1.31 (−35)	4.15 (174)
	Oil-fired power generation	0.59 (16)	−2.36 (−55)

[a]Change in GED ($ billion).
[b]Percent change from GED in previous period.

Table 13A.4   **GED tabulations using alternative mortality parameters**

	Total economy GED		
Model scenario	2002	2005	2008
Default	478[a]	428	351
Roman et al. (2009)	756	680	559
Mortality dose-response	(+58.2)[b]	(+58.9)	(+59.3)
$2 million	188	169	140
VSL	(−60.7)	(−60.5)	(−60.1)

[a]GED ($ billion).
[b]Percent change relative to default case.

References

Ayres, Robert U., and Allen V. Kneese. 1969. "Production, Consumption, and Externalities." *American Economic Review* 59:282–97.

Banzhaf, H. S., D. Burtraw, and K. Palmer. 2004. "Efficient Emission Fees in the US Electricity Sector." *Resource and Energy Economics* 26:317–41.

Bartelmus, P. 1999. "Green Accounting for a Sustainable Economy: Policy Use and Analysis of Environmental Accounts in the Philippines." *Ecological Economics* 29:155–70.

Bartelmus, P. 2009. "The Cost of Natural Capital Consumption: Accounting for a Sustainable World Economy." *Ecological Economics* 68:1850–7.

Bell, Michelle L., Adrian McDermott, Scott L. Zeger, Jonathan M. Samet, and Francesca Domenici. 2004. "Ozone and Short-Term Mortality in 95 US Urban Communities, 1987–2000." *Journal of the American Medical Association* 17:2372–8.

Burtraw, D., A. Krupnick, E. Manusr, D. Austin, and D. Farrell. 1998. "Costs and Benefits of Reducing Air Pollutants Related to Acid Rain." *Contemporary Economic Policy* XVI:379–400.

Fann, N., C. M. Fulcher, and B. J. Hubbell. 2009. "The Influence of Location, Source, and Emission Type in Estimates of the Human Health Benefits of Reducting a Ton of Air Pollution." *Air Quality Atmosphere and Health* 2:169–76.

Gundimeda, Haripriya, Pavan Sukhdev, Rajiv K. Sinha, and Sanjeev Sanyal. 2007. "Natural Resource Accounting for Indian States–Illustrating the Case for Forest Resources." *Ecological Economics* 61:635–49.

Henry, D., N. Z. Muller, and R. Mendelsohn. 2011. "The Social Cost of Trading? Measuring the Increased Damages from Sulfur Dioxide Trading in the United States." *Journal of Policy Analysis and Management* 30 (3): 598–612.

Ho, Mun S., and Dale W. Jorgenson. 2007. "Sector Allocation of Emissions and Damage." In *Clearing the Air: The Health and Economic Damages of Air Pollution in China*, edited by Mun S. Ho and Chris P. Nielsen, 279–330. Cambridge, MA: The MIT Press.

Leontief, Wassily 1970. "Environmental Repercussions and the Economic Structure: An Input-Output Approach." *Review of Economics and Statistics* 52 (3): 262–71.

Mendelsohn, Robert O. 1980. "An Economic Analysis of Air Pollution from Coal-Fired Power Plants." *Journal of Environmental Economics and Management* 7:30–43.

Muller, Nicholas Z. 2011. "Linking Policy to Statistical Uncertainty in Air Pollution Damages." *The B.E. Press Journal of Economic Analysis and Policy* 11 (1): Contributions, Article 32.

———. 2012. "The Design of Optimal Climate Policy with Air Pollution Co-Benefits." *Resource and Energy Economics* 34:696–722.

———. 2013. "Using Index Numbers for Deflation in Environmental Accounting." *Environment and Development Economics*, doi:10.107/S1355770X1300048X.

Muller, Nicholas Z., and Robert Mendelsohn. 2007. "Measuring The Damages of Air Pollution in the United States." *Journal of Environmental Economics and Management* 54:1–14.

———. 2009. "Efficient Pollution Regulation: Getting the Prices Right." *American Economic Review* 99 (5): 1714–39.

Muller, Nicholas Z., Robert Mendelsohn, and William D. Nordhaus. 2011. "Environmental Accounting for Pollution in the United States Economy." *American Economic Review* 101:1649–75.

Murty, M. N., and S. C. Gulati. 2006. "Natural Resource Accounts of Air and Water Pollution: Case Studies of Andhra Pradesh and Himachal Pradesh States of India." A report submitted to the Central Statistical Organization, Government of India. Institute of Economic Growth, University of Delhi, North Campus, December.

National Academies of Science, National Research Council (NAS NRC). 2009. *Hidden Costs of Energy: Un-priced Consequences of Energy Production and Use.* Washington, DC: National Academies Press.

Nordhaus, William D. 2006. "Principles of National Accounting for Non-Market Accounts." In *A New Architecture for the US National Accounts*, Studies in Income and Wealth, vol. 66, edited by D. W. Jorgensen, J. S. Landefeld, and W. D. Nord-haus. Chicago: University of Chicago Press.

Nordhaus, William D., and Edward Kokkelenberg, eds. 1999. *Nature's Numbers.* Washington, DC: National Academy Press.

Nordhaus, William D., and James Tobin. 1972. "Is Growth Obsolete?" In *The Measurement of Economic and Social Performance*, Studies in Income and Wealth, vol. 38, edited by Milton Moss. New York: National Bureau of Economic Research.

Pope, C. Arden, Richard T. Burnett, Michael J. Thun, Eugenia E. Calle, Daniel Krewski, Kazuhiko Ito, and George D. Thurston. 2002. "Lung Cancer, Cardiopulmonary Mortality, and Long-Term Exposure to Fine Particulate Air Pollution." *Journal of the American Medical Association* 287 (9): 1132–41.

Roman, H. A., K. D. Walker, T. L. Walsh, L. Conner, H. M. Richmond, B. J. Hubbell, and P. L. Kinney. 2008. "Expert Judgment Assessment of the Mortality Impact of Changes in Ambient Fine Particulate Matter in the US" *Environmental Science and Technology* 42:2268–74.

Tong, Daniel Q., Nicholas Z. Muller, Denise L. Mauzerall, and Robert O. Mendelsohn. 2006. "Integrated Assessment of the Spatial Variability of Ozone Impacts from Emissions of Nitrogen Oxides." *Environmental Science and Technology* 40 (5): 1395–1400.

United Nations. 2011. http://unstats.un.org/unsd/envaccounting/seea.asp.

United States Bureau of Economic Analysis. 2011. http://www.bea.gov/industry/gdp byind_data.htm.

United States Department of Energy, Energy Information Agency. 2008. http://www .eia.gov.

United States Environmental Protection Agency. 1999. *The Benefits and Costs of the Clean Air Act: 1990—2010.* EPA Report to Congress. EPA 410-R-99-001. Washington, DC: Office of Air and Radiation, Office of Policy.

United States Environmental Protection Agency. 2006. *National Emissions Inventory (NEI), 2002.* Washington, DC: Office of Air Quality Planning and Standards, Emissions Inventory Group; Emissions, Monitoring, and Analysis Division.

———. 2008. *National Emissions Inventory (NEI), 2005.* Washington, DC: Office of Air Quality Planning and Standards, Emissions Inventory Group; Emissions, Monitoring, and Analysis Division.

———. 2011. *National Emissions Inventory (NEI), 2008.* Washington, DC: Office of Air Quality Planning and Standards, Emissions Inventory Group; Emissions, Monitoring, and Analysis Division.

———. 2012a. Clean Air Markets Division. http://www.epa.gov/airmarkets/.

———. 2012b. Clean Air Interstate Rule. http://www.epa.gov/cair/.

———. 2012c. Heavy Duty Highway Diesel Program. http://www.epa.gov/otaq /highway-diesel/.

———. 2012d. Nonroad Diesel Program. http://www.epa.gov/nonroad-diesel/

Vardon, Michael, Manfred Lenzen, Stuart Peevor, and Mette Creaser. 2007. "Water Accounting in Australia." *Ecological Economics* 61:650–9.

Viscusi, W. Kip, and Joseph E. Aldy. 2003. "The Value of a Statistical Life: A Critical Review of Market Estimates Throughout the World." *Journal of Risk and Uncertainty* 27 (1): 5–76.

Human Capital Accounting in the United States
Context, Measurement, and Application

Michael S. Christian

14.1 Introduction

Research in human capital has experienced a resurgence over the past several years, with human capital accounts having been produced recently in Australia, Canada, China, Finland, New Zealand, Norway, Sweden, the United Kingdom, and the United States. Christian's (2010) account for the United States, using an approach based on that of Jorgenson and Fraumeni (1989, 1992), measured the human capital stock and human capital investment in both nominal and real terms over the period between 1994 and 2006. The account broke down net human capital investment among five components: investment from births, depreciation from deaths, investment from education net of the aging of enrolled persons, depreciation from the aging of nonenrolled persons, and a residual component that takes into account both migration and measurement error.

The discussion below adds to the work in Christian (2010) in three ways. First, it puts the results for the United States in international context by reviewing recent efforts in human capital around the world. Second, it updates the results to 2009 to reflect both the availability of new data and improvements to the data set using previously existing data. Third, it inves-

Michael S. Christian is assistant scientist at the Wisconsin Center for Education Research.

The author thanks Ana Aizcorbe, Barbara Fraumeni, Dale Jorgenson, Gang Liu, Rachel Soloveichik, two anonymous referees, and seminar participants at the Bureau of Economic Analysis and at the National Bureau of Economic Research for comments. An earlier version of this chapter was produced as part of a compensated consulting project with the Bureau of Economic Analysis of the US Department of Commerce, at which the author previously worked as a staff economist and which the author thanks for support. For acknowledgments, sources of research support, and disclosure of the author's material financial relationships, if any, please see http://www.nber.org/chapters/c12840.ack.

tigates the sensitivity of the results to alternative approaches to accounting for discounting and income growth, the measurement of taxes, the smoothing and imputation of data, and the classification of nonmarket activities as production.

A review of recent work finds that most work in human capital has focused on income-based approaches, particularly approaches based on lifetime income in the vein of Jorgenson and Fraumeni (1989, 1992). Using a lifetime income approach and assuming an income growth rate of 2 percent and a discount rate of 4 percent, the human capital stock of the United States in 2009 was equal to about three-quarters of a quadrillion dollars, split between market and nonmarket components by a ratio of about one-third to two-thirds. Net investment in human capital from education, net of the aging of persons enrolled in school, was equal to $7.0 trillion, split about evenly between its market and nonmarket components. The market component alone, equal to $3.7 trillion, is larger than the size of the education sector in the US national accounts by a factor of about four. While levels of human capital often change substantively with changes in the assumptions of the model, real growth in net investment in education, equal to 1.6 percent per year across both the market and nonmarket components, is quite robust to changes in the income growth rate, the discount rate, the treatment of taxes, the approach to smoothing and imputation, and the definition of nonmarket work.

14.2   Recent Efforts in the Measurement of Human Capital

Le, Gibson, and Oxley (2003) identifies three major approaches to measuring human capital: the cost-based approach, the income-based approach, and the educational-stock-based or indicators approach. This distinction has sufficient currency that it also appears in Liu and Greaker (2009), Gu and Wong (2010a), Li et al. (2010), Jones and Chiripanhura (2010), and Liu (2011). The indicators approach is the simplest; it uses an indicator or combination of indicators, such as years of schooling or the rate of literacy, to measure a country's human capital. The cost-based approach values the human capital stock at the cost of producing it. A frequently cited text on the cost-based method is Kendrick (1976), which measures human investment using the cost of rearing children, educating people, and other human-capital-related activities. A recent application of the cost-based approach is Kokkinen (2008), which estimates human capital in Finland.

The income-based approach values the human capital stock using the earnings of the persons in that stock. Jorgenson and Fraumeni (1989, 1992), which measure human capital using lifetime incomes in present discounted value, are seminal applications of the income-based approach. The income-based approach has been the most popular approach in recent applications, having recently been employed to create human capital measures for China

(Li et al. 2010), the United States (Christian 2010), the United Kingdom (Jones and Chiripanhura 2010), Canada (Gu and Wong 2010a), Australia (Wei 2004, 2008), New Zealand (Le, Gibson, and Oxley 2006), Sweden (Ahlroth, Bjorklund, and Forslund 1997), and Norway (Liu and Greaker 2009). The income-based approach is also being used for the human capital project at the Organisation for Economic Co-operation and Development (OECD), which aims to produce human capital accounts across countries for international comparisons (Mira d'Ercole and Liu 2010; Liu 2011). Abraham (2010) identifies the cost-based approach and the income-based approach as analogous to the income and production sides of a national income and product account but notes that, unlike the two sides of a national income and product account, cost-based and income-based human capital accounts should not necessarily lead to identical results.

Many implementations of the income-based approach limit the data set to the working-age population, to persons in the labor force, or to employed persons only. This limitation is described in Jones and Chiripanhura (2010, 46) as "consistent with the OECD's guidance on the measurement of physical capital which states that, 'be counted as part of the capital stock all that is required is that assets are present at production sites and capable of being used in production or that they are available for renting by their owners to producers.'" A human capital measure that is limited to the working-age population is denoted in Li et al.'s (2010) paper on China as "active human capital." Active human capital is measured in Gu and Wong's (2010a) study of Canada (working-age population), Le, Gibson, and Oxley's (2006) study of New Zealand (employed persons), Jones and Chiripanhura's (2010) study of the United Kingdom (employed persons), and Liu and Greaker's (2009) study of Norway (persons in the labor force). Wei's (2004) account for Australia presents results for both the working-age population as a whole and for people in the labor force only, and finds that the human capital stock for people in the labor force is about 80 percent the size of the human capital stock for the entire working-age population. Christian's (2010) paper on the United States, Ahlroth, Bjorklund, and Forslund's (1997) paper about Sweden, and Li et al.'s (2010) paper on China include results for the entire populations of the countries studied.

Most recent work focuses on the market component of human capital, which, under the income approach, is the component of human capital that is attributable to the value of a population's market work. The other component of human capital in Jorgenson and Fraumeni (1989, 1992), the nonmarket component, is attributable to the value of a population's nonmarket time. In some applications, the nonmarket component is excluded, sometimes purposefully under the premise that the market component alone is the preferable measure of human capital. For example, Le, Gibson, and Oxley's (2006, 595) paper about New Zealand states that "assuming equal value between a full-time worker and a nonparticipant is not justifiable, from an economic point of view." (See also Ervik, Holmoy, and Haegeland 2003; Gu and Wong 2010a.) Nonmarket human capital is included in Christian's (2010) paper about the United States and Ahlroth, Bjorklund, and Forslund's (1997) paper about Sweden.

Education is measured in the Jorgenson-Fraumeni approach using the number of years of education received. In the original Jorgenson and Fraumeni (1989, 1992) papers, people were classified as having between 0 and 18 years of education. This approach was particularly well suited for the demographic data available in US Census data at the time, which measured education levels in the US population in the same way. Most of the more recent work in human capital outside of the United States, however, has used data that measures education levels using qualifications earned (perhaps in part because of the existence of multiple educational tracks), and it is typically the case that these qualifications require more than a year to complete. As a result, many researchers outside the United States have adapted the Jorgenson-Fraumeni method to accommodate the circumstances in the country in which human capital is being measured. For example, Wei's (2004, 2008) account for Australia classifies people into four educational qualification groups: unqualified, skilled labor, bachelor's degree, and higher degree. The OECD comparative study (Liu 2011) used a set of educational categories defined by the International Standard Classification of Education (ISCED) 1997. In the United States, the census education variables changed in 1992 from individual years to degrees earned, although it is possible to recover individual years from the basic Current Population Survey (CPS) starting in 1997 (see Jaeger 1997, 2003). Christian's (2010) study of human capital in the United States imputed individual years of education.

One interesting difference that appears among studies is in approaches to deflating the stock of human capital over time to make comparisons across time possible. In some cases, the human capital stock is deflated using a consumer or labor price index (Wei 2004, 2008). Under this approach, changes in lifetime incomes relative to changes in prices remain after deflation. If human capital accounts purport to measure human capital stocks and investments as quantities, this approach implies that changes in real lifetime incomes reflect changes in the quality of human capital within age, sex, and education levels. In other cases, the human capital stock is deflated using prices for human capital itself, eliminating changes in lifetime incomes and leaving a quantity index based entirely on the number and distribution of persons by age, sex, and education (Gu and Wong 2010a; Christian 2010). The quality of human capital within age, sex, and education level is implicitly presumed to be constant over time.

Liu (2011) presents a set of cross-country comparisons from the first phase of the OECD human capital project, measuring the market component of active human capital across fifteen countries using the lifetime income approach. The study found that the market component of active human capital was typically between nine and eleven times the size of nominal GDP and between four and five times the stock of physical capital in 2006. Since the focus of the study was on cross-country comparisons, much of the focus was on human capital per capita, adjusted across national currencies using purchasing power parities. The study also measured the inequality of the distribution of human capital by gender, age, and education using Gini coefficients.

Several different approaches to disaggregating changes in the quantity of human capital from one year to the next into investment and depreciation are employed. Wei's (2008) disaggregation for Australia is especially novel, identifying (among several other things) human capital formation from postschool education and on-the-job investment, as well as depreciation of human capital formed by postschool education and on-the-job investment. Many human capital studies focus entirely on the stock of human capital and do not attempt to measure investment or depreciation.

Human capital accounting has particularly interesting applications for the measurement of the education sector. This application is specifically mentioned in the Atkinson (2005) report, which sets an agenda for measurement in the United Kingdom. Ervik, Holmoy, and Haegeland (2003) is an interesting application of human capital in that it focuses on the output of the education sector, to the extent that it does not present a measure of the stock of human capital. The authors find that the higher education sector in Norway is more than seven times larger when measured using the Jorgenson-Fraumeni methodology for human capital investment than when measured as it was in the Norwegian national accounts. Christian (2010) similarly finds very large values for investment in education in the United States. In contrast, Ahlroth, Bjorklund, and Forslund (1997) find measures of investment in education in Sweden that are often smaller than those measured in the Swedish national accounts.

Several applications of the income-based approach to human capital use measures of income other than lifetime income to value human capital. Haveman, Berdshadker, and Schwabish (2003) uses a measure of human capital denoted "earnings capacity," which measures the value of the human capital stock as the expected income in a single year of all working-age persons in an economy if all persons worked full-year, full-time. Earnings capacity is a measure of the potential annual rental value of human capital, in contrast to the asset value measured by the Jorgenson-Fraumeni approach. Since earnings capacity is based on current income (or, more accurately, potential current income, were persons working full-time, full-year) rather than lifetime income, it does not require assumptions about the discount rate or income growth rate to produce. O'Mahony and Stevens (2009) present a measure of the output of the education sector that aggregates enrollments across multiple levels of education using a weight based on the effects on earnings from completing each level of education.

14.3   Updated Measures for the United States

Updates of the human capital measures for the United States presented in Christian (2010) are presented in table 14.1 below for 2009 and for the each year between 1998 and 2009 in the appendix. The update introduces results for three more recent years (2007, 2008, and 2009), and also incorporates changes to the data set since Christian (2010). Both the account in Christian (2010) and this updated human capital account measure human capital by applying a method broadly similar to the Jorgenson-Fraumeni approach. The data set from which the account is produced uses the October school enrollment supplements to the Current Population Survey (CPS) to measure population and school enrollment, the March demographic supplements to the CPS to measure wages and hours worked, and the life tables of the Centers for Disease Control to measure survival rates. The account includes all persons, whether working age or not, with age topcoded at eighty and years of education topcoded at eighteen. When measuring lifetime incomes in present discounted value, an annual income growth rate of 2 percent and a discount rate of 4 percent is used. Measures of real growth are measured using quantity indexes of the population by age, sex, and education; consequently, all real growth measures are determined entirely by changes in the size and distribution of the population by age, sex, and education. The account is discussed in further detail in Christian (2010), with changes between the earlier account and the updated account discussed below.

While the approaches are very similar, there are several differences between the account presented here and the original accounts by Jorgenson and Fraumeni (1989, 1992). The most substantive is that investment in education is measured net of aging of persons enrolled in school. This decision was

Table 14.1   Human capital stock and investment, 2009

	Market	Nonmarket	Total
Stock of human capital (tril.)	$231.6	$525.4	$757.0
Net investment in human capital (tril.)	$2.6	$4.8	$7.4
Investment from births (tril.)	$4.0	$6.9	$10.9
Depreciation from deaths (tril.)	$0.4	$2.4	$2.8
Investment from education, net of aging of enrolled (tril.)	$3.7	$3.3	$7.0
Depreciation from aging of nonenrolled (tril.)	$5.3	$4.5	$9.9
Residual net investment (tril.)	$0.7	$1.6	$2.3
Real growth in stock (ann. 1998–2009)	0.8%	1.0%	0.9%
Real growth in net investment (ann. 1998–2009)	−0.8%	−1.8%	−1.4%
Real growth in investment from births (ann. 1998–2009)	0.4%	0.4%	0.4%
Real growth in depreciation from deaths (ann. 1998–2009)	0.2%	0.6%	0.5%
Real growth in net education investment (ann. 1998–2009)	1.7%	1.4%	1.6%
Real growth in aging of nonenrolled (ann. 1998–2009)	0.3%	0.5%	0.4%

made because attempts to measure gross investment in education were very large and sensitive to counterfactual assumptions (for more discussion on this decision, see Christian [2010]). There are also several other differences. The order in which different events take place within the economy—births, deaths, aging, education, and so forth—is slightly different in this account, and revaluation takes place after investment rather than before. The oldest age group in the sample in this account is eighty rather than seventy-five and, unlike the Jorgenson-Fraumeni accounts, people at the maximum age are able to earn income in this account. Market work is valued at its pretax wage in this account, rather than at the posttax wage as in Jorgenson-Fraumeni, so that market work is valued at its marginal product rather than at its return to the worker.

The OECD study by Liu (2011) estimates the market component of active human capital in the United States in 2006 at $153 trillion. When the account presented here is altered to make the results more comparable to those in the OECD study (by only including lifetime incomes of people age fifteen to sixty-four, setting income to zero for everyone age sixty-five and older, and setting the income growth rate to 1.32 percent and the discount rate to 4.58 percent), the market component of the stock of active human capital in 2006 is equal to $116 trillion. This is 24 percent lower than the OECD estimate, a discrepancy that is a subject for further investigation. One possibility is the difference in the treatment of education between the two studies; while this study measures educational attainment by the individual year, the OECD study uses categories from ISCED 1997.

14.3.1   Individual Years of Education

There are two major areas in which the data set in this account has changed since Christian (2010). First, the estimates in Christian (2010) were based on the October school enrollment supplements to the CPS, in which educational attainment has been measured since 1992 using qualifications earned rather than individual years of education (e.g., "some college but no degree" rather than thirteen, fourteen, or fifteen years of education; see Jaeger [1997]). To handle this, the accounts in Christian (2010) drew from, among other sources, lagged enrollments to impute the distribution of the population by individual years of education. The updated account recovers individual years of education by merging data from the publicly available basic CPS files, which since 1998 have included additional education questions from which variables that measure individual years of education can be created (Jaeger 2003). Because these variables are unavailable before 1998, the updated account only goes as far back as then. A human capital account for the United States that uses the Current Population Survey that includes the years 1992 (the first year of the switch from individual years of education to qualifications earned) through 1997 (the last year before the new education questions were added to the publicly available basic CPS) will still require imputation or adaptation to account for the absence of individual years of education.

One useful aspect of being able to measure individual years of education at the person level is that all of the variables used to measure human capital—wages, the employment rate, hours worked, school enrollment, and so forth—can vary by the individual year of education organically within the sample. In contrast, the imputations used in Christian (2010) made assumptions that limited that variability. In particular, the wage rate for any age and sex only varied across five broad educational groups—no high school diploma, high school diploma, some college, college degree, and advanced degree. One concern noted in Christian (2010) was that this might have led to inflated values of gross investment in education. The reasoning was that each year of education completed took on an immense gross investment value because, for many students, *not* completing a year of education meant falling behind the typical age-education progression (finishing high school at age eighteen, college at age twenty-two, etc.), which in turn substantially reduced the likelihood that one would finish a diploma or degree down the road. Since the imputations only put direct wage gains in the data set when one completes a diploma or degree, the gross investment value of each year of education would be inflated by not allowing for direct wage gains from the intermediate years of education in between. Indeed, gross investment in education measured in Christian (2010) was immense; the market component was $16.4 trillion in 2005. For this reason, Christian (2010) measured investment in education net of the aging of persons enrolled in school; since this measured the value of moving along the age-education progression rather than the value of not falling behind it, the results were of a more plausible magnitude. Interestingly, allowing wages to vary by individual year of education, as the new data set does by measuring individual year of education at the person level, does not seem to have alleviated the problem. In the new data set, gross investment in education remains very large, with a market component of $15.6 trillion in 2005. Given this magnitude, most of the discussion of education that follows will, like Christian (2010), focus on investment in education net of aging.

14.3.2   The Treatment of Taxes

Second, the estimates in Christian (2010) used the federal marginal tax rate variable in the CPS to compute the posttax wage used to value nonmarket time. The updated estimates compute the posttax wage using federal and state marginal tax rates from the Internet version (v9) of TAXSIM (Feenberg and Coutts 1993).[1] The posttax wage only affects measures of the nonmarket component of human capital; the market component of human

1. http://www.nber.org/taxsim/.

Table 14.2   Nonmarket human capital, 2009

	CPS	TAXSIM fed. only	TAXSIM fed. + state	Average fed. + state
Stock of human capital	$557.1	$550.4	$525.4	$515.7
Net investment in human capital	$5.2	$5.1	$4.8	$5.1
Investment from births	$7.3	$7.2	$6.9	$6.8
Depreciation from deaths	$2.4	$2.5	$2.4	$2.2
Investment from education, net of aging	$3.7	$3.5	$3.3	$3.9
Depreciation from aging of nonenrolled	$5.0	$4.8	$4.5	$4.9
Residual net investment	$1.7	$1.6	$1.6	$1.5
Real growth in stock	1.0%	1.0%	1.0%	1.0%
Real growth in net investment	−1.9%	−1.8%	−1.8%	−1.6%
Real growth in investment from births	0.4%	0.4%	0.4%	0.4%
Real growth in depreciation from deaths	0.6%	0.6%	0.6%	0.7%
Real growth in net education investment	1.5%	1.5%	1.4%	1.6%
Real growth in aging of nonenrolled	0.4%	0.5%	0.5%	0.3%

capital is measured using pretax wages to reflect the marginal return to labor received both by the workers themselves and by the government.

Table 14.2 presents selected human capital results for the nonmarket sector for 2009 using the CPS federal marginal tax rate variable, the federal marginal tax rate computed from TAXSIM, and federal and state marginal tax rates computed from TAXSIM. In all three of these cases, marginal tax rates are computed at the individual level: a separate tax rate is computed for each person in the sample used to compute human capital. A fourth set of human capital results are presented for 2009 using an average federal and state marginal tax rate that applies to all persons in a given year.[2] The fourth approach, unlike the previous three, eliminates progressivity in marginal tax rates. Only the nonmarket component is presented because the market component is unaffected by the choice of tax rate.

The inclusion of state taxes has a modest negative effect on nominal measures of nonmarket human capital. When the TAXSIM model is used, including state taxes as well as federal taxes reduces the nonmarket stock of human capital by 5 percent, nonmarket net investment in human capital by 5 percent, and nonmarket net investment in education by 7 percent. The disproportionately large effect on investment in education is likely a result of state taxes adding to the progressivity of the tax structure in the data set; as taxes become more progressive, the posttax wage return to education drops. In contrast, the inclusion of state taxes has only small effects on growth rates of real measures of nonmarket human capital.

Larger distortions take place when the progressivity of marginal taxes is

2. Published at the TAXSIM web site at http://www.nber.org/~taxsim/marginal-tax-rates/at .html.

ignored entirely and a single average marginal tax rate is applied to everyone. While the nominal human capital stock is for the most part unaffected, nominal measures of investment change more substantively. Total nonmarket net investment is 6 percent higher and, of particular interest, nonmarket net investment in education is 18 percent higher. Real growth rates in investment are also changed by the use of a flat marginal tax rate, with the rate of growth in total net investment higher by 0.2 percentage points and the rate of growth in net investment in education higher by (after rounding) 0.1 percentage points per year.

14.4   Discount and Income Growth Rates

The Jorgenson-Fraumeni approach to measuring human capital requires specifying an income growth rate (for projecting future annual incomes from current annual incomes) and a discount rate (for aggregating current and future annual incomes into lifetime incomes in present discount value). The income growth rate of 2 percent and discount rate of 4 percent used in Christian (2010) and in the account presented here are the same as those used in Jorgenson and Fraumeni (1989). Income and growth rates used in the primary results in other studies are summarized in table 14.3.

Compared to the other studies presented in table 14.3, a 2 percent income growth rate and a 4 percent discount rate seems more generous than tight-fisted. In table 14.4, results for the market component of human capital that assume a 1 percent income growth rate and a 6 percent discount rate are presented for contrast; this particular parameterization was also used as a robustness check in Jorgenson and Fraumeni (1989). A wider gap between the income growth rate and the discount rate should lead to smaller measures for human capital, since the lower income growth rate reduces future incomes and the higher discount rate reduces the present valuation of future incomes.

Abraham (2010) notes that one of the reasons that substantial differences exist between income-based and cost-based measures of investment in education is because the discount rate used in human capital accounts is typically much lower than the rate of return on education. This may reflect the difference between the rate of return on education required to make the investment worthwhile from a social perspective and the rate required to make the investment worthwhile from an individual perspective; while the latter is quite high due to uncertainty about the return an individual will eventually receive, the former is much lower since the return is diversified across individuals. To examine the extent to which this may contribute to the difference, the human capital account is reestimated using a very high discount rate, in this case 12 percent, alongside an income growth rate of 1 percent.

It should be unsurprising that the nominal measures of human capital

Table 14.3   **Discount and income growth rates used in human capital accounts**

Study	Country	Income growth rate	Discount rate	Notes
Jorgenson and Fraumeni (1992)	United States	1.32	4.58	Income growth rate is estimate of Harrod-neutral productivity growth; discount rate is long-term rate of return in private sector.
Ahlroth et al. (1997)	Sweden	1.89	5.44	
Ervik et al. (2003)	Norway	2.5	3.5	Discount rate is rate recommended for cost-benefit analysis by finance ministry.
Liu and Greaker (2009)				
Wei (2004)	Australia	1.32	4.58	
Le et al. (2006)	New Zealand	1.5	6	
Li et al. (2010)	China	4.11 (rural); 6 (urban)	4.58	Income growth rate is growth in labor productivity.
Jones and Chiripanhura (2010)	United Kingdom	2	3.5	
Gu and Wong (2010a)	Canada	1.7	5.1	Income growth rate is growth in labor productivity in business sector; discount rate is weighted average rates of return on equity and debt.
Liu (2011)	OECD countries	Varies by country	4.58	Income growth rate is based on historical growth and short-term projections by country, and is typically between 1.0% and 3.0%.

Table 14.4   Market human capital stock and investment under alternative income
                    growth rates and discount rates, 2009

	IG:2% D:4%	IG:1% D:6%	IG:1% D:12%
Stock of human capital (tril.)	$231.6	$135.4	$69.6
Net investment in human capital (tril.)	$2.6	$1.5	$0.8
Investment from births (tril.)	$4.0	$1.2	$0.2
Depreciation from deaths (tril.)	$0.4	$0.3	$0.2
Investment from education, net of aging of enrolled (tril.)	$3.7	$2.9	$1.7
Depreciation from aging of nonenrolled (tril.)	$5.3	$2.7	$1.1
Residual net investment (tril.)	$0.7	$0.4	$0.2
Real growth in stock (ann. 1998–2009)	0.8%	0.9%	1.0%
Real growth in net investment (ann. 1998–2009)	−0.8%	−1.8%	−3.3%
Real growth in investment from births (ann. 1998–2009)	0.4%	0.4%	0.4%
Real growth in depreciation from deaths (ann. 1998–2009)	0.2%	0.4%	0.6%
Real growth in net education investment (ann. 1998–2009)	1.7%	1.6%	1.7%
Real growth in aging of nonenrolled (ann. 1998–2009)	0.3%	1.2%	3.1%

investment fall substantially when the income growth rate is reduced and
the discount rate is driven upward. One interesting result is that measured
real growth in depreciation from aging of persons not enrolled in school
becomes greater as the gap between the income growth rate and the discount
rate rises. This, in turn, makes real growth in net human capital investment
more negative. Why is this the case? Between 1998 and 2009, there was a
substantial increase in the number of people between the ages of fifty-two
and sixty-three, henceforth referred to as late-career persons. The population of late-career persons grew by a total of 55 percent between 1998 and
2009, while the rest of the population grew by a total of only 6 percent. A
rise in the number of late-career persons means that the overall effects of
the aging of the population will increasingly reflect the specific effects of
the aging of late-career persons. This will generally lead to more depreciation since, from a human capital perspective, the effects of aging are more
severe among late-career persons. The aging of late-career persons is almost
entirely depreciation; as late-career persons age, they leave years of earnings
behind them. In contrast, the aging of younger persons has both depreciation and appreciation components. On one hand, younger persons leave
earnings behind as they age, causing depreciation; at the same time, younger
persons also get nearer and nearer as they age to the higher earnings they
will receive later in their careers, leading to appreciation. The appreciation
effect among younger persons becomes greater as the discount rate rises.
Consequently, the higher the discount rate, the greater the degree to which
depreciation from aging is more severe among late-career persons than it
is among younger persons. As a result, when the discount rate is high, a
shift in population toward late-career persons more substantially increases

depreciation from aging, which in turn leads to the higher measured growth rates in depreciation from aging that we see in table 14.4.

It is also interesting to note that even in the case where the income growth rate is set to 1 percent and the discount rate is set to 12 percent, the market component of net investment in education is equal to $1.7 trillion, which is still nearly twice the size of the $909 billion education sector measured in the cost-based National Income and Product Accounts.[3] Does this suggest that persons are receiving a substantial surplus from education? On the income side, while investment in the education sector net of aging is used in this account because it is easy to compute and because it relies on fewer counterfactual assumptions, a measure of gross investment in education that does not include the effects of aging while in school is what ultimately ought to drive personal decisions about education. This is because people will age regardless of whether they attend school or not; consequently, the decision to pursue education should be neutral to the effects of aging. Under traditional assumptions, gross investment in education is very large (even when the income growth rate is 1 percent and the discount rate is 12 percent, its market component is equal to $3.1 trillion), but this is primarily because the traditional model assumes that students who miss a year of education fall "off track" and face a much lower probability of completing diplomas and degrees down the road. In contrast, gross investment in education is more modest when one assumes that students who attended school would not have fallen "off track" had they missed a year of education, and instead would have enrolled in school a year later with the same probabilities as a year before. Under this counterfactual, explained in more detail in Christian (2010), the market component of gross investment in education is $1.18 trillion when the income growth rate is 1 percent and the discount rate is 12 percent.[4] However, the government claims a substantial part of the return to this investment in taxes. After accounting for taxes by adjusting the wage rate with an average tax rate and reestimating human capital, the market component of gross investment in education drops to $979 billion. Since the return to education is not enjoyed until a year later, this amount ought to be multiplied by 1.01 and divided by 1.12 to account for income growth and discounting; this further reduces the amount to $883 billion.

On the cost side, the cost to persons (as opposed to governments) of education includes both direct costs and foregone earnings. The direct costs of education to persons were $223 billion in 2009 while, using the data in the human capital account, the opportunity cost of time spent in school was

---

3. Author's calculation from the National Income and Product Accounts, adding personal consumption expenditures on education services ($223 billion, from table 2.4.5) to government consumption expenditures on education ($686 billion, from table 3.17).

4. This is smaller than investment net of aging because, in this particular case, depreciation due to aging is negative, likely because of the cases of children and young adults who come closer to their prime earning adult ages as they get older.

$377 billion. Adding the direct cost and time cost together yields a total personal cost of $600 billion, which, even at a very high discount rate, is substantially less than the $883 billion personal return to education. Even at these very high discount rates, the personal return to education is about half again as much as the personal cost.

It is useful to note that the above computation includes both elementary and secondary education as well as higher education. Elementary and secondary education is an interesting case, especially from the cost side, since much of it is compulsory, free of direct cost, and attended by students who (at least in this account) are too young to have an opportunity cost of time. Higher education, by contrast, is more characteristic of an economic decision. Applying the above computations to higher education alone yields a personal return of $440 billion (computed from a $648 billion pretax gross investment, adjusted after taxes to $488 billion, multiplied by 1.01 and divided by 1.12). The time cost to persons of higher education was $217 billion and the direct cost was $146 billion, combining to a total cost of $363 billion.[5] Comparison of the return and cost estimates suggests that the personal return to higher education is a little more than 20 percent greater than the personal cost, which in turn suggests that individuals receive a substantial surplus from education, even when the parameterization is conservative.

14.5   Smoothing and Imputation

The human capital model for Sweden produced by Ahlroth, Bjorklund, and Forslund (1997) was created from an annual survey of about 6,000. This sample is too small to estimate realistic means of wages, hours worked, school enrollment, and other variables for each age, sex, and education cell in the human capital data set; given there are 61 age groups, 2 sexes, and 18 levels of education in their model, there are up to 2,196 cells to fill. To fill these cells, the authors specified wages, probability of employment, hours spent at work conditional on employment, and probability of school enrollment as regression functions of sex, age, education, age squared, education squared, age times education, and age squared times education squared. The authors then estimated these regressions over their person-level sample (with log wages and hours spent at work as linear regressions and probabilities of employment and enrollment as logistic regressions) and used the estimated regression coefficients to impute values for these variables to each cell. These imputations make measuring human capital possible even with a small sample.

There are few problems from small samples in the United States, where the Current Population Survey regularly interviews more than 100,000 per-

---

5. Direct cost is measured from the National Income and Product Accounts, table 2.4.5.

sons each month. However, an approach that imputes the variables used to build human capital using a regression equation with age and education on the right-hand side has some interesting qualities. In particular, it smooths wages, hours, earnings, and enrollment, reducing jumps and spikes over age and education. For example, figure 14.1 presents two sets of school enroll-ment rates for men with eleven years of education between ages sixteen to twenty-two. The first uses rates computed directly from the Current Popu-lation Survey. The second uses rates imputed from a logistic regression of school enrollment on age, education, age squared, education squared, age times education, and age squared times education squared.

One substantive difference between the directly computed school enroll-ment rate and the imputed school enrollment rate is that the extent to which people are affected by falling off the typical age-education progression is reduced in the imputed case. Most Americans finish their twelfth year of education by the end of age eighteen, so persons who are nineteen years old but who have only finished eleven years of education have fallen off track. In the directly computed case, a man with eleven years of education faces a serious drop in the probability of continuing further education upon reach-ing age nineteen, with school enrollment rates dropping from 88 percent to 49 percent. However, in the imputed case, the school enrollment rate drops from 82 percent to 67 percent. This is still a substantial drop, but from the

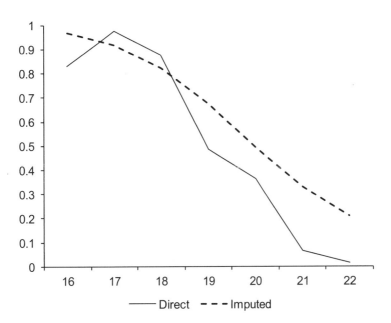

Fig. 14.1   School enrollment rates, 2009, men with eleven years of education, ages sixteen to twenty-two

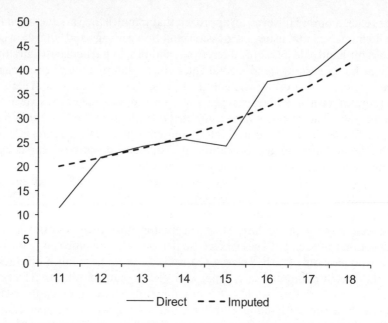

Fig. 14.2   Pretax wage rate, 2009, men age fifty, between eleven and eighteen years of education

perspective of years of education ultimately completed, the implication of missing a year of school is smaller.

A similar smoothing takes place in wages and earnings. Figure 14.2 plots the average pretax wage of men of fifty years of age and of between eleven and eighteen years of education, in both the direct case and the imputed case. In the direct case, the relationship between wages and education is jumpy, with evident sheepskin effects at the twelfth (high school diploma) and sixteenth (bachelor's degree) year of education. In the imputed case, the wage rate rises smoothly as years of education rise. This may also reduce the implication of missing a year of school. If missing a year of school reduces the probability of finishing a diploma or a degree down the line, the imputed approach may reduce the cost of missing a year of school by reducing the importance of degree and diploma years and increasing the returns to the intermediate years of education in between.

If, in the imputed case, not attending a year of school has smaller implications for later educational attainment and, potentially, for earnings, then it may also be the case that measured gross investment in education under traditional assumptions is also small because the cost of not attending a year of schooling and falling "off track" from the typical age-schooling progression is smaller. Table 14.5 compares results from the baseline human capital

Table 14.5   Market human capital stock and investment from baseline model and
model with substantial imputations, 2009

	Baseline	Imputed
Stock of human capital (tril.)	$231.6	$218.0
Net investment in human capital (tril.)	$2.6	$2.3
Investment from births (tril.)	$4.0	$3.7
Depreciation from deaths (tril.)	$0.4	$0.4
Investment from education, net of aging of enrolled (tril.)	$3.7	$3.9
Investment from education, gross, trad. assumptions (tril.)	$21.0	$16.8
Depreciation from aging of nonenrolled (tril.)	$5.3	$5.6
Residual net investment (tril.)	$0.7	$0.7
Real growth in stock (ann. 1998–2009)	0.8%	0.8%
Real growth in net investment (ann. 1998–2009)	–0.8%	–1.0%
Real growth in investment from births (ann. 1998–2009)	0.4%	0.4%
Real growth in depreciation from deaths (ann. 1998–2009)	0.2%	0.0%
Real growth in net education investment (ann. 1998–2009)	1.7%	1.4%
Real growth in aging of nonenrolled (ann. 1998–2009)	0.3%	0.5%

model with results from a model in which many of the relevant variables are imputed for the market component of the human capital stock.[6]

The imputations used in the alternative model are similar but not identical to those in Ahlroth, Bjorklund, and Forslund (1997). The right-hand-side variables in each regression were age, education, age squared, education squared, age times education, and age squared times education squared. However, rather than include sex among the right-hand-side variables, separate regressions were estimated by sex instead. For each sex and each year, three different school enrollment regressions for three different left-hand-side variables were run using logistic regression: full-time enrollment in grades one through twelve; full-time enrollment in postsecondary education; and part-time enrollment in postsecondary education. Logistic regression was also employed for a model with the probability of employment as the left-hand-side variable. Finally, hours worked conditional on employment, log pretax wage rate, and log posttax wage rate were imputed using ordinary least squares regression.

The imputations do have an effect on the market component of gross investment in education as measured under traditional assumptions; by using the imputation, the measured amount drops by a fifth, from $21.0 trillion to $16.8 trillion. However, this is still an enormous quantity that rivals the entire gross domestic product of the United States, a result that is in

6. These results will differ from the results in an earlier version of the paper (BEA Working Paper 2011-05) for having used the mean $\exp(X\beta + .5\sigma^2)$ rather than the median $\exp(X\beta)$ to impute wages from a log-linear regression $\log w = X\beta + \varepsilon$.

substantive contrast to Ahlroth, Bjorklund, and Forslund (1997), whose income-based measure of gross investment in education in Sweden was actually lower than the cost-based measure used in the Swedish national accounts. The rest of the results are for the most part unaffected by the use of imputation, which bodes well for human capital accounting in cases where sample sizes are small.

14.6   Valuation of Nonmarket Time

The human capital accounts presented here and in Jorgenson and Fraumeni (1989, 1992) include both a market and nonmarket component. The nonmarket component is measured under the assumption that time spent outside of work, school (assumed to be 1,300 hours a week for full-time enrolled students), and personal maintenance (assumed to be 10 hours a day) is spent in nonmarket activities that are valued at the posttax marginal wage. Some of these activities are undeniably work that leads to production of goods and services in the home, such as cooking, laundry, home repairs, and child care. Other activities, such as watching television, make a weaker case for being classified as nonmarket production; one can make such a case (the only way to draw any utility from a television, for example, is to actually spend time watching it), but the case is weaker.

It is possible, with time-use survey data, to put restrictions on which activities are valued in the nonmarket component of a human capital account and which activities are not valued. Using the American Time Use Survey, the time of individuals is split into categories that reflect the degree to which it ought to be considered home production. Time is split into six different kinds of activities: market work, school, nonmarket production, child and adult care, leisure, and maintenance. Nonmarket production includes housework, cooking, cleaning, laundry, home repairs and maintenance, home management, shopping, using services (going to the post office, for example), and religious and civic activities. Child and adult care includes not just basic child care (feeding, grooming, etc.), but also educational (helping with homework, etc.) and recreational (playing sports, etc.) child care as well. Leisure includes reading, sports, hobbies, entertainment, socializing, and watching television. Finally, maintenance includes not only sleeping, eating, and personal care, but also commuting to work. Commuting is included in maintenance because commuting only exists to support work, so the value of time spent commuting to work is already accounted for in earnings from market work. These categories borrow heavily from Aguiar and Hurst's (2007) classification of time into nonmarket work and leisure. They also correspond reasonably well with Abraham and Mackie's (2005) recommendations for identifying household production for a satellite account.

The American Time Use Survey is a smaller sample; it surveys about 13,000 individuals each year between 2003 and 2009. To incorporate the smaller sample into the human capital estimates, imputations based on regressions similar to those used in Ahlroth, Bjorklund, and Forslund (1997) are used. The proportion of total time spent in nonmarket production, child and adult care, leisure, and maintenance were each regressed on: (a) age, education, age squared, education squared, age times education, and age squared times education squared; (b) the proportion of time spent in market work and the proportion of time spent in school; and (c) the variables in (a) interacted with the variables in (b). These regressions were estimated separately by sex and year and used to predict time spent in nonmarket production, child and adult care, leisure, and maintenance under three different approaches. In the first approach, maintenance is still assumed to be 10 hours per day and full-time school enrollment is still assumed to be 1,300 hours per year. The remaining time outside of market work is divided among nonmarket production, child and adult care, and leisure in proportion to their predicted time from the above regressions. Only time spent in nonmarket work is valued in the human capital account. The second approach is the same as the first approach, except that both nonmarket work and child and adult care are valued. In the third approach, maintenance time is increased to 11.08 hours per day, and school time among those enrolled in school full-time is increased to 1,647 hours per year for elementary and secondary students and reduced to 1,105 hours per year for postsecondary students. This is in accordance with the average time spent on maintenance and schooling measured from the American Time Use Survey. Like the second approach, both nonmarket work and child and adult care are valued in the third approach. The results from the three approaches are presented in table 14.6.

Opting to only value time spent in specifically defined nonmarket work

Table 14.6   Nonmarket human capital stock and investment under alternative accounting for nonmarket time, 2009

	Base model	Nonmarket work only	Nonmarket w/child care	Maint., school from ATUS
Stock of human capital (tril.)	$525.4	$174.6	$210.6	$189.0
Net investment in human capital (tril.)	$4.8	$1.8	$2.1	$1.9
Investment from births (tril.)	$6.9	$2.3	$2.9	$2.6
Depreciation from deaths (tril.)	$2.4	$0.7	$0.8	$0.7
Investment from education, net of aging (tril.)	$3.3	$1.4	$1.8	$1.6
Depreciation from aging of nonenrolled (tril.)	$4.5	$1.7	$2.5	$2.2
Residual net investment (tril.)	$1.6	$0.5	$0.6	$0.6
Real growth in stock (ann., 2003–2009)	0.9%	0.9%	0.9%	0.9%
Real growth in net investment (ann.)	2.7%	3.9%	4.5%	4.4%
Real growth in investment from births (ann.)	0.2%	0.2%	0.2%	0.2%
Real growth in depreciation from deaths (ann.)	0.1%	0.2%	0.2%	0.2%
Real growth in net education investment (ann.)	1.3%	1.4%	1.4%	1.4%
Real growth in aging of nonenrolled (ann.)	0.3%	0.3%	0.2%	0.2%

has a very large negative effect on measures of the nonmarket component of the human capital stock, reducing it to one-third its value when all nonmarket, nonschool time outside of maintenance is included. Net investment is reduced in rough proportion, with the largest proportional drop in depreciation due to deaths and the smallest in net investment from education. This would be the case if older people spent relatively less time in nonmarket work and if people increase the amount of nonmarket time spent in nonmarket work as their levels of education rise. Real growth rates in the human capital stock are unchanged when only time spent in nonmarket work activities is valued, but real net investment in human capital grows considerably faster in the alternative accounting. Interestingly, this growth in real net investment does not come from the measured causes of investment (births, deaths, aging, or education), but rather from the residual component of net investment—the changes in population that are left over once calculations for births, deaths, aging, and education have been made. This residual includes migration and measurement error, and faster growth in residual net investment in the alternative accounting implies that growth in this residual was in groups that spent relatively more of their nonmarket time in household work.

When child and adult care is added to the nonmarket component of human capital, the most substantive effect for nominal human capital investment is on aging of persons not enrolled in school. This is a result of people spending less time on child and adult care as they become older. Real growth in net investment becomes faster, and this is again primarily in the residual component of net investment. Changing the number of hours spent in school conditional on enrollment and on maintenance reduces the components of the human capital stock and investment in rough proportion to each other and has very little effect on real growth in stock and investment.

The above analysis is merely a start at exploiting the possibilities for alternative measurements of nonmarket time in human capital. For example, this account and the account of Jorgenson and Fraumeni (1989, 1992) value time spent in nonmarket activities at the tax-adjusted marginal wage of the person performing the activity. This approach to valuating nonmarket tasks will value tasks more highly when they are performed by more educated persons, even in cases where the performance of the task is not likely to improve with education; this point is made in Rothschild (1989) and elsewhere. Consequently, valuing nonmarket tasks at market wage will yield a substantive nonmarket component of investment from education. Alternatives to valuating nonmarket tasks at market wages include valuing them at a replacement wage equal to the cost of hiring someone in the market to perform the task for you, possibly adjusted for differences in productivity between the amateurs working in the home and the professionals working in the market; this is the approach recommended for a satellite account for household production in Abraham and Mackie (2005). Abraham (2010) considers an approach that differentiates the relationship between education and productivity between different nonmarket activities.

14.7   Real Output of the Education Sector

One of the most frequently cited applications of a human capital account is the use of investment in education as a measure of the output of the education sector. This is the motivation for one of the original Jorgenson and Fraumeni (1992) papers, is recommended for a satellite account in the Atkinson (2005) report, and was discussed among possible approaches for the United States in Christian and Fraumeni (2005).

In an income-based human capital account, investment in education is equal to the sum of persons who are enrolled in school across sexes, ages, and levels of education weighted by the lifetime return in present discounted value to a year of education by sex, age, and level of education. If investment in education is measured in real terms using enrollments as quantities and lifetime returns as weights, then real investment in education is a volume-based measure of the real output of the education sector. A volume-based measure of the real output of the education sector measures real output using a measure of the amount of education services produced, which is typically identified as enrollments; examples of volume-based measures for the United States are presented in Fraumeni et al. (2009) and in Christian (2006).

On the other hand, if investment in education is measured in real terms by deflating a nominal measure of net investment in education using a price index such as the Consumer Price Index, then investment in education is an outcome-based measure of the real output of the education sector. The measure is outcome-based since it would not measure the amount of services produced, but rather the outcome of those services, namely the value of the amount of extra production and consumption of goods and services made possible by the education.

An alternative way to understand the CPI-deflated approach is as one in which higher lifetime returns to education, in terms of purchasing power, are understood as improvements in the quality of education. If this is the case, then the impact of higher lifetime returns to education ought to be reflected in the real growth in the volume of education, not in the price. This understanding would likely require an expansive understanding of the meaning of quality, since many things that drive changes in the return to education, such as skill-based technological change, are outside of the educational process itself.

Figure 14.3 presents comparisons between three measures of the real output of the elementary and secondary education sector between 1998 and 2009. The first is a simple count of students enrolled in school—a straightforward volume index with no adjustments for changes in the quality of

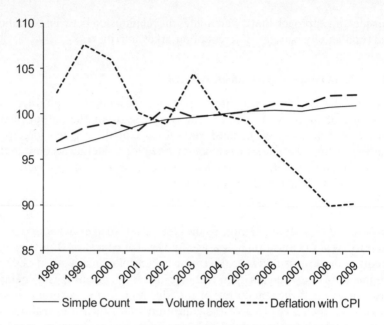

— Simple Count — — Volume Index ----- Deflation with CPI

Fig. 14.3   **Real elementary and secondary education output (2004 = 100)**

education over time. The second is growth in real investment in education net of aging of persons enrolled in school, using the baseline human capital account presented in table 14.1 and treating enrollments as quantities and lifetime returns as weights. This approach, like the simple count of students, also does not account for changes in the quality of education over time but, unlike the simple count of students, weights enrollments of students by sex, age, and level of education using their net investment values. The third measure is real investment in education net of aging of persons enrolled in school, also using the baseline human capital account presented in table 14.1 but computed by deflating nominal investment in education net of aging using the Consumer Price Index. This is a measure of the real purchasing power of the return to education and is an outcome-based rather than a volume-based approach. Both the market and nonmarket components of net investment in education are included.

We can see in figure 14.3 that the simple count and the volume index follow each other relatively closely. Both grew at an annual rate of 0.5 percent between 1998 and 2009, although the volume index grew more slowly in the 1998 to 2004 period (0.5 percent compared to 0.7 percent) and more quickly in the 2004 to 2009 period (0.4 percent compared to 0.2 percent). In contrast, nominal net investment deflated with the CPI presents a substantively different story, having declined at an annual rate of 1.1 percent between

1998 and 2009. This would be consistent with a decline in the lifetime return to elementary and secondary education in real terms over the period studied.

Figure 14.4 repeats this analysis for higher education, with the exception that the simple count of enrollments is measured in full-time equivalents rather than as an unadjusted headcount. All three series exhibit the same annual growth rate of 3.0 percent between 1998 and 2009, although there are wrinkles in growth between them in the intermediate years. In the 1998 to 2004 period, the simple count grows the fastest (3.3 percent), the volume index the second fastest (2.7 percent), and the CPI-deflated index the slowest (1.7 percent), indicating a shift in higher education enrollments toward persons with lower levels of return to education and also a general decline in the return to education by sex, age, and level of education. Both trends reverse completely in the 2004 to 2009 period, so that the simple count (2.5 percent) grows more slowly than the volume index (3.4 percent), which in turn grows more slowly than the CPI-deflated index (4.5 percent).

These results are consistent with those of Gu and Wong (2010b), who conduct a similar analysis comparing the growth in real output of the education sector between a cost-based approach and an income-based approach, with both approaches producing volume indexes based on the number of students enrolled. In their estimates for Canada, a simple count of students

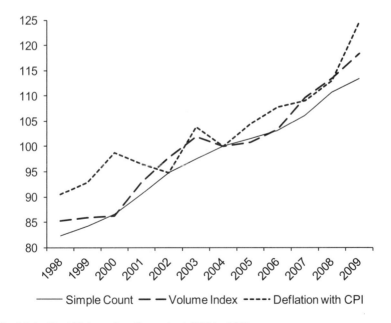

Fig. 14.4   Real higher education output (2004 = 100)

grew at a rate of 0.6 percent per year, a cost-based volume index grew at a rate of 0.9 percent per year, and an income-based volume index grew at a rate of 0.7 percent per year between 1996 and 2005.

From the perspective of national accounting, the framework of human capital can be used as an informative basis for a satellite account for the output of the education sector. Given that there are a substantial number of choices involved in measuring human capital using an income-based approach (the importance of which are discussed throughout this study), such an account should include alternative results under different assumptions.

14.8   Conclusions and Suggestions for Further Research

The findings above suggest that an income-based approach to measuring human capital in the United States similar to that of Jorgenson and Fraumeni (1989, 1992) yields a very large estimate of the stock of human capital. In 2009, using an income-based approach that assumes a 2 percent income growth rate and a 4 percent discount rate, the stock of human capital in the United States was about three-quarters of a quadrillion dollars, of which about one-third was market and two-thirds was nonmarket. The market component of net investment in education was $3.7 trillion, which is nearly four times as great than the $909 billion education sector measured in the National Income and Product Accounts. When the analysis focuses strictly on costs and returns to individual persons, there appears to be substantial consumer surplus from education even when the discount rate is increased to 12 percent.

Real growth in net investment from education, which was 1.6 percent per year between 1998 and 2009 is, for the most part, robust to changes in the income growth rate, the discount rate, the treatment of taxes, the approach to smoothing and imputation, and the valuation of nonmarket time. Other aspects of human capital are less robust. While it should not be surprising that changing the income growth rate, the discount rate, the treatment of taxes, or the activities classified as nonmarket production changes the levels of the human capital stock or human capital investment substantially, there are also some cases where real growth in investment in human capital is changed as well. For example, reducing the income growth rate and increasing the discount rate substantially reduces the growth rate in net investment, primarily by increasing the magnitude of depreciation from aging among persons aged in their fifties and early sixties.

In general, the human capital account as a whole was robust to using regressions to impute employment, school enrollment rates, and wages by age, sex, and education. This bodes well for measuring human capital from small data sets from which reliable sample means cannot be measured by age, sex, and individual year of education.

The work above lends itself to many extensions. Perhaps the most immediately interesting extension would be to extend the series further back in time. Haveman, Berdshadker, and Schwabish (2003) presents results for a potential-income-based model that go back to 1975, and readily available data from the Current Population Survey can be used to extend a human capital account for the United States as far back as 1968. This could be used to identify effects on human capital of long-run phenomena such as rising educational attainment and increased participation of women in market work. Extending the time series backward would also allow for empirical analysis of the differences between the lifetime-income-based approach of Jorgenson and Fraumeni (1989, 1992) and the potential-income-based approach of Haveman, Berdshadker, and Schwabish (2003).

It would also be useful to see if results generated from other data sets within the United States would generate results similar to those generated in the Current Population Survey. This might be especially useful for the purposes of measuring human capital from a small data set that requires regressions or similar approaches to impute wages, employment, and school enrollment by age, sex, and individual year of education. While measured human capital was for the most part robust to using regressions rather than sample means in the analysis of section 14.5, it is useful to note that this was the case when using regression coefficients from a large data set, the Current Population Survey, which, being large, will produce precisely measured regression coefficients. It would be useful to see if a human capital account generated entirely from a smaller data set would generate comparable results.

The alternative measures of the nonmarket component of human capital in section 14.6 is only a start to the application of time-use data to human capital accounts. The approach used was a model that uses regression techniques to impute the distribution of time using age, sex, education, and the extent of time spent in the market and in schooling. The robustness of these results to alternative assumptions about the function that determines the distribution of time across different activities is relatively low-hanging fruit. In addition, using alternative assumptions about the meaning of nonmarket work could yield further informative results. For example, in the results in section 14.6, the classification of activities as nonmarket work is a bright-line rule—either an activity is production or it is not. An alternative approach would allow that some activities are partially production and partially consumption. For example, Christian's (2007) account for household production of health care counted 20 percent of time spent in sports and exercise toward health-related production and the remaining 80 percent toward consumption. A third aspect of nonmarket production that suggests further investigation is the effect on the accounts from valuing of time spent in nonmarket activities at the wage of the person performing the activities rather than at the market cost of hiring another person to do it.

Abraham (2010) discusses a substantial number of important issues in human capital measurement, most of which focused on measuring the output of the education sector. The discussion sets out a plan for an satellite education account that includes both cost-based and income-based approaches to measuring human capital, mirroring the expenditure and income sides in the double-entry bookkeeping structure of a national account. Costs and income could include both market and nonmarket components, the latter of which would likely require further use of time-use data. Jorgenson (2010) elaborates on the relevant issues of a satellite account. Abraham (2010) also discusses fundamental questions about the attribution of income differences across different education levels to formal education itself. For example, persons who attain higher levels of education may have received more inputs not just from schooling but also from their families, and may also receive more on-the-job training. Income growth from technological change, even when skills neutral, will also amplify differences in lifetime earnings between different education levels, even though the technology is completely divorced from the education sector.

The usefulness of human capital ultimately comes down to its potential for practical application. This point is made by McGrattan (2010), who finds a disconnect between human capital accounting and applied economics research and recommends that research in human capital focus less on the size of the human capital stock and more on economic questions. The results on the real output of the education sector in section 14.7 are in part an attempt to connect human capital to an economic application, in this case to a related issue in the economics of education. Gu and Wong (2010b) conduct a similar analysis for the output of the education sector in Canada, comparing real growth in education output between cost-based and income-based approaches. Recently produced accounts in several countries discuss macroeconomic applications, with a particular focus on economic growth, sustainable development, and productivity (Kokkinen 2008; Le, Gibson, and Oxley 2006; Gu and Wong 2010a; Jones and Chiripanhura 2010; Li et al. 2010; Liu and Greaker 2009). The OECD project should facilitate international comparison (Mira d'Ercole and Liu 2010; Liu 2011). Wei (2008) mentions that the human capital framework can be particularly useful for studies of education, migration, and aging. Haveman, Berdshadker, and Schwabish (2003) makes use of disaggregations of a potential-income-based measure of human capital to analyze potential earnings and capacity utilization by race, age group, and education level. Jorgenson (2010) identifies human capital as one of the most important additions to accounting for nonmarket activities in national accounts. As human capital estimates become internationally more widespread and the number of researchers to whom they become available increases, the number of applications of human capital should increase with the collective creativity of its users.

Appendix
Human Capital, 1998–2009

Table 14A.1   Human capital, market and nonmarket combined, nominal ($trilllion)

Year	Stock	Net human capital investment						Revaluation
		Total	Births	Deaths	Education	Aging	Residual	
1998	478.7	6.3	6.6	1.9	4.9	6.7	3.4	15.3
1999	500.3	4.9	6.7	2.1	5.3	7.0	2.1	13.2
2000	518.4	6.3	7.2	1.9	5.5	7.9	3.3	18.0
2001	542.6	4.7	7.5	2.1	5.4	7.8	1.7	13.8
2002	565.1	5.1	7.9	2.2	5.4	7.8	1.8	22.8
2003	593.0	4.8	8.5	2.2	6.0	8.6	1.1	22.2
2004	620.0	5.3	8.8	2.4	5.9	8.3	1.3	19.1
2005	644.4	5.5	9.1	2.5	6.2	8.6	1.4	22.9
2006	672.8	7.3	9.9	2.5	6.3	9.0	2.6	27.1
2007	707.2	5.1	10.4	2.8	6.4	9.1	0.1	10.9
2008	723.1	5.2	10.6	2.7	6.7	9.6	0.2	28.7
2009	757.0	7.4	10.9	2.8	7.0	9.9	2.3	

Note: Net human capital investment from education is investment net of depreciation from aging of enrolled persons, while net human capital investment from aging is depreciation from aging of nonenrolled persons. Deaths and aging are depreciation rather than investment.

Table 14A.2   Human capital, market and nonmarket combined, real (2009 $trillion)

Year	Stock	Net human capital investment				
		Total	Births	Deaths	Education	Aging
1998	683.4	8.7	10.4	2.6	5.9	9.5
1999	692.3	6.7	10.4	2.7	5.9	9.8
2000	699.1	8.3	10.7	2.7	6.0	9.9
2001	707.4	6.1	10.6	2.7	6.1	9.9
2002	713.5	6.5	10.5	2.7	6.4	9.7
2003	720.0	5.8	10.8	2.8	6.4	9.8
2004	725.8	6.1	10.8	2.7	6.4	9.7
2005	732.2	6.0	10.9	2.8	6.4	9.8
2006	738.3	7.8	11.2	2.8	6.5	9.8
2007	746.3	5.3	11.4	2.8	6.7	10.0
2008	751.6	5.4	11.2	2.8	6.8	9.9
2009	757.0	7.4	10.9	2.8	7.0	9.9

Note: Net human capital investment from education is investment net of depreciation from aging of enrolled persons, while net human capital investment from aging is depreciation from aging of nonenrolled persons. Deaths and aging are depreciation rather than investment.

Table 14A.3   **Human capital, market only, nominal ($trillion)**

		Net human capital Investment						
Year	Stock	Total	Births	Deaths	Education	Aging	Residual	Revaluation
1998	153.2	1.9	2.4	0.3	2.6	3.9	1.1	3.5
1999	158.6	1.3	2.4	0.3	2.8	4.1	0.6	12.1
2000	172.0	2.0	2.7	0.3	2.9	4.5	1.2	−2.8
2001	171.2	1.2	2.7	0.3	2.8	4.3	0.4	3.8
2002	177.9	1.3	2.8	0.3	2.8	4.3	0.3	4.9
2003	184.2	1.3	3.0	0.3	3.0	4.5	0.2	3.4
2004	188.9	1.4	3.1	0.3	2.9	4.5	0.2	7.4
2005	197.7	1.4	3.2	0.4	3.0	4.7	0.2	9.9
2006	208.9	2.0	3.6	0.4	3.1	4.9	0.6	6.6
2007	217.5	1.2	3.8	0.4	3.2	5.0	−0.4	4.9
2008	223.6	1.3	3.9	0.4	3.4	5.1	−0.4	6.8
2009	231.6	2.6	4.0	0.4	3.7	5.3	0.7	

Note: Net human capital investment from education is investment net of depreciation from aging of enrolled persons, while net human capital investment from aging is depreciation from aging of nonenrolled persons. Deaths and aging are depreciation rather than investment.

Table 14A.4   **Human capital, market only, real (2009 $trillion)**

		Net human capital investment				
Year	Stock	Total	Births	Deaths	Education	Aging
1998	212.1	2.8	3.8	0.4	3.1	5.1
1999	214.7	1.8	3.8	0.4	3.1	5.4
2000	216.5	2.7	3.9	0.4	3.1	5.4
2001	218.9	1.7	3.9	0.4	3.2	5.4
2002	220.5	1.8	3.8	0.4	3.3	5.3
2003	222.1	1.7	4.0	0.4	3.4	5.3
2004	223.7	1.8	4.0	0.4	3.3	5.3
2005	225.3	1.7	4.0	0.4	3.4	5.3
2006	226.9	2.4	4.1	0.4	3.4	5.3
2007	229.1	1.3	4.2	0.4	3.5	5.4
2008	230.3	1.4	4.1	0.4	3.6	5.4
2009	231.6	2.6	4.0	0.4	3.7	5.3

Note: Net human capital investment from education is investment net of depreciation from aging of enrolled persons, while net human capital investment from aging is depreciation from aging of nonenrolled persons. Deaths and aging are depreciation rather than investment.

Table 14A.5　　　　Human capital, nonmarket only, nominal ($trillion)

Year	Stock	Total	Births	Deaths	Education	Aging	Residual	Revaluation
		\multicolumn{7}{c}{Net human capital investment}						
1998	325.5	4.4	4.2	1.6	2.3	2.8	2.3	11.8
1999	341.6	3.6	4.3	1.8	2.5	2.9	1.6	1.2
2000	346.4	4.3	4.6	1.6	2.6	3.5	2.1	20.8
2001	371.5	3.5	4.8	1.8	2.6	3.5	1.3	10.0
2002	387.1	3.8	5.1	1.9	2.6	3.5	1.5	17.9
2003	408.9	3.5	5.5	1.8	3.0	4.1	1.0	18.8
2004	431.1	3.9	5.7	2.0	3.0	3.8	1.1	11.7
2005	446.7	4.1	5.9	2.1	3.2	4.0	1.2	13.0
2006	463.9	5.3	6.3	2.1	3.2	4.1	2.0	20.5
2007	489.7	3.9	6.6	2.3	3.2	4.1	0.5	6.0
2008	499.6	3.9	6.7	2.3	3.3	4.5	0.6	21.9
2009	525.4	4.8	6.9	2.4	3.3	4.5	1.6	

Note: Net human capital investment from education is investment net of depreciation from aging of enrolled persons, while net human capital investment from aging is depreciation from aging of nonenrolled persons. Deaths and aging are depreciation rather than investment.

Table 14A.6　　　　Human capital, nonmarket only, real (2009 $trillion)

Year	Stock	Total	Births	Deaths	Education	Aging
		\multicolumn{5}{c}{Net human capital investment}					
1998	471.3	5.9	6.6	2.2	2.8	4.3
1999	477.5	4.9	6.6	2.3	2.8	4.5
2000	482.6	5.6	6.8	2.3	2.9	4.5
2001	488.4	4.4	6.7	2.3	2.9	4.5
2002	493.0	4.8	6.7	2.3	3.0	4.4
2003	497.9	4.1	6.8	2.4	3.1	4.5
2004	502.2	4.3	6.9	2.3	3.0	4.4
2005	506.8	4.4	6.9	2.4	3.0	4.5
2006	511.4	5.5	7.1	2.3	3.1	4.5
2007	517.2	4.0	7.2	2.4	3.2	4.6
2008	521.3	4.1	7.1	2.4	3.2	4.5
2009	525.4	4.8	6.9	2.4	3.3	4.5

Note: Net human capital investment from education is investment net of depreciation from aging of enrolled persons, while net human capital investment from aging is depreciation from aging of nonenrolled persons. Deaths and aging are depreciation rather than investment.

References

Abraham, Katharine. 2010. "Accounting for Investments in Formal Education." *Survey of Current Business* 90 (6): 42–53.

Abraham, Katharine, and Christopher Mackie, eds. 2005. *Beyond the Market: Designing Nonmarket Accounts for the United States.* Washington, DC: National Academies Press.

Aguiar, Mark, and Erik Hurst. 2007. "Measuring Trends in Leisure: The Allocation of Time Over Five Decades." *Quarterly Journal of Economics* 122 (3): 969–1006.

Ahlroth, Sofia, Anders Bjorklund, and Anders Forslund. 1997. "The Output of the Swedish Education Sector." *Review of Income and Wealth* 43 (1): 89–104.

Atkinson, Tony. 2005. *Atkinson Review: Final Report: Measurement of Government Output and Productivity for the National Accounts.* Basingstoke, UK: Palgrave MacMillan.

Christian, Michael. 2006. "Measuring the Education Function of Government in the United States." Presented at the Workshop on Measurement of Non-Market Output in Education and Health, London, England, October, 3–5.

———. 2007. "Measuring the Output of Health Care in the United States." *Survey of Current Business* 87 (6): 78–83.

———. 2010. "Human Capital Accounting in the United States, 1994–2006." *Survey of Current Business* 90 (6): 31–6.

Christian, Michael, and Barbara Fraumeni. 2005. "Measuring the Education Function of Government." Background materials for the meeting of the Bureau of Economic Analysis Advisory Committee, May 13.

Ervik, Astrid Oline, Erling Holmoy, and Torbjorn Haegeland. 2003. "A Theory-Based Measure of the Output of the Education Sector." Discussion Papers no. 353. Statistics Norway.

Feenberg, Daniel, and Elisabeth Coutts. 1993. "An Introduction to the TAXSIM Model." *Journal of Policy Analysis and Management* 12 (1): 189–94.

Fraumeni, Barbara, Marshall Reinsdorf, Brooks Robinson, and Matthew Williams. 2009. "Price and Real Output Measures for the Education Function of Government: Exploratory Estimates for Primary and Secondary Education." In *Price Index Concepts and Measurement*, Studies in Income and Wealth, vol. 70, edited by W. Erwin Diewert, John Greenlees, and Charles Hulten. Chicago: University of Chicago Press.

Gu, Wulong, and Ambrose Wong. 2010a. "Estimates of Human Capital in Canada: The Lifetime Income Approach." Economic Analysis (EA) Research Paper Series, Catalogue no. 11F0027M, no. 062. Ottawa: Economic Analysis Division, Statistics Canada.

———. 2010b. "Investment in Human Capital and the Output of the Education Sector in Canada." Presented at the 31st General Conference of the International Association for Research in Income and Wealth (IARIW), St. Gallen, Switzerland, August 22–28.

Haveman, Robert, Andrew Berdshadker, and Jonathan Schwabish. 2003. *Human Capital in the United States from 1975 to 2000: Patterns of Growth and Utilization.* Kalamazoo, MI: W. E. Upjohn Institute for Employment Research.

Jaeger, David. 1997. "Reconciling the Old and New Census Bureau Education Questions: Recommendations for Researchers." *Journal of Business and Economic Statistics* 15 (4): 300–9.

———. 2003. "Estimating the Returns to Education Using the Newest Current Population Survey Education Questions." *Economics Letters* 78 (3): 385–94.

Jones, Richard, and Blessing Chiripanhura. 2010. "Measuring the U. K.'s Human Capital Stock." *Economic and Labor Market Review* 4 (11): 36–63.

Jorgenson, Dale. 2010. "Human Capital and the National Accounts." *Survey of Current Business* 90 (6): 54–6.

Jorgenson, Dale, and Barbara Fraumeni. 1989 "The Accumulation of Human and Nonhuman Capital, 1948–84." In *The Measurement of Saving, Investment, and Wealth*, Studies in Income and Wealth, vol. 52, edited by Robert Lipsey and Helen Stone Tice. Chicago: University of Chicago Press.

———. 1992. "The Output of the Education Sector." In *Output Measurement in the Service Sectors*, Studies in Income and Wealth, vol. 56, edited by Zvi Griliches. Chicago: University of Chicago Press.

Kendrick, John. 1976. *The Formation and Stocks of Total Capital*. New York: National Bureau of Economic Research.

Kokkinen, Arto. 2008. "Human Capital and Finland's Economic Growth in 1910–2000." Paper prepared for the 30th General Conference of the International Association for Research in Income and Wealth, Portoroz, Slovenia, August 24–30.

Le, Trinh, John Gibson, and Les Oxley. 2003. "Cost and Income-Based Measures of Human Capital." *Journal of Economic Surveys* 17 (3): 271–307.

———. 2006. "A Forward-Looking Measure of the Stock of Human Capital in New Zealand." *The Manchester School* 74 (5): 593–609.

Li, Haizheng, Yunling Liang, Barbara Fraumeni, Zhiquiang Liu, and Xiaojun Wang. 2010. "Human Capital in China." Paper prepared for the 31st General Conference of the International Association for Research in Income and Wealth, St. Gallen, Switzerland, August 22–28.

Liu, Gang. 2011. "Measuring the Stock of Human Capital for Comparative Analysis: An Application of the Lifetime Income Approach to Selected Countries." OECD Statistics Working Paper Series no. 41, Statistics Directorate, Organisation for Economic Co-operation and Development, Paris.

Liu, Gang, and Mads Greaker. 2009. "Measuring the Stock of Human Capital for Norway: A Lifetime Labor Income Approach." Documents 2009/12. Oslo: Statistics Norway.

McGrattan, Ellen. 2010. "Comment on Michael Christian's 'Human Capital Accounting in the United States, 1994–2006.'" *Survey of Current Business* 90 (6): 37–41.

Mira d'Ercole, Marco, and Gang Liu. 2010. "The OECD Human Capital Project: Progress Report." Presented at the 31st General Conference of the International Association for Research in Income and Wealth (IARIW), St. Gallen, Switzerland, August 22–28.

O'Mahony, Mary, and Philip Stevens. 2009. "Output and Productivity Growth in the Education Sector: Comparisons for the US and UK." *Journal of Productivity Analysis* 31 (3): 177–94.

Rothschild, Michael. 1989. "Comment on 'The Accumulation of Human and Nonhuman Capital.'" In *The Measurement of Saving, Investment, and Wealth*, Studies in Income and Wealth, vol. 52, edited by Robert Lipsey and Helen Stone Tice. Chicago: University of Chicago Press.

Wei, Hui. 2004. "Measuring the Stock of Human Capital for Australia." Research Paper, ABS Catalogue no. 1351.0.55.001. Canberra: Australian Bureau of Statistics.

———. 2008. "Measuring Human Capital Flows for Australia: A Lifetime Labor Income Approach." Research Paper, ABS Catalogue no. 1351.0.55.023. Canberra: Australian Bureau of Statistics.

15

Measuring the Stock of Human Capital for International and Intertemporal Comparisons

Gang Liu

15.1 Introduction

Although the economics profession has long recognized that human beings and their acquired abilities are important components of the wealth of nations (Petty 1690; Smith 1776; Farr 1853; Engel 1883), it has only been with the seminal work done by Schultz (1961), Becker (1964), and Mincer (1974) that the concept of human capital has in a comprehensive way entered policy discussions and been used for addressing various research questions.

Several authors have underscored the critical role of human capital in driving economic growth (e.g., Romer 1986, 1989; Lucas 1988; Aghion and Howitt 1998; World Bank 2006a). In addition, people's material well-being is considered as encompassing not only their current income, but also the assets they own, including not only housing property and financial instruments but also human capital, since all these assets will generate income streams over their lifetimes.

The concept of human capital is a broad one: the Organisation for Economic Co-operation and Development (OECD) defined it as "the knowledge, skills, competencies and attributes embodied in individuals that

Gang Liu is a researcher at Statistics Norway.

This chapter builds on the work that was undertaken when the author led the Human Capital Project at the OECD. He wants to thank Marco Mira d'Ercole, Martine Durand, Paul Schreyer, Romina Boarini, Conal Smith, and many other former colleagues at the OECD for their great and continuous support. Special thanks go to Barbara Fraumeni and all the country correspondents of the OECD Human Capital Consortium for their constant help. The author is also grateful to Dale Jorgenson and Michael Christian for their valuable comments and suggestions on the paper. However, any remaining errors and omissions are the responsibility of the author. For acknowledgments, sources of research support, and disclosure of the author's material financial relationships, if any, please see http://www.nber.org/chapters/c12832.ack.

facilitate the creation of personal, social and economic well-being" (OECD 2001, 18).

This definition embraces a wide range of attributes of individuals (their formal education, but also the competencies that they have gained outside school settings, as well as people's health conditions) and a broad range of benefits stemming from it. These include not only the economic benefits that education delivers to individuals, but also noneconomic benefits in the form of improved heath conditions, longer life spans, better lifestyles, and even higher subjective well-being (Dolan, Peasgood, and White 2008), as well as the benefits that spill over to society at large, as in the case when education contributes to making people becoming better citizens, more tolerant and open to diversity, more willing to participate in democratic life, and better informed of environmental conditions.

While this broad definition is a useful reference point, all existing operational measures of human capital typically focus on a subset of these dimensions, or rely on different measures for its various aspects, with no ambition to bring all these aspects together into a single metric.

The notion of human capital is especially relevant for discussions on how to measure sustainable development. In recent debates on the subject, the UNECE/OECD/Eurostat working group on statistics for sustainable development suggested that a necessary condition for a country to grow along a sustainable development path is that its total capital stock (financial, produced, natural, human, and social capital) in per capita terms does not decline over time (UNECE 2009).

This "capital approach" implies that, to monitor sustainability, one should measure changes in different types of capital. Further, when these types of capital are deemed to be substitutable with each other in the production of different well-being outcomes, measures of different types of capital should be based on a common metric, so as to allow assessing whether declines in one type of capital are offset by increases in other types.

Despite this wide interest in human capital, there is no agreement on how to measure it, even when the broad concept of human capital mentioned above is narrowed down to formal education only.

Some analysts have relied on physical indicators, such as average school years, shares of the population having reached various levels of educational attainment, and measures of people's competencies. Others have focused on expenditures in the education system, and others yet have relied on measure of the stock of human capital based on the concept of lifetime earnings.[1] This diversity of approaches makes it hard to draw policy implications from comparisons of the stock of human capital across countries and calls for efforts to develop broader and more consistent methodologies.

---

1. All these approaches to measuring human capital have their pros and cons. For balanced discussions, see Stroombergen, Rose, and Nana (2002); Le, Gibson, and Oxley (2003); Fraumeni (2008); Liu and Greaker (2009); and Boarini, Mira d'Ercole, and Liu (2012).

The OECD has a long tradition in collecting and disseminating large sets of educational indicators,[2] as well as in developing methodologies for measuring the volume of education output within the System of National Accounts (SNA) (Schreyer 2010). What has been lacking until now is a framework suitable for measuring human capital in its own right, and for bringing together the wide range of factors shaping its evolution (e.g., demographic, education, and labor market factors). Further, even if such an accounting framework were in place, work would need to be done to identify the corresponding data requirements and the simplified assumptions required for making this accounting framework operational.

To initiate efforts along these lines, the OECD, together with the Fondazione Giovanni Agnelli (a leading Italian institution working on these issues), organized a workshop on human capital measurement in Turin in 2008[3] that gathered some of the leading researchers and practitioners in this field from several OECD and non-OECD countries. At that workshop, a consensus was reached that measuring human capital by the lifetime income approach was the best practical option. This conclusion was supported by the several national studies that had already applied the same approach.[4]

As a follow-up to the Turin workshop, a proposal to launch an "OECD human capital project" was presented to, and endorsed by, the OECD Committee on Statistics (CSTAT) at its meeting of June 2009. The purpose of this project was to identify common methodologies for measuring the stock of human capital for comparative analysis, both across countries and over time, and to implement these methodologies by means of existing OECD data.[5]

The OECD Human Capital Project started in October 2009 and took the form of an international consortium, consisting of sixteen OECD countries (Australia, Canada, Denmark, France, Israel, Italy, Japan, Korea, Mexico, the Netherlands, New Zealand, Norway, Poland, Spain, the United Kingdom, and the United States), Russia and Romania; Eurostat and the International Labor Organization (ILO) also participated in the consortium. The consortium was coordinated by the OECD Secretariat, thanks to support provided by Statistics Norway.

Up to this point, the OECD project has set up the databases and estimated

2. See various issues of *Education at a Glance*, OECD Publishing, Paris.
3. More information about the Turin workshop in 2008 is available at the following website: http://www.oecd.org/document/39/0,3343,en_2649_33715_41153767_1_1_1_1,00.html.
4. By the time of the Turin workshop, estimates of the value of human capital based on this methodology were available for the United States (Jorgenson and Fraumeni 1989, 1992a, 1992b); Sweden (Ahlroth, Björklund, and Forslund 1997); Norway (Ervik, Holmøy, and Hægeland 2003; Greaker and Liu, 2008); the United Kingdom (O'Mahony and Stevens, 2004); Australia (Wei 2004, 2007); New Zealand (Le, Gibson, and Oxley 2006); and Canada (Gu and Wong 2008).
5. Monetary estimates of the stock of human capital based on the lifetime income approach used in this project could both complement and benefit from direct measures of people's skills and competencies such as those that are being developed through the OECD Programme for the International Assessment of Adult Competencies (PIAAC) (for more information on the PIAAC program, see Schleicher 2008).

the value of human capital for sixteen participating countries (Australia, Canada, Denmark, France, Israel, Italy, Japan, Korea, the Netherlands, New Zealand, Norway, Poland, Romania, Spain, the United Kingdom, and the United States) over various observed years. All the detailed information on country databases and the corresponding estimates are available online at http://www.oecd.org/std/publicationsdocuments/workingpapers/.

This chapter summarizes the outcomes from the project. In doing so, the chapter also serves two other goals. First, it shows the feasibility of measuring human capital by applying the lifetime income approach based on data already available from the OECD statistical system. Second, it highlights some of the policy messages that can be drawn from analysis based on these measures of human capital stock.

The rest of the chapter is organized in the following way. Section 15.2 discusses the lifetime income approach that was used in this project, comparing these measures of human capital with those for conventional economic capital available within the SNA; this section also describes the scope of this project and details the implementation procedures of the lifetime income approach. Section 15.3 describes how the OECD database was constructed. Section 15.4 reports a number of empirical estimates, while section 15.5 concludes and identifies possible directions for future research.

15.2. Methodology

A monetary measure of the total stock of human capital can be derived either directly or indirectly. The indirect approach estimates human capital residually, based on the assumption that the discounted value of the benefits that the capital stock will deliver over its life will be equal, under certain assumptions, to the current monetary value of the capital asset. In the context of discussion on sustainable development, the total capital assets of each country may be thought of as generating a stream of benefits in the form of consumption goods in the future.

Hence, by taking the discounted value of the consumption streams, and subtracting from this amount the monetary value of those capital goods for which monetary estimates of their current stocks are readily available (i.e., financial and produced capital, market value of a range of natural assets), may provide an indirect (i.e., residual) estimate of the value of those capital stocks for which no monetary value can be observed on the market.

The World Bank has pioneered this approach, measuring the total stock of human capital as the difference between the total discounted value of each country's average consumption expenditures into the future (which is taken as a proxy for total wealth) and the sum of the tangible components of that wealth; that is, financial, produced, and natural capital (World Bank 2006a, 2006b, 2011; Ruta and Hamilton 2007). A similar approach has also been applied by Statistics Norway in the case of Norway (Greaker, Lokkevik, and Walle 2005).

While this indirect approach can be applied to a large number of countries based on limited statistical information, it has limits. First, it obviously ignores the nonmarket benefits of the various capital stocks. Second, this measure is affected by measurement errors in all the terms entering the accounting identities, resulting in potential biases in the resulting estimates of human capital. Third, it cannot explain what drives the observed changes of the stock of human capital over time.

Direct approaches derive a measure of the stock of human capital from information on its various components. Within this family of approaches, we can distinguish between parametric methods (which rely on econometric estimation of key parameters and are frequently used in academic research, see, e.g., Kyriacou 1991) and nonparametric methods (which are directly based on the available data and are more akin to the tools typically employed by national statistical offices). Most applications of the direct approach are of the nonparametric type; among these we can further distinguish a cost-based approach, an income-based approach, and an indicators-based approach.

- The cost-based approach measures human capital by looking at the stream of past investments, including investments coming from the individual, the family, employers, and governments (e.g., Schultz 1961; Kendrick 1976; Eisner 1985). This approach relies on information on all the costs that are incurred when producing the human capital. These costs include monetary outlays by each of the agents referred to above, but can also be extended to account for nonmarket expenditures (e.g., imputed values of the time devoted to education by both students and their parents).
- The income-based approach measures human capital by looking at the stream of future earnings that human capital investment generates (e.g., Weisbrod 1961; Graham and Webb 1979; Jorgenson and Fraumeni 1989, 1992a, 1992b). In contrast with the cost-based approach, which focuses on the input side, the income-based approach measures the stock of human capital from the output side.[6]
- The indicators-based approach measures human capital through various types of characteristics in the population such as literacy rates, school enrollment ratios, and average years of schooling (e.g., Ederer, Schuller, and Willms 2007, 2011; various issues of *Education at a Glance*). Unlike others, this approach usually relies on a variety of indicators that, though rich in information, lack a common metric and, as a result, cannot be aggregated into an overall measure. This makes the indicators-based approach less suitable for comprehensive comparisons

---

6. While the outputs from human capital investment are of many types (i.e., monetary and nonmonetary, private and public), the output measured by the lifetime income approach is limited to the private monetary benefits that accrue to the person investing in human capital. More discussions on this are provided in section 15.2.3 of this chapter.

of the total stock of human capital across countries and over time, and does not allow comparing the relative importance of different types of capital; that is, stocks of financial, produced, natural, and human capital (Stroombergen, Rose, and Nana 2002).

Although all of the approaches mentioned above have advantages and disadvantages, the (income-based) lifetime income approach was selected as the preferred methodology for the OECD Human Capital Project. This choice reflected the specific perspective used in this project, which focused on developing indicators that could be used to assess the intertemporal sustainability of a country's development path. The selection of this approach followed the discussion held at the 2009 OECD CSTAT meeting (OECD/STD/CSTAT(2009)8) and is consistent with the conclusions drawn from literature surveys (e.g., Liu and Greaker 2009; Fraumeni 2008, 2009).

15.2.1   The Lifetime Income Approach

The lifetime income approach, advocated by Jorgenson and Fraumeni (1989, 1992a, 1992b), measures the value of the total stock of human capital embodied in individuals as the total discounted present value of the expected future labor incomes that could be generated over the lifetime of the people currently living.

The choice of the lifetime income approach for measuring the total stock of human capital in the context of the OECD project reflects its advantages in bringing together, through a consistent accounting structure, a broad range of factors that shape the stock of human capital of the population living in a country: these factors include not only the total population and its structure (by age and gender) but also the expected life span of people (a measure that reflects health conditions), their educational attainment, and their labor market experiences (in terms of both their employment probabilities and the earnings they gain).

An additional advantage of the lifetime income approach is that changes in the stock of human capital during each accounting period can be described in terms of investment (such as formal and informal education), depreciation (such as deaths and net emigration), and revaluation (e.g., changes in the labor market premiums of education).[7]

While some of the existing applications of the lifetime income approach have provided estimates of the stock of human capital that include the lifetime income derived from both paid work (i.e., work sold on the labor market) and from nonmarket activities (i.e., household production and leisure time), measured through various imputations (e.g., Jorgenson and Fraumeni 1992b), the approach used in this chapter is limited to market work.

While the fact of providing a comprehensive monetary estimate of

---

7. One implication of the notion of human capital is that some of the expenditures that are currently classified as "consumption" within the SNA should rather be treated as "investment."

the stock of human capital is the main advantage of the lifetime income approach, this does not imply that the approach is immune from drawbacks, particularly the following:

- First, in order to calculate lifetime incomes, some judgments have to be made about discount rates and the real income growth that people currently living may expect in the future. The nature of these assumptions will obviously affect the final estimates, although their quantitative importance can be assessed through sensitivity analysis (see section 15.4.5).
- Second, there are many reasons to believe that labor markets do not always function in a perfect manner. In these cases, the wage rates by education used in this approach as a proxy for the monetary benefits provided by additional schooling will differ from the marginal productivity of a particular type of worker. Hence, this approach ignores the importance that other factors (such as workers' social background and innate abilities, or the effects of trade unions and industry of employment) may have on shaping wage differentials.[8]
- Third, by relying on observed market wages, the monetary stock of human capital may increase when the composition of employment shifts toward higher paid workers (e.g., from women to men, from migrants to natives, from less-educated to more-educated workers). Other indicators based on the lifetime income approach will, however, capture the effect of these compositional changes (see sections 15.4.3 and 15.4.4).

Despite these conceptual drawbacks, many researchers in this field share the view that compared to other methods, the lifetime income approach provides the most practical way to derive a monetary measure of human capital that is consistent with both economic theory and accounting standards (e.g., Abraham 2010). Further, as described below, the lifetime income approach is also the one that is closer to the assumptions used for measuring conventional economic capital/asset within the SNA (Fraumeni 2009).

15.2.2   Comparisons with the SNA Measures of Economic Capital

Standard investment theory underpins the measurement of both human and conventional economic capital (see Jorgenson 1963, 1967).[9] A single asset, no matter whether it is fixed capital (such as machines, buildings, and infrastructure) or human capital (such as knowledge, skills, and competen-

8. However, literature surveys on the returns to education (e.g., Card 2001) suggest that the ability bias in the cross-sectional relationship between years of school and earnings may not be substantial.

9. The term "economic capital," as compared to "human capital," is used here to refer mainly to produced capital (especially fixed capital) and natural assets that fall within the capital boundary of the SNA. Note that comparisons of the measurement in this section are made at the level of individual asset, i.e., among the single assets; therefore, the corresponding concepts of flow/stock should be understood within this context.

cies), can be used in production over several accounting periods (i.e., for more than one year). The value of the productive service that the asset can generate during each accounting period is a flow concept, while the value of the asset itself is a stock concept.

Both concepts are of significance for economic analysis: the value of the capital stock is a measure of "storage of wealth," while the value of its productive services is an input into economic production. In a well-functioning market, the stock value of a capital good would be equal to the present value of the productive services that the capital good generates over its lifetime.

In some circumstances, only the stock value (rather than the productive service value) of a capital can be observed from the market; in this case, the challenge for capital measurement might be of deriving an estimate of the corresponding service value from the observed stock value. The measurement of some traditional fixed capital (e.g., some types of machines, equipments, and buildings) corresponds to this situation; as many of these assets are usually sold and bought in markets, their prices (stock values) can be directly observed.

In other cases, however, the stock value of a capital good cannot be observed directly. One case is human capital, for the obvious reason that in modern societies human beings embodied with human capital are not sold and bought in the market. Nonetheless, even if the value of the stock of human capital cannot be directly observed on the market, a long stream of economic theory has argued that labor compensation can be considered as the service value that human capital provides during each accounting period. In these circumstances, the stock value of human capital can be derived by taking the present value of all the labor income streams over people's lifetime.

A similar reasoning applies to the measurement of many types of natural assets within the SNA. Clearly, the above-mentioned argument suggests that observing the stock value of one type of capital and then deriving its service value (as in the case of some fixed capital) or observing its service value first and then computing its stock value (as in the case of human capital and natural resources) are two sides of one coin. In principle, if capital markets are efficient, both accounting methodologies should be consistent with each other.

In practice, the two approaches face different challenges. To derive the service value from the observed market value of a fixed capital good, assumptions have to be made, for example, about the age-efficiency profile of the good in question (i.e., how fast the productivity of the machine considered will fall as it ages).[10] Similarly, to calculate the stock value of human capital

---

10. To aggregate the value of single asset across a cohort of assets, more assumptions are needed. For a deeper understanding on this subject, reference should be made to the OECD manual, *Measuring Capital* (OECD 2009a).

from its observed service value, assumptions have to be made about the income growth that each person with a given set of characteristics may expect in the future and on the rate used to discount these future earnings. No matter how these assumptions are made (e.g., either through empirical observations or through theoretical reasoning), they are exogenous in nature. As a consequence, different assumptions will affect estimates in different ways.

To fully develop the accounting structure of human capital estimates, further difficulties should be overcome. For instance, human capital is acquired by learning, studying, and practicing. But these activities cannot be undertaken by anyone else than the person considered. As these activities do not satisfy the "third-party criterion," the acquisition of knowledge cannot be considered as a process of production according to the production boundary of the SNA, even if the services produced by educational institutions are considered as a production activity (SNA 2008, 1.54).

Further difficulties would have to be addressed in order to extend the lifetime income approach to account for nonmarket activities.[11] All these considerations suggest that the construction of a human capital account (even one limited to formal education) should take the form of a satellite account, rather than of full integration in the currently standard SNA accounts.

15.2.3   Scope of the Project

Despite the broad definition of human capital provided above (i.e., "the knowledge, skills, competencies and attributes embodied in individuals that facilitate the creation of personal, social, and economic well-being"), a number of conceptual, methodological, and data limitations have restricted the scope of the project to measuring only *the personal economic well-being generated through market activities*. Such economic well-being is measured by the lifetime labor income that results from human capital investment and that accrues to individual persons themselves. This does not imply neglecting the wider range of benefits from human capital investment that accrue to the society at large, nor other noneconomic benefits that accrue to individuals, but simply recognizes that current valuation methodologies do not allow accounting for these other effects in a proper way.

Beyond the conceptual limitations of the lifetime income approach mentioned in section 15.2.1, some of the practical limitations of the approach implemented here include the following:

- First, while ideally the scope of human capital measurement should cover the whole population, data availability limits the possibility of

11. A first difficulty to extend the lifetime income approach to nonmarket activities is how to impute the value of the time devoted to learning (including both the students' own time as well as parents' and volunteers' time used for helping students). A second difficulty is the availability of detailed information on how individuals use their time.

implementing such a comprehensive approach. Thus, the measures presented here are limited to the population of working age (15 to 64).[12] This implies neglecting both the human capital embodied in children below age 15 and the possibility that elderly people will extend the "service life" of their own skills by staying longer in the labor market. The progressive increase (beyond the age of 65) of elderly people's labor market participation rates, partly due to pension reforms, implies that the monetary estimates of the stock of human capital presented here will be biased downwards.

- Second, the human capital measures presented in this chapter relate to the human resources *in use* (or *realized*) in a given country and year, rather than to the human resources that are *available*. For example, individuals' decisions to withdraw from the labor market, as well as institutional characteristics that affect earnings gaps between men and women, will affect the measures of realized human capital shown here.

- Third, the estimates of human capital shown in this paper, based on the earnings of workers classified by the highest level of education achieved, may confound the effects of different factors impacting on earnings.[13] For example, higher earnings due to better health conditions are indirectly included in the estimates shown in this chapter, whether or not these better health conditions are attributable to investment in education.

- Finally, as already mentioned, the estimates of human capital shown here are limited to market activities. In other terms, the potential effects of education in raising people's productivity in terms of household production (e.g., helping with children's study, making healthier food for family) are ignored.

15.2.4   Estimation Methods

Value of Human Capital

Implementing the lifetime income approach requires three major steps.

- First, a database containing the economic value of labor market activities for various categories of people needs to be compiled. This database should include, at minimum, information on the number of people, their earnings (when employed), as well as their school enrollment rates, employment rates, and survival rates. All these data should, ideally,

12. On the other hand, one may argue that if the research focus is on a country's current economic activities, the working age population (15–64), rather than the total population, might be more relevant, thus deserving a separate treatment.

13. Although formal education is the most important type of human capital investment, other factors (such as early parenting, on-the-job training, etc.) will affect individuals' earnings (Rosen 1989; Abraham 2010). However, distinguishing the effect from various factors would require econometric estimates drawn from earnings equations at the individual level.

be cross-classified by gender, age, and the highest level of educational attainment achieved.[14]

- Second, an algorithm needs to be constructed for calculating the lifetime income for a representative individual in each category in the database. The fundamental assumption applied here is that an individual of a given age, gender, and educational level will have in year $t + 1$ the same labor income (adjusted by the real income growth rate expected in the future and by the survival rate of each person) and other characteristics (e.g., school enrollment rate, employment rate and survival rate, etc.) of a person who, in year t, is one year older but has otherwise the same characteristics (e.g., gender and educational level). This assumption, which is unlikely to hold in practice,[15] simply reflects the nature of data used in this project, that is, cross-sectional data for different cohorts rather than longitudinal data following the same people over time.[16] Appendix A provides a more complete specification of the methodological assumptions and relevant equations used to estimate lifetime labor income for a representative individual in each category in the database.

- Third, the measures of lifetime labor income per capita estimated (through equations [A1] and [A2] as shown in appendix A) need to be applied to all individuals in each age/gender/education category to compute the human capital stock for that category. Summing up the stocks of human capital across all categories yields an estimate of the aggregate value of the human capital stock for each country.

Volume of Human Capital

Estimates of human capital values based on the methodology just outlined are in current prices. To monitor the evolution of human capital within a country, values in current prices are not enough, as changes of human capital values may be driven by changes in both human capital volumes and in price between two periods in time. Similarly, the difference of human capital value at one point in time between two countries may reflect both differences of human capital volumes and differences of the price levels in the two countries.

To compare human capital either across countries or over time, as required

---

14. In practice, most data on survival rates do not distinguish between different categories of educational attainment (i.e., survival rates differ only according to the age and gender of each person).

15. In other terms, the methodology used here ignores "cohort effects"; for example, there exists the possibility that a person born in the twenty-first century may expect different income flows in the future than a person born in the 1990s.

16. A natural modification of this approach would be to use not only cross-sectional but also time-series information in order to estimate the future earnings of various groups of people. For example, to smooth the short-term business cycle effects that cannot be removed by applying the original Jorgenson-Fraumeni approach (which relies on current cross-sectional information only), Wei (2008) relies on a cohort-based estimation method of future earnings.

in analyses of economic growth, productivity, and inflation, one needs to derive estimates of human capital *volumes* from the estimated human capital values, that is, to decompose changes of human capital at current prices into changes of price levels between two periods (or two countries) and changes of human capital volumes. Since there are two dimensions for comparisons (across countries and over time), two types of human capital indices (i.e., spatial volume and temporal volume indices) have been constructed.

Given the three terms of *value*, *volume*, and *price*, in principle any one can be derived from the other two. In practice, there are two approaches to deriving volume indexes. The first, which is more frequently applied, derives *volume* estimates by dividing *value* by a *price deflator*. The second directly constructs *volume* estimates and then derives *price* by dividing the *value* by such constructed *volume index*. This chapter applies the first approach for constructing human capital spatial volume index,[17] and the second one for constructing human capital temporal volume index.

Spatial Volume Index. The purpose of constructing spatial human capital volume index is to compare human capital in real terms between different countries at one point in time, since price levels for the same set of goods and services in different countries can differ. The approach used here is to simply divide estimated human capital values by the purchasing power parities (PPPs) for each country.

The OECD statistical system provides three types of estimates for purchasing power parities: (1) PPPs for GDP; (2) PPPs for private consumption; and (3) PPPs for actual individual consumption (which includes prices for the in-kind individual goods/services provided by governments and NPISHs [nonprofit institutions serving households] to households). Arguably, since incomes generated through human capital investment will flow to final consumption in the end, the PPPs used in this project are those for private consumption.

Depending on the purpose of the exercise, other PPPs could be applied. For instance, when evaluating human capital from an individual's perspective, the lifetime income they can earn should include not only wages and salaries after taxes, but also other payments and transfers (either in cash or in kind) flowing to them from other sources (e.g., employer's contribution to social security, government transfer); in this case, the relevant deflator may be the PPPs for actual individual consumption.

The income concept applied in this project is that of "wages and salaries" as defined in the SNA; this includes worker's own contributions to social security, but not those paid by employers. In part due to this, the PPPs for private consumption are used for constructing the spatial volume index.

---

17. To be more precise, the spatial index calculated as such is human capital *in real terms* across countries.

Ideally, the construction of spatial volume index needs to use as deflators the specific PPPs for *human capital* rather than the PPPs for *private consumption* as used in this chapter. Due to data constraint, the choice of the latter is just an approximation, which will lead to some biases when making country comparisons. However, it is challenging to make any judgments at this stage on whether the resulting biases are upwards or downwards for each project participating country. But this issue should be further investigated in the future.

Temporal Volume Index. To compare stocks of human capital in real terms over time, a temporal volume index needs to be constructed. This project relies on the Tornqvist index method,[18] whose methodology is outlined in Jorgenson, Ho, and Stiroh (2005) and has been applied in several national studies on human capital measurement (e.g., Gu and Wong 2010; Li et al. 2010).

According to this methodology, the growth rate of the temporal volume index of human capital is calculated as the weighted sum of the growth rates of the number of individuals in different categories of the population (such as age, gender, and educational attainment), using their shares of the nominal value of human capital as corresponding weights. In other terms:

(1)
$$\Delta \ln HCI = \sum_{age} \sum_{edu} \sum_{gender} \overline{VSH}^{edu}_{age,gender} \Delta \ln NUM^{edu}_{age,gender},$$

where HCI stands for the temporal human capital volume index, $NUM^{edu}_{age,gender}$ is the number of persons in the corresponding age/gender/education category, and Δ is the first difference operation between two periods of time, t and $t-1$.

Further, the weights in equation (1) are given by the share of each category of population in the total value of human capital averaged across the two periods, that is:

(2)
$$\overline{VSH}^{edu}_{age,gender} = \frac{1}{2} \{VSH^{edu}_{age,gender}(t) + VSH^{edu}_{age,gender}(t-1)\}, \text{ and}$$

(3)
$$VSH^{edu}_{age,gender} = \frac{LIN^{edu}_{age,gender} NUM^{edu}_{age,gender}}{\sum_{age} \sum_{edu} \sum_{gender} LIN^{edu}_{age,gender} NUM^{edu}_{age,gender}},$$

where $LIN^{edu}_{age,gender}$ refers to the lifetime income of a representative individual classified by age, gender, and educational level and is calculated by using equations (A1) and/or (A2) as shown in appendix A.

In principal, the more detailed the categories of population, the more accurate the volume index will be. At one extreme end, one could argue that

---

18. The Tornqvist index is a discrete approximation to a continuous Divisia index and has been shown to be an exact superlative index number (Diewert 1976).

each person should be treated differently from anyone else and thus be classified as a unique category; in practice, the data requirements to implement this approach are daunting, so that the approach is not practically feasible.

Despite this consideration, as long as data allows, the population should be classified with as much detailed category as possible. In this project, the working age population has been classified by three characteristics: age, gender, and educational level. With richer data, the classification might be extended to include more characteristics such as occupation, industry of employment, and so forth, as all these characteristics have important bearings in determining individuals' wages.

Equation (1) shows that the temporal volume index will increase if the composition of population shifts toward those categories of people having higher lifetime incomes. This may occur, for example, when more people attend higher education (which is generally associated with higher lifetime income) or when the composition of the working age population shifts toward younger people (because younger people have more remaining working years and so higher lifetime income, even if they usually have lower annual income at the time they enter into the labor market).

For some purposes, such as implementing sustainability assessment, more interest will be put on monitoring changes of human capital *per capita*. According to the notion of "weak sustainability," a necessary condition for a country to follow a sustainable path is that its total capital stock per capita does not decrease over time (UNECE 2009). The growth rate of human capital per capita is just the difference between the growth rate of the human capital volume (HCI) and that of population (NUM).

To account for the contribution of different characteristics (e.g., age, gender, and educational level) to the real growth of human capital per capita, first-order partial Tornqvist indices for each characteristic were derived. For instance, a first-order partial index for gender is defined as:

$$(4) \quad \Delta \ln HCI_{gender} = \sum_{gender} \overline{VSH}_{gender} \, \Delta \ln \left(\sum_{age} \sum_{edu} NUM_{age,gender}^{edu} \right), \text{ where}$$

$$(5) \quad \overline{VSH}_{gender} = \frac{1}{2} \{ VSH_{gender}(t) + VSH_{gender}(t-1) \}, \text{ and}$$

$$(6) \quad VSH_{gender} = \sum_{age} \sum_{edu} VSH_{age,gender}^{edu}.$$

The first-order partial volume index for gender as shown in equation (4) captures the shift of the population structure between men and women, while ignoring other shifts among age groups and educational categories within each gender. Similarly, the first-order partial volume indices for age (or educational attainment categories) measure the shift between age groups only (or between educational categories only).

In this approach, the contribution of each characteristic to the real growth of human capital per capita is defined as the difference between the growth of the first-order partial indices of human capital for each characteristic (age, gender, and educational level) and the growth of the number of individuals in the population.

It should be noted that the sum of these contributions across characteristics will differ from the overall growth of human capital per capita, as the sum of the contribution of the different characteristics represents only the first-order approximation to the growth of human capital per capita.[19]

15.3   Database Construction

Although the original lifetime income approach requires information by single year of age, all the data relevant for the implementation of this approach that are available within the OECD statistics system, as well as most data available to researchers in individual countries, refer to categorical data (i.e., data for people classified by either five-year or ten-year age groups).[20]

To develop a database suitable for this exercise, the OECD project has relied on a number of practical assumptions and imputation methods to generate data by single year of age. For example, data on the number of students by single year of age were estimated based on information on the average enrollment rate of a given age group, and on the number of people of each age. These assumptions and imputations obviously affect the quality of the estimates presented in this chapter.

A further factor shaping the estimates of the stock of human capital presented here is the quality of the underlying data in the various years. In general, the quality of the OECD Education Database, the principal data source for this project, is lower for the years preceding the mid-1990s, particularly in the following ways:

- School enrollment data for most countries are of better quality starting from 1998, partly reflecting changes in the International Standard Classification of Education (from ISCED 67 to ISCED 97) implemented around that year.
- Data on annual earnings by educational attainment categories are only available since 1997 for most countries participating in the project.
- Similarly, the OECD Education Database contains two educational attainment data sets: the first, with more detailed categories, starts for

19. Higher order partial volume indices and their corresponding contributions to the growth of human capital per capita have not been calculated in this study. For an example of such applications, see Jorgenson, Ho, and Stiroh (2005) and Fraumeni (2011).

20. In an effort to extend the 1992 Jorgenson-Fraumeni approach to measuring human capital and investments in education, Fraumeni (2008) proposed a streamlined approach that relied on a more limited database than the one used in the original 1992 study, combining categorical data and detailed data by single year of age.

most countries from the 1990s; and the second, with more aggregated categories, provides time series going back longer in time.

Because of these factors, it was decided that estimation of the stock of human capital would start from around 1997 for most countries, and that the project would use the educational attainment data set with more detailed categories.

For most of the countries participating in the OECD project, a database was established for each country.[21] This database for each country consists of the five data sets described below, covering the various elements that enter the estimation of the monetary value of the human capital stock based on the chosen lifetime income methodology.[22]

15.3.1   Survival Rates

The survival rate is the conditional probability that a person who is alive in year t will also be living in year $t + 1$. Information on survival rates, by gender and individual year of age, was mainly derived from country life tables published in the Human Mortality Database (http://www.mortality .org/). For a few countries that are not included in this database, data on survival rates were obtained through bilateral contacts with country correspondents.

Several studies show that people with higher educational attainment also have longer life-expectancy rates and higher survival rates. This may reflect a range of factors, such as having a healthier lifestyle (e.g., doing more exercise, having a healthier diet), having better working and living conditions, and having greater access to quality health care (e.g., OECD 2010a). Despite this evidence, it is difficult to find comparative data on the extent to which higher educational attainment improves survival rates in each country. For this reason, this project relies on the same survival rate for all people of a given age and gender. The use of differential survival rates by educational levels could be addressed in future research.

15.3.2   Educational Attainment

Educational attainment in each country participating in the project was based on the categories defined in the International Standard Classification of Education (ISCED 97) developed by UNESCO (2006) as shown in appendix B. It should be mentioned, however, that no country adheres exactly to this classification, and almost every country relied on detailed

---

21. Due to data constraints for Mexico and Russian Federation, the OECD Human Capital Project has so far only constructed databases for sixteen participating countries (Australia, Canada, Denmark, France, Israel, Japan, Italy, Korea, the Netherlands, New Zealand, Norway, Poland, Romania, Spain, the United Kingdom, and the United States). For the detailed information on the country databases, please refer to http://www.oecd.org/std/publications documents/workingpapers/.

22. More detailed and technical information on the construction of the five data sets are presented in Liu (2013).

codes that differed, to some extent, from those used by others: some codes were missing in many countries, and some countries combined two or more codes together. Furthermore, a few countries have detailed codes that are not specified in appendix B. In these cases, judgments have been used to translate the national classifications into the codes shown in appendix B.

When considering the transitions between educational levels, further information is needed both on the transition patterns from lower to higher education and on school duration (the length of school course) within each educational level. The transition patterns are displayed in appendix C. Country-specific information on school duration for each educational level is collected by the UNESCO's Institute for Statistics, the OECD, and Eurostat over sixty countries worldwide.[23]

This database provides information on school duration from 2000 to 2007, although data are not always available for all years. For missing years as well as for years before 2000, estimates were based on the assumption that school duration in each country was the same as that in the closest available year in the period of 2000 to 2007.

Information on the number of people by the highest educational attainment completed is available in the OECD Education Database. These data are mostly based on national Labor Force Surveys and are available by gender, educational level, and five-year (for most countries) or ten-year (for Japan) age groups; in addition, they typically refer to people between age 15 and 64.

Two adjustments to the data on number of people by educational attainment were applied. First, data on the working age population by educational attainment were benchmarked to the levels (by gender and five-year age groups) available within the OECD Demographic Database. This adjustment (which was small in most cases) was performed in order to assure the coherence between the educational and demographic information used in the project. Second, in order to obtain data by individual year of age from the available data referring to five-year or ten-year age groups, national data on the population by gender and individual year of age were used to interpolate across different educational categories.

Without additional information, it is difficult to fully assess the size of possible biases due to these adjustments. Collecting information on educational attainment by single year of age will be a natural way forward for future research.

15.3.3   Employment Rates

OECD data on employment rates by gender and educational level are based on the same source (national Labor Force Surveys) that was used for educational attainment data. Employment rates were calculated as the ratio

---

23. For methodological issues please refer to *2004 Data Collection on Education Systems— UOE Data Collection Manual* (OECD 2004).

of the number of employed persons to that of total population in each group classified by gender, age group, and educational attainment.

In the case of missing data on employment for some age groups, it was assumed that the corresponding employment rates were equal to 100 percent. Since missing data on employment rates occurred for very few and usually young age groups (in most cases, the age group of 15 to 19), while annual earnings for these groups are usually low, the assumption of full employment in early age will not affect substantially the accumulation of income over the rest of their lifetimes; as a result, the upward bias due to this assumption on the estimated value of the stock of human capital results is unlikely to be significant.[24]

Data on employment rates by five-year (for most countries) or ten-year (for Japan) age groups were broken down into data by individual years of age based on the assumption that the employment rate for each group applied equally to each single year within the corresponding age group.

15.3.4   School Enrollment Rates

Information on the number of students by gender and age (by single year of age up to 29, by five-year of age for the groups 30–34 and 35–39, and by one group for all people aged 40 and above) enrolled in different educational levels, classified according to ISCED 97 categories, is available in the OECD online databank (http://dotstat.oecd.org/wbos/Index.aspx).

Data on the number of students in each educational category, combined with data on the number of people by their highest educational attainment, allow computing school enrollment rates as needed for the purposes of this project; these are defined as the share of people who, having completed a given level of education, then enrolled in the level above. For simplicity, these school enrollment rates were computed only up to age 40. For people aged 30 and above, the assumption made to obtain data by individual year of age is that the enrollment rate for each single year within the age groups 30 to 34 and 35 to 39 is the same as that for the corresponding age groups.

In general, the quality of data on the number of students enrolled in different educational levels (as available in OECD.stat) varies across countries and over years. For instance, time series on enrolled students is shorter than the educational attainment data for Canada; as a result, for subsequent years, enrollment rates were held constant at the level of the last available observation. Similarly, in the case of Japan, no data on the number of students enrolled at above level 3 (upper secondary education) by age are available after 2000; consequently, other information has been used to make estimation of school enrollment rates for Japan.

---

24. The alternative option is to assume the employment rates for these age groups are zero, which will lead to downward bias. However, given that annual earnings for these groups are low, the resulted bias would not be significant either.

As many country-specific assumptions were used for constructing the data set of school enrollment rate, the potential biases due to the use of this data set should be kept in mind. Sensitivity analysis with respect to different assumptions for the construction of the data set of school enrollment rates could be conducted in the future.

15.3.5   Annual Earnings

Data on annual earnings by gender, age groups, and educational attainment are available through the OECD Education Database. The original sources of these data vary across countries (Labor Force Surveys, household income surveys, and other sources). Partially for this reason, the earnings concept used and the reference period for the earnings paid (i.e., annual, monthly, and weekly) may differ across countries. For example, while some countries provide estimates of annual earnings (based on the weekly and monthly data included in the original sources), other countries only provide monthly or weekly earnings data, as available in national sources.

The earnings data in the OECD Education Database may also reflect differences in how part-time and full-time workers (as well as students holding a paid job) were treated by the national correspondents providing these earnings estimates to the OECD. A more detailed assessment of these country differences in earnings' definitions (e.g., whether they include employers' social security contributions) is needed.

The data available in the OECD Education Database refer to both the number of "income earners" and the "total earnings" of each category of workers, classified by gender, age group (15–24, 25–29, 30–34, 35–44, 45–54, 55–64), and educational levels. This information is available for all countries participating in the project except Japan. For the latter country, information of annual earnings by gender, age group, and educational attainment was derived from national sources, and the way it was derived differs slightly from that used for other countries.

Because of differences in the exact definition of earnings used in the OECD Education Database, earnings data by educational attainment were benchmarked on the series "wages and salaries" per employee as available from the OECD annual national accounts. This implies that ratios between the earnings for different educational categories (from the OECD Education Database) were applied to the national account series of "wages and salaries" per employee. This procedure allowed deriving estimates of the value of annual earnings by gender, age, and educational levels that are consistent with the SNA totals.[25]

Two additional adjustments were then applied to the "benchmarked"

---

25. A similar adjustment method has been applied to align the earnings data from INES Network collection to those of national accounts (see "A proposal for indicators linking education to economic growth," OECD document, INES-LSO-WG-ECO (2011)1).

earnings data described above. First, in order to obtain earnings by single year of age, a parabolic curve was fitted through the observations of annual earnings by six age groups (15–24, 25–29, 30–34, 35–44, 45–54, 55–64) for most countries, and by nine age groups (20–24, 25–29, 30–34, 35–39, 40–44, 45–49, 50–54, 55–59, and 60–64) for Japan. Second, as the educational categories in the OECD annual earnings data sets do not always match those in the educational attainments data sets, imputations were used to generate annual earnings consistent with the educational levels shown in the educational attainment data sets.

15.4   Empirical Results

This section describes quantitative estimates from the project as they pertain to overall values of the stock of human capital, their distribution between people with various characteristics, and volume comparisons both across countries and over time. Due to data limitation, monetary estimates of the stock of human capital have been computed only for fifteen OECD countries (Australia, Canada, Denmark, France, Israel, Italy, Japan, Korea, the Netherlands, New Zealand, Norway, Poland, Spain, the United Kingdom, and the United States), and one nonmember country (Romania).[26] These estimates refer to the years for which data are available, as detailed in table 15.1.

The available years for most of the countries participating in the project are typically from around 1997 to around 2007, with a few countries missing specific years over this period. Other countries only have data covering a shorter time span. For country comparisons, the year 2006 has been chosen as benchmark since this is the year where country coverage is the most comprehensive.

Measuring the stock of human capital in each country based on the retained approach requires making assumptions on future earnings growth and discount rates. In this chapter, the annual discount rate was set at 4.58 percent for all countries (the same value used by Jorgenson and Fraumeni for the United States in their 1992 study).

Conversely, country-specific assumptions on real earnings growth in the future were based on the OECD medium-term baseline. This baseline is prepared by the OECD Economics Directorate based on historical data and short-term projections, and extended to the medium term based on

---

26. The estimated values of human capital for fifteen participating countries (Australia, Canada, Denmark, France, Israel, Italy, Korea, the Netherlands, New Zealand, Norway, Poland, Romania, Spain, the United Kingdom, and the United States) over the observed years (as shown in table 15.1) were first presented in Liu (2011). In 2012, estimates were also made for Japan over the period of 2002 to 2007. All the relevant estimates are available online at http://www.oecd.org/std/publicationsdocuments/workingpapers/.

Table 15.1   **Data availability for countries covered in the project**

Country	Data availability
Australia (AUS)	1997, 1999, 2001
Canada (CAN)	1997–1999, 2003–2006
Denmark (DNK)	1998–1999, 2001–2002
France (FRA)	1998–1999, 2002–2007
Israel (ISR)	2002–2007
Italy (ITA)	1998, 2000, 2002, 2004, 2006
Japan (JPN)	2002–2007
Korea (KOR)	1998–2007
Mexico (MEX)	No data
Netherlands (NLD)	2002, 2006
New Zealand (NZL)	1997–2007
Norway (NOR)	1997–1999, 2001–2006
Poland (POL)	1999, 2001–2002, 2004, 2006
Romania (ROU)	2002, 2006
Russian Federation (RUS)	No data
Spain (ESP)	2001–2002, 2004, 2006
United Kingdom (GBR)	1997–2001, 2003–2007
United States (USA)	1997–2000, 2002–2007

Source: OECD Human Capital Project.

assumptions about the growth of potential output in each country. This medium-term baseline is used by the OECD for much of its policy analysis (e.g., OECD 2009b).[27]

Using data from this medium-term scenario, the annual real income growth rate was computed as the geometric mean of real wages and salaries per employee for the total economy (including government workers) over the period 1960 to 2017 (as presented in figure 15.1). Due to lack of information on Israel and Romania in the OECD medium-term baseline, this parameter for these two countries was set at the level of 1.32 percent (the rate used by Jorgenson and Fraumeni for the United States in their 1992 study).[28]

27. Earlier estimates from this project relied on common assumptions for all participating countries, that is, an annual real income growth of 1.32 percent and an annual discount rate of 4.58 percent. These two values were those used by Jorgenson and Yun (1990) and Jorgenson and Fraumeni (1992b) in their estimations for the United States, and corresponded to their estimates of the annual growth rate of (Harrod neutral) productivity and of the long-run rate of return for the private sector of the economy. The choice of common assumptions for these two parameters was mainly based on the need of simplicity. Based on such simplified assumptions, preliminary estimates were presented in a "Project Progress Report" and in a paper presented at the CSTAT meeting of June 2010 (OECD/STD/CSTAT/RD(2010)3) and at the thirty-first IARIW conference (OECD 2010b), respectively.

28. The two decimals in the values of chosen parameters are not meant to suggest a high degree of precision in the estimates shown in this chapter; rather, they are just to show the consistency with the source data. For instance, the values of 1.32 percent and 4.58 percent were originally used by Jorgenson and Fraumeni (1992b).

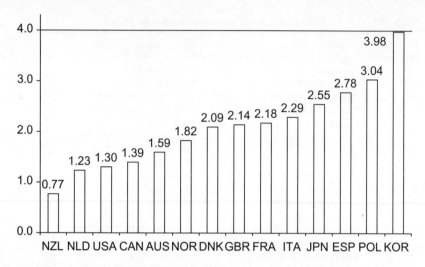

Fig. 15.1   Annual real income growth rates used in human capital estimation (%)
Source: OECD medium-term baseline.

15.4.1   Employment Rates and Survival Rates

A first set of estimates from the project relates to observations of country-specific employment rates and survival rates. These are shown here as they critically influence the human capital estimates reported later. Figure 15.2, which shows results for Canada in 2006, highlights patterns that hold for all countries covered in the project and that are in line with those reported in several national studies (e.g., Liu and Greaker 2009; Gu and Wong 2010), especially the following patterns:

- The higher the educational level, the higher the employment rate of each group; this pattern holds for both men and women, and for most age groups.
- The difference of employment rate between adjacent educational levels becomes smaller as the educational level increases.
- The employment rate is lowest at the two ends of working life. For women, and especially for those with lower education, a typical "M" shape pattern can be observed, with the lower employment rates at the bottom attained around age 25 to 39; that is, the age range where most women become mothers.
- Regardless of their educational levels, employment rates are higher for men than for women, except at some young ages. These gender differences are largest for people with less than upper secondary education (level 0/1 and level 2), and for younger cohorts (left lower panel in figure 15.2).

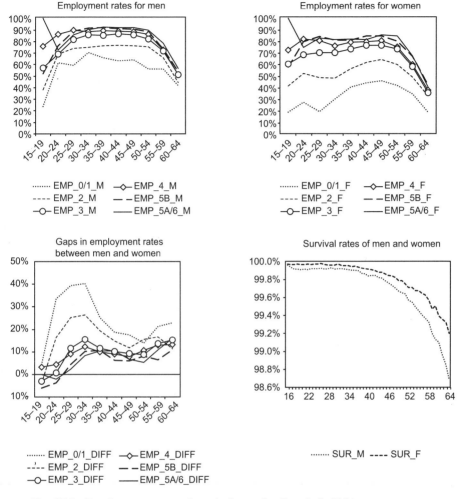

Fig. 15.2   Employment rates and survival rates for Canada in 2006
Source: OECD Human Capital Project.

- Survival rates decline with age, especially in older ages, for both men and women. At all ages, women have a higher survival rate than men (right lower panel in figure 15.2).

15.4.2   Annual Incomes and Lifetime Incomes

Earnings profiles by age and educational attainment have been computed separately for men and women, and are based on the two concepts of annual income and lifetime income, respectively. Figure 15.3 presents estimates for Canada in 2006; the upper panels refer to annual incomes and the lower pan-

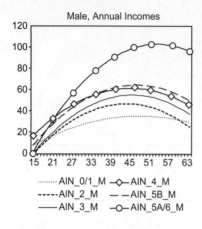
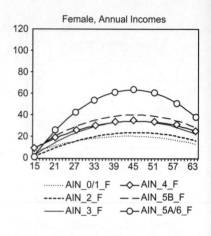

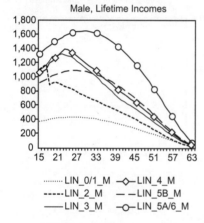
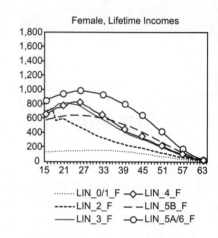

Fig. 15.3   Earnings profile for Canada in 2006 (current prices, in thousands Canadian dollars)

Source: OECD Human Capital Project.

els to lifetime incomes. These age-earnings profiles for Canada are similar to those prevailing in other countries covered by the project and to those highlighted in a range of national studies (e.g., Le, Gibson, and Oxley 2006; Liu and Greaker 2009; Wei 2004, 2007), particularly in the following ways:

- Both annual and lifetime incomes rise with age and then gradually decline, a pattern that holds for all educational levels. The peaks occur at younger ages for lifetime income than for annual income.
- Both annual and lifetime incomes are higher for people with higher levels of educational attainment.

- Both annual and lifetime incomes are higher for males than for females, at all levels of educational attainment.

15.4.3   Value of Human Capital

Level

To give an indication of the magnitude of the stock of human capital estimated by using the lifetime income approach, panel a of figure 15.4 shows the ratios between the value of the total stock of human capital and nominal GDP in 2006.[29] The ratios range between 8.3 in the Netherlands and 16.3 in Korea, with an average value of around 10.6. Cross-country differences are smaller when ignoring the four countries at both ends of the distribution (i.e., the Netherlands and Italy, at the lower end; and Poland and Korea, at the higher end), ranging between 9 and 11.

A second important feature highlighted by panel b of figure 15.4 is that the monetary value of the stock of human capital based on the lifetime income methodology is typically several times larger than that of produced capital in all countries for which relevant estimates of the latter are available.[30] The data shown in figure 15.4 indicate that ratios between human and produced capital range between 3.6 in the Netherlands and Italy and 7.0 in the United Kingdom, with a mean value of 4.7.

For some countries, the estimates of the stock of human capital based on the lifetime income approach described in this chapter can be compared with estimates derived from national studies that used a similar methodology. To allow more meaningful comparisons, the project estimates provided below have been based on assumptions that are as close as possible to those used by the selected national studies. For instance, comparisons are based on the same values for annual real income growth rate and discount rate as those used in the corresponding national studies.

- In the case of Norway, the differences between the estimates computed for this project and those presented in Liu and Greaker (2009) range between 1 percent (in 2001 and 2006) and 21 percent in 2003, with an average difference (across the period) of 8 percent.

29. For Norway, GDP data shown in figure 15.4 (as well as per capita GDP in figures 15.8 and 15.9) refers to "GDP Mainland Norway"; that is, GDP exclusive the oil and ocean transport industries.

30. The estimates of produced capital stock are drawn from OECD calculations based on investments data from member countries' national accounts data. These estimates are net figures as opposed to the *gross* estimates of human capital reported in this project, that is, living or human maintenance costs have not been deducted. There exist different views on whether these costs should be netted out from the gross estimates of human capital (e.g., Graham and Webb 1979; Conrad 1992). Another closely linked but different concern is that the gross estimates of human capital do not take into account the depreciation of human capital, such as deterioration in health and obsolescence of knowledge and skills (Conrad 1992); however, one may argue that these factors are implicitly reflected in the wage rates paid to individuals used in this approach.

Panel a. Stock of human capital to GDP

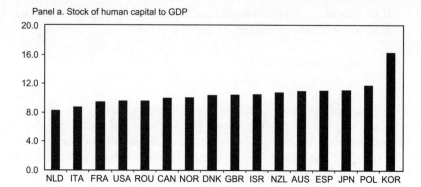

Panel b. Stock of human capital to produced capital

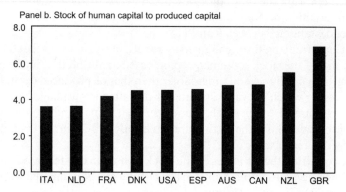

Fig. 15.4   Stock of human capital relative to GDP and to the stock of produced capital, 2006

Source: OECD Human Capital Project.

Note: Estimates for Australia refer to 2001; those for Denmark, to 2002.

- In the case of Australia, the difference relative to the results shown in Wei (2004) is about −2 percent (in 2001).
- In the case of New Zealand, the difference relative to the results shown in Le, Gibson, and Oxley (2006) is higher, at about 30 percent for 2001.
- In the case of the United States, Christian (2010) shows human capital values (limited to market earnings) for the whole population (age 0–80) in 2006 of USD 212 trillion. The estimate presented in this chapter, limited to the working-age population (age 15–64), is USD 153 trillion, implying a ratio between the two estimates of around 72 percent; this difference is fairly close to the ratio of the working-age population to the entire US population (67 percent).[31]

31. Based on own human capital data set and program for the United States, and by setting the income growth rate to 1.32 percent and the discount rate to 4.58 percent, and only including lifetime incomes of people aged 15 to 64, Michael Christian found that the estimated market

- In the case of Canada, estimates of human capital per capita for the total population, for men and for women reported by Gu and Wong (2009) for 2007 are C\$ 653,000, 795,000, and 511,000. These values compare to estimates in this project of C\$ 627,000, 799,000, and 453,000 in 2006, suggesting differences of –4 percent, 0.5 percent, and –11 percent, respectively.

To sum up, almost all national studies that have applied the lifetime income approach to measuring human capital share the same findings that the stock value of human capital is substantially larger than that of conventional economic capital, such as produced capital. The estimates produced as part of the OECD project, which are based on less detailed data than those typically available in the case of country-specific studies, are also broadly comparable to those produced by national research in the subject (with the partial exception of New Zealand).[32] Detailed differences between project and national estimates could be further investigated in the future.

Distribution

The estimates of the stock of human capital based on the lifetime income approach can also be compared across different groups of people within each country. The distribution of human capital across people classified by different dimensions within each country provides useful information for addressing issues related to inequality, poverty, and social cohesion. Taking 2006 as an example, this section describes the distribution of human capital between men and women (figure 15.5), among people with different educational attainment (figure 15.6), as well as among different age groups (figure 15.7) for the countries participating in the project.

To facilitate cross-country comparisons, the detailed (but differentiated) educational categories available for each country have been reclassified into three main groups; that is, "below upper secondary education" (denoted as EDU_0/1/2), "upper secondary education" (EDU_3/4), and "tertiary education" (EDU_5/6).[33] Data on individuals by single year of age have also been reclassified into three age groups; that is, young people (those aged 15 to 34, AGE_I), prime-age people (those aged 35 to 54, AGE_II), and older people (those aged 55–64, AGE_III).

---

component of the stock of human capital in the United States in 2006 is USD 116 trillion; while our calculation based on the OECD project database and with the same assumptions is USD 129 trillion, 10 percent higher.

32. In addition to these countries, unpublished estimates of the stock of human capital for Israel (based on monthly income across four educational levels for the years 1997–2007), elaborated by the national statistical office of that country, are also similar to our estimates presented in this chapter.

33. This classification holds for all participating countries except for Japan and Korea. For Japan, EDU_0/1/2 refers to levels 1, 2, and 3 combined, and EDU_3/4 corresponds to level 5B; while for Korea, EDU_3/4 refers to level 3 only and EDU_5/6 actually includes level 4.

For each figure, the upper panel on the left shows the distribution of the population among the various groups, while the upper panel on the right shows the share of human capital accruing to the groups considered. The lower panel on the left shows the ratios between the shares of human capital accruing to each group and their corresponding population share (with ratios larger than 1 implying that the group considered is "rich" in human capital, and with higher ratios indicating that the more better off the corresponding group is in terms of its holdings of human capital). Finally, proxy estimates of the Gini coefficient based on grouped data (computed on the basis of Lorentz curves plotting shares of the population against shares of their human capital) are reported in the lower panel on the right of each figure.[34]

Figure 15.5 provides information on the distribution of human capital between men and women in 2006. Although the population shares for men and women are in general very similar to each other (marginally higher in some countries and marginally lower for others, upper panel on the left), men dominate women in terms of their human capital holdings in all countries. This pattern is also confirmed by a visual inspection of the lower panel on the left of figure 15.5.

In almost all countries, men account for more than 60 percent of the total value of the human capital stock, with Korea, Italy, Japan, and the Netherlands recording values close to, or higher than, 70 percent. The exceptions are Romania and Poland, where men account for marginally less than 60 percent of human capital. Estimates of the Gini coefficient by gender vary between less than 0.10 to above 0.20 in Korea.

These gender differences in the distribution of human capital reflect a combination of lower labor force participation, lower employment, and lower wages for women than for men. As women usually do more housework than men, these gender differences in human capital would be lower if human capital estimates were to be extended to include nonmarket activities.

Figure 15.6 provides information on the distribution of human capital among people in the three main educational categories. In general, the higher the educational attainment of each person is, the higher will be their earnings and probability of having a job, and thus their measured human capital. However, because marginal returns to higher education (from EDU_0/1/2 to EDU_3/4 and from EDU_3/4 to EDU_5/6) vary across countries, human capital distribution by education varies as well. For instance, compared with other countries, the share of human capital held by more educated people

---

34. The Gini coefficient is a measure ranging between 0 (in the case of perfect equality; that is, the share of human capital accruing to each group is equal to its population share) and 1 (in the case of maximum inequality, e.g., all the human capital accrue to the richest group). While the Gini coefficient is generally based on individual records (with each person ranked according to their income or wealth level), the values shown here are based on broad categories that ignore within-group inequality.

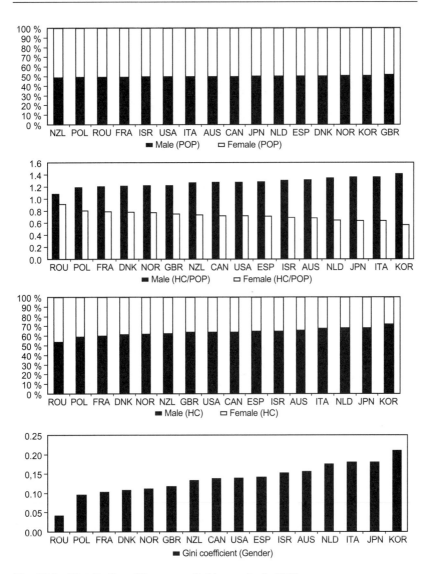

Fig. 15.5   Distribution of human capital by gender in 2006

Source: OECD Human Capital Project.

Note: Estimates for Australia refer to 2001; those for Denmark, to 2002.

is relatively low in Denmark and New Zealand, while it is relatively high in Italy and Spain. Estimates of the Gini coefficient by educational level range between less than 0.10 in Denmark, New Zealand, Poland, and Canada, and above 0.20 in Italy.

In theory, higher marginal returns from higher education are desirable

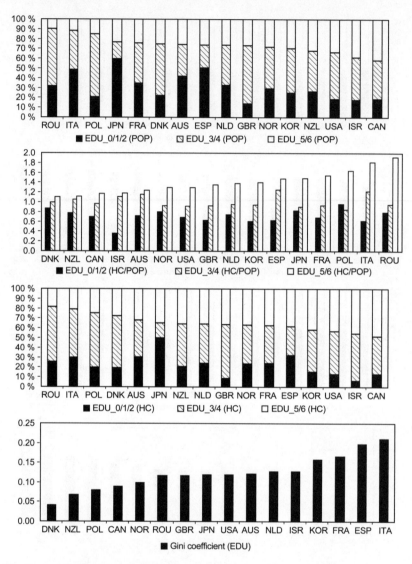

Fig. 15.6   Distribution of human capital by educational level in 2006
Source: OECD Human Capital Project.
Note: Estimates for Australia refer to 2001; those for Denmark, to 2002.

since they provide incentives for people to augment their investments in human capital. In this sense, larger Gini coefficients may imply that investment in human capital is encouraged. But higher Gini coefficients by educational attainment may also signal constraints in the possibility to access or complete higher education, which would point to the need for remedial policies in this field.

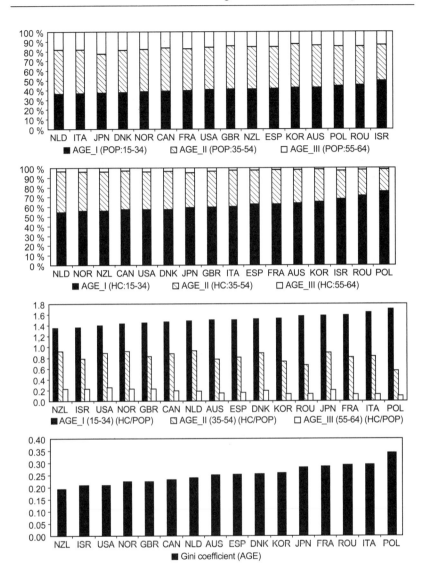

Fig. 15.7   Distribution of human capital by age group in 2006
Source: OECD Human Capital Project.
Note: Estimates for Australia refer to 2001; those for Denmark, to 2002.

Finally, figure 15.7 shows the distribution of human capital by age groups. The methodology used in this chapter implies that the younger people are, the more human capital they hold. The reason is that younger people have a longer remaining lifetime than their older counterparts, an effect that more than offsets their lower annual income compared to seniors. Conversely, higher unemployment rates for youths tend to lower the chance of their human capital to be employed in economic activities, implying that reducing youth unemployment rates is important not only to improve the current situation of youths but also to increase a country's (realized) human capital stock.[35]

One obvious limit of the methodology used in this chapter is that youths, as they age, are assumed to achieve the same earnings and employment probabilities of today's prime-age workers. To the extent that this assumption does not hold true (i.e., that today's youths could earn less as they age than prime-age workers earn today), the human capital holdings of young people will turn out to be much worse than depicted here.

15.4.4   Volume Measures of the Stock of Human Capital

Spatial Volume Index

County comparison based on the total value of human capital may be misleading due to two factors: first, because countries have different population sizes; and second, because countries may differ in terms of the purchasing power of people's earnings. Figure 15.8 addresses these two factors by showing information on countries' human capital values per capita in 2006. To take into account differences in price levels across countries, the estimates shown here are based on purchasing power parities (PPPs) for private consumption in each country, and expressed in terms of USD.

Based on the assumptions made here on the annual real income growth rate and discount rate, the estimates shown in figure 15.8 indicate that the values of human capital per capita range between USD 79,000 in Romania and USD 641,000 in the United States. Excluding the two ends of the distribution (Romania and Poland at the lower end, and the United Kingdom and the United States at the higher end), the differences of human capital per capita among other countries are, however, relatively small, comprised in a range between around USD 400,000 and USD 550,000.

For the purpose of country comparisons, values of GDP per capita in USD are also presented in the left upper panel of figure 15.8. Broadly speaking, countries with a higher GDP per capita also display a higher value of human capital per capita, but there are exceptions. For instance, despite relatively high GDP per capita in Italy and the Netherlands, their human capital per capita is relatively low. Conversely, Korea combines comparatively low GDP per capita and higher human capital per capita than most other countries.

Holdings of human capital per capita by gender, by educational level, and by age groups are also shown in upper-right, lower-left, and lower-right panels of figure 15.8, respectively. Country rankings in these panels are broadly

---

35. Given its importance, the youth employment rate is selected among the four human capital leading indicators by The Lisbon Council (Ederer, Schuller, and Willms 2011).

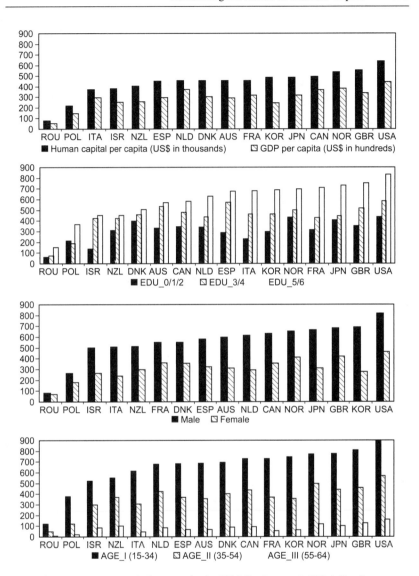

Fig. 15.8   Real human capital per capita in 2006 (in thousands US dollars)
Source: OECD Human Capital Project.
Note: Estimates for Australia refer to 2001; those for Denmark, to 2002.

similar to those shown for human capital per capita in the upper-left panel in the same figure. Nevertheless, due to differences in how human capital is distributed in various countries, the rankings are not exactly the same.

An alternative way of presenting the same type of information is conveyed by figure 15.9, which shows country human capital per capita in real terms

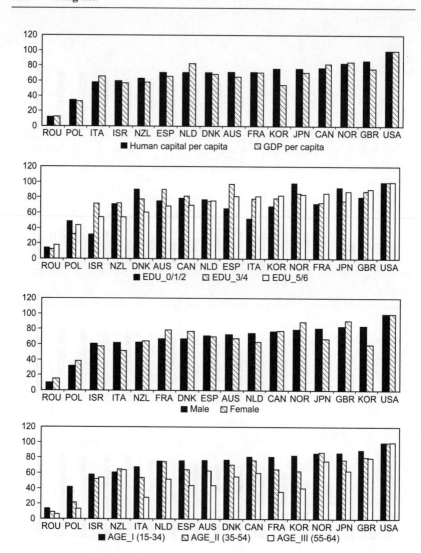

Fig. 15.9   Human capital spatial volume indices in 2006 (US levels equal to 100)
Source: OECD Human Capital Project.
Note: Estimates for Australia refer to 2001; those for Denmark, to 2002.

in 2006 relative to the level observed in the United States (set equal to 100). The upper left panel of figure 15.9 shows that the volume index of human capital per capita is only 12 for Romania and 38 for Poland, and over 60 for most other countries. This means that human capital per capita is larger in the United States than in any other participating countries. The same conclusion can be drawn from the other panels in figure 15.9 when looking at various population groups.

Temporal Volume Index

Information on how the stock of human capital in volume terms evolves in a country is of critical importance for policy decisions. In particular, from the perspective of assessing sustainability, a necessary condition for a country to grow along a sustainable path is that the volume of its total capital stock in per capita terms should not decline over time (UNECE 2009). While this argument underscores the importance of having a single measure of how the total capital stock of each country evolves over time (in real terms), information on the volume change in each capital stock of different types of capital is also important.

Though the observation of declining levels of human capital per capita would not necessarily imply that the development path for the country in question is "unsustainable," since this decline in human capital could be offset by raising stocks of other types of capital (as implied by the "weak sustainability" criterion, according to which different types of capital are assumed to be substitutable for each other; Pearce and Atkinson 1993), nonetheless, a decline in the real stock of human capital per capita will warrant policy attention.

Moreover, this argument is even more justified when applying the "strong sustainability" criterion, according to which critical capitals should not be allowed to fall below some minimum levels (Pearce and Atkinson 1993).

Figure 15.10 displays information on human capital temporal volume indices (denoted as "VOL"), population indices ("POP"), and human capital per capita indices ("HCPERCAPITA") for participating countries during their corresponding observation years.[36] For each country, the volume of human capital and the population in the base year were set as equal to 100.

Compared with the starting year, the total stock of human capital in real terms has increased for all countries except for Japan, though there were ups and downs for a few countries throughout the observation period. Even for countries that experienced increasing human capital volumes throughout the period, however, the rate of increase varied significantly across these countries.

The situation is strikingly different when looking at changes in the volume of human capital *per capita*. With the exception of Italy and Japan,[37] all countries experienced growing population during the period. The difference of the growth rate of human capital volumes index and that of population is the growth rate of human capital per capita. Relative to its starting year, three patterns are in evidence:

---

36. Due to data constraint, figure 15.10 shows human capital temporal volume indices only for thirteen OECD countries.

37. The working age population in Italy dipped around 2002 and picked up again since then; while that of Japan shrank monotonously during the observed period (2002–2007).

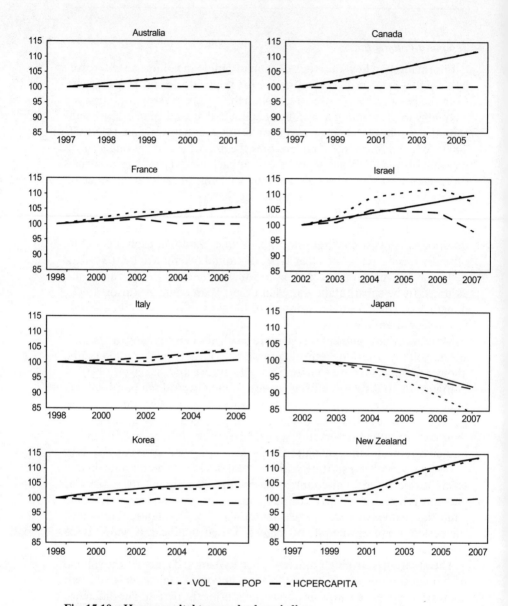

Fig. 15.10   Human capital temporal volume indices

Source: OECD Human Capital Project.

Note: The abrupt fall of human capital volume from 2006 to 2007 in Israel reflects a change of educational categories.

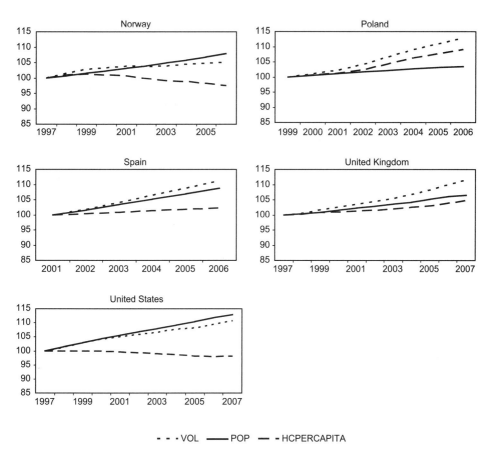

Fig. 15.10   (cont.)

- higher human capital volumes per capita in Italy, Poland, Spain, and the United Kingdom;
- broadly stable human capital volumes per capita in Australia, Canada, France, and New Zealand; and
- lower human capital volumes per capita in Israel, Japan, Korea, Norway, and the United States.

To explore why human capital volume per capita increased in some countries and declined in others, decomposition analyses can be used. Partial volume indices allow assessing the relative importance of the various factors at work. As outlined in section 15.2.4, these partial volume indices refer to the main population characteristics (i.e., age, gender, and educational attainment) and allow examining the contribution of these characteristics to the real growth of human capital per capita.

Figure 15.11 provides information on average annual growth rate of human capital per capita for each country throughout the observation period available (shown as "diamonds" in the figure). Contributions from first-order partial indices with respect to age, gender, and educational level are reported in the form of stacked bars: as mentioned already, the sum of the contribution that each characteristic makes to the growth of human capital per capita will not equal the overall growth in human capital per capita, as these contributions represent only first-order approximations.

Figure 15.11 indicates that, compared with the contributions from other two characteristics, the contribution of shifts of the population between gender was very small (positive for Israel, Italy, Japan, Korea, Poland, Spain, the United Kingdom, and the United States; negative for Australia, Canada, France, New Zealand, and Norway) and almost negligible for all countries. This means that during the observation period shift of population composition between men and women had little effect on the change of human capital per capita for all countries.

Similarly, for all countries the contribution from educational level was positive while that from age was negative. The former effect suggests that, during the period, more people attained higher levels of education, while the latter signals that all countries were experiencing population aging (since

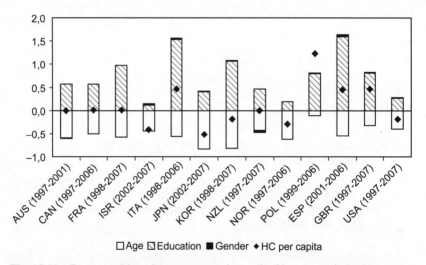

□ Age ⬚ Education ■ Gender ◆ HC per capita

Fig. 15.11 Decomposition of average annual growth of human capital volume per capita due to age, gender, and educational attainment (first-order partial volume index, %)

Source: OECD Human Capital Project.

Note: For many countries, the contribution from gender is too small to be discernible in the figure.

older people have fewer remaining working years and thus lower lifetime incomes).[38]

The magnitude of these two opposite effects varied across countries. For countries that experienced increased volumes of human capital per capita (Italy, Poland, Spain, and the United Kingdom), the positive contribution from education was larger than the negative effect from population aging. For countries that experienced broadly stable volumes of human capital per capita (Australia, Canada, France, and New Zealand), these two effects almost cancelled out each other. Finally, for countries that experienced decreased volumes of human capital per capita (Israel, Japan, Korea, Norway, and the United States), the contribution from age exceeded that from education.[39]

One obvious policy implication that can be drawn from these patterns is that some countries are not investing enough in education to offset the negative effect of population aging.

15.4.5   Sensitivity Analysis

The estimates of human capital presented in this project are subject to a number of assumptions, in particular assumptions about two key parameters, that is, the annual growth rate of real income of each age/gender/education categories in the future; and that on the discount rate. A number of national studies have shown that human capital estimates based on the lifetime income approach are sensitive to the choice of these two parameters (e.g., Wei 2004; Gu and Wong 2008, 2009; Liu and Greaker 2009; Fraumeni 2011).

In this project, sensitivity analysis has been implemented with respect to these two parameters. Taking the United States as an example, table 15.2 shows results of sensitivity analyses on human capital stock value and its distribution in 2006. In table 15.2, the baseline scenario is one where the annual real income growth rate is set at 1.30 percent and the discount rate is 4.58 percent, the values used for generating the estimates of human capital for the United States that have been shown above.

Since income growth rate and discount rate enter the estimation of the stock of human capital in multiplicative forms (see equations (A1) and (A2) in appendix A), what matters is the ratio between the two parameters; that

---

38. Recall that the focus of the current study is the working age (15–64) population. An aging working age population implies that the share of elderly people is increasing relative to that of younger people. This could happen when more prime age people (35–54) become older (55–64) and/or when less younger people (aged less than 15 years) enter the working age population.

39. Korea, a country where the contribution from education was larger than that from age, is an exception. This might reflect the fact that Korea is the only country that combines educational level 4 with level 5B in the original data source. As a result, the tertiary educational level (EDU_5/6) used for Korea in this project includes level 4; one consequence is that the contribution from first-order volume index with respect to education might be exaggerated.

Table 15.2 Sensitivity analysis on human capital stock value and distribution for the United States in 2006

| | | Level (trillions) | Distribution (%) | | | | | | | | |
| | | | Gender | | Education | | | Age | | |
Fixed annual discount rate (4.58%)	Annual income growth rate (%)	Total stock	Males	Females	EDU_0/1/2	EDU_3/4	EDU_5/6	AGE_I	AGE_II	AGE_III
Baseline	1.30	128,235	63.8	36.2	13.4	43.7	42.9	57.6	38.5	3.9
Scenario A	−2.10	86,131	63.7	36.3	11.2	42.4	46.4	50.6	44.1	5.3
		(−32.8)	(−0.2)	(0.3)	(−16.4)	(−3.0)	(8.2)	(−12.2)	(14.5)	(35.9)
Scenario B	1.11	125,009	63.8	36.2	13.3	43.6	43.2	57.2	38.8	4.0
		(−2.4)	(0.0)	(0.0)	(−0.7)	(−0.2)	(0.7)	(−0.7)	(0.8)	(2.6)
Scenario C	1.50	131,673	63.8	36.2	13.5	43.8	42.7	58.1	38.1	3.8
		(2.7)	(0.0)	(0.0)	(0.7)	(0.2)	(−0.5)	(0.9)	(−1.0)	(−2.6)
Scenario D	3.96	188,188	63.8	36.2	15.8	44.7	39.6	64.1	33.0	2.9
		(46.8)	(0.0)	(0.0)	(17.9)	(2.3)	(−7.7)	(11.3)	(−14.3)	(−25.6)

Source: OECD Human Capital Project.

Note: Changes (in percentages) relative to baseline scenario are shown in parentheses.

is, $\{(1 + r)/(1 + \delta)\}$. For this reason, the four scenarios shown in table 15.2 rely on the same annual discount rate (4.58 percent for all scenarios) while differing in terms of the real income growth rate that they use (-2.1% in scenario A, 1.11% in scenario B, 1.50% in scenario C, and 3.96% in scenario D), respectively; this implies setting the values of the parameter $\{(1 + r)/(1 + \delta)\}$ at 96.86%, 93.62%, 96.68%, 97.05%, and 99.41%, respectively.

Table 15.2 shows that the estimates of the total value of the stock of human capital are sensitive to the choice of the two parameters. Nonetheless, the distribution of human capital between men and women, among educational groups, and among age groups are relatively less sensitive.

Likewise, the growth of the volume of human capital is not very sensitive to the choice of the two parameters. As shown in figure 15.12, the curves of human capital volume for scenarios baseline B and C are almost identical; the same applies to the curves of human capital per capita.

One interesting pattern from figure 15.12 is that the curve referring to the volume of human capital in scenario A, which relies on a lower income growth rate than in the baseline, lies above that for the baseline scenario; conversely, in scenario D, which uses a higher income growth rate than in the baseline, the curve for the volume of human capital is below that of the baseline scenario. These counterintuitive results reflect the nature of the method used to estimate lifetime income in this chapter.

In terms of equations (1), (2), and (3) in section 15.2.4, the higher-than-baseline income growth rate (as in the case of scenario D) implies a higher share for the value of human capital held by younger people than for their older counterparts. Due to the population aging observed in the United States (and given that the sum of the value shares must equal one), the higher growth in the older population combined with a lower share of human capital held by this group, together with the lower growth in younger population weighted by a higher share of their human capital, lead to a growth of human capital volume that is smaller than in the baseline.

In addition, although the *level* of human capital volume is increasing due to higher income growth rate, the curve of human capital volume will be shifted down in order to keep the volume level at the starting year (1997) fixed at 100.

Therefore, in scenarios that have higher income growth rate than in the baseline, the lower growth rate of human capital volume, combined with the fixed starting value, will lead to curves of human capital volume that lie below the curve for the baseline. The opposite holds true for scenarios that have lower income growth rate (e.g., scenario A) than in the baseline.

While these paradoxical results stem from equations (1), (2), and (3), together with the population aging that is observed in the United States, it may also reflect a more fundamental constraint imposed by the basic assumptions made in this approach; that is, that annual real income growth

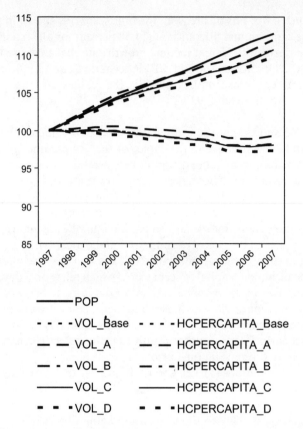

Fig. 15.12   Sensitivity analysis on human capital temporal volume index for the United States
Source: OECD Human Capital Project.

rate is exogenously given rather than derived from the model. The implications of this assumption can be gleaned when considering that, in a country experiencing aging population, its long-term economic growth would be affected since human capital, a critical asset for economic growth, is declining. This causal link from aging population to future income growth rate is neglected in the model for human capital measurement used in this project. Exploring how population aging will affect real income growth rate in the future is beyond the scope of this project.

15.5   Conclusions and Future Plan

Human capital is of significant importance for policymakers to address various issues such as economic growth, quality of life, social cohesion, and sustainable development. The OECD Human Capital Project is among the first attempts to measure human capital for comparisons both across countries and over time. To that end, an OECD database has been constructed for most of the project participating countries, containing information on the various elements that enter the human capital estimation, based on the lifetime income approach.

The results contained in the chapter show the feasibility of applying the lifetime income approach to measuring human capital for comparative analysis. They also highlight the feasibility of applying the methodology to categorical data (e.g., by five-year or ten-year age group) that are typically available within the OECD statistics system, rather than to more demanding detailed data that would be required by the original Jorgenson-Fraumeni methodology. The main results are the following:

- Despite of some differences, most of the estimates in this chapter are in line with those reported in national studies. In terms of the level of human capital value, almost all studies share the conclusion that, even when estimates are restricted to market activities, the value of human capital is substantially larger than that of conventional produced capital and is much larger than GDP (by a factor ranging from around eight to over ten times in this study).

- Within countries, the stock of human capital is not uniformly distributed across different groups of the population. The distributions of human capital indicate that men have a higher human capital than women. In addition, people with higher education are better off than those with lower education, and the same is true for younger people compared to their older counterparts, although the detailed patterns vary across countries.

- Adjusting for changes in price levels in each country shows that human capital volume increased for all countries (except for Japan) during the observed period. However, in some countries, the volume of human capital in per capita terms fell.

- Decomposition analysis of human capital volume indices shows that changes in the structure of the population between men and women had little effect on the change of human capital per capita in all countries. While more people attaining higher levels of education contributed positively to the change of human capital per capita in each country, in all countries population aging contributed negatively to this change over the observed years.

- The magnitude of these two opposite effects varied across countries. In Italy, Poland, Spain, and the United Kingdom, the positive contribution from higher educational attainment exceeded the negative effect of population aging, while the opposite was true in Israel, Japan, Korea, Norway, and the United States. it may imply that, when facing population aging, countries can invest more into education so as to offset this negative demographic effect.

- Finally, the sensitivity analysis confirms that estimates of the values of human capital are sensitive to the choice of the two key parameters in the estimation; that is, the annual real income growth rate and the discount rate. But within-country distribution of human capital and trends in human capital volume index in each country are less sensitive.

Country-specific assumptions of real income growth rates and a common discount rate have been used in this project to estimate human capital based on the lifetime income approach. Although there are reasonable arguments for these choices, there are also reasons in favor of different assumptions. This issue will have to be addressed in future research.[40]

In conclusion, it seems that, despite some deficiencies in the methodology used, the lifetime income approach, by bringing together the influence of a broad range of factors (demography, mortality, and educational attainment, as well as labor market aspects) allows comparing the relative importance of these factors and drawing useful policy implications from the estimates.

In the near term, the project could be expanded in two main directions: (1) improving the underlying statistical information (e.g., by using information from other sources to improve current data on school enrollment rates, by improving the comparability of educational categories, by improving the earnings concept used in the OECD database); and (2) extending the work to additional countries and years.

In the longer term, the OECD work on human capital based on the lifetime income approach could explore a number of more fundamental issues, including the following:

- Running simulations of future stocks of human capital, based on existing demographic projections.
- Constructing human capital accumulation accounts that will help explain changes in the stock of human capital over time in terms of investment, depreciation, and revaluation.
- Using the human capital estimates to construct an education satellite account, combining various inputs and outputs data on education.
- Extending the scope of the current accounting exercise to include children (below age 15), the elderly (above 65), and nonmarket activities.
- Examining how results on adults' competencies from PIAAC (the OECD Programme for the International Assessment of Adult Competencies) might be integrated into human capital accounting so as to produce "quality-adjusted" estimates.
- Identifying and reinforcing the structural links between human capital accounting and other economic entities in the SNA.

40. For more discussions on this issue, see Abraham (2010), Fraumeni (2011), and Liu (2013).

- Investigating potential possibilities for addressing more policy issues based on the human capital accounting exercise.

Appendix A

Methodological Assumptions and Relevant Equations Used for Estimating Lifetime Income

The OECD Human Capital Project distinguishes between three stages in the life cycle of an individual of working age (i.e., between 15 and 64 years of age): (1) "study-and-work" (15–40);[41] (2) "work-only" (41–64); and (3) "retirement only" (65 and above). Based on this assumption, the lifetime labor income of an individual can be computed using the following:

- For persons aged 65 and over (i.e., "retirement only" stage), their lifetime labor income is zero since, by assumption, these persons will not receive earnings after withdrawing from the labor market.
- For persons aged 41 to 64 (i.e., "work-only" stage), their lifetime labor income is estimated using the following:

(A1) $\quad LIN_{age}^{edu} = EMR_{age}^{edu} AIN_{age}^{edu} + SUR_{age+1} LIN_{age+1}^{edu} \{(1 + r)/(1 + \delta)\},$

where LIN_{age}^{edu} is the present value of lifetime labor income for a representative individual with educational level of "*edu*" at the age of "*age*"; EMR_{age}^{edu} is the employment rate for this individual; AIN_{age}^{edu} is his/her current annual labor income, if employed; SUR_{age} is the probability of surviving one more year given that this individual is at the age of "*age*"; r is the annual growth rate of the labor income (in real terms) of a person of these characteristics in the future; δ is the annual discount rate.

The lifetime income of a representative individual during the "work-only" stage is therefore estimated as the sum of two parts: the first part is the current labor income, adjusted by employment rate (the first term in equation [A1]); the second part is the lifetime income in the next year, adjusted by the corresponding survival rate, income growth rate, and discount rate (the second term in equation [A1]).

For persons aged 15 to 40 (i.e., "study-and-work" stage), their lifetime labor income is estimated using the following:

41. The cut-off at age 40 for the upper bound of the "study-and-work" stage is due to the fact that information on the number of students enrolled in different educational levels from the OECD database is available until age 40. Many countries have witnessed in recent years a quite significant increase in the number of adults (more than 40 years old) attending schools for further education (http://dotstat.oecd.org/wbos/Index.aspx).

$$(A2) \quad LIN_{age}^{edu} = EMR_{age}^{edu} AIN_{age}^{edu} + \left\{1 - \sum_{\overline{edu}} ENR_{age}^{edu-\overline{edu}}\right\} SUR_{age+1} LIN_{age+1}^{edu}$$

$$\cdot \{(1 + r)/(1 + \delta)\} + \sum_{\overline{edu}} ENR_{age}^{edu-\overline{edu}}$$

$$\cdot \left\{\left(\sum_{t=1}^{t_{edu-\overline{edu}}} SUR_{age+t} LIN_{age+t}^{\overline{edu}}\{(1 + r)/(1 + \delta)\}^t\right)/t_{edu-\overline{edu}}\right\},$$

where $ENR_{age}^{edu-\overline{edu}}$ is the school enrollment rate for a representative individual with educational level of "edu" pursuing studies into a higher educational level of "$\overline{edu}$"; $t_{edu-\overline{edu}}$ is the school duration for this individual with educational level of "edu" to complete a higher educational level of "$\overline{edu}$".

During the "study-and-work" stage, a representative individual in the next year will be confronted to two courses of action: the first is to continue his/her school and (after completing study and having gained a higher educational level) to receive income as $\{\sum_{t=1}^{t_{edu-\overline{edu}}}(SUR_{age+t} LIN_{age+t}^{\overline{edu}}\{(1 + r)/(1 + \delta)\}^t)/t_{edu-\overline{edu}}\}$, with the probability of $\sum_{\overline{edu}} ENR_{age}^{edu-\overline{edu}}$; the second is to start working (holding the same educational level as before) and earn income as $SUR_{age+1} LIN_{age+1}^{edu}\{(1 + r)/(1 + \delta)\}$, with the probability of $\{1 - \sum_{\overline{edu}} ENR_{age}^{edu-\overline{edu}}\}$. Therefore, his/her lifetime income in the next year is the expected value of the outcomes of these two courses of action (i.e., the sum of the second and the third terms in equation [A2]).

The empirical implementation of equations (A1) and (A2) is based on backwards recursion. With this approach, the lifetime labor income of a person aged 64 (i.e., one year before retirement) is simply his/her current labor income (the first term in equations [A1] and [A2]) because his/her lifetime labor income at 65 is zero by construction. Similarly, the lifetime labor income of a person aged 63 is equal to his current labor income plus the present value of the lifetime labor income of a person aged 64, and so forth.

In estimating lifetime labor income by using equations (A1) and (A2), several practical assumptions are made, some of which are used as well by other studies in the field (e.g., Gu and Wong 2008; Le, Gibson, and Oxley 2006; Liu and Greaker 2009; Wei 2004, 2007). The most important of these assumptions are the following:

- Individuals can only enroll in a higher educational level than the one they have already completed.
- No further enrollment is allowed for people having already achieved the highest educational level.
- Students enrolled in educational institutions requiring more than one year to complete are assumed to be evenly distributed across the total study period (school duration). This is equivalent to saying that, during each school year, the same proportion of all students will complete the study.

- No delaying, quitting, or skipping is allowed during the whole study period.

In formal terms, the total stock of human capital (HCV) is computed as:

(A3)
$$HCV = \sum_{age}\sum_{edu} LIN_{age}^{edu} NUM_{age}^{edu},$$

where NUM_{age}^{edu} is the number of persons in the corresponding age/education category. It should be noted that equations (A1), (A2), and (A3) are applied separately to both men and women; this allows computing the stock of human capital by gender.

Appendix B
Classification of Educational Levels in ISCED 97

The International Standard Classification of Education (ISCED) developed by UNESCO is based on standard concepts, definitions, and classifications, and aims to provide a tool suitable for assembling, compiling, and presenting comparable statistics on education both within countries and internationally. ISCED 97 covers primarily two cross-classification variables: (1) the level of education; and (2) the field of education. Due to data constraint, the OECD Human Capital Project only relied on the classification of educational levels, based on the following main categories:

- level 0: preprimary education
- level 1: primary education or first stage of basic education
- level 2: lower secondary or second stage of basic education
- level 3: upper secondary education
- level 4: postsecondary nontertiary education
- level 5: first stage of tertiary education
- level 6: second stage of tertiary education

Except for levels 0 and 1, the above-defined categories can be further subclassified according to the destination for which the programs have been designated, resulting in more detailed classifications. This information is used to determine the detailed transition patterns from lower to higher educational levels shown in figure 15A.1. In particular, the following should be noted:

- Level 2 encompasses sublevels 2A (designed to provide direct access to level 3 in a sequence that would ultimately lead to tertiary education, i.e., entrance to 3A or 3B); 2B (designed to provide direct access to 3C); and 2C (primarily designed to lead to direct access to labor market at the end of this level).

- Level 3 consists of sublevels 3A (designed to provide direct access to 5A); 3B (designed to provide direct access to 5B); and 3C (designed to lead directly to labor market or to level 4 or other level 3 programs).
- Level 4 consists of sublevels 4A (prepared for entry to level 5); and 4B (primarily designed for direct labor market entry).
- Level 5 includes sublevels 5A (theoretically based research and preparatory courses of history, philosophy, mathematics, etc., or giving access to professions with high skills requirements such as medicine, dentistry, architecture, etc.); and 5B (programs that are practical/technical/occupationally specific).

Appendix C

Transition Pattern in ISCED 97

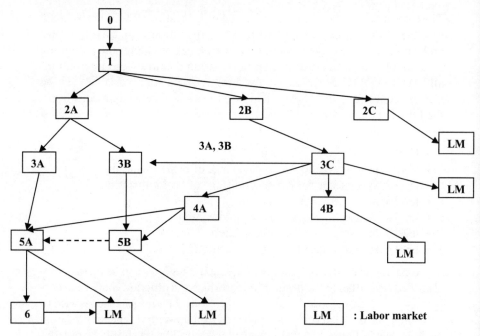

Fig. 15C.1   Labor market
Source: International Standard Classification of Education (ISCED) 97 (UNESCO 2006).

References

Abraham, K. G. 2010. "Accounting for Investment in Formal Education." *Survey of Current Business* June: 42–53.

Aghion, P., and P. Howitt. 1998. *Endogenous Growth Theory*. Cambridge, MA: MIT Press.

Ahlroth, S., A. Björklund, and A. Forslund. 1997. "The Output of the Swedish Education Sector." *Review of Income & Wealth* 43 (1): 89–104.

Becker, G. S. 1964. *Human Capital*. New York: Columbia University Press.

Boarini, R., M. Mira d'Ercole, and G. Liu. 2012. "Approaches to Measuring the Stock of Human Capital: A Review of Country Practices." OECD Statistics Working Papers, no. 2012/04, OECD Publishing, doi: 10.1787/5k8zlm5bc3ns-en.

Card, D. 2001. "Estimating the Return to Schooling: Progress on Some Persistent Econometric Problems." *Econometrica* 69 (5): 1127–60.

Christian, M. S. 2010. "Human Capital Accounting in the United States 1964–2006." *Survey of Current Business* June: 31–36.

Conrad, K. 1992. "Comment on 'Investment in Education and US Economic Growth' by D. W. Jorgenson and B. M. Fraumeni." *Scandinavian Journal of Economics* 94 (supplement): S71–S74.

Diewert, W. E. 1976. "Exact and Superlative Index Numbers." *Journal of Econometrics* 4 (2): 115–45.

Dolan, P., T. Peasgood, and M. White. 2008. "Do We Really Know What Makes Us Happy? A Review of the Economic Literature on the Factors Associated with Subjective Well-Being." *Journal of Economic Psychology* 29:94–122.

Ederer, P., P. Schuller, and S. Willms. 2007. *Innovation at Work: The European Human Capital Index*. The Lisbon Council Policy Brief, volume 2, number 3, Brussels.

———. 2011. *Human Capital Leading Indicators—How Europe's Regions and Cities Can Drive Growth and Foster Inclusion*. Brussels: The Lisbon Council.

Eisner, R. 1985. "The Total Incomes System of Accounts." *Survey of Current Business* 65 (1): 24–48.

Engel, E. 1883. *Der Werth des Menschen*. Berlin: Verlag von Leonhard Simion.

Ervik, A. O., E. Holmøy, and T. Hægeland. 2003. "A Theory-Based Measure of the Output of the Education Sector." Discussion Paper no. 353, Statistics Norway.

Farr, W. 1853. "Equitable Taxation of Property." *Journal of Royal Statistics* 16 (March): 1–45.

Fraumeni, B. M. 2008. "Human Capital: From Indicators and Indexes to Accounts." Paper presented at the OECD workshop on "The Measurement of Human Capital" in Turin, Italy, November 3-4.

———. 2009. "A Measurement Specialist's Perspective on Human Capital." Presentation at China Centre for Human Capital and Labour Market Research, Central University of Finance and Economics, Beijing, China, June 11.

———. 2011. "Human Capital Accounts: Choice of Rates and Construction of Volume Indices." NBER Working Paper no. 16895, Cambridge, MA.

Graham, J. W., and R. H. Webb. 1979. "Stocks and Depreciation of Human Capital: New Evidence from a Present-Value Perspective." *Review of Income and Wealth* 25 (2): 209–24.

Greaker, M., and G. Liu. 2008. "Measuring the Stock of Human Capital for Norway: A Lifetime Labour Income Approach." Paper presented at the OECD workshop on "The Measurement of Human Capital" in Turin, Italy, November 3-4.

Greaker, M., P. Løkkevik, and M. A. Walle. 2005."Utviklingen i den norske nasjonalformuen fra 1985 til 2004. Et eksempel på bærekraftig utvikling?" [Development of the Norwegian National Wealth 1985–2004. An Example of Sustainable Development?] Report 2005/13. Oslo: Statistics Norway.

Gu, W., and A. Wong. 2008. "Human Development and Its Contribution to the Wealth Accounts in Canada." Paper presented at the OECD workshop on "The Measurement of Human Capital," Turin, Italy, November 3-4.

———. 2009. "Human Development and Its Contribution to the Wealth Accounts in Canada." Paper presented at the International Symposium on Measuring Human Capital and Its Impact on Welfare and Growth, Beijing, China, October 9-10.

———. 2010. "Estimates of Human Capital: The Lifetime Income Approach." Economic Analysis Research Paper Series no. 062. Statistics Canada.

Jorgenson, D. W. 1963. "Capital Theory and Investment Behavior." *American Economic Review* 53 (2): 247–59.

———. 1967. "The Theory of Investment Behavior." In *The Determinants of Investment Behavior*, Conference of the Universities-National Bureau of Economic Research, 129–56. New York: Columbia University Press.

Jorgenson, D. W., and B. M. Fraumeni. 1989. "The Accumulation of Human and Non-Human Capital, 1948–1984." In *The Measurement of Savings, Investment, and Wealth*, edited by R. E. Lipsey and H. S. Tice, 227–82. Chicago: University of Chicago Press.

———. 1992a. "Investment in Education and US Economic Growth." *Scandinavian Journal of Economics* 94 (Supplement): 51–70.

———. 1992b. "The Output of Education Sector." In *Output Measurement in the Service Sectors*, edited by Z. Griliches, 303–41. Chicago: The University of Chicago Press.

Jorgenson, D. W., M. S. Ho, and K. J. Stiroh. 2005. *Information Technology and the American Growth Resurgence*, volume 3, *Productivity*. Cambridge, MA: Harvard University Press.

Jorgenson, D. W., and K.-Y. Yun. 1990. "Tax Reform and US Economic Growth." *Journal of Political Economy* 98: S151–93.

Kendrick, J. 1976. *The Formation and Stocks of Total Capital*. New York: Columbia University Press.

Kyriacou, G. A. 1991. "Level and Growth Effects of Human Capital: A Cross-Country Study of the Convergence Hypothesis." Economic Research Reports 19–26. C. V. Starr Centre for Applied Economics, New York University.

Le, T., J. Gibson, and L. Oxley. 2003. "Cost- and Income-based Measures of Human Capital." *Journal of Economic Surveys* 17 (3): 271–307.

———. 2006. "A Forward-Looking Measure of the Stock of Human Capital in New Zealand." *The Manchester School* 74 (5): 593–609.

Li, H., Y. Liang, B. M. Fraumeni, Z. Liu, and X. Wang. 2010. "Human Capital in China." Paper presented at the 31st General Conference of the International Association for Research in Income and Wealth, St. Gallen, Switzerland, August 22-28.

Liu, G. 2011. "Measuring the Stock of Human Capital for Comparative Analysis: An Application of the Lifetime Income Approach to Selected Countries." OECD Statistics Working Papers, no. 2011/06, OECD Publishing, doi: 10.1787/5kg3h0jnn9r5-en.

———. 2013. "The OECD Human Capital Project: A Technical Report." Unpublished Document. OECD Statistics Directorate.

Liu, G., and M. Greaker. 2009. "Measuring the Stock of Human Capital for Norway—A Lifetime Labour Income Approach." Documents, 2009/12. Statistics Norway.

Lucas, R. E., Jr. 1988. "On the Mechanics of Economic Development." *Journal of Monetary Economics* 22 (1): 3–42.

Mincer, J. 1974. *Schooling, Experience and Earnings.* New York: Columbia University Press.

OECD. 2001. *The Well-Being of Nations: The Role of Human and Social Capital.* Paris: OECD Publishing.

———. 2004. "2004 Data Collection on Education Systems—UOE data collection manual." Paris: OECD Publishing.

———. 2009a. *Measuring Capital OECD Manual,* 2nd edition. Paris: OECD Publishing.

———. 2009b. *OECD Economic Outlook,* volume 2009/1, no. 85. Paris: OECD Publishing.

———. 2010a. *Improving Health and Social Cohesion through Education.* Paris: OECD Publishing.

———. 2010b. "The OECD Human Capital Project: Progress Report." Paper presented at the 31st General Conference of The International Association for Research in Income and Wealth, St. Gallen, Switzerland, August 22-28.

O'Mahony, M., and P. A. Stevens. 2004. *International Comparisons of Performance in the Provision of Public Services: Outcome Based Measures for Education.* London: National Institute of Economic and Social Research.

Pearce, D. W., and G. D. Atkinson. 1993. "Capital Theory and the Measurement of Sustainable Development: An Indicator of Weak Sustainability." *Ecological Economics* 8 (2): 103–08. doi:10.1016/0921-8009(93)90039-9.

Petty, W. 1690. "Political Arithmetic." Reprinted in C. H. Hull (1899), *The Economic Writings of Sir William Petty.* Cambridge: Cambridge University Press.

Romer, P. M. 1986. "Increasing Returns and Long Run Growth." *Journal of Political Economy* 94 (5): 1002–37.

———. 1989. "Human Capital and Growth: Theory and Evidence." NBER Working Paper no. 3173, Cambridge, MA.

Rosen, S. 1989. "Comment on 'The Accumulation of Human and Nonhuman Capital,' by Dale W. Jorgenson and Barbara M. Fraumeni." In *The Measurement of Saving, Investment, and Wealth,* edited by R. E. Lipsey and H. Stone Tice, 282–85. Chicago: University of Chicago Press.

Ruta, G., and K. Hamilton. 2007. "The Capital Approach to Sustainability." In *Handbook of Sustainable Development,* edited by G. Atkinson et al., 45–62. Northampton, MA: Edward Elgar Publishing, Inc.

Schleicher, A. 2008. "PIAAC: A New Strategy for Assessing Adult Competencies." *International Review of Education.* DOI 10.1007/s11159-008-9105-0.

Schreyer, P. 2010. "Towards Measuring the Volume Output of Education and Health Services—A Handbook." OECD Statistics Working Papers, 2010/2, OECD, Paris.

Schultz, T. W. 1961. "Investment in Human Capital." *American Economic Review* 51 (1): 1–17.

Smith, A. 1776. *An Inquiry into the Nature and Causes of the Wealth of Nations,* Book 2. London: W. Strahan & T. Cadell.

Stroombergen, A., D. Rose, and G. Nana. 2002. "Review of the Statistical Measurement of Human Capital." Statistics New Zealand.

UNECE. 2009. *Measuring Sustainable Development.* Report of the Joint UNECE/OECD/Eurostat Working Group on Statistics for Sustainable Development, New York and Geneva.

UNESCO. 2006. *ISCED 1997—International Standard Classification of Education.* Paris.

Wei, H. 2004. "Measuring the Stock of Human Capital for Australia." Working Paper no. 2004/1, Australian Bureau of Statistics.

———. 2007. "Measuring Australia's Human Capital Development: The Role of

Post-School Education and the Impact of Population Ageing." *Statistical Journal of the IAOS* 24:183–91.

———. 2008. "Developments in the Estimation of the Value of Human Capital for Australia." Paper presented at the OECD workshop on "The Measurement of Human Capital," Turin, Italy, November 3-4.

Weisbrod, B. A. 1961. "The Valuation of Human Capital." *Journal of Political Economy* 69 (5): 425–36.

World Bank. 2006a. *Where Is the Wealth of Nations?* Washington, DC: The World Bank.

———. 2006b. *World Development Indicators 2006*. Washington, DC: The World Bank.

———. 2011. *The Changing Wealth of Nations: Measuring Sustainable Development in the New Millennium*. Washington, DC: The World Bank.

Developing a Framework for Decomposing Medical-Care Expenditure Growth
Exploring Issues of Representativeness

Abe Dunn, Eli Liebman, and Adam Hale Shapiro

16.1 Introduction

The large and growing share of GDP allocated to medical care has prompted greater focus on producing health statistics that provide more detailed information on the sources of expenditure growth and the value of those expenditures. One shortcoming of current national statistics is that they contain no information on medical expenditures by disease, even though the primary aim of purchasing medical-care services is disease treatment. This gap in our understanding of health expenditures has been noted by numerous academics and policymakers who have called for additional research in this area and the development of a national health-care satellite account that would help fill this void (see Berndt et al. 2000 and National Research Council 2010). More generally, the call for the development of a health-care satellite account is a critical part of a broader research agenda to expand economic accounts to better measure welfare (Abraham and Mackie 2005). There have been a number of case studies on the value of health spending that explore the costs and benefits of different treatments and technologies for particular diseases (e.g., heart attacks, depression, cataracts, and high cholesterol). However, only relatively recent research in this

Abe Dunn is an economist in the office of the chief economist at the Bureau of Economic Analysis, US Department of Commerce. Eli Liebman is an economist in the office of the director at the Bureau of Economic Analysis, US Department of Commerce. Adam Hale Shapiro is a senior economist at the Federal Reserve Bank of San Francisco.

The views expressed in this chapter are solely those of the authors and do not necessarily reflect the views of the Bureau of Economic Analysis, the Federal Reserve Bank of San Francisco, or the Board of Governors of the Federal Reserve System. For acknowledgments, sources of research support, and disclosure of the authors' material financial relationships, if any, please see http://www.nber.org/chapters/c12841.ack.

area has started to formulate statistical indexes that track the components of health expenditures by disease for a broad set of health conditions. For example, studying the full range of diseases, Aizcorbe and Nestoriak (2011) decompose expenditure per episode and service prices, and Roehrig and Rousseau (2011) focus on decomposing treated prevalence and expenditure per episode.[1] More recently, Dunn, Liebman, and Shapiro (2012), a companion piece to this chapter, decomposes each of these dimensions of health expenditure growth in a single framework.

This chapter focuses on health-care expenditures in the commercial insurance market, which is an economically important segment—accounting for more enrollees than Medicare and Medicaid combined. The importance of the commercial sector is set to grow with the implementation of the Affordable Care Act that is predicted to result in millions of uninsured individuals entering the commercially insured segment of the market. Many of the richest data sources for studying the commercial sector are convenience samples comprised of insurers and employers that contribute their employee or enrollee claims information.[2] Measurement issues may arise if these convenience samples are not representative and are evolving in a nonrandom fashion. For instance, estimates may not be representative of the US population if the sample is disproportionately from enrollees living in a particular geographic area. The work by Dunn, Shapiro, and Liebman (2013) shows there is large variation in medical-care expenditure levels across the United States, so it is conceivable that growth rates could also vary geographically. The age and sex distribution of the convenience sample may also be different from the actual US commercial population, leading to inaccurate estimates of expenditure growth. Finally, differences in the data contributors may also impact our estimates, as different groups with distinct populations (e.g., different employers or insurers) enter and leave the sample. In this setting, the application of population weights and an appropriately selected sample may be critical for obtaining meaningful estimates that are nationally representative. This chapter studies issues related to representativeness of the sample by examining how various weighting strategies and samples affect the components of spending growth.

To study this topic, we apply the full decomposition methodology outlined

---

1. There are a number of other studies that look at expenditures per episode and service prices. Dunn, Liebman, Pack, and Shapiro (2012) follow the methodology of Aizcorbe and Nestoriak (2011), but use an alternative data source. Aizcorbe and Nestoriak (2011) look at the decomposition between service price and expenditure per episode using national survey data. Other studies have also looked at the decomposition of prevalence and expenditures per case including Thorpe, Florence, and Joski (2004); Roehrig and Rousseau (2011); Roehrig et al. (2009).

2. Although several studies use the Medical Expenditure Panel Survey data, which is a representative sample of the civilian noninstitutionalized US population. The key limitation is that the sample size is relatively small (32,000 per year), which makes estimates from this data source greatly impacted by outliers and, given that this is a household survey, many diseases are potentially underreported.

in Dunn, Liebman, and Shapiro (2012) that looks at the various components of expenditure growth at the disease level. This decomposition starts with per capita spending, which is further broken into treated prevalence and expenditure per disease episode. Expenditure per disease is further broken out into a service utilization and service price component. Here we apply this methodology to study how different population weights and samples could impact the components of medical-care expenditure growth. Our study employs the MarketScan commercial claims data that is a convenience sample from health insurers and large employers for the years 2003 to 2007. There is no guarantee that the data that is provided by these contributors will reflect the overall commercial population. Moreover, additional data is added to the sample over time, with the number of enrollees increasing from around 7 million in 2003 to more than 13 million in 2007, which could influence our estimates.

Our primary strategy for dealing with the potentially nonrepresentative aspects of the data is to apply population weights, so that the weighted sample reflects the commercially insured population. We find that the unweighted MarketScan data produces qualitatively similar results to our weighted estimates along many dimensions. As in the work of Dunn, Liebman, and Shapiro (2012), we find that the main trends in spending growth are characterized by both increases in the underlying services price (e.g., price for a 15-minute office visit) and the growth in the treated prevalence of disease episodes. The utilization per episode of treatment is flat or is falling slightly over the period of study, which implies that conditional on having a disease episode, individuals are receiving approximately the same intensity of treatment over time.

We also investigate how changes in the data contributors (i.e., the insurers and employers providing the data) may impact our estimates. To address this issue, the sample is limited to those contributors that provide data for the whole sample period. Overall trends in this subsample are similar, although certain aspects of the fixed contributor estimates appear more plausible than those of the full sample. We discuss this issue in greater detail in the text. Although many of the qualitative findings do not change with the use of weights or alternative samples, there is evidence that the application of population weights may be of practical importance. In particular, the application of population weights produces spending and price growth figures that are more aligned to national benchmark estimates.

The qualitative finding that expenditure growth is driven by prevalence and service prices is interesting, but it is also worth highlighting that after adjusting for overall inflation, real medical-care expenditure growth is almost entirely caused by an increase in treated prevalence. Specifically, more than three quarters of the "real" growth in spending may be attributed to treated prevalence, with the remainder accounted for by expenditures per episode. This finding is robust across numerous estimates. This result contrasts sharply with estimates of Roehrig and Rousseau (2011), who find that growth is primarily driven by growth in expenditure per episode. Although we discuss some possible reasons for our different finding, more work is necessary to isolate the precise cause of this discrepancy.

The importance of population weights will partly depend on whether different demographic groups have distinct growth rates. For example, if younger individuals are overrepresented and have faster than average expenditure growth, then estimates of expenditure growth will be overstated. To see if the broadly observed trends apply to all segments of the population, we estimate the various components of expenditure growth for different subpopulations. Focusing first on subpopulations by age, we find the same general patterns of growth across all age groups, with expenditures primarily driven by service price and prevalence, but there also are some noteworthy differences among age groups. For instance, expenditure growth per person appears to be faster for children under 18 relative to other age segments. Also, service prices and utilization tend to grow more rapidly for younger populations, relative to older populations, although prevalence growth tends to be slower for younger individuals. Focusing next on the regional differences in growth, we find that spending patterns in three of the four regions follow a similar trend, but that spending in the South grows markedly slower. These findings hold for both the full sample and the sample with the fixed data contributors, although the differences among the growth rates in the different regions is less pronounced when using the information from the fixed data contributors.

Applying the estimates from this chapter to private health-care expenditures reported by the Center for Medicare and Medicaid Services (CMS), we can break total expenditure growth into a component attributable to population growth, another component to disease price growth, and the remainder due to real growth per capita. From 2003 to 2007, total expenditures in medical care for the commercial sector has grown by 26.3 percent.[3] Taking away the approximate 1 percent growth in the population leaves the growth in spending per capita to be around 25.2 percent.[4] Using the full sample and applying population weights, the disease-based price index grows by about 11 percent. This implies an approximately 13 percent real expenditure growth per capita. Changes in the demographics due to an aging population account for only a small fraction of this real growth (around 3 percent), and the remainder is caused by an increase in treated prevalence, holding the population demographics constant.[5] It is also worth highlighting that the growth rate of the disease price and the service price are quite

---

3. This figure is taken from the CMS national health expenditure accounts.

4. The population growth rate for the commercial sector is calculated based on Current Population Survey data.

5. These figures are all based on the full sample estimates. The relative magnitudes change only slightly when the sample of fixed data contributors is applied.

similar, indicating that using the disease price, rather than the service price, may not affect aggregate measures of inflation for the time period studied.[6]

There are several other methodological issues that arise when studying the components of expenditure growth that are not covered in this chapter. Some of these topics are covered in companion pieces to this work: (1) Dunn, Liebman, Rittmueller, and Shapiro (2014) examine different approaches for assigning medical services to disease categories and the effect on the components of expenditure growth; (2) Dunn, Liebman, and Shapiro (2014) examine alternative strategies for separating utilization and price, and look at how this affects the decomposition; (3) Dunn, Shapiro, and Liebman (2013) study the geographic differences in expenditure levels across MSAs (metropolitan statistical areas). Also, it should be noted that the primary focus of this chapter is to discuss samples and the application of population weights, so several interesting economic trends observed in our indexes are not discussed in detail here. See Dunn, Liebman, and Shapiro (2012) for a more in-depth economic analysis of medical-care expenditure trends. Each of these papers, including this one, offer essential contributions to the ultimate goal of developing a health-care satellite account for the US economy (see Rosen and Cutler [2007] and http://www.bea.gov/national/health_care_satellite_account.htm).

This chapter is divided into five sections. First, we discuss our methodology for medical-care expenditure construction. Next, we discuss the data used in our analysis and present some descriptive statistics. We then present our results and discuss the sensitivity of these results. In the last section, we conclude.

16.2   Methodology of Index Construction

The decomposition methodology of this paper borrows heavily from Dunn, Liebman, and Shapiro (2012) looking at expenditure growth. To begin, we start with a measure of expenditure per capita for disease d for time period t, which is

$$C_{d,t} = \frac{Total\ Expenditures_{d,t}}{Commercial\ Population_t}.$$

A measure of medical-care expenditure growth per capita from period 0 (the base period) to t is then the expenditure per capita index (ECI):

(1) $$ECI_{d,t} = \frac{C_{d,t}}{C_{d,0}}.$$

Since the denominator of the $C_{d,t}$ term is the full commercially insured population, this measure of expenditure growth does not take into account the health of the population. For instance, if expenditures are higher in the second period because more individuals develop heart disease, the $C_{d,t}$ will grow, even if the expenditure per heart disease episode do not change. Alternatively, $C_{d,t}$ may grow if the expenditure per heart disease episode increases, even if the population of individuals with heart disease remains unchanged.

16.2.1 Expenditure Per Capita Decomposition: Expenditure Per Episode and Treated Prevalence

Given the expenditure per capita index, we next decompose ECI into the prevalence of the condition and the expenditure per episode. We start by dividing $C_{d,t}$ into two components. One component of the expenditure per capita is the prevalence of treated disease, $prev_{d,t}$. Prevalence of treated disease d is the number of episodes treated in the population for disease d, $N_{d,t}$, divided by the commercially insured population:

$$prev_{d,t} = \frac{N_{d,t}}{Commercial\ Population_t}.$$

Note that prevalence includes only those instances where there is awareness of a disease and treatment was provided. It therefore excludes those instances where the individual is unaware of their condition.[7] The second component of expenditure per population is the expenditure per episode or average expenditure for treating disease d, $c_{d,t}$. The value $c_{d,t}$ may be calculated by dividing total expenditures of disease d by the number of episodes of disease d in period t,

$$c_{d,t} = \frac{Total\ Expenditures_{d,t}}{N_{d,t}}.$$

Distinct indexes may be constructed from each of these two components. One component is the growth in treated prevalence, relative to the base period:

$$PREV_{d,t} = \frac{prev_{d,t}}{prev_{d,0}}.$$

The second component is the change in expenditures per case relative to the base period:

$$(2) \qquad MCE_{d,t} = \frac{c_{d,t}}{c_{d,0}}.$$

---

7. Those individuals that have a condition but are unaware that they have a condition or do not seek medical attention for their condition would be considered in measuring the population's prevalence, but are not included in the treated prevalence figure.

These two components of expenditure capture distinct elements of its growth. Changes in the prevalence of a treated condition capture the changing health of the population, such as the growth in diabetes due to obesity. It may also reflect a growing awareness of a condition, such as the increase in awareness and diagnosis of high cholesterol. The second component may be viewed as the change in the price for treating the disease, d, which includes the prices of those services and also the mix and utilization of those services provided.

Using these equations, one can see that the expenditure per capita is then the cost per episode times the prevalence, $C_{d,t} = c_{d,t} prev_{d,t}$. From this we can see that the $ECI_{d,t}$ may be decomposed into the expenditure per episode index, $MCE_{d,t}$, and the treated prevalence index, $PREV_{d,t}$:

$$ECI_{d,t} = MCE_{d,t} + PREV_{d,t} + \frac{(prev_{d,t} - prev_{d,0})(c_{d,t} - c_{d,0})}{prev_{d,0}c_{d,0}} - 1.^8$$

This equation makes it clear that a population-based measure of expenditure for a particular disease will rise if there is either an increase in the prevalence of the disease or an increase in the expenditures per episode.

The indexes presented here are directly related to a simple and often reported figure, total medical-care expenditures per capita. To see this, we can create aggregate disease-specific indexes for the population-based measure, $ECI_{d,t}$. When $ECI_{d,t}$ is weighted by the national expenditure share for each disease in the base period, this becomes a measure of medical-care expenditures per person relative to the base periods' medical-care expenditures per person:

$$ECI_t = \sum_D ECI_{d,t}(\text{Expenditure Share}_0) = \sum_D \frac{C_{d,t}}{C_{d,0}}\left(\frac{C_{d,0}}{\sum_D C_{d,0}}\right)$$

$$= \frac{\sum_D C_{d,t}}{\sum_D C_{d,0}} = \frac{\text{Medical-Care Expenditures Per Capita}_t}{\text{Medical-Care Expenditures Per Capita}_0}.$$

This measure *includes* any change attributable to the prevalence of certain diseases. Thus this measure will grow along with disease prevalence. The measure may also reflect the changing demographics of the population, such as the growth from an aging population. As we will discuss later, we typically apply population weights that may change the meaning of these indexes. For instance, we may apply weights that hold the age, sex, and location characteristics of the population constant, so that changes in prevalence do not affect these demographic changes. Population weights will be discussed in greater detail in the following section. Next, we further decompose the disease expenditures per episode into a service price component and a service utilization component.

8. A decomposition using logs is: $\log(ECI_{d,t}) = \log(MCE_{d,t}) + \log(PREV_{d,t})$.

16.2.2   Expenditure Per Episode Decomposition: Service Price and Service Utilization

The MCE index is a measure of the medical-care expenditures for the treatment of an episode of care for a certain disease, and is defined as the dollar amount of medical care used until treatment is completed.[9] Since this index controls for the health of the population, it may be viewed as measuring the cost of treatment. Thus, if the $MCE_{d,t}$ is larger than one, it signifies that the expenditure for treating disease d is larger than the base period and if the index is less than one it signifies that the expenditure is less than the base period.

Our decomposition rests on the fact that the average expenditure, $c_{d,t}$, can be divided between a service price and service utilization component. This can be seen more easily by showing that the average expenditure is calculated by totaling dollars spent on all services to treat the condition and dividing those dollars by the number of episodes: $c_{d,t} = \Sigma_s p_{d,t,s} Q_{d,t,s} / N_{d,t}$, where $Q_{d,t,s}$ is the quantity of services for service type, s; $p_{d,t,s}$ is the service price for service type s; and $N_{d,t}$ is the number of episodes treated.

Measuring service utilization is not a straightforward task since the definition of a "service" is a bit ambiguous and there are a variety of ways that one could define it across various service types.[10] The approach taken here to define service utilization closely follows the methodology of Dunn, Shapiro, and Liebman (2013). Ideally, we would like the definition of a specific service to depend on how the price of that service is typically set and paid. For example, for physician services, individuals pay a unique price for each procedure done to them (i.e., the insurer and the patient together pay this amount). Therefore, we would like service utilization to reflect the amount of procedures done. Since not all procedures are equivalent, we weight each procedure by the average dollar amount paid for that procedure. This is a similar concept to a "relative value unit" or "RVU," which measures the approximate cost of each procedure and is used by Medicare to reimburse physicians for each procedure that is performed.[11] For prescription drugs, we define the unit of service as a prescription filled, albeit this is a bit of a misnomer since a prescription is really a "good," not a service. Because pre-

---

9. For example, for an individual with a broken foot, the episode of treatment will be defined by the dollar amount of medical services used to treat that condition from the first visit to a provider until the foot is healed. For medical conditions that are chronic, we interpret an episode as expenditure for services used to treat the chronic condition over a one-year period.

10. The key service types are inpatient hospital, outpatient hospital, general physician, physician specialist, and prescription drugs.

11. This framework has also been adopted by the commercial market. In a survey of twenty health plans conducted by Dyckman & Associates, all twenty health plan fee schedules were influenced by a resource-based relative value scale (RBRVS). There are deviations from the basic RBRVS methodology, so taking the average of observed prices in the market for each procedure is one measure used for capturing the typical "resources" used for a procedure.

scriptions vary depending on the active ingredient, the manufacturer, and strength, we weight each unique drug purchase by the average dollar amount we observe for that particular prescription across time periods. For hospital facility charges for inpatient stays, the prices paid to facilities are often set based on the disease and the number of visits to a facility. Therefore, for inpatient stays we define the unit of service as a visit. For outpatient facility services we also define the service as the visit itself. The exact construction of these measures is explained in more detail later in this chapter.

Given the definition of service and expenditure, the price for a particular service type and disease can be calculated by dividing its expenditure by the quantity of services provided: $p_{d,t,s} = c_{d,t,s}/Q_{d,t,s}$ where $c_{d,t,s}$ is the average expenditure on disease d for service type s at time t. For example, the price of an inpatient stay for treating heart disease is the total expenditure of inpatient treatment for heart disease in a time period, divided by the quantity of inpatient services for heart disease in that time period.

This decomposition allows us to create a service price and service utilization index. To simplify, let $q_{d,t}$ be a vector of services utilized for the typical treatment of diseases in a period t, $q_{d,t} = Q_{d,t}/N_{d,t}$, where the elements of the utilization vector for service type s is, $Q_{d,t,s}/N_{d,t}$. Also, let $p_{d,t}$ be a vector of service prices, where the elements of the vector for service type s is $p_{d,t,s}$. The service price index (SPI) is then calculated as:

$$SPI_{d,t} = \frac{p_{d,t}q_{d,0}}{c_{d,0}},$$

which holds the utilization of services fixed at a base period level, but allows prices to vary. Similarly, the service utilization index (SUI) may be defined as:

$$SUI_{d,t} = \frac{p_{d,0}q_{d,t}}{c_{d,0}},$$

which holds the price of services fixed while allowing the utilization of services to vary. Note that there is a precise relationship between these three indexes that is described by the following decomposition:

$$MCE_{d,t} = SPI_{d,t} + SUI_{d,t} + \frac{(q_{d,t} - q_{d,0})(p_{d,t} - p_{d,0})}{c_{d,0}} - \frac{p_{d,0}q_{d,0}}{c_{d,0}}.$$

Here the MCE index is equal to the service price index, $SPI_{d,t}$, plus the service utilization index, $SUI_{d,t}$, plus a cross term,

$$\frac{(q_{d,t} - q_{d,0})(p_{d,t} - p_{d,0})}{c_{d,0}}, \text{ and subtracting } \frac{p_{d,0}q_{d,0}}{c_{d,0}},$$

(which is close to 1). The cross term accounts for joint changes in both price vectors and utilization vectors and, in practice, the term is near zero. In the case where there are very few changes in utilization over time, $SUI_{d,t}$ is fixed near 1, then the $MCE_{d,t}$ will entirely be determined by service prices. Similarly, if there are very few changes in service prices over time, $SPI_{d,t}$ is near 1, and the $MCE_{d,t}$ will entirely be determined by utilization.

Both the $SPI_{d,t}$ and $SUI_{d,t}$ are Laspeyre indexes. By presenting the additive decomposition earlier that includes the Laspeyre price and utilization indexes, we allow the reader to calculate any of the standard indexes (such as the Laspeyre, Passche, or Fisher indexes) to examine the sensitivity of the results that are presented. Alternatively we could have reported a Laspyre price index and a Paasche utilization index:

$$SUI_{d,t}^{Paasche} = \frac{MCE_{d,t}}{SPI_{d,t}^{Laspeyre}} = \frac{p_{d,t}q_{d,t}}{p_{d,t}q_{d,0}},$$

but with this limited information, the reader would not be able to calculate other indexes of potential interest, such as the $SPI_{d,t}^{Paasche}$.[12]

16.3   Data

We use retrospective claims data for a sample of commercially insured patients from the MarketScan Research Database from Truven Health. The specific claims data used is the Commercial Claims and Encounters Database, which contains data from the employer and health plan sources containing medical and drug data for several million commercially insured individuals, including employees, their spouses, and dependents. Each observation in the data corresponds to a line item in an "explanation of benefits" form; therefore each claim can consist of many records and each encounter can consist of many claims.

We use a sample of enrollees that are not in capitated plans from the MarketScan database for the years 2003 to 2007. We also limit our sample to enrollees with drug benefits because drug purchases will not be observed for individuals without drug coverage. The MarketScan database tracks claims from all providers using a nationwide convenience sample of enrollees. Each enrollee has a unique identifier and includes age, sex, and region information that may be used when calculating population weights. All claims have been paid and adjudicated.[13]

The claims data has been processed using the Symmetry grouper from Optum. The grouper assigns each claim to a particular Episode Treatment Group (ETG) disease category.[14] The grouper uses a proprietary algorithm,

---

12. That is,

$$SPI_{d,t}^{Paasche} = \frac{MCE_{d,t}}{SUI_{d,t}^{Laspeyre}} = \frac{p_{d,t}q_{d,t}}{p_{d,0}q_{d,t}}.$$

13. Additional details about the data and the grouper used in this chapter are in Dunn, Liebman, Pack, and Shapiro (2012).

14. The ETG grouper allocates each record into one of over 500 disease groups. To ensure that we observe full episodes, we limit the sample to those enrollees that have a full year of continuous enrollment. In addition, we require that enrollees have one year of enrollment in the

based on clinical knowledge, that is applied to the claims data to assign each record to a clinically homogenous episode. The episode grouper allocates all spending from individual claim records to a distinct condition; the grouper also uses other information on the claim (e.g., procedures) and information from the patient's history to allocate the spending. An advantage of using the grouper is that it can use patients' medical history to assign diseases to drug claims, which typically do not provide a diagnosis. However, these algorithms are also considered a "black box" in the sense that they rely entirely on the expertise of those that developed the grouper software.

15.3.1 Service Price, Utilization, and Episodes

The number of episodes is a simple count of the total number of episodes of a medical disease for that calendar year. Total episode expenditures are measured as the total dollar amount received by all providers for the services used to treat an episode of a specific disease (including both out-of-pocket payments and amounts paid by insurance carriers).

We created utilization measures, which indicate the quantity of services per episode, based on the specific definitions of services. The service type categories are physician, inpatient hospital, outpatient hospital, prescription drug, and other. Using the definitions of the unit of service for each service type, the price of the service is calculated as the total expenditures for a particular disease and service category, divided by the quantity of services performed for that disease and service category. Furthermore, service utilization for a particular category is defined as the quantity of services divided by the total number of episodes for a particular disease. A listing of the service types and how the quantity of services is measured follows below.

Physician office: Expenditures from physician office visits are from procedures performed in a physician's office. We assign a measure comparable to an RVU for each procedure performed by the physician for that office visit. Specifically, for each Current Procedure Terminology (CPT) code and modifier code, we calculate a relative value unit by computing the average fee for that procedure performed in an office setting. The total amount of services performed in an office is calculated by summing over these calculated RVUs. Note that there is a simple interpretation of these amounts. For example, if the fees are the same as the average computed in our sample, then the total cost of office visit divided by the amount of the visit will be equal to 1.[15]

---

prior year and one year of enrollment in the following year to make sure that episodes occurring at the beginning or the end of a year are not truncated. This may be an overly conservative constraint on the sample of enrollees, and we are currently working on examining the sensitivity of our analysis to alternative assumptions on enrollment.

15. Although procedure codes are observed for 98 percent of physician office claim lines, in those cases for which we do not observe a procedure code we calculate the average price for a missing procedure code for patients with a particular disease. The results of the chapter do not change substantially if those claim lines missing procedure codes are dropped from the analysis.

Hospital inpatient: Inpatient hospital stays consist of both facility fees paid to the hospital and fees paid to the physician. For the portion of fees paid to the hospital, the amount of services is measured as the average dollar amount for an inpatient stay for the observed disease. For the portion of fees paid to the physician, we assign an RVU in the same way that we calculate an RVU in an office setting. The total amount of services performed in an inpatient setting is calculated by adding the physician and facility amounts.[16]

Hospital outpatient: Outpatient hospital visits are calculated in an identical fashion to the inpatient hospital visits. That is, the facility amount is calculated based on the average outpatient visit for that disease, and the doctor's portion of the total amount is calculated based on the average payment for the procedure codes.

Prescription drugs: The amount of the prescription drug varies based on the molecule, the number of pills in the bottle, the strength of the drug, and the manufacturer. To capture these differences, we calculate the average price for each National Drug Code (NDC), since each prescription is given a unique NDC. The average price for each NDC represents the amount of the service used. If the expenditure on a prescription is greater than this amount, it suggests that prices are above average in the given time period.[17]

All other: The other category primarily includes ambulatory care, independent labs, and emergency room visits. For these services, the amount of each category is measured as the average cost for a visit to that particular place of service, for example, the average cost of an ambulatory care visit to treat ischemic heart disease. For cases where procedure codes are available, we use the average cost of that procedure code for that place of service.

There are a few additional points to note. A small fraction of the procedures (less than 5 percent of the claims observations for nonfacility claim lines) are missing procedure codes. For these procedures we use the average price of the missing procedure codes for that service and disease type. Additional details regarding how the quantity of different services are measured are discussed in greater detail in Dunn, Shapiro, and Liebman (2013).

15.3.2 Population Weights and Samples

In an attempt to make the MarketScan convenience sample more representative, we apply poststratification population weights. Some of our estimates apply *fixed demographic weights* that hold the age and location distribution constant. Fixed population weights are important if one is interested in isolating the performance of the medical-care sector, rather

---

16. As an alternative, we have also examined changing this definition to consider the facility price per inpatient day. The results do not change significantly based on these two alternative measures of utilization.

17. An eleven-digit NDC uniquely identifies the manufacturer, strength, dosage, formulation, package size, and type of package.

than looking at the effects of an aging population on expenditures. As one example, we construct weights based on the four regions, age, and sex of the individuals, so that when the weights are applied, the population distribution corresponds to the US 2007 population in each year. The population estimates are specific to the privately insured population below 65, where the estimates are from the Current Population Survey (CPS).

In addition to the broadly defined area that apply regional weights, we also look at a more finely defined geographic area that fixes the population at the county level. Checking the estimates by applying county weights may be important, given that prior research has demonstrated significant variation in medical-care service prices and utilization across markets, even within a region (see Dunn, Shapiro, and Liebman 2013). When applying county weights, we use only those counties where we observe at least 2,000 individuals in the sample in each year. The weights are applied so that every county included in the study has an age and sex distribution identical to the 2007 US population. Each county contributes to the US and total estimates in proportion to the county's population.

While many researchers may be interested in the estimates from the fixed demographic weights, we also apply alternative population weights that match the changing population characteristics in each year. These weights are based on the location, age, and sex of individuals, so that the change in the weighted characteristics of the sample match the actual change in the population characteristics. We will refer to these as *changing demographic weights*. These weights will be important when trying to benchmark our spending estimates to other national estimates of health expenditure growth, such as commercial premium growth rates. Contrasting these estimates with the fixed population weights also helps us to better understand how the changes in the demographics of the population may impact spending growth figures. As discussed in greater detail in Dunn, Liebman, and Shapiro (2012), the difference between the changing demographic weights and the fixed demographic weights may be used to isolate the contribution of the changing demographics on the expenditure growth estimates.

In addition to the application of different population weights, we also explore alternative subsamples in the MarketScan data. One concern with the MarketScan data is that the data contributors are changing over time and, more specifically, the overall sample is growing considerably. For this reason, we study an alternative sample that focuses on a fixed set of data contributors. That is, those insurers and employers that contribute to the MarketScan data are selected if they contribute to the database in each year of the sample. When exploring this alternative sample, we also explore the use of different population weights on this subsample.

In all of our analysis, we exclude individuals that are in capitated plans and those that do not have drug benefits. These restrictions are important, since we have incomplete spending information on these individuals.

16.3.3   Descriptive Statistics

To better understand how the unweighted sample compares to the weighted sample, it is useful to compare the demographic characteristics of the actual commercial population with the unweighted MarketScan data. Table 16.1 reports a number of descriptive statistics for the commercial population and unweighted MarketScan data. The first thing to note about the MarketScan data is that the sample size is large and grows very rapidly over the period of study, with 7.0 million enrollees in the data in 2003 and 13.1 million in 2007.

The sample size is a major advantage of using the MarketScan data compared to a nationally representative survey, such as the Medical Expenditure Panel Survey, which is a survey containing the response of just 30,000 individuals in each year. Since many important and costly medical conditions are relatively rare and heterogeneous (such as cancers or heart attacks), a survey that has just 30,000 individuals may not be sufficient to be representative of the disease costs of many conditions, not to mention the typical

Table 16.1	Population levels and distributions for the commercial population and unweighted MarketScan data			
	Commercial population		Unweighted MarketScan	
	2003	2007	2003	2007
Number of enrollees (millions)	180.6	182.5	7.0	13.1
Gender (%)				
Male	49.5	49.6	47.9	48.5
Female	50.5	50.4	52.1	51.5
Age				
0 to 17	27.3	26.3	25.3	26.4
18 to 24	9.6	9.6	7.8	7.6
25 to 34	14.5	14.7	12.1	11.9
35 to 54	36.3	35.6	38.3	37.6
55 and over	12.2	13.8	16.6	16.5
Mean age	32.3	32.9	34.5	34.1
Region				
NE	19.3	18.9	11.5	12.0
MW	24.4	23.7	29.4	24.3
S	34.0	34.3	45.5	48.0
W	22.3	23.1	13.7	15.7

Notes: Commercial population estimates are taken from the CPS estimates of the commercially insured population, while unweighted MarketScan estimates are enrollee counts from the MarketScan data for individuals in noncapitated plans with drug benefits that are enrolled for the entire year.

challenges and limitations that arise when conducting consumer surveys. Despite the sample size, it is important to keep in mind that the MarketScan data is still a limited sample and represents just a fraction of the overall commercial population, between 3.8 and 7.1 percent of the total commercial population, over the period of study. Therefore, ensuring that the population characteristics reflect the national population of the commercially insured individuals may be vital for obtaining reasonable estimates.

The distribution of the demographics in the MarketScan data is roughly similar to the commercial population estimates, based on the age and sex distributions. However, it is important to highlight a few key differences that potentially have an impact on our expenditure decomposition estimates. First, the location of individuals in the commercial population and the unweighted population are quite distinct. The unweighted MarketScan data disproportionately draws enrollees from the South, with over 45 percent of the sample coming from that region, compared to 34 percent for the actual population. Second, the average age in the unweighted MarketScan data is higher than in the commercial population by two years, which could potentially lead to an upward bias on the unweighted data when looking at estimates of expenditure per capita. Third, the trends in the average age are distinct. The commercial population reflects the aging population in the United States, with the average age growing by 0.6 years, while the average age in the unweighted MarketScan data actually declines by 0.4 years over the period, leading to a total difference in the age growth of one year. This may lead to a downward bias in spending growth when using the unweighted MarketScan data.

Table 16.1 shows that the demographics of the MarketScan sample differ in some ways from that of the commercial population estimates. Next, we look at some basic per capita expenditure and expenditure growth estimates in table 16.2, where we contrast estimates when population weights are applied (the first three columns) to estimates when population weights are not applied (the last three columns). The weights applied here are changing population weights, which allow the population distribution to reflect the characteristics of the actual population in each year. These expenditures are broken into Major Practice Categories (MPC), where they are listed in order of 2003 per capita expenditures, and the bottom row shows per capita spending. We see average expenditures tend to be greater for the unweighted population, with average per capita expenditures in the unweighted sample about 12 percent greater in the unweighted sample than in the weighted sample in 2003. We also see that expenditure growth is over 6 percent greater in the weighted sample compared to the unweighted sample. The higher growth rates appear for some important disease categories that tend to increase with age. The category that stands out the most is the growth rate for the cardiology conditions that are 10 percentage points greater in the weighted sample

Table 16.2　Total annual per capita expenditures, shares, and growth by major practice category: Weighted and unweighted

Major practice category	Changing commercial population weights			Unweighted		
	2003 spending per capita ($)	2003 share of spending (%)	Growth 2003–2007	2003 spending per capita ($)	2003 share of spending (%)	Growth 2003–2007
Orthopedics and rheumatology	415.34	16.51	1.32	460.72	16.41	1.26
Cardiology	304.21	12.09	1.12	382.64	13.63	1.02
Gastroenterology	229.27	9.11	1.30	260.39	9.27	1.23
Gynecology	179.26	7.13	1.21	201.71	7.18	1.14
Endocrinology	166.12	6.60	1.42	193.35	6.89	1.35
Otolaryngology	159.57	6.34	1.16	166.47	5.93	1.16
Neurology	147.50	5.86	1.30	161.03	5.74	1.24
Pulmonology	121.08	4.81	1.16	138.85	4.95	1.10
Psychiatry	118.58	4.71	1.23	115.23	4.10	1.23
Dermatology	113.49	4.51	1.30	116.08	4.13	1.29
Obstetrics	111.29	4.42	1.22	96.51	3.44	1.18
Urology	90.53	3.60	1.24	103.81	3.70	1.17
Hematology	61.79	2.46	1.34	67.65	2.41	1.29
Hepatology	60.85	2.42	1.08	69.35	2.47	1.00
Preventive and administrative	57.25	2.28	1.73	60.96	2.17	1.70
Ophthalmology	40.00	1.59	1.25	46.24	1.65	1.18
Infectious diseases	35.45	1.41	1.37	38.61	1.38	1.35
Nephrology	34.32	1.36	1.26	40.96	1.46	1.20
Neonatology	25.26	1.00	1.39	40.92	1.46	1.30
Isolated signs and symptoms	18.67	0.74	1.13	19.20	0.68	1.11
Late effects, environmental trauma, and poisonings	13.72	0.55	1.24	14.83	0.53	1.18
Chemical dependency	11.80	0.47	1.58	12.09	0.43	1.50
Total	2,515.36	100.00	1.265	2,807.60	100.00	1.204

Notes: Commercial population per capita spending estimates by disease are calculated by multiplying disease expenditures by changing population weights, summing over spending, and then dividing by the full population. Unweighted MarketScan estimates are per capita expenditure estimates by disease category.

Table 16.3   **Per capita spending and premium benchmarks**

	2003–2007
Spending growth benchmarks	
NHEA-Private insurance	1.261
NHEA: All categories	1.246
BEA: All categories	1.222
Premium growth	
MEPS-Insurance component	1.265
Kaiser Employer Health Benefit Survey	1.332

Notes: The 2007 premium figures for the MEPS-Insurance component estimates are imputed from 2006 and 2008 estimates. Both the Kaiser premium estimates and the MEPS-IC estimates assume that 47 percent of employees are enrolled in a single plan and the remainder in family plans. The percentage was derived from the MEPS-Insurance Component 2003 estimates.

relative to the unweighted sample. However, more generally, the growth rates for most condition categories are greater in the weighted sample, relative to the unweighted sample.[18]

To check whether the spending growth rates are in a reasonable range, we compare the aforementioned growth rates with benchmark growth rates from other sources. When making this comparison, one should keep in mind that the estimate that we offer from the MarketScan commercial claims data set are unique and independent of the other sources, so we should not expect the benchmark estimates to precisely match the estimates that we are computing. However, the underlying factors affecting growth here should correspond to expenditures by private insurers from the National Health Expenditure Accounts (NHEA) and estimates of premium growth rates. We find that the growth rate in our weighted estimates match very closely with NHEA expenditures for private insurers and premium growth rates from the MEPS data, which are arguably the two most relevant data sources in this study (see table 16.3). Although the Kaiser Health Benefits Survey offers premium estimates, the estimate is based on a much smaller sample size of around 2,000 firms, compared with a sample of about 40,000 firms in the MEPS-IC data. The other spending growth benchmarks (i.e., the NHEA: all categories, and BEA: all categories) include other sources of payment, such as Medicare and Medicaid. Overall, the estimates from the weighted

18. In both the weighted and unweighted samples, about 13 percent of expenditures are not assigned to any ETG disease category. This includes screening for diseases and other records that cannot be assigned a disease category. Those claims that are not assigned disease categories are removed from our analysis. In most of the analysis we apply severity adjustment, which increases the share of ungrouped expenditures to 20 percent, since some episodes may be assigned a disease but not a severity level. As we will show later, similar results are found whether severity adjustment is applied or not, so removing those ungrouped claims that cannot be severity adjusted has little effect on our results. See Dunn, Liebman, and Shapiro (2012) for additional discussion regarding disease classification.

sample fall in a reasonable range to these benchmark estimates, while the unweighted sample falls a few percentage points below these benchmarks, which lends greater confidence to our weighted estimates. Matching expenditure growth rates to relevant expenditure benchmarks helps to bolster the case for applying population weights. In the next section, we focus on expenditure growth decompositions that apply age, sex, and location weights, although we continue to contrast our results with unweighted estimates.

16.4   Results

Table 16.4 compares the expenditure growth decomposition using the unweighted data to weighted data that allows the population distribution to reflect national population estimates and changes in the distribution of the population. We see that the weighted ECI grows at 26.5 percent, about 6 percentage points faster than the unweighted estimates. This expenditure growth difference reflects per capita spending changes that are also reported at the bottom of table 16.2. However, in table 16.4 we observe the sources of the expenditure growth differences in greater detail. The faster prevalence growth in the weighted data accounts for 2 percent of the difference in the ECI index and faster MCE growth (along with a cross-term difference) accounting for the remainder. Although we observe some differences in the weighted and unweighted estimates, there are also some interesting common patterns. In both sets of estimates we see utilization per episode remaining relatively flat or falling slightly, while expenditure growth is primarily driven by an increase in PREV and SPI.

Table 16.5 reports decomposition growth figures for some additional weighting strategies and samples, where each row of the table shows a dis-

Table 16.4	Decomposition of growth rates, 2003–2007 (weighted and unweighted)				
	ECI	PREV	MCE	SPI	SUI
Weighted: Changing comm. population					
2003	1.000	1.000	1.000	1.000	1.000
2004	1.070	1.039	1.033	1.028	1.007
2005	1.149	1.082	1.065	1.063	1.005
2006	1.211	1.106	1.100	1.104	1.003
2007	1.265	1.144	1.114	1.134	0.995
Unweighted					
2003	1.000	1.000	1.000	1.000	1.000
2004	1.066	1.042	1.026	1.024	1.004
2005	1.130	1.080	1.051	1.059	0.996
2006	1.159	1.085	1.074	1.095	0.988
2007	1.204	1.123	1.080	1.120	0.977

Notes: Estimates are computed using ETG severity adjustments. To save space, the cross terms from the different components of the decomposition are not reported.

tinct estimate of the growth decomposition for the 2003 to 2007 period. The first two rows repeat the unweighted and weighted estimates reported in table 16.4, but only shows the values of the index for 2007. The third row of the table holds the age, sex, and regional distribution constant to 2007 levels. As mentioned previously, many researchers may be interested in growth estimates that hold demographic factors constant to better isolate the trends in treatment patterns for similar populations. In Dunn, Liebman, and Shapiro (2012), this expenditure estimate is called the demographically adjusted expenditure per capita index (DECI). The difference in spending between the changing population weights and the fixed population weights is around 3.5 percentage points, with most of the differences in growth being driven by prevalence, as expected, since disease prevalence increases with age for many health conditions.[19] One concern with the application of regional weights is that focusing on regional weights may not capture the trends that are observed at a finer geographic level. Row 4 of table 16.5 reports estimates that fix the population distribution for each county to 2007 levels, rather than fixing the regional population.[20] The estimates applying county weights are nearly identical to the regional weight in every dimension, suggesting that the application of either county or regional weights may be appropriate for the study of the MarketScan claims data.

As mentioned previously, one might be concerned that changes in data contributors in the MarketScan data may have a measurable impact on our study in ways that are difficult to correct for. As an alternative estimate, we next focus on a subsample of the data that holds the data contributors fixed (including only those data contributors that are in the sample from 2003 to 2007). These estimates are shown in the bottom half of table 16.5. The qualitative estimates of this subsample are quite similar to the full sample that applies population weights. The key difference is that the growth rate using the fixed contributors from the MCE is 3 percentage points higher by 2007, and the prevalence index is 2 percentage points lower over this period. Although these differences are notable, we calculate that based on CAGR estimates, the difference in the various components of the decomposition are less than 0.007 percentage points for each component of the decomposition across the two samples. The same aggregate patterns hold for these alternative sets of estimates. All of the estimates imply that prevalence and service price growth are the key contributors to expenditure growth.

Focusing on the estimates that apply changing population weights, note that the fixed contributor sample appears in a reasonable range to our national benchmark spending growth estimates reported in table 16.3, but

19. In the paper Dunn, Liebman, and Shapiro (2012) the ECI reported in table 5 that applies the fixed population weight is referred to as the demographically adjusted expenditure per capita index, or DECI.

20. Recall that the sample is slightly different than the regional estimates, since we only keep those estimates that have at least 2,000 enrollees in each year of the sample.

Table 16.5   Decomposition of growth rates from 2003 to 2007 for different weights and samples

	ECI	PREV	MCE	SPI	SUI
Full MarketScan sample: Changing contributors					
Unweighted	1.204	1.123	1.080	1.114	0.971
Changing regional population weights	1.265	1.144	1.114	1.134	0.995
Regional weights, fixed demog.	1.231	1.118	1.110	1.132	0.993
County weights, fixed demog.	1.235	1.118	1.110	1.130	0.996
Fixed contributors					
Unweighted	1.247	1.114	1.124	1.153	0.989
Changing regional population weights	1.283	1.128	1.143	1.160	0.998
Regional weights, fixed demog.	1.250	1.103	1.139	1.159	0.996
County weights, fixed demog.	1.231	1.093	1.132	1.145	1.004

Notes: Estimates are computed using ETG severity adjustments. To save space, the cross terms from the different components of the decomposition are not reported.

about 1.8 percentage points higher than growth from the NHEA expenditure estimates. Another important set of national statistics that we may benchmark against are service price measures. The key benchmark price estimate is the BEA GDP health services price deflator, which shows a growth rate of 13.7 for the period of study. The SPI estimates that apply population weights centers around this figure, with growth rates ranging from 13.0 percent to 16.0 percent.[21]

Table 16.5 presents a range of estimates, but researchers should be aware of the trade-off to using the fixed contributor sample is that the sample size shrinks significantly in each year, with about 1 million fewer enrollees in 2003 (losing about 20 percent of the sample) compared to the full sample, and 5 million fewer enrollees in 2007. There are trade-offs when choosing between the full sample or the sample with fixed data contributors. The full sample contains more enrollees and more data contributors in each year, but may be influenced by changes in the type of data contributors across years. On the other hand, the sample with the fixed data contributors is a smaller sample size and may be more influenced by particular data contributors. Given this trade-off, in our work we look at both estimates and search for consistent patterns across each.

The results presented here may also be used to look at whether spending is growing due to treated prevalence or if spending is primarily rising due to growth in the MCE. Looking across the various estimates of table 16.5 that hold population fixed, the MCE growth accounts for between 46 per-

21. It should be highlighted that an important difference between our estimates and those of the BEA health services price deflator is that our estimates only contain private health insurance claims, while the GDP health services price deflator includes information on payments from all types of payers (e.g., private, Medicare, and Medicaid.). This could account for some of the difference.

cent to 55 percent of the expenditure growth, with prevalence (along with a cross term) accounting for the remainder. Therefore, growing prevalence and expenditure per case similarly contribute to overall spending growth. To compare these results to the analysis of Roehrig and Rousseau (2011), who perform a similar calculation, we first need to adjust spending and prices for overall inflation growth (which was 11.5 percent over this period). After making this adjustment, the "real" share of growth attributed to expenditure per case would actually range from 17.5 percent to –4.0 percent.[22] This result stands in stark contrast to the findings of Roehrig and Rousseau (2011) that use the Medical Expenditure Panel Survey data and find after adjusting for inflation that about 75 percent of spending growth may be attributed to expenditures per episode. Although Roehrig and Rousseau (2011) study a distinct period, 1996 to 2006, the work by Aizcorbe et al. (2011) that look at a more recent period (2001 to 2005) finds similarly rapid growth in expenditure per episode using the MEPS data. Additional work is necessary to better understand this discrepancy across the two data sources.

16.4.1   Heterogenous Trends in the Components of Expenditure Growth

The previous section focused on the aggregate trends in disease expenditure growth. However, there are differences in the growth rate for many disease conditions and their components, which is reported in table 16A.1 in the appendix. Differences in growth rates across diseases is discussed and analyzed in greater detail in Dunn, Liebman, and Shapiro (2012).[23] For instance, in that paper we find unique trends for different disease categories, showing that utilization for cardiology conditions are falling on average, while the prevalence of endocrinology conditions (like diabetes or high cholesterol) is growing rapidly. Another dimension in which growth rates could potentially differ is by the age group of individuals, which is particularly relevant for the application of population weights. For instance, if older individuals are overrepresented in the data, then trends will be more influenced by those diseases that tend to afflict older individuals, such as cardiology conditions.[24] However, if the general trends in the components of spending growth are common across age categories, then applying population weights will have less of an impact on the overall trend.

More generally, looking at the components of spending growth by age is informative, since it offers a check on whether the broad trends we observe in table 16.5 are true for all segments of the population, or if there is a particu-

---

22. The negative real growth arises because the expenditure per episode is rising slower than inflation for some estimates.

23. Table 16A.1 of the appendix is taken from Dunn, Liebman, and Shapiro (2012) and reports the components of spending growth for different disease categories. The heterogeneity in disease trends reported in table 16A.1 helps demonstrate the wide differences in the magnitudes of disease expenditures.

24. Clearly the type of diseases treated change with the age of the individual, as can be seen in table 16A.2 in the appendix, which charts expenditure shares as the population ages.

lar segment of the population that is driving spending growth that warrants further analysis. Table 16.6 reports trends in the different components of expenditure growth for the period 2003 to 2007 across different age groups, with each row representing a different age group. The top half of table 16.6 reports the full sample using a fixed population, regional weights. Below the results with the full sample, table 16.6 shows the components of spending growth using fixed contributors and a fixed population, regional weights. The left two columns of the table reports the population share in each age group, along with the expenditure share of that population.

The spending growth patterns for the different age groups in table 16.6 are similar to the patterns observed in table 16.5, for both the full sample and the fixed contributor sample. Utilization growth is relatively flat, and prevalence growth and price growth are the primary drivers of per capita expenditure growth for each age category. The common pattern in the components of expenditure growth is especially striking for age categories of 35 and above, which account for over 70 percent of the spending. Although there are many similarities in growth patterns, there are some noteworthy differences. First, those age categories below 25 tend to experience faster overall spending growth relative to the those over 25, which appears to be caused by both higher service price growth and higher utilization growth. Second, the SUI is growing for those below 35, but declining for those in age categories of 35 and above. Therefore, it appears that younger populations are receiving more

Table 16.6   Components of spending growth for different age categories applying regional fixed demographic weights, 2003–2007

Age group	Population share (%)	Spending share (%)	ECI	PREV	MCE	SPI	SUI
Full MarketScan sample: Changing contributors							
0 to 17	26	12	1.30	1.09	1.20	1.17	1.04
18 to 24	10	5	1.33	1.16	1.15	1.16	1.12
25 to 34	15	12	1.22	1.10	1.11	1.11	1.02
35 to 44	17	17	1.24	1.12	1.11	1.13	1.00
45 to 54	18	26	1.21	1.11	1.09	1.13	0.98
55 to 64	14	29	1.20	1.13	1.08	1.13	0.97
Fixed contributors							
0 to 17	26	12	1.28	1.06	1.21	1.19	1.04
18 to 24	10	5	1.33	1.13	1.19	1.41	1.04
25 to 34	15	12	1.21	1.07	1.14	1.16	1.02
35 to 44	17	16	1.24	1.10	1.14	1.20	1.00
45 to 54	18	26	1.24	1.11	1.13	1.16	0.99
55 to 64	14	29	1.25	1.13	1.11	1.15	0.98

Notes: The spending share is reported based on all five years of data. For both estimates, the population distribution is held fixed to 2007 levels, so regional shifts in population distribution have no effect on these estimates. These trends are computed based on the disease conditions for each age group. Many diseases are not observed across different age groupers.

Table 16.7   Components of spending growth for different regions, 2003–2007

	Pop. share (%)	Spending share (%)	ECI	PREV	MCE	SPI	SUI
		Full MarketScan sample: Changing contributors					
NE	19	18	1.38	1.10	1.26	1.24	1.04
MW	24	24	1.29	1.12	1.16	1.18	1.00
S	34	35	1.14	1.16	0.99	1.05	0.96
W	23	23	1.22	1.06	1.16	1.16	1.02
		Fixed contributors					
NE	19	17	1.34	1.11	1.21	1.21	1.04
MW	24	24	1.29	1.11	1.17	1.20	0.99
S	34	36	1.18	1.11	1.07	1.10	0.99
W	23	23	1.25	1.08	1.16	1.19	1.00

Notes: The spending share is reported based on all five years of data. For both estimates, the population distribution is held fixed to 2007 levels.

treatments for the same disease, relative to older individuals. This may partly reflect that younger individuals spend significantly less on cardiology conditions, a condition category that has seen a decline in utilization per episode.[25]

As with trends in age, similar issues may arise when considering differences in regional growth rates. Some regions may drive growth in different ways relative to others, leading to a bias in national estimates if a particular region is over- or underweighted. Analogous to the estimates presented in table 16.6, the expenditure growth rates and its components for each of the four regions are reported in table 16.7 using both the full sample and the sample with fixed contributors. There are a number of interesting patterns. First, growth in overall spending, as reflected in the ECI, is quite different across regions, ranging from around 38 percent growth in the Northeast to 14 percent growth in the South. The lower growth rate in the South appears to be due to both falling utilization levels and lower price growth, although prevalence growth is similar to or larger than the other regions.

Table 16.7 also shows that the components of growth in the South depend greatly on whether the full sample is used or only the fixed contributors. Prevalence growth differs by 7 percentage points across the full sample and fixed contributor sample, while the MCE growth differs by 6 percentage points. This suggests at least a couple of possibilities. Either the fixed sample is not representative of the population in the South or there is a data contributor entering in the South that greatly affects prevalence and utilization. Using the sample with fixed contributors, the growth rate in the South appears more in line with the other regions and the service price growth rate in the South is closer to the benchmark price growth levels. These trends in the South using the full sample appear far out of line with the other

25. See table 16A.2 that shows the expenditure share for each disease category by age group.

regional estimates and benchmark estimates, suggesting that the sample of fixed data contributors may produce more plausible figures. As a result, this fixed contributor sample is the focus of Dunn, Liebman, and Shapiro (2012). Although this is our current understanding of the data, it is difficult to be sure whether there is an actual bias without additional information.

Tables 16.6 and 16.7 suggest some interesting heterogeneous trends in growth rates that imply different contributions to overall growth. For instance, the slower spending in the South appears to greatly pull down national spending growth trends. Focusing on the fixed contributors sample, the South accounts for 36 percent of expenditures, but just 34 percent of the overall growth. Had the national trends followed the growth trends in the Northeast, national expenditures would be about 9 percent greater. Heterogenous trends by age group also contribute differentially to national growth rates. While those that are under the age of 24 account for 36 percent of the population, they account for just 17 percent of the spending. This low level of spending hides the fact that they contribute disproportionately to the growth rate. The growth rate for this younger population is about 30 percent over the sample period, compared to just 24 percent for the other age groups.

16.5   Some Alternative Approaches

Aside from the application of population weights, there are a number of other issues that researchers should keep in mind when studying expenditure growth. Here we focus briefly on two of these issues: (1) the classification of medical claims into disease episodes; and (2) using the panel structure of claims data.[26]

16.5.1   Disease Classification

Throughout this chapter, we have focused on a single approach for classifying medical claims into disease episodes (i.e., applying the ETG grouper with severity adjustment), but one may be concerned that a different classification strategy may have a large substantive impact on our analysis. Indeed, many research papers have proposed and applied a variety of strategies to classify medical claims into disease categories or disease episodes. In a companion piece to this chapter, Dunn, Liebman, Rittmueller, and Shapiro (2014), look at this issue in greater detail and explore the impact of numerous alternative classification strategies on the components of expenditure growth. They show that many of the key findings are similar across strategies and provide a range of estimates for disease expenditure growth. However,

---

26. Although we highlight these two points, there are some additional robustness checks that we also looked at prior to reporting the estimates in this chapter: (1) removing outlier disease episodes and (2) focusing on the more frequently observed disease episodes (e.g., a minimum of 10,000 observed episodes in the data).

Table 16.8   **Decomposition of growth rates from 2003 to 2007 for different weights and samples (not severity adjusted)**

	ECI	PREV	MCE	SPI	SUI
Full MarketScan sample: Changing contributors					
Unweighted	1.204	1.110	1.089	1.120	0.985
Changing regional population weights	1.265	1.130	1.125	1.133	1.004
Regional weights, 2007 fixed pop.	1.231	1.105	1.119	1.131	1.001
County weights, 2007 fixed pop.	1.235	1.111	1.118	1.129	1.002
Fixed contributors					
Unweighted	1.247	1.105	1.134	1.153	0.997
Changing regional population weights	1.283	1.117	1.155	1.160	1.008
Regional weights, 2007 fixed pop.	1.250	1.093	1.149	1.159	1.004
County weights, 2007 fixed pop.	1.231	1.085	1.141	1.144	1.011

Notes: Estimates are computed using ETG without applying the severity adjustment. To save space, the cross terms from the different components of the decomposition are not reported.

they primarily focus on a single weighting strategy. Similarly, in this study, it is difficult to tell if an alternative classification strategy may have a distinct effect on the estimates, depending on the weighting strategy that is applied.

To provide some range of estimates, we present results using a slightly different disease classification approach, ETG grouping without severity adjustment. Note that severity adjustment accounts for related complications, comorbidities, and demographic factors that may influence the expected utilization of services needed to treat a condition of a particular severity. Therefore, removing severity adjustment produces more aggregate disease categories. Table 16.8 shows these results. There is a very clear and systematic effect from applying nonseverity adjusted ETGs across all estimates: (1) the utilization growth increases slightly (by about 2 percentage points); (2) the MCE grows by about 2 percentage points; and (3) prevalence growth falls by about 2 percentage points. The likely reason for this difference is that there is a growth in the severity of illness within each broad ETG category, leading to more service utilization when collapsing across severity categories. Although we observe some differences, the main qualitative findings remain unchanged.

Since we are primarily interested in understanding the treatment for identical conditions, applying the severity adjustment is our preferred methodology.[27] It should also be noted that when applying a completely different methodology for grouping diseases, the MEG grouper, we find estimates that are consistent to those reported in table 16.8. See Dunn, Liebman, Rittmueller, and Shapiro (2014) for additional discussion.

---

27. As an additional check, we also look at alternative weights using the MEG grouper, and we obtain similar results.

16.5.2   Panel Analysis: Death and Selection Issues

The MarketScan data is a panel data set that tracks individuals over multiple years. This feature of the data is shared by other commercial claims data sets, and there are potentially great advantages from exploiting the panel aspects of the data to study health expenditure growth, where the health condition of each individual may have unique idiosyncrasies that are specific to that individual.

Although the panel aspect of the data appears potentially useful, in this subsection we show how using the panel dimension of the data may actually lead to significant bias. The key problem is that in the first year that an individual enters the panel, we know that those individuals are selected to live at least one more year. In contrast, for the last year that an individual is in the panel, it is not clear whether the individual will be in the data the following year or not, and they could potentially exit the sample through death. In other words, the first year of the panel contains only those individuals that live one additional year, while the last year of the panel includes some individuals that may die in the following year. This fact, combined with the knowledge that the health care for individuals is typically much more expensive in the last year of life, leads to a potentially large and positive selection bias in expenditure growth.

To demonstrate this point, we estimate spending levels for two populations of individuals in 2006: (1) the continuing sample, which includes those individuals that are in the data for the additional full year of 2006; and (2) the exiting sample, which includes those individuals that do not have full enrollment in the following year. We focus on population weighted spending estimates, so the total population and age distribution of the two samples is identical.[28] We find that the per capita spending for the exiting sample is 21 percent higher than the spending for the continuing sample. The allocation of spending also appears distinct. Specifically, for the exiting sample, a greater share of spending is allocated to potentially fatal diseases. For example, the exiting sample allocates 9.9 percent of spending to malignant cancers, while the continuing sample allocates 5.8 percent of spending. We also find more spending on severe conditions in the exiting sample with 14.9 percent of spending on severity 3 or severity 4 conditions, compared with 11.9 percent of spending on these conditions for the continuing sample.

Further investigation reveals that the difference between the exiting sample and the continuing sample may have major effects on expenditure growth, leading to a large overstatement of the expenditure index and its components. Therefore, researchers studying expenditure growth should be mindful of this selection issue when using panel data. Despite these issues,

---

28. In this analysis we do not study 64-year-olds, since 64-year-olds typically enter the Medicare program and leave private insurance when they turn 65.

there are potentially significant gains in our understanding of expenditure growth from exploiting the panel dimension of these data, but more research is necessary to better understand how to account for potential selection bias.

16.6   Conclusion

Researchers examining spending growth in the commercial sector often use convenience claims data, which may not be representative of the full commercially insured population. In this paper, we analyze the MarketScan commercial claims data and apply various weighting strategies to correct for the potential nonrepresentative aspects of the data. In general, we find that spending growth is primarily driven by price growth and a growth in prevalence, with utilization per episode staying relatively flat. Although this main qualitative finding holds, even when no weights are applied, we find that the application of population weights to reflect the population distribution of the United States produces spending growth figures that are more aligned with other benchmark estimates of price and expenditure growth from national statistics. In general, the results in this chapter complement those reported in Dunn, Liebman, and Shapiro (2012) by showing how alternative weighting strategies impact key results and trends.

To further understand the components of spending growth and how they may be influenced by population weights, we look at growth rates for different subpopulations. In particular, we look at growth rates by age group and by geography. We find that a similar general pattern of spending growth holds across age groups, but we also find some interesting differences across age groups. Spending growth appears to be increasing most rapidly for the population below 25, primarily due to higher service price growth and utilization growth. Prevalence appears to be increasing most rapidly for the population over the age of 18. Looking at regional growth differences, we find that growth rates are slower in the South, due to both lower price and lower utilization growth.

Overall, we recommend applying population weights for studying expenditure growth in all circumstances when attempting to make national projections using a convenience sample. However, another important consideration is the changing mix of data contributors, which could introduce a bias. Comparing estimates when the data contributors are fixed to those estimates when the data contributors vary over time produce similar estimates, although prevalence growth rates tend to be lower and price growth trends tend to be higher for the fixed contributor sample. There are trade-offs with using either the full or the fixed sample. In this study and in our related studies, even if we focus on one set of estimates, we examine estimates from both samples and search for consistent patterns across each.

There are several important areas for future research. First, it would be useful to look at other convenience samples to see if we observe similar patterns using alternative data sources. Second, there are interesting panel aspects of these claims data that could potentially be useful for obtaining more precise estimates, but researchers must first figure out how to deal with the selection issue caused by the most unhealthy people potentially exiting the sample through death. Third, this chapter is entirely descriptive of the trends, but does little to explain the observed trends. Future research may benefit from trying to understand the underlying health and economic factors that may have cause these observed differences and changes over time.

Appendix

Table 16A.1   Sources of growth, 2003–2007 (fixed demographics, full sample, regional weights)

	ECI	PREV	MCE	SPI	SUI
Infectious diseases	1.338	1.421	1.162	1.087	1.081
Endocrinology	1.366	1.305	1.068	1.152	0.937
Hematology	1.298	1.125	1.152	1.196	0.976
Psychiatry	1.235	1.141	1.083	1.129	0.994
Chemical dependency	1.572	1.500	1.079	1.110	1.018
Neurology	1.275	1.103	1.159	1.189	0.983
Ophthalmology	1.190	1.148	1.036	1.084	0.965
Cardiology	1.054	1.028	1.019	1.120	0.922
Otolaryngology	1.165	1.057	1.104	1.124	1.006
Pulmonology	1.117	1.004	1.122	1.169	0.963
Gastroenterology	1.260	1.124	1.135	1.140	1.000
Hepatology	1.053	1.018	1.033	1.098	0.951
Nephrology	1.209	1.423	0.864	0.851	1.025
Urology	1.189	1.113	1.083	1.112	0.983
Obstetrics	1.227	1.061	1.158	1.119	1.038
Gynecology	1.194	1.024	1.162	1.147	1.014
Dermatology	1.283	1.103	1.164	1.154	1.023
Orthopedics and rheumatology	1.290	1.145	1.129	1.121	1.026
Neonatology	1.277	1.135	1.129	1.122	1.002
Preventive and administrative	1.715	1.362	1.261	1.134	1.111
Late effects, environmental trauma, and poisonings	1.222	0.969	1.268	1.230	1.035
Isolated signs and symptoms	1.124	1.018	1.104	1.106	1.010

Table 16A.2   Distribution of spending by age group: Average, 2003–2007

	0 to 17	18 to 24	25 to 34	35 to 44	45 to 54	55 to 64
Spending per capita	$1,428	$1,587	$2,424	$2,802	$3,998	$5,899
Spending share by disease for each age group						
Infectious diseases	2%	1%	1%	2%	2%	1%
Endocrinology	4%	4%	5%	7%	8%	9%
Hematology	3%	3%	2%	2%	2%	3%
Psychiatry	9%	8%	5%	5%	4%	2%
Chemical dependency	0%	1%	1%	1%	1%	0%
Neurology	6%	7%	6%	6%	6%	5%
Ophthalmology	2%	1%	1%	1%	1%	2%
Cardiology	4%	3%	4%	8%	14%	20%
Otolaryngology	16%	8%	6%	5%	4%	3%
Pulmonology	7%	3%	3%	3%	4%	5%
Gastroenterology	6%	8%	8%	9%	11%	10%
Hepatology	1%	2%	2%	3%	3%	2%
Nephrology	0%	1%	1%	1%	2%	2%
Urology	2%	3%	3%	3%	3%	5%
Obstetrics	1%	12%	22%	5%	0%	0%
Gynecology	1%	5%	8%	11%	8%	5%
Dermatology	8%	8%	5%	4%	4%	3%
Orthopedics and rheumatology	13%	16%	14%	18%	19%	18%
Neonatology	8%	0%	0%	0%	0%	0%
Preventive and administrative	7%	3%	3%	3%	2%	1%
Late effects, environmental trauma, and poisonings	1%	1%	1%	1%	1%	0%
Isolated signs and symptoms	1%	1%	1%	1%	1%	0%
Total share	100%	100%	100%	100%	100%	100%

References

Abraham, Katharine G., and Christopher Mackie, ed. 2005. *Beyond the Market: Designing Nonmarket Accounts for the United States.* National Academies Panel on Conceptual, Measurement and Other Statistical Issues in Developing Cost-of-Living Indexes. Washington, DC: The National Academies Press for the National Research Council.

Aizcorbe, Ana, Ralph Bradley, Ryan Greenway-McGrevy, Brad Herauf, Richard Kane, Eli Liebman, Sarah Pack, and Lyubov Rozental. 2011. "Alternative Price Indexes for Medical Care: Evidence from the MEPS Survey." Bureau of Economic Analysis, Working Paper.

Aizcorbe, Ana, and Nicole Nestoriak. 2011. "Changing Mix of Medical Care Services: Stylized Facts and Implications for Price Indexes." *Journal of Health Economics* 30 (3): 568–74.

Berndt, Ernst, David Cutler, Richard Frank, Zvi Griliches, Joseph Newhouse, and Jack Triplett. 2000. "Medical Care Prices and Output." In *Handbook of Health Economics,* vol. 1A, edited by Joseph P. Newhouse and Anthony C. Culyer, 119–80. Amsterdam: Elsevier Science B.V.

Dunn, Abe, Eli Liebman, Sarah Pack, and Adam Shapiro. 2012. "Medical Care Price Indexes for Patients with Employer-Provided Insurance: Nationally-Representative Estimates from MarketScan Data." *Health Services Research.*

Dunn, Abe, Eli Liebman, Lindsey Rittmueller, and Adam Shapiro. 2014. "Defining Disease Episodes and the Effects on the Components of Expenditure Growth." Bureau of Economic Analysis, Working Paper.

Dunn, Abe, Eli Liebman, and Adam Shapiro. 2012. "Decomposing Medical-Care Expenditure Growth." Bureau of Economic Analysis, Working Paper.

———. 2014. "Implications of Utilization Shifts on Medical-Care Price Measurement." *Health Economics*, forthcoming.

Dunn, Abe, Adam Shapiro, and Eli Liebman. 2013. "Geographic Variation in Commercial Medical-Care Expenditures: A Framework for Decomposing Price and Utilization." *Journal of Health Economics* 32 (6): 1153–65.

National Research Council. 2010. *Accounting for Health and Health Care: Approaches to Measuring the Sources and Costs of Their Improvement.* Washington, DC: The National Academies Press.

Roehrig, Charles, George Miller, Craig Lake, and Jenny Bryant. 2009. "National Health Spending by Medical Condition, 1996–2005." *Health Affairs*, February. Web Exclusive.

Roehrig, Charles, and David Rousseau. 2011. "The Growth in Cost Per Case Explains Far More of US Health Spending Increases Than Rising Disease Prevalence." *Health Affairs* 30 (9): 1657–63.

Rosen, Allison, and David Cutler. 2007. "Measuring Medical Care Productivity: A Proposal for US National Health Accounts." *Survey of Current Business* 87: 54–58.

Schreyer, Paul, Alain Gallais, Sandra Hopkins, Francette Koechlin, Luca Lorenzoni, and Seppo Varjonen. 2010. "Towards Measuring the Volume of Health and Education Services." Draft Handbook. Paris: OECD.

Thorpe, Kenneth, Curtis Florence, and Peter Joski. 2004. "Which Medical Conditions Account for the Rise in Health Care Spending?" *Health Affairs*, August. Web Exclusive.

Experimental Measures of Output and Productivity in the Canadian Hospital Sector, 2002 to 2010

Wulong Gu and Stéphane Morin

17.1 Introduction

Health care is an important economic activity in Canada (CIHI, 2011b). As a share of gross domestic product (GDP), health-care expenditures rose from 7.0 percent in 1975 to 11.7 percent in 2011.

Recent discussions about health-care spending have focused on two issues: (1) the extent to which the increase is due to an increase in the *quantity* as opposed to the *price* of health-care services, and (2) the efficiency and productivity of health-care providers.

For example, the Canadian Institute for Health Information (CIHI) examined sources of the increase in hospital expenditures between 1998 and 2008. Using the GDP price index as a proxy for the price index of hospital expenditures, CIHI (2012b) reported that total hospital expenditures rose 6.7 percent annually over the period, 2.8 percent of which was due to price changes. The remaining 3.9 percent was due to an increase in the quantity of hospital services as a result of factors such as population growth, population aging, and technical progress and innovation. In a related study, CIHI (2011a) examined factors behind the increase in total health-care expenditures.

Wulong Gu is senior advisor and assistant director of the Economic Analysis Division at Statistics Canada. Stéphane Morin is an economist in the Economic Analysis Division at Statistics Canada

We thank Ana Aizcorbe, John Baldwin, Ernie Berndt, Carol Corrado, Mary O'Mahony, Tim Prendergast, Art Ridgeway, Luke Rispoli, Michelle Rotermann, Claudia Sanmartin, and Paul Schreyer for their helpful comments. We also thank Sara Allin and Ruolz Ariste at the Canadian Institute for Health Information for helpful discussions. For acknowledgments, sources of research support, and disclosure of the authors' material financial relationships, if any, please see http://www.nber.org/chapters/c12842.ack.

With regard to the efficiency and productivity of health-care providers, Sharpe, Bradley, and Messinger (2007) noted that accurate measures of health-care output and productivity are essential and recommended that more resources be allocated to develop better measures for Canada's health-care sector.

The key to addressing both issues is a direct output measure of health-care services—a measure that does not currently exist. In the national accounts, output of the health-care sector is measured by the volume of inputs, which includes labor costs for physicians, nurses, and administrative staff, consumption of capital, and intermediate inputs (Statistics Canada 2001). An input-based output measure assumes that there are no productivity gains in the health-care sector.[1] As a result, it does not provide a measure of productivity performance, nor does it allow a decomposition of total health-care expenditures into price and output quantity components.

The main objective of this chapter is to develop an experimental direct output measure for the Canadian hospital sector. The focus is on the hospital sector because hospitals make up the largest component of health-care spending, and the data are readily available. Hospital expenditures totaled $60.5 billion in 2011 and accounted for 29.2 percent of total health spending that year (CIHI 2011c).[2]

The direct output measure developed here is based on the number of "activities" in hospitals, with activities defined as episodes of treatment of diseases and conditions. Because the treatment of different diseases/conditions involves different types of service, weights must be applied to construct the direct output measure. Previous studies have proposed two alternative weights: one based on the unit costs of treatments, and the other based on the value of treatments to patients (the effect on the patient's health outcome) (Atkinson 2005; Dawson et al. 2005; Schreyer 2010). These studies acknowledge that the former is the most practical. Accordingly, this analysis constructs a direct output measure of the hospital sector using unit costs as weights—the cost-weighted activity index.

The cost-weighted activity index, when calculated inappropriately, introduces a bias in the estimate as a result of a shift from inpatient treatment toward cheaper outpatient treatment with improved or similar health outcomes (Schreyer 2010, 2012). The index will show a decline in the volume of hospital care, which is contrary to intuition that, because of the substitution of one mode of treatment for another, the volume of hospital care increased, or at least, did not change.

This chapter examines the substitution bias in the cost-weighted activity index as it is often calculated. It also examines aggregation bias or the effect

---

1. The input-based output measure implies that no multifactor productivity growth occurs in the health-care sector.
2. Other health-care expenditure categories include physicians, drugs, and other health institutions.

of using various levels of aggregation of case types to calculate the direct output measure. This is relevant because countries often classify case types at a high level of aggregation to overcome problems that are created by changes over time in classification at a detailed level.

Two previous Statistics Canada studies developed direct output measures for hospital care. Kitchen (1997) constructed a direct output measure for the hospital sector as the cost-weighted sum of the number of treatments for inpatients, outpatients, and chronic care during the 1986 to 1992 period. Statistics Canada (2001) extended the estimate for inpatient care to take into account differences in unit costs across 500 categories of inpatient treatments.

This study is related to Yu and Ariste (2009), who constructed a direct output measure for the hospital sector as a cost-weighted activity index for the periods 1996 to 2000 and 2003 to 2005. The present analysis differs in that it attempts to correct for substitution and aggregation biases.

The rest of the chapter is organized as follows. Section 17.2 outlines the methodology used to construct the direct output measure. Section 17.3 describes the data sources. Section 17.4 presents an estimate of hospital sector output and examines potential bias in the estimate. Section 17.5 concludes.

17.2   Methodology

This section summarizes the approaches used to measure the output of hospital sector and highlights challenges, issues, and data constraints that national statistical agencies encounter in implementing the various approaches.

This study employs the approach in the Organisation for Economic Co-operation and Development (OECD) handbook on measurement of the volume of output of education and health services (Schreyer 2010). That approach is similar to those proposed by the Atkinson review of the measurement of government output and productivity for the national accounts (Atkinson 2005), the US National Research Council (2010), and Eurostat (2001). It has been adopted by a number of countries to develop a direct output measure of the health-care sector (Schreyer 2010).

The Systems of National Accounts (SNA) 1993 (CEC et al. 1993) and SNA 2008 (EC et al. 2009) recommended an output-based approach for measuring the volume of health sector output.[3] Eurostat (2001) made similar recommendations and provided detailed guidance toward implementation in its *Handbook on Price and Volume Measures in National Accounts*. The

---

3. The principles for constructing the output-based measures of nonmarket services, including health care, go back to work by Hill (1975).

handbook became European law, obliging member states to implement the recommendations.

Measurement of direct output starts with a definition of the unit of output and weights used for aggregation. For the goods-producing business sector, the unit of output and the weights used for aggregation are straightforward. For example, to construct the direct output measure of the automobile manufacturing sector, the unit of output is defined as the number of cars manufactured, and market prices are used for aggregation. The hospital sector, however, is less straightforward.

Schreyer (2010) defines the unit of health services as the treatment of a disease or condition. Ideally, the unit of output should capture the complete treatment, encompassing the path a patient takes through heterogeneous health-care institutions to receive full and final treatment. This definition of the target measure, known as a disease-based estimate of health-care output, is similar to that used by the Eurostat handbook (2001), Berndt et al. (2001), Aizcorbe and Nestoriak (2011), and Triplett (2001).

Implementation of this ideal definition requires tracking individual patients across health-care institutions to measure complete treatment; existing data rarely allow such linkages. In addition, the concept of "complete treatment" is problematic if the objective is to construct a direct output measure for specific institutions such as hospitals. For practical reasons, Schreyer (2010) proposes a working definition of the unit of health-care services—activities relating to an episode of treatment of a disease/condition provided by specific institutions.

Because episodes of treatment of different diseases/conditions involve different types of service, weights must be applied to construct the direct output measure. Typically, market prices provide such weights, but because there are no market prices for most hospital services, Schreyer (2010) proposes that unit costs be used to obtain the cost-weighted activity index. The Atkinson report (Atkinson 2005) and Dawson et al. (2005) recommend that the marginal value of a treatment be used to derive a value-weighted activity index as the ideal output measure, where the marginal value is based on the effect of the treatment on the patient's health outcome. .

In Canada, the public sector (federal, provincial, and municipal governments) provides and finances 90 percent of hospital services. If well-functioning markets existed for hospital services, unit costs of treatments would tend to be the same as their value to patients, and market prices (which tend to be equal to unit costs and value to patients) should be used for aggregation. But because there are no markets for most publicly financed hospital services, unit costs of treatments may be different than values to patients, and consequently, the choice of weights matters for the direct output measure.

Because the effect of a treatment on health outcomes is often not available, the Atkinson report (Atkinson 2005) and Dawson et al. (2005) conclude that the *cost-weighted activity index* is a practical approach for constructing the direct output measures for the hospital sector. However, a cost-weighted activity index might introduce a substitution bias (Schreyer 2010, 2012). Substitution bias arises when a shift from inpatient to outpatient treatment occurs, and inpatient treatment and outpatient treatment are assigned to different case types with different unit costs even though they both have the same effect on outcome. If outpatient treatment is less expensive, a cost-weighted activity index will indicate a decline in the hospital sector's volume of output. This is counterintuitive, since the volume of hospital service under the above assumption does not change when outpatient and inpatient treatments have same effect on health outcomes and are valued equally by patients.[4]

This counterintuitive result derives from an implicit assumption in the cost-weighted activity index: a treatment with lower unit costs has lower quality than a treatment with higher unit costs. But if treatments have a similar effect on health outcomes, they should have the same quality.[5] An appropriate measure for the example chosen would show no change in the volume of hospital output and a decline in the price of that output as a result of the shift toward cheaper outpatient treatment.

The bias can be removed by grouping treatments with similar health outcomes in the same case types (Schreyer 2010, 2012). This is not always feasible, as outpatient and inpatient cases are often assigned to different case types using different classification systems. And in some instances, there is no classification of case types for outpatient treatments.

Substitution bias arises from *quality* changes in hospital care that come from shifts between case types that the cost-weighted activity index does not capture. A *value-weighted activity index* captures such quality changes and does not suffer from substitution bias. For a value-weighted activity index, weights for aggregating treatments are based on the effect of treatments on health outcomes. To the extent that shifts from inpatient treatment to less expensive outpatient treatment have no effect on health outcomes, a value-weighted index will show a decline in the price of the hospital output but no change in the volume of hospital output.

To construct a cost-weighted activity index, treatments are assigned to various case types. The level of detail in the classification of treatments may introduce a bias when more aggregated levels of classification are used. This is referred to as aggregation bias in this chapter.

4. The substitution bias also exists in the relative price level of hospital services that the OECD constructed in its pilot study, because inpatient and outpatient treatments were assigned different case types and different unit costs were used as weights for the two types of service (Schreyer 2010; Koechlin, Lorenzoni, and Schreyer 2010).
5. Quality is defined as characteristics of a product that consumers value. For treatment of a disease, "quality" is the effect on health outcomes. Triplett (2006) provided an extensive discussion of quality adjustment.

The objective of this chapter is to construct a cost-weighted activity index for the hospital sector and examine the magnitude of substitution and aggregation bias. Hospital sector output includes both inpatient and outpatient care. The unit of output is defined as the number of episodes of treatment that patients received in hospitals—specifically, the number of discharges by case type (patient statistics are derived from hospital discharge registers). In this chapter, the terms "case," "treatment," and "discharge" are used interchangeably.

The cost-weighted activity index of the volume of hospital sector output Q is expressed as a Tornqvist aggregation of the number of patient cases, by case type, using unit costs as weights:

(1) $$(\ln Q_t - \ln Q_{t-1}) = \sum_i \bar{s}_i (\ln q_t - \ln q_{t-1})$$

$$s_i^t = \frac{c_i^t q_i^t}{\sum_i c_i^t q_i^t}, \quad \bar{s}_i = \frac{1}{2}(s_i^t + s_i^{t-1}),$$

where q_i is the number of cases for case type i, c_i is the unit cost per treatment for case type i, and s_i is the share of case type i in total costs.[6]

The volume index of the hospital sector output is then used to derive the price index of the hospital sector output.

An alternative approach is to construct the price index of hospital services and derive the volume index as deflated total expenditures of the hospital sector. The choice between the two methods is mainly driven by data availability. For example, Germany and Denmark use the deflation method and construct the price index of hospital services, while the Netherlands constructs the volume index of the output of hospital care (Schreyer 2010). The Bureau of Labor Statistics (BLS) uses the deflation method to construct the producer price index (PPI) of hospital expenditures for the United States (Carton and Murphy 1996). The BLS samples the costs of inpatient and outpatient treatments and derives the price index of hospital expenditures as the weighted sum of unit costs of inpatient and outpatient treatments, using their cost shares as weights.[7]

Unlike other countries, the unit cost for a case type in Canada is not a monetary value. Rather, the unit cost (resource intensity weight) represents the relative resource intensity of inpatient and outpatient cases compared with the average inpatient case, which has a value of 1.0. Therefore, the deflation method is not feasible using Canadian data.

To examine the substitution bias in the cost-weighted activity index, inpatients and outpatients in the same case types are combined, and the

---

6. In the estimation below, the case type for inpatients is further disaggregated based on the age of patients and the severity of the disease to obtain more homogeneous groups of patients with similar unit costs when that information is available.

7. Because the BLS also makes a distinction between inpatient and outpatient treatments, its hospital price index may introduce a substitution bias similar to that examined here.

same unit costs are used to weight inpatients and outpatients belonging to the same case types. The resulting estimate is compared with the estimate derived from classifying inpatient and outpatient cases as distinct activities, and then weighting them using different unit costs.

The approach adopted for the present study has been suggested by Schreyer (2010, 2012), but has not previously been implemented because classifications for outpatient treatments are often not the same as those for inpatient treatments, or are lacking altogether.

An alternative is to assume that, without the shift toward outpatient treatment, the growth of inpatient and outpatient care would be similar. Therefore, the relatively faster increase of outpatients would be entirely due to substitution. Growth of outpatient cases that exceeds the growth of inpatient cases is weighted using the unit costs for average inpatients to derive an alternative direct output measure. This assumes that outpatient treatment yields the same health-care services as inpatient treatment. The difference between the new and original estimates provides a measure of substitution bias.

17.3   Data

Hospitals are involved in inpatient care, outpatient care, and activities such as research, education, and social services. Inpatient and outpatient services accounted for 92.5 percent of total hospital expenditures in 2007, down slightly from 94.6 percent in 1999 (CIHI, 2012b).

The direct output measure of the hospital sector constructed in this chapter covers all provinces except Quebec, for which consistent time-series data are not available.[8] The nominal value of the hospital sector is estimated as total hospital expenditures, which are obtained from the income statements of all hospitals in the Canadian MIS Database (CMDB).

The data on inpatient and outpatient cases are from the hospital discharge register. The volume index constructed in this chapter covers inpatient and outpatient treatment, but not other hospital activities, which account for only about 5 percent of total hospital expenditures.

The databases used for estimating the nominal value and the volume index of the output of the hospital sector have the same coverage of hospitals (CIHI 2011a).[9] The volume index of the hospital sector output estimated from the hospital discharge register can be compared with total hospital expenditures from the CMDB to derive a price deflator for hospital sector output.

8. Outpatient data are not available for Alberta, and so are excluded from the estimates.
9. Hospitals in the DAD can be linked to the Canadian MIS Database, which contains hospital income statements and balance sheets.

17.3.1   Total Hospital Expenditures

Total expenditures for Canadian hospitals are from the CMDB, maintained by CIHI (CIHI 2011a). The CMDB includes financial information from hospital balance sheets and income statements.[10] Total hospital expenditures are published in *National Health Expenditure Trends* (CIHI, 2011b), and constitute the source data used to estimated the gross output of the hospital sector in the Canadian System of National Accounts.

17.3.2   Inpatients

Data on inpatient treatment are from the Discharge Abstract Database (DAD), maintained by CIHI (CIHI 2012a). The DAD contains administrative, clinical, and demographic information on hospital inpatients in all provinces except Quebec.

The DAD assigns inpatients to one of twenty-one Major Clinical Categories (MCCs) (table 17.1) based on their "most responsible" diagnosis. Inpatients in each MCC are further assigned to one of about 600 Case Mixed Groups (CMGs), which aggregate cases with similar clinical and resource utilization characteristics. These data may be further disaggregated by patient age or disease severity to obtain more homogeneous groups of patients with similar resource requirements. For 2009, there are twenty-one MCCs and 570 CMG categories. The number of age groups and complexity/comorbidity categories changed slightly over time: for the 2002 to 2004 period, four complexity levels and three age groups; after 2004, more detailed age groups and six comorbidity levels (CIHI 2007a).

Unit costs, or resource intensity weights (RIW), are calculated for inpatients in a specific CMG, age group, and complexity/comorbidity category.[11] All RIWs are relative to an average inpatient case, which is assigned an RIW of 1.0. For example, a patient with an RIW of 2.0 would require twice as many resources during the course of hospital treatment as the average inpatient.[12]

The RIW is used to estimate the cost per weighted case that measures the relative cost-efficiency of a hospital's inpatient care. This indicator compares a hospital's total inpatient care expenses to the weighted number of inpatient cases. The result is the hospital's average cost of treating average inpatients.

In this chapter, RIWs are used to aggregate inpatient cases across case types to derive the volume index of inpatient care in hospitals.

10. In provinces and territories where hospitals are part of a regional health authority, regional hospital data are submitted to the CMDB.
11. Resource intensity weights (RIW) is a measure of the relative amount of hospital resources used to treat an inpatient or outpatient. RIW are calibrated annually so that the average inpatient acute care case in Canada has a value of one (CIHI 2007a).
12. Unit costs for atypical cases (which include acute care transfers, sign out, and death) are calculated using a per diem-based approach. Unit costs for atypical cases are then expressed relative to that for an average case (CIHI 2007a).

Table 17.1   **Major Clinical Category (MCC)**

Number	Title
1	Diseases and Disorders of the Nervous System
2	Diseases and Disorders of the Eye
3	Diseases and Disorders of Ear, Nose, Mouth and Throat
4	Diseases and Disorders of the Respiratory System
5	Diseases and Disorders of the Circulatory System
6	Diseases and Disorders of the Digestive System
7	Diseases and Disorders of the Hepatobiliary System and Pancreas
8	Diseases and Disorders of the Musculoskeletal System and Connective Tissue
9	Diseases and Disorders of the Skin, Subcutaneous Tissue and Breast
10	Diseases and Disorders of the Endocrine System, Nutrition and Metabolism
11	Diseases and Disorders of the Kidney, Urinary Tract and Male Reproductive System
12	Diseases and Disorders of the Female Reproductive System
13	Pregnancy and Childbirth
14	Newborns and Neonates With Conditions Originating in the Perinatal Period
15	Diseases and Disorders of the Blood and Lymphatic System
16	Multisystemic or Unspecified Site Infections
17	Mental Diseases and Disorders
18	Burns
19	Significant Trauma, Injury, Poisoning and Toxic Effects of Drugs
20	Other Reasons for Hospitalization
99	Miscellaneous CMG and Ungroupable Data

Source: Canadian Institute for Health Information (2007a).

17.3.3   Outpatients

Data on outpatient services for all provinces except Ontario, Quebec, and Alberta are also from the DAD. Outpatient data for Ontario are from CIHI's National Ambulatory Care Reporting System (NACRS). Outpatient data for Alberta and Quebec are not available for the period covered in this chapter.

The DAD makes a distinction between inpatient and outpatient treatments. Inpatient and outpatient cases are assigned to the same case types at the aggregate level of classification, but to different case types at more detailed levels. Outpatient cases and day procedures are assigned to one of twenty-one MCCs at the aggregate level, and to one of around 100 Day Procedure Groups (DPGs) at the detailed level according to the principal procedure recorded. Those assigned to the same DPG constitute a homogeneous group with similar clinical episodes and requiring similar resources.

Outpatient cases and day procedures in the NACRS are assigned to one of about twenty Major Ambulatory Clusters (MACs) at the aggregate level, and to one of about 300 case types using the Comprehensive Ambulatory Classification System (CACS). The CACS provides a more detailed classification of outpatient cases than DPGs in the DAD, but the classifications are similar, and MACs can be mapped to MCCs.

Each outpatient case is assigned an RIW. Because the RIW for outpatient cases is comparable to the RIW for inpatient cases (Hicks and Zhang 2003), the volume index of inpatient and outpatient cases can be combined to derive the volume index of the output of the hospital sector.

This study focuses on 2002 to 2010, because the data are consistent and no major changes in the classification of inpatient and outpatient cases were made during the period.[13] The two hospital register databases used in this analysis pertain to the April–March fiscal year; the data were converted to calendar years based on the month of patient discharge.

17.4   Direct Output Measures

This section presents direct output measures of the hospital sector for 2002 to 2010 for all provinces except Quebec,[14] for which consistent data are not available. Because outpatient data are not available for Alberta,[15] it was assumed that growth in the volume index of outpatient care in Alberta is equal to the average growth of outpatient care in the other provinces.

From 2002 to 2010, the number of inpatient cases rose slightly from 2.36 million to 2.41 million (figure 17.1). However, the number of outpatient cases and day procedures nearly doubled from 1.18 million to 2.02 million, an increase that has been attributed to a shift in elective surgeries from an inpatient to a day-surgery setting (CIHI 2007b).

This analysis first presents the cost-weighted activity index of hospital sector output when inpatient and outpatient cases are assigned to different case types, and different unit costs are used to aggregate inpatient and outpatient cases. Specifically, the index is estimated by aggregating inpatient and outpatient cases at the most detailed classification level. Inpatient cases are further disaggregated by patient age group and by disease/condition severity. Substitution and aggregation biases are then examined. Finally, the estimate is compared with the estimate from the Canadian System of National Accounts.

17.4.1   Cost-Weighted Activity Index: Inpatient and
Outpatient Cases Assigned to *Different* Case Types

Table 17.2 presents the volume index of hospital sector output for the 2002 to 2010 period that results when inpatient and outpatient cases are assigned to different case types and different unit costs are used to weight them.

The volume index of *inpatient* care increased 0.6 percent per year. This

---

13. The classification of case types at the detailed level changed for 2004/2005. The volume index for that year was estimated based on the higher level of aggregation.
14. Quebec accounted for about 20 percent of hospital expenditures over the 2002 to 2010 period.
15. Alberta accounted for about 12 percent of hospital expenditures over the 2002 to 2010 period.

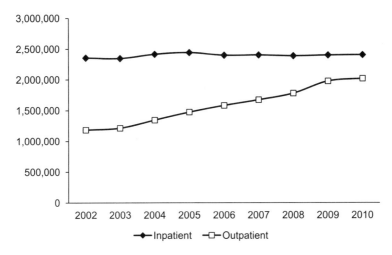

Fig. 17.1   Number of hospital inpatient and outpatient cases, Canada, 2002 to 2010
Source: Authors' estimate from the CIHI data.

Table 17.2   **Direct output measure of hospital sector, Canada, 2002 to 2010**

	All		Inpatient		Outpatient	
Year	Volume index of output	Number of cases (in thousands)	Volume index of output	Number of cases (in thousands)	Volume index of output	Number of cases (in thousands)
2002	100.0	3,541	100.0	2,357	100.0	1,184
2003	100.0	3,563	99.5	2,349	104.2	1,215
2004	103.2	3,760	100.8	2,416	122.2	1,345
2005	105.3	3,917	101.3	2,443	137.1	1,474
2006	103.7	3,980	98.3	2,399	148.4	1,581
2007	105.9	4,076	99.6	2,403	158.3	1,673
2008	108.3	4,168	100.7	2,389	170.9	1,779
2009	112.4	4,376	103.2	2,401	188.9	1,976
2010	114.8	4,424	105.2	2,406	194.1	2,018
	Average annual growth (%), 2002 to 2010					
	1.7	2.8	0.6	0.3	8.6	6.9

Source: Authors' estimates from the CIHI data.
Notes: Excludes Quebec. The volume index of output is set equal to 100 in 2002.

growth was faster than the increase in the unweighted number of inpatient cases (0.3 percent). The difference signals a change in the nature of inpatient cases toward those that are more resource intensive (e.g., elderly patients, CIHI 2007b), as a result of the aging of the population. Other factors contributing to the difference include an increase in cases that involve resource-intensive technologies and the general shift from inpatient to outpatient care.

The volume index of *outpatient* care rose 8.6 percent per year. This growth, too, was faster than the increase in the unweighted number of outpatient cases (6.9 percent), and reflects more use of resource-intensive technologies.

The volume index of the *hospital sector* overall is obtained by aggregating the volume indices of inpatient and outpatient care using their relative cost share as weights.[16] The volume index of the hospital sector increased 1.7 percent per year, which was slower than the increase in the total number of inpatient and outpatient cases (2.8 percent). The difference is mainly due to compositional shifts in hospital care toward outpatient treatment, which is less resource intensive, and therefore, less expensive than inpatient treatment. Thus, the shift, or "substitution," reduced the growth of the volume index of hospital care.

Using the same databases, Yu and Ariste (2009) constructed a cost-weighted activity index for the hospital sector (excluding Quebec) for 1996 to 2000 and for 2003 to 2005. The estimate for 2003 to 2005 in the present analysis is almost identical to theirs: both indicate growth of 2.6 percent per year in the volume index of the hospital sector output (data not shown).

For the table 17.2 estimates, inpatient and outpatient cases were assigned to detailed case types. To assess the effect of level of aggregation, an alternative estimate is derived by using a higher level of aggregation—the Major Clinical Category (MCC). The unit cost of an MCC is calculated as an average of unit costs among the detailed case types that comprise the MCC. Differences in unit costs between age groups and disease/condition severity are not taken into account.

Use of higher levels of aggregation reduced the growth in the volume index of the hospital sector by 0.6 percentage points per year (table 17.3). This aggregation bias appears in both inpatient and outpatient care, reducing annual growth in the volume index of inpatient care by 0.6 percentage points, and in the volume index of outpatient care by 0.4 percentage points.

17.4.2   Cost-Weighted Activity Index: Inpatient and Outpatient Cases Assigned to Same Case Types

To the extent that inpatient and outpatient treatments of the same disease/condition have a similar effect on health outcomes but there has been a shift towards less expensive outpatients, the cost-weighted index will underestimate growth.

To assess the substitution bias that occurs when inpatient and outpatient cases are assigned to *different* case types, they are grouped using the *same* classification and assigned to one of twenty-one MCCs. Relative unit costs for inpatient cases are used as weights to aggregate inpatient and outpatient

---

16. The share of total costs attributable to day procedures is calculated from RIW in the DAD. It was 11.7 percent in 2002 for the eight provinces whose statistics on both inpatient cases and day procedures are included in the DAD (Quebec and Alberta are excluded).

Table 17.3   **Effect of level of aggregation on direct output measure of hospital sector, Canada, 2002 to 2010**

	Annual average growth (%)		
	Detailed level	Broad level	Difference
All			
Volume index of output	1.7	1.2	–0.6
Number of cases	2.8	2.8	0.0
Composition	–1.1	–1.6	–0.6
Inpatient			
Volume index of output	0.6	0.0	–0.6
Number of cases	0.3	0.3	0.0
Composition	0.4	–0.2	–0.6
Outpatient			
Volume index of output	8.6	8.2	–0.4
Number of cases	6.9	6.9	0.0
Composition	1.6	1.2	–0.4

Source: Authors' estimates from the CIHI data.

Notes: The detailed level of aggregation consists of about 600 case types for inpatients, and 100 to 300 case types for outpatients. The broad level of aggregation consists of about twenty categories for both inpatients and outpatients.

treatments belonging to the same case type. This is compared with the cost-weighted activity index of the hospital sector when different unit costs for inpatient and outpatient cases belonging to the same MCCs are used for aggregation. The difference between the two estimates is a measure of the substitution bias in the cost-weighted activity index.

The substitution bias is considerable (see table 17.4). Removal of the bias increased the growth of the volume index of the hospital sector output during the 2002 to 2010 period by 2.6 percentage points.

The substitution bias can be regarded as resulting from quality changes in hospital service that the normal cost-weighted activity index fails to capture (Schreyer 2010, 2012), because it assumes that outpatient treatments with lower unit costs have lower quality than do inpatient treatments of the same disease/condition. Thus, the cost-weighted activity index will show a decline in volume of output when treatment shifts from inpatient to outpatient care. If inpatient and outpatient treatments have similar effects on health outcomes, a cost-weighted activity index that was adjusted for quality measure would show no decline in volume of output.

To remove substitution bias and capture quality changes from shifts in treatments between case types, Schreyer (2010, 2012) recommends that inpatient and outpatient cases be grouped together if they have a similar contribution to health outcomes. In practice, this is not always feasible, because inpatient and outpatient cases are often assigned to case types using different classification systems. And sometimes, outpatient cases are not classified at

Table 17.4   Substitution bias in direct output measure of hospital sector, Canada, 2002 to 2010

	Annual average growth (%)		
	Distinct grouping	Same grouping	Difference
All			
Volume index of output	1.2	3.7	2.6
Number of cases	2.8	2.8	0.0
Composition	−1.6	0.9	2.5
Inpatient			
Volume index of output	0.0	0.0	0.0
Number of cases	0.3	0.3	0.0
Composition	−0.2	−0.2	0.0
Outpatient			
Volume index of output	8.2	7.4	−0.8
Number of cases	6.9	6.9	0.0
Composition	1.2	0.5	−0.8

Source: Authors' estimates from the CIHI data.
Notes: "Distinct grouping" refers to assignment of inpatient and outpatient cases to distinct Major Clinical Categories (MCCs) with different unit costs. "Same grouping" refers to assignment of inpatient and outpatient cases to the same MCCs using the same unit costs.

all. In such instances, a cost-weighted activity index may seriously underestimate the volume index of the hospital sector when there is a large shift toward outpatient treatment, as has occurred in Canada.

17.4.3   Cost-Weighted Activity Index from a Counterfactual

The magnitude of substitution bias has been examined using a broad level of disaggregation of patient cases in section 17.4.2. Ideally, it should be examined using a more detailed level of disaggregation. To assess the robustness of the estimated substitution bias, this section provides an alternative estimate at a more detailed level using the assumption that the growth of inpatient cases and outpatient cases would be similar without the substitution. Therefore, the difference in the growth rates of outpatient and inpatient cases is entirely due to the substitution.[17] The growth of outpatient cases exceeding the growth of inpatient cases is weighted using the unit cost for average inpatient cases. The difference between the new estimate and the original estimate provides an assessment of the substitution bias in the cost-weighted activity index of the hospital sector.

The results of this counterfactual reveal a similarly large substitution bias in the cost-weighted activity index (table 17.5). The estimated volume index of the hospital sector from the counterfactual increased 4.0 percent per year

17. CIHI (2007a) attributes the relative growth difference between inpatient and outpatient cases mostly to a shift in elective surgeries from an inpatient to a day-surgery setting.

Table 17.5   **Alternative estimates of direct output measure of hospital sector**

	Average annual growth (%)		
	Volume index of output	Price index of output	Nominal expenditure
Detailed level of distinct case groups for inpatients and outpatients	1.7	5.2	7.0
Broad level of distinct case types for inpatients and outpatients	1.2	5.8	7.0
Broad level of same case types for inpatients and outpatients	3.7	3.3	7.0
Counterfactual estimate	4.0	3.0	7.0
Preferred estimate	4.3	2.7	7.0

Source: Authors' estimates from the CIHI data.
Note: Average annual growth in percent, 2002 to 2010, Canada.

during the 2002 to 2010 period, compared with 1.7 percent per year for the cost-weighted activity index.

17.4.4   Productivity Growth of Hospital Sector

Table 17.5 summarizes the alternative estimates of the direct output measure of the hospital sector and presents both volume and price indices. The price index is derived by dividing total hospital expenditures by the volume index of output.

The preferred estimate is the cost-weighted activity index based on the detailed case type aggregation and corrected for substitution bias. Growth in this quality-adjusted cost-weighted activity index of hospital sector output can be calculated as the growth in the volume index estimated from using different classifications for inpatient cases and outpatient cases at a detailed level (1.7 percent per year) plus the substitution bias in that estimate (2.6 percent). Alternatively, it can be calculated as the sum of the estimate from using the same classification for inpatient and outpatient cases at a broad level (3.7 percent) plus the aggregation bias in that estimate (0.6 percent).

The quality-adjusted estimate of hospital sector output over the 2002 to 2010 period rose 4.3 percent per year. The price index of hospital sector output derived from the quality-adjusted volume index measure increased 2.7 percent per year. Growth in the price of the hospital sector is slightly higher than growth in the price of gross domestic product over that period (2.5 percent per year).

Table 17.6 compares the quality-adjusted estimate of the direct output measure of the hospital sector with the output measure from the input-based approach in the Canadian System of National Accounts for the 2002 to 2008 period. Because the direct output measure of hospital sector examined in

Table 17.6   Comparison of national accounts estimates of hospital sector output with direct output measure of hospital sector, Canada, 2002 to 2008

	Average annual growth (%)	
	National Accounts	Experimental estimates
Volume index of output	4.1	4.2
Price index of output	2.7	2.8
Nominal hospital output	6.8	6.9

Source: Authors' estimates from the CIHI and Statistics Canada data.

this chapter does not include Quebec, Quebec is also not included in the estimate in the national accounts.

Nominal gross output of the hospital sector in the national accounts is estimated from total hospital expenditures in the Canadian MIS Database. Nominal gross output of the hospital sector is about 10 percent higher than total hospital expenditures, a difference that is quite stable over the period. The growth rate of nominal gross output in the hospital sector is similar to the growth rate in total hospital expenditures. The direct output measure of the hospital sector increased 4.2 percent per year, while the output measure of the hospital sector estimated as the volume index of inputs in the national accounts increased 4.1 percent per year.

Figure 17.2 displays an estimate of labor productivity (ratio of the volume index to hours worked) based on the quality-adjusted direct output measure constructed in this chapter. Hours worked for the hospital sector is obtained from Statistics Canada's Labour Productivity Program (Maynard 2005), estimated as total employment times average hours worked per worker. The employment data are from the Survey of Employment, Payrolls and Hours, which collects administrative information on employment for all establishments. The data on hours worked are from the Labour Force Survey, a monthly household survey that collects employment data for all workers.

Labor productivity in the Canadian hospital sector increased 2.6 percent per year over the 2002 to 2010 period. This represents annual growth of 4.3 percent for output and 1.7 percent for hours worked.

Based on the growth accounting framework of Solow (1957) and Jorgenson and Griliches (1967), table 17.7 decomposes growth in labor productivity from 2002 to 2008 into the contribution from investment (capital deepening), the contribution from intermediate input deepening, and multifactor productivity growth.[18] The contribution of capital deepening is estimated as the growth in capital per hours worked times the share of capital income in nominal gross output. The contribution of intermediate input deepening is estimated as the growth in intermediate input per hours worked times the

18. The data on gross output and intermediate input were available up to the year 2008.

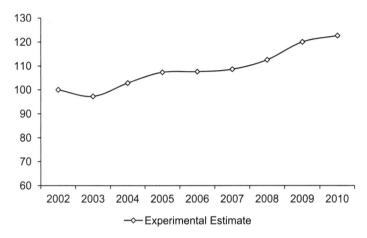

Fig. 17.2   Labor productivity in Canadian hospital sector, 2002 to 2010
Source: Authors' estimates from data from the CIHI and Statistics Canada.

Table 17.7   **Sources of labor productivity growth in hospital sector, Canada, 2002 to 2008**

	(%)
Labor productivity growth	2.0
Contribution of:	
Capital deepening	0.1
Intermediate input deepening	1.6
Multifactor productivity growth	0.3

Source: Authors' estimates from the CIHI and Statistics Canada data.

share of intermediate inputs. The residual component is multifactor productivity growth, which captures the effect of changes in technologies and organizations that are not embodied in investment in medical equipment.

Capital stock for the hospital sector is estimated from investment using the perpetual inventory method. The data on investment are from the annual Survey of Capital and Repair Expenditures, which collects data on capital expenditures for all business and government entities. The data on intermediate inputs are from the input/output accounts of Statistics Canada.

Labor productivity growth was largely due to intermediate input deepening, which includes expenditures on drugs. Multifactor productivity increased 0.3 percent per year over the 2002 to 2008 period.[19]

19. Because the capital income of the hospital sector in the national accounts includes only the consumption of capital, not the returns on capital, the share of capital income and the contribution of capital deepening are underestimated.

17.5   Conclusion

This chapter constructed an experimental volume index of hospital sector output by aggregating inpatient and outpatient cases using their cost share as weights. This cost-weighted activity index was corrected for substitution bias and aggregation bias. Substitution bias arises when a shift from inpatient to outpatient treatment occurs, and inpatient and outpatient cases are assigned to different case types and aggregated using their respective unit costs as weights. Aggregation bias arises when the index is constructed using a case-type classification at a high level of aggregation.

The analysis reveals a large substitution bias in the index when inpatient and outpatient cases are aggregated using their respective unit costs as weights. The substitution bias represents quality improvements stemming from shifts toward outpatient care that are not captured in the normal cost-weighted activity index.

The results of this study are consistent with the OECD recommendation that inpatient and outpatient cases not be separated for estimating the cost-weighted activity index (Schreyer 2010). Rather, they should be grouped together if they make a similar contribution to health outcomes. However, this is not always feasible, because they are frequently assigned to different case types using different classification systems. In such instances, the cost-weighted activity index may seriously underestimate the volume index of hospital services when there has been a shift toward cheaper outpatient treatment that yields similar or improved health outcomes.

The quality-adjusted estimate of the direct output measure of the hospital sector increased 4.3 percent per year over the 2002 to 2010 period. The price index of the output of the hospital sector increased 2.7 percent per year, slightly faster than the growth in the price index of gross domestic product. Labor productivity in the hospital sector based on the direct output measure increased 2.6 percent per year.

This chapter focuses on quality changes in the hospital sector as a result of the trend toward outpatient treatment of diseases/conditions that formerly had been handled on an inpatient basis. The study does not address the effect of quality improvements within the same types of treatments on the volume index. Dawson et al. (2005) found evidence of quality improvement within the same type of treatments, but the effect was not nearly as large as that arising from the substitution of outpatient for inpatient treatment described in this chapter.

References

Aizcorbe, A., and N. Nestoriak. 2011. "Changing Mix of Medical Care Services: Stylized Facts and Implications for Price Indexes." *Journal of Health Economics* 30 (2): 568–74.

Atkinson, A. B. 2005. *Atkinson Review Final Report: Measurement of Government Output and Productivity for the National Accounts.* New York: Palgrave Macmillan.

Berndt, E. R., D. M. Cutler, R. G. Frank, Z. Griliches, and J. P. Newhouse. 2001. "Price Index for Medical Care Goods and Services—an Overview of Measurement Issues." In *Medical Output and Productivity*, Studies in Income and Wealth, volume 62, edited by D. M. Cutler and E. R. Berndt, 141–98. Chicago: University of Chicago Press.

Canadian Institute for Health Information (CIHI). 2007a. *CIHI DAD Resource Intensity Weights and Expected Length of Stay for CMG+2009.* Ottawa: Canadian Institute for Health Information.

———. 2007b. "Trends in Acute Inpatient Hospitalizations and Day Surgery Visits in Canada, 1995/1996 to 2005/2006." Ottawa: Canadian Institute for Health Information.

———. 2011a. *Canadian MIS Database—Hospital Financial Indicators, 1999–2000 to 2000–2010.* Ottawa: Canadian Institute for Health Information.

———. 2011b. *Health Care Cost Drivers: The Facts.* Ottawa: Canadian Institute for Health Information.

———. 2011c. *National Health Expenditure Trends, 1975–2011.* Ottawa: Canadian Institute for Health Information.

———. 2012a. *Data Quality Documentation for External Users: Discharge Abstract Database—Multiyear Information.* Ottawa: Canadian Institute for Health Information.

———. 2012b. *Hospital Cost Drivers Technical Report—What Factors Have Determined Hospital Expenditure Trends in Canada?* Ottawa: Canadian Institute for Health Information.

Carton, B., and B. Murphy. 1996. "Hospital Price Inflation: What Does the New PPI Tell Us?" *Monthly Labor Review* 24:24–31.

CEC, IMF, OECD, UN, and World Bank. 1993. *Systems of National Accounts, 1993.* New York: Commission of the European Communities-Eurostat, International Monetary Fund, Organisation for Economic Co-operation and Development, United Nations, and World Bank.

Dawson, D. H. Gravelle, M. O'Mahoney, A. Street, M. Weale, A. Castelli, R. Jacobs, et al. 2005. *Developing New Approaches to Measuring NHS Outputs and Productivity.* Final Report to the Department of Health, Centre for Health Economics (York), and National Institute of Economic and Social Research.

EC, IMF, OECD, UN, and World Bank. 2009. *Systems of National Accounts, 2008.* New York: European Commission, International Monetary Fund, Organisation for Economic Co-operation and Development, United Nations, and World Bank.

Eurostat. 2001. *Handbook on Price and Volume Measures in National Accounts.* Luxembourg, Germany, European Communities. Luxemberg: Office for Official Publications of the European Communities.

Hicks, V., and J. Zhang. 2003. *Hospital Price Index Feasibility Study.* Ottawa: Canadian Institute for Health Information.

Hill, T. P. 1975. *Price and Volume Measures for Non-Market Services.* Report to the Statistical Office of the European Communities. Brussels.

Jorgenson, D. W., and Z. Griliches. 1967. "The Explanation of Productivity Change." *Review of Economic Studies* 34 (3): 249–83.

Koechlin F., L. Lorenzoni, and P. Schreyer. 2010. "Comparing Price Levels of Hospital Services across Countries." OECD Health Working Papers no. 53, OECD, Paris.

Kitchen, G. 1997. "Measuring the Constant Dollar Output of Hospitals and Education." *Proceedings of Business and Trade Statistics Conference.* Ottawa: Statistics Canada.

Maynard, J. P. 2005. *Annual Measure of the Volume of Work Consistent with the SNA: The Canadian Experience.* Economic Analysis Methodology Paper Series: National Accounts no. 005, Statistics Canada Catalogue no. 11F0026MIE. Ottawa: Statistics Canada.

National Research Council. 2010. *Accounting for Health and Health Care: Approaches to Measuring the Sources and Costs of Their Improvement.* Washington, DC: National Academic Press.

Schreyer, P. 2010. *Towards Measuring the Volume Output of Education and Health Services: A Handbook.* OECD Statistics Directorate Working Paper no. 31, STD/DOC(2010)2, OECD, Paris.

———. 2012. "Output, Outcome, and Quality Adjustment in Measuring Education and Health Services." *Review of Income and Wealth* 58 (2): 257–78.

Sharpe, A., C. Bradley, and H. Messinger. 2007. *The Measurement of Output and Productivity in the Health Care Sector in Canada: An Overview. Report Prepared for the Canadian Medical Association (CAM).* Ottawa: Centre for the Study of Living Standards.

Solow, R. 1957. "Technical Change and Aggregate Production Function." *Review of Economics and Statistics* 39:312–20.

Statistics Canada. 2001. *A Guide to Deflating Input/Output Accounts: Sources and Methods.* Statistics Canada Catalogue no. 15F0077GI. Ottawa: Statistics Canada.

Triplett, J. E. 2001. "What Is Different About Health? Human Repair and Car Repair in National Accounts and in National Health Accounts." In *Medical Output and Productivity*, Studies in Income and Wealth volume 62, edited by D. M. Cutler and E. R. Berndt, 15–96. Chicago: University of Chicago Press.

———. 2006. *Handbook on Hedonic Indexes and Quality Adjustments in Price Indexes: Special Application to Information Technology Products.* Paris: OECD.

Yu, K., and R. Ariste. 2009. *Comparisons of Hospital Output in Canada: National and International Perspectives.* Unpublished Paper. Lakehead University and Canadian Institute for Health Information.

18

Innovation Accounting

Carol A. Corrado and Charles R. Hulten

> We will be more likely to promote innovative activity if we
> are able to measure it more effectively and document its role
> in economic growth.
> —US Federal Reserve chairman Ben S. Bernanke, May 2011[1]

The National Income and Product Accounts (NIPAs) are one of the most important achievements of the field of economics. They provide a time-series record of the volume of economic activity and its major components, one that is reasonably consistent over time. The NIPAs thus provide a quantitative framework for understanding the magnitude and sources of past economic growth and a framework for diagnosing current economic problems. It is hard to imagine the formulation of recent economic policy without the information contained in the national accounts.

This is precisely what policymakers had to confront during the Great Depression. Nascent GDP estimates first rose to prominence during World War II, where they played a critical role in resource planning. First published in the late 1940s, the US NIPAs have evolved to include dozens of tables that incorporate a vast quantity of data from a large number of sources.

For all this impressive effort, the national accounting system has come under criticism from a number of directions. It is essentially an account of the sources and uses of the nation's productive capacity as represented by its market activity. While such data are of great importance for addressing critical economic issues and trends, they do not address other important issues.

Carol A. Corrado is senior advisor and research director in economics at The Conference Board and a senior policy scholar at the Georgetown University Center for Business and Public Policy. Charles R. Hulten is professor of economics at the University of Maryland and a research associate of the National Bureau of Economic Research.

For acknowledgments, sources of research support, and disclosure of the authors' material financial relationships, if any, please see http://www.nber.org/chapters/c12837.ack.

1. Quote from keynote address at an international conference on intangibles held at Georgetown University in Washington, DC., in May 2011.

For example, they omit important nonmarket activities, like those arising in the household sector of the economy, and more generally, the various activities associated with the use of time. The effect upon the environment is also an area in which the national accounts have traditionally had little to say. Finally, there is dissatisfaction with the use of gross domestic product as the summary statistic of national living standards. This concept is said to be too easily confused with economic well-being, perhaps even with happiness, which depends, among other things, on the way GDP is distributed among people and on the choices people make about nonmarket uses of time.

These issues provide the subject matter of much of this conference and proceedings. Our contribution takes a different look at the problem of GDP as a market concept. Within the general framework of the sources and uses of a nation's productive capacity as presented in the accounts, we ask whether GDP as currently measured provides a sufficient account of the forces causing GDP to grow over time. Our focus is on the processes of innovation that have both greatly affected the growth and composition of US GDP in recent decades and been a persistent long-run driver of rising living standards. Our previous work (Corrado, Hulten, and Sichel 2005, 2009; Corrado and Hulten 2010) on this topic focused mainly on how much of an economy's aggregate resources is directed to innovation.

One of the most important purposes of the national accounts is to provide a long-term historical record against which to judge trends in economic growth, and present data with which to explain these trends. Table 1.1.6 of the US national accounts, for example, indicates that real GDP in 2005 stood at $976 billion in 1929, the first year for which GDP data are available, and that this figure rose to $2 trillion in 1950 and then to $13.3 trillion in 2011. These estimates imply an average annual growth rate of more than 3.2% over the 1929 to 2011 period as a whole. When viewed against the backdrop of these estimates, the 1.6 percent rate of growth since 2000 and 0.2 percent growth rate since 2007 are particularly weak. But what do we infer from this slowdown and the accompanying slowdown in productivity growth? The usual footprints of a prolonged and deep recession—or the economy's innovation processes grinding to a halt?

Accounting practice has traditionally linked inputs of capital and labor to the output of consumption, investment, net exports, and government output in the context of the circular flow of products and payments. No explicit account was taken of the innovations in technology and the organization of production that led either to a greater quantity of output from a given base of inputs or improvements in the quality of the inputs and outputs. This situation has changed dramatically with the *System of National Accounts 2008* (European Commission et al. 2009) decision to capitalize certain types of research and development expenditure in the national accounts framework. Research and development (R&D) is unquestionably an important part of the innovation process, but it is by no means the only part or even the most important part. We have found, in our previous research, that a very broad definition of innovation investment—commonly referred to as "intangibles"—has been the largest systematic driver of economic growth in business sector output over the last fifty years (Corrado and Hulten 2010), and that US businesses currently invest more in intangibles than they do in traditional fixed assets (figure 18.1). Most of these intangibles are currently omitted from both national and financial accounting practice.

This chapter describes some of the steps involved in building a more comprehensive national innovation account as a satellite to the main national accounting framework. A complete national innovation account would necessarily span intangible investments by businesses, households, and government. Our previous work has been almost entirely on the first category and the bulk of our comments here will continue to be directed at business intangible capital and its measurement. We emphasize the importance of the quality dimension of intangible investment, an issue heretofore largely absent from the intangibles literature. Our most recent work places this issue

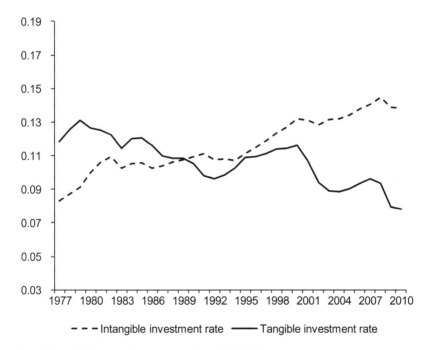

Fig. 18.1   US business investment rates, 1977–2010

Source: Update using methods originally set out in Corrado, Hulten, and Sichel (2005, 2009) modified to include the BEA's estimates of performer R&D and entertainment and artistic originals (Moylan and Robbins 2007 and Soloveichek 2010, respectively), and the revised method for estimating investment in new financial products reported in Corrado et al. (2012).

Notes: Ratio to business output adjusted to include new intangibles. Figures for recent years are preliminary estimates.

in the foreground of intangibles analysis (Hulten 2010a, 2010b, 2012; Corrado, Goodridge, and Haskel 2011).

18.1 Expanding the Existing Accounts

National income and product accounting is a familiar and well-established field of economics, as is growth accounting. Innovation accounting is not, though the SNA 2003 decision to capitalize software and artistic originals followed by, as previously mentioned, the same move for R&D in SNA 2008 are important steps in that direction. There are, of course, many innovation metrics in the innovation literature (e.g., number of patents), but they are not integrated into an internally consistent framework linked to a common performance measure. Because economic innovation is valued in large part because of its effects on income and wealth, embedding an innovation account within the larger GDP and growth accounting framework makes sense. A natural way to proceed, therefore, is to ask how the existing product, wealth, and growth accounts might be supplemented or expanded to accommodate this objective.

The growth accounting model already contains a rudimentary innovation account in the form of total factor productivity (TFP). TFP is generally associated with costless "technical change," which is one manifestation of innovation. The problem with this approach to innovation accounting is that TFP is typically measured as a residual, a fact that has earned it the name "the measure of our ignorance." Moreover, because TFP is a partial indicator of innovation outcomes, it is not a complete basis for innovation accounting itself.

The residual TFP model developed by Solow (1957) and extended by Jorgenson and Griliches (1967) is nonetheless the starting point of the analysis that follows. In the Solow-Jorgenson-Griliches model, production, Q_t, takes place under constant returns and Hicks's neutral productivity change, A_t:

$$(1.1) \qquad Q_t = A_t F(K_t, L_t).$$

Under the conditions of competitive equilibrium, the value of the marginal products of labor and capital, L_t and K_t, equal corresponding factor prices P_t^L and P_t^K, and the GDP/GDI identity can be derived from the production function. Moreover, the growth rate of output can be decomposed into the contributions of labor and capital, weighted by their respective income shares, plus the growth rate of the Hicksian efficiency term:

$$(1.2) \qquad \frac{\dot{Q}_t}{Q_t} = \left[\frac{P_t^K K_t}{P_t^Q Q_t}\right]\frac{\dot{K}_t}{K_t} + \left[\frac{P_t^L L_t}{P_t^Q Q_t}\right]\frac{\dot{L}_t}{L_t} + \frac{\dot{A}_t}{A_t}.$$

Expressions with overdots are rates of growth. The first two terms on the right-hand side of (1.2) are the contributions of capital and labor to the growth in output, interpreted as a movement along the production function, while the last term in the output growth occurs as a result of productivity change, interpreted as a shift in the function.

In the following subsections, we will consider the modifications and additions needed to expand the basic growth accounting framework to be a more comprehensive and explicit framework for measuring innovation. This involves four general steps, some of which have already been undertaken (in part or in whole):

- introducing innovation inputs such as R&D into the underlying model
- making product quality change an explicit component of real GDP
- making quality change in the inputs of labor and capital more explicit
- making process improvements that lower unit costs and prices more explicit

We discuss each of these topics and then turn our attention to measurement.

18.1.1   Capitalizing Intangibles Reveals Investments in Innovation

The link between productivity, intangible investments, and innovation has roots in numerous literatures. R&D has been part of neoclassical growth accounting since the 1970s (Griliches 1973, 1979) and innovation was made explicit in endogenous growth models beginning in the 1990s (e.g., Romer 1990, Aghion and Howitt 2007).

Corrado, Hulten, and Sichel (2005, 2009) examined the question of how the amount spent on innovation in each year is represented in the current price GDP accounts. This involves two separate adjustments, one to output for the amount spent in each year and the other to factor inputs for the capitalized value of this spending. R&D tops the list of items included in this spending, but the list is in fact much longer, as emphasized in our earlier work with Sichel as well as some preceding studies (e.g., Nakamura 2001). In short, a broad concept of R&D is needed to fully represent the innovation process. Innovation involves coinvestments in marketing, worker training, and organizational development. As noted in the introduction, the items on this longer list of innovation-related expenditures have come to be called "intangible capital."

Including intangible capital in the fundamental national accounting identity involves adjustments to both GDP and gross domestic income, GDI. To keep things simple, we examine the case in which a single intangible is capitalized and added to the national accounting identity. The value of aggregate output is represented by $P_t^Q Q_t$, but now nominal-price investment in the intangible, $P_t^N N_t$, is added to the other components of final demand $(P_t^C C_t + P_t^I I_t)$ to obtain GDP. On the income/input side, the gross income accruing to the stock of intangibles, $P_t^R R_t$, is treated as a component of GDI.

The expanded accounting identity now has the form:

$$(1.3) \qquad P_t^Q Q_t = P_t^C C_t + P_t^I I_t + P_t^N N_t = P_t^L L_t + P_t^K K_t + P_t^R R_t.$$

The corresponding growth accounting equation then has the form

$$(1.4) \quad \frac{\dot{Q}_t}{Q_t} = \left[\frac{P_t^K K_t}{P_t^Q Q_t}\right]\frac{\dot{K}_t}{K_t} + \left[\frac{P_t^R R_t}{P_t^Q Q_t}\right]\frac{\dot{R}_t}{R_t} + \left[\frac{P_t^L L_t}{P_t^Q Q_t}\right]\frac{\dot{L}_t}{L_t} + \frac{\dot{A}_t}{A_t},$$

where the output index now includes real investment in the intangible asset

$$(1.5) \quad \frac{\dot{Q}_t}{Q_t} = \left[\frac{P_t^C C_t}{P_t^Q Q_t}\right]\frac{\dot{C}_t}{C_t} + \left[\frac{P_t^I I_t}{P_t^Q Q_t}\right]\frac{\dot{I}_t}{I_t} + \left[\frac{P_t^L N_t}{P_t^Q Q_t}\right]\frac{\dot{N}_t}{N_t}.$$

The stock of intangible capital R_t is the accumulated real intangible investment N_t via the perpetual inventory model (PIM): $R_t = N_t + (1 - \delta)R_{t-1}$. The term δ is the rate of decay of appropriable revenues from the conduct of commercial knowledge production.

The accounting algebra of intangible capital is relatively straightforward. The interpretation, however, is less so.

Enter Demand

First, unlike tangible capital and labor, intangible capital is not a direct input to production, in the sense that an increase in R&D or marketing does not necessarily have a direct impact on the production of the goods made for sale. This raises a question about the interpretation of the share weights in equation (1.4). The literature has generally adopted the position that intangible investment affects output indirectly via the efficiency shift term, A_t. This is a reasonable assumption for many types of intangible capital, but not all types. Product R&D and marketing are not directed at increasing the efficiency of production but, rather, to the design and sale of goods and services. Hulten (2012) provides one solution to this problem by introducing demand-side considerations into the growth accounting framework and, following Nerlove and Arrow (1962), making the income-share weights depend, in part, on the elasticity of product demand. This solution implies that the introduction of intangibles into the accounting framework involves a basic shift in the perspective away from a pure production function foundation.

. . . and Market Power

Models in which innovation is explicit treat it as a source of market power, which also introduces demand-side elements to the model. Romer (1990) assumed innovators were, in effect, a separate sector of the economy (he called it the design sector) who practiced monopoly pricing. In Romer the innovator's price is given by $P = \gamma MC$, where MC is the marginal cost of producing a new good and γ is the producer markup, a function of the good's price elasticity of demand (Romer 1990, unnumbered equations at the top of page S87). Romer goes on to formulate the intertemporal zero-profit constraint, whose solution equates the instantaneous excess of revenue over marginal production cost as just sufficient to cover the interest cost of the innovation investment (equations 6 and 6', page S87).

In a two-sector neoclassical growth model where the two sectors are a production sector and an R&D sector, Romer's solution for producers' markups can be shown to be a transformation of the factor share of intangible capital (Corrado, Goodridge, and Haskel 2011, 12). Let this ratio be denoted as s^R, which is $P^R R / P^Q Q$ from above, time subscripts ignored. When intangible investment is equated to Romer's "innovation investment" and variable production costs C are equated with marginal costs,[2] Corrado, Goodridge, and Haskel (2011) showed that the Romer producer markup equals $1/(1 - s^R)$; that is, that it must be sufficient to generate revenue that covers the "interest cost" of innovation.

The existence of market power in the innovation sector stems from a host of underlying business dynamics that are suppressed for the sake of simplicity in an aggregate model. Commercial knowledge is modeled as nonrival and appropriable in these models—but in reality new products and processes constantly come and go, each with a finite period of appropriability. Commercial knowledge may be thus represented as a single asset being produced and "sold" at a monopoly price in all periods in these models, but the underlying dynamics involve overlays of case after case of Romer's intertemporal zero-profit solution.[3]

Romer notes that the design sector can of course be in-house, consistent with the fact that most business intangibles are produced and used within the confines of a firm and therefore do not generate an externally observable price and quantity. This is not a problem for theory, which can appeal to shadow prices in the place of market-determined prices, but it poses serious problems for the measurement of these intangibles. Measurement is discussed in a separate section below.

18.1.2   Real Output Includes Quality Change

GDP is a measure of the volume of output flowing through markets, valued at current market prices. This is a source of strength as well as a source of weakness. It is a strength because market flows are observable by the statistician and market valuations are an arm's-length indicator of the value

---

2. Variable production costs exclude the costs of R&D labs.
3. One implication of this solution is that value of own-produced intangibles in a given industry at a given point in time includes an innovator markup, $\mu_{i,t} \geq 1$, that may be modeled as a multiple of the competitive factor costs of the inputs used up in the innovation process. Variants of such a formulation entered BEA's R&D satellite account (Moylan and Robbins 2007), the calculations in Hulten and Hao (2008), and Corrado, Goodridge, and Haskel's (2011) suggested method for calculating R&D price deflators. Like s^R, in the Corrado, Goodridge, and Haskel (2011, unnumbered equation, p. 18) model, the parameter μ is related to the price elasticity of demand, and ignoring time and industry subscripts, the producer markup γ then becomes $1/(1 - \mu s^R)$.

of the transaction to both seller and buyer. GDP growth also has important implications for employment and personal incomes. On the other hand, aggregate GDP does not address the question of how the gains from innovation are shared in the population, nor does it address nonmarket activity.

The greatest potential weakness from the standpoint of innovation accounting is that it may not capture the full benefits of new or greatly improved products. The point was forcefully made by William Nordhaus (1997, 5–55) when he argued in his paper on the history of lighting that "official price and output data may miss the most important revolutions in history," because they miss the really large ("tectonic") advances in technology.[4] The importance of quality change and the potential for measurement bias are underscored by Bils and Klenow (2001), who use Engel curve analysis to estimate the rate of quality upgrading in a cross-section sample of sixty-six consumer durables over the years 1980 to 1996. They found that quality growth in their sample occurred at an average annual rate of about 3.7 percent, and concluded that BLS price estimates "did not fully net out the impact of quality upgrading" (p. 1029), missing some 60 percent of the quality effect.[5]

Quality change can occur both through upgrading of existing products and through technological breakthroughs that result in new goods, and both offer the possibility of measurement bias. This bias tends to lead to an overstatement of the growth in prices and a corresponding understatement in the growth in real output, measured in units of effectiveness rather than transaction units (e.g., a personal computer measured in units of computing power versus the physical computer sold). When an adjustment for quality is made, an increase in the effectiveness of a good is measured in terms of the equivalent quantity of the older vintage of the good needed achieve the same result. In other words, "better" is treated as "more."

The translation of "better" product into "more" can be incorporated into the growth accounting framework in the following way. Following Hulten (2010a, 2010b), let output in effectiveness units be denoted by Q_t^e and the

---

4. The issues involved with output quality adjustment can be illustrated by the following example. There are two countries, A and B, each with two workers who can produce one unit of output each (widgets). Labor productivity in both countries is thus equal to one. Country A then deploys one worker that is employed in research aimed at increasing productivity while the other worker remains in production and now produces three widgets. Labor productivity rises to 1.5. Country B does almost the same thing, but its researcher is employed in improving the quality of widgets so that one new widget is the equivalent of three old ones. If country B's new widgets are not adjusted for quality, then the measure of labor productivity will appear to have fallen to 0.5. On the other hand, if a quality adjustment is made, labor productivity in B is the same as in country A. Failure to make a quality correction thus leads to a biased comparison of growth in the two countries.

5. On the other hand, Greenlees and McClelland (2011) use a hedonic characteristics approach and find that, in the case of packaged food, BLS likely has *underestimated* price change. The complexity of the quality measurement issue is discussed in greater detail in appendix B of this chapter.

corresponding transaction-based quantity by Q_t. The corresponding prices are P_t^e and P_t. Because the total amount spent on acquiring the good V_t is invariant to the units of measurement, we have:

(1.6) $\qquad\qquad V_t = P_t Q_t = P_t^e Q_t^e$, and $Q_t^e = V_t / P_t^e$.

In the hedonic model, Q_t^e is viewed as a bundle of characteristics (faster processor, more memory, etc.), and an increase in Q_t^e is seen as an increase in one or more of the characteristics. The overall amount of the increase is determined by computing the hedonic price of each characteristic using regression techniques and using the results to determine the implied Q_t^e. This procedure makes Q_t^e depend on customers' valuation of the innovation.

The implication for growth accounting is that the growth in output in effectiveness units—that is, inclusive of product innovation—has two components: a pure production quantity component and a quality component based on prices,

(1.7) $$ \frac{\dot{Q}_t^e}{Q_t^e} = \frac{\dot{Q}_t}{Q_t} + \left[\frac{\dot{P}_t}{P_t} - \frac{\dot{P}_t^e}{P_t^e} \right]. $$

There is a reasonable argument for both concepts of output as the appropriate variable for the production function (1.1). This argument disappears in favor of Q_t^e when product-oriented R&D is made an explicit input in the production function as per the discussion of investments in innovation in the previous section (after all, why would funds for this purpose be expended?). The TFP residual then becomes

(1.8) $$ \frac{\dot{A}_t^e}{A_t^e} = \frac{\dot{A}_t}{A_t} + \left[\frac{\dot{P}_t}{P_t} - \frac{\dot{P}_t^e}{P_t^e} \right] $$

The algebra of product quality may be straightforward, but like the issues that arise when analyzing intangibles as investments in innovation, the conceptual framework requires a shift from a purely supply-side view of growth accounting to one in which output is both produced and sold, and involves elements from the demand side.

18.1.3   Other Elements in the TFP Residual

Product-oriented innovation is reflected in the price terms of the quality-corrected real GDP identity, equation (1.7), and in TFP, equation (1.8). It is there that the profusion of new or improved products arising from the IT revolution is reflected. However, the IT revolution has also had major impacts on process innovation. Advances in computing and software and Internet engagement are widely acknowledged as sources of ongoing productivity-enhancing business process improvements (e.g., from moving B2B transactions to the Internet, to adopting whole new systems for supply-chain and inventory management). These impacts operate through two different channels involving the $\dot{A}_t / A_t$ term in equation (1.8). This term is a function of the amount of process-oriented intangible capital, and increases as the stock increases. This is the direct efficiency effect of intangibles. There is also an indirect effect associated with spillovers from the original innovator to other users. This is the lower cost (sometimes no cost) externality effect, akin to the manna from heaven formulation of the original Solow residual. There is also a component of the efficiency term that arises from autonomous "tinkering" and learning effects. These effects serve to increase output per unit input and lower unit costs.

The reallocation of resources between efficient and inefficient firms is also a source of aggregate efficiency gain in the A_t parameter. Empirical research has shown that this is an important effect (Foster, Haltiwanger, and Krizan 2001), particularly when the reallocation is due to young, rapidly growing innovators displacing incumbent firms. Reallocation also has an important international dimension, and innovators in the United States and Europe outsource the production segment of the international value chain to foreign countries. A complete account of innovation would thus involve both a domestic industry and firm level of detail, as well as a global dimension.

18.1.4   Real Inputs and Quality Change

The preceding formulation implicitly implies that quality change affects final goods and services (i.e., output). An adjustment to this model is needed when quality change occurs in investment goods because capital is also an input to the production process.

Quality Change and Capital Goods

The capital services term that appears as an input into the production function must be adjusted for the quality change embodied in the successive vintages of investment that comprise its underlying net stocks. Solow's 1960 model of capital-embodied technical change is one way to proceed. In this model, investment goods are measured in both effectiveness and transaction units that are linked by an efficiency index: $H_t = \Phi_t I_t$. As with the consumption goods model, the efficiency index is equal to the price ratio P_t^I/P_t^H. The capital stock in any year is built up using a perpetual inventory equation for both the efficiency and transaction unit denominated stocks.

Hulten (1992) shows that the resulting efficiency stock (Solow's "jelly" stock J_t) is proportional to the transaction-based stock, K_t, implying that $J_t = \Psi_t K_t$. The proportionality factor, Ψ_t, is the weighted sum of the past efficiency indexes, Φ_t, and the corresponding capital-embodied growth accounts can therefore be expressed as a quality-modified version of equation (1.2):

$$(1.9) \quad \frac{\dot{Q}_t}{Q_t} = \left[\frac{P_t^K K_t}{P_t^Q Q_t}\right]\frac{\dot{K}_t}{K_t} + \left[\frac{P_t^L L_t}{P_t^Q Q_t}\right]\frac{\dot{L}_t}{L_t} + \frac{\dot{A}_t}{A_t} + \left\langle \left[\frac{P_t^K K_t}{P_t^Q Q_t}\right]\frac{\dot{\Psi}_t}{\Psi_t} - \left[\frac{P_t^I I_t}{P_t^Q Q_t}\right]\frac{\dot{\Phi}_t}{\Phi_t}\right\rangle.$$

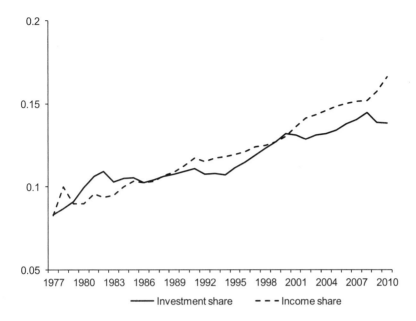

Fig. 18.2   Intangible investment and capital income
Note: Ratio to business output adjusted to include new intangibles.

As before, the correction for quality change involves additional terms in the growth account. From a practical standpoint, the efficiency terms can be estimated using a hedonic price model and the corresponding price equations are: $\Phi_t = P_t^I / P_t^H$ and $\Psi_t = P_t^K / P_t^J$. (Note that for simplicity's sake, we show Q, not Q^e in this equation.)

If improvements in efficiency proceed at a constant rate along the optimal consumption path of a Golden Rule steady state, capital income and investment shares are equal. The terms in (1.9) that correct for quality change cancel out in this special case, including the terms in intangible capital, not shown in (1.9), but which parallel those for tangible capital. The shares for intangible capital are shown in figure 18.2, which illustrates that while these shares run close to one another, the term generally is a source of change.

The Composition of Labor Input

The single labor term in the production function (1.1), L_t, assumes that labor is a homogenous input. If there are N categories of workers, this single variable must be replaced with the hours worked in each of the j different categories $H_{j,t}$. In this case, the production function is assumed to have the form

(1.10) $$Q_t = A_t F(L(H_{1,t}, \ldots, H_{N,t}), K_t),$$

where $L(H_{1,t}, \ldots, H_{N,t})$ is an index of the different types of labor. If each type is paid the value of its marginal product, the growth rate of the labor index is equal to the growth rate of the hours worked by each type of labor, weighted by its share in the total wage bill:

$$(1.11) \qquad \frac{\dot{L}_t}{L_t} = \sum_{j=1}^{N} \frac{w_{j,t} H_{j,t}}{\sum_j w_{j,t} H_{j,t}} \frac{\dot{H}_{j,t}}{H_{j,t}}.$$

Following Jorgenson and Griliches (1967), the left-hand side of this equation can be decomposed into two components, one representing total hours worked by all types of worker, $H_t = \sum_j H_{j,t}$, and another the share-weighted change in the relative composition of hours worked:

$$(1.12) \qquad \frac{\dot{L}_t}{L_t} = \frac{\dot{H}_t}{H_t} + \sum_{j=1}^{N} \left[\frac{w_{j,t} H_{j,t}}{\sum_j w_{j,t} H_{j,t}} \right] \left[\frac{\dot{H}_{j,t}}{H_{j,t}} - \frac{\dot{H}_t}{H_t} \right].$$

The first term on the right-hand side represents the change in labor input due to increases in total hours worked, while the second term measures the increase in effective labor input as the composition of total hours worked shifts to higher productivity (wage) categories. For this reason, the composition term is sometimes called labor "quality." The Jorgenson-Griliches labor decomposition (1.12) can thus be inserted into the growth accounting equation (1.4) to yield yet another "effectiveness" correction.

The labor composition adjustment does not involve innovation per se. In practical applications of the model, workers are often disaggregated along education and occupation dimensions. And an important finding in the literature is that increases in educational attainment have been a significant contributor to the growth in output per worker in the United States, especially in the last three decades. Thus, while not innovation per se, the labor composition term is generally regarded as the *direct* channel through which the impact of human capital accumulation on economic growth occurs.

As may be seen in the accompanying chart (figure 18.3), when the growth in US labor input is broken down into just three skill-based categories, the contribution of high-skilled labor dominates the picture of the past fifteen years. The contribution of skilled workers and managers to economic growth via the accumulation of intangible capital *within* firms (and thereby owned and exercised *by* firms) is over and above the direct influence of private returns to such workers in the labor composition, or labor "quality," term, plotted in figure 18.3.

18.2.   Implementation and Measurement

The theoretical problems of establishing an innovation account even in the limited sense of this chapter present many difficulties, but the issues of implementation present equally great, or perhaps even greater, difficulties. A

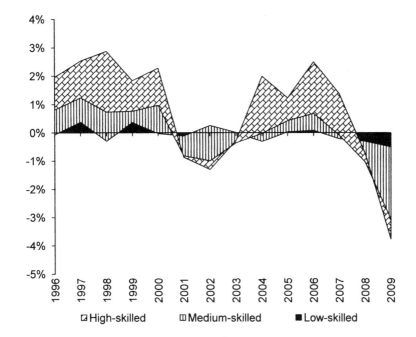

Fig. 18.3   Labor services contributions by skill type, 1996–2009
Source: Author's elaboration of data from the World Input-Output Database, available at www.wiod.org.

major problem arises from the fact that much innovation occurs within the confines of the firm and the processes giving rise to the innovation are hard to observe. Indeed, firms usually have a strong interest in preventing them from being observed in order to protect intellectual property. In some cases, these processes may be imperfectly seen or understood by the managers of the firm (the financial crisis and the role of new financial instruments). In this section, we also examine the implications for innovation accounting of some of the measurement issues that arise in these areas.

18.2.1   Extending the Asset Boundary

When questioned about the relevance of the existing asset boundary for intangibles in national accounts more than six years ago, US BEA director Steve Landefeld answered, "No one disagrees with [the capitalization of intangibles such as R&D] conceptually. The problem is in the empirical measurement."[6] Since then researchers and practitioners at national statisti-

6. Reported on page 66 of "Unmasking the Economy," *Business Week* (February 13, 2006, pp. 62–70), by Michael Mandel.

cal offices and international organizations have done much to remedy "the problem in empirical measurement."[7]

The discussion and equation (1.3) above suggests that to estimate intangible capital and analyze its role in economic growth as per equations (1.4) and (1.5), we need:

- a list of intangible assets to be measured
- magnitudes for the nominal investment flows $P_t^N N_t$ for each asset type
- a means to separate these flows into price P_t^N and quantity N_t components
- service lives of each asset to enable the compilation of net stocks R_t
- a means to estimate P_t^R

We briefly review the state of measurement in these areas. Many more details and discussion are found in Corrado et al. (2012, 2013).

Asset Types Anchor the Framework

In broad terms, as of a March 2012 OECD (Organisation for Economic Co-operation and Development) expert meeting on the measurement of intangibles, the list of intangible asset types proposed by Corrado, Hulten, and Sichel (2005) remained the main framework for measurement (table 18.1). By contrast, methods used to estimate the nominal investment flows and develop an understanding of the underlying innovation processes represented by intangible assets are evolving and advancing. A major reason for the forward progress on measurement is intense interest by The Conference Board, the European Commission, and the OECD (among others) to better understand the macroeconomic impact and underlying nature of the innovation investments needed for knowledge-based economies to continue to grow and compete effectively in current global markets.

We will not discuss the asset categories in table 18.1 here in detail, except to note that assets fall into three broad categories: computerized information, innovative property, and economic competencies, and that these categories are populated with nine asset types (the rationale for each subcategory is discussed in detail in Corrado, Hulten, and Sichel 2005, 2009). The list is surprisingly similar to that in the IRS guide for reporting the value of financial assets following a corporate merger or acquisition, though the two frameworks were developed independently.[8] It is notable that both embrace

7. This section draws liberally from an elaboration and "harmonization" of what was learned from work under two projects funded by the European Commission (COINVEST and INNO-DRIVE, which concluded late 2010/early 2011, respectively) and the ongoing work on intangibles at The Conference Board. See Corrado et al. (2012) at http://www.intan-invest.net/ for further details.

8. The US tax code specifies twelve intangible assets to be valued and listed as financial assets following a merger or acquisitions, including the value of the business information base, the workforce in place, know-how (listed along with patents and designs), and customer and supplier bases. (See US IRS *Publication 535, Business Expenses*, 2–31).

Table 18.1	Knowledge-based capital of the firm (a.k.a. intangibles) by asset type	
Asset type		Included in national accounts?
Computerized information		
1. Software		Yes
2. Databases		?[a]
Innovative property		
3. Mineral exploration		Yes
4. R&D (scientific)		Satellite for some[b]
5. Entertainment and artistic originals		EU-yes, US-no[c]
6. New product/systems in financial services		No
7. Design and other new product/systems		No
Economic competencies		
8. Brand equity		
a. Advertising		No
b. Marketing and market research		No
9. Firm-specific resources		
a. Employer-provided training		No
b. Organizational structure		No

Source: Corrado et al. (2012, 13).

[a]SNA 1993 recommended capitalizing computerized databases. The position of most national statistical offices is that databases are captured in current software estimates.

[b]R&D satellite accounts are available, or under preparation, in many countries. Results for Finland, the Netherlands, United Kingdom, and the United States are publicly available.

[c]The US BEA plans to include entertainment and artistic originals and R&D as investment in headline GDP in a revision in 2013.

modern business realities and value assets whose ownership is not typically protected by legal covenants.

Alternative Approaches to Estimating Nominal Investment Flows

There are at least two basic models for how to proceed to estimate nominal intangible investment flows for each of the asset types in table 18.1, which are data from deep within firms. The first is to use a survey instrument, such as the R&D surveys that are run in most industrialized countries. Businesses are accustomed to this survey, and its long and successful history suggests that a survey approach to measuring innovation costs for business functions that are separate, identifiable departments within a company is a reasonable way to go. Note also that these surveys distinguish between own company costs and purchased R&D services, as well as license payments to and from other companies.

The second approach is to follow the "software" model; that is, use data on purchases from a regular industry survey (combined with information on exports and imports) and estimate production on own-account using information on employment and wages in relevant occupations. Both approaches thus boil down to the same idea, namely, that one needs to obtain measures for *both* in-house and purchased components of intangible investment. A general expression for estimating nominal intangible investment flows was set out in Corrado et al. (2012) and Corrado and Hao (2013). Further details are shown in an appendix.

A number of other developments in the measurement of investment flows are also noteworthy. First is the pioneering work on Japan (Fukao et al. 2009) that disaggregated intangible investment according to manufacturing and nonmanufacturing. Since then the Japanese (Miyagawa and Hisa 2013) and researchers in Australia (Barnes 2010), and the United Kingdom (Dal Borgo et al. 2011) have experimented with industry-level estimates of intangibles, as such disaggregation can be important for policy analysis. Box 18.1 highlights some of the hurdles that need to be crossed to develop accurate data on intangibles by industry for the United States.

Second is the emerging survey work on investment in intangible assets in the United Kingdom (Awano et al. 2010). The UK survey goes beyond R&D and asks companies for information on own-account expenses and purchases of intangibles for five major categories of intangibles (software, R&D, new product development expenses not reported as R&D, information on investments in worker training, and likewise for organizational development). The approach relies on firms being able to report spending in certain categories that lasts more than one year and contrasts with the approach in innovation surveys (the "community innovation surveys" popular in Europe and elsewhere) that require firms to know what innovation is, which in turn requires defining innovation and assuming firms interpret the questions and instructions in a consistent manner.

Third is the research that has used detailed information of occupations and/or microdata to study the link between intangibles and performance at the firm or industry level. This research has yielded insights on the value of the parameters that appear in equation (A1.1) of the appendix and it has identified new or improved sources for indicators used for components. For example, an improved own-cost indicator for investments in new financial products was developed, first, in the COINVEST project funded by the European Commission, and then by Corrado and Hao (forthcoming) using a grouping of occupational codes identified for the analysis of financial innovation; for further details and comparative results using this new indicator for twenty-seven European countries plus Norway and the United States, see Corrado et al. (2012, 2013). The move notably lowered estimates of investment in new financial products but did not otherwise change the comparative analysis of saving and economic growth with intangibles in these countries.

Another line of work uses linked employee-employer microdata, including data on firm performance; such data sets have been used to study human capital formation and its link to market performance in the United States as, for example, in Abowd et al. (2005). The INNODRIVE project funded

Box 18.1
Industry analysis of intangibles a tough haul for the United States

Analysis of innovative activity with establishment-based industry data presents certain difficulties in the United States. With the implementation of the NAICS (North American Industry Classification System) nearly fifteen years ago in the United States, some of the country's most innovative firms (Apple, Cisco, Nvidia, and other so-called factoryless makers, including certain pharmaceutical companies) were regarded as resellers of imported goods (imagine!) and placed in the wholesale trade sector.* The headquarter operations of many companies (which may include marketing and IT departments) were placed in a separate sector (Management of Companies), and company-owned but separately located R&D labs were lumped with independent producers of R&D services in the R&S services industry. Because the BLS did not necessarily implement NAICS in the same way as did the census, industry-level productivity analysis, particularly for IT industries, has been hampered by the switch to NAICS (National Research Council 2006).

The difficulty that arises in the analysis of intangibles is that the fruits of innovative activities (profits) cannot be easily linked to the costs of innovation in industry data with head offices and R&D labs sometimes (but not always) split off. This complicates what is already a difficult problem, which is the usual disconnect between company and establishment-based industry data systems. In the United States, the Statistics of Income provide data on advertising by industry, but this is on a company basis.

The BEA worked to surmount the R&D lab location issue in developing its R&D satellite account, and the periodic Economic Census began to collect information on industries served for the Management of Companies sector in 2007 (such data were unavailable since 1997), suggesting fewer such hurdles going forward. We also speculate that industry-level estimation of intangibles is less challenging in countries where IT and pharmaceutical production outsourcing has been less abrupt and/or prevalent and classification systems did not split head offices and R&D labs from operations until very recently.

*Obviously we do not have direct knowledge of how the census classifies any given firm, but they confirm that factoryless producers are placed in wholesale trade. For the R&D survey, which is conducted by the Census Bureau for the National Science Foundation (NSF), the NSF instructs the census to classify firms by the primary line of sales for the company as a whole (i.e., on a global basis). In BLS surveys, firms more or less self-classify.

by the European Commission built linked data sets for six European countries, and one of its first findings shed light on the relative value of the intermediate and capital costs of own-account organizational capital production (Görzig, Piekkola, and Riley 2010); that is, the $P_j^M M_j$ and $P_j^K K_j$ of equation (A1.1) of Appendix A. Their findings suggest these costs are consequentially different from zero, the implicit assumption in the Corrado-Hulten-Sichel (CHS) framework.

Piekkola (2012) then pointed out that, when allowing for imperfect competition and markups, such data sets can be used to estimate both the marginal product *and* output elasticity of an asset type. He used the Finnish data set in an exercise that, among other purposes, evaluated the 20 percent assumption embedded in the CHS estimates of own-account organizational capital.[9] On balance, Piekkola found that 21 percent of the wage costs of those doing managing, marketing, and administrative work with a tertiary education can be considered as investment in organizational capital. Organizational capital is the largest component of the CHS broad category, economic competencies, and it is rather remarkable (and we do not say this lightly) that a rigorous study confirms the basic approach of CHS to estimation.

Updated Estimates of Nominal Intangible Investment Flows

The composition of US intangibles for the major categories of table 18.1 are shown in figure 18.4, which is a disaggregation of the intangible investment trend shown in figure 18.1. These estimates reflect many of the advances noted above, to the extent possible. Several points are noteworthy. First, R&D is a rather small fraction of the total intangible investment rate. The recent move by the BEA to capitalize R&D is a major step in the direction of a national innovation account, but it is a first step. The most important subcategory in terms of size is economic competencies. It is also responsible for much of the growth in the total rate.

Net Stocks of Intangible Capital and the Perpetual Inventory Method

The estimates shown in figure 18.4 are annual rates of investment. The corresponding annual investment flows determine the size and growth rate of the stocks of each type of intangible asset, in conjunction with the rate of depreciation of the existing stocks. The conventional perpetual inventory method used to estimate the stocks of tangible assets is the logical starting point for the estimation of intangible capital stocks from these annual investment series (recall, here, the discussion of equation [1.5]) However, technical and data issues confront this approach. At the conceptual level, use of the perpetual inventory method (PIM) presumes that the contributions of dif-

9. This refers to the assumption that managers devote roughly 20 percent of their time to strategic functions, and therefore that 20 percent of managerial compensation can be used as an estimate of organizational capital investments on own-account.

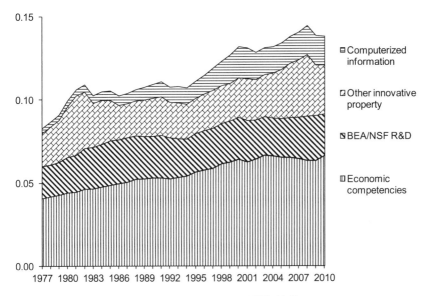

Fig. 18.4   Intangible investment by broad type, 1977–2010
Source: See source note to figure 18.1.
Note: Ratio to business output adjusted to include new intangibles.

ferent vintages of investment are separable, which is a strong assumption to impose on investment in knowledge capital (Hulten 2012).[10]

The most empirically important problem is perhaps the recognition that a model of economic depreciation reflects two distinct processes, discards and economic decay (a topic discussed extensively in Corrado et al. 2012). A design might exhibit no "economic decay" (i.e., it will never "wear out" in a quantity sense) but might be "discarded" as, for example, fashions change. The geometric depreciation rate δ in the PIM must capture the net effect of both these terms.[11] Similarly, worker training may earn long-lasting returns

10. It is not unreasonable to measure the stock of, say, vehicles, at any point in time as the sum of past purchases, adjusted for retirements and wear and tear. This is the conventional PIM approach. It is quite a different matter to assume that annual R&D expenditures by a research laboratory are highly independent, or "strongly separable" in the terminology of aggregation theory.

Moreover, the unexpected nature of returns to certain investments in intangibles and the nonrival nature of knowledge capital challenges the plausibility of the PIM when applied to intangibles. Patent protection and business secrecy give the innovator a degree of protection from the nonrivalness problem, but the value of the investment to the innovator is limited to the returns on the investment that can be captured, which in turn provides the basis for calculating net stocks. See, for example, Pakes and Schankerman (1984).

11. The geometric depreciation rate is given by $\delta = d/\bar{T}$, where $\bar{T}$ is an estimate of the service life of an asset and, intuitively, d is a parameter that reflects the degree of convexity (or curvature) of the age-price profile. Higher values of d are associated with higher discards/lower survival rates.

Table 18.2   Depreciation rates for intangible assets

Asset type	Depreciation rate
Computerized information	
1. Software	.315
2. Databases	.315
Innovative property	
3. Mineral exploration	.075
4. R&D (scientific)	.150
5. Entertainment and artistic originals	.200
6. New product/systems in financial services	.200
7. Design and other new product/systems	.200
Economic competencies	
8. Brand equity	
a. Advertising	.550
b. Market research	.550
9. Firm-specific resources	
a. Employer-provided training	.400
b. Organizational structure	.400

Source: Corrado et al. (2012, 25).

to the firm making the investment, conditional of course on the probability that the worker stays with the firm (the "survival" factor again). The Bureau of Labor Statistics (BLS) reports that the average tenure of employees in the United States is between four and five years, and this forms the basis for setting a "service life" for employer-provided training.

Direct estimates of life lengths from surveys are a relatively new source of evidence. Surveys conducted by the Israeli Statistical Bureau (Peleg 2008a, 2008b) and by Awano et al. (2010) with the UK Office of National Statistics ask about the "life length" of investments in R&D (by detailed industry in Israel) and intangible assets (R&D plus five other asset types in the United Kingdom). The bottom line is that the Israeli survey supports lengthening the service life for R&D (as does a good bit of the R&D literature), while the UK survey confirms that the very fast depreciation rates CHS assumed for economic competencies are about right. As a result, in terms of depreciation rates, the main change that has thus far been made to the original CHS rates is to use a depreciation rate of .15 for R&D (see table 18.2), which is the central estimate of the depreciation rate for R&D adopted by BEA in its satellite account (Moylan and Robbins 2007).[12]

---

12. One complication here is that technical knowledge and design investments are not only "inputs" to the production of goods and services, they are also inputs to the production of further intangible capital. One implication is that some knowledge investments may have a longer useful life.

Prices for Intangible Investments and Assets

Intangible investment in real terms—obtaining each N_j—is a particular challenge because units of knowledge cannot be readily defined. Although price deflators for certain intangibles (software, mineral exploration) are found in national accounts, generally speaking, output price measures for intangibles have escaped price collectors' statistical net.

An exception is the emerging work on price measures for R&D. The US BEA (Bureau of Economic Analysis) offered an R&D-specific output price in its preliminary R&D satellite account (Moylan and Robbins 2007; Copeland, Medeiros, and Robbins 2007; and Copeland and Fixler 2009). A contrasting approach is in the recent paper by Corrado, Goodridge, and Haskel (2011), which casts the calculation of a price deflator for R&D in terms of estimating its contribution to productivity. The solution hinges importantly on the decomposition of productivity change, which depends on parameters such as the producer and innovator markups discussed in section 18.1.1, the degree to which quality change is captured in existing GDP (section 18.1.2), and the extent to which the current growth path deviates from the "maximal" consumption path (illustrated in figure 18.2).

Applying their method to the United Kingdom yielded a price deflator for R&D that *fell* at an average rate of 7.5 percent per year from 1995 to 2005, and thus implied that real UK R&D *rose* 12 percent annually over the same period. This stands in sharp contrast to both the science policy practice of using the GDP deflator to calculate real R&D (the UK GDP deflator *rises* 3.75 percent per year in the comparable period) and the results of applying the BEA method to the UK data (the UK BEA-style deflator rises 2.1 percent on the same basis).

The link between the price of an investment good in any year, in this case our P_t^N, to the price of its corresponding capital services (user cost), in this case our P_t^R, is a forward-looking discounted expected value:

$$(2.1) \qquad P_t^N = \sum_{\tau=1}^{\infty} \frac{(1-\delta)^\tau E(P_{t+\tau}^R)}{(1+r)^\tau},$$

which brings to light several valuation issues relevant to intangible assets. One is that expectations are not so easily reduced to an annual intertemporal valuation (and revaluation) of an asset's marginal product; in reality, the evaluation/revaluation often takes place within a strategic planning cycle. And in some circumstances, investments are made without specific expectations of a given use.

Intangible investments as firm-strategic investments suggests that they derive value from the options they may open or create (or do not rule out) down the road. It is therefore unsurprising that a literature and practice of "real" options and risk-adjusted R&D project evaluation has emerged. This literature, associated with Lenos Trigeorgis, among others (e.g., Trigeorgis 1996), will not be reviewed or evaluated here in detail, except to say that in the practice of capital budgeting by firms, only special circumstances give rise to the situation in which the value of R&D is equal to conventionally calculated net present value (NPV) based on expected cash flows.

NPV as conventionally calculated ignores the strategic value (i.e., the option values) of the flexibility of R&D assets to respond to changes in the marketplace or technology outlook—and this implies that returns to ordinary capital cannot be compared with returns to R&D unless the option values of R&D are factored in.[13] We cannot be sure of the size of the unobserved option values, of course, but it is not uncommon in case studies of "medium" risk projects for real asset values to *double* after taking account of option values (Boer 2002). These findings and line of work are an important topic for future work on intangible investment prices for and thinking about the δ in equation (2.1) and the PIM.

The managerial flexibility offered by intangible capital also implies that current market developments are unlikely to impact the present value calculation of all vintages equally. In vintage capital models (e.g., Hall's 1968 analysis of quality change in pickup trucks) this possibility and the identification problem it presents that, in turn, prevents complete analysis is acknowledged. Not only must the same (and then some) be said of intangible capital, but also the possibility that the same shocks may not affect capital and wealth equally. The latter depends on the degree of financial intermediation, the transparency of the intermediation process, and agents' perceptions of firm balance sheets. The valuation of wealth, W_t, and of capital, $P_t^I K_t + P_t^N R_t$, occurs in different sectors with different agents, and a disconnect can arise when such valuations diverge (and/or when measurements diverge from reality). When this happens, we have

$$(2.2) \qquad P_t^I K_t + P_t^N R_t = q_t W_t,$$

where q_t is Tobin's average q ratio. This possibility (and the underlying reasons for it, measurement or reality) is important for the study of innovation and its impact because the rush of new products and processes in the financial sector has been implicated in the recent financial crisis, and the q ratio did indeed fluctuate (Corrado and Hulten, forthcoming).

18.2.2   Implications of Intangible Capital for Growth Accounting

Table 18.1 showed that current national accounting systems in the United States and European Union capitalize just some of the knowledge-based assets of firms. A more complete list is needed to represent how modern

---

13. A common approach that integrates real options and NPV for project evaluation was quantified by Trigeorgis as: NPV of real asset investment = NPV of estimated cash flows + Option Values.

business allocates revenue between current expenditures and investments in future capacity. Given the very substantial effort needed to extend the national accounts to include the more complete list of intangible assets, it is reasonable to ask what is gained from the effort. Clearly the level of GDP increases, as does the overall rate of investment, but what of the growth rate of real GDP, the basis for improvements in living standards? The following two tables address this question.

Table 18.3 shows results of capitalizing the investments listed in table 18.1 on the sources of growth in output per hour in US private industries. It is the empirical counterpart of the growth equation (1.4). The results were generated using estimates of intangible investment from the BEA (R&D and entertainment and artistic originals) and our own prior work (Corrado, Hulten, and Sichel 2005, 2009; Corrado and Hulten 2010) as revised and updated for INTAN-Invest (2012) (Corrado et al. 2013).

Table 18.4 shows comparably calculated results using the existing asset

Table 18.3   Sources of growth in US private industry output per hour, including intangibles, 1980–2011

	1980–2011 (1)	1980–1990 (2)	1990–2001 (3)	2001–2007 (4)	2007–2011 (5)
1. Output per hour	2.25	2.20	2.58	2.24	1.44
	Contribution of:				
2. Capital deepening	1.18	.96	1.38	1.13	1.27
3. Tangible[a]	.53	.40	.70	.45	.49
4. Intangible	.66	.56	.69	.68	.77
a. Computerized information	.17	.12	.23	.15	.16
b. Innovative property	.25	.26	.19	.25	.42
c. Economic competencies	.23	.18	.26	.27	.19
5. Labor composition	.29	.31	.32	.19	.34
6. TFP	.77	.94	.88	.92	−.16
	Memos—Percent of line 1 explained by:				
7. Intangible capital deepening	27.0[b]	25.5	26.6	30.3	—
8. Total capital deepening	49.5[b]	43.6	53.6	50.7	—
9. TFP	38.5[b]	42.5	34.1	41.0	—
10. Total capital deepening *without* new intangibles[c]	36.7[b]	30.8	41.8	35.1	—
11. TFP *without* new intangibles	49.8[b]	53.3	44.6	55.3	—

Sources: Elaboration of output, hours, and fixed asset data from the BEA; labor composition index is from the BLS. Estimates of intangibles not capitalized in the US national accounts as of May 2013 are based on data from the BEA (R&D and entertainment and artistic originals) and INTAN-Invest (2012).

Notes: Private industry excludes education, health, and real estate. Figures are annualized percent change calculated from natural log differences. Contributions are in percentage points and independently rounded. Column (2), (3), and (4) periods are between years with business cycle peaks as defined by the NBER.

[a]Excludes land (but includes inventories).

[b]Calculated from 1980 to 2007.

[c]Based on results shown in table 18.4.

Table 18.4   Sources of growth in US private industry output per hour, existing asset boundary, 1980–2011

	1980–2011 (1)	1980–1990 (2)	1990–2001 (3)	2001–2007 (4)	2007–2011 (5)
1. Output per hour	2.22	2.13	2.60	2.20	1.45
		Contribution of:			
2. Capital deepening	.88	.66	1.09	.77	1.01
2a. ICT	.55	.46	.76	.44	.37
2b. Non-ICT[a]	.33	.20	.33	.33	.64
3. Labor composition	.33	.34	.35	.21	.39
4. TFP	1.02	1.14	1.16	1.22	.06
		Memos:			
5. Output	2.92	3.53	3.82	2.56	−.51
6. Hours	.70	1.40	1.22	.36	−1.96

Sources: See sources for table 18.3.

Notes: See notes for table 18.3, except only intangibles in the current asset boundary, computer software and mineral exploration, are included.

boundary, and is the empirical counterpart of the growth equation (1.2). Periods shown correspond to periods between business cycle peaks, except the last, which extends from the most recent peak to the most recent full year of data (2011).

As in our prior work, one of the main results of extending the asset boundary to include investments in innovation is that capital deepening becomes the dominant factor explaining the growth of labor productivity (line 8 compared with line 10 of table 18.3). Moreover, intangible capital deepening has been the dominant component of total capital deepening for the last forty-plus years. Intangibles *alone* explain about one-fourth of the growth in output per hour between 1980 and 2007—nearly one-third from 2001 to 2007 (line 7 of table 18.3).

Total factor productivity growth averaged more than .9 percent per year from 2001 to 2007 but has contracted, on balance, since then (table 18.3). Using the existing asset boundary (table 18.4), total factor productivity shows roughly the same declining pattern after 2007 as the corresponding estimates of table 18.3, which includes all intangibles. The decline in TFP starts from a higher rate in table 18.4, however (1.22 percent over the period 2001–2007, compared to 0.96 in table 18.3). The recent productivity results do not, of course, signal a new underlying trend due to the incomplete nature of the economic recovery, although the poor results to date have been interpreted with much pessimism (e.g., Gordon 2012).

Absent from Gordon's discussion, of course, are the trends shown in figure 18.1 (intangible investment did not slow as sharply as did tangible investment in recent years) and figure 18.3 (spending on industrial R&D remained relatively strong)—both reasons for a certain degree of optimism about prospects for US productivity in the medium term. On the other hand, the trend in output per hour declines even when intangibles are included in the analysis.

However, before too much is made of this finding, the Nordhaus point about the inability of conventional statistics to capture the effects of "tectonic" innovations should be revisited. The IT revolution surely qualifies as tectonic, with major structural changes affecting businesses, consumers, and markets (e-commerce is just one example, "workerless" factories and driverless autos are others). The tectonic revolutions of the past were subject to a downward bias in estimated real GDP, according to Nordhaus, but given the intangible nature of information and knowledge and the difficulty in even defining the units in which they are measured, the tectonic bias associated with the IT revolution may be larger. Sorting this out is a priority for future research and for the development of an innovation account. Some further thoughts on this subject are offered in appendix B of this chapter.

18.3   Conclusion

Innovation accounting requires recognizing that innovation is not costless, that innovation is a source of market power, and that innovation accounting requires a shift in thinking from the pure production model to one that factors in elements of demand. Building on previous work, we have described a national innovation account that incorporates a broad range of intangible assets (based on the Corrado-Hulten-Sichel framework) and that separately identifies the quality component in price change, and thereby the direct contribution of product innovation to economic growth. A corresponding decomposition of conventional TFP follows (based on Hulten 2010a, 2010b), one in which the same component is used to decompose productivity into product and process innovation.

The innovation accounting discussed here focuses mainly on business activity. But it emphasized the importance of thinking about how innovation improves welfare through increasing consumer surplus on the one hand, and growing income faster than price change on the other—issues related to the theme of this conference.

The analysis and material developed in this chapter have two natural extensions. The first is an extension of the accounting model to include the effects of globalization. This is not a simple matter of considering an open economy in the usual way. Indeed, the simple abstraction that all firms operate globally would be an important first step to developing an understanding of the relatively higher rate of private investment in intangible assets by the United States compared with other advanced countries (van Ark et al. 2009) and changes in incomes and costs in the US economy in recent decades.

Second, a complete set of national accounts that include explicit time use, household, and human capital components could be further expanded using elements introduced in this chapter. Linkages between the activities of business, including the benefits that flow to consumers from innovation (including lower costs of production abroad) and the benefits that flow to business from education, seem essential ingredients to forming strategies that promote economic growth and competitiveness of advanced economies. Although these components exist in part or in whole (Christian 2009, Bridgeman et al. 2012), building this larger system is a complicated endeavor beyond the scope of this chapter.

Appendix A

The Corrado et. al. (2012) model is based on the following equation, shown below as in Corrado and Hao (2013):

$$
(A1.1) \quad P^N N_t = \sum_{j=1}^{J} \mu_j (P^L L_{j,t} + P^K K_{j,t} + P^M M_{j,t})
$$

$$
= \sum_{j=1}^{J} \mu_j^{shadow} (P^L L_{j,t} + P^K K_{j,t} + P^M M_{j,t})^{own-account} + P_j^N N_{j,t}^{purchased}
$$

$$
\cong \sum_{j=1}^{J} \sum_{s=1}^{S} (\mu_{s,j}^{shadow} (P^L L_{s,j,t} + P^K K_{s,j,t} + P^M M_{s,j,t})^{own-account}
$$

$$
+ P_j^N N_{s,j,t}^{purchased})
$$

$$
= \sum_{j=1}^{J} \sum_{s=1}^{S} (\mu_{s,j}^{shadow} \gamma_{s,j}^{own-account} \lambda_{s,j}^{own-account} OwnCost_{s,j,t}^{Indicator}
$$

$$
+ \gamma_{s,j}^{purchased} \lambda_{s,j}^{purchased} Purchased_{s,j,t}^{indicator}).
$$

In this equation, $P^N N$ is first expressed as an aggregate of J assets using terms set out for the model of section 18.1.1 above (but here we of course include the intermediate inputs used in the production of the intangible). A closed economy is assumed.

The parameter $\mu \geq 1$ is a measure of the degree of market power, the "innovator" markup over competitive factor costs of inputs used up in the innovation process. This parameter varies of course across industries as it depends on customers' price elasticity of demand for an industry's products.

The first line of equation (A1.1) holds whether an economy's intangibles are self-produced or marketed purchases. What changes when investment moves from the former to the latter is the origin of the innovator markup, namely, whether it is an imputed "shadow" value or a factor embedded in transactions data (i.e., embedded in P^N). To underscore this equivalence, the second line of equation (A1.1) expresses intangible investment in terms of both sources of supply. The superscript "own-account" denotes intangibles produced and consumed *within the same firm*.

The third line is a more general expression where aggregation now is over a subset of private domestic sectors (S). This line is conceptually equivalent to the first two lines in the absence of public investments and international trade in intangibles and underscores that, to date, most work on measuring intangibles has concentrated on private, not public, investments.[14] As to the internationalization of intangibles, very little is known, with the exception of R&D. As a practical matter, *net* international trade in R&D remains relatively small for the United States but is consequential for other countries, such as Finland. In general, trade in services, especially business and professional services, is expanding rapidly (e.g., Jensen 2011), and the internationalization of intangibles is an important topic for future work. Here we simply note that, in reality, when intangibles are capitalized, the adjustments to production and gross domestic capital formation need not be identical as implied by the discussion in section 18.1.1.

The variables $OwnCost_{s,j,t}^{Indicator}$ and $Purchased_{s,j,t}^{Indicator}$ in the fourth line are time-series indicators of the actual in-house intangible production or purchased intangible assets in each sector. The parameters $\lambda_{s,j}$ and $\gamma_{s,j}$ are sector- and asset-specific capitalization factors that adjust the indicators to benchmarks for each asset and sector. The first factor adjusts the indicator to business spending (in the case of using compensation as an own-cost indicator, the factor used transforms it to gross output); the second adjusts spending to a measure of investment if, say, an indicator were a mix of short- and long-lived expenditures. As previously mentioned, sector cost indicators could be derived from employment surveys (or firm-level microdata as in Piekkola et al. 2011), and sector purchased indicators could be obtained from input-output relationships, from which historical time series can be derived.

Appendix B
Measuring Quality Change and Accounting for Business Dynamics

Each term in (1.8) helps frame dimensions along which businesses innovate and compete, and thus subsumes many phenomena addressed in the industrial economics, consumer demand, and microproductivity literatures. In what follows we make a modest attempt to link innovation accounting via equation (1.8) to some of these phenomena, and to do this we need to shift our focus to the industry level and discuss the creation of consumer welfare and introduce certain aspects of price measurement.

Product Innovation at the Industry Level

The output of each industry or sector in the economy is modeled as consisting of two groups of products in a given period. The first group

14. An example of an exception is the van Ark and Jaeger (2010) study of public intangibles in the Netherlands.

consists of the same products the industry or sector produced in the previous period, and the second group consists of products that are new to the market. The latter encompasses a wide range of innovations of course, from the introduction of simple new varieties, to substantially new designs, to "truly new" goods. Such distinctions will be consequential to our analysis in a moment, but for now we assume the new-to-the-market grouping of products is homogeneous at the industry or sector level. We also assume no exiting products.

Let v_i be the i-th industry's share of total revenue (V_i) originating from new-to-the-market products in a period (time subscripts are ignored). Then effective price change for an industry over the period can be expressed as a weighted average of price change for its new products ($\dot{P}_i^{new}/P_i^{new}$) and price change for its continuing products, which is the simple change in unit value or transactions price ($\dot{P}_i/P_i$):

$$(A2.1) \qquad \frac{\dot{P}_i^e}{P_i^e} = (s_i^{new}) \frac{\dot{P}_i^{new}}{P_i^{new}} + (1 - s_i^{new}) \frac{\dot{P}_i}{P_i},$$

where the variable s_i^{new} is the Divisia weight for new-to-the-market product price change, which equals $.5 * v_i$ from the above. This equation yields an operational expression for the quality component term on the right-hand side of equation (1.8) of the previous section, namely,

$$(A2.2) \qquad \frac{\dot{P}_i}{P_i} - \frac{\dot{P}_i^e}{P_i^e} = s_i^{new}\left(\frac{\dot{P}_i}{P_i} - \frac{\dot{P}_i^{new}}{P_i^{new}}\right).$$

This equation states that the quality component term for an industry is differential price change between continuing and new products, weighted by half the revenue share of new products.

The term ($\dot{P}_i^{new}/P_i^{new}$) is not in the static choice set of the standard neoclassical growth accounting model, but the microtheoretic underpinnings of ($\dot{P}_i^{new}/P_i^{new}$) were set out by Hicks in 1941 and can be used as a starting point. Because prices of new products in a previous period are by definition nonexistent, an estimate of the "virtual" price—the price that sets demand to zero in the previous period—must be used in the calculation of ($\dot{P}_i^{new}/P_i^{new}$) at $t = 1$, the period of introduction of the new product or service.

Various methods are available to generate such estimates. Without going into details and therefore generally speaking, different approaches may be used depending on just where the new product or service is along a "newness" continuum. After all, product differentiation is as much about the introduction of new varieties, product replacement cycles, and the like as it is about the introduction of truly new goods and services. And although both ends of the "newness" continuum generate gains in consumer welfare as per equation (A2.2), it is sensible to make some distinctions because the different ends are captured in statistics in different ways.

Consider first the "routine" model turnover/new variety phenomenon that affects many types of goods and services. Statistical agencies have established generally accepted methods for dealing with this; for a review, see Greenlees and McClelland (2008). High rates of item replacement and flat price profiles for items priced are little-appreciated facts of life for price collectors in dynamic economies. Noncomparability (the inability to form $(\dot{P_i}/P_i)$ from one month to the next) is in fact a pervasive issue even for technologically stable goods such as packaged food (Greenlees and McClelland 2011). In some sense this is the flip side (or dual) of a large body of work that has used census microdata to study business entry and exit, productivity, and worker dynamics (e.g., Dunne, Roberts, and Samuelson 1988; Davis, Haltiwanger, and Schuh 1996; and Foster, Haltiwanger, and Krizan 2001).

Much quality change (the "garden variety" change) is therefore deeply embedded in our price statistics. Greenlees and McClelland (2011) use the characteristics data collected along with Consumer Price Index (CPI) price quotes since the start of the twenty-first century to analyze and evaluate how well BLS has fared in its monthly linking of items that cannot be matched from one period to the next. For the class of goods they studied (packaged food), they found that BLS likely has *underestimated* price change. Needless to say, this line of research is exceedingly important for improving the accuracy of our price statistics. But it also shows that BLS has the wherewithal to decompose its monthly chained consumer price index according to equation (A2.1) for feeding into the operational expression (A2.2) for the quality component term in the "new" real GDP identity.

Innovation accounting even without the precise identification of "garden variety" quality change can still proceed, however. Consider now the time period of analysis. We have been implicitly assuming equations (A2.1) and (A2.2) refer to *monthly* price change, and s_i^{new} for many new-to-the-market products and services will in all likelihood be quite small. For example, Apple's iPhone was an immense success as a product innovation (it accounted for nearly 60 percent of the company's revenue in 2012) but in the quarter of introduction (2007:Q3), it accounted for just 2.5 percent of its total sales. Because industries that routinely innovate through introducing new products will have higher fractions of total revenue originating from new products over longer periods of time, a business cycle, five years, or even a decade, would appear to be a more informative period for innovation accounting.

In fact, BEA's Moulton and Wasshausen (2006) have done just that. Using data on PC prices from 2000 to 2005 and assuming $s_i^{new} = 1$, they estimated the computer industry's ongoing quality component term using a procedure equivalent to equation (A2.2). Their result (11.5 percent per year) was not the full drop in quality-adjusted PC prices (16.4 percent) because unit prices for PCs were found to have fallen nearly 5 percent per year. And because computer final sales are but 0.8 percent of GDP in the United States, the contribution of quality change for computers was calculated to be less than 0.1 percentage point of average annual real GDP growth during the period they studied.

Although Moulton and Wasshausen's result is small in the aggregate (more on why this is the case in a moment), their decomposition adds a small piece to the puzzle of why income and employment generated by computer production grew so much less than the quality-adjusted real value added by the industry. Quality-adjusted price change *is* an indicator of consumer welfare, but with product innovation (and in the case of PCs, falling unit prices also) the welfare increase is not necessarily tied to an increase in the real personal disposable income of workers in the industry or locality in which production takes place. Decomposing the extent to which process innovation has allowed incomes (costs) to grow faster than unit price change would be a helpful addition to the productivity and welfare analysis toolkit.

Price Change at the "Truly New" End of the Continuum

Consider now the opposite end of the continuum from which we started. Price change for new products is equal to the change in welfare due to the introduction of the new products (with, of course, a reversal of sign). Equivalently, as shown by Hausman (1981), the welfare gain is the change in expenditure that holds utility constant with the introduction of the new product, otherwise known as the compensating variation (CV), or consumer surplus.

As an operational matter, Hausman (1999) also provided an approximation to the $(\hat{P}_i^{new}/P_i^{new})$ term requiring the unobserved Hicksian "virtual" price in the period prior to introduction. The CV can be used to capture price change from this point to the period when the market share of the new good has stabilized, that is, a period like the five years for innovation accounting studied by Moulton and Wasshausen. Hausman showed that the CV from new goods can be approximated, in our notation, as

$$(A2.3) \qquad CV \approx (.5 * \upsilon_i * V_i)/\alpha_i,$$

where α_i is the own-price elasticity of demand for the i-th industry's products. The equation is a lower-bound linear approximation to the actual demand curve. Using it only requires an estimate of the price elasticity of demand (PED) along with data on revenue of new products for each industry (i.e., it does not require estimation of the demand curve).

Equation (A2.3) is useful for innovation accounting because it illustrates how new products that gain significant demand (V_i) can lead to large measured gains in productivity—and just how large depends on the own-price elasticity of demand (α_i). New goods that are very similar to existing ones (i.e., new varieties) will have high own-PEDs, and thus their contribution to welfare change will be considerably smaller than the contribution of products that have relatively low PEDs and experience high demand.[15] The former category may include a new model year car, whereas the latter category might include a new statin drug, such as Lipitor, which was introduced in 1997 and by 2003 became the best-selling pharmaceutical in history.[16]

The analysis of equation (A2.3) also suggests that firms will exercise market power when PEDS are low and demand is high, especially when the situation was created by a firm's own customer savvy, mastery of technology, and marketing. Nor should we be surprised to see that firms that innovate on the variety margin must also compete on the cost margin; high PEDs (and the availability of substitutes) are frequent in these situations, and the demand for new "brands" often must be stimulated by lowering costs or by advertising. This underscores that innovation accounting needs to acknowledge the presence of imperfect competition (as per section 18.1.1)—and also that estimates of intangible investment at the industry level are needed (as per box 18.1 in section 18.2.1) so that the dynamics of costs, prices, and intangible spending can be analyzed more fully.

References

Abowd, John M., John Haltiwanger, Ron Jarmin, Julia Lane, Paul Lengermann, Kristin McCue, Kevin McKinney, and Fristin Sandusky. 2005. "The Relation among Human Capital, Productivity, and Market Value: Building Up from Micro Evidence." In *Measuring Capital in the New Economy*, Studies in Income and Wealth vol. 65, edited by C. Corrado, J. Haltiwanger, and D. Sichel, 153–98. Chicago: The University of Chicago Press.

Aghion, Philippe, and Peter Howitt. 2007. "Capital, Innovation, and Growth Accounting." *Oxford Review of Economic Policy* 23 (1): 79–93.

Awano, G., M. Franklin, J. Haskel, and Z. Kastrinaki. 2010. "Investing in Innovation, Findings from the UK Investment and Intangible Asset Survey." NESTA Working Paper, July.

15. To fix this idea, assume innovation accounting is performed for a five-year period for an industry whose change in unit costs is zero and whose product line completely turns over. In other words, after five years, products being produced and sold are not the same as those at the end of the previous five years, which implies $v_i = 1$. Now assume $V_i = 10$, $V = 1,000$, and $\alpha_i = 2.5$, where the latter is a relatively high value for the price elasticity of demand (hereafter, PED). A table of estimates for selected products is available at http://en.wikipedia.org/wiki/Price _elasticity_of_demand. Equation (A2.3) then states, after taking into account the relative size of the example industry, that product innovation in the industry contributes 0.2 percentage points per year to aggregate productivity change (recall we assumed the change in unit costs to be zero). But if the PED was a much larger value, say 4, the contribution of product innovation in this industry would be much smaller, less than 0.1 percentage point on an annual basis (more or less equivalent to the Moulton and Wasshausen analysis).

16. Again, to be concrete, if the gain in demand were the same magnitude as the example in the previous footnote and the PED was, say .5, the contribution of the innovation would be estimated at 1 percentage point per year, which is very large indeed.

Barnes, Paula. 2010. "Investment in Intanagible Assets and Australia's Productivity Growth—Sectoral Estimates." Productivity Commission Staff Working Paper.

Bils, Mark, and Peter J. Klenow. 2001. "Quantifying Quality Growth." *American Economic Review* 91:1006–30.

Boer, F. Peter. 2002. *The Real Options Solution: Finding Total Value in a High-Risk World.* New York: John Wiley & Sons, Inc.

Bridgeman, Benjamin, Andrew Dugan, Mikhael Lal, Matthew Osborne, and Shaunda Villones. 2012. "Accounting for Household Production in the National Accounts, 1965–2010." *Survey of Current Business* 92 (May): 23–36.

Christian, Michael S. 2009. "Human Capital Accounting in the United States, 1994 to 2006." https://www.bea.gov/papers/pdf/human_capital_accounting_in_the _united_states_1994_2006_christian.pdf.

Copeland, Adam, and Dennis Fixler. 2009. "Measuring the Price of Research and Development Output." BEA Working Paper WP2009-2, February.

Copeland, Adam M., Gabriel W. Medeiros, and Carol A. Robbins. 2007. "Estimating Prices for R&D Investment in the 2007 R&D Satellite Account." BEA Working Paper, November.

Corrado, Carol, Peter Goodridge, and Jonathan Haskel. 2011. "Constructing a Price Deflator for R&D: Estimating the Price of Knowledge as a Residual." The Conference Board Economics Program Working Paper EPWP no.11-03, August.

Corrado, Carol, and Janet X. Hao. 2013. "Brands as a Productive Asset of the Firm: Concepts, Measurement, and Global Trends." Report prepared for the World Intellectual Property Organization, June 18. New York: The Conference Board.

———. Forthcoming. "Innovative Labor in Business: Measuring Intangible Investment at the Sectoral and Industry Level."

Corrado, Carol, Jonathan Haskel, Cecilia Jona-Lasinio, and Massimiliano Iommi. 2012. "Intangible Capital and Growth in Advanced Economies: Measurement Methods and Comparative Results." Working Paper, June. http://www.intan -invest.net.

———. 2013. "Innovation and Intangible Investment in Europe, Japan, and the United States." *Oxford Review of Economic Policy* 29 (2): 261–86.

Corrado, Carol, and Charles R. Hulten. 2010. "How Do You Measure a 'Technological Revolution'?" *American Economic Review* 100 (5): 99–104.

———. Forthcoming. "Financial Intermediation in the National Accounts: Asset Valuation, Intermediation, and Tobin's *q*." In *Measuring Wealth and Financial Intermediation and Their Links to the Real Economy*, Studies in Income and Wealth vol. 73, edited by Charles R. Hulten and Marshall Reinsdorf. Chicago: University of Chicago Press.

Corrado, Carol, Charles Hulten, and Daniel Sichel. 2005. "Measuring Capital and Technology." In *Measuring Capital in the New Economy*, Studies in Income and Wealth vol. 65, edited by C. Corrado, J. Haltiwanger, and D. Sichel, 11–14. Chicago: University of Chicago Press.

———. 2009. "Intangible Capital and US Economic Growth." *The Review of Income and Wealth* 55 (3): 661–85.

Dal Borgo, Mariela, Peter Goodridge, Jonathan Haskel, and Annarosa Pesole. 2011. "Productivity and Growth in UK Industries: An Intangible Investment Approach, 2011-06." Imperial College Business School Working Paper.

Davis, Steven J., John C. Haltiwanger, and Scott Schuh. 1996. *Job Creation and Destruction.* Cambridge, MA: MIT Press.

Dunne, T., M. Roberts, and L. Samuelson. 1989. "The Growth and Failure of US Manufacturing Plants." *Quarterly Journal of Economics* 104:671–98.

European Commission, International Monetary Fund, OECD, United Nations, and World Bank. 2009. *System of National Accounts, 2008.* New York: United Nations.

Foster, L., J. Haltiwanger, and C. J. Krizan. 2001. "Aggregate Productivity Growth: Lessons from Microeconomic Evidence." In *New Developments in Productivity Analysis*, edited by E. Dean, M. Harper, and C. Hulten, 303–418. Chicago: University of Chicago Press.

Fukao, Kyoji, Tsutomu Miyagawa, Kentaro Mukai, Yukio Shinoda, and Konomi Tonogi. 2009. "Intangible Investment in Japan: Measurement and Contribution to Growth." *Review of Income and Wealth* 55 (3): 717–36.

Gordon, Robert J. 2012. "Is US Economic Growth Over? Faltering Innovation Confronts the Six Headwinds." NBER Working Paper no. 18315, Cambridge, MA.

Görzig, B., H. Piekkola, and R. Riley. 2010. "Production of Own Account Intangible Investment: Methodology in Innodrive Project." Innodrive Working Paper no 1.

Greenlees, John S., and Robert McClelland. 2008. "Addressing Misconceptions about the Consumer Price Index." *Monthly Labor Review* August: 3–19.

———. 2011. "Does Quality Adjustment Matter for Technologically Stable Products? An Application to the CPI for Food." *American Economic Review* 101 (3): 200–05.

Griliches, Zvi. 1973. "Research Expenditures and Growth Accounting." In *Science and Technology and Economic Growth*, edited by B. R. Williams, 59–95. London: MacMillan.

———. 1979. "Issues in Assessing the Contribution of Research and Development to Productivity Growth." *Bell Journal of Economics* 10 (1): 92–116.

Hall, Robert E. 1968. "Technical Change and Capital from the Point of View of the Dual." *Review of Economics Studies* 35:34–46.

Hausman, Jerry. 1981. "Exact Consumer Surplus and Deadweight Loss." *American Economic Review* 71:662–76.

———. 1999. "Cellular Telephone, New Products, and the CPI." *Journal of Business & Economic Statistics* 17 (2): 188–94.

Hulten, Charles R. 1992. "Growth Accounting When Technological Change Is Embodied in Capital." *American Economic Review* 82 (4): 964–80.

———. 2010a. "Decoding Microsoft: Intangible Capital as a Source of Company Growth." NBER Working Paper no. 15799, Cambridge, MA.

———. 2010b. "Growth Accounting." In *Handbook of the Economics of Innovation*, chapter 23, edited by Bronwyn H. Hall and Nathan Rosenberg, 987–1031. Amsterdam: Elsevier-North Holland.

———. 2012. "Intangible Capital, Product Innovation, and the Theory of the Firm." Unpublished Manuscript, University of Maryland, June.

Hulten, Charles R., and Janet X. Hao. 2008. "What Is a Company Really Worth? Intangible Capital and the 'Market to Book Value' Puzzle." NBER Working Paper no. 14548, Cambridge, MA.

Jensen, J. Bradford. 2011. *Global Trade in Services: Fear, Facts, and Offshoring*. Washington, DC: Peterson Institute for International Economics.

Jorgenson, Dale W., and Zvi Griliches. 1967. "The Explanation of Productivity Change." *Review of Economic Studies* 34 (July): 349–83.

Miyagawa, Tsutomu, and Shoichi Hisa. 2013. "Estimates of Intangible Investment by Industry and Productivity Growth in Japan." *Japanese Economic Review* 64 (1): 42–72.

Moulton, Brent R., and Dave Wasshausen. 2006. "The Role of Hedonic Methods in Measuring Real GDP in the United States." Paper presented at the 31st CEIES Seminar, The Role of Hedonic Price Measurement on Productivity, October. http://www.bea.gov/papers/pdf/hedonicGDP.pdf.

Moylan, Carol, and Carol Robbins. 2007. "Research and Development Satellite Account Update." *Survey of Current Business* 87 (October): 49–92.

Nakamura, Leonard. 2001. "What Is the US Gross Investment in Intangibles?

(At Least) One Trillion Dollars a Year!" Federal Reserve Bank of Philadelphia Working Paper no. 01-15, 2001.

National Research Council. 2006. "Improving Business Statistics through Interagency Data Sharing: Summary of a Workshop." Caryn Kuebler and Christopher Mackie, Rapporteurs. Committee on National Statistics. Washington, DC: The National Academies Press.

Nerlove, Mark, and Kenneth J. Arrow. 1962. "Optimal Advertisting Policy under Dynamic Conditions." *Economica* 39:129–42.

Nordhaus, William D. 1997. "Do Real Output and Real Wage Measures Capture Reality? The History of Lighting Suggests Not." In *The Economics of New Goods*, Studies in Income and Wealth vol. 58, edited by Timothy Bresnahan and Robert J. Gordon, 29–66. Chicago: University of Chicago Press.

Pakes, Ariel, and Mark Schankerman. 1984. "The Rate of Obsolescence of Patents, Research Gestation Lags, and the Private Rate of Return to Research Resources." In *R&D, Patents, and Productivity*, edited by Zvi Griliches, 73–88. Chicago: University of Chicago Press.

———. 2008a. Reported in "Examples of Surveys on Service Lives of R&D." *The OECD Handbook on Deriving Capital Measures for Intellectual Property Products (2010)*. Paris: OECD.

Peleg, S. 2008b. "Service Lives of R&D." Central Bureau of Statistics, Israel.

Piekkola, Hannu. 2012. "Intangibles: Can They Explain the Unexplained?" INNO-DRIVE Working Paper.

Piekkola, H., M. Lintamo, R. Riley, C. Robinson, K. Geppert, B. Gorzig, A. Neumann, et al. 2011. "Firm-Level Intangible Capital in Six Countries: Finland, Norway, the UK, Germany, the Czech Republic, and Slovenia." In *Intangible Capital—Driver of Growth in Europe*, edited by H. Piekkola. http://www.inno drive.org/attachments/File/Intangible_Capital_Driver_of_Growth_in_Europe_ Piekkola(ed).pdf.

Romer, Paul M. 1990. "Endogenous Technological Change." *Journal of Political Economy* 98 (5) Part 2: S71–S102.

Soloveichik, Rachel. 2010. "Artistic Originals as a Capital Asset." *American Economic Review* 100 (5): 110–14.

Solow, Robert M. 1957. "Technical Change and the Aggregate Production Function." *Review of Economics and Statistics* 39 (3): 312–20.

———. 1960. "Investment and Technical Progress." In *Mathematical Methods in the Social Sciences*, edited by K. J. Arrow, S. Karlin, and P. Suppes, 1:48–93. Stanford: Stanford University Press.

Trigeorgis, Lenos. 1996. *Real Options: Managerial Flexibility and Strategy in Resource Allocation.* Cambridge, MA: MIT Press.

van Ark, Bart, Janet X. Hao, Carol A. Corrado, and Charles R. Hulten. 2009. "Measuring Intangible Capital and Its Contribution to Economic Growth in Europe." *European Investment Bank Papers* 14 (1): 62–93.

van Ark, Bart, and Kirsten Jaeger. 2010. "Intangible Capital in Europe and Its Implications for Future Growth." Working Paper, The Conference Board.

Panel Remarks

J. Steven Landefeld

We have heard from Federal Reserve Board chairman Ben Bernanke; Council of Economic Advisers member Katharine Abraham; former Treasury secretary Larry Summers; officials of the US FRB and Treasury, the European Central Bank (ECB), and the International Monetary Fund (IMF); and representatives of the financial industry about the importance of the statistics we produce and the urgent need to address the measurement issues highlighted by the recent recession. These issues include developing and better integrating measures of economic welfare and sustainability into our national accounts as well as developing better and more comprehensive measures relevant to key long-term issues confronting the nation, such as health care and investments in human capital.

We are also all aware of the daunting fiscal challenges that we confront in statistical agencies in the United States and abroad. In many cases, existing statistics are confronting elimination as a result of budget cuts. How do we then cut and improve at the same time? The seeds of the solution are, I believe, contained in the papers and topics that we have discussed—and will continue to discuss—at this and future CRIW meetings. The papers presented at this meeting highlight how through new methods and source data we can do more with less. Three examples may be particularly important.

The first example is the integration of micro and macro distributional

J. Steven Landefeld is director of the Bureau of Economic Analysis at the US Department of Commerce.

For acknowledgments, sources of research support, and disclosure of the author's material financial relationships, if any, please see http://www.nber.org/chapters/c12845.ack.

data. We have had several excellent papers by Jorgensen and Slesnick, Schreyer and Diewert, and Carroll on the concepts and methods and important results that can be produced through such integration. Traditionally, the work supporting such integration has relied on large-scale and challenging exact and statistical match studies—matching household survey to tax data to adjust for underreporting, misreporting, and family size. However, as the papers by Fixler and Johnson and by McCully suggest, use of adjustments using aggregate household, tax, and national accounts data can produce estimates of the distribution of income and spending that are likely to be close to the results from more detailed micro studies. Also, using the latest national accounts data on growth in incomes and spending by type, it should be possible to extrapolate from the latest microdata benchmark to produce more timely and reasonably reliable data on broad trends in the distribution income than is available from tabulations of the microdata with significantly fewer resources than those required by micro studies.

Second, in the financial area, we have heard proposals for important new data collections that would fill gaps in coverage and develop new methods for better measurement of risk and sustainability in financial markets. If such collections by financial regulators and central banks are designed so as to provide data that meets both the microdata needs of regulators and the aggregate data needs of investors, policymakers, and business, statistical agencies may be able to incorporate such data at a relatively low cost. While this process will require better coordination, through better access and standardization, statistical agencies should be able to piggyback on regulatory information rather than developing expensive new surveys.

These new data collections can supplement ongoing work presented by Cagetti et al. on how the integration of existing and extended flow of funds and national accounts data can fill gaps and provide key information including ratios, or leading indicators, of unsustainable trends (bubbles) in asset prices, liabilities, saving, and consumer spending.

Third, as illustrated by the chapter by Dunn, Liebman, and Shapiro, existing commercial, administrative, and Internet data—in this case health insurance records—can be used by statistical agencies to address measurement problems that cannot be easily addressed by surveys, at a fraction of the cost of surveys. Use of such "big data" will require the development of new IT systems, work on assessing the coverage and reliability of such data, as well as agreements and standards on confidentiality, access, and control. Such data seem to offer a major tool for updating, extending, and improving official statistics. Possible uses include weighting and benchmarking big data for use as extrapolators to produce more timely and accurate early GDP and other estimates. The US national accounts have always made extensive use of private data as extrapolators, and there are important opportunities to update and improve the accounts. No doubt, as the BEA learned from its work on health care, there is a front-end investment that is required, but such investment will produce significant gains to the statistical system in the future.

Shirin Ahmed

It is a pleasure to be here and to talk about the National Income and Product Accounts from the perspective of the economic programs area at the US Census Bureau.

With respect to the national accounts, our primary role is to provide useful and relevant source data that allows the BEA to accomplish its their mission. We work very closely with the BEA staff to continually improve what we are doing. My remarks cover our work in providing information to fill data gaps, creating new opportunities with data sharing, and strategically aligning priorities across agencies.

Filling Data Gaps

In terms of filling data gaps, our key area of focus has been providing more data about the services sectors of the US economy.

We received funding in mid-2010 to expand the industry coverage of both the Quarterly Services Survey (QSS) and the Service Annual Survey (SAS) with the goal of providing complete coverage of receipts across all of the services sectors of the US economy, which are estimated to be 55 percent of GDP. Previously, only the Economic Census provided this kind of coverage every five years. At the time, the QSS was only covering 17 percent of the services sector and the SAS was covering about 30 percent.

The funding allowed QSS to expand over a two-year period, starting with new quarterly statistics on ambulatory health-care services and social assistance, and then adding in other industries covering transportation, warehousing, finance, and so on, with the expansion fully implemented by March 2011. This timing coincided with the release in January 2011 of the full set of services industries for SAS for the 2008 survey year. At this point, the industry expansion allowed the Census Bureau to produce complete coverage of consumer spending for the BEA annually.

To provide complete coverage quarterly for consumer spending, plans are underway to add the accommodations sector to the QSS with the collection of data this fall as part of the business surveys redesign. Every five years, after an Economic Census, the business surveys undergo a major sample revision process that gives the Census Bureau an opportunity to fill new

Shirin Ahmed is assistant director for economic programs at the US Census Bureau.

For acknowledgments, sources of research support, and disclosure of the author's material financial relationships, if any, please see http://www.nber.org/chapters/c12843.ack.

data needs. Other initiatives as part of the business sample revision process include new QSS revenue detail for the financial industry—giving BEA quarterly estimates of items such as interest income, noninterest income, commission fees, and so forth. In the SAS, the new sample will collect and publish additional product-level detail for the newly expanded services industries. The new product data will be published by January 2013.[1]

Similarly, the expansion of services industries extended to another economic indicator, the Quarterly Financial Report (QFR). The QFR data are a primary source for current estimates of corporate profits, taxes, and dividends for the gross domestic income accounts. In the first quarter of 2010, we provided to the BEA new estimates covering the information and the professional and technical services sectors. We are now getting ready to further expand to include the following four service sectors: health care and social assistance, real estate and rental and leasing (except lessors of nonfinancial intangible assets), administrative and support and waste management and remediation services, and accommodation and food services. We will begin collecting the additional data from about 1,400 corporations with assets of $50 million or more in October 2012. We will provide the data to BEA on a trial basis. Publication of the data will begin in March 2014 with the release of data for the fourth quarter of 2013. With this expansion, the QFR will cover 35 percent of the services sectors, and will provide detailed financial data for the largest services sectors of GDP.

Later this fall, we will field our 2012 Economic Census. The BEA and Census Bureau staffs have spent about two years working on content and review of questionnaires for the 2012 Economic Census. Because of its comprehensive nature, new inquiries are added about the sources of revenue for intellectual property and about activities for contract manufacturing services performed domestically and at locations outside the United States.

New for the 2012 Economic Census will be data products devoted to enterprise statistics that reflect both these new inquiries as well as the repurposing of existing business register and Economic Census data that shows the specialization and diversification of US businesses. Prototype tables using 2007 Economic Census data were released last month. With the new enterprise statistics, we also developed the Enterprise Classification System (see http://www.census.gov/econ/esp/).

Lastly, as part of the 2012 Economic Census of Island Areas, we have added critical content about capital expenditures necessary to fill gaps in BEA's preparation of GDP for the island areas.

Data Sharing

Let me turn now to data sharing. Earlier this year, the BLS and the Census Bureau signed a memorandum of understanding (MOU) to share multiunit

1. Preliminary unpublished tabulations are being provided to BEA staff this summer.

data, which is also referred to as data for multilocation establishments. This data is typically free from the IRS, or Title 26 data, which has been one of our challenges with data sharing among the BEA, BLS, and Census Bureau agencies.

This is the first time the Census Bureau will be sharing business microdata with the BLS. Since the early 1990s the Census Bureau has received industry classification codes from BLS for new business births, which has improved our business register. The sharing of these new data will provide many advantages to both agencies to improve and to make more consistent their business registers, and corresponding statistical products. This will benefit the BEA, which has the challenging work of integrating data from both agencies in the production of the national accounts. Additionally in this world of global activity, we are working on an MOU with BEA to receive their data about multinational enterprises to improve the overall coverage of the business register at the US Census Bureau. Currently our business register covers enterprise activities within the United States.

Statistical Priorities and Infrastructure Improvements

Finally, let me make a couple of comments about statistical priorities and infrastructure improvements. Over the years, the BEA and Census Bureau have worked closely together and, as we look to the future, we see the need to strategize more given the current budget climate and the need to continue to improve our respective programs to keep pace with the changing economy. Senior staffs at both agencies started meeting this year to understand strategic priorities and to meet high-level operational needs for both agencies. From these meetings, we have cross-agency teams reviewing seasonal adjustment practices and another group evaluating ways to meet new content/ data needs on more of a flow basis rather than at revision or census periods. Lastly, we created a team to bring together the Census Bureau, the BEA, and the Producer Price Index Program at the BLS to reach agreement on an approach for collecting and reporting data for industry product outputs that are more consistent, comparable, and usable for the BEA, BLS, and Census Bureau. Thank you.

John W. Ruser

It is a pleasure for me to describe some of the initiatives of the Bureau of Labor Statistics (BLS) related to the themes of this conference. I would like to start by talking about some of the important ongoing work to improve and redesign the Consumer Expenditure Surveys (CE). As you know, the CE

John W. Ruser is associate commissioner for productivity and technology at the US Bureau of Labor Statistics, US Department of Labor.

For acknowledgments, sources of research support, and disclosure of the author's material financial relationships, if any, please see http://www.nber.org/chapters/c12846.ack.

is a key input into the Consumer Price Index, but it is also a valuable tool for studying household consumption patterns. This venerable survey has not undergone substantial redesign since the early 1980s and has come under some criticism for measurement error and respondent burden. Recently, CE staff worked with staff from the Survey of Consumer Finance and from the American Community Survey to make improvements to the income, assets, and liabilities sections of the CE questionnaires. These changes will be implemented in 2013. The CE staff is also developing a process to impute federal and state income tax estimates using the NBER TAXSIM model. This will also be implemented for the 2013 data.

Beyond these short-run enhancements, the CE program has a major redesign initiative underway called the Gemini project. This project is examining ways to redesign the CE surveys from scratch to improve the estimates, reduce burden, and improve data quality. As part of the Gemini project, the BLS has held several workshops and symposia to reach out to stakeholders and to explore a variety of topics, including data capture technology, data users' needs, and survey methods. A data users forum collected input from a broad range of users about how they use CE data and the extent to which their data needs are being met. Information collected during the forum will assist the CE program in evaluating alternative redesign options. The objectives of the CE methods workshop were to identify: (a) existing knowledge and experience that can inform redesign decisions on key topics, and (b) specific research projects, both small and large, to address outstanding issues. The key methodological topics covered in the workshop included global questions, interview structure, proxy reporting, recall period, and split questionnaire methods. The workshop featured practical, solution-based discussions that will allow the BLS to move forward with the redesign process in an informed manner.

As part of the Gemini project, the CE program contracted with the National Research Council, through its Committee on National Statistics (CNSTAT), to convene an expert panel to contribute to the planned redesign. The panel held several meetings and hosted both a Household Survey producers workshop and a redesign options workshop. In late August 2012, CNSTAT will deliver a draft copy of its report regarding redesign recommendations to the BLS entitled "Measuring What We Spend: Toward a New Consumer Expenditure Survey." A public meeting to discuss the report will be hosted by CNSTAT in October 2012. The purpose of the meeting will be to discuss panel activities, recommendations for changing the CE, CE research and plans for the future, as well as specific recommendation topics, such as the use of respondent incentives.

The health-care sector, a subject of this conference, is receiving considerable BLS research attention, including research to improve health-care price measurement and the measurement of output and productivity in hospitals.

At the recommendation of prominent health economists and the CNSTAT report *At What Price*, both the Consumer Price Index and Producer Price Index programs have computed medical price indexes by disease. The initial CPI disease-based indexes were published in the February 2010 edition of the *Monthly Labor Review*. PPI indexes have just been computed and are under review. Disease-based price indexes are a part of an interagency effort (with the BEA) to publish medical data by disease. The BLS constructed the PPI indexes to assist the BEA in deflating nominal disease expenditures. Unlike medical service price indexes, disease-based indexes estimate, through weight adjustment, the savings that occur from substituting more expensive medical services to less expensive ones and thus yielding a more accurate measure of health-care inflation.

Another health-care-related project deals with new challenges for BLS's medical price data collection brought by changes in the medical industry and in medical privacy laws (HIPAA). These changes have increased the proprietary nature of medical prices and medical data in general. This could be impeding the goal of collecting representative price samples, as BLS price collectors report a rise in medical outlet refusals to disclose prices. The BLS is purchasing a proprietary private medical insurance claims database and will compare it to collected prices to determine if this increasing refusal incidence is generating sample selection bias.

The BLS has heard from informal sources that, over time, physicians are conducting more procedures per patient visit. Using the purchased claims database, the BLS plans to investigate if physicians are actually providing more procedures per visit over time. If this is true, we plan to determine if this improves healing by significantly reducing the time length of illness episodes. If there are no significant reductions to healing time or other evidence of better healing, the payments for these additional procedures might be considered inflationary.

The BLS is also undertaking research similar to the Canadian study presented in this conference on measuring output and productivity in hospitals. The research compares results based on three possible measures of output:

1. a "treatment" approach, based on a weighted aggregation of annual inpatient stays and outpatient visits (weighted by associated charges by disease-related group, DRGs);

2. a "procedures" approach, based on a weighted aggregation of the number of procedures undertaken for each DRG (weighted with the associated DRG charge/cost data); and

3. a deflated revenues approach.

The first two approaches utilize data from the Nationwide Inpatient Sample (NIS), sponsored by the Agency for Healthcare Research and Quality (AHRQ) in HHS. The NIS provides a wealth of information on health care utilization and charge data, including patient discharge data, with annual data available starting in 1988. The 2010 database contains information on approximately 8 million hospital stays from over one thousand hospitals in forty-five states.

Preliminary results suggest that the "treatment" approach is the most viable because of data limitations with the other two approaches. The research also attempts to "quality-adjust" the treatment-based output measure using data on survival rates by DRG but finds that this adjustment has no real effect on the output measure. The BLS will continue to explore ways that these data may be used to measure hospital output in BLS measures of productivity.

The BLS has been collaborating with the BEA on a set of industry-level production accounts. These accounts incorporate BEA industry measures of gross output and intermediate inputs—including energy, materials, and purchased services—and labor and capital input measures by industry from the BLS. The accounts present contributions of KLEMS inputs and multifactor productivity to gross output growth at roughly the three-digit NAICS level of industry detail based on a gross-output production accounting framework. A joint BEA-BLS working paper describing the prototype accounts is being presented in August 2012 at the Second World KLEMS conference at Harvard. A research spotlight will be published in the BEA's Survey of Current Business and the final working paper will be posted on both the BEA and BLS websites.

Finally, related to the conference agenda topics of household production, leisure, and living standards, 2012 respondents to the American Time Use Survey currently are being asked a module of questions about well-being. This module, sponsored by the National Institute on Aging, asks respondents to rate how they felt (sad, stressed, happy, tired, in pain) during three activities they engaged in "yesterday" (the core of the ATUS is a time diary about how people spent their time on the day before the interview). A similar module ran in 2010. More information about the ATUS well-being module is available on the BLS website (www.bls.gov).

Adelheid Burgi-Schmelz

To begin with, I would like to thank the organizers of this panel for having invited me. I will start by repeating the Sherlock Holmes/Sir Arthur

Adelheid Burgi-Schmelz is a special advisor to the Swiss Federal Department of Home Affairs. She is the former director of the Statistics Department at the International Monetary Fund.

The views expressed herein are those of the author and should not be attributed to the IMF, its executive board, or its management. For acknowledgments, sources of research support, and disclosure of the author's material financial relationships, if any, please see http://www.nber.org/chapters/c12844.ack.

Conan Doyle quotation cited by Federal Reserve chairman Ben Bernanke at the opening of this conference: "It is a capital mistake to theorize before one has data." And, I might add, if data are not readily available, then data gaps need to be filled. Hence, filling data gaps is at the core of my panel remarks.

This conference extensively covered, among other topics, issues focusing on well-being, distribution of income, household production, information for macroprudential policy, integrating real and financial accounts, sustainability, human capital/education, and health. What these topics have in common is that there are lots of data gaps that may prevent "theorizing" comprehensively.

The IMF Statistics Department is spearheading a global effort to plug some data gaps that became critical in the financial crisis. I will now provide you with some information on this work. Please consider this information more as teasers than as in-depth studies, make extensive use of the references provided, and contact me or my colleagues at the IMF if you have follow-up questions.

So where are these data gaps?

I will point to the following two examples:

First, let's look at the following balance sheet view of data needs and sources, as shown in figure P4.1.

This figure shows how IMF data collections such as Standardized Report Forms (SRFs), International Investment Positions (IIPs), and the Coordinated Portfolio Investment Survey (CPIS) or joint efforts with other international organizations—such as QEDS or JEDH—cover the checkered fields on holders of liabilities versus issuers of liabilities.

Second, we live in an interconnected world! The IMF started to analyze financial interconnections outside the traditional banking systems in 2010. Figure P4.2 shows the idea.

It is important to note that the size of these flows has become almost as large as the size of flows within the traditional banking system, but the flows connect different nodes than the banking system nodes.

These are just two examples. In order to plug the gaps, the G20 and the IMFC mandated the Data Gaps Initiative in early 2009. The initiative is based on twenty recommendations with annual progress reports, as shown in table P4.1.

Among these recommendations is recommendation #16, which covers information on the distribution of household income, a topic that this conference discussed thoroughly.

The Data Gaps Initiative is based on close collaboration of international agencies, as shown in figure P4.3.

The backbone is the Interagency Group on Economic and Financial Statistics (IAG), which is composed of BIS, ECB, Eurostat, IMF (chair), OECD, the UN, and the World Bank. The IAG jointly runs a website with

Issuer of liability (debtor) \ Holder of liability (creditor)	Central bank	General government	Other depository corporations	Other financial corporations	Nonfinancial corporations	Other resident sectors	Nonresidents
Central bank	(shaded)	1. SRF 1SR (Liabilities)	1. SRF 1SR (Liabilities) 2. SRF 2SR (Assets)	1. SRF 1SR (Liabilities)	1. SRF 1SR (Liabilities)	1. SRF 1SR (Liabilities)	1. SRF 1SR (Liabilities) 2. IIP 3. JEDH
General government	1. SRF 1SR (Assets)	(shaded)	1. SRF 2SR (Assets)	1. SRF 4SR (Assets)	n.a.[1]	n.a.[1]	1. IIP 2. QEDS
Other depository corporations	1. SRF 1SR (Assets) 2. SRF 2SR (Liabilities)	1. SRF 2SR (Liabilities)	(shaded)	1. SRF 2SR (Liabilities)	1. SRF 2SR (Liabilities)	1. SRF 2SR (Liabilities)	1. SRF 2SR (Liabilities) 2. IIP 3. QEDS
Other financial corporations	1. SRF 1SR (Assets)	1. SRF 4SR (Liabilities)	1. SRF 2SR (Assets)	(shaded)	1. SRF 4SR (Liabilities)	1. SRF 4SR (Liabilities)	1. SRF 4SR (Liabilities) 2. IIP 3. QEDS
Nonfinancial corporations	1. SRF 1SR (Assets)	n.a.[1]	1. SRF 2SR (Assets)	1. SRF 4SR (Assets)	(shaded)	n.a.	1. IIP 2. QEDS 3. JEDH
Other resident sectors	1. SRF 1SR (Assets)	n.a.[1]	1. SRF 2SR (Assets)	1. SRF 4SR (Assets)	n.a.	(shaded)	1. IIP 2. CPIS[2]
Nonresidents	1. SRF 1SR (Assets) 2. IIP 3. CPIS	1. IIP 2. CPIS	1. SRF 2SR (Assets) 2. IIP 3. CPIS	1. SRF 4SR (Assets) 2. IIP 3. CPIS	1. IIP 2. CPIS	1. IIP 2. CPIS	(shaded)

Fig. P4.1 A balance sheet view of data needs and sources

[a]Contributor: Mr. Alfredo Leone, International Monetary Fund.

[1]This data gap can in the future be filled with data from the public debt data template (which also covers assets), which is being piloted in some countries.

[2]CPIS data can be used to derive other resident sector's claims as residual.

An interconnected world

The financial links between the United States, the United Kingdom, and Luxembourg are especially strong.
(countries with largest number of connections with other countries)

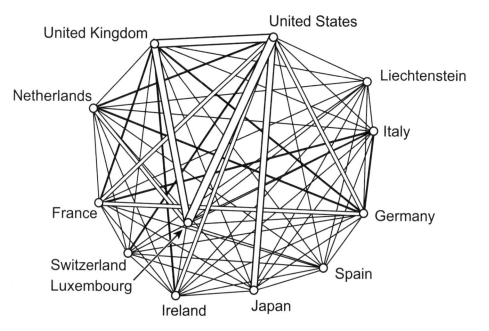

Fig. P4.2   **Financial interconnections outside of the traditional banking systems**

Sources: Lipper (Thomson Reuters); and IMF staff calculations (2010). http://www.imf.org/external/np/pp/eng/2010/100410.pdf; http://www.imf.org/external/np/pp/eng/2010/100510a.pdf.

Notes: An interconnected world: The financial links between the United States, the United Kingdom, and Luxembourg are especially strong. (Countries with largest number of connections with other countries). Thicker lines signify greater exposure among countries.

Principal Global Indicators (www.principalglobalindicators.org/default.aspx).

The website is continuously expanding the data sets covered and upgrading its methodology. In the first days of this month, for example, balance of payments and international investment position data based on BPM6 were published for the first time.

Another result of the collaboration of the IAG are the quarterly G20 growth aggregates, as shown in figure P4.4.

I had better stop here before you are completely overwhelmed by my

Table P4.1   Data gaps

	Existing conceptual/ statistical frameworks and ongoing collection	Conceptual/statistical framework needs further development
Build-up of risk in the financial sector	# 2 Financial soundness indicators (FSIs) # 5 Credit default swaps # 7 Securities	# 3 Tail risk in the financial system # 4 Aggregate leverage and maturity mismatches # 6 Structured products
Cross-border financial linkages	# 10, #11, #12 Coordinated portfolio investment survey, international banking statistics, international investment positions	# 8 and # 9 Global network connections and systemically important global institutions # 13 and #14 Financial and nonfinancial corporations' cross-border exposures
Vulnerability of domestic economies to shocks	#15 Institutional sector accounts # 17 Government finance statistics # 18 Public sector debt #19 Real estate prices	#16 Distributional information
Improving communication of official statistics	#20 Principal global indicators (PGI)	

Sources: http://www.imf.org/external/np/g20/pdf/063011.pdf;   http://www.imf.org/external/np/g20/pdf/053110.pdf;   http://www.imf.org/external/np/g20/pdf
/102909.pdf.

Notes: The column in the middle refers to statistics that exist already, but that should be improved or expanded. The column on the right-hand side lists items that did not exist at the outset of the financial crisis. Moreover, in order to develop them, a framework needs/needed to be developed first before data collection could start.

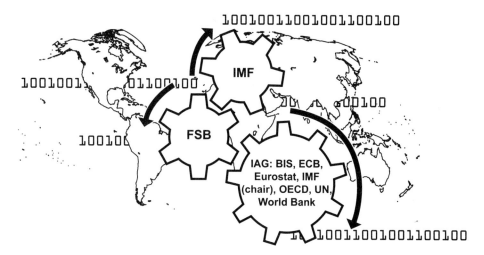

Fig. P4.3   Collaboration in the G20/IMFC Data Gaps Initiative

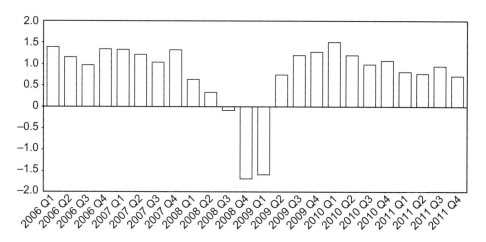

Fig. P4.4   Example: G20 GDP growth aggregates

Source: http://stats.oecd.org/index.aspx?queryid=33940.

Notes: G20 quarterly GDP in volume terms. Percentage change on the previous quarter, seasonally adjusted data.

enthusiasm. There is plenty of more information to be found on the website of the IMF (www.imf.org/external/data.htm).

I thank you, the audience, for bearing with me, and I am grateful that the staff of the IMF Statistics Department has produced or coproduced all these wonderful results that I highlighted today!

Contributors

Katharine G. Abraham
Department of Economics and
Joint Program in Survey Methodology
1218 LeFrak Hall
University of Maryland
College Park, MD 20742

Shirin Ahmed
US Census Bureau
4600 Silver Hill Road
Washington, DC 20233

Ben S. Bernanke
Brookings Institution
1775 Massachusetts Ave NW
Washington, DC 20036

Adelheid Burgi-Schmelz
Swiss Federal Department of Home
    Affairs
Iselgasse 1
Bern, Switzerland 3003

Marco Cagetti
Research and Statistics
Board of Governors of the Federal
    Reserve System
20th Street and Constitution Avenue,
    NW
Washington, DC 20551

Christopher D. Carroll
Department of Economics
440 Mergenthaler Hall
Johns Hopkins University
Baltimore, MD 21218

Michael S. Christian
Wisconsin Center for Education
    Research
1025 W. Johnson Street
Madison, WI 53706

Carol A. Corrado
The Conference Board
845 Third Avenue
New York, NY 10022-6679

W. Erwin Diewert
Department of Economics
University of British Columbia
#997-1873 East Mall
Vancouver, BC V6T 1Z1 Canada

Abe Dunn
Bureau of Economic Analysis
1441 L Street NW
Washington, DC 20230

Dennis Fixler
Bureau of Economic Analysis
1441 L Street NW
Washington, DC 20230

Susan Fleck
Immigrant Investor Program
US Citizenship and Immigration
    Service
20 Massachusetts Avenue, NE
Washington, DC 20529

Wulong Gu
Economic Analysis Division
Statistics Canada
RHC Building, 18H
Ottawa, Ontario
Canada K1A 0T6

Edward Harris
Tax Analysis Division
Congressional Budget Office
Second and D Streets, SW
Washington, DC 20515-6925

Alice M. Henriques
Board of Governors of the Federal
    Reserve System
20th Street and Constitution Avenue,
    NW
Washington, DC 20551

Elizabeth Ball Holmquist
Research and Statistics
Board of Governors of the Federal
    Reserve System
20th Street and Constitution Avenue,
    NW
Washington, DC 20551

Joanne W. Hsu
Board of Governors of the Federal
    Reserve System
20th Street and Constitution Avenue,
    NW
Washington, DC 20551

Charles R. Hulten
Department of Economics
University of Maryland
Room 3114, Tydings Hall
College Park, MD 20742

David S. Johnson
US Census Bureau
Room 7H174
Washington, DC 20233-8500

Dale W. Jorgenson
Department of Economics
Littauer Center Room 122
Harvard University
Cambridge, MA 02138

J. Steven Landefeld
Bureau of Economic Analysis
1441 L Street, NW
Washington, DC 20230

Eli Liebman
Bureau of Economic Analysis
1441 L Street, NW
Washington, DC 20230

Gang Liu
Statistics Norway
P.O. Box 8131
Dep. N-0033
Oslo, Norway

Lisa Lynn
Bureau of Economic Analysis
1441 L Street, NW
Washington, DC 20230

Clinton P. McCully
Bureau of Economic Analysis
1441 L Street, NW
Washington, DC 20230

Susan Hume McIntosh
Research and Statistics
Board of Governors of the Federal
    Reserve System
20th Street and Constitution Avenue,
    NW
Washington, DC 20551

Stéphane Morin
Economic Analysis Division
Statistics Canada
RHC Building, 18H
Ottawa, Ontario
Canada K1A 0T6

Nicholas Z. Muller
Department of Economics
Warner Hall, 305D
Middlebury College
303 College Street
Middlebury, VT 05753

Steven Rosenthal
Office of Productivity and Technology
Bureau of Labor Statistics
2 Massachusetts Avenue, NE
Washington, DC 20212-0001

John W. Ruser
Bureau of Labor Statistics
2 Massachusetts Avenue, NE
Washington, DC 20212-0001

Matthew Russell
Industry Economic Accounts
Bureau of Economic Analysis
1441 L Street, NW
Washington, DC 20230

Frank Sammartino
Congressional Budget Office
Second and D Streets, SW
Washington, DC 20515-6925

Paul Schreyer
Deputy Director
OECD Statistics Directorate
2, rue André Pascal
75775 Paris Cedex 16 France

Adam Hale Shapiro
Federal Reserve Bank of San Francisco
101 Market Street
San Francisco, CA 94201

Manik Shrestha
International Monetary Fund
700 19th Street, NW
Washington, DC 20431

Daniel T. Slesnick
Department of Economics
University of Texas
Austin, TX 78712

Erich H. Strassner
Industry Economic Accounts
Bureau of Economic Analysis
1441 L Street, NW
Washington, DC 20230

Lisa Usher
Office of Productivity and Technology
Bureau of Labor Statistics
2 Massachusetts Avenue, NE
Washington, DC 20212-0001

David Wasshausen
Bureau of Economic Analysis
1441 L Street, NW
Washington, DC 20551

Author Index

Abowd, J. M., 610
Abraham, K. G., 27, 28, 29, 81, 81n68,
  90n1, 93n4, 470, 478, 480, 485, 486,
  502, 536n40, 545
Accardo, J., 222
Aghion, P., 493, 599
Aguiar, M. A., 117, 128, 187, 478
Ahlroth, S., 463, 464, 465, 474, 477, 478,
  479, 495n4
Ahmad, N., 90n1, 105, 106, 107, 109
Aizcorbe, A. M., 28, 33, 34, 546, 546n1,
  549n6, 565, 578
Aldy, J. E., 432, 440
Allen, M., 387n13
Antoniewicz, R. L., 245, 261n23, 263,
  263n27, 264n29
Ariste, R., 577, 586
Armour, P., 188, 217n5, 220
Arrow, K. J., 600
Atkinson, A. B., 36, 46n16, 182n1, 465,
  481, 576, 577, 578
Atkinson, G. D., 527
Attanasio, O., 71, 71n62, 128, 141, 187
Avery, R. B., 245, 263
Awano, G., 610, 614
Ayres, R. U., 433

Banzhaf, H. D., 434
Barnes, P., 610
Barnett, W., 94n7
Bartelmus, P., 430, 433
Barten, A. P., 47n24

Battistin, E., 128, 141
Becker, G. S., 47n20, 91, 92, 93n3, 96,
  100n12, 493
Bee, A., 141
Bellamy, V., 222
Benson, D., 246n6
Berdshadker, A., 465, 485, 486
Berg, A., 238n30
Bernanke, B. S., 18n1
Berndt, E. R., 34, 545, 549n6, 578
Bils, M., 117, 128, 187, 602
Bjorklund, A., 463, 464, 465, 474, 477, 478,
  479, 495n4
Blinder, A., 216
Blundell, R., 119
Boarini, R., 494n1
Boer, F. P., 616
Bond, C. A., 278n2
Bosworth, B., 141, 247n10
Bound, J., 223
Boushey, H., 216
Bradley, C., 576
Bradley, R., 33
Bricker, J., 245n2, 247n10, 252, 253n15
Bridgman, B., 90n1
Broda, C., 117, 221
Brown, C., 223
Brown, M., 249n12, 267
Browning, M., 247n8
Brumberg, R. H., 235
Bucks, B., 266
Budd, E., 222

647

Subject Index